The IB Career-related Programme (CP) Core

Rebecca Austin Pickard, Becky Duffy,
Paige Freeborn, Angie Nastovska,
Lola Robledo, Susan Stewart,
Marjorie Vautrin

hachette
LEARNING

To order, please visit www.HachetteLearning.com or contact Customer Service at education@hachette.co.uk / +44 (0)1235 827827.

ISBN: 978 1 0360 1443 8

First published in 2025 by Hachette Learning,
An Hachette UK Company
Carmelite House
50 Victoria Embankment
London EC4Y 0DZ
www.HachetteLearning.com

The authorised representative in the EEA is Hachette Ireland, 8 Castlecourt Centre, Dublin 15, D15 XTP3, Ireland (email: info@hbgi.ie)

Impression number 10 9 8 7 6 5 4 3 2 1
Year 2029 2028 2027 2026 2025

Cover photo © JBLANCO_PHOTO/stock.adobe.com
Illustrations by DC Graphic Design Limited
Typeset in ITC Berkeley Oldstyle Std 10/14pt by DC Graphic Design Limited, Hextable, Kent.
Printed and bound in Great Britain by Bell & Bain Ltd, Glasgow

A catalogue record for this title is available from the British Library.

Contents

How to use this book

This book will help you throughout the IB Career-related Programme, building your skills every step of the way. Each chapter looks at a different aspect of the Career-related Programme in detail.

The following features will help you to consolidate and develop your understanding.

INQUIRY QUESTIONS

Questions which provide focus to your reading and understanding of each section. By the end of the section you should able to answer the questions.

Key terms

◆ Provide explanations of important terms.

LEARNING ENGAGEMENTS

These activities allow you to test your knowledge and strengthen your understanding.

Top tip!

These tips appear throughout the book and provide guidance on steps you can take to improve your understanding and key things you should consider.

REAL-WORLD EXAMPLE

These present examples of how theoretical knowledge is put into practice in the wider world.

Reflection and reflexivity

Activities and questions providing an opportunity to reflect on the knowledge you have learned.

Learning journal

Activities which help you to develop your learning journal.

'Lightbulb' moments

Provide general guidance and support throughout.

Learner profile

Highlights where content aligns with the IB learner profile.

Common pitfalls

These demonstrate common mistakes that you may encounter and how to avoid them. Watch out for these!

LINKS

These appear throughout the book to highlight where there are links/connections between the components and aspects of the IB Career-related Programme:

- language and cultural studies (LCS)
- community engagement (CE)
- personal and professional skills (PPS)
- the reflective project (RP)
- approaches to learning (ATL) skills
- international-mindedness
- IB learner profile.

About the authors

Becky Duffy is a passionate advocate for the IB Career-related Programme (CP), serving as both a CP Coordinator and PPS teacher at a high-achieving, comprehensive high school in Pennsylvania. As a subject matter expert, she has dedicated extensive effort to developing the PPS curriculum, the PPS teacher support materials, and the IB PPS workshops for new and veteran teachers alike. She has over 21 years of teaching, instructional coaching and educational leadership experience.

Dr Angie Nastovska is an innovative educational leader committed to transforming learning through inquiry, equity and authentic practice. She currently serves as the Director Of Curriculum And Assessment at iLEAD Schools, an Adjunct Professor at United States University, a global consultant for the IB and an IB workshop leader. Dr Nastovska designs and implements programs that empower both educators and students, drawing on her expertise in curriculum development, project-based learning, competency based education and systemic school transformation. Her work focuses on cultivating future-ready, compassionate learners equipped with the transversal skills needed to thrive in a rapidly changing world.

Lola Robledo is a highly experienced IB educator with over 35 years of teaching experience in Spain, Portugal, Venezuela and Switzerland. She has held the position of MYP Service Action, DP CAS and CP Service Learning Coordinator, as well as IB DP World Languages Coordinator at the International School of Geneva in Switzerland. She teaches Spanish and has extended experience as an IB examiner and workshop leader.

Marjorie Vautrin is an experienced IBDP and IBCP teacher. She is a French B, TOK and LCS teacher, as well as an Extended Essay Coordinator. She is passionate about education and leads IB workshops to share her expertise and passion with the IB educators' community.

Paige Freeborn is a highly experienced IB educator with expertise across the MYP, CP and DP programmes. She teaches at Brockton School, an inclusive IB World School in North Vancouver, Canada, where her work centres on arts education, CE, and social, emotional and ethical learning. Throughout her career, Paige has demonstrated a deep commitment to fostering intercultural understanding and socio-ecological responsibility through both her scholarship and educational practice. She has contributed to the development of IB's CE curriculum and associated workshops, supporting educators and students in building meaningful connections within and beyond the classroom.

Rebecca Austin Pickard is an experienced IB educator working extensively across both the CP and DP programmes. She was IBCP Coordinator in the early pilot stages of the CP and has supported many schools globally establish the CP. Nowadays, she works full-time as a consultant, workshop leader and developer for the IB, as well as the author of ThinkIB's CP site.

Susan Stewart has lived and worked in South Africa, Thailand, the UAE, Belgium, Oman, Sweden and the UK, and speaks, to varying degrees, English, French, Dutch, German, Afrikaans, Swedish, Arabic and BSL. Susan has a background in international education, leading multilingual language programmes in IB World Schools. Susan was a curriculum developer for the new LCS course. She has a particular interest in language policy as a driving force in promoting multilingualism within families, schools and on a national level.

Welcome to the CP Core

INQUIRY QUESTION

- Where will CP take me?

How do we flourish in a difficult world?

Being a human is extraordinary, but no easy endeavour. We are constantly made aware of how complicated and chaotic the world can be, and if you are young, you have the added 'gift' of people older than you constantly telling you how much worse it is now than it was in their youth. A gift wrapped up with a final bow of how uncertain the future is too. Well, the writers of this book are all firmly in agreement that you can absolutely flourish in this crazy world of ours. The key is in having the tools to do so—and that is within everyone's grasp. Especially yours, by holding this book.

■ The world is a busy and complicated place.

So how do we flourish in a complex world? Let's start as we mean to go on by talking about thinking. The term 'stubborn optimism' was coined by Christiana Figueres and Tom Rivett-Carnac in response to the challenges posed by climate change, centred on the idea that in a complex world where many of us feel a lack of control, the most powerful thing we can do is change how we behave as individuals and use ourselves as a catalyst for change. As a movement, this means that you can be a positive and energetic driving force behind your actions and beliefs, starting with understanding yourself as an individual. This then impacts those around you and ripples out to change even wider aspects of society. Imagine if we all took on this challenge and the impact it could have.

The good news is, you don't have to take this at face value as a nice idea. You can start now with the International Baccalaureate Career-related Programme (CP). This course encapsulates the notion that we do not wait for life to happen to us; we create and shape the life we want. Therefore, the aim of this book is simple: you will learn how to flourish, adapt, bounce back and thrive in your studies and your life beyond them, both now and in the future. That might sound ambitious, but you can start to get excited about the possibilities that await you. Just be prepared to be positive, patient and open-minded.

You might find the prospect of embarking on your CP course a little overwhelming, never mind your future career. You could be reading the words 'flourish' and 'thrive' and think the world 'survive' is more apt. This is understandable as you are anticipating some important decision-making ahead. Certainly, our world can be convincingly scary at times, but with a mindset of 'stubborn optimism', you will develop a solid and adaptable skillset to navigate the many different areas of your life with strength, kindness and hope. In short, you have so much to enjoy now and to look forward to.

Take a step back and think

'What I like about the world is simply that everybody is different.'

(Anne, charity sector, Newcastle, UK)

Before delving into the course, take a moment to reflect. When was the last time you stopped to think about what is amazing about the world around us? You may think this is a bit of a cliché question—you are undoubtedly right. However, we spend much of our lives immersed, if not drowning, in the media. The narrative can often be dominated by what is wrong in the world, what other people think we should be doing or what we should be scared about this week. It makes sense, if only for a moment's peace of mind, to think about how remarkable the world truly is.

How would you answer the questions 'Why is the world amazing?' and 'What is the most amazing thing about the world to you?' Well, I asked over fifty individuals, aged 15–80, from different backgrounds, careers and pathways (and inadvertently one commercial-radio drive-time show presenter) these questions. The responses were varied, with most people finding it a good if rather a big question. There were some philosophical mini-essays, one-word answers; most serious, some not at all. Some found it a little embarrassing; some needed no encouragement at all. All were revealing.

We are going to look at the responses in a learning engagement with two distinct parts.

LEARNING ENGAGEMENT

Part 1

Firstly, before you look at the responses on the next page, think about how you would answer these two questions:

- Why is the world amazing?
- What is the most amazing thing about the world to you?

Write, draw or doodle your first thoughts.

Now look at the responses below, taking your time to consider what each person has said and why they might have said it. How many of these do you agree with? Do some of them make more sense to you than others? Feel free to add to your initial ideas.

The world is amazing because one is so unbelievably insignificant in it, but at the same time you can build a significant life in your corner of it.

Georgina, global head of design agency, London, England

What I like about the world is simply that everybody is different.

Anne, charity sector, Newcastle, England

Everywhere I've travelled (especially in the poorest countries), I've been struck by how deeply people care for one another … And what's even more powerful is the kindness they extend to outsiders too. That quiet generosity is everywhere if you look for it … and it's one of the most human things about us.

Harriet, PR and marketing specialist, New York, USA

The planet's resilience is amazing despite what humans do to it … The most amazing thing is there is still a lot of the unknown to explore.

Elise, educator, France

The perpetual welcoming surprise that there's always something new on the horizon—you just need to keep an eye open and never lose your inner child in relation to the sense of wonder; keeping an open mind about where your learning comes from.

David, rail industry specialist, Sevenoaks, England

Laughter and, particularly, our ability to laugh in the face of adversity. Literally the sound of laughter and the joy that comes from it, even for those who aren't laughing.

Lara, company director, Belfast, NI and San Diego, California, USA

I would say the biggest thing in the world is the human mind. When used positively, it creates amazing things, making the world even greater, and to add to the palpable things it creates, we have the ability to learn from what we read and do even greater things, or enjoy literature and communicate with others.

Pedro, educator, Uruguay and Wales

There is always the window of possibility. In that space between the beginning and the end is a place that has as much joy as if dreams were realized. For me, that is the part that remains untouched by all the stresses in life.

Lucy, author, Broadstairs, England

Art, theatre, music, anything we can make … this is what is amazing about the world. Even if this comes from pain and suffering, people have a way of expressing this so beautifully and it adds so much meaning to the world.

Anna, 21-year-old student at Royal Holloway, University of London, England

The relationship between humans and their animals is a daily joy. Raising a child. Friendship. The beauty of a clear, starry night and a full moon. Classical music blows me away and moves me to tears.

Sue, primary teacher, Kent, England

Looking at your ideas and the thoughts on this page, perhaps share them with your peers and teacher. What similarities can you find? Look at the role of community, culture, communication and connection at play, not to mention the power of the human mind.

How might you link this to other Core components and your DP and career-related studies courses?

LEARNING ENGAGEMENT

Part 2

Now we are going to look closer at the survey and evaluate its validity a little further.

Look at who answered these questions and where they come from. Of course, the full cultural backgrounds of all who responded are not fully included here but there could be a perceived bias towards European/US perspectives. Consider these questions:

- Do you think people from other countries and different cultural backgrounds might respond differently to these questions?
- Why might people from different cultural backgrounds have different perspectives on these questions?
- How might you find opportunities to speak to people from different cultural backgrounds about these questions to seek multiple perspectives?

Consider whether you could carry out your own informal survey, asking classmates, family and teachers the same questions. You might find something interesting about the impact of the question on the person you ask.

From that original survey of over fifty people, I noticed that the process of thinking about the question became as important as the answer itself and what this revealed about the person. People connected with their families as they discussed it. More than that, there seemed to be a real sense of calm as they took a step back to pause and consider the big picture. Ask the right questions and it becomes as much about the journey as it does the destination.

It is this ability to develop your understanding of yourself and about the impact of your actions and beliefs that runs like a backbone through the CP. This is central to keeping your well-being front and centre.

The future is yours

Congratulations for choosing a pathway that has you, your development and your right to make choices as the central focus of your learning. It is a great time to be a CP student! With over a quarter of the twenty-first century behind us already, we know so much about education—the different ways we learn, the best ways to teach. We also know far more about how we can best prepare for a future which looks so different to the last century. This is why, when you tell people about the course you are studying, you will often find adults saying, 'I wish I had that when I was at school'.

It can sound daunting to hear that jobs and careers are changing rapidly and there is uncertainty as to what they will look like. But let's reframe it into something empowering from the start. With this course, you can step out of school ready for the next steps, where you can do almost anything. You can have the confidence to use skills in multiple ways and differing environments. You will be able to speak up for yourself as well as interact with and understand the world around you. Most importantly, you can be reassured that you are armed with something so much more powerful than just knowledge—you have self-awareness, adaptability and a skillset which you know is only going to grow throughout your life. Let's look at some of the ways the CP will support your long-term development.

Encouraging you to be a lifelong learner

Let your mind grow.

> **Key term**
>
> ◆ **Growth mindset:** When you have the belief that your capacities and talents can be improved over time with effort.

> **Top tip!**
>
> The term 'growth mindset' was coined by Carol Dweck. She's worth researching as her ideas are really accessible, evidence-based and inspiring.

We started this book with the term 'stubborn optimism' as a belief in the power of an individual's attitude and behaviour to shape the future. This links with the IB's core principle of developing committed, lifelong learners who understand themselves with a **growth mindset**. You will hear this term at times throughout this book, as working towards and adopting a growth mindset has such a far-reaching impact, on both our physical and mental well-being. It's a very practical and accessible way of feeling in charge of our learning. It means that our skills are not set in stone at birth; such is the physiological way our brain works that skills can be developed constantly. Obviously, we are all different and we will all find developing skills easier or more difficult in certain areas and at different times of our lives.

If you are in an IB classroom right now, there is a good chance you will see the IB learner profile on the wall, which lists the ten attributes we strive to develop throughout our lives in our commitment to being a locally and globally minded, empathetic contributor to the world's community. These attributes are: balanced, risk-taker, caring, open-minded, communicator, knowledgeable, principled, inquirer, reflective and thinker. But this is not a checklist. Throughout our lives, our relationship with these attributes changes and strengthens in meaning; at times we will feel like experts and at other times like complete novices. Think back to the initial exercise with our survey of responses from people about what they found amazing about the world. How many of the learner profile attributes did they demonstrate by answering that one question alone? How many of the attributes seem to be relevant when engaging with the world? It's important to realize that the learner profile is a tool and not just a poster on the wall.

Designed with your future in mind

Let's look at the reasons why being a CP student matters and explore some of the research it is built upon. Many students globally are not studying at school what they need for the future. The CP is a course designed with the intention to align with what a range of trusted and peer-reviewed research says young people need for future readiness. It is not just important to develop skills but to know how your skills can transfer to different contexts for different purposes.

At the heart of this are the approaches to learning skills areas of thinking, communication, social, self-management and research. You will find that you use many skills in these areas across your DP, CRS and Core components. You can explore the ATL skills and how they link to the programme and Core components in Section 5, but let's now look at why skill development is so important.

This understanding is not unique to the CP. The Skills' Builder Partnership is a global movement working with educators, employers and organizations with their skill builder framework (**www.skillsbuilder.org/impact**). Their research came to the conclusion that 'essential skills support higher wages, greater job and life satisfaction, and reduction in the likelihood of being out of work or training'.

They identified eight essential skills for future working practices: listening, speaking, problem-solving, creativity, staying positive, aiming high, leadership and teamwork.

From an IB perspective, what is interesting is that all these aptitudes and skills are already present in the ATL skills. And it is these that are developed in so much detail in the CP Core.

Globally, we are in the middle of a shift in the way we work, but it's important to investigate how the types of jobs that there will be in the future may change. The World Economic Forum's research in 2023 predicted that there will be *plenty* of jobs in the future, but that 23% of today's jobs will change because 'technology is expected to create 69 million new job roles and displace 83 million current roles'.

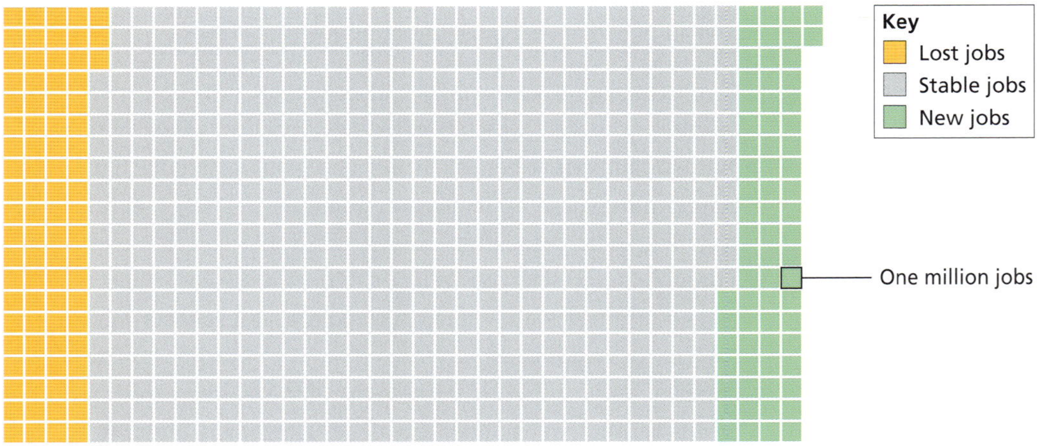

World Economic Forum projections for total global job growth and loss, 2023–27 (Source: WEF, Future of jobs report 2023)

> *'The days of learning one trade for a lifetime are gone. To stay relevant in today's job market, workers need to embrace continuous learning and reskilling. With 44% of job skills expected to change within five years, it's essential that both individuals and companies invest in lifelong learning.'*
>
> (Source: WEF, www.weforum.org/stories/2024/10/jobs-skills-work-digital-economy)

So if there are going to be plenty of jobs, then what does the WEF predict they will be? And what are these jobs that are in decline? Table 1 outlines the largest growing and declining jobs across the world by 2030.

Table 1 Top 10 largest growing and declining jobs globally by 2030 (Source: WEF, Future of jobs report 2025)

Largest growing jobs	Largest declining jobs
Agricultural workers	Cashiers and ticket clerks
Delivery services drivers	Administrative assistants
Software and app developers	Building caretakers and cleaners
Building tradespeople	Material-recording and stock-keeping
Shop salespersons	Printing trades workers
Food-processing workers	Accounting and book-keeping
Car, motorcycle and van drivers	Accountants and auditors
Nursing professionals	Transportation attendants and conductors
Food and beverage serving workers	Security guards
General and operations managers	Bank tellers

LEARNING ENGAGEMENT

Why does this matter to me?

Let's look at yourself, your context and ideas first and not make what everyone else is doing and thinking your first line of research.

1 First, look at the source above and think about what *you* find surprising and unsurprising. You might grab a piece of paper and a pen or make a voice note on your phone. Try to expand your reasons as to why certain job sectors are on the right or the left. What industries are you connected with? This may be through family or professional links you already have through school and experiences you have had personally.
2 Now create a visual that shows jobs in the future; think about what will still be familiar and what will be unfamiliar. This could be a mind map, a sketch cartoon, Venn diagram or whatever works for you. Aim to create your own version first, rather than using artificial intelligence (AI). Compare your responses and look for similarities and differences.
3 Feel free to share your responses with your peers and class too. Another important part of placing yourself at the centre of your learning is considering other perspectives and reflecting on how they may or may not affect what you think and believe.

Academic integrity and artificial intelligence

> *'The goal of academic integrity is to make knowledge, understanding and thinking transparent. Students must also master the technical components of academic integrity, which includes learning how to correctly reference and ethically use information, opinions and artificial intelligence (AI) tools.'*
>
> (IBO, academic integrity policy)

What does this mean for you as a student? Responsibility, accuracy and honesty.

This means you commit to your responsibility to produce honest and genuine work, whether individual or group-based. You accurately reference your sources and acknowledge others' work and ideas. You also use IT and social media responsibly and you are ethically principled in the way you take part in the examination process.

You probably will have heard the term '**agency**' already at your stage of school career. To act with agency means you have the ability to take action—and choose how you act. If we add integrity into the mix, we are talking about being transparent and honest in the way you take action. There is no better time to talk about acting with agency than when it comes to using artificial intelligence (AI) in your learning.

Artificial intelligence has certainly added a complexity to the world. Until recently, the only AI we referred to in IB education was 'academic integrity' (or 'applications and interpretations' in maths). Now we have another AI to include and you must have a very clear understanding of the role both academic integrity and artificial intelligence play in your life before you start your course, and keep hold of that understanding the whole way through. This is at the heart of being an open and honest student and transfers to the way you live your life.

Research is important in every aspect of the CP Core, culminating in the reflective project. Academic integrity is all about transparency and artificial intelligence can be a great tool in supporting that transparency. Remember to remain the main protagonist in cultivating what you think and believe—everything else can, at best, be a helpful assistance tool.

> *'[S]tudents need to be aware that the IB does not regard any work produced—even only in part—by such [AI] tools to be their own. Therefore, as with any quote or material from another source, it must be clear that any AI-generated text, image or graph included in a piece of work has been copied from such software. The software must be credited in the body of the text and appropriately referenced in the bibliography. If this is not done, the student would be misrepresenting content—as it was not originally written by them—which is a form of academic misconduct.'*
>
> (IBO, academic integrity policy)

Agency and building your future

Key term

◆ **Agency:** A philosophical, sociological and psychological idea that acknowledges humans as active participants in their own lives with the capacity to initiate intentional action. (Adapted from IB LCS guide, p.50)

You have the capacity to think, work and make choices independently through being organized and, through developing reflective and reflexive practice, you can become self-regulating and adaptable. You will get things wrong, you already have—we all have. That is the messiness of being human. But you are more than ready to shape your future with intention and heart.

> *'You know, I don't know about you, coach, but I hope that either all of us, or none of us, are judged by the actions of our weakest moments, but rather by the strength we show when, and if, we're ever given a second chance.'*
>
> (Ted Lasso, American football coach)

How will you know if you are successful? First of all, you need to learn how to learn about yourself. We look at this later in this section, but the first step in having agency and a growth mindset is establishing what success actually looks like. People often think this is an upward trajectory of growth with no bumps in the road, but this is unrealistic and totally inaccurate. Real success is acknowledging that there will be surprises and setbacks, but that you have the tools to bounce back and adapt.

What does it mean to be a CP student?

A CP student is at the centre of their educational experience.

Being a CP student means being a fully conscious learner. You work with others to carve out and build your own understanding of your courses and experiences. Crucially, a CP student connects their subjects and experiences through the transfer of shared ideas and skills. A CP student is able to do this is because they do not just study career-related studies and DP subjects; there is a whole Core programme with four different elements designed for you to be able to make connections, not just in your course, but in many different contexts beyond the classroom.

There are four components of the Core: language and cultural studies (LCS), community engagement (CE), personal and professional skills (PPS) and the reflective project (RP). While each have their own identity, you will easily find clear connections between them all.

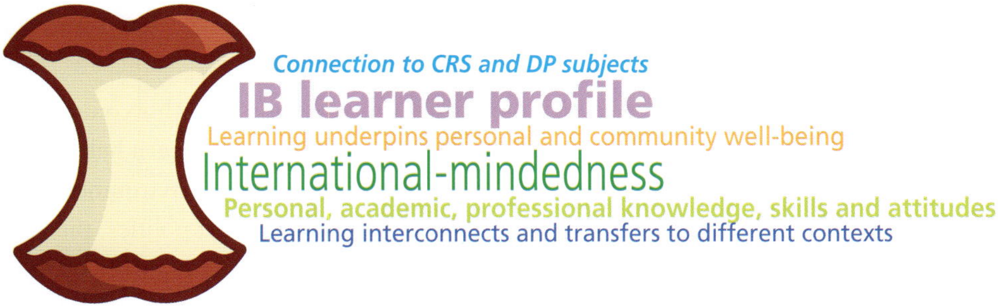

■ Common features across the CP Core

Links

Start looking early in your course for connections between subjects and how you are using the same skills in different areas. The personal and professional skills (PPS) course will explore transversal skills in detail, but a general tool that links all your subjects together is the ATL skills categories of research, self-management, communication, social and thinking skills, which provide a general way of seeing how everything connects.

You will explore and develop a number of identities in your role as a CP student. Think of them as hats you will wear at different times. We have established that the CP is a holistic, interconnected course, so it makes sense to consider how all the elements come together in shaping you over your time in school and beyond right from the start. You will shift between certain roles as needed, which enables you to practise resilience and adaptability. These roles are explored below.

LEARNING ENGAGEMENT

CP identities

If possible, complete this exercise as a group where you divide up the roles of the 'curious explorer', 'skill practitioner', 'ethical decision-maker', 'community change-maker', 'internationally minded communicator' and 'lifelong learner'.

Each of you should read your section in the text with its two parts and pick out 5–10 words and phrases that you think capture what that means in the CP.

Together, discuss your findings and create a visual (e.g. a sketch, mind map or table) that captures these different identities you will take on during your programme.

If you are working in a smaller group, you can take on more than one section and feedback your findings in the way described above. Alternatively, you can build up an understanding through reading together and discussing the words and phrases before building a visual collaboratively.

The curious explorer

The phrase 'be curious, not judgemental' is often misattributed to the poet Walt Whitman; its origin is actually unknown. Irrespective of this, it does capture in a simple way an essential approach to life. Think of an open or closed door. If you are curious, you are open to possibilities and prepared to be surprised by what there is to know about the world. Being judgemental, however, closes you off and any chance of a conversation or connection ends there. You are content to be just as you are and put up barriers and negativity towards anything new. Do not be mistaken—being curious does not stop you from being decisive or knowledgeable, but it is a confident stance that says 'I know and embrace that neither I, nor anyone else, can know everything'.

Be curious to the point of nosiness about yourself—this could be relationships, ambitions, problems. This is not a chaotic curiosity—you will learn habits of mind and systems of thinking that will enable you to navigate complex environments and situations. Then think big too—be curious about life locally and globally; politics, the environment, science, the arts, the news, people on the other side of the world, and so on.

■ The curious explorer experiencing the CP

When I started the CP, I noticed that each subject introduced concepts—these were big, universal ideas that my teachers said would help me understand the subject more and make links to the world around me. I wasn't sure at first as they seemed like such large topics—it was hard to know what to think as I just seemed to have more questions than answers. I shared this with my teacher and they seemed delighted I didn't have any answers yet as it meant I was keeping an open mind. However, I started noticing that LCS and PPS talked about similar ideas, just with a different focus and context. Community engagement in particular made me realize that these ideas were connected with the world and they really mattered.

CP student, India

Skill practitioner

The second hat you will wear on the CP is that of skill practitioner (or its more accurate title—'*skilled* skill practitioner'). Developing skills has often been associated with something particularly essential to the twenty-first century, but actually this is not really true. For example, it has been known for a long time how important the skills of communication, problem-solving, critical thinking and self-management are. Skills are malleable and transferable. It is not enough to develop skills or even enough to know the level of ability you are achieving; what matters and represents true mastery is using skills in various contexts. This is why we talk about transversal skills and why they are central to the PPS course in particular.

The skill practitioner experiencing the CP

In PPS, I started asking questions and building inquiries with my teachers and classmates and that really helped me get to know the different skills I needed, both now and in the future. I saw that I move within multiple contexts, such as career-related studies, DP subjects and other Core areas as well as my personal life and work outside school. The skill domains in PPS focus on me as the learner; how I understand myself, relate to the world around me, the systems thinking I can use as well as how to develop intercultural understanding.

The PPS class focuses on transversal skills and how they might work in different parts of the course from the very start, so I was able to make connections from my own experience. For example, I found that language and cultural studies is all about communication skills and thinking about yourself as a communicator. These communication skills were helpful in community engagement, as I had to arrange meetings and write letters to start my community projects. Once the projects started, they were not straightforward and some problems arose; it was helpful to be able to apply systems thinking with my group to be able to solve this.

The reflective project starts a little later in the first year and I think it sounds like hard work with all the research, ethical thinking and project management. Though I have read a bit about it and noticed there are a lot of links with PPS in my portfolio; for example, delivering presentations, how to listen and give effective feedback.

CP student, Germany

Ethical decision-maker

Key term

◆ **Ethics:** The study of right and wrong, as well as any system or code of moral rules, principles or values. Understanding why something is right or wrong helps to inform and guide our choices, actions and behaviours.

The third hat you will wear is that of the ethical decision-maker. You will have to make many decisions throughout your life—some seemingly small and inconsequential—and you will find yourself at times debating the right way to proceed and articulate where you stand. You will find that the words 'moral' and 'ethical' are often used interchangeably, but there is an important distinction. Morals are your personal beliefs of right and wrong while **ethics** concern society and differing standards of right and wrong behaviour. Therefore moving confidently within and adapting successfully to different environments demands an understanding of yourself and the world around you. Exploring different ethical frameworks will help, as this enables you to build the sensitivity and self-knowledge to make sound choices that are good for you and those around you. By exploring ethical issues and dilemmas in CP, you will become someone who realizes that all actions have consequences.

The ethical decision-maker experiencing the CP

I'm beginning to think there are ethical issues and dilemmas everywhere; now we've been introduced to what these are, they seem to run through every part of the course. CRS is great because the ethical issues and dilemmas that come up are directly related to the world and my studies, and these might be interesting ideas for my reflective project. Saying that, it's not the only area I found that has interesting issues. Community engagement is raising some interesting local organizations and issues right on my doorstep in the guided learning phase; I am going to have to work out how to navigate these problems as there are a lot of people involved.

Still, I am beginning to appreciate in Language and cultural studies (LCS), how culture plays an important role in ethical decisions—what seems a really obvious solution at times would be very insensitive in some cultures. It's hard to know what to think, but at least the discussions and group presentations I have already done on ethical dilemmas in PPS are helping. I am getting better at arguing my ideas, but I don't always find it easy to see alternative perspectives. However, it seems not just okay to question and challenge, but it's actually expected. These words 'reflective' and 'reflexive' seem to be everywhere too, which gets you really thinking about your actions and beliefs and how this affects the world around you.

CP student, Hong Kong

Community change-maker

Another hat? Yes, but it's an important one: community change-maker. A community is a physical space we inhabit; however, community also refers to social interactions, relationships and making connections with others. Just what are the impacts of our actions within a community? It's also important to take a step back from what is happening around us and consider how community relates to something much bigger and more complex. CP students understand that truly being part of a community involves taking part in a two-way conversation, as well as the ability to listen to the needs of those around us. Being a true community member requires hard work, stepping out of one's comfort zone and committing to consistency of effort and communication.

The community change-maker in the CP

I was hoping that my first idea of having a bake sale and raising money for a charity might be enough for my first community engagement project, but then i realized it was not. CE is about getting to know a community first and talking with them to understand their needs and your own before deciding what to do. I always knew that different cultures and my home language played a part in my family life, but I hadn't realized that I could build on that to make a difference in my school community.

In PPS, I noticed that I love helping out with events in my community outside school, but I keep school life separate. So, I am planning with my classmates a cultural day with students, parents and staff where we celebrate many different languages and cultures in the school through talks, performances, food and art. I am not sure where it is going yet, but I know it can have a big impact for everyone involved as we don't just get to share what we know, we get to find out so much more about other people's backgrounds too.

CP student, Australia

Internationally minded communicator

The hat of being an internationally minded communicator is more than knowing that different cultures are interesting. The last sentence of the IB mission statement captures international-mindedness by saying 'that others with their differences can also be right'. Therefore, being internationally minded is being a critical thinker, as critical thinking demands that we explore multiple perspectives which contribute to being able to form a position. It demands a mindset open to equitable, authentic relationships founded on fairness and reciprocity. Internationally minded communicators seek a more peaceful world, but they are not afraid to use their voice—and the power of communication can never be understated. With both ethical and critical thinking, the values of international-mindedness can travel more easily to different contexts and lead to a greater appreciation for the way others can lead their lives.

The internationally minded communicator in the CP

As part of my career-related studies, we looked at the ethics of the fashion industry, with a particular focus on fast fashion. As I discovered more and more, I found my views contrasted with my actions. I love buying clothing that's cheap because it gives me more options and I can keep up to date more easily, but I am looking at the effect on the planet with the amount of waste and on people in developing countries being able to earn a living wage through these big companies, and I am wondering what to do.

I am writing to local environmental charities to see if I can get some work experience and find out the most effective way to use my voice. I am working on shaping a research question for my reflective project on an ethical dilemma centred on the fashion industry so I can understand it better. I know that I can create a podcast which might be a great way to express my ideas.

CP student, UAE

Lifelong learner

An IB education is centred around being a lifelong learner, so it makes sense that this appears here as the last hat. In fact, all the CP hats will last a lifetime and serve you well. Curiosity, connection and open-mindedness will guide you throughout your life. Communities will always be a place to participate in, advocate for and learn from. You will spend a lifetime finding out what you think or seeking to understand why your ideas have changed. You will expect nothing less than for your beliefs and biases to be constantly challenged as the world changes around you. You will find making decisions easy at times and challenging at others, especially when more seems at stake. And lastly, you know that being a lifelong learner means understanding yourself, your aspirations and not being frightened to challenge yourself and set goals. You understand that the more you step out from what is familiar and embrace multiple perspectives from around the world, the more of a multidimensional human being you become.

The lifelong learner in the CP

I am learning a lot about myself on this course. The most valuable thing I am learning is that we are all a work-in-progress and never a finished product. The more I get into the course, the more I find out about skills I never knew I had—who knew I could keep calm under pressure and solve problems quickly? (I found this out at my eventually successful, but not uneventful, community engagement project!) The most important part of the CP is when you realize that everything connects; it makes adapting to new challenges so much easier because you know you already have skills you can use. You will also never stop being surprised and interested at what else you can learn about yourself, other people and the world around you. I can adapt to change and also be the change. I'm just getting started.

CP student, Malta

Leading your own learning

So far, if you think the CP is all about being the protagonist in your own story, then you would be right. You lead your learning and can certainly learn to be your own coach. Learning is not a quiet endeavour; yes, it is about 'cognitive' skills (what we commonly refer to as **thinking skills**) but, more than that, it is about your understanding of how and why you learn the way you do. This is what we call 'metacognitive' skills and they are central to being a self-aware learner. You cannot even begin to be successful if you do not look after yourself mentally and physically, and this is where 'affective' skills come in. It is important for learners to understand that behaviour and attitude can influence whether they are able to adopt the mindset to work effectively.

Key term

◆ **Thinking skills:** These involve cognitive processes that we use to solve problems, make decisions, ask questions, plan, organize and create. Critical and creative thinking, problem-solving and information literacy consistently top the list of skills necessary to successfully navigate our ever-changing world in a variety of contexts.

Practical steps to lead your own learning

There are some understandings and habits you can establish from the start of your course which will set great self-management skills in motion. See these as something you do for yourself to make everything easier in the long term as progress is not immediate. Through your CP course you will learn techniques and systems that will help in each area which will build your ability to self-motivate, persevere and know what working habits work well for you.

Build on prior learning and ask questions

The way your courses are designed, from your CRS and DP subjects to the four Core components, is to build on prior knowledge. They do this on purpose to make you feel secure in what you know already before then adding on new learning. If at any time you feel uncertain with something new and how it connects to your existing understanding, take a moment to reflect. Work out what your questions are and ask. Even if it is asking for a pause, a recap or simply acknowledging, 'I don't get it yet'.

Set goals

It's important to personalize your learning right from the start. Do not just set long-term, big dreams without working out how you will get there. It's important to have a vision of where you want to go, but remember this is just a statement of intent. What are the steps to get you there? No matter how incremental and small they may be, when you see them stack up, it becomes impressive and satisfying.

Connect your experiences

This section has already discussed how everything in your CP course connects, but it is up to you to make those connections. There is no one answer for you to find as it is a subjective experience. You may connect experiences and ideas in a way that is completely different to someone else. That's exactly the point.

Trust the process

In connection with this last point, remember that the purpose of connection is not to compare yourself as better or worse than someone else. This is an exercise in patience, which can be frustrating (there are scientific reasons for this connected to the teenage brain, but let's stay focused here). You will find that with all the different parts of the CP, when they come together, the process is the purpose, not the product. You could have a student blindly working their way through courses, acing tests and coming out of school without an ounce of self-awareness, or ability to bounce back from mistakes or any idea about their skillset and how to use it. The aim of the CP is knowing yourself and moving forward, which could look like many different things.

Reflection and reflexivity

What is a successful learning process meant to look like?

This leads us on to the question: what is a successful CP experience? Think about the picture here, which has something to say about what it's like to go through a learning process. Think about your learning engagements so far from school and your whole CP experience ahead of you. Reflect on these questions:

- What do you most relate to?
- What surprises you?
- What message is being communicated here?
- Does it challenge your existing position on what progress means?

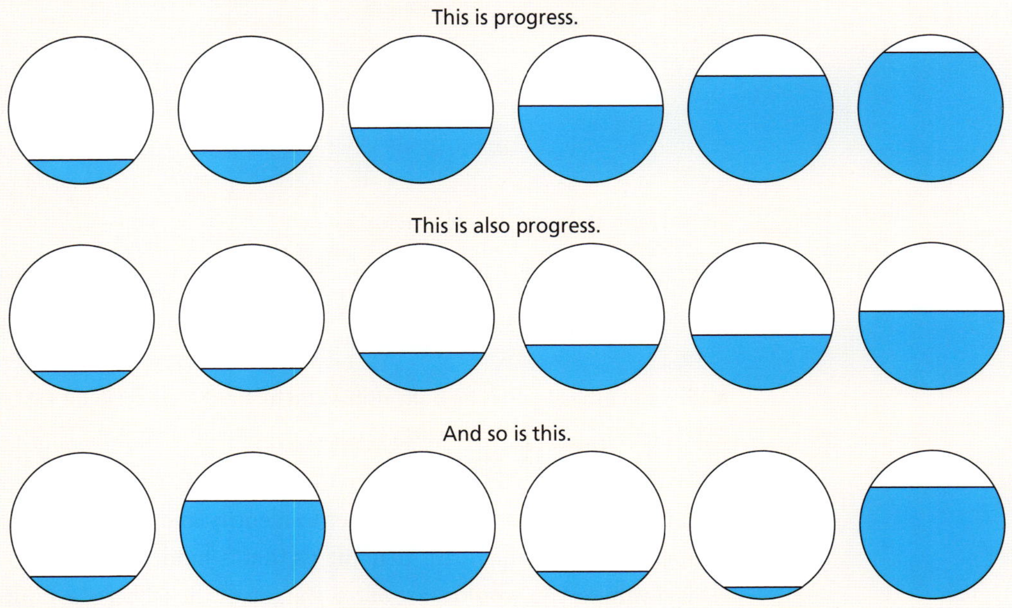

■ What does progress look like?

The answer? Well, hopefully you have concluded that success and progress look like many things, as long as you place yourself as the learner at the heart of the learning journey. And by that we mean a fully engaged, proactive, reflective, resilient learner who can learn equally from the setbacks as they can from the successes.

Most of all, lead your own thinking

So far in this introduction, we have seen how the values of international-mindedness and the learner profile inform the whole of the CP. A common thread throughout the CP Core is that by understanding yourself and those around you, ethically and culturally, you can navigate the many contexts you live and work in and advocate for yourself and others.

This can be a complex process, but use all the Core elements to develop your thinking in different ways. Understanding values and understanding yourself and those around you properly can only happen by considering how many different factors directly contribute to this. You will encounter a motif in this book used in different ways in LCS, CE and RP. Whatever the focus, the iceberg demonstrates how some ideas/factors/values are far more obvious than others (those above the surface), but the more we explore them and build up a portrait of understanding, the deeper we can go in our thinking (below the surface). Just as an iceberg, what is above the surface can look huge, but actually it is just a small mass compared to the massive base below; critical thinking involves surface-level observations and a far deeper level of analysis and reasoning.

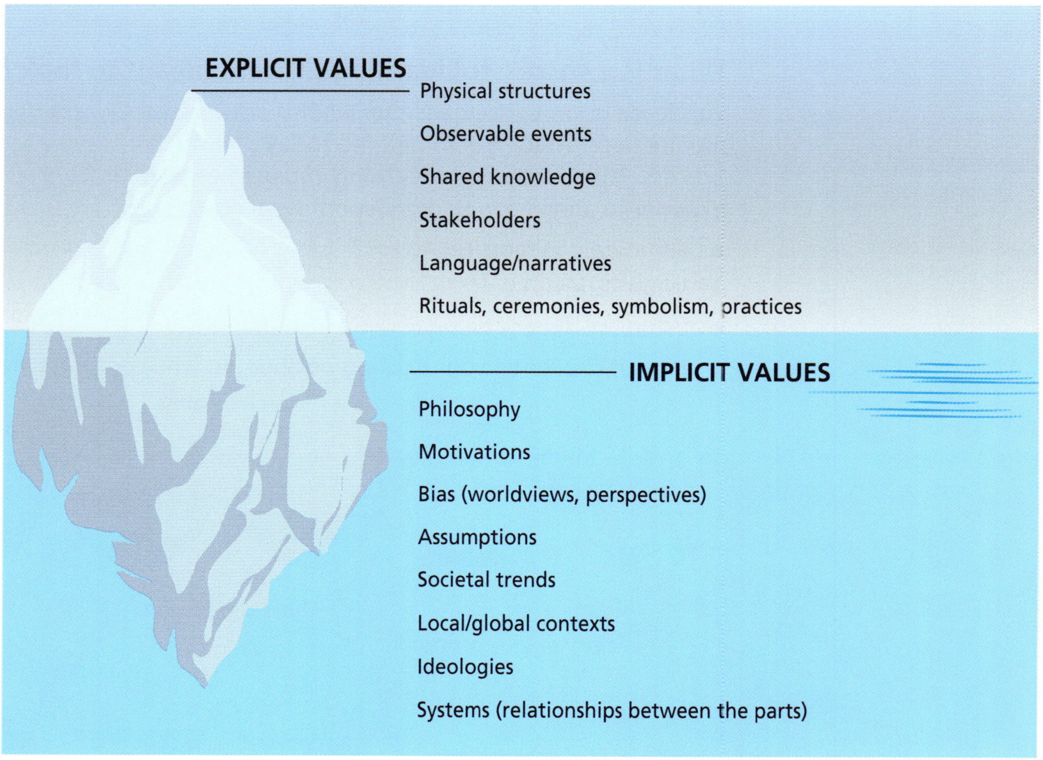

How can ethical values be both visible and hidden? (Source: IB RP TSM, p.39)

An iceberg model is used in 'systems thinking' as a way of analysing what affects us as individuals in the world around us. It is an analogy that works because it enables us to understand what is visible and easier to identify and then work, step by step, towards a deeper understanding of what is influencing us that is hidden. So, here, if we consider understanding ethical values, you would start out at the top of the iceberg, asking 'What's happening?' and 'What's happening over time?' as you look at the behaviour and actions around you and whether these stay the same or change over time. Then you start to consider what is less obvious and requires deeper thinking; you might ask 'What is influencing me/people to act like that?' and then look deeper at culture, asking 'What beliefs do I/people have that promotes that?'

For example, let's take a school community's attitude towards reducing plastic waste.

REAL-WORLD EXAMPLE

What's happening?

A group of students—the Zero Wasters—have campaigned in their school for there to be zero plastic bottle use with a ban in school. They want all schools in the local area to do the same.

What's happening over time?

The Zero Wasters wanted to understand the culture of waste in the school and monitored the amount of plastic waste generated by the school over time with a community engagement project. They found out that it was mainly students causing the waste proportionally, which was surprising as a survey revealed that the students supported doing something about the waste in the school. What also changed over time was the number of students who seemed to know about plastic waste and wanted to do something positive about it. This was reinforced with some of their studies in sciences, geography and environmental systems and societies as well as community projects.

What is influencing people to act like this?

The school is in a coastal local community. School initiatives, such as beach clean-ups, have shown the impact of plastic waste on their local environment, which many students have spoken about. So, the Zero Wasters discovered a desire for change on environmental issues among the student body, but students thought it was pointless as it wouldn't change anything. A closer look at some of the students' social media use and general media consumption does reveal support of action on climate change and not enough being done.

What beliefs do people have that promotes this?

A recent documentary revealed the way social media can make young people anxious with the sheer volume of information available. Perhaps that made the young people think it was pointless to act? The Zero Wasters found that interesting, but the wider global issue that concerns everyone is that plastic waste is a major contributor to climate change with carbon emissions. This is such a huge problem, it can be hard to feel positive when you don't feel you can do anything. The Zero Wasters concluded that if you could see a change immediately in your local community and the positive effect it might have, then this might not only change behaviour, but also create a more positive attitude towards acting on ethical values.

LEARNING ENGAGEMENT

Applying systems thinking to an ethical issue

Following this example of the 'Zero Wasters', consider an ethical issue that affects your school community. It might also be plastic waste or it might be a different issue. For example, you could consider: over-use of cars/under-use of public transport or bikes by parents and staff, ethically sourced food in your school canteen, limitations on access to education for the wider community or equal opportunities in sporting activities based on gender or age.

Use the same questions:

- What's happening?
- What's happening over time?
- What is influencing people to act like this?
- What beliefs do people have that promotes this?

Create a mind map of your possible ideas. What possible outcomes and solutions might this mind map suggest? Remember to use the example to help you consider different perspectives and ways of considering this.

The purpose of this exercise is not to have all the answers immediately but to see where your thinking might take you and how many stakeholders there are to consider in different communities. Not only this, it will also help you see what starts seemingly small and local, can connect to global concerns.

This opportunity will come up time and time again throughout your CP as you will have opportunities to engage in lots of different thinking skills—analytical, critical, creative, ethical, reflective and reflexive. This will sometimes be challenging and uncomfortable as it takes us out of our comfort zones, but by doing this, we are willing to question what we think is true rather than accept it without question.

In CE, this can lead you to a greater respect for cultural influences so we can make the right choices and take the right courses of action for our communities. In LCS, we can analyse language and culture in our individual values and how we can leverage that to impact our future. In PPS, you will reflect on how values and ethics work differently and similarly across different contexts and use strategies to align yourself and adapt. In the RP, you will draw upon all elements of your course to think critically about an ethical dilemma and form your own position.

Key terms

◆ **Reflection:** Metacognitive and process reflection involve examining past experiences and actions to improve future practice (focused on the 'how' of actions).

◆ **Reflexivity:** Critical and self-reflexivity involve examining our thoughts and beliefs, where they come from and the impact they have.

Reflection and reflexivity

You have already read that it is important to lead your own thinking in the CP and that you will engage in lots of different types of thinking. So it is important to spend some time here introducing you to another connecting feature through all the Core elements: **reflection** and **reflexivity**.

It may be that some of you have studied the IB before at MYP, or you may well be completely new to it. If it's the former, you may feel familiar with the term 'reflection' and know what it's all about; if the latter—well, you may feel a little baffled. Whatever you bring to this, have a completely blank slate and open mind to this section. This is all about finding new ways of thinking about thinking and thinking about our actions, and it's likely that you have not considered reflexivity before, whether you have already had experience of the IB or not.

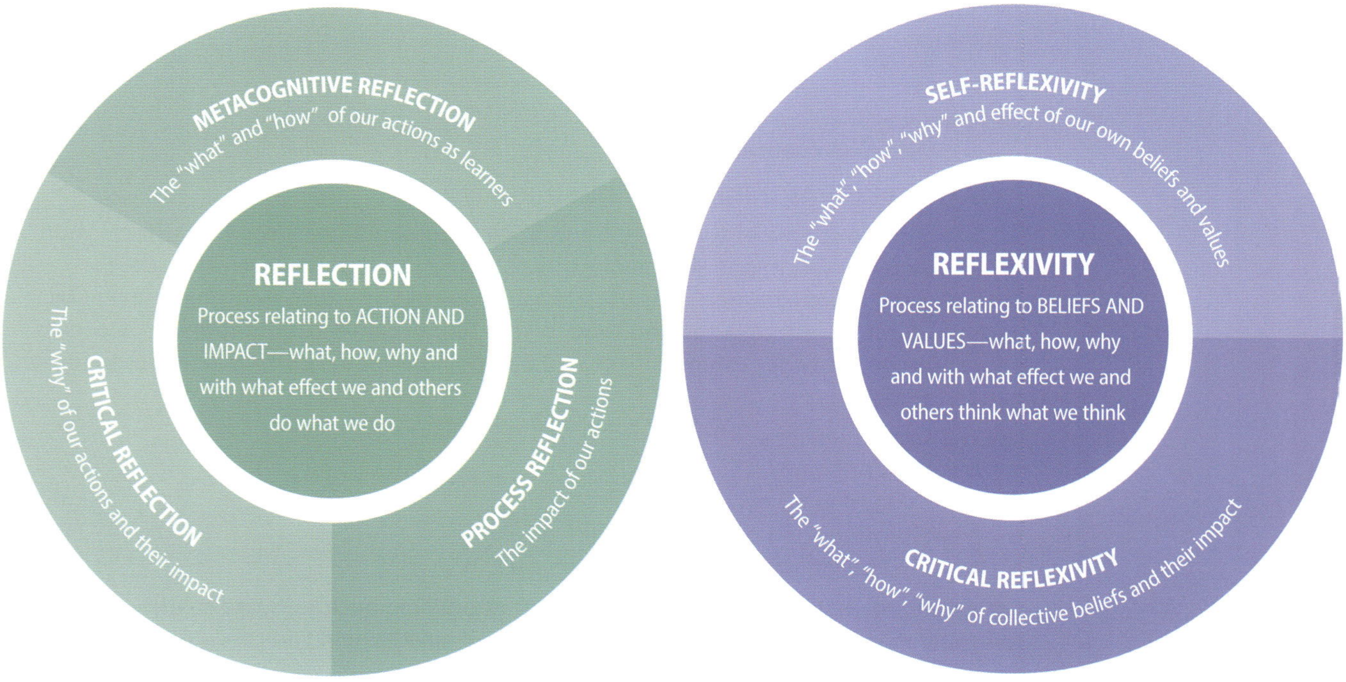

■ Reflection and reflexivity: Ways to widen and deepen your thinking (Source: IBO 2025b, p.28)

- **Metacognitive reflection** builds an awareness of one's own cognitive/learning processes and examines one's thinking, actions and goals, which leads to self-regulated learning.

  What does this look like? You consider the 'what' and 'how' about your actions as a learner.
- **Process reflection** starts with an experience and leads to new or changed understandings, insights and/or actions.

  What does this look like? You reflect on the impact of your actions.
- **Critical reflection** links reflection with analytical and critical thinking, encouraging students to focus on experiences and actions within a broader, systemic context.

  What does this look like? You think about why you took those actions and why they might have had an impact—and the implications of this.
- **Self-reflexivity** involves considering one's positionality, identifying and questioning one's own assumptions, biases and attitudes, understanding how they influence one's own responses and actions, and how they impact others, given the complexity and interconnectedness of roles and relationships.

  What does this look like? This means you identify what your own or others' beliefs are, how and why they have developed and the effect they have had on yourself and others.
- **Critical reflexivity** involves critically examining and challenging collective assumptions, values and frames of reference, understanding their contexts (e.g. cultural, societal, historical), how they shape perceptions and actions, how they impact others and how they might change in the future.

  What does this look like? You think past individual beliefs and consider whole systems, such as communities and cultures, and ask what and how they believe what they do and why this has the impact and implications it does.

(Source: IB RP guide (2025), p.60)

Reflection and reflexivity are not something new, introduced by the IB. The value of reflective and reflexive practice in business globally has long been recognized as a way to invest in the development of people and sustain organizations in the long term. This is beneficial for many reasons but generally, a commitment to reflective and reflexive practice forges new and deeper understandings of yourself and the people around you. With more understanding comes greater empathy and creativity as you are adaptable to your own and others' needs. Your reflective and reflexive skills are your internal compass, which you can use and develop in every aspect of your life. This tool helps you make sense of your experiences, choices and growth; in short, you can learn how to be your own coach and champion. Through reflective and reflexive skills, you will focus on the impact of actions and beliefs on individuals, groups and wider aspects of society.

LEARNING ENGAGEMENT

All this could sound complicated, but it does not have to be. Look at the following table and revisit your response to the learning engagement on p.xxiv. Identify where you looked at each stage of the table in your learning engagement mind map.

Table 2 Reasons for being reflective and reflexive

It helps you think critically about lived experiences happening both now and in the past.
It deepens thinking about actions and beliefs, helping you identify biases and assumptions you and others might hold.
When you understand yourself and others better, you are able to change.
Enables you to adapt as you understand why your and other's actions and beliefs might have the impact they have.

Making thinking easier

The first step in widening our understanding of reflection and reflexivity is to expand the vocabulary around it and link it to the skills you are already practising. What could being reflective and reflexive look like? When you know just how many diverse approaches you can take to thinking in this way, the more relevant it will be for you and you will see why it takes place so much in your CP course. You will notice that many of the ways we understand our actions and beliefs are actually things we are doing already; we just haven't thought about them that way or connected them to personal development. Reflective and reflexive questioning and thinking is not easy and involves deep introspection at times. However, Table 3 lists the aspects of learning that this type of thinking does make much easier.

Table 3

Self-awareness	Getting to know yourself so you can see when your own biases and assumptions are playing a part in your thinking.
Analytical thinking	Where you break down complex ideas and experiences into parts to identify possible patterns.
Critical thinking	Being able to analyse information objectively, breaking down assumptions and critiquing solutions without one's own biases getting in the way.
Evaluative thinking	Builds upon critical thinking and is a structured approach to inquiry that leads you to make decisions.
Problem-solving	Finding challenges, exploring possible solutions and making changes.
Adapting to change	Adjusting your approach as a response to new information.
Open-mindedness	A mindset of being responsive and non-judgemental to new ideas and perspectives.
Empathy	Considering the feelings of others and the value in doing so.

Reflection and reflexivity enable you to:

- assess your performance critically
- respond to failure and bounce back
- explore the strengths and weaknesses of arguments and your performance
- analyse your own and others' thoughts, feelings and behaviours
- identify and question assumptions, biases and values
- explore the connection between experiences and beliefs with actions and decisions
- consider multiple perspectives and possible solutions
- adapt and change approaches with confidence.

LEARNING ENGAGEMENT

Even though you may be at the start of your programme, it is a useful exercise to think about how you have already been using different types of reflective practice and where you might use it in the future. Using the table and bullet-point list above, discuss with a partner where you have used these skills already in your school career, and where you anticipate using them in the whole CP.

This learning engagement could be the type of activity you use in PPS as you explore different contexts and how you use skills.

How do I ask reflective and reflexive questions?

The following questions and question stems give you a feel for how each particular area of reflection or reflexivity can sound. You can use these to discuss all sorts of aspects of your course, such as: process, topic, research, ethical dilemma, format, learning, understanding, thinking, culture, language, community, skill, context, concept, actions, decisions or beliefs. This list is not exhaustive!

Table 4

Type of reflection/ reflexivity	Description	Questions
Metacognitive reflection	'What' and 'how' of actions	• What is your goal? • How could you approach this project/topic/research/ challenge/process? • What resources will I need? • How will I know I have been successful?
Process reflection	Effects of actions	• What did you learn from …? • How has this changed your thinking? • What are the next steps? • What would you do differently next time?
Critical reflection	'Why' of actions and effects	• Why did you choose this …? • Why did you act in this way/take this decision? • How have your actions/decisions had an impact on …? • How could you have acted differently or changed the outcome?
Self-reflexivity	Effect of belief of self on others	• How did your values/assumptions/biases affect the approach you took to this? • How could your values/assumptions/biases affect others?
Critical reflexivity	How/why these beliefs came about, and how/ why they have the impact they do	• Where do you think your bias about … comes from? • How has the process changed your understanding and your thinking? • What has influenced your perspective now?

Creating, experiencing, documenting and curating your experiences

One of the best ways to make reflective and reflexive practice part of your life is through journaling. Each element of the Core requires you to keep a centralized learning space, which you will use in different ways. In LCS, CE and RP this is referred to as the learning journal and in PPS it is called the portfolio. This is mandatory for completing each part of the Core and completion is verified and assessed by your school.

Top tip!

Reflection is not:

- **Objective:** The learning journal is a place to be refreshingly subjective.
- **Told in the third person:** You should write in the first person—this is all about what *you* think.
- **Descriptive:** No 'dear diary' entries here.
- **What you think you should write:** No performance journalling needed. Write down every thought, no matter how unrefined you might think it is. The worst that could happen is you give yourself something to laugh at when you look back on it.
- **Pointless:** Giving yourself even five minutes to gain some insight into what you have done and why you might believe something is never wasted.

Thinking can be messy

The nature of this centralized learning space differs depending on the subject; however, there is much in common which allows you freedom to find out what works for you. Take ownership of the learning journal or PPS portfolio—this is not something that is happening to you. You are creating it, and it is an opportunity to be practical and creative. Now that you have read about what can be involved in reflective and reflexive thinking, you know that this journal is not about performing and writing a superficial diary. This is a place for honesty, exploration, uncertainty and finding patterns in your own learning and thinking.

Approaches to journaling and keeping a portfolio

Your IB teachers may have a system in place for you to use, which undoubtedly will be about making this as accessible for you as possible. Schools often will set up or ask students to create a digital folder for journaling, which is great as it's also a place where you can keep resources, such as a question and activity bank for ways to use and interact with your work. You are not limited to digital, however, as there are many fans of physical journals as well. Many students keep both a notebook and a digital journal as it gives lots of choice for how you want to respond. After all, very few of us want to do things in one way all the time. However, you should ensure that whatever tools you use, there is one centralized space that acts as the gateway that outlines your learning journey. You can use the digital learning space as your central area where you can upload any notes, mind maps and diagrams from your physical journal. If you use a physical journal as your central space, then you can use tools such as QR codes to link to digital evidence.

Top tip!

You can make reflective and reflexive practice interesting by varying different aspects: the way you respond, who you work with on it and the setting you are working in.

The way you respond

You might choose a mixture of written, oral, visual and digital responses and move between them in your journal. Each of these are different modes of responding and you are encouraged to use different modes (multi-modality) in your CP course. There are good reasons not to get stuck in one way of responding.

For example, typing can be efficient but we can delete things so easily that we don't keep a record of our thought processes as well as handwriting and all its messiness can convey. Equally, writing can be a lot when you are trying to work out your thoughts, so voice notes can be really effective at capturing where your thoughts are at. Lastly, not only might you find drawing and visuals the best way to capture your thinking rather than blocks of writing, but you may find a cartoon, graph or painting which captures exactly what you want to say.

Who you work with

Reflections can be the result of your own independent work, but more often than not you will have worked with others. You might be reflecting on pair/group work where you all had very different perspectives or you were given feedback on some work. Equally, you might have taken part in a whole class debate in person or a discussion on a forum which has left you with challenges to your thinking.

The context of your experience

You might be reflecting on experiences from different contexts: school, course, professional or personal. You might be reflecting on informal learning engagements or formal assessments. Furthermore, you might be drawing upon your experiences with different people, be this teachers, family or experts from the wider community (e.g. leaders in a work-experience setting).

Using your journal in the Core

All aspects of the Core use a journal or portfolio, and there will be much shared practice. It's good to consider the unique nature of each Core element, however, so the journal or portfolio's role can start to take shape in your mind. This is another part of finding a system that works for you and making the most of it. You might use the same digital platform divided into different sections for all the Core components or have a physical journal that does the same. As long as you have a clear space for each area of the Core, it will work.

■ Learning isn't a straight road; your path will vary.

LEARNING ENGAGEMENT

Using the information below on the Core components, create a visual that clearly captures the similar different ways you will use a journal or portfolio to support your learning journey in each Core component. For example, this could be a mind map or a Venn diagram.

■ Language and cultural studies

The learning journal in LCS documents the whole learning journey and your specific learning story. It evidences your participation, any instruction you received and assessment. It is, moreover, a place for reflection and multiple perspectives as you paint a picture of your linguistic and cultural repertoire over the CP course. The LCS section will give you lots of ideas on how to keep your journal, but initial ideas could include your initial language and cultural portrait, ongoing reflections as you revisit this portrait and embark on new research and learning engagements, as well as review points with your supervisor. Your supervisor will monitor the learning journal but will not tell you exactly how to keep it, so you can be creative in the way you do it.

■ Community engagement

In CE, the learning journal informs your assessment; that means you use it as a place to record ongoing experiences, whether that be working on your project or informal conversations you have outside of them. It is also a place to inform and document specific review points with your teacher and class where you can take a step back and consider your learning journey. CE is very much about dialogue and sharing, so expect to use your learning journal as a companion to conversation and a place for all your thoughts that develop about yourself and your relationship with the concept of community.

Personal and professional skills—Portfolio

Through an inquiry process of 'focus, explore, act, reflect and share', the PPS portfolio has two purposes: it serves as a place where you create responses to your inquiries, but it is also a place where you curate your learning engagements as a final assessment. When you explore this section of the book, there will be lots of ideas on how you might use the portfolio, but the overriding idea is that you first use it as a holding folder of all the work, conversations, experiences and, of course, reflections you have over the 100-hour course. However, progressively throughout the course you will be asked to self-assess and present on specific learning goals, culminating in a final curated portfolio where you evidence your achievement through the requirements of the PPS learning outcomes.

Reflective project

In the RP, it possibly will not come as a surprise that the learning journal is for your reflections on your research and process, as well as a place to signpost how your beliefs and values are changing and being challenged. When you come to write your written reflection (up to 1,000 words for the reflective project—final reflection form), you will use your learning journal to track your process and how your thinking has changed and deepened over the course. One of the most important functions of the learning journal is that it serves to authenticate your reflective project as your own work. It provides the basis for your discussions with your supervisor and for your presentations to your peers, as well as a place to record feedback. It is not formally assessed by the IB, unlike your project, but it is a mandatory part of the process. Without the learning journal, your work cannot be verified as your own.

Summary

All learning journals and the PPS portfolio are a place for:

- revision and refining goals
- gathering evidence and artefacts
- recording feedback (from teachers, peers, others)
- making reflections
- understanding and engaging with concepts
- demonstrating learning outcomes.

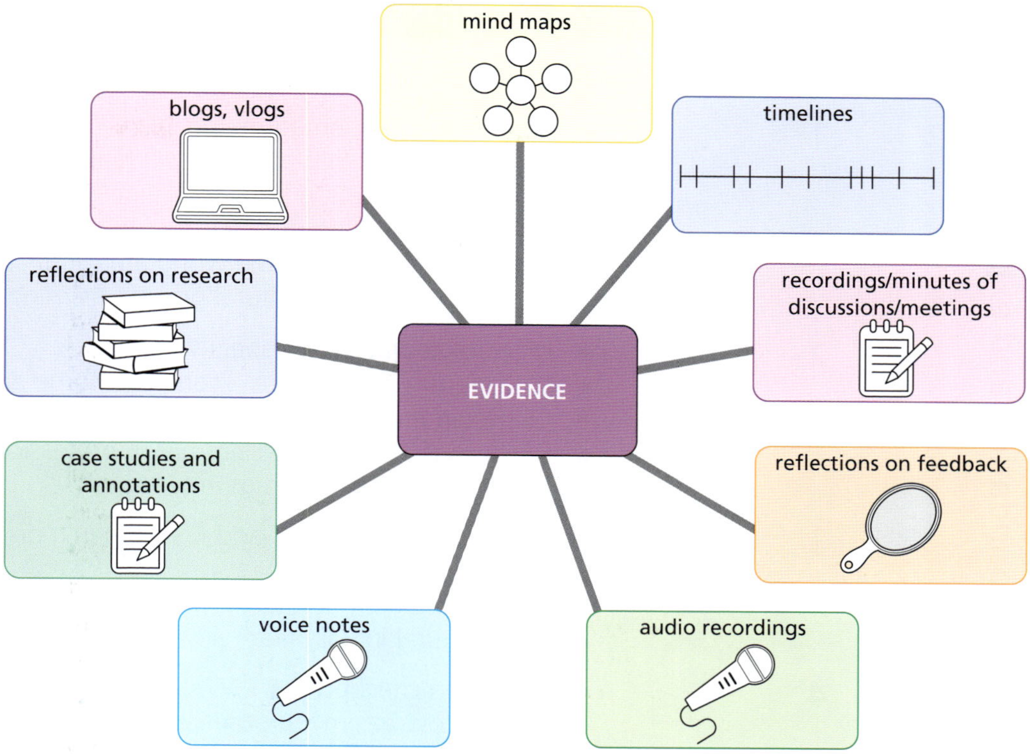

■ Digital or physical evidence (or both!) could take all sorts of forms

Using this CP Core textbook

This is not a manual; it's a companion. You don't have to read it from cover to cover. You can jump around, return to certain sections when you need inspiration and guidance and use this book as a mirror and a map.

■ Create your own adventure

Each section of this book is designed to be a complete companion for you as a student through specific aspects of the CP Core. Your teachers have Core guides and teacher support material available from the IB ready to use, and this book supports you as the student and helps you to get the most out of your experience. With that in mind, remember that:

- You may use the LCS, CE, PPS and RP sections simultaneously and move around between them.
- All of the sections are designed not just to support your transversal skill development, but to enable you to be increasingly independent over the course of the two years you are taking the CP.
- Your teachers and mentors will also find this book useful as it enables them to see the course from your perspective and what will help you.

Table 5 An example two-year overview for RP, PPS, CE and LCS

Year	Month	Activities
1: Foundation and exploration	1	• Welcome and orientation: Intro to CP Core and learning journals • Theme/concept: Self-awareness, identity, agency, optimism • PPS: Communication skills and team-building • CE: Explore definitions of 'community' • Activity: 'What makes the world amazing?' student reflection • LCS: Start language/cultural portrait learning engagement
	2	• PPS: Collaboration, perspective-taking • LCS: Identity and culture—compare home and host cultures • CE: Begin mapping local community connections • RP: Intro to ethics and dilemmas in professions • Activity: Mind-map community issues
	3	• RP: Ethical case studies and first research discussions • PPS: Ethical reasoning • CE: Choose area of interest for engagement • LCS: Cultural inquiry (interviews, exploration)
	4	• Reflection checkpoint #1: What have I discovered about myself so far? How has my mindset shifted? • CE: Design an initial engagement plan • RP: Shortlist potential dilemma topics
	5	• RP: Develop possible research questions • PPS: Time management and mindset for long-term success • CE: Begin first round of engagement • LCS: Explore language and worldview
	6	• RP: Choose ethical dilemma and refine working question • Workshop: Research skills (bias, source credibility, AI use) • CE: Reflect on early engagement experiences • LCS: Learning journal check-in
	7	• RP: Source gathering and journaling • PPS: Emotional intelligence and conflict resolution • CE: Systems awareness in local contexts • Activity: Interview someone in your career field
	8	• RP: Develop argument structure • CE: Continue/expand engagement • LCS: Review point 2 • PPS: Transferable skills reflection
	9	• RP: Outline or concept map due • CE: Peer-sharing of progress • Reflection checkpoint #2: What values have shaped my actions? What do I want to build towards? • LCS: Showcase a learning journal artefact
	10	• Year-end reflection and planning ahead: • Journal reflection and goals for the year ahead • RP: Summer thinking task (optional prep work) • CE: Final check-in or celebration of Phase 1 • LCS: Optional student-led presentations

Year	Month	Activities
2: Agency and completion	1	• RP: Finalize plan and research question • Begin writing (intro and structure) • CE: Re-engage or pivot based on feedback • PPS: Reflection on motivation and purpose
	2	• RP: Draft 1 of main body • CE: Apply feedback from previous year • PPS: Critical thinking and resilience • LCS: Focus on area of exploration
	3	• RP: Draft 2 submitted—feedback and edits • PPS: Reflexivity, bias, and clarity in writing • CE: Document personal and collective growth and impact • LCS: Link cultural learning to aspirations connected to area of exploration
	4	• RP: Final revision, citation check, bibliography • PPS: Communication and professionalism • *Viva voce* preparation begins • CE: Final reflection writing
	5	• RP: Final submission • *Viva voce* presentation • PPS: Looking ahead—careers and transitions • CE: Prepare evidence of impact and learning
	6	• PPS: Resilience, change and global awareness • LCS: Global cultural issues in your field • CE: Optional creative expression of project

	7	• Learning journal synthesis:
		  • Reflective project
		  • CE and LCS intersections
		  • Self- and systems-learning
		• PPS: Future-ready skills
		• Final reflections:
		  • What changed in how you think?
		  • How have your actions evolved?
		  • What do you value most now?
		  • Share project journey with peers

	8	• Programme showcase or celebration • Portfolio and journal finalization • Student-led presentations, community sharing or CP exhibition • Optional peer-led well-being reflections

Suggested CP Core monthly timeline

You might wonder how the CP Core could build together and work over two years. It's most important to stress that the CP process can look like many different things—that is the beauty of the flexibility of the CP. So Table 5 (on the following spread) is not set in stone or a requirement of the CP in any way. It is merely to help you visualize how the course might connect together and develop over the two years.

LEARNING ENGAGEMENT

Using this example of a core timeline, make a note of what excites you, what you have further questions about, and what you are curious to know more about. Think about this first by yourself and then share with a partner or as a class to compare and contrast your responses. From here, you can discuss ideas you might have to explore further and how you can all contribute to the programme's success.

Conclusion

We may have reached the end of the opening section, but this is just the start for you.

Remember the 'stubborn optimism' and 'growth mindset' with which we started this section? This weaves its way through your whole CP experience as you embark on becoming the lifelong learner who is so many things: the curious explorer, the skill practitioner, the ethical decision-maker, the community change-maker, the internationally minded communicator. As you build skills over the next two years of the CP, remember that it is never about perfection, but about how much you can learn about yourself and the world through all the ups and downs of the whole process. An authentic and relevant education with you at the very centre of it.

1 Community engagement (CE)

1.1 Understanding CE

INQUIRY QUESTIONS

- What is CE and how does it fit into a CP and IB education?
- What are the aims of CE?
- What are the key guidelines of CE?
- What is the role of the learning journal in CE?
- How does CE connect to the other CP components?
- How does CE connect to the other IB frameworks?
- What are the CE requirements?
- How do you approach reflective and reflexive practice in CE?
- How is CE assessed?
- How can you take care of your well-being while engaged in CE?

1.1.1 What is community engagement?

Community engagement (CE) is an active process of working collaboratively with communities in order to create meaningful solutions to complex issues that affect them. This includes learning in partnership with representatives from the community, helping to develop the ability of a community to solve problems and achieve tasks. It includes building relationships and making decisions with the community.

CE is one of the four components of the CP Core. It is a requirement for all CP students and takes place over the two years of your studies. Together with the other three Core components—language and cultural studies (LCS), personal and professional skills (PPS) and the reflective project (RP)—CE supports you in developing and embodying the attributes of the learner profile.

CE offers you opportunities to learn *in*, *from* and *with* communities. It teaches you how to ethically apply knowledge and skills by using both your cognitive and affective learning. It invites you to engage with communities in **dialogic**, **reciprocal**, reflective and reflexive ways, and expand your understanding of complex **systems**. By engaging in inquiry-based processes, you will learn to explore CE dimensions, prepare for community engagements, foster community relationships grounded in ethical actions, and evaluate and share your work with others.

Key terms

◆ **Dialogic:** A reciprocal style of communication where different perspectives and viewpoints can arise, people can openly respond, and inquiry and the co-construction of knowledge are centred.

◆ **Reciprocal:** Reciprocal communication and relationships are built on respectful, shared efforts with mutual, two-way contributions that benefit everyone involved.

◆ **Systems:** Sets of interacting or interdependent elements that use processes or procedures to work towards a common purpose. Social, economic, political and ecological systems provide a lens for exploring structure, interdependence, complexity and change in the human and natural worlds.

Top tip!

CE is not meant to be approached in a linear way. It is a process-based journey that will require you to revisit each of the CE sections in this book multiple times. The CE aims and learning outcomes are deeply interconnected, which requires a well-rounded approach to thinking and doing. You can support a well-rounded learning process by understanding CE sections as having a modular and non-linear structure. This means that the chapters are divided up into distinct parts and you do not have to engage with them in a set order. Headings and summaries will help you locate CE concepts and chapter themes.

Relational ways of being that lead to ethical action

Community engagement

Community engagement aims

In CE, you will gain a deeper understanding of how you can positively impact the communities you belong to, both now and in the future. Through CE, you learn how to ethically engage with the community in compassionate and informed ways.

The aims of CE are for you to:

- build relationships and engage in reciprocal collaborations that contribute to individual and collective well-being
- develop awareness of the complexity of, and appreciation for, the diverse ways of knowing, doing and being
- cultivate compassionate integrity, ethical solidarity and **active hope**
- embrace reflective and reflexive practice as tools for building a cognitive and affective foundation that supports lifelong learning and global citizenship.

Central to your CE journey are the relationships you develop with the community. CE places value on respect and collaboration leading to ethical action. You will need to approach community engagements with a spirit of humility, openness and critical curiosity. Through CE experiences and relationships, you will grow as a person and develop your academic, civic, social, cognitive and affective skills. You will also cultivate an attitude of openness, solidarity and **compassion** for your communities and the larger social and environmental systems in which they are embedded.

Throughout this process, you will:

- develop and apply critical- and creative-thinking skills, social and affective skills, and ethical reasoning
- reflect on your background and ways of thinking, developing the ability to create caring relationships and engage in place-based learning
- gain a deeper understanding of local and global issues, and develop the ability to understand and ethically engage with complexity
- develop a sense of individual and collective responsibility, and the capacity to become an active participant in realizing individual and collective goals.

Key terms

◆ **Active hope:** Authentic, action-oriented hopefulness that combines criticality and a clear view of reality with identification of what we truly long for and the determination to act and move in that direction.

◆ **Compassion:** The capacity to both understand conceptually and empathetically what it is like to be an actor in a system, combined with the intention to act in support of others who might be impacted by the unintended consequences of human behaviour within larger, interconnected systems.

Key guidelines

These guidelines will give you a deeper understanding of CE.

CHOICE OF ENGAGEMENTS

Student driven: You are required to be an active participant in your own learning process. While your teachers will offer support and guidance, it is expected that you will use your voice throughout your CE journey so that you can co-create, share and collaborate with the community.

1 **Relevant opportunities or challenges:** It is essential that you research challenges and opportunities that are relevant to you and the community. The importance of the engagement needs to be clearly and explicitly defined by you *and* the community, keeping in mind that there needs to be a common understanding of the opportunity, and a shared vision of the desired outcomes. If these outcomes change over time, there must be continued mutual understanding between you and your community partners.

2 **Dimensions and principles:**

   a Your engagements need to include different parts of the community: personal connections, relationships with others, and how everything works together as a whole, including different environmental and/or social systems. You can't engage ethically with a community without acknowledging these complex and interconnected layers. Your engagements need to reflect an understanding that communities overlap, intersect or are nested within each other; individuals identify with, and participate in, multiple communities. Communities themselves are embedded and operate within larger systems. In some cases, the meaning of 'community' may be straightforward, and in other cases, it may require more thought and deliberation before you come to a full understanding of the meaning of 'community'.

   b You must bring an actively respectful communication and reflective and reflexive thinking to your community engagements.

LEARNING AND PARTICIPATION

1 You are the one responsible for shaping your CE journey, with your teacher's support.
2 You are required to participate in the guided-learning time organized by your school.
3 Your active engagements need to be sustained over the course of the two years of the programme.

ASSESSMENT

1 You are required to maintain a learning journal in a format that you decide upon and discuss with your teacher.
2 You need to prepare for and participate in the three review points throughout the two years of the programme.
3 Through your engagements, you will need to demonstrate the four learning outcomes.

> The four learning outcomes articulate what you are able to do at some point during your community engagement journey. They are derived from and embed with the principles of engagement and the dimensions of a community (see Section 1.1.6).

1.1.2 The learning journal

You are required to keep a learning journal throughout the two years of your CE learning journey, which must be sustained throughout the two years of the programme. It is important you understand the value of the learning journal, and it is a good idea to set it up and contribute to it early on. Your teacher will explain the fundamentals of the learning journal so you can set it up and have it ready for the learning engagements that happen throughout this section.

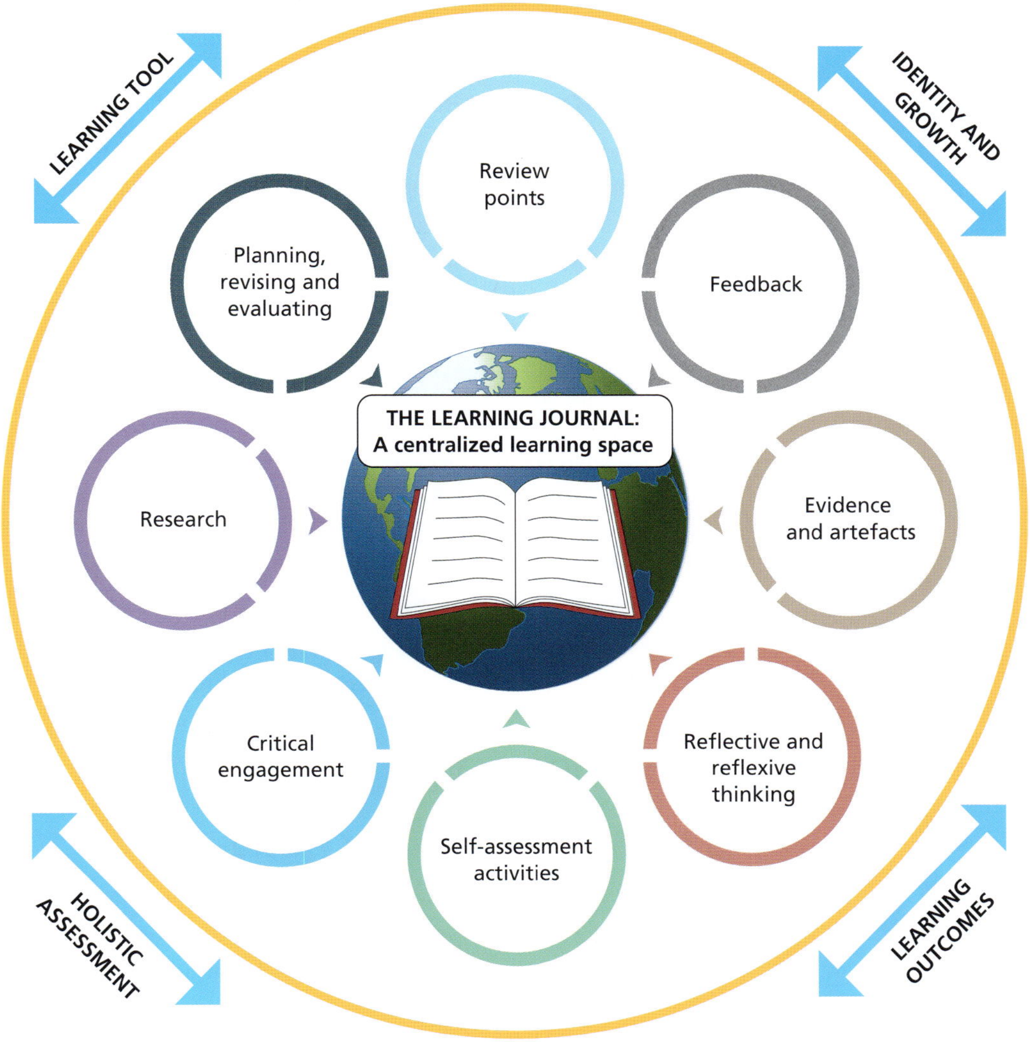

■ An overview of the learning journal

The learning journal is a centralized learning space where you will show evidence of your sustained engagements and your demonstration of the learning outcomes. The learning journal will help you hone your approaches to learning (ATL) skills, connect more deeply with the learner profile, understand your identity and growth, and help you prepare for assessments that reflect not just one competency or skill but what you have learned overall. You will use it for planning, exploration, reflection and reflexivity, and it will house meaningful information about your CE explorations.

The learning journal will help you become a more independent learner and the more you add to it, the more it becomes 'yours'—your own place to explore creativity, innovation, analysis, research and complex ideas. The artefacts you place in your learning journal will contain evidence of your learning and growth. Artefacts include things like annotated photographic evidence, letters, artwork, reflections, research, reports and digital presentations. These artefacts will provide you and your teacher with essential feedback on your learning. You want your learning journal to reflect varied numbers and types of artefacts that demonstrate your reflective and reflexive thinking. You will also want to track your constructive feedback in your learning journal as this will help you see your growth over time.

What format can the learning journal take?

Your teacher may set learning journal guidelines to support your individual development and/or your school's local context. It is important that you update your learning journal on a frequent basis so it authentically captures your CE journey. You also need to construct it in a way that allows for oversight by the school and being amenable to submission to the IB, if required. You may choose the format and style of your learning journal, and this may include:

Table 1.1

Multimodal	A digital learning journal with photographic and video evidence.
	A physical learning journal with tools such as QR codes to link to digital evidence, such as videos.
	Combining physical and digital elements to benefit from a range of modes that enable you to best express yourself in personal and creative ways, and to effectively capture your learning.
Multilingual	Multilingual elements, such as the primary language of your school/school's location and/or your first or best language.

Maintaining your learning journal will be a continuous process of observation, documentation and reflection, and you are expected to highlight both strengths and challenges.

1.1.3 Connecting CE

Connecting CE to the CP Core

CE supports the rest of the CP Core by helping you to develop a deeper sense of ethics, reflection and reflexivity, reciprocity and systems awareness. Throughout this section, you will have many opportunities to improve your understanding of these topics and how you can apply this to the rest of the CP Core.

Links to language and cultural studies (LCS), personal and professional skills (PPS), and the reflective project (RP) can be found in Table 1.2 (on pp.8–9).

Connecting CE to other IB frameworks

All four IB programmes emphasize developing lifelong learners who can make a difference and have a positive impact on the world. The following concepts are central to all IB programmes and they help students embody the IB mission:

1 **International-mindedness** 'is a multifaceted concept that captures a way of thinking, being and acting characterized by an openness to the world and a recognition of our deep interconnectedness to others' (IBO 2019, p.2). It requires curiosity and a willingness to show interest in people, places, things and issues that might, at first, seem different,

unfamiliar or challenging. Internationally minded people approach the unknown with curiosity and inquisitiveness rather than making quick judgements or retreating to what is familiar. They see learning as lifelong and life-wide, and they develop the skills and dispositions needed for effective research and inquiry.

2 The ten attributes of the **learner profile** underpin and are central to understanding what it means to be internationally minded (IBO 2019, pp.3–4).

3 **Approaches to learning** (ATL) **skills** support students in cultivating the dispositions, strategies and practices that foster international-mindedness, ensuring that students have the skills required to embody the learner profile.

CE and international-mindedness

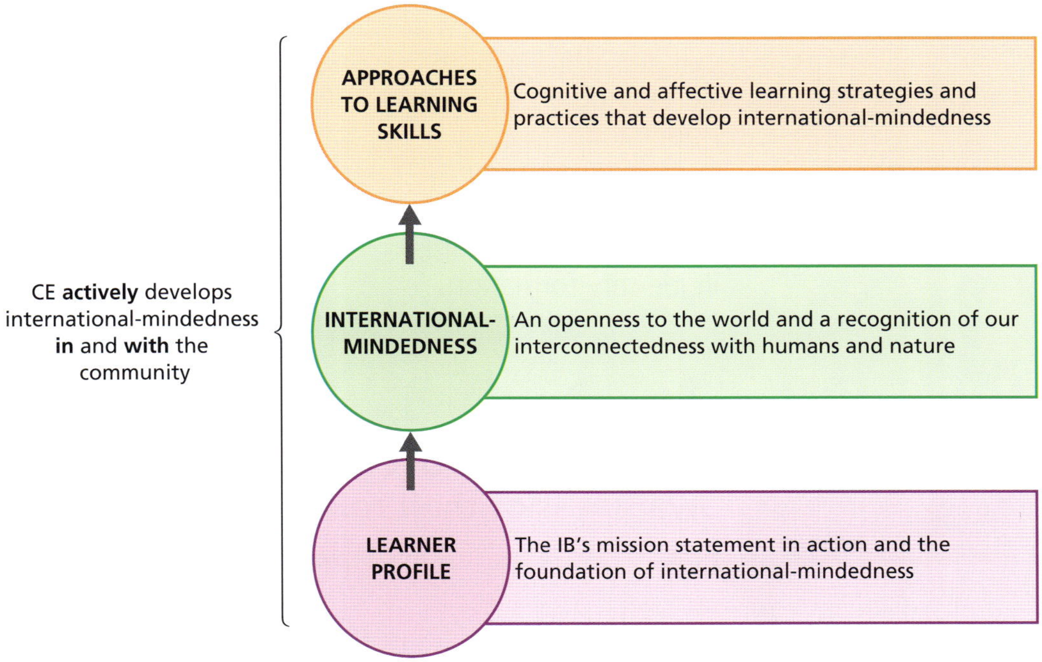

■ Ways in which CE develops international-mindedness

International-mindedness involves open-minded inquiry into diverse perspectives, a critical appreciation of multiple points of view, and a desire for positive action.

CE allows you to engage with local and global issues and to practise intercultural understanding, as well as developing respect through interaction with diverse communities. This includes working with communities to collaboratively explore and respond to relevant issues while fostering an appreciation and understanding of diversity and justice. CE challenges you to critically consider **power** and **privilege** and become aware of the complex nature of local and global challenges, cultivating a sense of responsibility towards the wider world.

As an internationally minded student, you respect and value differences in others, actively learning about local, national and global issues. You show empathy for others and care about the world around you. You seek harmony and understanding when interacting with people from cultural contexts different from your own, and you are open-minded enough to realize that there are always opportunities to learn from others. International-mindedness is part of all aspects of the IB curriculum and it is incorporated into what you learn and how you are taught through concept-based inquiry approaches.

Key terms

◆ **Power:** This refers to the hierarchical structures, relations and processes that are formed by social, cultural, political, economic and historical factors, and that involve a person's or group's capacity to exert influence, domination or control over other individuals and groups. Power is not equally distributed in all contexts.

◆ **Privilege:** A social advantage that only one person or group of people have, usually as a result of their social, economic, sexual, racial, identity, position or viewpoints.

Table 1.2 Linking CE to LCS, PPS and the RP

CE LEARNING OUTCOME 1: Foster reciprocal and dialogic engagement		
LCS	**PPS**	**RP**
CE supports you in skilfully negotiating an understanding of meaning in diverse situations within and across languages/ cultures. This includes developing an understanding and appreciation of the mediating role of languages and cultures in identity formation.	CE supports you to develop more effective communication skills as you seek to open dialogue that fosters reciprocal and ethical engagement when participating with and contributing to communities.	CE supports you to practise reciprocity in structured dialogues, such as interviews and *viva voces*.

CE LEARNING OUTCOME 2: Explore systems and develop awareness of their roles within these		
LCS	**PPS**	**RP**
CE deepens your knowledge and understanding of systems thinking. Language is a system and a social practice. When using language, you will be engaging with relational/cultural/ social systems and this may include exploring larger local/global systems.	CE helps you identify, analyse, and explore relational/ social systems and understand your roles within systems. This will support you to develop strategies and practices to navigate, challenge and thrive within those systems, both personally and professionally.	CE supports your knowledge and understanding of personal, relational and larger systems. This supports your RP work, which asks you to consider an **ethical dilemma** arising within the context of human and/or ecological systems.

Key term

◆ **Ethical dilemma:** A choice between two (or more) conflicting values or courses of action, where each alternative has its own drawbacks or may lead to undesirable consequences. Because neither alternative provides an ideal solution, there is no clear-cut answer and an ethical decision is difficult to make.

CE LEARNING OUTCOME 3: Develop, articulate and enact ethical thinking and action

LCS	PPS	RP
CE will help you develop a deeper knowledge and understanding of ethical philosophies and paradigms, and this will influence your decision-making processes as you apply ethics in community engagements. This will support your explorations of ethics and ethical practices within the context of language and culture.	CE supports PPS by asking you to draw on interpersonal and intrapersonal skills, such as ethics, as you collaborate with the community, particularly within diverse settings.	While developing your CE engagements, you will learn about the nature of ethical dilemmas through real-life, community based situations. This will support your ability to view your ethical dilemma from diverse perspectives.

CE LEARNING OUTCOME 4: Engage in reflective and reflexive practice

LCS	PPS	RP
CE and LCS invite you to engage in ongoing reflection and analyses of your positionality, perspectives, and biases as you engage with wider cultural/social factors and contexts. Both Core components require you to challenge your own perspectives and remain open to changing them. This helps cultivate the ability to hear others' perspectives and understand diverse contexts.	CE and PPS offer you ongoing opportunities for reflection and reflexivity, practised in community, personal or professional settings. It is essential to reflect on your own actions and impact in personal and professional settings while also examining your beliefs and values. This will help you ethically navigate sensitive topics and build bridges across differences.	CE and RP ask you to explore various perspectives on ethics and ethical dilemmas, which is an essential part of deeper investigations, investigating multiple perspectives and making skilful decisions.

LEARNING ENGAGEMENT

An internationally minded student

Individual reflective practice

Here are some personal characteristics that have been identified as essential in an internationally minded student:

- knowledge, understanding and appreciation of different cultures
- self-awareness
- empathy
- an ability to collaborate with people from different backgrounds
- an ever-deepening knowledge and understanding of global issues
- an ability to see oneself as interconnected with other beings on the planet, including humans, non-humans and the natural world
- language skills.

The table below lists the IB learner profile attributes. Try to connect these with the list of characteristics given above by adding the characteristics to the relevant section of the column on the right.

Table 1.3

Inquirers	They develop their natural curiosity. They acquire the skills necessary to conduct inquiry and research and show independence in learning. They actively enjoy learning and this love of learning will be sustained throughout their lives.	
Knowledgeable	They explore concepts, ideas and issues that have local and global significance. In so doing, they acquire in-depth knowledge and develop understanding across a broad and balanced range of disciplines.	
Thinkers	They exercise initiative in applying thinking skills critically and creatively to recognize and approach complex problems, and make reasoned, ethical decisions.	
Communicators	They understand and express ideas and information confidently and creatively in more than one language and in a variety of modes of communication. They work effectively and willingly in collaboration with others.	
Principled	They act with integrity and honesty, with a strong sense of fairness, justice and respect for the dignity of individuals, groups and communities. They take responsibility for their own actions and the consequences that accompany them.	
Open-minded	They understand and appreciate their own cultures and personal histories, and are open to the perspectives, values and traditions of other individuals and communities. They are accustomed to seeking and evaluating a range of points of view, and are willing to grow from the experience.	
Caring	They show empathy, compassion and respect towards the needs and feelings of others. They have a personal commitment to service and act to make a positive difference to the lives of others and to the environment.	
Risk-takers	They approach unfamiliar situations and uncertainty with courage and forethought, and have the independence of spirit to explore new roles, ideas and strategies. They are brave and articulate in defending their beliefs.	
Balanced	They understand the importance of intellectual, physical and emotional balance to achieve personal well-being for themselves and others.	
Reflective	They give thoughtful consideration to their own learning and experience. They are able to assess and understand their strengths and limitations in order to support their learning and personal development.	

CE and the learner profile

Through a deepening understanding of the IB learner profile, CE supports the development of your international-mindedness. The learner profile attributes reflect the well-rounded nature of an IB education and highlight the importance of nurturing curiosity, cultivating compassion, and developing the knowledge and skills needed to care responsibly for our planet. By developing connections within the community, including human-to-human and human-to-non-human/nature, you will examine your own identity and values through the lens of the learner profile. CE will give you a greater ability to be able to reflect on your thinking and actions in relation to the learner profile.

LEARNING ENGAGEMENT

CE and the learner profile

Collective reflexive practice

1. With a peer, discuss each of the attributes of the IB learner profile and how they relate to your own identity, beliefs and values.
2. Next, discuss how each IB learner profile attribute will support you throughout your CE journey.
3. Share back with the whole group.
4. Record your thoughts in your learning journal, noting if any of your perspectives and viewpoints about CE and the learner profile have changed.

Approaches to learning in CE

CE supports you to develop your own set of skills to become a self-regulated learner who can ask good questions, pursue their aspirations, set effective goals and foster the resilience, commitment and determination to achieve them. These skills help to support your ability to make decisions and take action, encouraging you to see your learning as an active and dynamic process. They underpin your ability to engage in dialogic, reciprocal and reflexive ways, and to develop a better understanding of what the community needs. The ATL skills are given in Table 1.4 below.

Table 1.4 ATL skills

Communication	Exchanging thoughts, messages, and information effectively through: • interactions, including effective communication, intercultural understanding, non-verbal and digital literacy, collaborative engagement and digital participation • language, including critical reading and research, effective writing, structured and logical organization of academic work, mathematical and symbolic literacy, and academic integrity and citation.
Social	Working effectively with others through: • respectful and compassionate engagement • collaboration and teamwork • conflict resolution and decision-making • leadership and advocacy • constructive communication.

Self-management	**Organization skills:** Managing your time and tasks effectively through: • effective planning and organization • strategic learning productivity • appropriate technology use and preparedness. **Affective skills:** Managing your state of mind through: • mindfulness • perseverance • emotional management • self-motivation • resilience. **Reflection:** (Re)considering what has been learned, and choosing and using the ATL skills through: • reflective and adaptive learning • thoughtful inquiry • analytical reasoning and problem-solving • ethical awareness.
Research	**Information literacy:** Finding, interpreting, judging and creating information through: • information gathering and analysis • effective processing and presentation • research and communication literacy. **Media literacy:** Interacting with media to use and create ideas and information through: • research and information management • critical awareness and perspective • effective communication and analysis.
Thinking	**Critical thinking:** Analysing and evaluating issues and ideas through: • critical observation and problem-solving • argument formulation and evaluation • creative thinking and perspective-taking • solution generation and analysis • complex systems exploration. **Creativity and innovation:** Developing things and ideas that never existed before through: • creative ideation and problem-solving • innovation and design • critical and flexible thinking • conceptual thinking. **Transfer thinking:** Utilising skills and knowledge in multiple contexts through: • cross-disciplinary learning and application • knowledge integration and creation • adaptation and transfer.

The following questions can help you consider how the approaches to learning (ATL) skills can be developed in CE. As you read them, you might want to record your thoughts in your learning journal.

Communication skills:

- How can you evaluate the effectiveness of your communication skills? How does self-awareness impact your ability to effectively communicate with people in the community?
- How can you develop your active listening abilities to be able to consider different perspectives?
- How can effective communication help develop intercultural understanding?
- How can you consider digital literacy in your CE work?
- How do you understand the role of non-verbal communication in dialogues?

Social skills:

- How can you use your collaboration skills to help create a safe classroom environment—one that allows diverse perspectives to be explored in respectful ways?
- How can your relationships in the classroom be a model for the relationships you develop within the community?
- How can you develop and maintain collaborative relationships within the community?
- How can you use constructive and respectful communication in conflict resolution and decision-making processes?

Self-management skills:

- What inspiring examples of community initiatives could motivate you to participate in CE in an active and sustained way?
- How can you use your affective skills (mindfulness, perseverance, emotional management, self-motivation and resilience) when you experience disagreements, discomfort and challenges in CE?
- How can you use reflective practice to support your learning?

Research skills:

- How can research help you identify, explore and understand opportunities and challenges in CE?
- How can you take into account bias and AI-generated materials when researching?

Thinking skills:

- Through critical thinking and flexible perspective taking, how can you understand your roles and responsibilities within the communities you are a part of?
- What different perspectives can you apply to understand relevant issues?
- How can you use flexible thinking to understand different perspectives?
- How do you know you are making ethical decisions that support the community?

LEARNING ENGAGEMENT

CE and the ATL skills

One way of developing your ATL skills is by mapping how they can be applied in CE. With a peer, your teacher or a group of students, create a visual representation of the ATL skills. You may choose to create a mind map, table, puzzle, collage, compass or something else that represents your thinking. The objective is to connect the ATL categories (and possibly subcategories) to what you currently understand about the aims, dimensions and principles of CE. This activity is meant to spark your initial thinking and imagination around the development and application of the ATL skills in relation to future community engagements. You can revisit this representation in the later stages of your CE journey to see if and how your thinking has changed.

1.1.4 CE requirements

CE relies on learning and engagements that happen both in the classroom and within the broader community. Your learning process will include a mix of *guided-learning time* in the classroom, as well as *active engagements* beyond the classroom. These contexts are distinct, yet interrelated and interconnected.

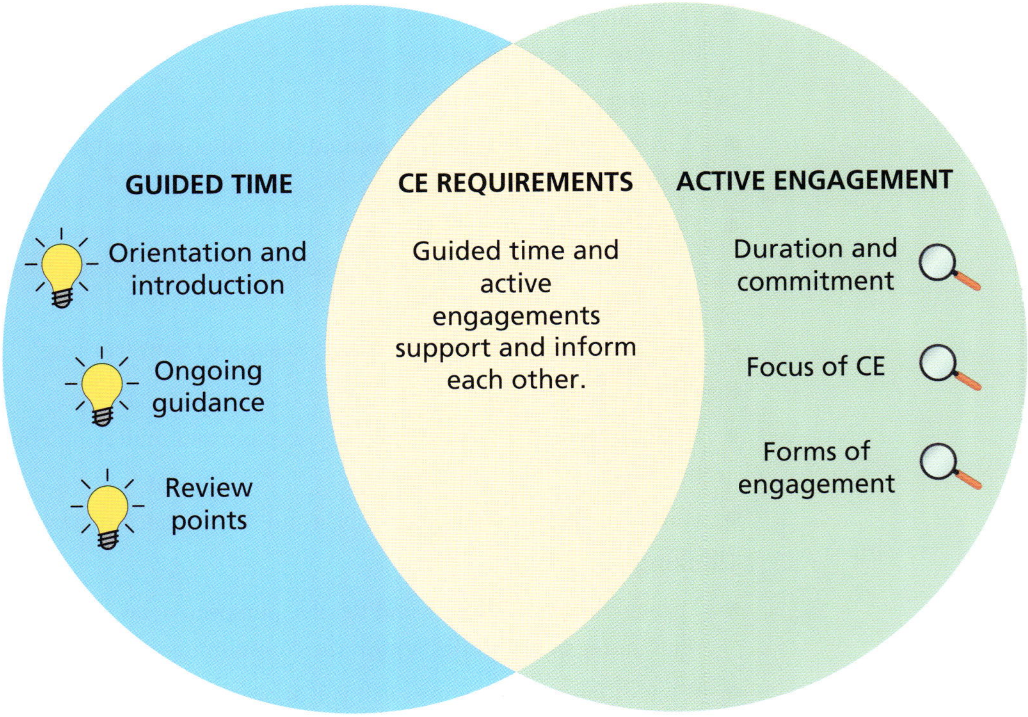

■ The CE learning process is a mix of guided learning and active engagements.

As you apply your skills and knowledge in new and/or unfamiliar CE contexts, you will gain new perspectives and connect to the concepts you have studied in your guided-learning time. Applying your knowledge and skills in guided-learning time and active engagements, and considering how these CE requirements support and inform one another, will help foster a more purposeful and impactful CE experience.

Guided-learning time

During guided-learning time at your school, you will explore the nature of CE, its aims and learning outcomes and how it relates to the rest of your CP Core. You will investigate the nature of community challenges and opportunities with the intention of engaging compassionately with the community. You will also have the opportunity to engage in respectful conversations and practise reflection and reflexivity.

Classroom discussion is an essential part of sharing ideas and perspectives.

CE is not an extracurricular activity. Rather, it is the ongoing study and application of concepts and practices that support the community. CE is deeply connected to the rest of the CP Core, your subject areas, your co- and extracurricular activities, and your life outside of school. As you work in class with your peers and teacher, you will develop your understanding of how to respectfully engage with diverse communities, values and belief systems, and participate in conversations that allow for a broad range of perspectives and ideas. You will inquire into topics of personal, local, and global significance, and examine issues of identity, power and ethics. Your guided-learning time will provide you with opportunities to check your understanding and give and receive feedback.

Active engagement

Active engagement is an essential part of building relationships with the community.

Active engagement refers to the time you spend outside of the classroom, working in and with the community. This can include engaging in advocacy initiatives online, helping out at a local charitable organization, or contributing to a research project with community partners. While these direct interactions with the community will be related to what you discuss during guided-learning time, they will go beyond that. All active engagements must be designed and carried out in ways that align with CE guidelines and requirements. You will need to carefully consider the forms of engagement you choose and their relationship to the learning outcomes. Your active engagements must be reflected in your learning journal. Examples of engagements include decision-making and organizing activities, participation in community events, advocating for community needs, and engaging in learning and research that benefits the community.

While all students engage in classroom guided-learning time, active engagements in the community may vary widely, depending on students' interests, the authentic needs of the community and the community connections that are developed. Depending on the nature of the engagement, you may need to obtain special permissions from your school, and you will need to follow the safety and risk protocols that are in place at your school.

Sustained engagements

You will be encouraged to aim for longer-term, sustained engagements that enable you to develop respectful partnerships within the community. Sustained engagements provide the necessary time to explore issues, create collective understandings and visions, and collaboratively plan, act, reflect, evaluate and share. Sustained engagements may include long-term relationships with the same community over time, with perhaps a different focus at different times. Engagements may also involve different community partners, depending on the focus area within which the community challenge or opportunity is identified.

Shorter-term engagements

In certain contexts, shorter-term engagements may be appropriate and allow for flexibility. For example, in the case of crises or natural disasters, you may want to offer solidarity to the community by providing immediate responses and support. It is important that you consult with your CE teacher when you have questions about the nature and length of your engagements.

CE is complex and, at times, the process may be 'messy'. Sometimes, despite everyone's best intentions, aligned with logical action sequences, it is not possible to see hoped-for outcomes. When intentional and well-planned engagements do not come to fruition and/or result in shorter-term engagements, this will be an important part of your learning journal reflections.

Reflection and reflexivity

Guided time and active engagements

In your learning journal, reflect on the following questions. You may choose to share with your teacher, a peer or the whole group.

- How do your individual learning and thinking styles support your own growth and development during guided-learning time and active engagements?
- How do your individual learning and thinking styles support the community during active engagements?
- What intentions and goals would you like to set for guided time and active engagements?
- How will you use your ATL skills and the learner profile attributes to support others during guided-learning time and active engagements?
- What potential challenges and benefits might arise from guided-learning time and active engagements?
- What are you most excited about when it comes to guided-learning time and active engagements? Is there anything you are concerned about?
- What more would you like to know and understand about guided-learning time and active engagements?

1.1.5 Reflective and reflexive practice in CE

The concepts of reflective and reflexive practice will be woven throughout your CE component. These ideas are explored in Table 1.5 below. Reflective practice involves looking back at past experience to improve future learning, while reflexive practice deepens this lens by asking you to examine your thoughts, feelings and biases, and understand how these influenced your actions and impacted the community.

CE asks you to review your thinking and actions, examining your views and assumptions, and being open to having your perspectives challenged and even changed. You will discover more about reflection and reflexivity as you journey through these sections; however, at the start of your CE explorations, it is useful to have a basic understanding of how reflection and reflexivity support the principles of CE and contribute to international-mindedness through ethical engagement. Although reflection and reflexivity are deeply related, it is important to understand how they are distinct from each other.

Table 1.5 Comparing reflective and reflexive practice

Reflective practice **(looking back to improve future goals and actions, and manage change)**	**Reflexive practice** **(turning the mirror back on ourselves, opening to changing our perspectives, and examining what we take for granted)**
• Examining your past experiences and actions to improve future practice • Examining your thinking and actions as they relate to your personal goals • Looking back at your own learning, thinking and actions/processes to discover new or changed understanding and insights, and applying these to your engagements within broader contexts • Linking critical thinking and questioning and interrogating your active engagements while understanding systemic causes, structural concerns and the connections between power, knowledge and identity	• Considering where you come from and how this influences how you habitually think and interact with others • Questioning your own attitudes, thought processes, values, assumptions, prejudices and habitual actions • Understanding how your assumptions, biases, attitudes, responses and actions influence and impact others • Understanding your roles and responsibilities in relation to others • Challenging collective assumptions and values, understanding how they drive perspectives and actions, and how they impact systems • Being open to collectively changing assumptions, biases and perspectives • Examining individual assumptions in relation to collective social, cultural and historical narratives

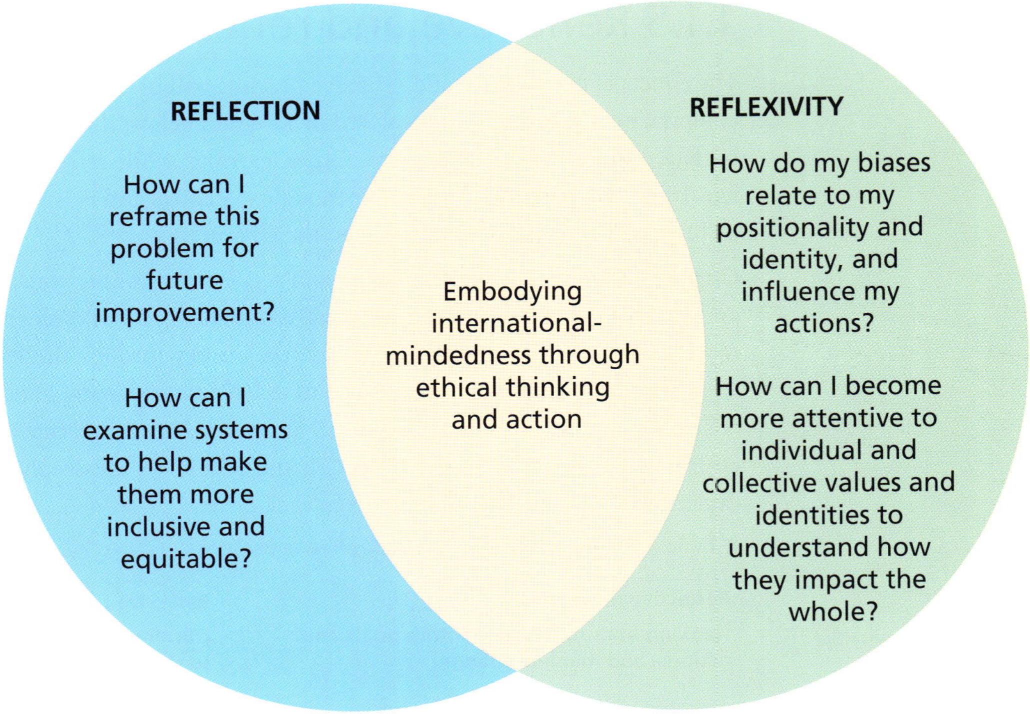

■ Reflection and reflexivity combine to embody international-mindedness.

Reflection and reflexivity

With your teacher or a peer, discuss what you have learned about reflection and reflexivity, noting their similarities and differences. Then share your thoughts with the whole group. Reflect on your learning and growth in your learning journal.

- How do reflection and reflexivity develop international-mindedness so that you can all contribute to a more peaceful world?
- How do reflection and reflexivity contribute to ethical interactions with the community?
- How can reflection and reflexivity help create positive and sustainable change?
- How can you examine your own assumptions and biases, even when you think you are 'right'?
- What is most exciting about becoming a more reflective and reflexive learner? Are there any concerns about reflection and reflexivity?
- How does reflexivity extend the concept of reflection, which is featured in both the learner profile and the ATL skills?

REAL-WORLD EXAMPLE

Developing individual and collective capacities

Early on in their CE learning, students gather at a lunch break to discuss their work in the community. They all want to engage with community partners whose work revolves around environmental protection. Two students debate the need for human economic progress over certain environmental protections. One student shares their belief that in order to protect the environment in the long term, human jobs must be secured; in this way, humans will be able to develop more green technologies. They mention that marginalized communities should have a chance to develop economically, and it is not fair that they should continue to suffer. The other student agrees with the comment about marginalized communities and argues that everyone needs to ramp up their protection of the environment, and that by placing human progress and well-being at the top of the priority list, we will keep doing what we are doing to the planet, and nothing will ever change. They note that humans in certain places have become accustomed to luxuries at the expense of the environment, and we need to see faster change. The two students' conversation becomes the only focus in the room, and the remaining students find it hard to contribute to the conversation. A third student speaks up, reminding everyone that they are meant to be working together to determine processes around reaching out to potential community partners. She expresses a need for a more calm and structured reflection process and several other students nod their heads in agreement. The two students apologize and end their debate, asking what should happen next.

LEARNING ENGAGEMENT

Have a look at the list of words and the hexagon diagram below. Working with your teacher, a peer or in a small group, fill in each hexagon with a key term, making sure each term links with the neighbouring hexagons and discussing how and why the different words connect. Each hexagon can connect to up to six others. Arrange them until you are comfortable with the connections. Your teacher may ask you to explain to others why you have created these connections.

Table 1.6 Word bank

perspectives	assumptions	biases	ethical	respectful	agreement
co-creation	support	collectively	open	actions	systems
change	societal worldview	cultural worldview	power	power dynamics	attentive
insights	community	beliefs	roles	responsibilities	critical questioning
values	prejudice	interconnectedness	engagement	knowledge	identity

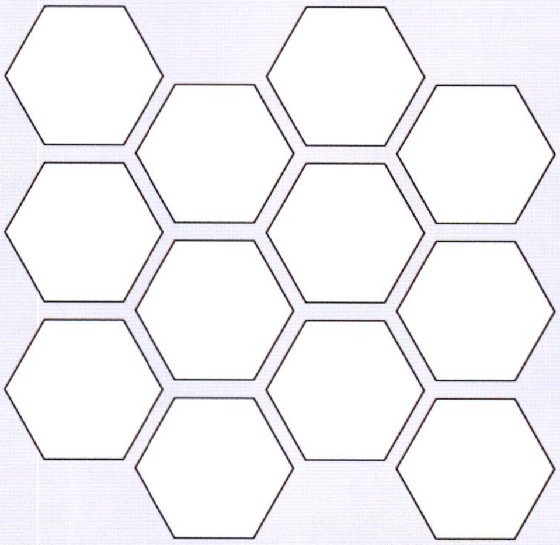

Template hexagon diagram

Reflection and reflexivity

With your teacher or a peer, discuss the following questions. You can add further questions before sharing your thoughts with the whole group.

- How can we discuss our perspectives, assumptions and biases in ethical and respectful ways?
- What shared understandings and group agreements can we co-create to support and include everyone?
- How will we know if we are spending too much time on less important things while missing out on what is most important?
- How can we collectively respond to changes as they happen?
- As we discuss our biases, how can we remain open to them changing over time? How will we know when and if they change over time?
- How do we understand how our affective states impact our actions and the systems we are a part of?
- How can we collaboratively unpack societal/cultural worldviews and mental models?
- How can we understand power dynamics as always present and ever-changing?
- How can we become more attentive to quieter voices and leaders, ensuring that they have time to share their valuable insights?

1.1.6 How is CE assessed?

The learning outcomes

Assessment in CE is represented in the form of a continuum, rather than a fixed journey. It is ongoing and focuses on providing evidence of learning and engagement centred on the four learning outcomes (LO). You will find more detailed information about assessment in Section 1.5.

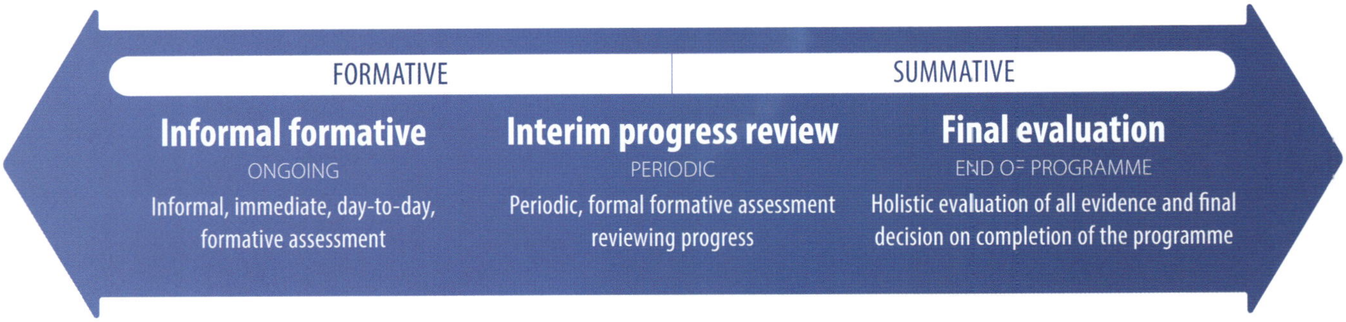

■ Assessment in CE (Source: IBO 2025a, p.21)

To complete this Core component successfully, you will need to demonstrate and provide evidence that you have met the learning outcomes LO1–LO4, described in Table 1.7.

Table 1.7 CE learning outcomes

Learning outcome		Descriptors
LO1	**Foster reciprocal and dialogic engagement**	Students are able to develop reciprocal and respectful partnerships with a chosen community, engage in dialogue with their community partners throughout, and undertake responsive, collaborative action that positively contributes to themselves and the community.
LO2	**Explore systems and develop awareness of their role within these**	Students are able to undertake inquiry-based activity and analyse the structures and impact of systems, becoming aware of their complexity and interdependence. They recognize themselves and their communities as part of larger social and natural systems. They articulate an awareness of their positions and roles within these systems and an understanding of how their choices and behaviours are both shaped by and can have an impact on them.
LO3	**Develop, articulate and enact ethical thinking and action**	Students are able to understand the importance of ethical thinking at a personal, relational and systemic level, and to demonstrate this through their actions. They understand the ways in which different ethical considerations overlap and sometimes contradict each other, and that what they think is right may not always be what is right for someone else.
LO4	**Engage in reflective and reflexive practice**	Students are able to formulate and engage in CE experiences in a reflective and reflexive manner. They engage in a range of reflective and reflexive practices as part of a process of understanding the self and others.

Reflection and reflexivity

Think about these questions individually and then share your thoughts with your teacher, peers or in a small group. It is important that you give your reasons or thoughts.

- How do the CE learning outcomes relate to the LOs in the other Core components?
- Which learning outcome concepts, ideas and/or terms are new for you?
- Which learning outcomes are you most excited about and why?
- Do you feel concerned about any of the learning outcomes at this time? If so, why?
- How can you imagine yourself applying these learning outcomes to hands-on situations and future learning?

The role of the learning journal

Your learning journal will not be given a grade; however, throughout the two years of your programme, your learning journal could demonstrate:

- evidence that highlights your understanding of the learning outcomes
- thoroughness and depth of reflections
- self-awareness and contextual/situational awareness of the issues encountered when engaging with the community
- evidence of creative and critical thinking
- practices and questions that arise from reflective/reflexive processes, accumulated over time, with the intention to learn (i.e. not purely descriptive reflections)
- a meaningful selection of personal learning artefacts that accurately represent your approaches to CE and your overall CE journey.

The learning journal plays an important role across the continuum of assessment activities. The three review points are more formal evaluation events in your CE journey, when you will need to outline key moments of learning and growth. For these review points, you will have to select and share evidence from your learning journal in ways that will help you tell your authentic CE story. The learning journal will also support the final decision on your completion of the CE.

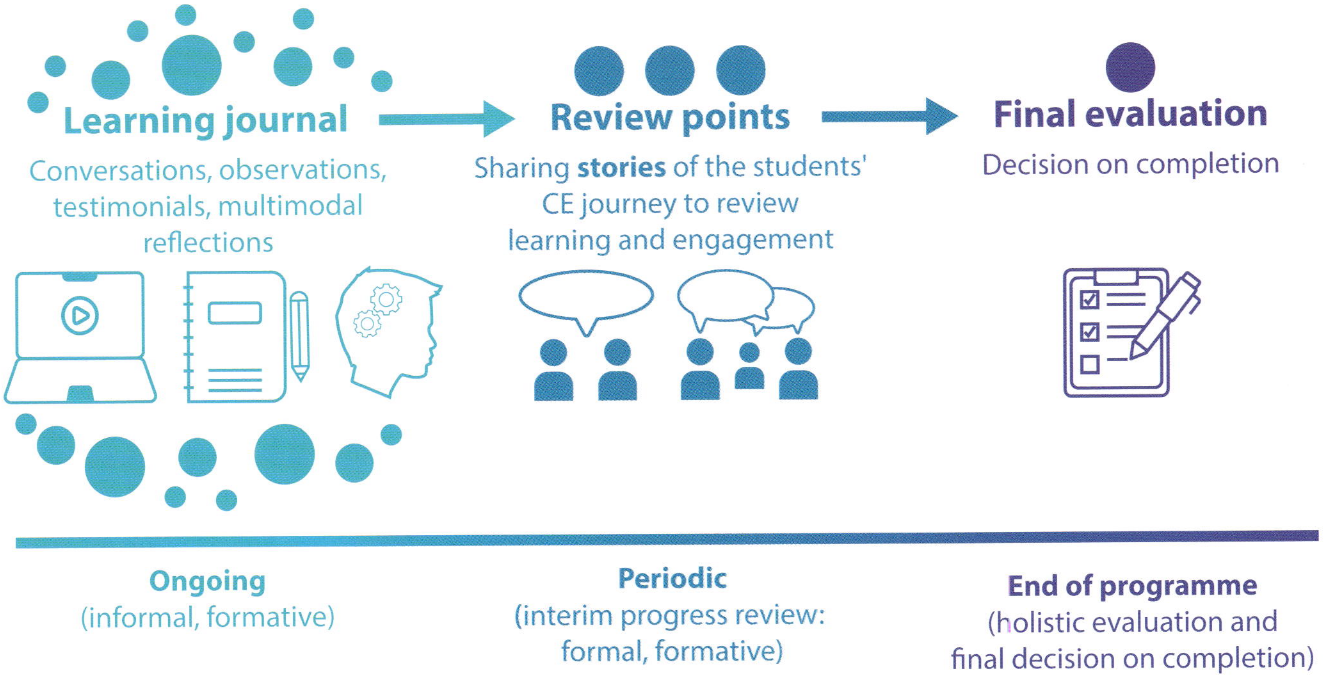

■ How does the learning journal inform and support assessment? (Source: IB CE guide, p.35)

What types of evidence should you add to your learning journal?

Your learning journal will be developed over a period of time and it will include reflective and reflexive responses to questions, showing the development of your learning and growth over time. As you add evidence into your learning journal, you will reflect on your own responses to engagements in and with the community, including questions that these experiences have raised for you. As you work to create your learning journal, it is important to ask yourself: 'Which evidence should I pay more attention to and prioritize? Why?'

Learning journal evidence should:

- be a meaningful, authentic and relevant reflection of your learning, understanding and growth
- reflect a well-rounded and ethical approach to your CE journey, rather than a checklist of completed and uncompleted tasks
- provide varied details, explanations, context and connections
- come from different sources and perspectives
- cover all dimensions of communities (personal experiences, relationships, knowledge and understanding of ecological and social systems)
- include specific and notable examples of the principles of engagement (dialogue, reciprocity, reflection and reflexivity)
- demonstrate your ability to analyse biases, perspectives and assumptions in a balanced way
- be closely related to—and show your knowledge of—the learning outcomes.

In the following table, you will find different types of evidence and examples that you can include in your learning journal to demonstrate that you have met the learning outcomes.

Table 1.8 Types of evidence to include in your learning journal

Evidence type	Examples
Planning, revising and evaluating engagement	Mind maps, timelines, communication charts, voice notes, recordings or minutes of discussions and meetings
Research	Research into proposed community engagements
Critical engagement	Case study material and/or other material from the guided learning, as designed by your school
Self-assessment activities	Reflection upon the IB learner profile attributes and their interaction with systems and ethical thinking in relation to community activities
Reflective and reflexive thinking	Self in the context of community; personal growth and development in written and oral forms (e.g. audio recordings, voice notes); multimodal forms; self and/or community in the context of larger systems
Evidence and artefacts	Evidence from your CE activities, such as annotated photographic evidence, letters, etc.
Feedback	Sharing and responding to feedback from teachers, peers and community partners
Review points	Preparation, documentation and reflection upon review points

LEARNING ENGAGEMENT

Learning journal evidence

With a peer, your teacher or in a small group, look at the list below and decide which pieces of evidence might be considered strong learning journal examples, and which pieces of evidence would be considered insufficient learning journal examples. Discuss how you could transform an insufficient piece of evidence into a strong piece of evidence. Your teacher may ask you to share your thoughts with the whole group.

- A photo of the soup kitchen where you have been going regularly to cook
- A short essay describing what you did in one experience of an engagement
- A letter of advocacy for a precise human rights issue
- A document crediting your participation in a race in your local village/town
- A plan of action created by you and other members of the community
- A screenshot of a blog you have created
- A reference to an article downloaded from the internet about a global issue
- Notes from an interview with your school principal about a strategic decision your school wants to implement
- A poem/song written by you
- A meme
- A phone number for a potential community contact

Learning journal artefacts

Learning journal artefacts will help you prepare for and reflect on your review points, conversations with community partners and class/community demonstrations. Growth-over-time maps, mind maps, stock and flow, and systems icebergs can be very helpful, among other types of artefacts (see systems thinking in Section 1.2.2 for more information on stock and flow and systems icebergs).

Growth-over-time maps

A growth-over-time map is an effective way to show your growing awareness of the CE learning outcomes. Conceptually, they are quite simple, involving *x*- and *y*-axes. The *x*-axis represents time, while the *y*-axis represents your growth in a particular area (e.g. ethics, self-management, resilience, reflexivity and systems thinking). The following example outlines a student's growth over time in their understanding of ethics.

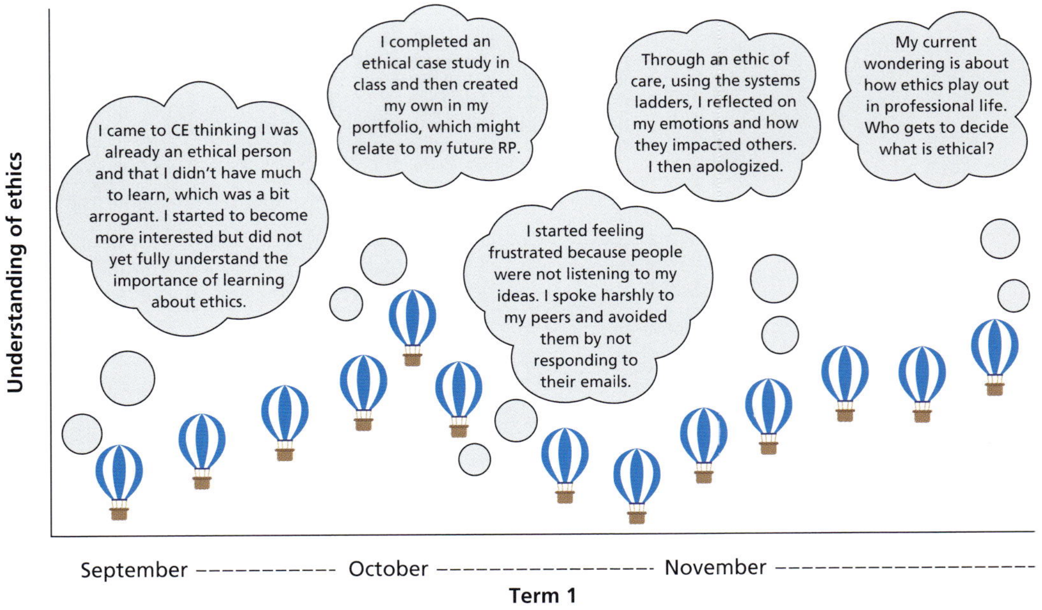

■ Example of a growth-over-time map

Mind maps

Mind maps support your understanding of the various community partners that impact and/or are impacted by a particular issue. As a CE student, it can be useful to create a mind map that houses important contact information and brainstorming ideas about how you might work with them to address an opportunity or help solve a community challenge. Mind maps are useful for your initial brainstorming process because they help you get a better understanding of complex topics through visual connections.

When creating mind maps, access your thinking skills and stay open-minded about new and unexpected connections. Allow your creativity to flow freely, pausing to reflect on new connections. Notice what happens as you identify areas of interest and begin to refine your ideas. These can be significant moments of reflection and reflexivity.

The following template can be useful to support your initial explorations of your chosen CE topic. You can use or adapt this template to support your learning.

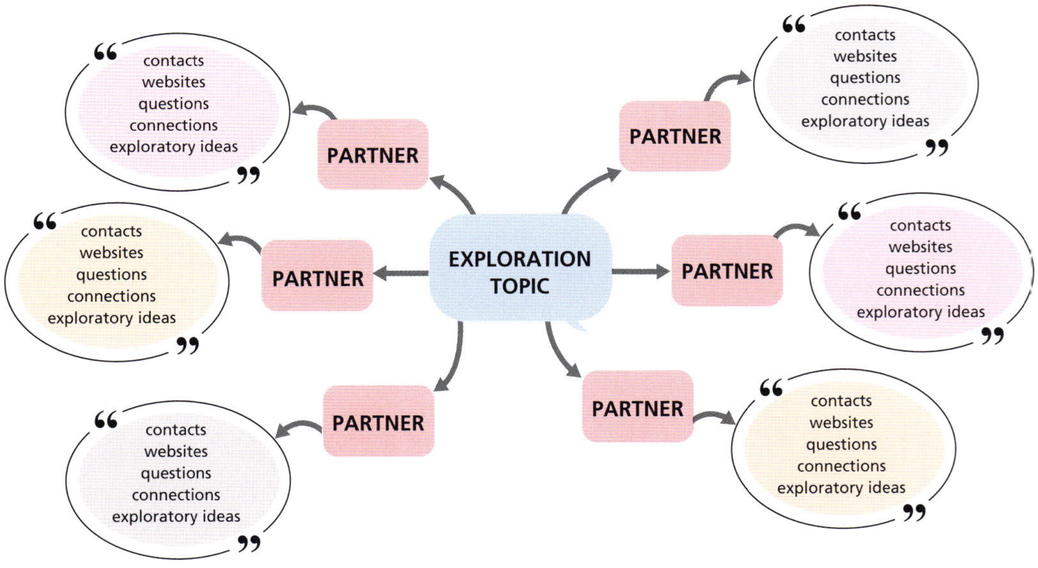

■ A possible mind-map template as you begin exploring potential CE partners

Mind maps can be created in a variety of ways, and you can discuss various online tools with your teachers and/or peers (e.g. Coggle, MindMeister, Lucidchart, Google drawing/slides, Microsoft slides, Mural and Miro). As you create your maps, it is important to keep the following in mind:

- Clarity and focus—ensure every community partner is directly related to the topic at hand.
- Question the links and connections between community partners, as this will help you gain further clarity on the systems dimensions of the topic you are interested in.

Notice the level of detail in the following example mind map, which focuses on some of the key concepts and stakeholders involved in addressing homelessness. While this map presents a range of interconnected themes, you may want to narrow your focus to a particular aspect or cluster on the map. However, it is essential that you develop an understanding of the relationships between all relevant stakeholders, no matter what community opportunity or challenge you are exploring.

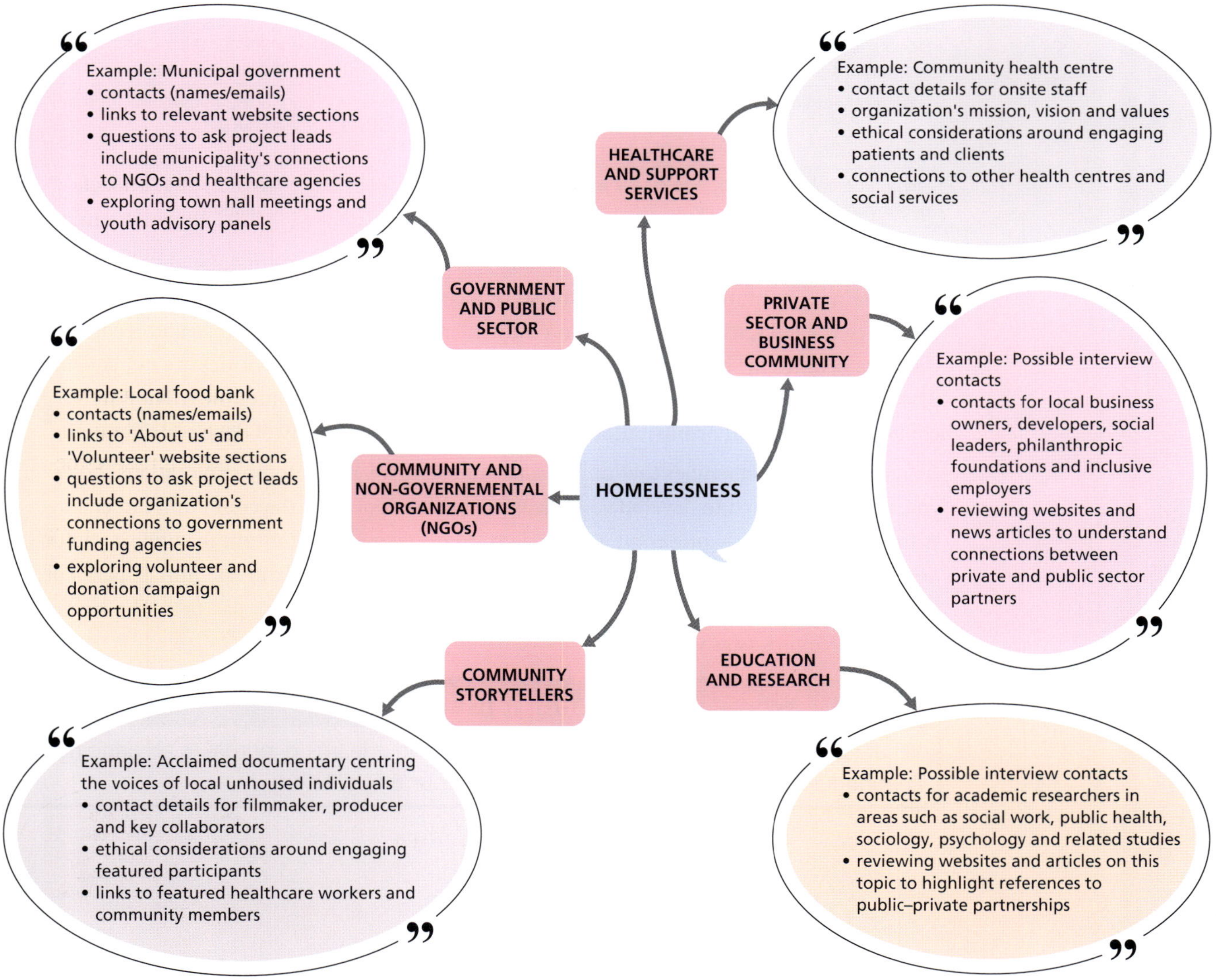

■ Preliminary mapping of key concepts and stakeholders in addressing homelessness

There are various types of community partners that you can consider when creating your mind maps. Some partners are directly and/or indirectly affected by the topic under exploration, and some support the topic. The following table can help you create your mind maps.

■ **Table 1.9** Types of community partners (Adapted from Visible Network Labs, 2023)

Partner type	Partner role	Examples
Local community	Core partners directly affected by engagement. Contribute local knowledge and insights	Residents, homeowners, tenants, families, children
Government	Act as regulators and facilitators. Provide funding, enforce regulations, offer platforms for dialogue	City council, environmental agency
Local businesses	Provide resources and have a vested interest in community well-being. Contribute to economic development	Local shops, corporate offices
Non-profit organizations	Facilitators, mediators, or implementors. Bring expertise and focus on specific issues	Food banks, educational charities, advocacy groups
Educational institutions	Offer knowledge and expertise. Engage in research projects, offer educational opportunities	Local schools, colleges, universities
Activists and community leaders	Serve as thought leaders or catalysts. Accelerate pace of change by drawing attention to issues	Community organizers, bloggers, grassroots organizations
Media	Inform the public about community issues, actions and results. Advocate for change and accountability	Local newspapers, TV stations, influencers
Donors and foundations	Provide financial resources crucial for initiation and continuation of community engagement activities	Philanthropic organizations, individual donors
Ecological entities	Create functioning ecosystems and biodiversity. Create ecological balance to protect our planet's health	Plants, animals, microorganisms, ecosystems
Environmental and geophysical elements	Provide critical resources required for planetary survival	Water, soil, air, climate, land formations

While it may seem unusual to include 'ecological entities' or 'environmental and geophysical elements' as community partners, doing so reflects ecocentric worldviews. Such perspectives recognize the land, water and other non-human entities as relational beings and recognize their importance in shaping our communities and decisions. These entities are not considered passive resources, but rather an integral part of the health of the community. They are considered community contributors and their well-being is worthy of deep consideration.

It is important to remember that mind maps are useful for initial topic explorations; however, you are also expected to develop your ideas in collaboration *with* the community to ensure your ideas reflect authentic community needs. Mind maps are not meant to support you in developing your ideas in isolation. Rather, they are intended to help create initial sparks of exploration and inquiry to support you in reaching out to community partners who have some of the same interests as you.

Learning journal

What have you learned about the importance of your learning journal as an ongoing, continuous and creative process? Note down your thoughts.

1.1.7 Your well-being is important

■ It is important you look after your own well-being during your CE experience.

It is important to understand that sometimes our CE work does not turn out as we had hoped. Sometimes, despite our best efforts, we do not see the desired results. This may lead to feelings of disappointment, confusion, stress, guilt, overwhelm and doubt, which can sometimes lead to decreased motivation, fatigue, anxiety or hopelessness. While all feelings and emotions are a natural part of the human experience, and are equally valid, sometimes they can be difficult to manage. Naming your thoughts and feelings can help reduce stress and open you to new perspectives.

Reflecting back on the ATL skills, we can see that emotional awareness is a key part of our self-management affective skills. Emotional awareness can help us understand our feelings and emotions, and once we understand what is happening, we can take steps to support ourselves. There are many ways to practise resilience, including reflecting on your feelings, adjusting your mindset, finding new strategies to help you stay on track, and maintaining persistence and flexibility.

REAL-WORLD EXAMPLE

Recognizing and responding to the emotional aspects of CE

Eileen came into CP CE knowing she wanted to become more involved with local organizations that support families dealing with childhood cancer. Her brother spent much of his childhood in and out of the hospital, and Eileen feels grateful for the care he and her family received.

Since beginning the CP, Eileen has reached out to several local organizations and has met with representatives from each one. She has chosen to get more deeply involved with one organization and, through this organization, she has completed a volunteer training program, supported a volunteer recognition day and family orientation days, and provided support during community outings for children who are well enough to attend. Eileen has been learning more about what this organization does and she has been researching the impacts of childhood cancer.

Recently, Eileen has started to feel a little overwhelmed after her visits to the organization. She has learned that a few of the children she met are not doing well, and that they will no longer be well enough to attend group outings. She has also seen some distraught parents while visiting the organization. Eileen cancelled her last three visits to the organization and she feels badly for not having the motivation to follow through with her CE commitments.

Eileen approaches her CE teacher to explain what is happening, saying she feels guilty. Her teacher reassures her that she has done nothing wrong, and that there are moments when her CE work may feel overwhelming, especially when working with vulnerable communities. She suggests Eileen speak with a school counsellor or a trusted adult to talk through her feelings. Eileen meets with the school counsellor and creates a plan for continuing with the organization.

A few months later, Eileen reflects on her CE work. She realizes that processing her feelings and emotions has helped her to develop more resilience and greater compassion for those impacted by childhood cancer. She wants to go into pediatric nursing and she knows that her CE work will help her provide more support to families in the future.

Eileen now feels more settled in her work, and she is better able to meet and attend to emotional challenges. In her learning journal, she reflects that she is feeling more balanced and that she has an even deeper sense of purpose.

As you care for yourself and your community, you will develop more empathy and compassion. While this can feel very nourishing, sometimes it can also lead to feeling overwhelmed or emotionally drained. When you are experiencing mental-health challenges, it is essential to find ways to recharge and prioritize your well-being so that you can maintain your ability to engage with—and show care within—the community. Maintaining a balance between the outward energy you use to care for others and caring for yourself is an important part of your CE work. Here are some ways you can care for yourself as you learn and grow:

- Acknowledge your feelings. It is okay not to be okay, and at times you may need to take a break from a challenging situation.
- Celebrate successes, such as learning a new skill, making new friends, connecting with your values and acting in alignment with your ethics.
- Think about your efforts as an opportunity to learn, and if things do not go as planned, try to focus on positive solutions.
- If you find yourself becoming discouraged, caught in negative thinking cycles or feeling alone, reach out to a trusted person.
- Find positive ways of coping, which may include:
    - listening to music
    - watching your favourite movie or TV show
    - talking with a trusted person
    - getting a hug from someone you trust
    - spending time in nature
    - hugging a tree
    - gentle movement, stretching or exercise
    - reducing online screen time
    - meditating or praying
    - being with pets
    - calling a loved one
    - cooking
    - volunteering and being of service to others
    - writing or journaling
    - doing a creative activity
    - practising gratitude
    - engaging in breathing exercises.

LEARNING ENGAGEMENT

Calming exercise

Slow, deep breathing is one of the most effective ways to calm the body. When you are feeling anxious or overwhelmed, try following some or all of the steps below.

- Sit in a comfortably upright position. You can also stand with your feet shoulder-width apart, with your hands relaxed and hanging by your sides.
- If it feels comfortable, close your eyes. However, if closing your eyes does not feel okay, you can soften your eyes and gently cast your gaze at about a 45-degree angle downward, focusing on a point 1–2 feet in front of you.
- Tune into your body and notice how you are feeling. Are there any thoughts arising? Do you notice you are breathing?
- Connect with your feet and feel their weight on the floor. Notice if there is more weight on one foot or on one part of the foot. Try to even out the weight between the bottom of your heels, the inside (big-toe side) of each foot and the outside (little-toe side) of each foot. If you are sitting with your legs crossed and your feet off the floor, you can sense into the weight of your legs.
- Connect with your body by taking three slow, deep breaths. Focus on the flow of your inbreath and outbreath, aiming for a complete outbreath before breathing in again. If your mind takes you away from your breath, this is completely normal. Once you notice that your mind has wandered away from following the breath, you can gently redirect your focus back to your inbreath and outbreath. It does not matter how many times you need to do this.
- Once you have taken a series of inbreaths and outbreaths, you can slowly open your eyes if they have been closed or slowly lift up your gaze if your eyes are open.
- Refocus on your surroundings by engaging your senses: What do you see, hear, smell, taste and feel? Are some senses more prominent than others? There is no correct answer, and the point is to simply notice what you notice without judging your experience.
- If at any point you feel uncomfortable, feel free to pause or stop. It may take some time for this practice to feel intuitive and comfortable.

Learning journal

What have you learned about self-care as it relates to CE? In your learning journal, can you capture this in a growth-over-time map or in some other format?

1.1.8 Summary

- CE is a compulsory element of the CP Core, driven entirely by you with your teacher's guidance.
- Your engagement in and with the community has to be informed by the three principles (dialogue, reciprocity, reflection and reflexivity) and the three dimensions of community (personal, relational, systems).
- You are required to engage in a sustained way during the two years of your CP programme.
- You are required to keep a learning journal with evidence of the learning outcomes.
- You are required to participate in at least 30 hours of guided learning.

1.2 The building blocks of CE

INQUIRY QUESTIONS

- What are the building blocks of CE?
- How do you define community?
- What are the dimensions of a community?
- What is systems thinking in CE?
- What are the principles of engagement?
- How do you define reflection and reflexivity in CE?

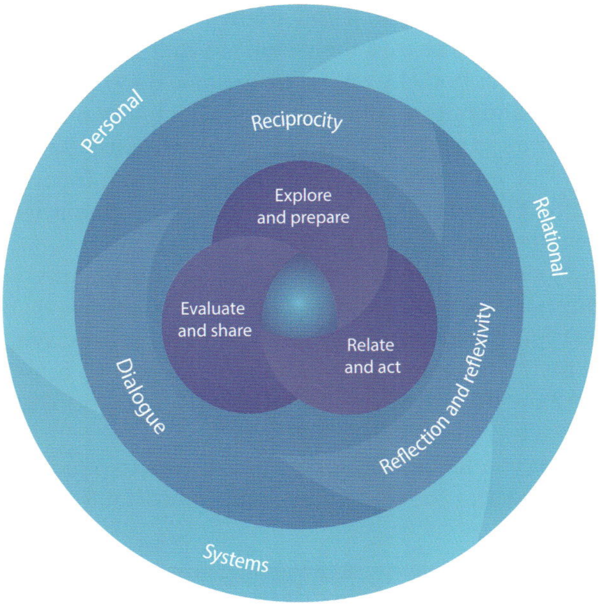

■ The learning and engagement process interacts with the dimensions and principles of CE (Source: IB CE TSM)

Community engagement revolves around building and sustaining collaborative relationships with communities to respond to relevant opportunities or challenges and contribute in constructive, generative ways (IBO 2025a, p.13). It involves respectful dialogue, reflexive practice and reciprocity, and processes that foster openness and balanced power dynamics across the community. To understand and engage with CE, it is necessary to understand the ideas of both 'community' and 'engagement'.

In CE, you will view community in three interrelated dimensions: personal, relational and systems. These three dimensions will enable you to expand your awareness and understanding of CE, and will inform and inspire your engagements.

The partner to community is engagement, and this is underpinned by a set of three principles: dialogue, reciprocity, reflection and reflexivity. These principles will help you effectively navigate your community engagements in ethical ways.

The dimensions of community and the principles of engagement both inform and drive the CE learning and engagement process, which is formed through inquiry-based learning. In CE, you will actively practise thinking and acting in alignment with these dimensions and principles (see Section 1.4).

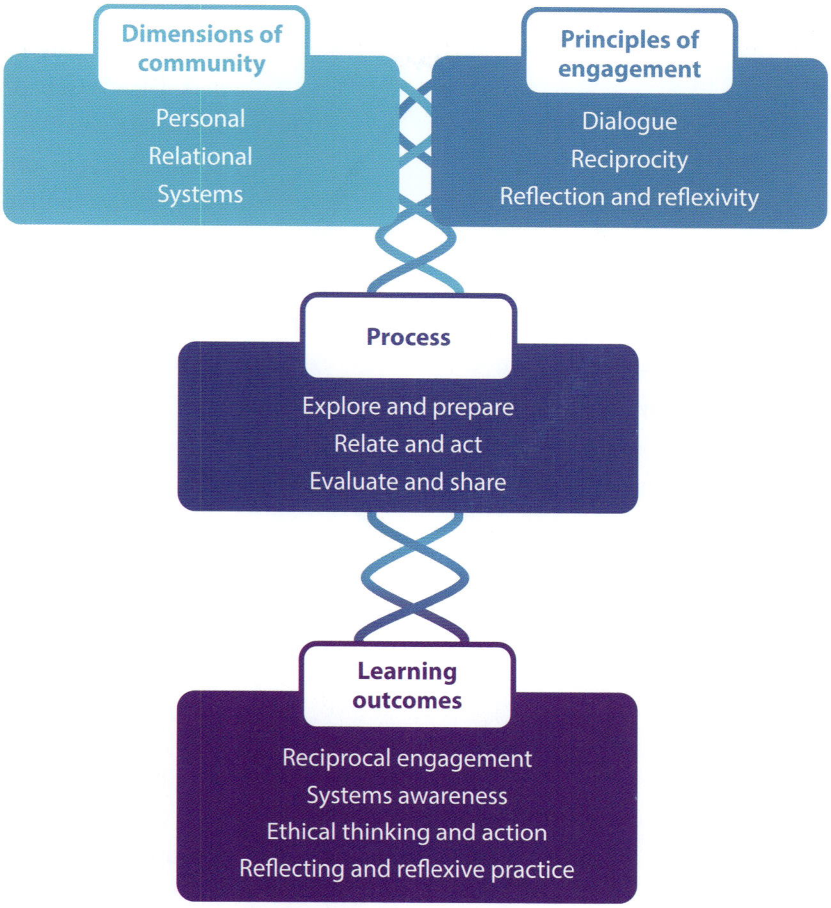

■ The building blocks of CE (Source: IB CE guide, p.14)

1.2.1 Defining community

'Community' is a broad term used to describe a dynamic system that brings people together through sharing common experiences, interests, geographical spaces, goals and/or identities. A community can be as close as a local neighbourhood or as vast as a worldwide online group, and it can range from a family group to an entire society. When you feel you are part of something, you feel connected, you feel that you belong; and in the context of community, belonging means that you have the ability to be an active co-creator of the community.

You may find a strong sense of community in your connections with a group of people who share a similar cultural identity, or you may feel deeply connected to ecological systems (nature). Perhaps you feel a sense of connection with other people who care about ecological well-being and share the worldview that nature must be protected, as we are all an integral part of nature. Or perhaps you feel a strong sense of community with people who care about the same social issues as you, are experiencing similar achievements and/or challenges in life, or enjoy a similar lifestyle to yours. A community is woven together from different elements, and understanding what weaves a community together is important to understanding how the community functions.

Examples of communities

Communities can be identified in different contexts: *Personal* (your parents/guardians/caregivers, family, elders, friends, school or learning community); *local* (the place where you live, a religious or social community you participate in, other groups with which you interact locally); *global* (online communities, memberships in international movements or organizations); *professional* (groups or organizations with which you engage through work placements or internships).

Take a moment to consider the image on the left, which is not an exhaustive list. What communities do you already belong to? What communities would you like to belong to? What communities are missing from the figure?

LEARNING ENGAGEMENT

Understanding community

Before you explore the personal, relational and systems dimensions of a community, work with a peer, your teacher or in a small group to explore your idea of community. Follow the steps below. Your teacher may ask you to share your thoughts with others.

1. Write the word 'community' at the centre of a page (digital board or paper). Think about the words that come to mind when you hear 'community', share them with others and record them. Each word recorded needs to be different. Space the words around the page so they are not all gathered in one place.
2. Add onto someone else's word with a new word or phrase. You can write your word or phrase alongside someone else's, then draw a line connecting the words and explain the connections.
3. Make additional connections between the ideas on the page. You can use lines, arrows and colours to indicate the connections or add notes on the page.
4. Each participant will then add a question about 'community' to the page based on what has emerged thus far. Discuss these questions to strengthen your understanding of community and engage with different perspectives.
5. Write a definition of 'community' using the ideas generated.
6. Discuss the definitions. As the definitions are shared, look for similarities and differences between them.
7. Now discuss the following questions:
   - In what ways can a class, such as this one, be a community?
   - What is an example of a community that you belong to?
   - What makes you feel as if you are part of this community?
   - How do the communities you belong to support you?
   - How do you support the communities you belong to?
   - What roles do time and culture play in defining community?
   - What duty, if any, do individuals have to their communities?

Learning journal

Record your idea of community in your learning journal. Make a point of revisiting your initial ideas in the future to show your growth over time and your developing understanding of community.

1.2.2 Dimensions of community

A community has many layers and, in order to understand how a community functions, it is important to explore the three interconnected community dimensions: personal, relational and systems. Developing an awareness of these dimensions will help you better understand who you are, the relationships you develop with others, and how larger social and ecological systems function in an interconnected way. As you journey through CE, you will deepen your knowledge and understanding of how these dimensions function within your own life and the lives of others, and this will inform and inspire your engagement and actions within communities.

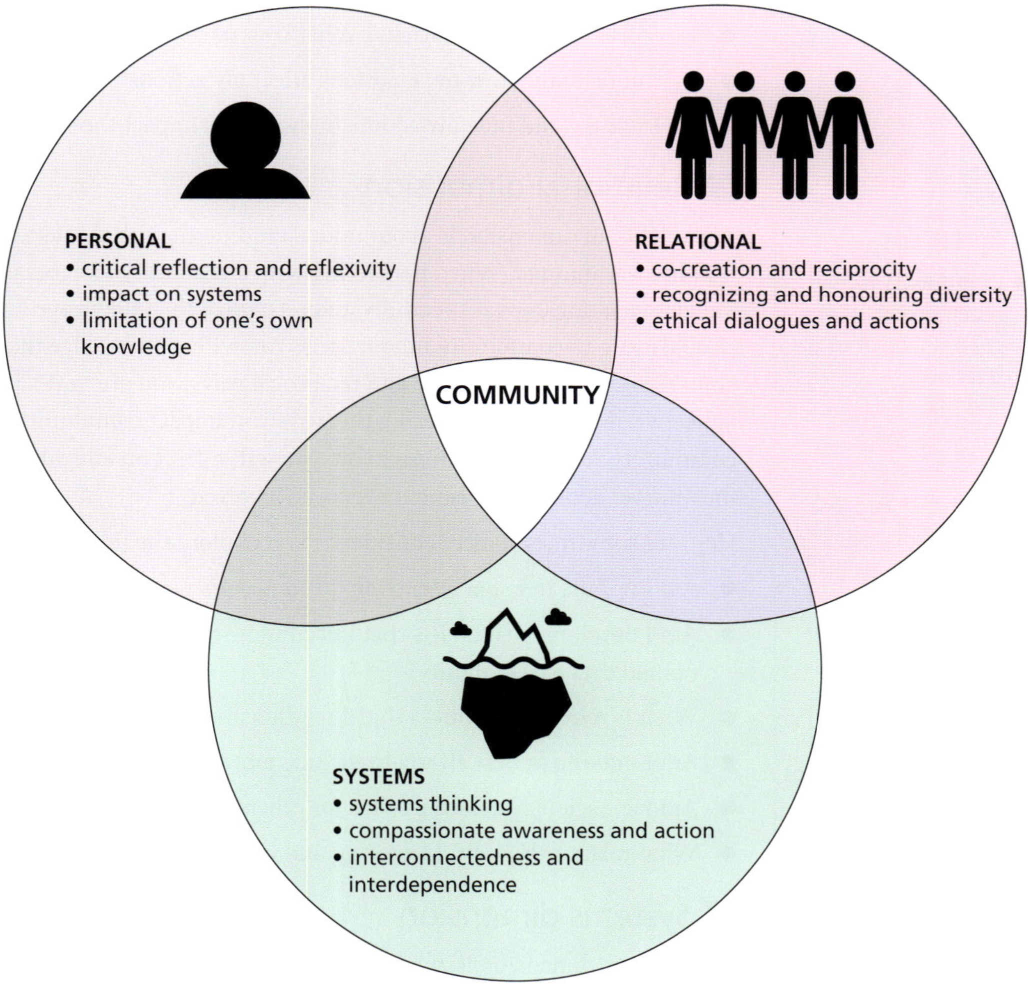

■ How do the community dimensions relate to each other?

Personal dimension

The personal dimension allows you to explore who you are and how you relate to the context of the community. You will reflect on how you develop compassion, resilience and motivation through successes and setbacks. You will also examine what shapes your perspectives and values, where they come from, how they change over time, and to what extent you are aware of the limitations of what you know.

Exploring the personal dimension will help you understand how you impact the systems around you and, in turn, how these systems impact you. As you notice the way your personal dimension impacts the relational dimensions and the larger systems around you, you will gain a clearer understanding of what motivates your decisions and the ethics of your actions.

Here are some questions that might help you explore the personal dimension:

- How do I understand myself in relation to my social identities (e.g. religion, faith, class, cultural background, gender, race, ethnicity and geographical location)?
- Do I understand how my social identities shape my views of the world? Do I understand how they influence the actions I take in the world?
- What motivates me? Why?
- How do I respond to setbacks? What frustrates, confuses or challenges me?
- Do I understand how my emotions affect my actions?
- Do I understand how my actions/non-actions impact the systems I am part of?

Relational dimension

The relational dimension is about understanding the social interactions and relationships within a community. When partnering with community members, you will learn how to navigate relationships respectfully and recognize the knowledge and wisdom that diverse people bring to community interactions. You will acknowledge that by engaging with the community in compassionate and reciprocal ways, you are developing both individual and collective agency. By considering the ways you impact community relationships, and the ways community relationships impact you, you will reflect on ethical issues that guide you toward meaningful actions that benefit everyone involved.

Here are some questions to consider as you explore the relational dimension:

- Am I willing to listen attentively to someone's perspective, even if I disagree with them?
- Am I developing the skills that I need to respectfully disagree with others in ways that uphold everyone's dignity?
- What is required to build ethical relationships?
- Am I making honest efforts to include more diverse voices?
- Am I consciously creating space for others to tell their stories?
- What relationships am I fostering and nurturing? How am I doing this?

Systems dimension

The systems dimension is about understanding that communities function as systems themselves while also being a part of larger, more **complex systems** (e.g. ecological, social, economic and political). In CE, you will focus on complex systems, which are understood through **complexity theory**, a framework that explains how systems with many interacting

Key terms

◆ **Complex systems:** A system made up of many connected parts that influence each other. These systems can change over time, and small actions in one part can lead to big or unexpected changes in the whole system. Examples include ecosystems, communities and societies.

◆ **Complexity theory:** 'Complexity theory helps to grasp the non-linear nature of [...] processes, including how [...] choices have unintended consequences or how small [actions] can cause large-scale systemic changes.' (IB Global politics TSM 2024, p.18)

parts behave in unpredictable and dynamic ways. In complex systems, cause and effect are hard to predict, and the same action will not always lead to the same result (Kurtz and Snowden, 2003). Complex systems are always changing and the different parts influence each other in unexpected ways. Sometimes small actions have a big impact and sometimes big actions result in little change (Tapsell and Woods, 2010). For example, you might organize a small community clean-up, expecting only a few people to join. However, your actions could inspire a long-term environmental initiative. On the other hand, a big event might not create the change you hoped for because of shifting or unmet community needs. In complex systems, even small actions can have surprising outcomes, both big and small. We often only understand what happened after the fact and sometimes we never fully understand it at all.

This is where systems thinking becomes important. In CE, systems thinking helps you move beyond simple explanations for complex issues and become more comfortable with the reality of unpredictability and non-linearity. Instead of assuming that one action leads to one predictable outcome (linear thinking), systems thinking encourages you to explore how different parts of a system (people, relationships, environments and organizations) are connected and influence one another in dynamic and often unexpected ways.

How you respond to the outcomes of your actions or inactions matters. By showing open-mindedness, resilience and flexibility, you can revise your plans, reflect on what you have learned and adapt your actions to better meet the needs of the community and your shared goals.

Understanding your place and role within complex systems is a key part of CE. This includes an examination of the intended and unintended impacts of your actions and inactions. It also involves understanding how community members collaborate around challenges and opportunities within larger social and ecological systems. Throughout CE, you will become aware of the need for adopting a compassionate systems perspective to help address local and global challenges. Through analysis, reflection and reflexivity, you will gain a greater sense of how ethics informs your actions.

Here are some questions that might help you explore the systems dimension:

- In what ways is a community a system?
- How are community systems interconnected?
- How do systems work? What do I understand about systems thinking?
- Do I understand how CE relates to complex systems?
- How does the way I think and act—or not act—impact the systems I am part of?
- How can I change the structures, processes or patterns of a system?
- How can I best focus on helping to relieve the suffering I see in systems?

Systems thinking

A system is any group of interacting, interdependent or interconnected parts that form a complex whole with a common and specific and/or shared purpose.

By acknowledging the dimensions of a community, you will learn that one way of approaching community challenges is by looking at them as interconnected and interrelated systems. This is called systems thinking, and it is a way of asking yourself how various elements within a system influence and interact with each other. In systems thinking, you will look for patterns and root causes, and you will ask about relationships within the system.

Systems thinking is a purposeful approach for analysing challenges and opportunities more comprehensively, and it is important to do this before taking action. Systems thinking allows you to ask more thoughtful questions before jumping to conclusions, and it requires your curiosity, clarity, compassion, choice and courage, as well as the willingness to see a situation more thoroughly. It will help you acknowledge and understand the interconnectedness of community dimensions, and the importance of taking into account varied and valid perspectives, which is a key part of reflexivity.

Key term

◆ **Systems iceberg:** A visual tool that helps support deeper explorations of systems issues through understanding the underlying causes of events. The systems iceberg model consists of four levels: events, patterns and trends, underlying structures and mental models.

Because systems thinking is, by definition, a holistic approach to CE, you need to approach it in an open-minded way. One helpful systems thinking model is the **systems iceberg** (which you first met in the Introduction), a tool that allows you to shift your perspective and see beyond the immediate events that everyone notices. As you may be aware, approximately 10% of an iceberg's total mass is above the water, while approximately 90% of its mass lies underwater. However, the part of the iceberg that lies underwater is acted upon by ocean currents, and this impacts the iceberg's behaviour at its tip. Addressing complex problems only at the event level—the tip of the iceberg—is not enough, as the root causes of the problem are hidden from plain sight. You will need to search deeper within the system. Bringing a sense of curiosity and active listening skills will help, and there are several tools that you can use to deepen your understanding of systems thinking. An iceberg metaphor is often used to describe systems thinking, meaning that we can easily see what lies above the water, although the vast majority of the iceberg lies underneath the water.

Links

You will notice that the iceberg metaphor is used in other CP components to explore different ideas. Although the way it is used may differ, the idea of the iceberg is consistently applied to help us think about what is and isn't immediately visible in any given situation.

As Schroeder and Rowcliffe (2019) note, social and ecological justice issues are like icebergs. The top of the iceberg is shaped by 'undercurrents' that are not immediately visible on the surface. In social and ecological systems, these undercurrents can build up over many years, and it takes effort, attention and critical thinking to disentangle the interconnected patterns, trends, structures, processes, values and beliefs that lie beneath the iceberg. The iceberg model consists of four levels: events, patterns and trends, underlying structures and mental models.

The event level is the level at which we typically perceive the world and look for answers to the questions: 'What happened? What is it about this problem that I don't understand?' For instance, imagine you wake up feeling tired and anxious after a series of increasingly sleepless nights. On this particular morning, you are feeling more anxious and irritable than normal, so much so that you want to avoid seeing your family members or going to school. At that moment, you may think you can fix this problem by going to sleep earlier that evening; however, the iceberg model will invite you to think more deeply about your sleep issue.

Below the event level, you may begin noticing some patterns and ask: 'What has been happening over time?' This layer of the iceberg asks you to examine situations that have been going on for a while which perhaps you had not noticed before. For example, you may realize that your lack of sleep and anxiety have worsened after increasing your time on social media before bed. By observing this layer of the iceberg, you may start to see a way out of this problem.

Below the pattern level lies the structure level. Here you will ask yourself: 'What is influencing these patterns? Where are the relationships between the parts?' The answer might come from different places or circumstances, and in the case of sleep patterns, perhaps you start to realize that the amount of time you spend on social media before bed is directly related to the amount of peer and academic stress you feel throughout the day at school. Perhaps you become aware that you are increasingly upset about your homework and think your peers and teachers don't value your contributions in class. At this level of the iceberg, you notice the connections between social media, sleep and school routines. You can see that spending more time on social media results in less sleep, which creates more stress at school the next day, which in turn creates more anxiety in the evening and the instinct to engage more with social media.

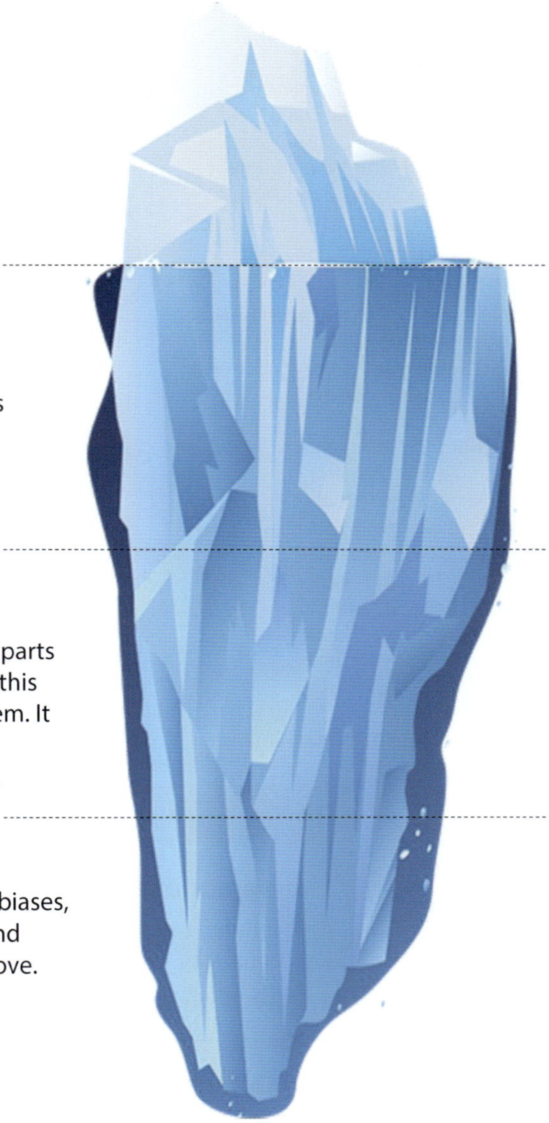

■ The four levels of the systems iceberg (Source: IB CE TSM)

The bottom layer of the iceberg contains the mental models that underlie the entire issue. These are the attitudes, beliefs, expectations, values, biases, perspectives, assumptions and worldviews that have allowed the structures to continue functioning as they are. The essential question you will ask yourself here is: 'What beliefs keep the system in place?' In the case of sleep patterns, one mental model might be the belief that pushing through at all costs or 'toughening up' is what it means to be a successful person. A related mental model may be equating productivity with self-worth and not considering yourself to be as worthy a person unless you achieve academic success. (Both of these beliefs are misguided, by the way!) By uncovering and examining these underlying mental models, you will be able to start addressing the root causes of the issue.

Systems icebergs and the three community dimensions

Systems icebergs can be designed and used in many ways. They can frame a discussion, feature as an artefact in your learning journal, become a focus for review points and be included in presentations.

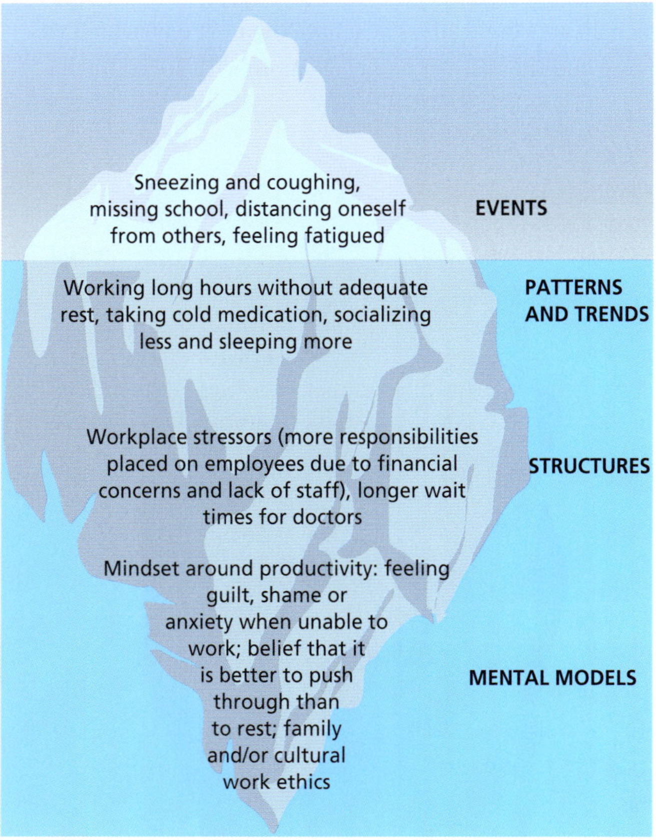

■ A systems iceberg of the personal dimension

As you engage with community partners and gain more knowledge and understanding about community needs, you can create or co-create icebergs to visually represent systems challenges, which makes complex systems easier to access. By uncovering systemic layers, you will begin to find positive and hopeful ways to actively respond to systems challenges.

The personal dimension

You can also use systems icebergs when examining the personal dimension. This is the dimension that allows you to connect with your own experiences, assumptions and emotions while hearing and considering the perspectives of others. It helps you develop your ability to be open to feedback, which allows you to adapt your approaches as new systems insights emerge. Deepening understanding of this dimension helps you develop meaningful and compassionate relationships with yourself and others, which can help foster collective understanding. Self-awareness, self-reflection, empathy and mindfulness help bring the personal system into balance. See the example of how you can use the systems iceberg within the personal dimension.

Reflection and reflexivity

The personal dimension

Answer some or all of the following questions in your learning journal and/or share them with a peer or your teacher. Your teacher may also ask you to share with a larger group.

- How do you nurture your own body, heart and mind?
- Do you think you have a responsibility to act in service of the greater good?
- How committed are you to act with sincerity, honesty and integrity?
- How willing are you to expose your vulnerabilities when embracing action?
- How ready are you to be in reflective and reflexive contact with your own thoughts, feelings, values and perspectives?
- Are you willing to examine your habits and the impact they have on yourself and others?

LEARNING ENGAGEMENT

The personal dimension

The following collaborative activity is meant to support you in developing more open-mindedness, which will help you become a more reflective and reflexive learner.

Working with a peer, your teacher or in a small group, brainstorm the different roles you may take on in a discussion. The roles below are suggestions, and you are encouraged to expand on these ideas in ways that are meaningful for you. These roles are not fixed categories, but flexible lenses. You may not identify fully or at all with any single role and that's okay. You can move between roles depending on the group, the discussion, the context and your own growth, blending, adapting or inventing new ones that suit your way of contributing to dialogues. Consider the question, 'Do you think you have a responsibility to act in the service of the greater good?' and brainstorm how you might contribute to a discussion through the lenses of various roles.

Reflecting on your speaking and listening habits, are there some roles you are more comfortable or less comfortable with? Do certain roles leave you feeling more confident or vulnerable? If so, do you know why? You can also choose to create your own role-play cards to use in various role-play scenarios for discussion. You can capture your reflections in your learning journal.

Facilitator
Moderate team discussion, keeping the meeting on track and supporting good communication.

Challenger
Challenge ideas and assumptions, not people. Present and argue a counter-opinion.

Harmonizer
Mediate the differences between members of the team. Relieve tensions.

Innovator
Contribute new and alternative ideas and perspectives to the discussion.

Recorder
Record key decisions, solutions and action points discussed by the team.

Prioritizer
Make sure the group keeps focused on the most important issues and points of the discussion.

■ Suggested role-play cards for discussion

The relational dimension

The relational dimension encourages empathy, cooperation, solidarity and mutuality. Compassion arises in the relational dimension as people interact with one another, hear one another's perspectives and act with respect. The relational system is strengthened through an **ethic of care**. It is also strengthened through an **ethic of community**, which centres collective needs, reinforcing an understanding of interconnectedness. The relational dimension reminds us that the well-being of the collective—which includes humans, non-humans and the natural world—impacts the individual. In turn, the well-being of individuals impacts the collective.

Key terms

◆ **Ethic of care:** An ethic of care places caring relationships at the centre of what it means to lead an ethical life. Rather than a strict adherence to universal principles, the focus is on compassionate, reciprocal and caring relationships that are grounded in relevant contexts.

◆ **Ethic of community:** An ethical framework emphasizing the importance of contributing to the well-being of the larger community. Loyalty, responsibility, compassion, social justice and the well-being of the greater good are central themes.

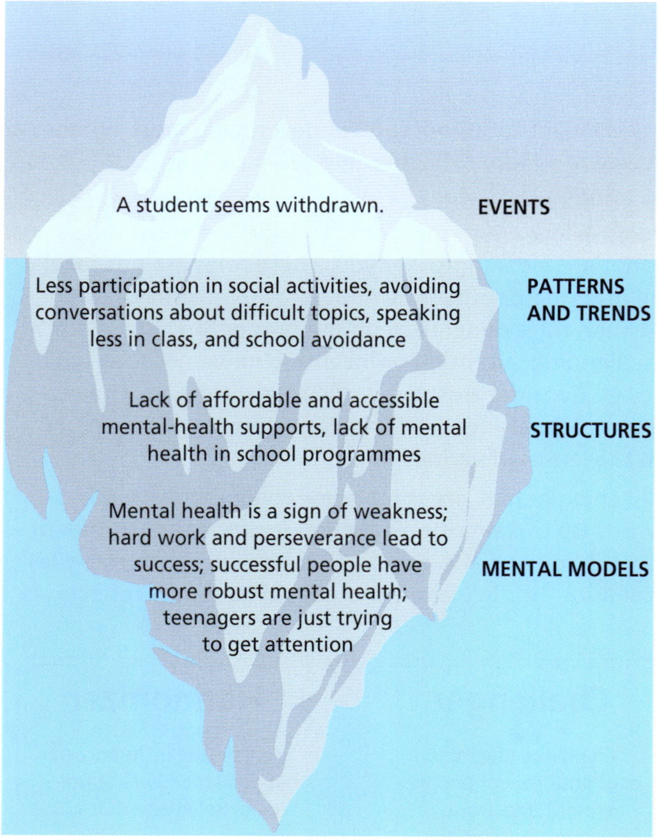

■ A systems iceberg of the relational dimension

LEARNING ENGAGEMENT

The relational dimension

1. With a partner, decide which of the following terms you want to focus on in this learning engagement. You can choose some or all of the following:
   - compassion
   - transformative action
   - connected community
   - worldviews
   - socio-ecological systems
2. Write your own definitions for these terms.
3. Share your definitions with your partner, then rewrite the definitions using both people's ideas.
4. Your teacher may ask you to share your definitions in order to develop class definitions. (The following activity might help you with this.)

Reflection and reflexivity

The relational dimension

Answer some or all of the following questions in your learning journal and/or share them with your teacher or a peer. Your teacher may also ask you to share with the whole group.

- How can your relations with others help you develop a sense of appreciation and compassion?
- To what extent can the sense of being connected with a community help you value its members and recognize their knowledge and worldviews?
- How can your relations with others help you develop the ability to engage in transformative action?
- How can relational systems positively impact the larger socio-ecological systems around us?
- What is important to remember and do when there is discomfort in relational systems?

The systems dimension

This dimension concentrates on larger local and global socio-ecological structures, such as cultural, economic, political and environmental systems. Analysing systems dimensions with tools such as the systems iceberg can help us understand where the barriers to compassion are within a given system. These barriers can include cultural norms, institutional structures or systemic inequalities. Systems icebergs can help when you are trying to identify the underlying causes of persistent social or ecological problems. By analysing the root causes of the issue, you can better focus on working towards longer-term systems change.

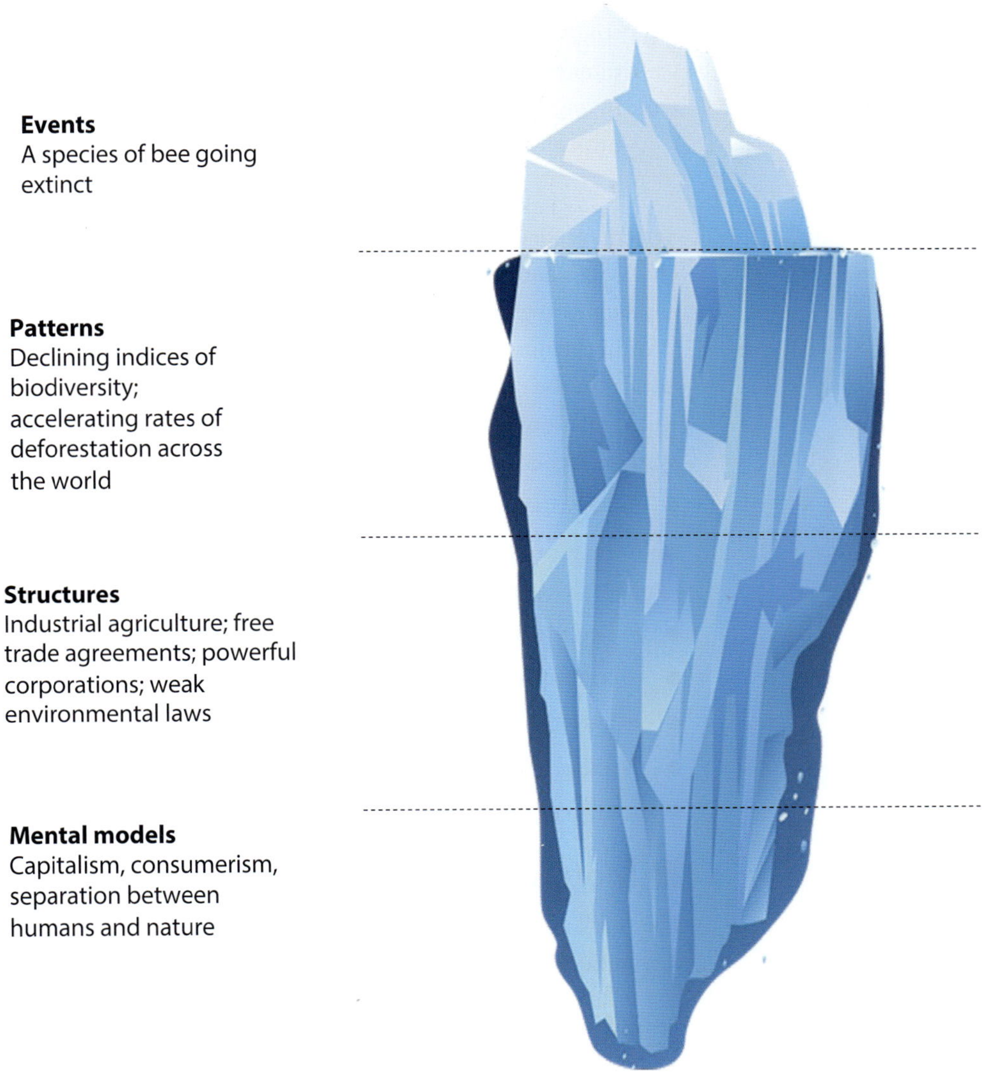

■ A systems iceberg: Examining bee extinction (Source: IB CE TSM)

Reflection and reflexivity

The systems dimension

Answer some or all of the following questions in your learning journal and/or share them with your teacher or a peer. Your teacher may also ask you to share with the whole group.

- What methods or tools could you use to identify the events or facts in a system?
- What might you do to identify what is working or not working well in a system?
- What attitudes, beliefs, expectations, values, assumptions or personal circumstances might shape the way you approach a system?
- Why is it important to understand and consider all three interconnected systems dimensions in community engagement?
- In what ways do the learner profile and ATL skills interconnect to support you in ethically addressing systems opportunities and challenges?

Systems icebergs can be helpful tools throughout your CE journey, as they help you to notice challenges and analyse the causes of those challenges. Within the systems dimension, they can help you gain clarity around the breadth and depth of social and ecological challenges. Within the personal dimension, they can help illuminate individual patterns that are hard to notice. In the relational dimension, they can help explain how cultural and systemic forces shape relationships and cause ongoing tensions or conflicts. Some of the ways that you can use systems icebergs in your learning journal are:

- to identify and explore a social or ecological topic in more detail
- to better understand your personal habits, biases, patterns and assumptions when you are experiencing challenging feelings, emotions and circumstances
- to better understand conflicts or tensions that arise in group-based processes
- to frame group and community discussions
- as a teaching tool
- as a tool in community sharing
- as an artefact in your CE review points.

More systems tools: stock and flow

The stock and flow systems tool provides an additional source of understanding, reflection and inspiration as you move through your CE journey.

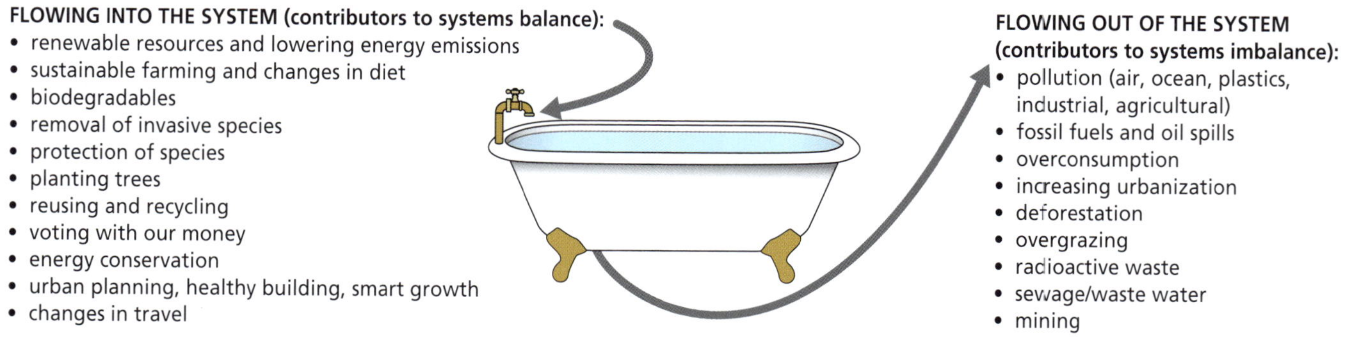

A stock and flow diagram for environmental well-being (Based on IB CE TSM, p.22)

Stock and flow diagrams provide another way of analysing systems by exploring the interconnectedness of a system's parts. 'Stock' refers to anything that accumulates or reduces over time; this provides us with information about the state of the system, helping us make connections about the system's behaviour. Flows are the activities or processes that change the stock through inflows (which add to it) and outflows (which subtract from it). A stock increases when inflow exceeds outflow and decreases when outflow exceeds inflow.

The information collected from observing the relationship between stock and flow can help us in decision-making processes. A helpful metaphor for stock and flow is a bathtub. The water sitting in the tub represents the stock or accumulation within the system at any point in time. The faucet represents the inflow, which adds to the system, while the drain represents the outflow, which removes from or depletes the system.

LEARNING ENGAGEMENT

Stock and flow

Working with a peer, look at the environmental well-being stock and flow image and work through the steps below. Your teacher may ask you to share with the whole group.

1. What does the stock represent in this system (e.g. environmental well-being)?
2. What is the current state of the stock?
3. What happens to environmental well-being when outflows exceed inflows?
4. What are the risks or consequences if this imbalance continues over time?
5. What do you know about the types of inflows and outflows that affect environmental well-being?
6. What choice, voice or agency do you have to influence the inflows and outflows in this system?

Shorter- and longer-term systems solutions

When addressing community challenges, systems thinkers consider both shorter- and longer-term solutions. Shorter-term solutions bring relief to an issue in the short term, while longer-term solutions reach deep into the iceberg to address the root causes of the issue. Review the following real-world example and complete the questions in the learning engagement below.

REAL-WORLD EXAMPLE

Poverty and homelessness

Students living in an urban area are considering how they want to engage with the community. They all want to help those living below the poverty line, and they are particularly interested in reaching out to organizations that provide food to those in need, especially those with no homes. As the students begin discussing the roles of various community partners, it becomes clear that there are differing perspectives within the group. One student says they don't want to tackle shorter-term solutions, such as working with a local soup kitchen, because this will do nothing to solve the underlying problem. This student is concerned that by giving 'handouts' to homeless people, they will not be motivated to get jobs and the governments will be less likely to help solve the problem. Another student counters these ideas, saying that they can't just ignore the suffering of people living on the streets while they wait for long-term change; by helping people find adequate nutrition, they are more likely to have the energy required to address their challenges. The rest of the students try to hear both perspectives, and suggest that perhaps there is a way the group can address both shorter- and longer-term solutions.

LEARNING ENGAGEMENT

Poverty and homelessness

With your teacher, a peer or in a small group, discuss the following questions about the real-world example above. Your teacher may ask you to share with a larger group.

1. What are the potential benefits and challenges of advocating for shorter-term solutions?
2. Considering the systems iceberg model, what longer-term solutions will help reduce or eradicate poverty and homelessness in the community? Are these solutions realistic? Why, or why not? What would need to change to make them viable?
3. How can these students balance the immediate needs of people within the community while also setting personal and collective goals around addressing the root causes of these challenges?
4. Accessing the perspective of the student who is concerned about shorter-term solutions, what are some of the assumptions that are being made? How could you address and challenge these assumptions in respectful ways?
5. How can these students find out how community partners are approaching shorter- and longer-term solutions?
6. How will students know if their actions are contributing to shorter- and/or longer-term systems change?

Key terms

◆ **Anthropocentric:** The belief that humans are the most important beings on the planet, and that their needs take priority over the needs and rights of non-humans, ecosystems and the rest of life on the planet.

◆ **Ecocentric:** The belief that the welfare of ecosystems must be protected for the sake of all life on Earth. This belief focuses on the interconnectedness of ecosystems, including living and non-living elements, and prioritizes actions that will bring about overall ecological health and balance.

◆ **Biocentric:** The belief that non-human beings have inherent value, and that their welfare should be considered as equally important to that of humans. This belief focuses on the well-being and rights of non-human life as a moral imperative for humanity.

Learning journal

In your learning journal, capture your developing knowledge and understanding of systems thinking in a growth-over-time map or in some other format.

REAL-WORLD EXAMPLE

Applying systems thinking: Rights of Nature

As part of their CE work, three students decide to approach local government representatives about starting a Rights of Nature (RoN) movement in the community. The RoN movement represents 'a fundamentally different approach to the relationship between human activities and the natural environment in that the main focus is the health of ecosystems in its own right' (Kahui et al., 2024, p.2). Beginning in the twenty-first century, the RoN movement fought for the idea that nature has inherent rights. Since then, progress has happened through court rulings and bylaws reflecting non-human beings and natural entities (e.g. animals, rivers and ecosystems) as holders of rights (Wood, 2023).

The students care about environmental protection and they have been researching RoN movements in Africa, Asia, Antarctica, Europe, North America, Oceania and South America. They have learned that in 2006, Ecuador was the first country to affirm support for RoN at the level of its constitution (Kahui et al., 2024). They have also learned that Te Urewera, a national park in New Zealand, and the ancestral home of the Tūhoe people, is now 'a legal entity and has all the rights, powers, duties and liabilities of a legal person' (Tūhoe, 2025). In Africa, there are communities of people who have created collaborative RoN learning networks in the service of supporting African people and organizations to advocate for nature rights (The Rights of Nature, 2022). The students have realized that there are competing worldviews around the world, with some people coming from a **ecocentric/biocentric** worldview, and some coming from an **anthropocentric** worldview. These diverging views have raised questions about various ways to move forward.

In preparation for their meetings with community government representatives, the students consult with community mentors who have experience with making proposals to local governments. These mentors coach the students to address the dominant worldviews in the community. The students mention to the community members that they would like to form a youth advisory committee. To fully prepare for their meetings, the students seek further consultation on how they can address various challenges and worldviews.

LEARNING ENGAGEMENT

Applying systems thinking: Rights of Nature

With your teacher, a peer or in a small group, imagine you are the ones preparing for meetings with community government representatives to discuss the issues in the real-world example above. You want to make a compelling case and you know that solid preparation will be the key to success. Copy and complete the table below, adding new questions if you wish. Then review the questions below the table. Your teacher may ask you to share with a larger group.

Table 1.10 (Adapted from Pashby et al., 2020)

Area to consider	Key question
Background	What have been the main causes of this situation?
Perspectives	What are the different viewpoints on this situation?
Fairness	Who is the most impacted by this issue?
Leadership	Who is in the best position to make a change for everyone? If engaging with government officials isn't your preferred approach, what other methods do you believe are effective for leading systemic change?
Responses	What is one good option for improving this situation?
Future	How do you think this issue might change in the future?

1 Consider what you would include in this example for each of the iceberg levels (events/symptoms, patterns/trends, underlying structures and mental models).
2 What are the opposing mental models that are causing issues? Can you define/articulate them in some detail? Where do they come from? How old are they?
3 How do certain worldviews spread to become culturally dominant? How can you question dominant views?

Systems thinking and ethics

As you engage with the community to address relevant opportunities and challenges, you will identify the ethical dimensions of complex issues such as poverty, environmental sustainability, human rights, peace and conflict. As you better understand systemic challenges and opportunities within the community, you will connect your research process with ethical actions. As you do this, you will open yourself up to more diverse perspectives and viewpoints, learning to bridge differences with respect and a sense of shared well-being. Systems thinking through ethical and compassionate lenses will support you in probing deeper into underlying ethical questions so that you can make decisions that will positively impact the community.

It is important that you connect your growing sense of systems thinking and ethics to the rest of your CP Core and subject areas. Your reflective project (RP) offers you an opportunity to engage with an ethical dilemma arising from a systems challenge. Personal and professional skills (PPS) provides you with an opportunity to consider how the personal, relational and systems dimensions are supported through ethical actions across a variety of professional contexts. And your language and cultural studies (LCS) component provides you with opportunities to consider how language and cultural nuances impact community dimensions and support ethical actions across different community contexts.

Reflection and reflexivity

Systems thinking and ethics

Answer some or all of the following questions in your learning journal and/or share them with a peer. Your teacher may also ask you to share with the whole group.

- How does it support your ethical actions when you consider the community dimensions from a systems lens?
- What happens to larger socio-ecological systems when personal and relational systems are healthy and in balance? How does this inspire you to take care of yourself and act ethically with others?
- Why is it important to think about complex systems in compassionate and ethical ways? What possibilities emerge when you do this? What happens when you don't do this?

LEARNING ENGAGEMENT

Systems thinking and ethics

Systems thinking and ethics encourage a move towards a more relational approach to living in an interconnected world. Review the table below and work with your teacher or a peer to complete the right-hand column ('Ethical challenges'). You can also think of more topics to add to the table.

Table 1.11

Topic	Systems thinking and ethics	Ethical challenges
Technology and AI	Designing AI systems	Transparency of algorithms; data privacy
Economics and finance	Designing economic systems that prioritize sustainability, equity and long-term ecological health over short-term profit maximization	Inequality; resource depletion; financial instability
Public health	Addressing health pandemics by considering the cultural and socio-economic contexts of countries	
Urban design	Designing cities that promote sustainability, social equity and human well-being	
Fashion design	Creating global fashion systems that take greater care of the environment	

Active hope in systems thinking

'Passive hope is about waiting for external agencies to bring about what we desire. Active hope is about becoming active participants in bringing about what we hope for. Active hope is a practice. Like tai chi or gardening, it is something we do rather than have.'

(Source: Macy and Johnstone, 2012, p.3)

When engaging in CE research, you may feel worried, powerless or overwhelmed. This could stem from concerns about the economy, global relationships, climate change or the erosion of human rights. Often by acknowledging these concerns, we start to feel more hope and inspiration to want to move things forward in positive ways.

As the term implies, active hope involves actions that lead to hope and, in turn, this leads to more hopeful actions. Active hope can help people face systems challenges by finding ways to positively engage in their community, personally and collectively. Active hope begins with a clear understanding of the situation. You can then identify personal and collective values and connect these values to a larger vision. By taking values-aligned action, systems change can begin. Complex systems are dynamic, not static. Through ethical decision-making and a compassionate stance, you can positively influence systems, even in challenging times. This inspires hope and action that aligns with one's core values.

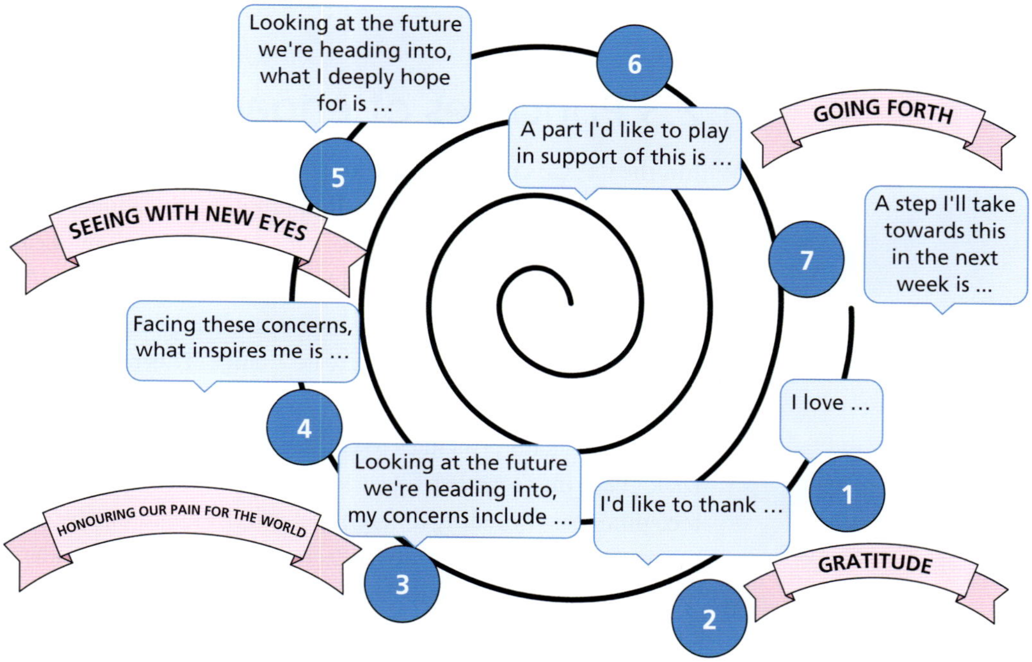

■ Active hope can be represented in a spiral. (Adapted from C. Johnstone, *Active Hope*, 2020)

LEARNING ENGAGEMENT

Active hope

Considering the spiral above, connect it to a systems challenge you care about, such as increasing heat waves and forest fires, ocean pollution, homelessness or human rights violations. Make sure you relate each statement to your chosen system challenge. Once you have completed the statements, you may choose to share your work with others.

1 I love …
2 I would like to thank …
3 Looking at the future we are heading into, my concerns include …
4 Facing these concerns, what inspires me is …
5 Looking at the future we are heading into, what I deeply hope for is …
6 A part I would like to play in support of this is …
7 A step I will take towards this in the next week is …

Reflection and reflexivity

Active hope

With your teacher or a peer, discuss the following questions. Your teacher may ask you to share with a larger group.

- How do you respond to setbacks? How can you strengthen your ability to respond to setbacks and challenges through active hope? When you find it challenging to access active hope, how do you feel?
- How can you foster active hope in your relationships and partnerships? When you do this, how might it impact yourself and others? When you find it challenging to access active hope, how does this impact your relationships and community partnerships?
- As you go about changing mental models to change the structures, processes, patterns, trends and events within the system, how can you cultivate active hope?

1.2.3 Principles of engagement

Within the CP, CE creates a space for students to engage in and with the world, and highlights 'the focus on action [that exists] in all IB programmes: a focus on moving beyond awareness and understanding to engagement, action and bringing about meaningful change to make a more peaceful and sustainable world for everyone' (IBO 2019, p.2).

Engaging in and with a community happens when groups and individuals share a common interest and then come together to create change. This requires courage, knowledge, willingness and resilience.

There are three main principles to consider when engaging with communities:

1. Dialogue brings together voices in the community. By listening with attention and respect, recognizing and holding different perspectives, and uncovering underlying norms and assumptions, the community collectively creates shared understanding and goals.
2. Reciprocity helps to develop ethical solidarity and creates an environment of inclusivity. In a reciprocal environment, the knowledge of individual community partners is valued, and communities are recognized as holding knowledge. Power and responsibility are equitably distributed.
3. Reflection and reflexivity develop your learning and self-knowledge. They ask you to critically examine your own positions, feelings, attitudes, assumptions, biases and values so that you can become a more engaged and compassionate community member.

The three principles of engagement provide a framework that you can use to build and maintain relationships with the community. The three principles of engagement infuse all stages of the learning process and, although they are separate concepts, they also interact and support one another. True engagement cannot happen without these three elements interacting with each other.

In your work with the community, you can actively practise the principles of engagement by helping build trust, respect and integrity. This includes:

- developing and maintaining reciprocal relationships
- actively valuing the wisdom, knowledge and skills of the community members
- developing an awareness of the power imbalances that exist within the community and taking action to ethically address them
- positively contributing to community dialogues and interactions
- critically reflecting on equity issues to better understand the needs of the community
- understanding that small steps and actions have an impact on the community
- understanding that non-action can have an impact on the community
- understanding that despite your best efforts, sometimes CE does not go as planned, and 'failure' is also an important part of your learning and growth, in dialogue with your teacher and the community.

Dialogue

Once you have identified the community you want to work with, your engagement will need to include the different voices and perspectives that make up that community. Initially, you will need a dialogue with relevant community members to get to know them. It is important to understand what the community values and what their challenges and opportunities are. You will bring your own perspective to community dialogues, and it is important that you listen to other perspectives. If you are hosting or facilitating a meeting, it is important to ensure that relevant perspectives are welcomed and heard. This helps foster an environment where people can respectfully explore one another's experiences and viewpoints. When participants approach the space with openness and a willingness to listen and learn, it supports the development of cultural safety and mutual respect.

Healthy dialogues are founded upon collaboration, empathy and commitment, and they honour everyone involved, whether people choose to speak or actively listen. The role of both speaker and listener are equally important and healthy dialogues offer an opportunity for new perspectives to emerge. From this, community members can decide on their purpose and shared values. When community members share a purpose and values, and take ethical actions, this can create systems change. It is important to note that sometimes structured dialogues can help people feel safer in showing their vulnerability and sharing their authentic ideas and feelings. Structured dialogues are facilitated interactions that require planning, clear communications and shared agreements.

Although in-person communication is generally considered more helpful, sometimes (depending on people's locations and/or schedules) dialogues and decision-making processes need to happen through email or other digital channels. If you find yourself in the position of facilitating an online dialogue, make sure guidelines are clearly established in advance and agreed upon by all participants. Clarity, inclusion, accessibility and intercultural understanding need to be fostered from the beginning to allow smooth interactions. Consideration of time zones, recording protocols, chat functions, access to technology, communication styles and skilfully managing misunderstandings are important. It takes good preparation and technology skills to create respectful digital dialogue spaces where everyone can feel supported, actively listen and adapt when needed.

Reflection and reflexivity

The importance of healthy dialogues

It is important to prepare well for community dialogues, particularly if you are the one convening, facilitating or hosting them. Working with your teacher, a peer or in a small group, discuss some or all of the following questions. Your teacher may ask you to share with a larger group.

- When engaging in dialogue, what do you think should be the main focus of the exchange?
- Why and how would you put yourself in someone else's shoes?
- What type of questions do you think would make the other person feel less defensive and more included?
- When engaging in dialogue, what do you think is the best way to practise patience and non-judgemental awareness?
- What approaches and strategies can you use to include and hear all voices?
- How do you foster dialogue in a group?
- How do you keep the communication channels open?
- How do you address conflicts or divergences of opinions and perspectives?
- How open are you to accepting other people's perspectives, especially when they are different from your own?
- Why do you think some people feel uncomfortable when they are challenged with a new perspective?
- How ready are you to accept the potential change that might arise from dialogue?
- To what extent can one understand the entirety of another person's experience?
- To what extent might your assumptions be tied to your identity?
- To what extent do unequal power relations influence our everyday social interactions?
- What strategies do you think you could put in place to move from 'agreeing and disagreeing' to 'mutual understanding'?
- What comes more naturally to you: mindful speaking or mindful listening? Why? How can you practise honing your skills in your more non-dominant dialogic areas?

Top tip!

Capture your current understanding of the principles of engagement in a growth-over-time map or in some other format. This will help prepare you for your review points.

Compassionate and inclusive dialogic processes

■ Compassionate conversations include active listening, reflection, ethical actions and intentional speaking.

Throughout your CE journey, you need to clearly define the purpose of your actions before you engage with community members. You are encouraged to carefully explore community opportunities and challenges through dialogue with the community members.

There are different ways to create spaces where dialogues can take place and where community members can express varied insights, voices and perspectives. The remainder of this section will explore compassionate and inclusive approaches to dialogues which you can encourage at your school and/or in your local community.

In compassionate dialogic spaces, people are able to speak and listen openly and respectfully, without interruption. If people are uncomfortable sharing, they can choose to listen mindfully, which helps create a compassionate relational dimension. Remember that conversations do not always lead to actions or agreed outcomes. A central part of creating compassionate relational spaces is learning to embrace questions rather than answers, understanding that learning and transformation do not always appear linear.

As you prepare to engage in community dialogues, consider the following points:

- Be authentic and present, speaking from a place of honesty and self-awareness.
- Reflect: 'Why am I engaging in this conversation? What outcome am I hoping for?'
- Consider how open you are to hearing other perspectives and engaging meaningfully.
- If you are not emotionally ready to engage and/or contribute respectfully, consider postponing, taking a step back or taking on the important role of an active listener.
- Understand the purpose of the dialogue and ensure your understanding aligns with others'.
- Avoid assumptions as these can lead to misunderstandings and disconnection.
- Ask clarifying questions.
- Practise supportive non-verbal communication, communicating with respect and care.
- Listen with the intent to understand rather than to respond.
- Reflect on any biases or assumptions you may be bringing into the conversation.
- Use 'I' statements and avoid making generalizations or assumptions.
- Allow silence and space for people to think and reflect.
- Acknowledge emotions as a natural part of human connections, understanding that they provide you with important information.
- If you feel challenging emotions, try becoming curious rather than furious.
- Be open to changing your perspectives, learning new things and admitting when you are wrong or do not know something.

REAL-WORLD EXAMPLE

Applying dialogic protocols: Returning to the Rights of Nature

A group of CE students wants to start a Rights of Nature (RoN) movement in their community. After seeking support from local community mentors, they put together a proposal for local government representatives. This proposal includes the formation of a youth advisory committee, which will work alongside government representatives, researching and consulting from a youth-based perspective. Upon receiving the proposal, local government representatives invite the students to attend a community meeting where other environmental advocacy groups will be presenting.

The CE students prepare as well as they can for the meeting, including a presentation rehearsal for their CE class. At the meeting, they are given five minutes to present their ideas. As their presentation begins, the students realize that their slideshow is not working, and their speaking notes are located within this slideshow. Although they are feeling flustered, they do their best to express their thoughts. After their presentation, a few of the other participants tell them that while they appreciate the students' efforts, these are very naïve and impractical ideas. The students argue that RoN movements are happening in other countries, and the response is that these dreams are meant to spark dialogue, but they will never translate into nature having the kinds of rights the students envision. The students are encouraged to drop their RoN idea and join an existing youth activism group. As the meeting ends, the students feel deflated and stressed.

Throughout the following week, the students consider giving up on their RoN ideas. However, after a class discussion with their CE teacher and peers, they decide to regroup and examine the ways they can create a more compassionate space, strengthen connections with the adults in their community, and create a more open and curious approach, hopefully with more success.

LEARNING ENGAGEMENT

Applying dialogic protocols: Returning to the Rights of Nature

With your teacher or a peer, reflect on the real-world example above and discuss the following questions. Your teacher may ask you to share with a larger group.

1 Considering what you know about compassionate community dialogues, how do you think these students could have acted differently?
2 What learner profile attributes and ATL skills could these students have drawn upon as they engaged in the RoN community dialogue?
3 If you were a part of this CE student group, how would you help plan the next community dialogue? Consider space, place, timing and format, along with possible responses to challenging feedback and questions.

Learning journal

Capture your current understanding of compassionate dialogues in your journal through a growth-over-time map or in some other format. This will help you prepare for your review points.

Talking circle protocols

For centuries, Indigenous peoples from around the world have used talking circles as a way to engage in respectful dialogues that build trust, respect and empathy in communities (Darling and Horrigan, 2012; Pranis, 2005). Talking circles are a structured dialoguing tool rooted in Indigenous traditions. In CE, they support the development of social and emotional intelligence and ethical leadership by promoting active listening, respect for diverse perspectives and a deeper understanding of complexity.

An Indigenous talking circle at the Dehcho First Nation Assembly in the NWT (Canada)

While simple to create, talking circles require participants to engage in a process that is clear, structured and equitable. Inclusive and well-facilitated talking circles build community, provide support, generate understanding and create stronger relationships (Ball et al., 2010). Talking circles often include a circle of chairs with no tables. Circles are inherently non-hierarchical and everyone can see everyone else. Circles often have a talking object, a facilitator and clear guidelines. Sometimes circles lead to collective decision-making and sometimes they are spaces in which people can share authentically and respectfully, even when there are different perspectives and no decision is reached.

In talking circles, everyone is recognized as an equal participant and an equally valued member of the community. When all members of the circle have a chance to speak and be heard, the circle becomes a rich source of collective information, identity and interaction. The following guiding principles are adapted from Kay Pranis' work on circle processes (2005), which draws inspiration from Indigenous approaches to dialogue and community building. Talking circles help facilitate processes that:

- honour the presence and dignity of every participant
- value the contributions of every participant
- emphasize the connectedness of all things
- support emotional and spiritual expression
- give equal voice to all
- ensure respect, inclusion and non-coercive approaches.

Table 1.12 Talking circle protocols (Source: IB CE TSM, p.24)

Setting up	While it may be tempting to skip the set-up process, setting up the circle—together—with chairs (often with no tables) is essential. Participants can also sit on the floor. Ensure everyone is seated within the circle, paying attention to and supporting those with mobility challenges.
Welcoming	It is important to take the time to welcome everyone to the circle, even if there are no new participants. Warmly welcome new participants to the circle by sharing the intention of the circle. Give new participants a chance to introduce themselves.
Grounding rituals	Circles can start with a simple ritual, such as a check-in, a poem, a mindfulness practice or by placing a meaningful object in the centre of the circle to focus people's attention.
Guidelines	It is important to remind everyone of the circle guidelines each time. Students can co-create these guidelines, focusing on respectful speaking and listening. It is everyone's responsibility to practise mindful listening. When it is their turn, people can choose to speak or pass. All members of the circle are reminded to listen attentively, whether they choose to speak or not.
Talking object	Often an object is chosen to denote when someone has a turn to talk. The object is passed around the circle and only the person holding the object may speak at any one time. This slows the pace of the conversation and encourages attentive listening and reflection. It reminds people to avoid interrupting others and avoid cross-talk (speaking out of turn with someone close or further away in the circle).
Facilitator	The facilitator may speak without the talking object, but does so sparingly. Their role is to encourage a respectful space. The goal is not to reach a consensus or drive towards solutions, although this may happen.
Speaking norms	People speak in the 'I' and do not refute or challenge other people's stories and contributions. People can say 'I pass' without judgement, if they do not want to speak. Everyone has a responsibility to listen without interrupting the speaker.
Closing	The facilitator (or someone else) closes the circle by acknowledging and honouring all participants. There may be a reflection question, such as: 'What resonated most for you in this circle today?'

Reflection and reflexivity

Talking circles

Answer the following questions in your learning journal. Then, share your thoughts with a peer, your teacher or a larger group.

- When you look around your local and global communities, what do you notice about intentional dialogic processes?
- Do they happen often, and are they mostly compassionate?
- Are they sometimes harmful and, if so, why and how?
- What types of dialogic approaches bring belonging and inclusion to communities? Does this belonging and inclusion need to include everyone in the community? If so, why? If not, why not?
- When, where and why do you think talking circles could be helpful as you journey through CE?
- What are some of the barriers to using talking circles in your community, and how can these be overcome?

Fishbowl activity

The fishbowl activity is a variation on a talking circle that can be useful for larger groups where complex issues are being considered. Often, the space is set up with two circles of chairs—an inner circle and an outer circle. An alternate configuration might be a single circle of chairs with people standing in an outer circle. The people inside the 'fishbowl' (inner circle) actively debate a topic, while the people outside the fishbowl listen carefully to evaluate the information they are hearing and reflect on new insights gained. People take turns in these roles to allow them to be both contributors and listeners in the conversation, and it is important that all of the people inside the fishbowl feel safe and comfortable in this role. The fishbowl activity can be useful when you want to make sure that everyone has an opportunity to participate in the discussion. It helps develop everyone's listening, speaking and observation skills.

The key steps are:

- Determine a theme or topic.
- Set up an inner and outer circle. The inner circle is the 'fishbowl' while the outer circle is a space for observation.
- Ask an open-ended question. Some background information may be read aloud at the beginning to help set the context.
- Invite volunteers to sit in the inner circle. Only people in the inner circle may speak.
- People in the outer circle listen attentively and may take notes.
- The facilitator (teacher or student) is not in either circle. Their role is to pose questions and ensure every voice in the inner circle is heard.
- Let participants know ahead of time that people will rotate in and out of the inner circle.
- Once everyone has had a chance to participate in the fishbowl, ask participants to discuss some reflection questions.

Reflection and reflexivity

Fishbowl activity

With a peer or your teacher, discuss some or all of the following questions. Your teacher may ask you to share with others as well.

- How does the fishbowl activity promote active listening?
- What is the value of asking open-ended questions?
- What actions can you take to foster an inclusive environment during the fishbowl activity?
- What types of discussions might be best suited to the fishbowl activity?
- How does the fishbowl activity promote open-mindedness?

Conversation cafés

A conversation café is an informal yet structured method of dialogue that invites people to engage in open, respectful conversations about meaningful issues. The process encourages active listening, equal participation and thoughtful reflection in a welcoming environment. Much like a talking circle, conversation cafés help you develop the ability to listen and respond in constructive dialogues, particularly those that involve complex or debatable issues. This helps develop skills in all areas of the three CE principles (reciprocity, dialogue and reflection/reflexivity).

A conversation café should bring people together in a process that helps generate new connections, strategies, ideas and shared understandings. It is not meant to be a problem-solving, action/resolution-based activity, although actions and resolutions may stem from these conversations and some problems may be solved.

The key steps for a conversation café are:

- Approximately five to seven people sit in a circle around a table with a talking object placed in the centre. Pens and paper may be available for participants to jot down thoughts. One person serves as the 'host' of the table.
- Someone reads aloud the group's collective agreements, such as listening without interrupting, speaking from personal experience and respecting diverse views. The host gently reminds participants of these agreements as needed.
- The theme or topic is posed as an open-ended question. The host may also introduce a challenging problem or question with no easy answers to stimulate deeper collective thinking.
- Participants are invited to write or draw their thoughts on the shared paper as part of their reflection.
- People move into four rounds of dialogue (while everyone is welcome to talk, they can also choose to listen):
  - **Round 1:** The talking object is used. Each participant has roughly one minute to share their initial thoughts, feelings or experiences related to the topic.

- **Round 2:** The talking object is used. Having had an opportunity to listen to each person, the participants have one further minute each to share their thoughts and feelings.
- **Round 3:** A more open group conversation takes place and the talking object becomes optional.
- **Round 4:** The talking object is used again. Each participant reflects on the Round 3 conversation, its impact on them and what they are taking away from it.
- Optional variation: After the first café, participants (except one host) may rotate to different tables at timed intervals to further share ideas.

(Adapted from Lipmanowicz and McCandless, 2014)

LEARNING ENGAGEMENT

Conversation cafés

Complete the following in your learning journal. You may choose to share your thoughts with others.

- When, where and why do you think a conversation café could be helpful in the community?
- What are some of the barriers to enacting a conversation café in your local context, and how could these be overcome?
- What skills would you need to co-host a conversation café, and how can you develop, strengthen and enact these skills?

The 'nine whys' activity

Nine whys

The 'nine whys' activity helps individuals uncover the deeper purpose behind their work—what truly matters to them. It can also support clearer communication of personal motivations and, when shared, contribute to collective understanding within a group. This activity is typically done in pairs, with one person (Partner A) asking the questions and the other person (Partner B) responding to them. This activity can be adapted in creative ways, and the facilitator can wrap up the partner activity by posing questions to the whole group. This may then move into a circle dialogue or another collective reflection format.

The key steps for the 'nine whys' activity are:

- Two people, Partner A and Partner B, sit facing each other.

  Partner B states a focus area, what they are doing or something they care about (e.g. 'I am working on ...' or 'I am passionate about ...').

  Partner A asks: 'Why is that important to you?'

  Partner B answers.

  Partner A continues to ask 'Why?' up to nine times or until Partner B reaches a core insight.
- The partners then switch roles and repeat the process.
- After each partner has had a chance to pose and respond to questions, they may share with the group.
- The facilitator may record and highlight commonalities, differences or emerging themes across the pairs (e.g. do any common themes, purposes or visions emerge?).

(Adapted from Lipmanowicz and McCandless, 2014, www.liberatingstructures.com/3-nine-whys)

LEARNING ENGAGEMENT

Nine whys

Consider the 'nine whys' activity and answer the following questions in your learning journal. Your teacher may ask you to share with the whole group.

- When, where and why do you think the 'nine whys' activity could be helpful in the community?
- How can this process help make underlying values, beliefs and perspectives clear?
- What are some of the barriers to enacting a 'nine whys' activity in your local context, and how could these be overcome?
- What skills would you need to facilitate a 'nine whys' activity, and how can you develop, strengthen and enact these skills?

Learning journal

Capture your understanding of dialogic processes in your learning journal through a growth-over-time map or in some other format. This will help you in your review points.

REAL-WORLD EXAMPLE

Initiation and persistence in CE

Hassan has noticed that a large group of students in his year group get very anxious about exams. After informally collecting some information by chatting with his friends, he decides that he would like to organize a mindfulness club at this school to help reduce stress and improve the focus and overall well-being of his classmates. He holds a meeting for those interested in participating in some of these mindfulness sessions.

During the meeting, Hassan begins to feel increasingly uncomfortable. He realizes that he didn't have time to plan well for the meeting, and more people turned up than he had expected. While he tries his best to facilitate an open discussion, only a few people speak up while others stare at their phones or engage in side conversations. One student who arrives late tries to speak up and she is interrupted several times. She thinks that others in the group are laughing at her and she ends up in tears. Another student says he thought the mindfulness sessions were going to be run by a professional, and he questions what he can get out of a student-run stress reduction group.

After this initial meeting, Hassan feels overwhelmed. The task seems more daunting than he initially thought, and he is not sure he wants to continue with it. He discusses it with his teacher and some of his peers. He comes to realize that while the first meeting did not go well, there is still a chance to bring people together for a healthy and inclusive discussion. He decides that he will continue with the initiative, recognizes this as a moment of growth and reflects on it in his learning journal. He includes his hopes for these community engagement sessions and comes up with approaches and strategies that may help make this initiative a reality. These include:

- crafting a clear and respectful communication to thank people, admit his mistakes and call for another meeting with a clear agenda and communication protocols
- speaking with school stakeholders, including the extracurricular advisor and student services team, inviting them to the meeting
- organizing the next meeting using talking circle protocols
- practising introducing the talking circle with a focus on inclusion, empathy, fairness and care.

LEARNING ENGAGEMENT

Initiation and persistence in CE

Working with your teacher or a peer, review Hassan's experience then answer the questions below. Your teacher may ask you to share with a larger group.

1. If you were in Hassan's situation, why might you feel overwhelmed after the first meeting? What challenges and concerns would you identify?
2. Looking at the final list of bullet points in the real-world example, how would you approach each of these steps?
3. How would you apply the principles of engagement to Hassan's initiative?

Reciprocity

Reciprocity is a central part of CE interactions. It refers to actions that are mutually respectful and caring, meaning that you give to others not just to be nice or get something in return, but to develop a relationship where care and support flow both ways. In human relationships, reciprocity benefits all people in a relationship, and this has an incredibly positive impact on the community. Reciprocity happens in exchanges where each person gives and receives something from the other in a genuine and non-transactional manner. This develops respectful relationships based on trust, respect, empathy and shared purpose. Through reciprocal actions, people can produce something new together—something that did not exist before.

It is also essential to consider human relationships with non-human beings; for example, humans' relationships with plants, animals and the lands they live on. As Peruvian archaeoastronomer and Indigenous activist Carlos Milla Villena notes, 'the concept of reciprocity is totalizing ... that is, it occurs not only among the members of the community, but also among them with Nature, in all its expressions' (Villena, 2005 as cited in Doe, 2023, as cited in Distin, 2024).

Reciprocity requires intention, effort, timing and awareness. When you pay attention and notice someone putting effort into something, or notice another being experiencing challenges, you can ask: 'How can I help?' Reciprocity also includes paying attention to other humans' successes so that you can recognize them and celebrate with them. Responding and giving to other beings takes time and effort, along with an awareness of what will best support them in any given moment.

Important points to remember about reciprocity are:

- Observe and listen with empathy so that you understand what other beings are feeling and needing.
- Act with the intention to truly help rather than trying to only benefit yourself.
- Allow other beings to teach you things and remain curious and open.
- Give without the expectation of receiving anything back; reciprocity is not about keeping score or track of who has done what.
- Be open to feedback if someone asks you to focus on helping them in a different way.
- Openly give constructive feedback when asked.

Practising reciprocity in CE

There are many ways that you can practise reciprocity in CE. For example, in human interactions, you can show reciprocity by learning about someone's work before meeting with them. Reviewing a person or organization's biography, website and examples of their work ahead of time will show them that you care and that you are genuinely interested. You can then use your professional skills to effectively manage meetings and communications and, in this way, you support others. Other examples of human reciprocity in practice include:

- taking the time to learn about a community partner's vision, mission and values, and actively listening to them speak about their passion areas
- showing respect and understanding by learning about the cultural values, ways of knowing and approaches that shape your community partners' work.
- asking community partners what they need, rather than what you personally find easiest or more enjoyable to do
- actively listening for the purpose of understanding, rather than responding or reacting
- continuing to check in with community partners to ensure that their needs haven't shifted
- sharing your knowledge with community partners
- giving back to your school or broader community by teaching others
- treating younger and older people with respect and care
- actively showing appreciation in person and/or through follow-up communications
- giving purposefully, not just for the sake of giving, but for the sake of appreciating and recognizing someone's needs
- reflecting on your reciprocal thoughts and actions
- following through with your commitments
- clearly communicating around lack of follow-through or failed plans
- practising reflexivity to see where you have challenges or lack insight around reciprocity.

Learning journal

In your learning journal, capture your current understanding of reciprocity. Reflect on what you could do to specifically practise reciprocity and record this in your notes.

In the following learning engagement, you will explore reciprocity from the perspective of humans' relationship with the natural world, as well as human-to-human relationships.

LEARNING ENGAGEMENT

Understanding reciprocal relationships with nature

All living beings are interconnected, and we need to acknowledge the importance of living in reciprocity with the land to ensure that all living beings (including animal and plant species) thrive.

1. With a peer or teacher, discuss the following questions and make a note of your thoughts in your learning journal.
   - How are we related to the plants, animals, and land around us?
   - Who (including the animals, plants, air and land) do we take for granted?
   - How can the energy we put into something affect it?
2. Next, create three columns on a piece of paper. In the first column, make a list of some products you are highly dependent on in your daily life. In the second column, write down the natural source of these products. In the third column, record how you give back to or care for the natural sources of the products you have listed.

Reflection and reflexivity

Discuss the following questions with your teacher, a peer or in a small group. Reflect your discussion in your learning journal.

- How can you maintain a positive and sustainable relationship with the natural sources on which you depend?
- What are more environmentally safe alternatives to some of the products you use?
- How can you give back to the land that provides for you?
- What would it look and feel like if humans were in a reciprocal relationship with the natural world?
- How does reciprocity relate to sustainability?
- In what circumstances or relationships do you show reciprocity? How does this strengthen and support your relationships? What happens in relationships when reciprocity is not enacted?
- How can you practise reciprocity in unfamiliar circumstances and/or communities? What would you need to understand about the community to be able to show reciprocity in a way that is meaningful for that community? How will you know your actions are meaningful for that community?

1.2.4 Reflection and reflexivity

CE requires *ongoing* reflection and reflexivity. When you engage in reflection, you will think back to events and try to work out what you think happened, how you felt about it and why you responded the way you did. Your analysis of events will include who said and did what, how, when, where and why. By reviewing experiences, you will bring them into focus and look for important details that may have eluded you before. You will make an effort to understand what happened in the past, which impacts your plans for future learning and growth, in solidarity with your community.

Through reflexivity, you will make an effort to challenge your own perspectives, habits and assumptions, understanding how they impact the personal, relational and systems dimensions of CE. This will help you enter reciprocal dialogues with a greater ability to set aside your own assumptions and usual ways of thinking and being so that you can create more space for the feelings and perspectives of others. Learning to be reflexive allows you to increase your awareness and compassion for yourself and others, and it enhances your sensitivity to complex issues. Reflexivity requires you to place yourself *within* a system so that you can be critically conscious of how you are impacting that system. It is about examining your own biases and, in order to do this in a non-judgemental way, you will need to accept that human bias is a natural part of life. You need to be aware that when bias goes unrecognized or is misunderstood, it can influence decision-making and behaviour, potentially leading to unintended and even harmful consequences. By non-judgementally examining the connections between your biases, values, identities, behaviours and beliefs, you will understand how they interconnect, interact and intersect with others in the community.

Reflective and reflexive practices do not only happen at the end of a unit, nor are they tick-box exercises. They should be organic, continuous, systematic and critical reviews of what you are learning, leading to deeper understandings about how you engage with the dimensions and principles of CE. Insights arise in different ways and at different times, and you need to identify key moments during your learning and engagement process that inspire reflection and reflexivity. In this way, reflective and reflexive practice can happen authentically and by choice, with a deeper focus on quality versus quantity.

Reflection and reflexivity are practices, meaning they require consistent attention and thoughtful application. These practices help you to process information, critically examine how you will put that information to use, and apply it to your community engagements. Reflection and reflexivity practice can involve independent work in your learning journal, working with a peer or working within a larger group. It can include facilitated dialogues, self- and peer feedback, and community presentations. Reflection and reflexivity, as learning outcomes, must be evidenced during guided-learning time and informal conversations, during your active engagements and at the formal review points. It is essential that you document your reflection and reflexivity growth over time.

LEARNING ENGAGEMENT

Reflection and reflexivity

With your teacher or a peer, discuss the following questions. Your teacher may ask you to share with others.

- How can I include diverse ways of knowing and being, even/especially when I hold a different perspective?
- What am I learning about myself through the engagements?
- Where are my biases and assumptions, and how do I know? Are they changing over time? Where do they come from?
- Are there parts of my identity, belief system and/or life experiences that I am ignoring or completely missing?

Learning journal

Capture your current understanding of reflection and reflexivity in your journal through a growth-over-time map or in some other format. This will help you in your review points.

The wheel of positionality

As you are learning in CE and LCS, perspectives are constructed in cultural and societal contexts, and it is important that you practise reflection and reflexivity in relation to the dimensions of your social identity. This will help you understand how you see others, how others see you and how this impacts the relational systems you are part of.

When you reflect on your social identity, you are examining your positionality. Positionality helps you understand who you are and how your identity affects your connection to the people, systems and power structures that surround you. Your positionality is tied to your values, beliefs and hopes, and it influences how you perceive and filter information. Your skills, abilities, resources and lifestyle are shaped by the culture and society you live in, and it is important that you are aware of this, especially as you engage with people and communities that are different from your own.

The wheel of positionality is a helpful tool to help you examine how your identity connects to the way the community is structured, what is expected of different people within the community, and how individuals are supported or not supported within the community. Your positionality may shift depending on your local or global context and it may change throughout your life, even if your external environment remains the same.

■ The wheel of positionality

As you learn in LCS, power refers to the amount of control and influence one has in a group or society. Power is deeply connected to culture, history, social norms and economic factors, which impact a person's or group's ability to exert influence, control or domination over another person or group. Power is not equally distributed within the community, and 'individuals' and communities' choices and actions can influence, or be influenced by, power structures and relations' (IB LCS guide, p.18). For example, looking at the wheel, consider a recent immigrant. If they do not speak the dominant language/s of their community, would they have the same access to power and resources as someone who is fluent in the dominant language/s? If they are not citizens in their new country, would they have the same access to power and opportunities as those with citizenship? And how would financial stability or insecurity impact this immigrant when it comes to some of the other spokes of the wheel?

Understanding how the various parts of the wheel overlap and interconnect is an essential part of reflexivity, and it helps develop intellectual and cultural humility. This wheel will help you better understand why you do or do not have certain opportunities in the community, and it will give you a better understanding of others' circumstances, which can deepen empathy and understanding.

LEARNING ENGAGEMENT

The wheel of positionality

This learning engagement will be completed in your learning journal, and your teacher may ask you to share parts of it with others, to the degree that you are comfortable.

Look at the wheel of positionality and consider:

- Which parts of my identity have I understood for the longest time?
- Which parts of my identity impact how others see me?
- Which parts of my identity impact how I see others?
- Which parts of my identity place me in a greater or lesser position of power and influence within my community?
- Why is it important for me to understand why I and others have or do not have as much power and influence within the community?
- How can an understanding of this wheel help me become more knowledgeable, open-minded, caring and principled as I take action in and with the community?

Types of reflective and reflexive practice

As discussed, reflection and reflexivity are related, but are separate processes. In this section, you will explore a broader and more nuanced approach to understanding reflection and reflexivity through the concepts of metacognitive reflection, process reflection, critical reflection, self-reflexivity and critical reflexivity. While it is not necessary for you to memorize the details of these different types of reflective and reflexive practice, they are included here so that you can see the multiple lenses through which it is possible to view reflection and reflexivity.

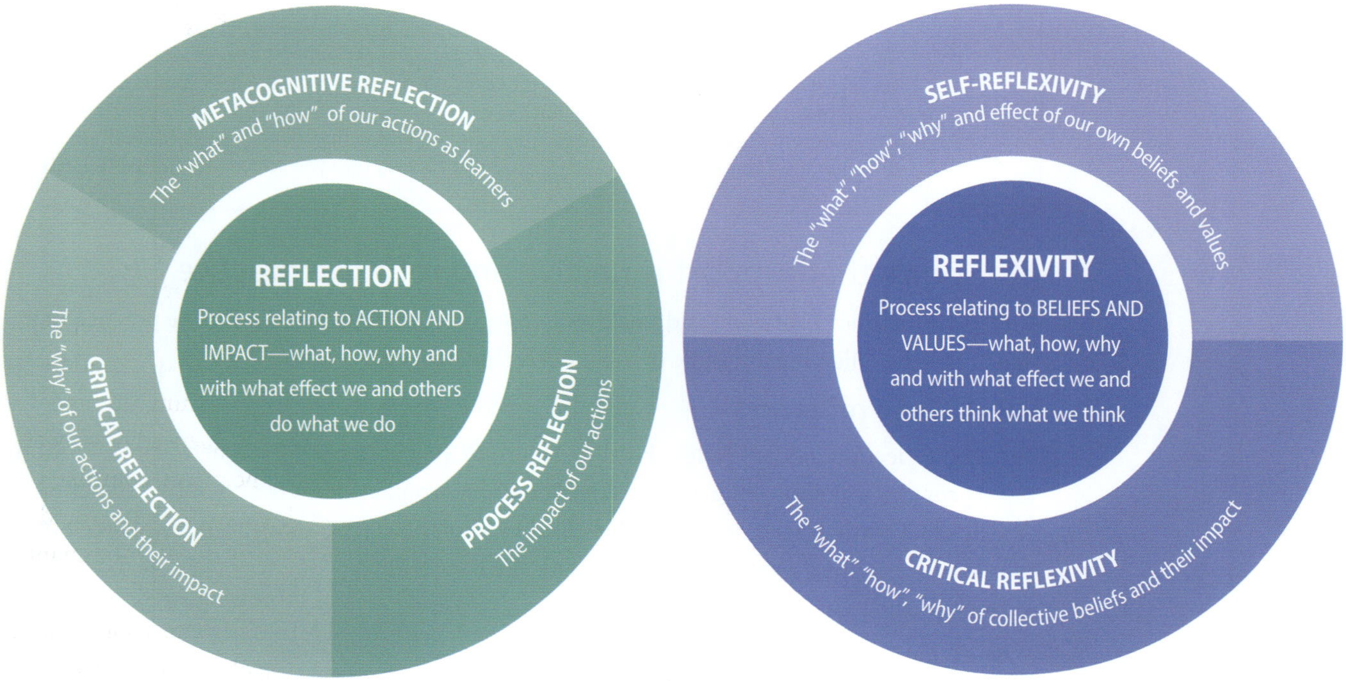

Types of reflective and reflexive practice (Source: IBO 2025b, p.28)

Table 1.13

Reflection type	Description	Possible applications
Metacognitive reflection	Metacognitive reflection enhances your awareness of your own learning process and *how* you learn. It involves examining your own thinking, actions and goals. This leads to self-regulated learning.	Reflecting on community engagements, consider how you have learned and processed new concepts and ideas, made assumptions, goals and decisions, and interacted with others.
Process reflection	Process reflection starts with an experience and leads to new or changed understandings, insights and/or actions. This requires looking at different situations from many angles to gain new insights.	After a community engagement, you examine how the process unfolded, how people responded, what was learned and what can happen differently next time.
Critical reflection	With critical reflection, you look inward to analyse your thoughts and actions so that you can grow from an experience. You think deeply about your assumptions, actions, reactions, decisions and beliefs to understand what you think, why you think it and how you act in given situations.	After challenging or confusing conversations with community members, consider your assumptions, biases, reactions and decisions. Learn to own your mistakes, see different perspectives and continually grow from your experiences. Be open to having your views challenged and consider how you can foster deeper ethical engagement.
Self-reflexivity	With self-reflexivity, you look inward and focus on how your personal perspectives are shaped by your identity and life experiences. You analyse your own background, beliefs and identity to help you understand why you think and act the way you do.	Self-reflexivity is important when entering a new community or cultural experience. It causes you to be more aware of your own thinking and how your biases and assumptions are showing up. This enables you to take a step back before speaking or moving into action, which can minimize misunderstandings. You can make better decisions about how you want to respond to the community you are engaging with.
Critical reflexivity	Critical reflexivity asks you to zoom out and connect your personal perspectives to larger systems, such as culture and power. This helps you understand how your perspectives connect with others' perspectives in the community. It asks you to examine situations through lenses of power, fairness and identity. It explores how the world around you shapes your experience and how you shape the world around you.	Critical reflexivity is helpful when learning about sensitive situations, such as social injustices It helps you understand why your biases exist, how they show up, how they are influenced by your society/culture, how they impact others and how you can act ethically. In your community engagements, connect your experiences to your identity, roles and social position within the community. Consider how these may give you certain advantages or cause blind spots.

Models that support reflective and reflexive practice

Models help reduce confusion and uncertainty by giving reflective and reflexive practice more structure. The following are some of the models that may help.

The ABCs of reflection

The ABC reflection model (Welch, Plaxton-Moore, 2019, based on Hondagneu-Sotelo, Rashoff, 1994) provides a generic template for reflection. It incorporates both the cognitive and affective aspects of CE, which are also reflected in the ATL skills. The ABC model can be included in your learning journal as you work in and with the community.

- **Affect:** What and how you feel.
  - What were you feeling during the process?

- **Behaviour:** The ways you behave before, during and after the experience.
  - Can you think of a time you had to work with someone else in a similar situation?
  - What did you do?
  - With this new insight, how might you behave in the future?
- **Cognition:** What you learned.
  - What concepts/terms from class discussions/readings reflect this process?

The DEAL model

The DEAL model (Ash and Clayton, 2009) provides a structured approach to critical reflection. It can be included in your learning journal as you work in and with the community.

- Describe the experience objectively and in detail, making sure there are important elements that are in line with the learning outcomes.
  - Where and when did the experience occur?
  - Who was there and who was not?
  - What actions did you/others take?
  - Who did not speak/act?
  - What goals did you want to work on in this engagement?
  - How did you act or communicate differently in this experience compared to previous experiences?
- Examine the experience from different perspectives/through different lenses.
  - How did the experience enhance your understanding of a concept/theory?
  - How does this experience highlight the relationship between the community and larger systems?
  - Did you enter the engagement with expectations/assumptions and were these confirmed or refuted?
  - What surprised you about the experience and why?
  - What skills or knowledge from previous experiences did you draw on and how did this influence how you acted?
  - What strengths helped you and did you identify gaps in your knowledge/skills that you intend to address?
  - Did you uncover biases or attitudes as a result of the experience and do you need to address these?
  - In what ways did power differentials emerge in this experience?
  - What are the sources of power in this situation; who benefits and who is harmed?
  - What privileges did you/others bring to this situation? What are the sources of such privilege?
  - What specific elements of your CE lessons/discussions relate to this experience?
  - How were you able to apply a skill, perspective or concept related to CE or other elements of the CRS (CP)?
- Articulate learning. Using your responses in the describe and examine phases, summarize your learning as a result of the experience and reflection. Set goals and future directions for learning that can be applied in subsequent experiences.
  - What did you learn?
  - Why does it matter?
  - What should be done in light of it?
  - How has your understanding of concepts changed as a result of the experience and reflection?
  - What goals do you intend to set for yourself for future experiences?

Ladder of inference

The ladder of inference is a model that was first introduced by Chris Argyris and Peter Senge (D'Eon, 2022) and it helps us understand why we interpret things the way we do. It helps us examine our preferences, biases, habits and opinions, which are rooted in our own mental models and which are, in turn, influenced by our positionality within the community. By taking a more reflective and reflexive approach to understanding how we interpret and act on information, we can avoid drawing incorrect and/or incomplete conclusions about people and circumstances.

The ladder helps us examine how we take in data through our senses and how thoughts form in relationship to the data we sense. The bottom of the ladder, 'observations', refers to that which we take in through our senses (seeing, hearing, tasting, touching and smelling). This observable data has not yet been filtered through our own mental models.

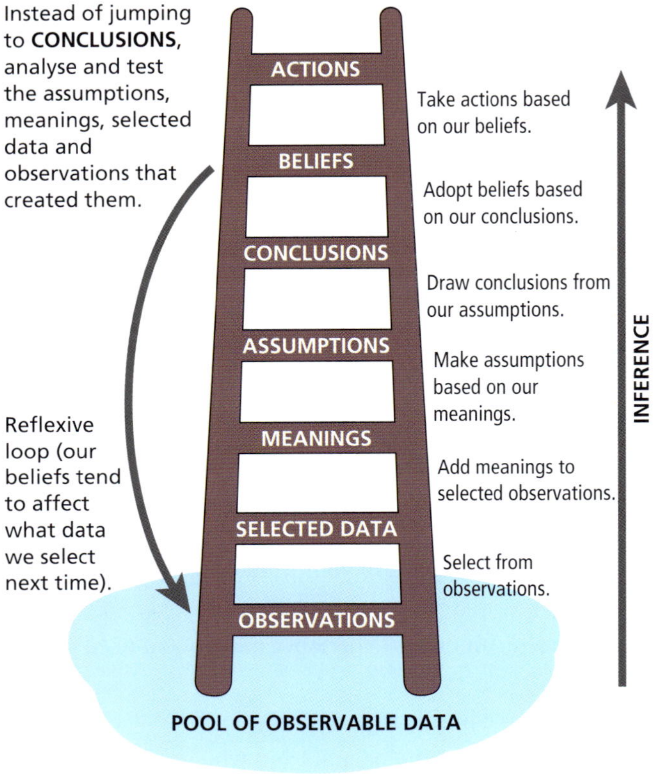

■ The ladder of inference (Based on the model by Chris Argyris, 1923–2013)

Our mental models, which are informed by our biases, worldviews, perspectives, values, beliefs and experiences, determine how we filter the observable data that comes in through our senses, and it is here that assumptions and beliefs can begin to affect our observations. Biases are like mental shortcuts, and they are a part of everyone's life. They can help us avoid danger and become more efficient in our thinking. However, they can reduce our ability to be empathic and open-minded, and result in oversimplifications and stereotyping.

The ladder can help us reduce misunderstandings and misinterpretations, gain knowledge and understanding, and become more compassionate and effective communicators and leaders. The bottom of the ladder is where we neutrally observe data, rather than imbuing it with our own habitual meanings and biases. As we move up the ladder, we begin interpreting information more subjectively, based on our own thoughts, opinions, habits and beliefs, and this can lead to false assumptions and conclusions, which further impact and solidify the beliefs that brought us up the ladder in the first place. Through reflexive practice, we can begin to examine our assumptions and move down the ladder to a place of observing incoming data through a more neutral awareness. This allows us to be open to new ways of understanding, and often this leads to more connection with others. Depending on the situation, it can also lessen our own emotional distress.

As D'Eon (2022) notes, there are reflective and reflexive steps we can take to ensure we do not unconsciously climb up the ladder without recognizing our biases, possibly hurting ourselves or others along the way.

■ Table 1.14

Sixth rung	When moving into action, ask yourself, 'Am I acting on my constructed narrative or on what is really happening?'
Fifth rung	When coming to conclusions, examine the beliefs that are behind those conclusions.
Fourth rung	Ask yourself if you are basing your assumption on the facts that you have witnessed or on what you believe. Perhaps you will want to investigate further.
Third rung	Be critical of your own thought process, becoming aware of your brain assigning meaning to things. Do not believe everything you think. Ask yourself if you need more information.
Second rung	Do not dismiss any information, even when it does not align with your perspective.
First rung	Observe the facts as objectively as possible. Do not make judgements or assumptions. Record what you see and hear.

LEARNING ENGAGEMENT

The ladder of inference

Answer the following questions in your learning journal.

- Identify a time when you became upset in a conversation that had escalated and later regretted your response. Perhaps someone challenged your thoughts and beliefs or did something you considered offensive. Perhaps you felt agitated and responded from a place of heightened emotional reactivity (e.g. anger). Remember how your body felt and the thoughts that went through your mind.
- Thinking back to what happened, examine it as neutrally as possible. What was actually said and done at that moment? What was the incoming data (e.g. something you heard or saw)?
- Moving up the ladder, consider how you selected certain data (perhaps becoming fixated on the other person's body language, tone of voice or word choice).
- Next, examine how you made meaning of what was happening, and how this led to assumptions and conclusions. It can take just seconds to move up the ladder.
- Did you adopt new beliefs based on your conclusions, or did this situation reinforce long-held beliefs about another person or the circumstance?
- What actions did you take that you later regretted? How could you have self-managed to ensure you had time to reflect on the situation and examine your responses from a place of more emotional stability and mental clarity?
- What did you learn from this situation, and how would you like to act in similar circumstances in the future?

Ladder of connectedness

CE is focused on the quality of our relational connections and sometimes, despite our best intentions, it can be hard to connect with someone else. This may be because of personality differences or it may be for other reasons that are, at first, unnoticed or not fully understood. Like the ladder of inference, the ladder of connectedness (Senge, 2018) is a model that will help you practise reflection and reflexivity on a deeper level. Both ladders help you unpack your own biases so that you can examine them in relation to the CE community dimensions and principles of engagement.

The ladder of connection challenges you to examine why you feel disconnected from others or lack empathy for them. Feeling disconnected is a natural part of the human experience; however, it is important to know why disconnection is happening.

Beginning at the top of the ladder, when you are emotionally disconnected from others in the community, you can recognize the ways in which you depersonalize and/or deprioritize them. Moving down the ladder, you can notice when empathizing with others leads to feelings of personal distress, causing you to disconnect so that you do not feel discomfort.

In-group empathy refers to showing preferential treatment to those community members who have similar lifestyles, beliefs, worldviews and values as you. Cognitive empathy refers to intellectually understanding others' experiences without having an emotional connection with them. Altruism refers to connecting on both a cognitive and emotional level, which spurs the desire to take action to help. Neutral awareness refers to your ability to empathize with others while maintaining a sense of personal balance; this allows you to emotionally support others in the community without moving into your own personal distress.

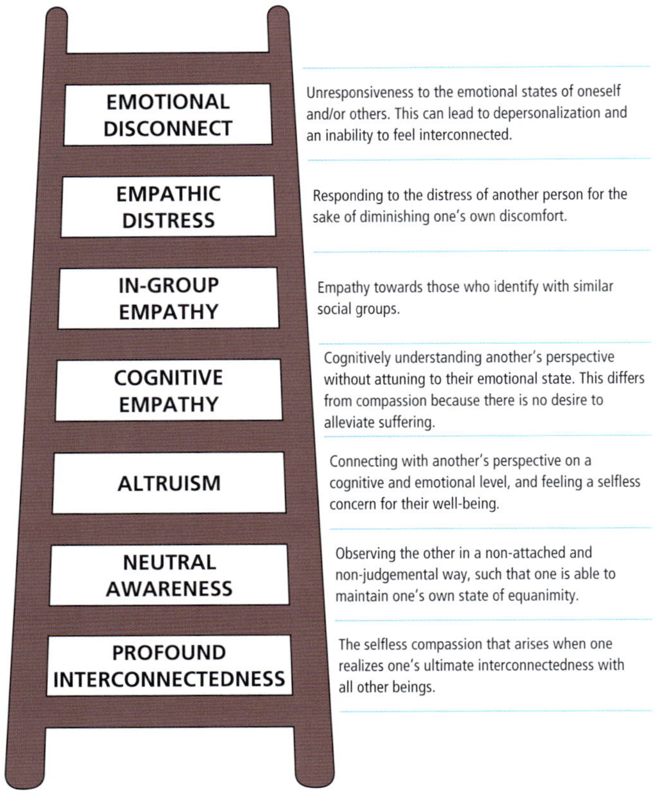

■ The ladder of connectedness (Based on Senge, 2018)

The bottom rung of the ladder is profound interconnectedness, which happens when you realize that all beings in the community, and all communities, are connected in some way. This interconnectedness happens when you don't see yourself as separate from others and the world around you, and it is beautifully expressed through the African concept of Ubuntu. When explaining Ubuntu, Archbishop Desmond Tutu says it 'is the essence of being human. It speaks of the fact that my humanity is caught up and is inextricably bound up in yours. I am human because I belong to the whole, to the community, to the tribe, to the nation, to the Earth. Ubuntu is about wholeness, about compassion for life' (Amnesty International, 2010).

Reciprocity relies on connection, and you can consciously cultivate connections with others that are grounded in trust and mutual respect, even when you don't know them well or like them. Through self-reflexivity, you can notice where you are on the ladder, examine what is happening and choose to move down the ladder. This allows you to make conscious adjustments in your interactions with others to support your overall ethical intentions. Healthy communities reflect people's willingness to be reflective and reflexive in their connections with others, honour their shared humanity and uphold everyone's dignity, regardless of personal preferences.

REAL-WORLD EXAMPLE

Applying the ladder of connectedness

A CE teacher, Mr Carnahan, notices that one of his students, Emma, is having challenges relating to the other students. She is not joining in on class discussions and she tends to work on her own, even when she is invited to join a peer group. Emma is new to the school and she comes from another country where the school environment was quite different.

Mr Carnahan approaches Emma and gently asks how she is doing with her peer group. Emma explains that she misses her friends and feels shy around new people. She shares that collaborating with new people can be a challenge for her sometimes.

Mr Carnahan introduces Emma to the ladder of connectedness. Together, they consider some of the terms and concepts that Emma can further explore. Mr Carnahan encourages Emma to reflect on the most relevant parts of this ladder in her learning journal. After the discussion with her teacher, Emma realizes that she wants to become more of a risk-taker and collaborate with her new peers. She notes that she feels care and empathy in class discussions, that she would like to get to know her peers' perspectives better, and she would like to openly share more of her own perspectives as well.

LEARNING ENGAGEMENT

Applying the ladder of connectedness

With your teacher or a peer, discuss the following questions about the real-world example above. Your teacher may ask you to share with a larger group.

1. What reciprocal actions can Emma take with her new peers and how might this help her create more of a connection with them?
2. What parts of the ladder connect to the IB learner profile and ATL skills?
3. What would it be like to feel truly connected with your community, not only with other people, but with nature and everything else around you? How could that kind of connection bring you a sense of hope, joy and belonging?
4. Are there any approaches or beliefs that would need to change for you to feel more connected in your community, both in and outside of school?

More on reflexivity

When you interact in and with the community, you will see what an important role social relationships play. The relationships you create with members of the community, be it in or outside of school, are influenced by what you bring with you into these relationships (e.g. your race, gender or social class). These factors determine your position in relation to others, shape the way you think and approach the community, and inform the power balance and privileges that are alive in your engagements.

Examining your positionality is important when engaging with the community and this requires reflexive practice. Understanding your positionality will help you understand how and why you think and act the way you do. It will help you pause to consider whose voices are dominant, whose are not, whose need to be heard and how your own voice is involved.

(If you need to, refer back to 'self-reflexivity' and 'critical reflexivity' in Table 1.13.)

Reflection and reflexivity

With your teacher or a peer, discuss the following questions. Your teacher may ask you to share your thoughts with others.

- What relevant identities and prior experiences do you bring to your community engagements?
- How does your own positionality motivate which engagements you want to be a part of?
- What beliefs or assumptions about the community do you have and how do these shape your engagements with the community?
- To the best of your knowledge, what might be some of the social identities of the people you are engaging with? How can you make sure to show respect and support for everyone you are engaging with, regardless of how your social identities interact?
- How do you understand your biases and perspectives as socially constructed?
- Where are your biases? How do they relate to your positionality and identity and influence your actions in the community?
- Do you understand where your attitudes or responses come from? How are these tendencies related to your cultural context and positionality?
- How does your positionality impact your ability to consider divergent worldviews and narratives?

1.2.5 Summary

- CE is viewed through three interrelated dimensions: personal, relational and systems.
- Engagement is underpinned by three principles: dialogue, reciprocity and reflection/reflexivity.
- Systems thinking is a holistic approach to CE. We can understand and analyse complex systems through various systems tools.
- Active hope can help us face complex systems challenges.
- Ongoing and diverse reflective and reflexive practice is a way of understanding how we interact with the world and how we understand the impact of our actions/non-actions on the systems we are a part of.

1.3 Ethics

INQUIRY QUESTIONS

- How do ethics infuse your entire CE journey?
- How can you explore ethics in CE?
- How can you explore ethical concepts, lenses and paradigms in CE?
- How can you connect ethics to the rest of the CP Core?
- How are ethics connected to other worldviews?

Key terms

◆ **Ethical thinking:** Ethical thinking involves thinking critically about, and applying, ethical values to navigate our personal and professional lives. It fosters moral development and enables us to make responsible choices and be accountable for our decisions. Self-reflexivity supports ethical thinking as it enables us to identify and examine our personal values to guide us in our actions and decisions.

◆ **Ethical issue:** A situation or topic that raises questions of what is right or wrong for individuals, organizations, communities or society as a whole, and which requires consideration from an ethical or moral perspective. Ethical issues may be encountered in all areas of life (e.g. personal, social, professional, economic, environmental) and may relate to questions of fairness, honesty, justice, human rights or the rights of nature.

1.3.1 Understanding and exploring ethics in CE

Ethics are a key part of CE. Ethics may be defined differently across cultural contexts and, therefore, ethical actions are contextual and are shaped by the social and cultural circumstances in which they happen. A range of concepts are tied to **ethical thinking** and action, including social and ecological justice, power, care, agency, and individual and collective responsibility.

When working with the community, ethical thinking and actions require you to be open-minded towards different values and beliefs. This will help you approach conversations in ways where everyone can feel included and have an equal opportunity to participate, strengthening community health and belonging. Ethics help you determine what is fair and just while considering the well-being of non-humans and the natural world. As you partner with community members and interact with humans, non-humans and the natural world, ethics will help guide you toward your best intentions, particularly when facing challenging choices.

Ethical thinking asks you to consider value systems, perspectives, ways of knowing and being, contexts, and systemic nuances and complexities. As you encounter **ethical issues**, *ethical action* asks you to actively participate in addressing these issues through a caring and critical lens, bearing in mind the IB's commitment to international-mindedness and intercultural understanding and respect. Reflecting in an informed, critical and compassionate manner will help you further develop your personal value system and clarify the ethical principles that underlie individual and collective decisions.

The connection between ethics and worldviews

People worldwide do not share a universal code of ethics. Ethics are influenced by cultural elements, family, faith, values and traditions, all of which shape our worldviews. Our actions reflect our ethics, which in turn are shaped by our worldviews. For example, some cultures focus more on individualistic worldviews, including individual well-being and prosperity. In contrast, some cultures focus more on collectivism, which refers to worldviews and decision-making processes that centre the needs of the whole community.

It is also essential to consider other worldviews in CE. An anthropocentric worldview places a high value on human needs and sees humans as the top of nature's hierarchy. An anthropocentric worldview often sees natural resources as something to be used and controlled by humans for the benefit of humans, and environmental issues are addressed only when they directly impact humans. In contrast, an ecocentric worldview considers nature and ecosystems to have intrinsic value, regardless of their usefulness to humans. An ecocentric worldview sees all ecosystems as profoundly interconnected and all living beings as inherently valuable. In this worldview, humans are seen as equal to (and a part of) nature. Closely related to an ecocentric worldview is a biocentric worldview, which focuses on the intrinsic value of all life forms.

Understanding your own worldviews will help you understand your decisions and actions and why you make your ethical choices. Understanding your own worldviews will also help you critically question your values, beliefs, perspectives, biases and assumptions. A central part of CE is understanding that even if you hold a different worldview than someone else, you can still treat them with respect, act with integrity and show an *ethic of care* (Noddings, 2016). An ethic of care is when you show concern for another person's well-being, even though your ways of knowing and being may differ. Community well-being is also considered an ethic—an *ethic of community*—which is put into action when you focus on centring the needs of the entire community (Furman, 2004). As you reflect on your own worldview and values, it is helpful to explore some of the broader dimensions of ethical thinking. The visual below offers a way to understand how ethics can be shaped by multiple influences, including personal beliefs, community needs and global perspectives.

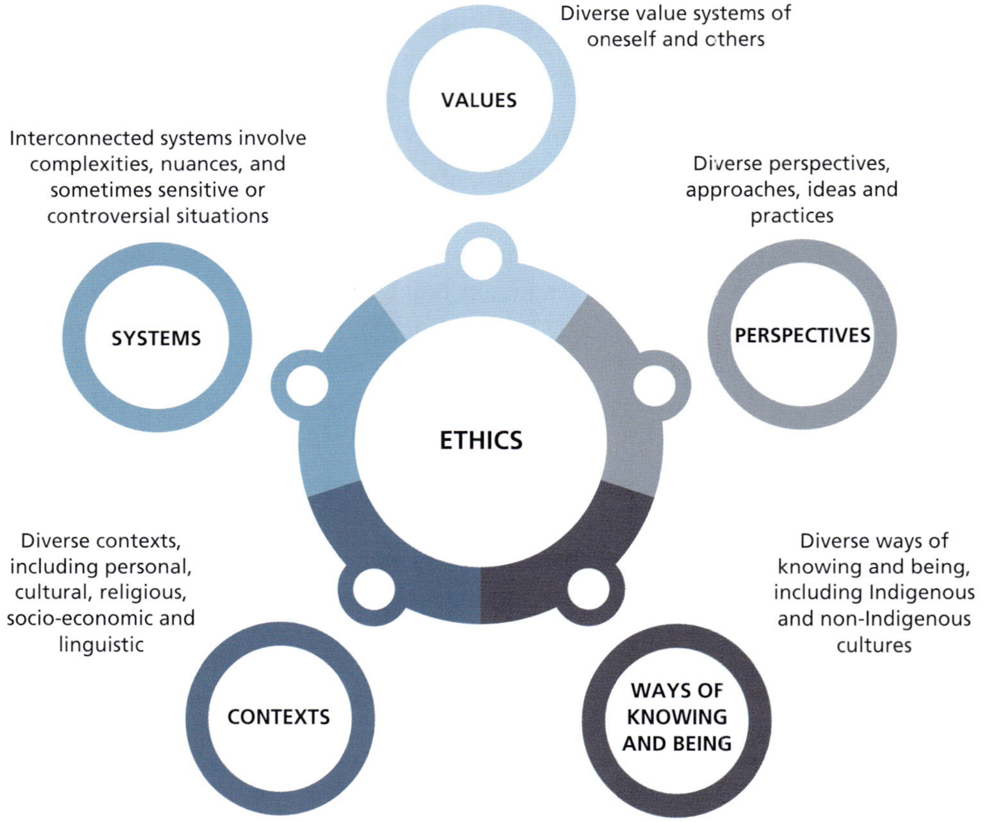

■ The many balanced aspects of ethical thinking

Top tip!

By reflecting on your knowledge and understanding of ethics, you will map your growth over time (see growth-over-time maps in Section 1.1.6). This is a valuable way to show your developing knowledge and understanding of this learning outcome at review points and community demonstrations.

Reflection and reflexivity

Ethics

Reflect on the following questions in your learning journal.

- In what other school contexts have you engaged with and/or reflected on the concept of ethics?
- In what other school and/or non-school contexts have you needed to ensure your actions are respectful and beneficial to the community?
- In the past, how have you navigated ethical dilemmas with careful consideration?
- In the past, have you consulted with mentors and community leaders when considering ethical dilemmas?
- Discuss your current ability to articulate ethical considerations in project planning and execution.

Ethical space

As you move through CE and develop higher-level reflection and reflexive skills, you will be asked to deepen your knowledge and understanding of the importance of diversity. This may happen through dialogues with peers and community partners or as you learn more about communities that are different from your own.

As Ermine (2007) notes, one definition of ethics is 'the capacity to know what harms or enhances the well-being of living beings'. He describes an *ethical space* as being 'formed when two societies, with disparate worldviews, are poised to engage each other' (p.193). This description highlights how ethical space can open possibilities for respectful engagement across differences.

Ethical space, however, is not limited to interactions between whole societies. It can also emerge whenever people, groups or communities with different identities, backgrounds or perspectives come together. In this space, ideas can be explored openly, even when disagreements arise, with the shared intention that each person speaks and acts with empathy and respect.

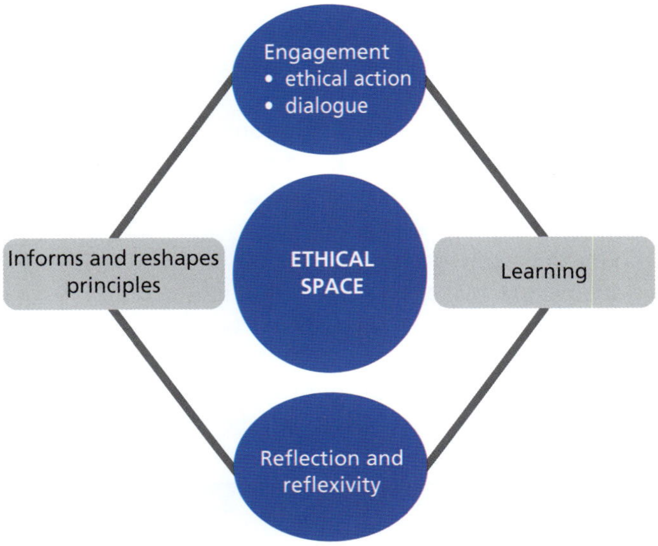

■ Ethical spaces positively impact individuals and relationships. (Adapted from Nikolakis and Hotte, 2021)

Throughout your time in CE, you can set out to create ethical spaces. Through dialogue and collaboration with peers, teachers and community partners, you will encounter and learn from people with different ways of knowing and being. You are asked to respond respectfully in challenging situations where differing approaches and perspectives emerge. Rather than avoiding complex topics and conversations, you are invited to contribute to ethical spaces where discussions can be facilitated through caring and critical lenses. By understanding and using the dimensions of community and principles of engagement, you will hone your communication, thinking, collaboration and reflection skills, which will help you strengthen your ethical decision-making.

Consistently practising ethical thinking will help you build meaningful and authentic relationships, which will help you contribute to the common good. As a part of your ethical thinking, it is essential to avoid approaches that are simplistic, salvationist or paternalistic, when looking at community challenges. As Andreotti (2012) notes, *simplistic approaches* focus too much on the events level of the systems iceberg and they avoid the complexity of issues—they do not address the root causes of problems. This can often lead to 'quick fixes' or uncomplicated solutions that distract people from what is really going on. *Salvationist approaches* reinforce the idea that one person or group is better or wiser because they have more resources. This can create an 'us versus them' mentality, where one person or group acts in the role of the 'saviour' while the other person or group is considered the 'victim'. While some salvationist approaches come from generosity and good intentions, they can end up causing harm because they ignore the wisdom, knowledge, strengths, experiences and skills of the community members they are trying to help. *Paternalistic approaches* position the 'helper' as someone who knows best, much like a parent who makes decisions for a child without involving them in the decision-making process. Paternalistic approaches include making decisions for the community without consulting the community, which undermines community members' agency, independence and autonomy. It is important to note that ill-thought-out approaches to CE can cause harm to the communities they are trying to support and reinforce harmful stereotypes. Engaging in ethical thinking and actively contributing to ethical spaces for learning, dialogue and reflection will help you become more reflexive about your own individual approaches, as well as the collective approaches that you are a part of.

Considering ethics from multiple perspectives and engaging in continuous reflection will support you to open your heart and mind to new ways of knowing and being. The ethical concepts and models you will be introduced to in this section will help you develop and refine your collaboration, research and thinking skills to contribute to ethical spaces positively. Throughout this process, it is essential to commit to ongoing learning, which will inform and possibly reshape your principles and beliefs. Reflect on the moments when you realize that you are engaging with perspectives, contexts and concepts in new ways. Then, through your learning journal, document your reflexive journey.

LEARNING ENGAGEMENT

Discuss the following with your teacher or a peer. Your teacher may also ask you to share with a larger group.

Describe a time when you entered an ethical space and tried to understand someone else's perspective, even though you disagreed with them.

- How did you feel? Were there challenging feelings and/or emotions present?
- Did you experience any changes in mood? How did they affect the interaction?
- How did you become aware of your mind–body connection and self-regulate?
- What role did respect and humility play in the interaction?
- How did you address tension and try to encourage open dialogue?
- What helped you to understand the perspective of another in that interaction?
- If applicable, how did you follow up with the person or people after the conversation?
- How did you reflect on this discussion with attention to your own habits, biases, perspectives and worldviews?

Learning journal

What have you learned about ethics so far? Capture this in a growth-over-time map or in some other format in your learning journal.

1.3.2 Exploring ethical concepts, lenses and paradigms

Key terms

◆ **Ethical concepts:** The core ideas or 'ingredients' of ethical thinking, such as identity, integrity and power, that help you explore what is right or wrong in a situation.

◆ **Ethical lenses:** The perspectives or values you use to interpret ethical situations. Like a pair of glasses, different lenses can help you see an issue in a new way and lead to different decisions.

◆ **Ethical paradigms:** The broader cultural or philosophical systems that shape how you understand ethics. Your paradigm influences which voices you prioritize and how you align your values with your actions.

As you explore ethics, it will be helpful to have models that help you analyse, structure and refine your thinking. This becomes especially important when you are faced with challenges and difficult decisions. Ethical concepts, lenses and paradigms, while deeply interconnected, are also distinct models to support you in becoming more thoughtful and purposeful in your ethical thinking and actions.

Ethical concepts can be thought of as distinct components or 'ingredients' for ethical thinking; examples include the concepts of identity, integrity and power. *Ethical lenses* help you combine these ingredients (concepts) into a more cohesive set of ideals that frame your perspectives and inform your decisions and actions. Much like a set of glasses, you can change your ethical lenses to give you a new perspective on an issue, challenge or solution. This is especially important when considering difficult or impactful decisions, as changing ethical lenses can offer new perspectives that may lead to different outcomes. And finally, *ethical paradigms* consider the larger cultural and/or philosophical contexts from which you are operating. This impacts which perspectives and voices you prioritize, which choices and actions you consider ethical, and how you choose to align your worldviews, values and actions.

■ Ethical concepts

Ethical concepts present distinct ideas about what constitutes skilful decision-making. These ideas can be considered on their own or combined with other ideas to help you understand the focus of your ethical explorations and guide your thinking. The figure on the next page describes eight ethical concepts that contribute to the community's well-being when considered alone and together. For example, understanding identity and perspective strengthens reflective and reflexive practice, leading to a greater understanding of what motivates ethical actions. Equity, integrity and care promote personal and collective responsibility, and systems thinking (covered in Section 1.2.2) clarifies connections between community dimensions (personal, relational and social/ecological). Power encourages recognizing how influence and control impact the well-being of all members of the community.

Learning journal

In your learning journal, reflect on the most and least familiar ethical concepts to you. As you reflect, consider your personal and family history and culture, and any other subject areas or ideas you have thought about when exposed to local and global information.

PERSPECTIVE

Is it possible to be neutral in your attitudes and decisions?

How can we decide what is ethical when different individuals/communities have different, and possibly divergent, perspectives and beliefs?

IDENTITY

How do you communicate with people with different identities?

How do you avoid reducing others to a single, one-dimensional identity?

EQUITY

How do you make sure that the engagement is fair and equitable for all involved?

How are you thinking and acting in ways that promote and support respect, solidarity, understanding and reciprocity?

RESPONSIBILITY

How do you assess whether behaviour and actions are responsible in the context of your community engagement?

How do you balance individual and collective responsibility in the engagement?

ETHICAL CONCEPTS

CARE

What is required for the engagement to contribute in a constructive way to the community's well-being?

What caring attitudes and actions are present in your engagement with the community?

SYSTEMS

Why do you think you need to be a systems thinker in community engagement?

How can systems thinking inform ethical action?

POWER

How do you share power with the community?

How can you empower others to share their wisdom, knowledge, voices, challenges, creativity, ideas, hopes, concerns and actions?

INTEGRITY

How do you make sure that all parties are acting with integrity in the engagement?

How reliable and trustworthy is your engagement with the community?

■ Some questions you can ask yourself when considering different ethical concepts in CE (Based on the IB CE toolkit)

Reflection and reflexivity

Ethics, perspectives and identities

Discuss the following questions with your teacher or a peer. Your teacher may ask you to share your ideas with a larger group. You are encouraged to identify other relevant concepts when exploring ethics and formulate questions and possible responses. Additional concepts may include choice, honesty, justice, respect, truth, change, ecological justice and rights.

- How do perspectives influence which ethical concepts are most important to you at any point in time?
- What do you understand about how your identities shape your views of the world and the actions you take in the world?
- How do you understand yourself in relation to your social identities (religion, faith, class, cultural background, gender, race, ethnicity, geographical location)?
- How can you become more attentive to individual values and identities and how these impact the whole community?
- How can you understand biases and perspectives as socially constructed?
- In what ways can power be understood as complex?
- What factors might cause power to change within a community, and how will you know it has changed?
- How do you understand who has power, agency and voice, and why? Will everyone share your perspectives on this? Why, or why not?
- How can you help make systems more equitable?

Ethical lenses

As mentioned earlier, an ethical lens is a viewpoint through which we analyse ethical issues. Ethical lenses may include multiple ethical concepts, such as honesty, integrity and care. Ethical lenses are another tool you can use to strengthen your understanding of situations, particularly when there are differing viewpoints and things to consider. Like wearing a new pair of glasses, ethical lenses support you to see new perspectives more clearly. Balancing perspectives is an essential part of arriving at fair and equitable decisions that benefit individuals and the community as a whole.

LEGAL SYSTEMS

This lens opens perspectives about laws, legal systems, norms, rules, regulations, policies and rights, including the rights of non-humans. This lens prompts questions such as:

- What are the laws that govern this society?
- Who created these laws?
- In what socio-historic context were they created?
- Whose voices were present/absent when these laws were created?
- Who has the power to influence/enforce laws?
- Who benefits from them and whose voices are silenced?
- How does what is 'legal' relate to what is 'ethical'? How does it relate to what is 'just'?

JUSTICE

This lens opens perspectives about the different types of justice and addresses what humans and non-humans need to survive and thrive in various contexts. It invites examination of injustice and inequity. This lens prompts questions such as:

- What is justice?
- Who decides what is just?
- What systems and structures create and/or perpetuate ongoing inequalities and inequities?
- How are justice issues evolving?
- How are justice issues approached, discussed and managed when there are differing social, historic and cultural perspectives?

PROFESSION

This lens opens perspectives towards the ethics of various professions, recognizing that professional codes of ethics are continually evolving. This lens prompts questions such as:

- Who creates professional ethics?
- Whose voices are dominant, whose voices are silenced and why?
- What informs professional ethics?
- What is the process of changing and evolving professional ethics?
- How are professional ethics related to justice and legal systems?

COMMUNITY/ COMMON GOOD

This lens offers perspectives on the value and resonance of life in community as something good in and of itself. It centres the community as a whole and examines how actions contribute to the life of the community, highlighting mutual concern for the shared interests of all members of the community.

- How can people reach conclusions through reciprocal community participation and decision-making processes?
- What will best serve the community as a whole?
- What happens when community well-being risks the well-being of non-humans and the natural world (e.g. the climate as a common good)?
- What is the balance between what is best for the individual and what is best for the collective?

RIGHTS

This lens opens perspectives about rights and dignity. The ethical action is the one that best protects and respects the rights of those affected. Rights are also often understood as implying the duty to respect others' rights and dignity.

- What is a right? Who decides?
- Is something a right if it is not in the law?
- In what socio-historic contexts have different rights been acknowledged?
- What happens if different rights 'clash'?
- What could happen if humans centred the rights of non-humans and the natural world? Whose voices would need to be a part of creating this change?
- What would happen to human harmony and well-being if non-human and environmental rights were protected? What systems would protect these rights?

CARE

This lens opens perspectives to empathy, care and compassion for individuals, as well as more broadly for all life and the planet.

- Who will benefit from what I decide?
- Who/what living being will be hurt by my actions?
- What are the long-term effects of a decision I/we make today?
- Which option appropriately takes into account the relationships, concerns and feelings of humans and non-humans?
- How can I care for myself as a part of living systems?
- How can humans come into more awareness of the bio-intelligence of systems to foster more caring and compassionate actions?

■ Ethical lenses (Adapted from the IB CE TSM)

REAL-WORLD EXAMPLE

Homelessness in the community

Homelessness continues to be a significant issue across a particular heavily populated urban area, and local politicians hold a community meeting to discuss approaches to this complex issue. Five politicians speak about their approach to the problems at the meeting, which is well-attended by people of various ages, including students. Three politicians think this issue should be tackled through an ethic of care. Understanding that there are many interconnected issues, they want to increase services for homeless individuals. They also believe that supporting individuals will benefit the community, meaning they see things through an ethic of community. One politician focuses on the legal system, noting that some homeless people are breaking the law by sleeping on the streets and using illegal drugs. This politician wants the community to take a tougher stance on crime. The last politician is focused on equity issues, offering statistics about the number of homeless people related to historically marginalized populations. This politician thinks that local community councils need broader representation to ensure everyone's voice will be heard.

LEARNING ENGAGEMENT

Homelessness in the community

Read through the real-world example above and answer the questions, which ask you to apply ethical lenses. You can approach this independently, with a peer or as part of a more extensive group discussion.

1. In your learning journal, create a mind map of the stakeholders involved in this issue.
2. Beside each stakeholder, explore the different ethical lenses that could support a critical examination of ethical considerations. For example, which stakeholders will focus more on care for individuals or the legal rights of various community members?
3. Consider the following:
   a. Historically, who has made and enforced the laws and policies impacting the homeless population?
   b. Who has the power, who has been silenced, who benefits from this issue, and why?
   c. When the community does not meet homeless peoples' needs, where are the barriers to empathy, compassion and understanding, and why does this happen?

Ethical paradigms

Ethical paradigms are more comprehensive than ethical lenses and are used to categorize ethical orientations and guide ethical reasoning. Paradigms are philosophical models that reflect a broader worldview. They often align with ethical theories such as **utilitarianism**, **deontology** or **virtue ethics**. Western philosophy has been rooted in such ethical theories, which may have some thematic similarities to approaches found in non-Western traditions.

Other ethical paradigms have arisen from or been further influenced by feminist, Indigenous and critical scholarship. For example, **care ethics** are found in diverse global perspectives, such as African communitarian worldviews, Indigenous ways of knowing and being, Confucianism and Buddhism. As with ethical concepts, the intention of understanding paradigms is to help open up different perspectives that can be included in personal reflections and community dialogues.

Key terms

◆ **Utilitarianism:** Doing what creates the greatest good for the greatest number of people.

◆ **Deontology:** Doing what is right based on rules or duties, no matter the outcome.

◆ **Virtue ethics:** Making choices based on being a good person with strong character traits (e.g. honesty or courage).

◆ **Care ethics:** Making decisions by caring for others and focusing on relationships, empathy and compassion.

VIRTUE ETHICS	CONSEQUENTIALISM (E.G. UTILITARIANISM)	DUTY-BASED ETHICS (E.G. DEONTOLOGY)	ETHICS OF CARE
Central themes: Virtue and qualities. What is right is what makes us the best person we can be.	**Central theme:** The consequences of our actions. What is right is what generates the best outcome for the largest number of people.	**Central themes:** Rights and duties and how actions conform to intentions. What is ethical is what follows from absolute moral duties and imperatives, no matter what the current challenges are.	**Central themes:** Relationality, care and compassion for all human beings, and for all life and the planet. What is right is that which promotes healthy relationships, well-being and interdependence.

■ The core themes of some well-known ethical paradigms (Source: IB CE TSM)

Learning journal

If you are working on an ethics growth-over-time map, what can you add to it now?

The connection between ethics and worldviews

Earlier in this section, you explored the idea of worldviews and how they shape your ethics. You started reflecting on your own worldview and how other perspectives (such as anthropocentric, ecocentric and biocentric worldviews) influence the ethical choices people make. To deepen this understanding, compassionate community dialogues, including those in your classroom or school, will invite a range of perspectives and value systems. Learning to listen to and understand these diverse worldviews will help you further explore how ethics are formed and how they guide decision-making in different community contexts.

Reflection and reflexivity

Before you read the next section, take some time to think about these questions. You might want to share your answer with others or keep it in your learning journal:

- What is your cultural background? This might include your parents, caregivers, grandparents, ancestors or other people, places and traditions that have shaped who you are.
- What are your cultural traditions and beliefs?
- What are some of the traditions, beliefs and assumptions of your culture that may seem unusual or different to someone from outside your culture?
- What traditions, beliefs and assumptions from other cultures do you find interesting or unusual?

Within CE, you are asked to recognize dominant worldviews and critically engage with them rather than take them for granted. Some of these worldviews are deeply embedded in the cultural fabric of society. However, just because some claim that everyone shares a perspective in the culture/society, this might not be the same for everyone. A critical question is, 'Does this dominant worldview tell the whole story?' As the IB learner profile reminds us, knowledge is embedded in local and global contexts, and it is important to inquire into different knowledge systems rather than making assumptions or privileging your own system over others.

REAL-WORLD EXAMPLE

Ayu's experience

Ayu recently arrived at her new school, which is located in a wealthy area of Western Europe. She was born in Pakistan where she attended an IB school and she completed a Middle Years Programme project on the dangers of fast fashion. She feels very passionate about the problems of the fast fashion industry, notably the water pollution that results from clothing dyes entering local water systems and destroying drinking water and aquatic ecosystems. Ayu is also deeply concerned about the impacts on clothing factory workers, including harmful working conditions, child labour, gender-based violence and unfair wages.

Ayu meets with some of her new CE peers to discuss how they can launch an important initiative to help local refugees in their community. They discuss providing refugees with care packages that include local nutritious food, baby supplies and clothing. Ayu's peer suggests they buy cheap T-shirts from a local store to put in the care packages and Ayu strongly disagrees with this idea. She explains that cheap T-shirts in local stores are often made in countries such as Pakistan and Bangladesh, where the fast fashion industry can harm local environments and communities. Some other students mention that the fast fashion industry provides employment for people, and that affordable clothing is important since not all families can buy clothes without cheaper options.

Ayu says she can't be part of a project that perpetuates the dominant culture's ideas of convenience and excessive consumption at the expense of social and environmental issues. She suggests they search in second-hand stores and ask people in the school community to donate clothing they no longer wear. Another student explains that some people don't like wearing other people's clothing, and it is only fair to provide refugee teens with the same styles their peers are wearing, as this will help them fit in. They point out that this is also about belonging and well-being, since it is important for newcomers to feel accepted as they enter a new society.

LEARNING ENGAGEMENT

Ethics

In your learning journal, answer the following questions (adapted from Pashby and Sund, 2020). You may wish to work with your teacher, a peer or in a small group to answer some or all of these questions. Your teacher may also guide you to choose from other topics.

1. Considering the issue of fast fashion in your local context, answer these questions and share your answers with the group:
   - What do you know about this issue?
   - What ideas have you heard about it before?
   - Where have you heard/read these ideas from (e.g. school, media, friends, etc.)?
   - What views would you consider culturally/societally dominant?
   - Do any of these views differ from what you thought about the issue?
2. In a small group, locate a few sources that highlight views on fast fashion in your local area. These can include social-media posts, podcasts, TEDx talks and news articles.
   - What or whose story dominates the narrative about the issue?
   - Do they all reinforce a similar message, or do they differ?
   - What stereotypes or generalizations are evident in the messages?
   - What or whose story is missing? Why?
3. With the group, map the culturally/societally dominant and culturally/societally marginalized views. Then answer the following:
   - Sort them into topics (e.g. those addressing political, social or economic considerations), then consider which category gets the most attention.
   - Who decides which opinions are heard or valued?
   - What inequalities are evident in this issue?
   - Who could provide an alternative perspective or viewpoint?

Indigenous worldviews

There is an increasing global awareness of the historical and ongoing injustices that many groups of Indigenous peoples have faced, and of how threats to Indigenous societies can lead to a loss of traditional knowledge and cultural diversity. For example, in 2007, the UN adopted the 'United Nations Declaration on the Rights of Indigenous Peoples', which includes the statement that 'Indigenous peoples have the right to maintain, control, protect and develop their cultural heritage, traditional knowledge and traditional cultural expressions, as well as the manifestations of their sciences, technologies and cultures.'

Understanding Indigenous worldviews is essential to CE, allowing us to reflect on holistic and reciprocal perspectives around human, non-human and natural life cycles. Table 1.15 contains some examples of Indigenous worldviews. However, it is essential to recognize that Indigenous communities worldwide are diverse, and their worldviews are rooted in their distinct lands, languages and histories.

Table 1.15 Examples of Indigenous worldviews

All things are animate; all life is valued	Everything has spirit and knowledge, including humans, more-than-humans and the natural world; therefore, everything is a part of everyone's relations (Little Bear, 2000). Humans are stewarding the lands left for them by their ancestors and that they have a moral responsibility to continue caring for the lands. For example, in Indigenous African cultures, 'there is no controversy in traditional Africa that the living generation, in as much as they are protected by their ancestors, have a duty to conserve the communal resources for their successors' (Owolabi, 2022, p.14). Remembering the wisdom of other cultures can be invaluable when engaging in advocacy work.
Holistic and cyclical	Some Indigenous peoples understand time as cyclical, rather than linear. The earth has a natural, holistic order, and patience and respect are fundamental to community, relational and ancestral processes (Bohanon, 2006).
Intergenerational	Elders and Knowledge-keepers transmit cultural knowledge and values, creating intergenerational solidarity and community well-being (Viscogliosi et al., 2020). Indigenous peoples are caretakers of the earth. They understand that every generation must take responsibility for the Earth's balance to ensure that balance is sustained for the seventh generation (Clarkson et al., 1992).
Right relations	Taking responsibility for being in relationships with other humans, species, more-than-humans and the land. This involves deep listening, respect, reciprocity, just actions, self-reflexivity, learning, unlearning and an openness to engage with discomfort and uncertainty (Gram-Hanssen et al., 2022).
Honesty and generosity	Wholeness, strength and balance are created through sharing, kindness and generosity; this ensures positive relationships with all beings (Little Bear, 2000).
Land and place-based	In Indigenous cultures, the land is understood as ontologically alive and an extension of the body. 'We are part of a web of interdependent human and other-than-human beings … land is life, because without land there is no life (human or otherwise)' (Ahenakew, 2017, p.82). Land is 'the first and most essential teacher and community member and the origin of Indigenous cultures' (Cajete, 2015, p.46). People are here to steward the lands left for them by their ancestors and they have a moral responsibility to continue caring for the lands. For example, in Indigenous African cultures, the current generation is tasked with protecting the land left to them by their ancestors, and by protecting these lands, they will conserve life-giving resources for future generations (Owolabi, 2022).
Oral knowledge and wisdom	Oral history 'makes invisible histories visible' (Mustonen, 2018, p.35) and is an essential part of recognizing the wisdom and knowledge that Indigenous peoples have passed along through oral traditions for millennia.
Balance	Balance is considered through the spiritual, emotional, mental and physical realms (Hunter et al., 2006).

LEARNING ENGAGEMENT

Indigenous worldviews

Consider the following questions and how they inspire different perspectives and ways of sharing the planet. Record your answers in your learning journal.

■ Table 1.16

Nature	What is your own relationship with the natural environment? What can you learn from Indigenous worldviews about your interconnectedness with nature, and how could this influence your actions or decisions?
Values	What Indigenous worldviews resonate the most with your value systems and why?
Community	How do Indigenous worldviews balance the needs of the community with the needs of individuals' rights? What can you learn from this balance? How does a focus on community respect and reciprocity challenge the norms of the communities you belong to? What does it look like when local and global communities are guided by Indigenous worldviews?
Oral storytelling and knowledge	Does this differ from how you have been taught to learn and share your knowledge?
Challenges	How can Indigenous peoples' wisdom and perspectives help us address climate change and biodiversity loss?
Cultural appropriation	How do you think we can learn about Indigenous cultures without appropriating them or misrepresenting them?
Policies and laws	How can communities ensure that the rights and voices of Indigenous peoples are respected?
Ethical responsibilities	What responsibilities do non-Indigenous people have in honouring Indigenous worldviews and preserving Indigenous cultures?
Personal actions	Through your actions, how can you support Indigenous communities? How can you actively incorporate Indigenous principles into your life?
Education	How can the education system change perspectives about Indigenous cultures to promote reconciliation with Indigenous peoples?

■ More worldviews from around the world

The following worldviews come from South American, African, Indian and Chinese contexts. After reviewing these worldviews, complete the learning engagement questions that follow in your learning journal.

BUEN VIVIR

Coming from a South American context, *buen vivir* is 'interpreted as integrative and collective well-being' (Chaves et al., 2018). Emerging from Indigenous worldviews, it is a conceptual framework for understanding social and ecological commons, positioning the community as the centre point of well-being (Gudynas, 2011). This worldview is community-centric, biocentric, ecologically balanced and culturally sensitive, and it calls into question the ontological roots of Western-Eurocentric development stories, which propagated 'the division between nature and society, a colonial distinction between modern and non-modern Indigenous peoples, the myth of progress as an unidirectional linear path, and a strong confidence on Cartesian science' (p.447).

UBUNTU/ BOTHO

Ubuntu is an African/South African Indigenous worldview that can be translated as humanness (Gade, 2011) which, in the Xhosa language, is expressed as *umuntu ngumuntu ngabantu* meaning 'people are people through people' (Truth and Reconciliation Commission, 1998). In Africa and South Africa, ubuntu is a philosophy and a way of life. It is centred around solidarity and communalism, coexistence and mutual interdependence, compassion and caring, and respect and dignity (Ngubane and Makua, 2021). *Ubuntu* is related to the African concept of *botho*, which possesses qualities that reflect the good side of human nature, including 'humaneness, compassion, gentleness, hospitality, generosity, empathy, kindness, friendliness' (Sodi et al., 2021). These qualities help communities thrive through interconnectedness and shared spirituality.

■ Some examples of different worldviews (Source: IB CE TSM)

ECO-SWARAJ

Eco-swaraj, which originated in India, focuses on alternative models for socio-ecological development. It is grounded in an ethic of responsibility towards other humans and nature, with a focus on ecological wisdom and resilience, social well-being and justice, direct or radical political democracy, economic democracy, and cultural knowledge and plurality (Kothari, 2018). *Eco-swaraj* is holistic and 'encompasses physical, material, socio-cultural, intellectual and spiritual dimensions ... [placing] collectives and communities at the centre of governance and economy' (p.50).

CONFUCIANISM

Confucianism is an ancient Chinese system focusing on personal ethics and a 'profound commitment to humaneness and civility' (Grim and Tucker, 2014, p.117). Confucianism can also be interpreted as an eco-ethical principle that understands humans as interconnected, interdependent and intertwined with the cosmos (Yao, 2014). In other words, Confucianism understands humans as 'anthropocosmic beings in relationship, not anthropocentric individuals in isolation ... the metaphor of humans as forming a triad with the cosmos and Earth (Grim and Tucker, 2014, p.121). This worldview has great implications for helping to create socio-ecological well-being (Yao, 2014).

■ Some examples of different worldviews (Source: IB CE TSM)

LEARNING ENGAGEMENT

More worldviews from around the world

With your teacher or a peer, discuss how these worldviews encourage us to:

- think differently about sustainability
- address local and global challenges, such as climate change and loss of biodiversity
- reconsider our views about leadership.

Two-eyed seeing

Two-eyed seeing/*etuaptmumk* (Mi'kmaw) means 'learning to see from one eye with the strengths of Indigenous knowledges and ways of knowing, and from the other eye with the strengths of Western knowledges and ways of knowing—and learning to use both of these eyes together for the benefit of all' (Elder Albert Marshall, as cited in Littlechild and Sutherland, 2021, p.7). Two-eyed seeing helps us critically consider our own identity and how our identities are woven into a much greater, cyclical, and reciprocal whole, encouraging more respectful, ethical and reciprocal relationships between ourselves and the wider community.

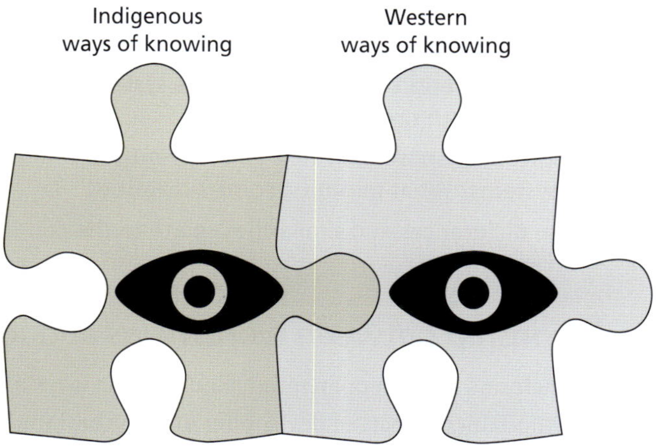

■ Seeing the world from multiple perspectives: Indigenous and Western ways of knowing

One way of considering two-eyed seeing is in relation to Indigenous knowledge systems and Western sciences. Although Indigenous knowledge systems and Western sciences stem from different worldviews, they also share things in common, such as a focus on patterns and observations, a quest for understanding, their ability to reflect complex systems, tracking changes over time and experimentation (Fischer et al., 2022). Western sciences are a 'dominant, institutionalized form of scientific understanding … which centre scientific rationality as the foundation' (Stein et al., 2024, p.2), while Indigenous sciences are approached in 'more holistic, integrative and relational ways that have social, political, ecological and spiritual implications' (Stein et al., 2024, p.3).

> *'It makes sense that the people who have lived on the land the longest, who have watched the environment and climate grow, shift and change, would have an intense and deeper level of understanding and knowledge versus individuals who had only been studying the same area for decades.'*
>
> (Source: Miller, 2025)

Top tip!

When researching Indigenous ways of knowing, you must ensure that your sources are centring and honouring Indigenous voices. You can access Indigenous viewpoints online, through academic and non-academic sources, including Indigenous oral traditions, creation stories and teachings. Focus on information shared by Indigenous people.

The above quote is from Coralee Miller, a Syilx (Okanagan) artist from Canada. Through her artwork, Coralee explores the concept of cultural identity and how Indigenous cultural values and beliefs can evolve modern understandings of the interconnectedness of all beings. In this quote, Miller highlights the importance of seeing environmental challenges from both an Indigenous and a Western perspective, each relying on the other to strengthen knowledge, understanding and ethical actions. Through understanding the interconnectedness of shared natural resources, humans may be inspired to act in ways that support environmental well-being.

LEARNING ENGAGEMENT

Diverse perspectives on the treatment of natural resources

Working in a small group, collectively choose a natural resource, such as water, trees or soil. Next, consider how this resource may be viewed through different perspectives within Indigenous and Western viewpoints. Your teacher may ask you to engage in research and/or summarize your thoughts in your learning journal.

Reflection and reflexivity

Natural resources

With your teacher, a peer or in a small group, discuss the following questions. Your teacher may ask you to share with a larger group.

- How can Indigenous and Western knowledge systems work together to ensure the well-being of the Earth's natural resources?
- How might natural resources be viewed differently in Indigenous and Western knowledge systems? What might be some similarities?
- How do these differences and similarities relate to the concept of worldviews?

The relationship between worldviews and identity

Two-eyed seeing helps us keep an open mind about diverse ways of knowing and being in the world, which is a fundamental part of developing intercultural understanding. It inspires us to consider our identity in relation to the broader context of local and global communities and ecosystems, prompting us to further consider how we can develop a more ethical relationship with the world around us.

When considering your own and others' worldviews, it is important to reflect on your own identity. Worldviews and identity are interconnected because the way you see the world shapes how you view yourself and how you relate to those around you. Your belief systems, values and perspectives on the world are a part of your identity, and they can be informed by things like your cultural background, life experiences, geographical location, access to resources, personality traits, social interactions, education, religion or spirituality and media influences. Pausing to consider how your identity and worldviews interact is an important part of understanding what ethical frameworks and values guide your actions and decision-making processes.

Learning journal

Connecting identity and worldviews

In your learning journal, explore the following questions. You are invited to express your learning in whatever way suits you, including reflection, artwork, mind maps, infographics or creative storytelling. Once you have considered your own viewpoints, your teacher may ask you to discuss your ideas with others.

- How can I tell a story about who I am, where I come from and what I believe in?
- How do I express my identity through the lens of my worldviews? Does this change in different contexts? If so, why and how?
- How does my identity shape the way I perceive and interact with the world around me?
- Is a relationship with the lands around me a part of my identity? How does this impact my views on reciprocity with non-humans and the natural world?
- How do my individual values influence my worldviews and identity? How do the collective values that surround me influence my worldviews and identity?
- How does social media impact my worldview, identity and how I treat other beings and the natural world?

Ubuntu

Ubuntu has its roots in humanist African philosophy and it cultivates a deep sense of community belonging. It means 'a person is a person through other persons' (Tutu, 1999), emphasizing that people come to know themselves through community. Ubuntu reflects the values and practices of solidarity, respect, care, dignity and compassion, which leads to more happiness and harmony (Seroto, 2016).

Ubuntu also reflects the importance of intercultural understanding as a way to deepen community belonging. It 'strongly emphasizes the interconnectedness of people [and] speaks to the ethic of humanity as part of a collective, whilst simultaneously recognizing uniqueness and difference' (Letseka, 2016, p.vii). This philosophy aligns with an open-minded and empathic attitude towards aspects of culture that are different from one's own, 'emphasizing that we can see commonalities from each other as human beings at a deeper level' (Lee, 2024, p.89). From a space of shared commonalities, respectful community connections are strengthened.

LEARNING ENGAGEMENT

Ubuntu

There are many credible texts and videos available, both online and offline, that explore the topic of Ubuntu. Find a source that is meaningful for you, and as you engage with it, take notes in your learning journal. Notice what thoughts, feelings and emotions you connect with.

LEARNING ENGAGEMENT

Ubuntu

Working with your teacher, a peer or in a small group, think about a lesson plan that you could develop for younger students focusing on learning more about the Ubuntu worldview. Choosing one or more of the topics below, think about how you could create some simple learning objectives and activities, along with clear instructions and inquiry questions, to engage these younger students. What resources would you provide for them? How would you ask them to share their learning in a creative way? How could you start introducing them to the concept of reciprocity, in developmentally appropriate ways, and connect this to aspects of the learner profile? How could you challenge them to take action in their community in developmentally appropriate ways?

Topics:

- Global inequalities
- Social justice/human rights
- Ecological well-being/nature rights
- Racism/racial segregation
- Protest/courage
- Spirit/intergenerational connections
- Activism
- Peace and freedom

After outlining a basic lesson plan, you can consider presenting your ideas to a Primary or Middle Years Programme teacher in your school.

Shifting perspectives

Consider consciously shifting your perspective as you learn about something new. Changing our perspective requires humility, reciprocity and engagement with new and/or less familiar knowledge (e.g. traditional knowledge).

The quote below comes from Dr Robin Wall Kimmerer, a Native American scholar, scientist, professor and author. Dr Kimmerer is a member of the Citizen Potawatomi Nation, and her influential work sits at the intersection of Indigenous and Western science. Dr Kimmerer believes that two-eyed seeing is necessary for the future health of our planet. In her writing, she explains how Indigenous environmental knowledge, which has been handed down through generations, is based on scientific methods, including observation and experimentation. While Indigenous interactions with nature are approached through a different worldview, modern science can benefit tremendously from Indigenous knowledge.

> *'Because we can't speak the same language, our work as scientists is to piece the story together as best we can. We can't ask the salmon directly what they need, so we ask them for experiments and listen carefully to their answers. We stay up half the night at the microscope looking at the annual rings in the fish ear bones in order to know how the fish react to water temperature. So we can fix it. We run experiments on the effects of salinity on the growth of invasive grasses. So we can fix it. We measure and record and analyse in ways that might seem lifeless but to us are the conduits to understanding the inscrutable lives of species not our own. Doing science with awe and humility is a powerful act of reciprocity with the more-than-human world … Science can be a way of forming intimacy and respect with other species that is rivaled only by the observations of traditional knowledge holders. It can be a path to kinship.'*

(Source: Kimmerer, 2013, p.252)

LEARNING ENGAGEMENT

Shifting perspectives

Working with your teacher, a peer or in a small group, consider Dr Kimmerer's quote above. Next, discuss some or all the following questions. Any questions you would like to consider on your own can be included in your learning journal.

1 What does Kimmerer mean by 'a powerful act of reciprocity'? What does 'reciprocity' mean?
2 What does 'humility' mean? Can you identify a time when you felt this while learning?
3 Identify a moment when you felt awe and/or humility while learning something new. How do awe and humility—or conversely, arrogance—influence the research and application of scientific knowledge?
4 How can humility, awe and reciprocity guide our human decisions about using scientific knowledge?
5 What does Kimmerer mean by 'traditional knowledge holders'? What are some examples of traditional knowledge holders?
6 What are some examples of moments where Western science learned from and in relation to traditional knowledge holders?
7 What are some examples of moments in which Western science has not learned from and in relation to traditional knowledge holders, to detrimental effects?
8 In what ways is science a 'path to kinship'?

(Adapted from J. Mogyoros, *Guided inquiry prompts: Weaving Indigenous and Western sciences*)

Reflection and reflexivity

Shifting perspectives

In your learning journal, reflect on your collaborative discussions.

- As you engaged in the discussions on shifting perspectives, which points did you agree with and differ on?
- When you noticed different perspectives arising, how did you respond?
- Did you try to understand what other people were saying, listening to understand rather than responding?
- Were you reflexive in recognizing your worldviews and biases?
- How did you share your viewpoints in thoughtful and respectful ways?

REAL-WORLD EXAMPLE

Working with Indigenous communities

In one of their IB courses, Matteo and Zahara have been researching traditional Indigenous healing ceremonies. They are learning that Canada's Indigenous communities have holistic views of health, which are connected to their culture, community, ancestry, and the lands they live on. Matteo and Zahara are inspired by how Indigenous communities approach the spiritual, physical, mental, and emotional dimensions of health, and they want to learn more. As they consider reaching out to Indigenous partners, they want to be culturally sensitive.

The students reach out to a local organization via email and the executive director (ED), Lydia, responds that she would be happy to work with the students. In their first meeting, Lydia mentions that an important part of her organization's work is teaching healthcare professionals about culturally responsive practices. These are centered on trusting relationships, reciprocity, and respect for Indigenous knowledge systems. Matteo and Zahara bring up the idea of a school presentation on Indigenous health and Lydia says she would be happy to speak with some Elders in her community to see if they would like to present. Matteo and Zahara are excited when they hear back from Lydia who tells them two Elders will be joining them for the assembly. Both Elders were in the residential school systems in Canada. These Elders give school presentations on Indigenous culture and spiritually and their connection to the health and well-being of their community.

The day of the presentation arrives, and Matteo and Zahara follow through with the last stages of the setup, including chairs, a sound system, and putting out some light refreshments. They have sent a clear email to Lydia in advance to let her know where to park and what to do when they enter the school. They warmly welcome their guests at the door to the school, thanking them for their time and generosity. They ensure the Elders are seated comfortably and provide them with refreshments, letting them know they can ask for anything they need. As the presentation begins, Matteo and Zahara begin with a Land Acknowledgement to show their recognition and respect for the Indigenous Nations who are the original stewards of the lands on which their school resides.

The Elders share their stories and speak about the purpose and importance of community healing ceremonies. Near the end, a new student challenges parts of their stories, saying it seems like a waste of time to focus on traditional healing when 'real doctors' and regular medical care could be prioritized. They express concern about young people not getting the help they need. The Elders respond with generosity and patience. One Elder thanks the student for sharing their perspective and explains that Indigenous communities do go to doctors and hospitals, but they also care for their health through traditional cultural practices, which are a form of medicine. The Elder shares that healing ceremonies are about strengthening relationships, spirits and communities, and that this kind of balance is essential for well-being. The other Elder adds that Western and Indigenous medicines can work alongside each other, each contributing something valuable to community health. Even so, the student insists they still believe these practices are not useful or modern. Matteo and Zahara feel worried and uncomfortable, and they do not like how the presentation ends.

After the presentation, Matteo and Zahara apologize to their guests, asking Lydia if they can follow up with a conversation. Lydia agrees and they meet the following week. Matteo and Zahara bring up the questions that were asked to the Elders saying they were inappropriate, and they feel embarrassed. Lydia encourages Matteo and Zahara to see this as a moment of learning and growth, encouraging them to continue learning through the wisdom of Elders' stories. She shares how Indigenous communities hear Elders' stories with respect and a deep understanding of their cultural and spiritual significance, reminding Matteo and Zahara that education around Indigenous culture is an ongoing process as reflected in the country's Truth and Reconciliation Calls to Action. She hopes they will continue exploring and remain open-minded about new ways of understanding holistic health through an Indigenous lens.

Matteo and Zahara ask Lydia if it would be ok for them to personally apologize to the Elders and Lydia asks them to send a written or recorded message, which she will pass along. As they end the call, Matteo and Zahara commit to raising more awareness about the importance of Indigenous ways of knowing as a path to truth and reconciliation. Lydia encourages them to stay in touch as they create another plan of action, and she provides additional resources for them to explore.

LEARNING ENGAGEMENT

Working with Indigenous communities

With your teacher, a peer or in a small group, consider the real-world example above and discuss some or all of the following questions:

1. How can Matteo and Zahara work to raise awareness around Indigenous ways of knowing in their school?
2. How did the Elders reference the concept of two-eyed seeing in their response to the student's comments?
3. Beyond Elder presentations, how can Matteo and Zahara continue their work with the organization that Lydia directs?
4. If you were Matteo and Zahara, how would you have responded had you been in the Elders' presentation?
5. Is there anything Matteo or Zahara could have done differently to prepare other students for this presentation?
6. When discomfort arises, how can we use ethical speech and actions to respond?
7. What lessons will you take away from this case study that might strengthen your relationships with both Indigenous and non-Indigenous community members?

Learning journal

Consider adding to an ethics growth-over-time map, reflecting your awareness and understanding of Indigenous worldviews.

1.3.3 Ethics and the connection to the rest of the CP Core

Ethics are an important consideration in each part of your CP Core. Each CP Core component provides you with a distinctive way of viewing and applying ethics, and when these components are considered together, they provide you with a deep and nuanced understanding of ethics that you will carry forward into real-world contexts. As you read the following paragraphs, consider how the rest of your CP Core supports and informs your understanding of CE ethics. Also consider how CE ethics support and inform your understanding of the rest of the CP Core.

LCS and CE

Language and cultural studies (LCS) provides a foundation for considering perspectives and how individuals construct or attribute meaning. Skills and understandings developed in LCS can be used in CE; they help enhance your knowledge of issues and support you in engaging within different contexts in an ethical way. Demonstrating a genuine interest in communicating with community members in their languages/language varieties helps to develop authentic relationships. Because LCS offers you a lens through which to explore ethics within the context of language and culture, LCS experiences can also inspire CE. By evaluating how language and culture influence the perspectives of different community members within societal systems, LCS will help you gain valuable insight into the intricate interplay between ethics, language and culture.

PPS and CE

Through personal and professional skills (PPS), you will further develop and learn to apply critical and self-reflexive thinking. As you engage with the community, you will continuously seek awareness and understanding. Ethical thinking and intercultural understanding help inform how you approach relationships, opportunities and challenges. Approaching community endeavours from a place of ethical and intercultural understanding will help you establish and maintain authentic relationships and community partnerships. Underlying these partnerships will be practical communication skills, which will support you as you seek to open dialogue that fosters reciprocal and ethical relationships.

The RP and CE

CE fosters an exploration and understanding of the community's needs. It asks you to examine the complexities of social interactions and the importance of mutual collaboration while learning about the nature of ethical dilemmas through real-life situations. In both CE and reflective project (RP), you will need to use excellent research and communication skills, along with strong reflective and reflexive practices, which will help you make ethical decisions. CE projects can inform and nurture the RP through meaningful connections between research, theoretical perspectives and authentic social experiences connected to career-related studies (CRS). While you engage with communities to address relevant challenges or opportunities, you will be able to identify the ethical dimensions of complex issues such as environmental sustainability and human rights, and build meaningful connections between the research process, ethical critique and the experience of diverse, multiple and divergent perspectives. The ability to identify these ethical dimensions will help you further understand how systemic challenges impact the community.

1.3.4 Summary

- Ethics infuse your CE journey and are the key to developing reciprocal and respectful relationships with the community.
- Different ethical concepts and lenses can help you frame an issue from a particular perspective.
- Ethical reasoning and decision-making can be guided by ethical paradigms.
- An essential part of developing intercultural understanding is understanding and honouring diverse ways of knowing and being.
- Ethics inform and reflect different worldviews that need to be explored in your engagements.

1.4 The learning and engagement process in CE

INQUIRY QUESTIONS

- How are teaching and guidance approached in CE?
- What are the three stages of the learning and engagement process?
- What is guided learning?
- What counts as CE?
- How long should your engagements last?
- How do you identify challenges and opportunities in the community?
- How can you gather information about the community?
- What are the different forms of engagement?

1.4.1 The structure of learning and teaching

CE relies on learning and engagement that happen both in the classroom and in the community. You will experience a range of guided learning activities in class with your teachers and peers, together with active engagement in the community. Your guided learning time will provide you with foundational CE knowledge and give you a chance to apply CE knowledge and understanding through reflections, activities and discussions. Your teacher will provide ongoing guidance for your work within the community, your three review points and your community sharing. Through sustained active engagements within the community, you will apply your CE knowledge and understanding and enact the three principles of engagement.

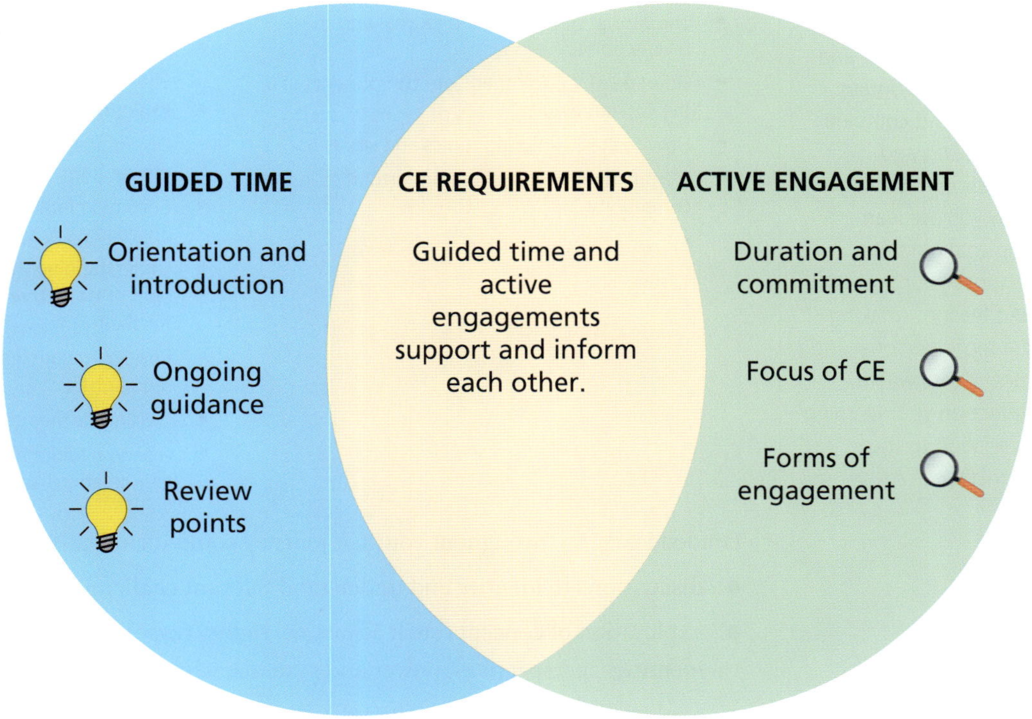

CE is made up of both guided time and active engagements.

Guided learning

During your guided-learning time, you will explore CE in ways that are relevant to your school and local context. Your teacher will provide structural support to help you navigate the complexities that arise from CE, and you will build key skills and understanding to help you engage critically and ethically with your work. This guided-learning time allows you to learn in a supported environment before working in and with the community. It also gives you a safe and supported space to reflect on and interpret experiences. In line with IB requirements, your school must dedicate a minimum of 30 hours for teaching, supervision and guidance. How these hours are allocated across the timetable will be determined by your school's context.

In your guided-learning time, you will take part in independent and collaborative activities that deepen your awareness and understanding of the learning outcomes. You will explore the meaning of community, identity, power, ethics, conflict management, meeting challenges, as well as deepening reflection and reflexivity by looking at relevant concepts and issues. You will also engage respectfully with collaborative reflection and dialogue, and have the opportunity to give and receive feedback. You will reflect on the idea of building healthy relationships with your teachers and peers, and use this to model healthy relationships within the community. Two distinct parts of your guided time are introduction and orientation, and ongoing guidance.

Table 1.17 Differences between introduction and orientation, and ongoing guidance

Introduction and orientation	Ongoing guidance
• The nature, aims, and LOs • The general expectations and requirements • What 'community' and 'engagement' mean • The process of engagement: the principles and dimensions of the process of engagement • Building an understanding of what constitutes completion of CE • Exploring your positionality • The format of the learning journal and the review points • How to link CE to other Core components and the CP framework • How to start exploring topics and issues • Identifying challenges and opportunities in the community	• Being supported and guided in a sustained manner • Understanding the complex and systemic nature of the challenges and opportunities • Engaging critically and ethically with local and global issues • Managing and examining your CE journey • Discussing topics for your engagement • Continuing the building of knowledge required to demonstrate the four LOs • Consolidating and practising the principles and dimensions of the CE process • Exploring relevant concepts • Diving deeper into ethics and exploring a range of ethical frameworks • Becoming familiar with and practising different approaches to systems thinking • Understanding the purpose of the review points (and of **narrative assessment**), and preparing for them • Reviewing your learning and engagement on a regular basis • Getting further guidance and encouragement • Having additional chats, check-ins or conversations as necessary

Key term

◆ **Narrative assessment:** A way to monitor, evaluate and share your progress over time. It combines storytelling and reflection to show you how you are learning and changing. It includes your thoughts and feelings, making it a more personal and meaningful way to reflect on your learning in relation to the four LOs.

Guided learning throughout your CE journey could include:

- discussions to identify and understand relevant challenges and opportunities
- exploration of concepts such as justice, rights, responsibility, interdependence, change, identities, perspectives, power and systems, which are related to other parts of the CP Core
- explorations of ethical frameworks
- understanding the purpose and format of the review points.

You will prepare for review points as you reflect on these topics with your teacher and peers. These are distinct points in your CE journey where you can share chosen stories, perspectives, progress and insights with your teacher. Your teacher will then provide further guidance, feedback and support. The review points will be supplemented with additional check-ins or conversations with your teacher, as required.

You will have three review points sessions throughout the two years of the programme. Here is what these review points will look like. You will find more guidance within Section 1.5 of this book, on assessment.

Table 1.18 Purpose of each review point

Review points	Purpose/aims
1	• Provide support and feedback. • Reflect on initial plan of action in relation to the LOs.
2	• Reflect on how your community engagements are unfolding and what and how you are learning. • Provide evidence of LOs. • Answer the question: 'What now?'
3	• Final story-telling moment. • Reflect on your CE journey in relation to the LOs.

Although the three review points are mandatory, more formal and more structured, you will undoubtedly have many informal check-ins and review points with your teacher.

Active engagement

Your CE journey will be unique to you, your community context and your interests. It may include:

- engaging with communities individually or as part of a group
- engaging with people you know (e.g. family, community elders)
- engaging with professionals (e.g. through internships or work placements)
- engaging with local organizations (e.g. neighbourhood associations)
- engaging with global organizations (e.g. international youth councils)
- selecting from several different forms of community engagement.

You are responsible for shaping your own CE journey, both independently and with support from your teacher. The number of hours that you dedicate to actively engaging with the community outside of the guided hours organized by your school is not specified. It will depend on your own approach to engaging in and with the community to support the four learning outcomes.

What counts as CE?

So, what counts as CE? How do you determine if your engagement can be considered appropriate or not? Here is a set of guiding questions to support you in determining its appropriateness.

If you and your CE adviser can justify and answer 'yes' to each of the following questions, the engagement can be considered appropriate.

1. Does the engagement stem from a student's personal interest and relevance, as well as community interest and relevance?
2. Does it allow for engaging with and demonstrating the four learning outcomes?

3 Is there active engagement as opposed to passive engagement? Active engagement means you are practising the three principles of engagement: dialogue, reciprocity, and reflection and reflexivity. Passive engagement means you are involved but not fully participating (e.g. by not contributing meaningfully through reciprocal actions, dialogue or thoughtful reflection).
4 Is it informed by understanding the community through the three dimensions: relational, systems and personal?

How long should your community engagement last?

Your learning and participation will be determined by the nature of your community engagement over the two years of your CP programme. Aim for sustainability in your engagements, making sure your actions align with your ethical intentions and goals. Longer-term or more sustained engagements will help you form and maintain reciprocal partnerships where you have the time to explore issues, co-create visions, collaborate, decide on plans of action (or inaction), reflect and evaluate together with the community.

The process of engaging with and in a community might not be straightforward and, at times, it might even look a bit 'messy'. You may find that even with a well-designed initial plan of action, the final duration of your engagement changes. Sometimes, a longer-term engagement is not achievable, as specific contexts call for different approaches and flexibility to respond to specific challenges. In these cases, shorter-term engagements may be appropriate. For example, you might want to respond to an immediate natural disaster, or you might need to adapt to new and unforeseen circumstances in the community or in your own life. In such cases, a shorter-term engagement may work better despite the recommendation that you aim for longer or more sustainable engagements.

LEARNING ENGAGEMENT

Shorter- or longer-term engagements

Discuss the following questions with your teacher, a peer or in a group. Then, summarize the main points in your learning journal.

1 Why do you think longer-term engagements are recommended?
2 When would a combination of shorter and longer term be a good idea?
3 In which circumstances could you combine shorter- and longer-term engagements?

1.4.2 The three stages of the learning and engagement process

CE is a process- and inquiry-based learning journey. You will move through the three stages of learning and engagement, and it is the interaction between these three stages, the CE dimensions and the CE principles of engagement that will help you to demonstrate your understanding of the learning outcomes. The process of engaging with and in a community is cyclical and adapted to the knowledge, experience and feedback you gain throughout your journey. Engagement is driven by the three principles of community (dialogue, reciprocity, and reflection and reflexivity), which help expand your understanding of the three dimensions of community (personal, relational and systems).

The engagement process is grounded in inquiry-based learning and geared towards action. It is structured in three stages and should be considered as ongoing, with the three stages being repeated as needed. The three stages are interconnected and may even take place at the same time. You will likely engage with these stages multiple times at different points during your CE journey. The three stages are: explore and prepare, relate and act, evaluate and share.

These different stages are reviewed in more detail in the following sections.

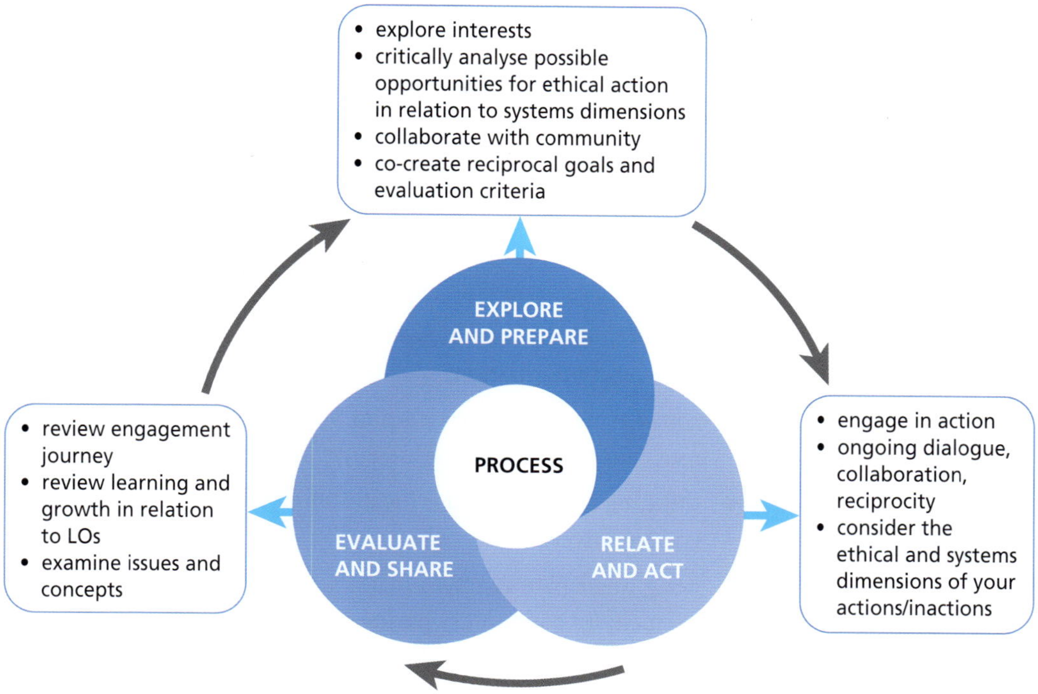

Stages of your CE journey

1 Explore and prepare

As discussed, CE is a process- and inquiry-based learning journey. You must begin cycles of CE inquiry with the explore and prepare stage before taking action within the community. Too often, students rush into action, only to discover later on that they should have taken more time to explore their topic and make preparations to take action. Unfortunately, this can lead to confusion for the students and community partners. In some cases, it can lead to students not following through with their commitments, and then community partners may be left in a difficult position.

By exploring your interests and aspirations and aligning them with community-based opportunities and challenges, you will help ensure that your future actions are meaningful and supportive, both for yourself and the community. You will spend this stage researching the topic and your context's specific opportunities and challenges. You will also ensure that your action plans are not developed in isolation from the community; instead, they must be rooted in respectful and reciprocal collaborations with the community. This includes clarity around people's roles, responsibilities and willingness to take action.

In the explore and prepare stage, you must be mindful of your assumptions and seek clarity from community partners. As the Irish playwright George Bernard Shaw once said, 'the single biggest problem in communication is the illusion that it has taken place' (Lyman, 2024). Therefore, before taking action, ensure that communications are clear and understood by everyone involved. Ensure you return to the explore and prepare stage whenever you consider new community partnerships, and be clear and timely with your communications.

Challenges and opportunities

During the first stage of the process, and before you embark on any type of engagement, you need to explore both your interests and relevant opportunities and challenges within the community. Consider what you would like to contribute and respond meaningfully to by:

- thinking about the local or global issues you are passionate about
- reaching out to the community to investigate meaningful, authentic and relevant community concerns, hopes, challenges and opportunities
- learning about the background and socio-cultural context of the community you are considering partnering with
- exploring your positionality: who you are, your place within the community, the powers and privileges you hold and your past experiences
- researching opportunities and challenges in the community using diverse methods and sources of information
- considering the importance and function of systems dimensions, analyse the issues and root causes that might be affecting the community
- thinking creatively and critically about ideas to address challenges or opportunities collaboratively
- designing a plan of action that:
  - **i** includes community partners
  - **ii** aims for a mutual understanding of what the challenges, opportunities and goals are
  - **iii** explores the ethical issues underlying community challenges
  - **iv** explores the root causes and broader social forces that contribute to those challenges using a systems thinking approach
  - **v** maintains timely and respectful communications with community partners, ensuring they are well-informed and aware of any plans of action.

Where do you start? What might inspire you to engage?

When you start exploring the focus of your engagement and looking for inspiration, some ideas will come from your own experiences and interests. In contrast, others may come from a unit of inquiry you have studied. You might have learned something at school that has sparked your interest, or you might have some experiences you enjoyed when participating in activities inside and outside school.

LEARNING ENGAGEMENT

Finding your inspiration

Look at the following table and fill in some ideas that might interest you in each area. Consider which of these might inspire you to engage. No matter your area of interest, the most important thing is that you feel inspired and motivated to get involved sustainably.

Table 1.19

Personal interests and experiences	Prior learning or prior engagement	Learning in other parts of the CP programme	Participation in an internship	Other sources

How do you identify an opportunity or challenge?

■ Examples of the topics you might want to explore in more depth in relation to your CE

CE should happen in response to a relevant opportunity or challenge, where you and the community decide together what needs to be done. Once you determine your general areas of interest, you can explore the topics that those areas are related to. Sometimes, you will find these opportunities and challenges relate to the areas shown in the image on the left; however, it is essential to recognize that this is not an exhaustive list. You can add other topics you are interested in or would like to learn more about through your engagements.

Don't forget! The relevance of the opportunity or challenge will need to be **jointly** decided by you **and** the community.

You must consider the three dimensions of community as you explore and prepare. Read the following real-world example, which shows how you can consider the community dimensions in your exploration and preparation processes.

REAL-WORLD EXAMPLE

Considering the dimensions of community

Maryam, a CE student, wants to partner with a community organization focusing on food security. The organization focuses on shorter- and longer-term solutions to food insecurity and how this intersects with climate changes in the local area. The organization works with various stakeholders, including regional and national governments, refugee organizations and organizations that support the city's homeless population. They also have relationships with local farmers and farmers' markets, urban green space organizers, nutritionists and mental-health counsellors working with vulnerable populations.

As a part of her explore and prepare stage, Maryam writes an initial email to this community partner, and one of the programme managers responds asking, 'Exactly what type of work are you interested in? Once we understand what you are thinking, perhaps we can discuss ways for you to get involved.' The programme manager encourages Maryam to discuss specifics with the lead volunteer coordinator. Maryam reaches out to the volunteer coordinator and books a 20-minute online meeting.

Maryam wants to be well-prepared for this meeting. She knows the volunteer coordinator's schedule is hectic, and she doesn't want to ask questions that she can find on the organization's website. She studies the website as part of her research and takes notes in her learning journal. Maryam knows she must consider the three dimensions of community in her explore and prepare stage, so she visually represents her thinking in her learning journal. In the personal dimension, she notes she is interested in the individual stories of those involved, including those who work at the organization and those the organization helps. More specifically, Maryam is interested in the psychological and emotional impacts on everyone involved. She includes a brief reflection outlining her reasons for getting involved and how this relates to her identity and worldviews. In the relational dimension, she notes the relationships between various stakeholders and wonders how they collaborate, build trust and include new people in their initiatives. In the systems dimension, she notes the importance of researching the underlying causes of food insecurity and the connections between different community systems, such as education and healthcare. Maryam wonders if all stakeholders share a similar viewpoint.

Once Maryam has completed her explorations in her learning journal, she seeks out her teacher to ask for advice. Maryam wants to ensure her communications are clear and respectful and reflect the principle of reciprocity and systems thinking. In her online meeting with the volunteer coordinator, she wants to discuss some of the general ideas she outlined in her learning journal, and she also wants to ensure that she leaves room for the community partner to share their needs and wishes with her.

LEARNING ENGAGEMENT

Considering the dimensions of community

Place yourself in the role of Maryam's CE teacher and consider how you would support her in preparing for this online meeting. Remember that Maryam wants to express her ideas clearly while supporting the community partner's needs.

The following questions are meant to provide support as you consider this topic; however, you can also record your responses in your own way. Your teacher may ask you to share with the whole group.

1 Understanding that Maryam wants to prove to this community partner that she is authentically interested in the scope and depth of their work, what details would you encourage Maryam to share in her online meeting? Are there any details you would advise Maryam not to share?

2 How important is it for Maryam to share her knowledge of the community dimensions noted in the above real-world example? What would you advise her to share?

How can you gather information about a community?

Once you have identified the community you want to work with, you need to gain a deeper understanding by gathering relevant information. You can gather information about the community you have chosen to engage with in many ways, including:

- consulting websites, paying attention to an organization's mission, vision and value statements (often this will give you a sense of the community's perspectives around social and/or ecological approaches and worldviews)
- reviewing people's biographies online
- speaking with a member of the community
- researching the people, groups or organizations the community is connected to (as Maryam did when she was exploring the relational dimension)
- searching for news articles, documentaries and articles that discuss the community's work
- attending a community meeting or orientation session
- looking at the community's social media channels
- taking a tour of the community's local site
- reviewing the minutes of the community meetings.

Learning journal

Gathering information about a community

In your learning journal, answer the following questions, then discuss them with your teacher, a peer or in a small group.

- Which community am I planning to engage with?
- Who leads the community?
- Who could be my contact point(s) in the community?
- Where (or from whom) can I learn more about the challenges and opportunities of this community?
- What is the story of the community?
- What is essential to the community? How do I know?
- What opportunities and challenges already exist in the community?
- What is the underlying cultural and socio-economic story of the community?
- What is my connection with the community? What do I share in terms of identity, experience, etc.?
- What local and/or global issues does this particular opportunity/challenge connect to?
- How am I going to create and agree on a shared goal?
- How do I intend to co-design an action plan?
- Have I reflected on my positionality within the community? How does it influence how I situate myself in the context of the community and how I relate to the community?
- How will I know to what extent my actions and/or non-actions address the factors involved in the opportunity and/or challenge?
- What does the community know about this engagement? Have I informed them about my expectations or asked about theirs?

LEARNING ENGAGEMENT

Are you ready to act?

1 Look at the checklist below and, in your learning journal, review what you have done in each of these areas, noting:
   - how each area connects to the learning outcomes
   - what you can do to explore further and/or improve
   - what you will need to learn and/or do to gain clarity on what comes next in your process
   - how you feel about your process and progress.

- ☐ individual or groupwork
- ☐ community definition clear
- ☐ community identified
- ☐ information gathered
- ☐ clear challenges/opportunities
- ☐ dialogue with community established
- ☐ community clear about expectations
- ☐ thoughts/ideas in learning journal
- ☐ chat with teacher
- ☐ willing to engage

2 Next, reflect on what you have learned about the CE learning and engagement process. Your teacher may ask you to record your thoughts in your learning journal or discuss them with a peer or the whole group.
  a Can you add something related to learning and engagement in one of your growth-over-time maps or in some other format?
  b How have you grown in understanding, awareness and practising ethics, reflection, reflexivity, reciprocity and/or complex systems thinking? Can you identify specific events or circumstances that sparked this growth?

Forms of engagement

Now that you have a clearer idea of some of the pathways your CE journey may take, you will engage in and with the community. As you engage with the community, you will develop more awareness and form new connections. There are many ways of engaging in and with the community, and your own experiences, preferred ways of learning and personality traits will undoubtedly inform your approach to community partnerships. As you embody the learner profile and practise your ATL skills, reflective and reflexive practice will help you identify how to take appropriate risks, become more curious about other ways of engaging and practise skills that may be new and/or less intuitive and familiar.

LEARNING ENGAGEMENT

How might you engage with a community?

Look at the questions below to explore what forms of engagements are most appropriate for you at this point in time. Remember that your engagements will take many forms and as you become more connected with the community, you may want to engage in new ways.

Table 1.20 What forms of engagements are right for you at this time?

How might you engage with the community in meaningful ways?					
Take some time to think about how you might engage with the community in a way that will help you meet the learning outcomes in a sustainable way.					
On a scale of 1–5 (max.), rate where your interest lies.	**1**	**2**	**3**	**4**	**5**
You love working with others in a team.					
You thrive when you work with others who share the same interests as you.					
You are very comfortable with making decisions and helping to organize teams.					
You love participating in community activities.					
You love participating in voluntary work.					
You always show your commitment to work.					
You prefer campaigning to direct participation.					
You feel more comfortable with advocating for change than with direct participation.					
You prefer co-designing with the community.					
You love researching issues and looking at possible co-created plans of action.					

Read the descriptions of the forms of engagement in Table 1.21 while reflecting on the previous learning engagement. Think about what forms of engagement you are interested in, in line with community challenges or opportunities. What forms of engagement are a good fit for both your interests and the needs of the community, and why?

■ **Table 1.21** Forms of engagement provided in the CE guide (Source: IBO 2025a, p.22)

Form of engagement	Description
Community-building and organizing	Bringing people together to pursue a shared interest and work collaboratively towards change; enhancing a social group or sense of community among groups/individuals who live in the same area or have common interests through engaging in decision-making and organizing to act collectively to address issues.
Participation	Participating in the formal or informal work of communities, voluntary organizations, etc., to work towards achieving goals related to issues that are relevant to both communities and students, and showing commitment to contributing as individuals and as members of a group.
Advocacy	Acting individually or collectively—with the consent of, and in collaboration with, the community—to publicly support positive social, environmental or humanitarian change through tangible products or engagements that use persuasion and dispersal of accurate information, and aim to lead others into taking action.
Community learning and research	Recognizing community partners as knowledge holders and actively and dialogically engaging with them to learn from them and/or collaboratively carry out research with the community that creates and disseminates knowledge and/or creative expression. It is intended to apply the newly acquired knowledge and understandings to further illuminate issues that are relevant to the student and community partner and possibly inform further action.

■ **Table 1.22** Some examples of forms of engagement from the CE guide (Source: IBO 2025b, pp.1–3)

Form of engagement	Characteristics	Examples	Non-examples
Community-building and organizing	• There is a shared interest/goal between the student and the community partner(s). • The student is an active member and possibly a facilitator involved in, for example, decision-making, organizing activities, etc. • The student identifies as a part of the community they are engaging with in this form.	• Setting up a school or local basketball club aimed at students who want to play for fun or for health reasons, rather than competitively (which is currently the only option available in the school or local community) • Organizing a fair with local religious leaders intended to both celebrate a local religious community and seek to raise awareness and engagement with a wider community • Acting as youth representative on the local town council; engaging with local youth to act as their representative (e.g. setting up a school forum; creating a social media page or website to encourage ideas); and prioritizing and supporting proposals and projects in the council that respond to youth interests (e.g. a cultural centre)	• Giving out toys during a Christmas charity event • Being a player on a school/local basketball team • Being a member of a church choir
Participation	• The student shows long-term commitment. • The student's role in the engagement can be clearly Identified. • The student does not have to identify as part of the community. • The student does not have to be actively involved in the decision-making process to achieve the identified goals/outcomes. • The student may be involved in activities where they are engaging directly with the individuals or groups benefiting from/impacted by the work, or they may take on support roles in this work.	• Regular peer tutoring in partnership with a primary school or community centre in the community • Participating in activities organized for the elderly on a regular basis (e.g. IT lessons, tax preparation) • Joining a local food bank as a long-term volunteer, facilitating partnerships with local farmers to increase the supply of fresh, healthy, local food for food insecure individuals or families and also to support local farmers	• Attending a play organized by the local theatre • Passively attending a community fair • Participating in a charity run • Sending a monetary donation to a charity

Form of engagement	Characteristics	Examples	Non-examples
Advocacy	• Wherever possible/appropriate, the student creates or supports creating a space for community voices to be heard, and possibly joins the community voice rather than speaking for the community. • Whenever the student speaks/acts on behalf of a (marginalized) community or individuals, they do so with the knowledge, consultation and consent of the community/individuals, who see them as a partner and ally. • The student shows clear awareness of the ethical issues involved in representing someone else's voice, and is able to justify their engagement as a representative for the community/individuals. • The student undertakes research to support claims and make a compelling case. • Target audience: Often policymakers or lawmakers, sometimes businesses or corporations.	• Setting up and participating in an online campaign (e.g. blog, website, social media) to raise awareness of human, civil or environmental rights • Producing a media or arts presentation (e.g. short film, photography exhibition, podcast, street theatre, mural on a prominent street/building) as part of a campaign to advocate in conjunction with a local community organization (e.g. a rewilding project, support for carers, inclusion campaign) • Collaborating with a local community to set up and participate in a campaign to raise awareness of an endangered language, advocate for education in the language in the town/region, and lobby the school leadership and local authorities for changes in language policy and provision	• Purely performative social-media posts • Buying jewellery from a local small business • Following a diet/lifestyle choice (e.g. veganism) based on ethical principles
Community learning and research	• There is clearly identified knowledge and/or skills. • Clear permission and consent is given by the community partner to share the identified knowledge and/or skills. • There is acknowledgement (and, where appropriate, compensation) of the community whenever the knowledge is applied further. • The learning and research may be more informal in nature, practising open-minded, attentive listening as a compassionate, relational activity, or it may follow a more formalized participatory community-based research approach. • The learning and research is characterized by a collaborative process between students, faculty and community members.	• Starting a birdwatching club at school, in collaboration with the local community or a local organization, to learn about and help raise awareness about local wildlife • Taking lessons from a henna artisan in preparation for a local fair (and engaging in research around the cultural significance of this tradition) • Undertaking community-based research on water supply in the local area or on seeds and organic farming, aiming to gain insights that could inform possible approaches to improving the water supply or for setting up a seed exchange programme in the local area • Organizing regular beach or park clean-ups in collaboration with local users and documenting the primary forms of waste to inform relevant local bodies that organize waste removal and/or recycling	• Using knowledge from an online community to beat a high score in a video game • Undertaking community-based learning/research in completion of a diploma programme (DP) subject • Undertaking community-based learning/research for the primary reason of personal/company financial gain (e.g. for market research where the research/questions are pre-determined by the company)

LEARNING ENGAGEMENT

Forms of engagement

Review Table 1.22 for ideas of potential CE engagements. With your teacher, a peer or a small group, brainstorm more opportunities to add to each form of engagement. Your teacher may ask you to share your ideas with a larger group.

When deciding on an engagement, you need to consider meaningful, relevant and authentic forms of engagement that will meet the needs of the community. It is also critical to consult with your community partner(s) regarding forms of engagement they think will be most skilful and supportive. Sometimes, despite the best of intentions, you may choose a form of engagement that will not be accessible or relevant to the community partner(s), so it is essential to remain flexible, adaptive, open to feedback and consciously aware of the principles of complex systems change (non-linearity and unpredictability). When you receive feedback about your forms of engagement, engage in reciprocal and respectful dialogues with your community partner(s) to ensure your actions and plans are aligned with their needs. This is an ethical approach to CE.

A word on advocacy

One often misunderstood form of engagement is advocacy. Traditionally, this has been seen as a profusion of posters on school walls, with logos and slogans advocating for human and/or ecological rights. While it is true that advocacy focuses on supporting a cause, it is also about taking actions that consciously address the systemic issues that underlie that cause. For example, promoting an 'International Day of ...' gives you and your peers a chance to have your voices heard and perhaps raise awareness of an issue within the community. However, this alone does not address the root causes of the problem (why the international day is needed in the first place).

Addressing the root causes of the problem and educating others can lead to lasting systems change rather than just superficial solutions. Advocacy does not always have an immediate impact on the system that it is addressing. As we learned with systems thinking (Section 1.2.2), complex (human and ecological) systems are non-linear, and causes and effects are unpredictable. For example, similar stimuli can cause very different effects within the system, and a small stimulus can cause a disproportionately large disruption in another part of the system or vice versa.

While some forms of advocacy, such as #BlackLivesMatter, may have a noticeable and/or immediate impact on larger systems, smaller acts are also necessary, such as speaking out to try and stop bullying while encouraging others to do the same. Just as necessary are the research processes that you carry out in your school community, such as learning about the use of plastics and organizing student-administration communication channels to try and change how single-use plastics are handled. Another example is working with an NGO and writing letters to local and/or global governments to promote human rights.

Here are some helpful guidelines for advocacy work. Make sure you begin with research, as you need to get a deep understanding of the topic that you want to explore. Do some research on the topic's background as well as its social and political contexts. Here is a non-exhaustive list of questions.

Table 1.23 Research questions to get you started

Background	• What is the issue? • When did the issue begin? • Who is involved in the issue? • What are some of the social implications of this issue?
Social context	• Which community/communities are impacted by the issue? Why, when, where and how? • What social and cultural considerations might influence the issue? • What engagement has already occurred around the issue?
Political context	• Who are the rule makers, and how are decisions made? • Whose voices are included and excluded from decision-making processes? • How can people engage with the decision-makers? • How are voices represented within the community?

Engagement in virtual spaces

Using technology, you can extend your local action to global action through partnerships with students and communities in other parts of the world. While these virtual spaces and digital tools can support and enhance your learning and engagement, you must reflect critically on the ethical dimension of the engagement and its learning purpose.

Additionally, while digital engagements can be extremely helpful, you must follow the digital citizenship and safety guidelines outlined by your school. These include carefully researching those you will meet online, especially if you do not know them well, creating strong passwords and protecting your accounts, being wary of who you share your personal details with, and carefully considering what you choose to share about your personal life. You may also ask a teacher or other adult to attend some or all of these online meetings. Before you embark on virtual engagements, consider the following questions:

- How private and safe is this space? How do I know?
- Is any personal information going to be shared? How and who is sharing this?
- Is this exchange going to be recorded? By whom? What for?
- What kind of organizational ethics and privacy laws/policies are in place?
- How do I know AI does not generate this exchange?
- What strategies will I to use to navigate the vast amounts of content on the internet?
- How do I intend to uphold academic integrity and adhere to IB principles?
- How will I communicate respectfully and responsibly in this space?

LEARNING ENGAGEMENT

Enhancing forms of engagement

With your teacher, a peer or in a small group, look at the table below and decide what could be considered an appropriate form of engagement. Discuss the actions that would be regarded as inappropriate or that would not support a deeper understanding of the learning outcomes. Discuss how you could change these 'non-examples' in ways that would turn them into meaningful forms of engagement.

Table 1.24

Community building and organizing	**Yes**	**No**
Working with the senior leadership team in the school to address issues within the school community		
Baking cookies for a bake sale		
Giving out toys during a Christmas drive		
Setting up a school or a local basketball team		
Teaching the local language to newly arrived children at a refugee centre		
Participation		
Joining the plastic-free school campaign and participating actively		
Peer tutoring		
Taking pictures of a community engagement with no clear purpose		
Learning to cook		
Creating and performing a puppet show to teach primary school pupils about an environmental issue		
Advocacy		
Hanging campaign posters on the school walls		
Posting pictures from a bake sale on your social media profile		
Setting up and participating in a letter-writing campaign to raise awareness of human rights		
Starting an anti-bullying campaign at school		
Organizing a walk to raise awareness about a local issue		
Community-based learning and research		
Watching bee hotels in a communal garden to make sure that they work		
Learning the local language to get a job		
Partnering with a local community to design and run a green spaces protection campaign		
Surveying the community to learn about homeless people and then setting up a knitting club for winter months		
Producing a list of potential local partners and then adding it to your learning journal		

LEARNING ENGAGEMENT

Where are you now?

It is essential to continuously review your CE explorations and preparations before taking action within the community. This ensures your interests, hopes, dreams and intentions are aligned with the purpose and aims of CE. Working with a peer, review what you have done so far. The following is by no means an exhaustive list; however, it will help you orient and re-orient back to the purpose and aims of CE. If you discover missing ideas, plans, goals, actions, intentions and concepts, speak with your teacher.

■ **Table 1.25**

Sources of inspiration	**Yes**	**No**
I am choosing to explore topics and/or causes that are important to me.		
I have reflected on these topics/causes in relation to my identity, positionality and worldviews.		
Topics		
I have prepared for the following CE stage (relate and act) by properly researching my topics.		
I have connected my research to community opportunities and/or challenges.		
Community		
I have identified people and/or organizations within the community I would like to connect with.		
As a part of my explorations and preparations, I have researched these people and/or organizations. This will give me the best chance of acting in ways that respect the time and expertise of those in my community.		
Dimensions of community		
I have explored the dimensions of community in relation to my topic and the people/organizations I would like to work with. This includes a consideration of how I care for myself (personal), how I can care for the community (relational), and how social and/or ecological issues are impacting the community (systems). I have also considered how others care for themselves, the community, and social and/or ecological systems.		
I have recorded my ideas on the dimensions of community in my learning journal, as this will support my overall work and my CE review points.		
Principles of engagement		
I have explored the principles of engagement (dialogue, reciprocity and reflection/reflexivity) and considered my strengths and growth areas within each.		
In my preparations, I have tried to engage in ethical and reciprocal dialogues in my preparations. I have reflected on my ideas and actions, and I have considered how my perspectives, biases and assumptions impact my thinking and actions.		
Forms of engagement		
I have reflected on the various forms of engagement and understand that I may engage with one or more of these forms at any given time.		
I have explored topics, community partners and/or community organizations that will allow me to engage authentically and meaningfully for the purpose of collectively addressing a community opportunity and/or challenge.		
Information gathered		
I have gathered information in a logical and organized way, and this is clearly reflected in my learning journal.		
In my learning journal, I have organized the information in a way that will allow me to easily add, update and/or reflect on it as needed in the future.		
Ethics		
I have connected ethical concepts, lenses and paradigms to my explorations and preparations.		
Throughout my explorations and preparations, I have remembered to honour diverse ways of knowing and being, and this has led me to expand my thinking and/or research.		

2 Relate and act

Your exploration and preparation stage leads to developing relationships within the community as you take action. Remember that you will need to work with the community in a partnership, and you must critically reflect on your own actions and thoughts. You must also engage in respectful and ethical dialogues and ongoing communications.

What might you be doing during this stage of the process?

1 Building and maintaining reciprocal relationships:
   - When you are building relationships, focus on seeking connections, mutual understanding, equity and reciprocity.
   - Focus on your positionality, as this will help you reflect on your perspectives and roles while balancing the inclusion of multiple and diverse voices.
   - Act in ways that help to develop and maintain open dialogic channels.
   - Use ethical decision-making before, during and after taking action and/or deciding not to take action.

2 Taking action in partnership with the community by:
   - engaging in the actions with them
   - listening mindfully and carefully to their needs and feedback
   - maintaining communication and collaboration in a sustained way, as co-determined by you and your community partner
   - engaging in ongoing reflection and reflexivity.

Top tip!

Before taking action in partnership with the community, you must ask yourself if that action counts as CE. To refine your understanding of your engagement, you must view the three stages of the process as interconnected (a process you build on, learning from each part of the process). Your actions alongside communities may lead you to explore further or even evaluate the path that you have undertaken, and you may want to adjust your plans and actions accordingly.

Reflection and reflexivity

Some thoughts before moving on

Select five of the questions below and reflect on them in your learning journal. Next, share your ideas with your teacher or a peer. Your teacher may ask you to share with a larger group.

- How are you nurturing relationships with the community?
- How are you maintaining dialogue? What strategies are you developing to foster dialogue with the community?
- In what ways are you and your community practising respect, empathy and care?
- How are you and your community dealing with disagreement?
- How have you planned to deal with possible failure, conflict or mistakes?
- How are you enacting cultural humility?
- What ethical frameworks are you using to decide your actions or inactions? How, how often and where are you reflecting on this?
- How are your values and beliefs changing because of your actions and interactions?
- How is systems thinking helping you and your community understand the engagement?
- Is your community concept changing due to your relationships and actions? If so, how?
- Is your understanding of the opportunity changing due to your relationships and actions? If so, how?
- What is working well and what is not working so well?
- What expectations have been met so far and which ones have not?
- What are some sources of satisfaction and frustration for the members of the community and how have they communicated with you about this?
- How have you had to pivot or adapt your plans to meet emerging and evolving community needs? What role did you play in this through specific actions?

Maintaining reciprocal relationships

There are many ways to foster reciprocal and respectful relationships with the community, and creating sustainable partnerships takes time, commitment and practice. The visual below displays a non-exhaustive list of the various ways you can show respect for your community partners. Respect develops trust, which in turn motivates community members to work together in skilful ways.

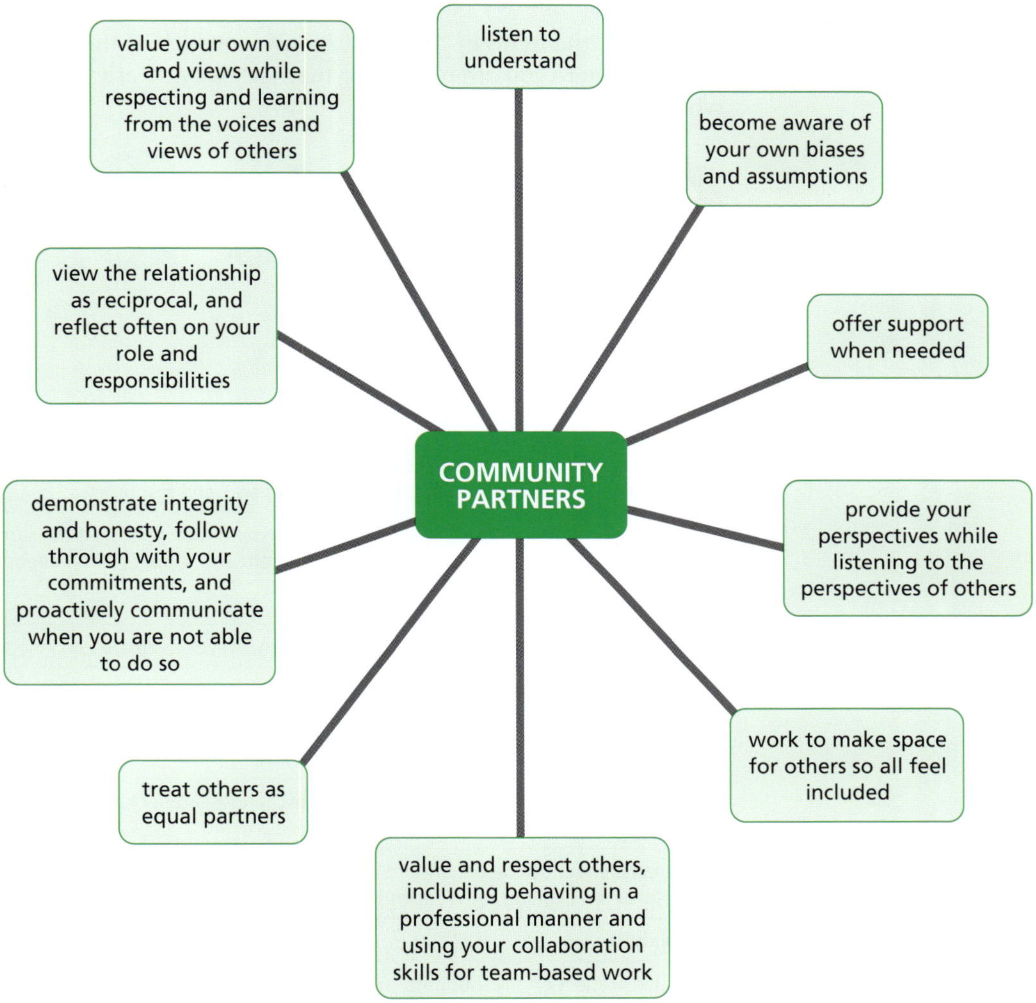

■ Ways to act as a reciprocal community partner

Reciprocity starts at the beginning of your relationship with your community partner. Whether engaging in formal or informal work, it is essential that you prioritize reciprocal actions, such as building trust and maintaining effective communications. Help your community partner understand where you are coming from and what CE is about, letting them know what you have learned about the topic in a clear and effective way. This way you will foster a mutual understanding of the challenges and/or opportunities encountered.

LEARNING ENGAGEMENT

Where are you so far?

It is essential to continuously review how you are relating and acting within the community. This ensures that you engage 'in action alongside community members, with ongoing communication and dialogue, collaboration and reciprocity, and being mindful of context'. It also ensures you consider 'when it is responsible and ethical to take action, and when it might be more appropriate not to take action' (IBO 2025a, p.26).

For each of the items in Table 1.26, consider which of the icons given below most closely matches where you are now. Your teacher may also ask you to share with a peer or the whole group.

Table 1.26 How do I feel about my progress?

Reciprocity	**Your progress**
I am reciprocal when relating to community members and taking action within my community. I do this by helping others and acting in ways that will benefit others. I try to find a good balance of giving and receiving in my community partnerships. This includes sharing things like support and resources.	
I check in with my community partners to understand their needs. At the same time, I try to understand my needs and ask for help and support when needed.	
Dialogue	
I use dialogue to relate to community partners and develop trust and connection.	
When discussing ideas and problem-solving, I consider not just ideas and solutions but also the needs and feelings of others.	
Reflection	
In my learning journal and during in-person exchanges, I reflect on my actions to improve them for the future.	
I regularly reflect on the dimensions of community and principles of engagement to ensure I am aligning my work with the nature and aims of CE.	
Reflexivity	
I regularly reflect on my thoughts, actions, biases and perspectives. I challenge myself to consider any assumptions I bring to a situation and how this impacts the relational systems I am a part of.	
I regularly reflect on my roles and question the power dynamics involved in different situations, noting how they affect my actions. I question whether my actions are aligned with community needs and whether they support the health of social and/or ecological systems.	
Ethics	
I consider whether my actions are responsible and ethically sound.	
I challenge myself to consider different ethical concepts, lenses and paradigms and relate these to my community engagements.	

3 Evaluate and share

As previously stated, the three stages of the engagement process are interrelated. While preparing and acting, you also evaluate and share thoughts and insights with your peers, community and teachers. The evaluate and share stage allows you to review your CE journey, evaluate your engagements and examine and articulate milestones, impacts and outcomes. It will also allow you to share what you have learned with others.

Assessing the progress of your journey can be one of the best ways to help you stay motivated. Reflecting on your progress also allows you to highlight it, meaning others will be inspired and may want to join you in your work. Even if you think that you were not as successful as you would have liked, evaluating your progress can help you understand why you were not successful and what you can do better next time, as well as assessing the impact of your work.

During this stage, you will be doing some of the following:

1. Reviewing and evaluating your engagements, examining and articulating milestones, impacts and outcomes with a focus on:
   - assessing your CE journey, including issues, concepts, processes and relationships you have encountered, both individually and collectively. Have you created any tangible products, such as a website, social media campaign, an event, exhibition or publication?
   - examining the impact on yourself and the community. What have you learned from stepping into unfamiliar situations or perspectives? What changes have occurred in people's knowledge, understanding or attitudes? What new insights, skills or perspectives have you developed through this experience? Have your engagements led to any changes in practice, either inside or outside your school community?
   - evaluating the outcomes of your engagement. How has the issue or topic you explored come to be understood or approached differently? How did your emotional responses (e.g. joy, discomfort) influence your engagement and learning? In what ways did your engagement align with your interests, values or sense of purpose?
   - exploring intentional and unintentional consequences of your actions
   - reflecting on transformations that have occurred as a result of your actions or inactions, including any shifts in your worldview, assumptions or relationships.
2. Sharing your journey with your peers, teachers and community members by:
   - assessing, reflecting and sharing your CE stories in ways that are appropriate to your school context and audience
   - recognizing and celebrating your journey.

Table 1.27 provides some questions you can use to help you evaluate your work within the community and decide which parts you want to share.

Table 1.27 Guiding questions to help you evaluate your work

Reciprocity	• How did I maintain dialogue with the community throughout my engagements? Were there essential agreements with the community partner to keep open and active dialogue? If not, how did I do my best in this regard? • What assumptions and emotions did I bring to dialogues within the community? • How complex was the creation of shared understandings? Did misunderstandings occur around logistical and/or conceptual matters? If so, what actions did I take to try to resolve them? • What essential knowledge did I learn from the community? What did the community learn from me? • Can I create a visual depiction of my understanding of reciprocity and how I have grown with this principled action over time?
Ethics	• What did I do to cultivate compassion, respect others and work together from a place of shared values? • To what extent has my approach to people and situations been defined by openness, open-mindedness, humility and a willingness to ask questions and think critically? • Can I create a visual depiction of my understanding of ethics and my ethical growth over time?
Reflection and reflexivity	• How did I cope with discomfort when taking action? • What did I do to learn about my positionality before approaching the community? • How did I reflect on this throughout my engagements? How can I show my reflexive growth over time? • How have community engagements impacted me? What have I learned, unlearned and/or relearned? • Can I create a visual depiction of my understanding of reflection and reflexivity and my growth in these areas over time?
Community dimensions	• How can I evaluate my knowledge and understanding of the community dimensions? • How can I share this knowledge and understanding with the community in age- and context-appropriate ways? • Can I create a visual depiction of my understanding of the community dimensions and my growth in this area over time? How could this benefit the community?
Succession planning	• How am I engaging in succession planning with my engagements? How does this relate to an ethic of care for the community? • How can I contribute to the sustainability of CE within my community?

Learning journal

Your journey

As you reflect on your engagements and think through reflexive lenses, you will define your journey's story. To help you evaluate your work and prepare to share it with the community, choose one or two questions from each of the categories in Table 1.27 and answer these questions in your learning journal. Your teacher may ask you to share your thoughts with others.

Different ways to share your journey

Sharing your journey and the processes you went through to develop and sustain healthy community relationships is a key part of the CE process. Your school may have in place some ways of sharing your journey; however, you can also be proactive and seek other opportunities to share your stories. Here are some things you can consider:

- **School assemblies:** An assembly can be a great way to highlight parts of your journey, and you can invite community partners to attend the assembly and contribute. Your community partner may also help you prepare assembly presentations.
- **Written communication channels**, such as school newsletters, newspapers or magazines. Sharing your CE can inspire others, and well-presented research and materials are another form of advocacy.
- **Social-media posts:** Through official school channels, you may have options for developing social-media posts that focus on your and your peers' CE work. This must be done in an ethical way, taking into account privacy and consent issues. You must first discuss featuring your CE work on social media with your teacher.

Sustainability and succession planning

If your engagement work has a strong foundation, there is a greater likelihood that the work will continue flourishing. Working with your community partner, you can put a plan in place that communicates a thorough understanding of your engagements, associated goals and outcomes, strengths, areas for improvement, insights into various approaches and strategies, and possible next steps. As you prepare to complete your CE journey, you can also speak with your teachers, family members, peers and younger students to brainstorm ways to keep this work going into the future.

In some circumstances, students maintain relationships with community partners and/or continue working with them after high school. As you reach the completion of your CE journey and find a way to express your gratitude to your community partner or partners, you may also want to inquire about future volunteer, internship or work opportunities.

The importance of academic integrity in every CE stage

Throughout your CE journey, you must ensure the credibility of all sources, both online and offline. Use your ATL skills to ensure your sources are reliable and accurate, and when accessing media sources, note how the media's interpretations of events may be skewed by bias. Whenever possible, use primary sources. Some questions to consider are:

- **Who:** Who published the information and why?
- **What:** What is the main idea? Does the evidence back up the claims?
- **Where:** Where did you find the information? How do you know if it is a reputable place to find information about your topic area?
- **When:** When was the information published and written?
- **Why:** What was the reason behind publishing this information?

Whether engaging in research as a part of your explore and prepare stage, supporting the community through research-based activities in your relate and act stage, or giving presentations to the community in your evaluate and share stage, you must interrogate your sources to ensure the information you are using is credible. Using unreliable information can lead to the spread of misinformation, disinformation or fake news.

Extenuating circumstances

Some students face difficult and extenuating circumstances as they journey through their Career-related Programme. Some students find themselves in a situation where they must gain employment to support themselves and/or their loved ones, while other students may be dealing with a long-term illness or hospitalization, or need to act in a caregiving role for family members. Other students may have a unique social entrepreneurship opportunity for their career-related studies. In such rare and/or exceptional circumstances, your school will guide you. Engaging in legal employment, caregiving, entrepreneurship or internships that may or may not be directly related to your schooling may be a valid form of CE under certain conditions.

Should you find yourself in an exceptional or extenuating circumstance, your teacher will support you in adapting your CE journey using the information from the IB's guide, 'What counts as CE?', and will discuss ways to meet the learning outcomes successfully. This may involve adjusting your initial plans to ensure that your modified engagement strategies will meet the requirements for CE.

Throughout your CE journey, it is essential to discuss your ideas with your CE coordinator and/or CE advisor to ensure they will support the community and help you demonstrate your knowledge and understanding of the learning outcomes. Demonstrating the necessity of the engagement, your ethical approaches to the engagement, and a substantial and sustained commitment will be a part of your discussions with your CE coordinator and/or CE advisor. You must share how you will:

- engage in a CE learning and engagement process characterized by dialogue, reciprocity, reflection and reflexivity
- develop knowledge and understanding of personal, relational and systems dimensions in relation to the activities you undertake
- demonstrate that the activities you undertake will enable you to engage with the CE learning outcomes meaningfully
- demonstrate a clear awareness of ethical considerations associated with your participation in alternate forms of approved engagements (e.g. working in a professional setting, caregiving, focusing on your healing with medical support, or entrepreneurial endeavours that may include remuneration).

1.4.3 Summary

- Your teachers will help guide you throughout your CE journey.
- There is a difference between the structured time built into your school schedule (guided time) and all the time you devote to the CE component (learning hours).
- The process of CE consists of three stages: explore and prepare, relate and act, and evaluate and share.
- Reflective and reflexive practice that leads to the development of ethical ways of knowing and being is the driving force of your engagements.

1.5 Assessment in CE

INQUIRY QUESTIONS

- How is CE assessed?
- What is the nature of CE assessment?
- What are the different types of assessment?
- What are the review points?
- What is narrative assessment?
- What are the key features of narrative assessment?
- What is the role of the learning journal in CE assessment?
- How can you complete CE?

1.5.1 The nature of CE assessment

The aim of any assessment is to generate evidence of how a student is developing according to the learning outcomes of a programme. Assessment can range from an informal conversation with a teacher to a more formal review point, and there are different purposes for assessment:

- **Assessment for learning:** When your teachers use evidence to infer your development with the purpose of impacting the effectiveness of their teaching (formative assessment).
- **Assessment as learning:** When you use evidence to reflect on and monitor your ongoing development with the purpose of impacting your learning (formative assessment).
- **Assessment of learning:** When teachers use evidence of your learning to make judgements on your development at a specific point in time against goals and standards (summative assessment).

In assessment *for* learning, your teacher will evaluate your progress in an ongoing and informal manner. The information will come from various sources and will include observations and self-reflection. Its main aim is to provide you with timely feedback so that you can improve and deepen your understanding of CE.

Assessment *as* learning is also a type of formative assessment that focuses more on the process of learning than the product. Its main aim is to support your learning process. In this type of assessment, you are expected to take an active role in your learning and assessment; for example, by reflecting on your understanding of the engagement process or by evaluating your progress. It will generally be present in class activities.

Assessment *of* learning is about evaluating your progress when acquiring knowledge, skills and competencies. Its main aim is to determine the extent to which the CE learning outcomes have been met. In CE, the assessment of your learning will happen at the end of the programme, when a holistic evaluation is made to determine whether or not you have met the learning outcomes and completed the programme.

CE offers you opportunities to learn in, from and with communities, and to apply knowledge and skills acquired in other areas of your learning. Your engagement will be assessed throughout the two years of the programme, with a clear emphasis on the *quality* of the entire journey and how it has contributed to your learning and development.

You are required to provide evidence for whether or not you have met the learning outcomes. Some of them will be demonstrated many times, while others will be only occasionally explicit, but you must show evidence of every outcome.

■ Table 1.28

Through meaningful and purposeful engagement with community, you will be able to:	
LO1	Foster reciprocal and dialogic engagement.
LO2	Explore systems and develop an awareness of their role within these.
LO3	Develop, articulate and enact thinking and action.
LO4	Engage in reflective and reflexive practice.

Assessment can be approached in different ways. While all are equally valid, some are more effective than others. Your school context will determine which methods and strategies are most appropriate to support assessment and will monitor your progress in relation to the learning outcomes. You will need to find which ones work best for you, but it is recommended that you use as many different methods and strategies as possible.

1.5.2 Types of CE assessment

Assessment is a vital tool to understand your progress. It is repeating, circular and continuous by nature, and it provides you and your teachers an opportunity to reflect on your engagement while acknowledging that this process is not always straightforward. During guided time, you will have the opportunity to learn about the purpose of this evaluation and what methods will be used to help you navigate your CE journey.

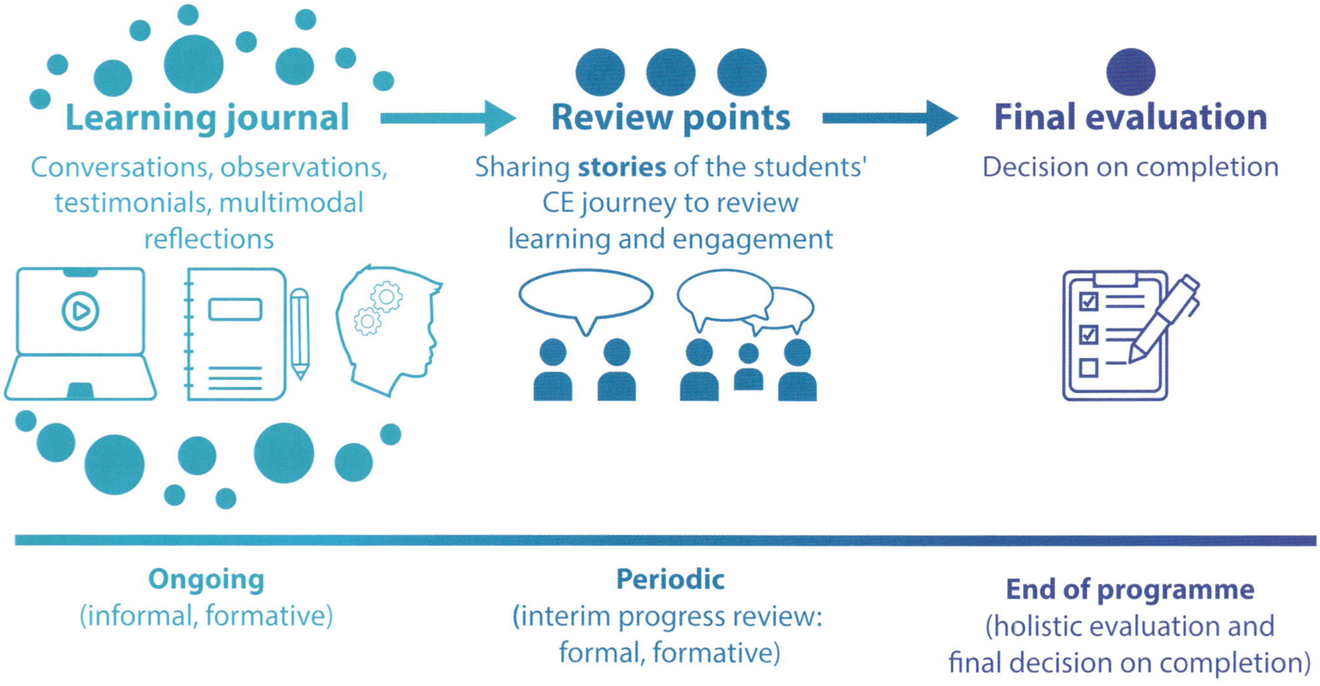

■ Continuum of assessment in CE (Source: IBO 2025a, p.21)

Assessment in CE is best represented in the form of a continuum, and the methods used will give you an idea of how you can craft your CE journey and map your learning journey.

Informal formative assessment

This refers to the ongoing evaluation of your learning and it is actionable, meaning that you can make real-time adjustments to your engagement based on ongoing conversations and dialogues with your teacher. This type of assessment provides your teacher with important information so that they can help you meet your learning goals.

In CE, informal formative assessments include (but are not limited to) the following:

- teacher observations that happen during guided time
- teacher observations that occur within the context of a classroom or out-of-school activities
- in-class presentations
- self-reflections that happen throughout your engagement and are visible to your teacher
- evidence your teacher can see in your learning journal
- unplanned opportunities for teacher–student dialogue that provide you with immediate feedback through questions or clarifications.

You can also use peer assessment or self-assessment to take a more active role in your learning and identify the next steps needed to make progress. Peer assessments will strengthen your collaboration skills through making decisions with others, problem-solving activities, and analysis and evaluation of information. You can discuss with your teacher the expectations around peer assessment, including the use of appropriate language and processes.

Interim progress reviews

Interim progress reviews are a more systematic method of evaluating your learning, growth over time, skills and competencies. In the case of CE, these moments emphasize dialogue and reflection, and the aim is to provide a space where you can tell the story of your unfolding CE journey.

While the review points may be conducted in a group, it is beneficial for the first two—or all three—to be done individually to ensure that you and your teacher can adequately focus on your progress and ensure you are meeting the learning outcomes. You will select evidence from your learning journal to support discussions in the review points, and it is up to you to carefully select and arrange which pieces of evidence you will share.

> Your learning journal reflects time, energy, growth and learning, and it can support post-secondary and scholarship applications. It may also help future employment opportunities, and you should ensure you can take your learning journal with you upon graduation. Speak with your teacher about transferring files from school to personal accounts.

Review points

It is recommended to approach the three review points through narrative assessment to demonstrate your learning against the four learning outcomes (see Section 1.5.3 for more information about narrative assessments).

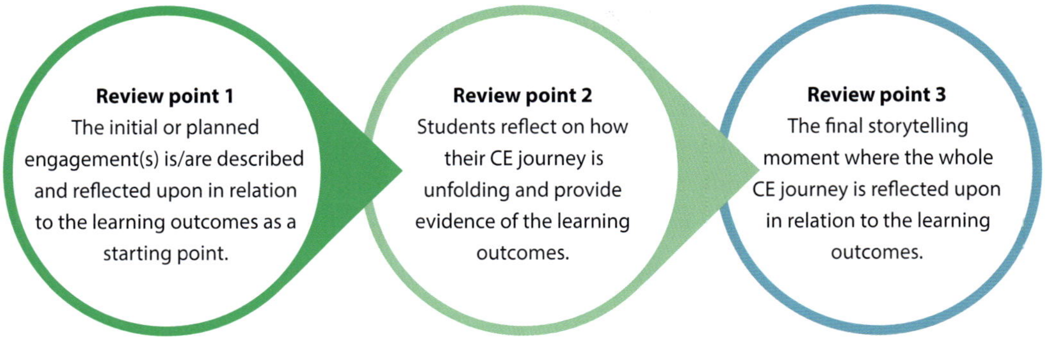

■ The narrative assessment expectations for each review point (Source: IB CE TSM)

The first review point

Your first review point will occur when you clearly understand CE aims, learning outcomes and requirements. At this point, you will be in the beginning stages of your active engagements with the community, having started planning or moving forward with initial engagements. You will also be in the initial stages of applying ethical systems, reciprocal, reflective and reflexive lenses to your CE work. The main focus of this review point is: 'How am I embarking on my CE journey?'

The following table will support you in preparing for your first review point.

■ **Table 1.29** (Adapted from IB CE toolkit)

LO1	Foster reciprocal and dialogic engagement: ● How am I planning to build relationships with community members based on respect, mutuality, solidarity and understanding? ● What steps am I taking to ensure that my engagement with the community is dialogic, involving attentive listening in addition to speaking and acting? ● How am I preparing to be open to learning from the community's knowledge and experiences?
LO2	Explore systems and develop awareness of their roles within these: ● How am I understanding and engaging with the three CE dimensions: personal, relational and systems? ● How am I identifying and learning about the different systems (social, economic, ecological) that influence the community with which I am engaging? ● As I start my CE journey, what steps am I taking to understand my role and impact on systems? ● How will I use systems awareness to inform my approach to CE? ● At the end of my CE journey, what would I like the community I work with to say about me, my work and the impact I have had on various community systems?
LO3	Develop, articulate and enact ethical thinking and action: ● What ethical considerations should I consider as I embark on my CE journey? ● How do I set intentions to act through an ethic of care to support my own and the community's well-being? ● In what ways am I planning to seek consent and feedback from the community to guide my engagement activities? ● How will I respond skilfully and ethically if I do not receive the feedback I want from the community or my teachers?
LO4	Engage in reflective and reflexive practice: ● How will I document my thoughts, feelings, insights and learning throughout my CE journey? ● How am I reflecting on my assumptions, biases and perspectives? How can I understand others' assumptions, biases and perspectives? How does this influence how I engage with communities? ● What strategies will I use to critically assess my engagements' impact on myself and the community? ● How will I ensure that my reflections lead to actionable changes in my approach to CE? ● What difficulties do I think I will encounter during my CE journey, and how can I positively reflect on these difficulties?

REAL-WORLD EXAMPLE

The first review point

Kenji feels nervous about his first review point, a one-on-one meeting with his teacher. Kenji has a basic understanding of ethics, which connects closely to his family's faith system. He is interested in systems thinking but hasn't yet created systems thinking artefacts for his learning journal. He hopes to develop a systems iceberg for the topic he wants to address with the community: plastics in the ocean.

Ahead of the meeting, Kenji creates a PowerPoint presentation with slides devoted to each learning outcome. Reflecting on the first learning outcome, he says his shyness holds him back from initiating dialogues and he is unsure of his growth in this area. His ethics slide features a mind map connecting his spiritual beliefs to ethical paradigms, with highlighted areas showing where his thinking has changed. His reflection and reflexivity slides show entries from his learning journal including his anxiety around being a more active participant in reciprocal dialogues. Kenji ends with his plans for using systems thinking tools to tackle ocean plastics, sharing research and expressing his concern about meeting community partners. He sets personal learning goals like asking for help, practising positive self-talk and improving his learning journal organization.

Kenji's teacher reflects on Kenji's passion for his topic and his strong ethic of care towards nature. His teacher asks him to outline his plans for contacting community partners and suggests he connects with his PPS teacher to gain insight into constructing timely communications with community partners. His teacher also encourages him to continue developing his collaboration skills through human-to-human interactions.

Kenji feels relieved. He has perfectionist tendencies and has worked hard to build the confidence to share his incomplete work with his teachers. Kenji also feels anxious about upcoming meetings with community members. He is grateful for his teacher's reminders that his teachers will support him throughout this process.

In preparation for your first review point, try to respond to the questions from Table 1.29 in your learning journal, and make sure you show your knowledge and understanding in whatever creative ways work best for you. This may include mind maps, growth-over-time maps, systems tools, a video, podcast, infographic or annotated drawings/photos. If you choose to create a presentation for your review points, your teacher will provide guidance around appropriate presentation tools, methods and formats. This may be the same or different from the other review points, depending on what your teacher has determined will work best for your school context. You can also note/explore other ideas, thoughts or feelings that come to your mind when preparing for your review points, and you may want to develop your own questions related to the learning outcomes.

Being well-prepared is essential for effective dialogue with your teacher at your review point. You must be ready to share, listen, receive constructive and compassionate feedback, and ask follow-up questions. Your teacher will encourage you to speak openly about your journey, and you can support yourself by using your ATL skills to embody the attributes of the learner profile.

Reflection and reflexivity

Preparing for the first review point

In your learning journal, consider the following questions. Your teacher may ask you to share your thoughts with others.

- How would you like to share your developing knowledge, growth and understanding of the learning outcomes in your first review point?
- What key stories, milestones, challenges and successes are important for you to share? Why do you consider these significant parts of your CE journey?
- What concerns do you have as you head into your first review point? How can you self-advocate and/or seek support to alleviate these concerns?
- What are you most excited about sharing at the first review point?

The second review point

Your second review point will happen after you have had time to grow community plans and ideas together. The main focus of this review point is: 'Where am I in my CE journey?'

The following table will support you in preparing for your second review point.

Table 1.30 (Adapted from IB CE toolkit)

LO1	Foster reciprocal and dialogic engagement: • How have my relationships within the community evolved to become more reciprocal and dialogic? • What evidence can I provide to show that my engagements have been based on mutual respect and understanding? • In what ways have I adjusted my approaches to ensure more effective two-way communication with the community? • Is there any information I do not yet have? How will I obtain this information? • How have I/can I respond skilfully and ethically when/if the community has not been able or willing to engage reciprocally with me? How can this still be a reflective/reflexive learning engagement for me?
LO2	Explore systems and develop awareness of their roles within these: • How am I applying the three dimensions (personal, relational and systems) to my guided learning and active engagements? Which dimensions do I tend to focus more and less on? How can I reflexively examine the reasons for this? • What new insights have I gained about the systems affecting the community, and how has this knowledge influenced my role within these systems? • How have I considered various systems lenses based on equity and inclusion? • Can I identify any changes in my perception of my impact within these systems since the beginning of my CE journey? • How have I applied my understanding of systems to enhance the appropriateness and effectiveness of my CE efforts?
LO3	Develop, articulate and enact ethical thinking and action: • What ethical issues or dilemmas have I encountered during my CE journey, and how have I addressed them? • How has my understanding and practise of ethical engagement evolved over time? • What feedback have I received from the community regarding the ethics of my engagements, and how have I responded to it? • Do I have any relevant and timely feedback to give to the community I am working with about ethical engagement and action? If so, is it possible, helpful and appropriate to communicate this feedback skilfully and ethically? Can the feedback be heard, and do I need someone to support me in giving this feedback?
LO4	Engage in reflective and reflexive practice: • What forms of engagement am I involved with? Do I enjoy these engagements? Why or why not? Is there anything I can identify as particularly beneficial, satisfying or rewarding? • What frustrates, confuses or challenges me so far in my CE journey? Have I found anything particularly useful to manage this? What have I learned by reflecting on my biases, assumptions and positionality in relation to challenging moments? • How can I learn and grow from setbacks, boredom, discomfort and frustration? Can I recognize these as equally important parts of my journey? How do I find hope, possibilities and agency even where there are personal, relational and/or systemic tensions? • What key lessons have I learned from reflecting on my CE activities, and how have they influenced my approach? • How have my reflections led to changes in my thoughts, emotions and/or actions in CE? What insights have I gained about my own and others' assumptions, biases and perspectives? How has this influenced how I engage with communities? • Can I provide specific examples of how reflective and reflexive practice has helped me to overcome challenges, choose different strategies to support changing contexts, enhance my engagements with the community and/or change the nature of my community engagements?

REAL-WORLD EXAMPLE

The second review point

Kenji feels more confident at the second review point. Through a PowerPoint presentation structured similarly to his first review point, Kenji reflects on his learning in CE. He has reached out to several local organizations and attended a webinar hosted by a global organization working to reduce global plastics. Kenji had hoped to partner with a local organization working to assess the impact of microplastics in the ocean; however, after a meeting with their community coordinator, he realized the organization doesn't work with teenagers on research or advocacy.

Kenji has started meeting with a multi-generational climate action group that includes teens, university students, retired individuals and other concerned citizens. He tells his teacher he is enjoying this group and enjoys speaking with the elders in the group. He relates this to his LCS, noting that the elders speak different dialects.

Currently, Kenji is co-designing a project to present in schools and, at a planning meeting, he shared a systems iceberg he created. The group discussed underlying mental models and Kenji expressed a desire to become more politically engaged. In his learning journal, he drafted infographics and sample letters to send to local politicians.

Kenji shares that he becomes quiet when he senses others are not as passionate about climate change. He understands nature as interconnected and feels a responsibility to protect it. After speaking with his parents, he is working to keep an open mind when engaging with people who have different outlooks and priorities. Kenji is intrigued by Indigenous worldviews and the concept of 'right relations' with nature.

■ Kenji's systems iceberg

Kenji's teacher commends him for his involvement in the broader community and his sustained attention to the CE learning outcomes. He challenges Kenji to think more about reciprocity in his group and encourages him to speak with another CE group working on climate activism. The meeting ends with the teacher asking Kenji to create specific learning goals to help him engage more openly in discussions.

Being well-prepared is essential for effective dialogue with your teacher at your second review point. You must be ready to share, listen, receive constructive and compassionate feedback, and ask follow-up questions. Your teacher will encourage you to speak openly about your journey, and you can support yourself by using your ATL skills to embody the attributes of the learner profile.

At the second review point, you will be expected to show a deeper understanding of the four learning outcomes and their interconnectedness. By this point, you will have more authentic, community-based examples to share, and you can reference these real-world examples as you demonstrate your growth in reciprocity, reflection, reflexivity, systems thinking and ethics. Using relevant, experience-based personal examples, try to reference the three dimensions and the three principles of engagement.

In preparation for your second review point, try to respond to the questions from Table 1.30 in your learning journal; you may also want to develop your own questions related to the learning outcomes. As with the first review point, make sure you show your knowledge and understanding in whatever creative ways work best for you. This may include mind maps, growth-over-time maps, systems tools, a video, podcast, infographic or annotated drawings/photos. If you choose to create a presentation for your review points, your teacher will provide guidance around appropriate presentation tools, methods and formats. This may be the same or different from the other review points, depending on what your teacher has determined will work best for your school context.

Reflection and reflexivity

Preparing for the second review point

In your learning journal, consider the following questions. Your teacher may ask you to share your thoughts with others.

- Since your first review point, how have you grown in your knowledge and understanding of the learning outcomes? What evidence can you provide to show this growth?
- What key stories, milestones, challenges and successes are important for you to share? Why do you consider these significant parts of your CE journey? How do these relate to what you shared in your first review point? Have you needed to adapt, change or pivot substantially? If so, how did you do this and how did this contribute to your growth?
- What concerns do you have as you head into your second review point? How can you self-advocate and/or seek support to alleviate these concerns?
- What are you most excited about sharing at the second review point?

The third review point

Your third review point will happen before the end of the course, after you have engaged in the programme in a sustained manner and are ready to share your whole experience with CE.

The main focus of this review point is: 'How am I rounding off my CE learning journey, what will I take from it into the future and how can my CE work continue to benefit the community?'

The following table will support you in preparing for your third review point.

■ **Table 1.31** (Adapted from IB CE toolkit)

LO1	Foster reciprocal and dialogic engagement: ● What have been the most impactful moments of reciprocal and dialogic engagement throughout my CE journey, and how will I apply these lessons in future interactions? ● How has my ability to engage in meaningful dialogue evolved, and in what ways will I continue to develop this skill beyond my CE context? ● What have been the most effective strategies I have found to build mutual respect and understanding, and how can these be adapted to other areas of my life? ● How can I help amplify and support the community partners who have helped me throughout my CE journey?
LO2	Explore systems and develop awareness of their roles within these: ● How has my understanding of systemic influences on communities changed, and how will this awareness influence my future actions and decisions? ● What are my engagements' intended or unintended impacts on myself and the community? How do I/will I know? ● What role do I see myself playing in addressing systemic issues based on my CE experience, and how can I prepare for this? ● How will I continue to educate myself about the systems I am a part of?
LO3	Develop, articulate and enact ethical thinking and action: ● What ethical principles have guided my CE journey, and how will I ensure these principles continue to guide my future endeavours? ● How have I navigated ethical issues and dilemmas during my CE journey, and what strategies will I use to do this in the future? ● In what ways has my CE experience deepened my commitment to ethical action, and how will I manifest this commitment moving forward?
LO4	Engage in reflective and reflexive practice: ● What have been the key takeaways from my reflective and reflexive practice during my CE journey, and how will I integrate this into my future learning and development? ● How has reflexive practice influenced my CE experience, and how do I plan to use this approach to navigate future opportunities and challenges? ● What methods or tools have I found most useful, and how will I ensure that reflection and reflexivity continue to be part of my approach to future endeavours? ● How will my developing reflective/reflexive practice support me in co-creating healthier and more equitable systems in the future? ● Does the way I have conducted myself and shared my CE journey affect the future involvement of students, teachers, parents or community partners? ● Do I want to continue working with any of the community partners I have been involved with? If so, why? How can I do this? If not, why not?

REAL-WORLD EXAMPLE

The third review point

Kenji feels happy walking into his third review point. He has created strong community connections and he looks forward to continuing his work with the climate action group after he graduates. Kenji has also helped create a youth advisory council for the original organization he contacted. Working alongside some CE peers, he is designing a workshop on ocean plastics for younger students and he feels confident when teaching others.

Kenji is thinking of going into education and he believes his career-related studies (CRS) in environmental sciences will benefit him. He discusses connections to his RP which, while not focused on ocean plastics, looks at environmental protection laws. Kenji has learned that environmental legal protections are more complex than he originally thought and he is balancing his idealism with practical considerations.

Kenji wants to learn more about two-eyed seeing from a science point of view and he is following Indigenous scientists from Brazil, Ethiopia, Kenya and Australia on social media. He highlights some social-media posts, saying that they bring him hope. He shares growth-over-time maps around the learning outcomes and he thinks he has grown in ethics and systems thinking, but he needs to work on trusting others.

Kenji's teacher commends him for his CE. He asks for more detailed plans about the workshops Kenji is planning for younger students, reminding Kenji that he will need to communicate plans to the teachers of these younger students and seek feedback to ensure the content and delivery methods are appropriate. He asks Kenji to speak about his vision for the CE-sharing evening and shows him some resources on active hope. The teacher notes that Kenji seems hopeful and engaged when discussing his passion topics. He asks Kenji to complete a self-assessment rubric, which will be a discussion topic in class.

As you learned in your first and second review points, good preparation is essential for effective dialogue with your teacher. You must be ready to share, listen, receive constructive and compassionate feedback, and ask follow-up questions. Your teacher will encourage you to speak openly about your journey, and you can support yourself by using your ATL skills to embody the attributes of the learner profile.

The questions in Table 1.31, along with the real-world example above, will help you prepare for your third review point. To ensure you can show your understanding of all four learning outcomes, make sure you answer some or all questions from each learning outcome in your learning journal. You can also note/explore other ideas, thoughts or feelings that come to mind when preparing for your review points, and you may want to develop your own questions related to the learning outcomes.

As per your preparation for your first and second review points, make sure you show your knowledge and understanding in whatever creative ways work best for you. This may include mind maps, growth-over-time maps, systems tools, a video, podcast, infographic or annotated drawings/photos. If you choose to create a presentation for your review points, your teacher will provide guidance around appropriate presentation tools, methods and formats. This may be the same or different from the other review points, depending on what your teacher has determined will work best for your school context.

Reflection and reflexivity

Preparing for the third review point

In your learning journal, consider the following questions. Your teacher may ask you to share your thoughts with others.

- Since your second review point, how have you grown in your knowledge and understanding of the learning outcomes? What authentic evidence can you provide to show this growth?
- What key stories, milestones, challenges and successes are important for you to share? Why do you consider these significant parts of your CE journey? How do these relate to what you shared in your second (and/or first) review point? Have you needed to adapt, change or pivot substantially? If so, how did you do this, and how did this contribute to your growth?
- What concerns do you have as you head into your third review point? How can you self-advocate and/or seek support to alleviate these concerns, and what tools, strategies and approaches will you use to do this?
- What are you most excited about sharing at the third review point? How will you be able to summarize your entire CE journey in a concise and memorable way? What lessons will you carry forward with you into the future?

1.5.3 Narrative assessment

Narrative assessment is the recommended holistic approach to evaluate your progress in your CE journey. It focuses on **what** happened, **how** it happened and **why** it happened. Narrative assessment will support you to find an authentic and meaningful way to communicate your CE experiences to your teacher through storytelling.

Narrative assessment focuses on the collection, interpretation and communication of detailed, qualitative descriptions of your CE experiences through storytelling. Storytelling supports systems change by changing 'how [individuals] see themselves, their communities and their broader context. Systems change when people change: how they relate to others, who they are in relationship with and what they believe they are capable of doing' (Snow et al., 2025b). Narrative assessment will help you develop empathy, see new perspectives, gain new insights and highlight how things are changing within the community dimensions and principles of engagement.

Narrative assessment will show you how significant learning is taking place, and it will enable you to engage in the kind of transformative learning that will positively impact you in the future. This begins with inner transformation (the personal dimension), leading to a positive transformation in relationships (the relational dimension) and positively impacting larger socio-ecological systems (the systems dimension). Through narrative assessment, you are encouraged to connect these community dimensions in constructive, insightful and compassionate ways.

Through storytelling, you will make sense of your experiences and decide how to give them meaning. You will choose which stories to share, how to tell them, and own 'the interpretation of [your] stories and observations' (Snow et al., 2025a, p. 8). When preparing for the three review points, narrative assessment will help you decide how you want to talk about your experiences, the knowledge you have acquired, the skills you have learned and/or put into practice, the challenges and opportunities you have encountered, the decisions you have made or not made and the strategies you followed. Your narrative assessment is not a story of success, but rather what you have experienced and how you interpret your experiences in relation to the CE learning outcomes.

In a narrative assessment, it is important to connect your learning to the community context in which your engagements happened. You will need to describe what you have done and learned in ways that are detailed and convincing and that properly reflect the contexts you were in. When your CE work has not produced the results you had hoped for, or when your actions or inactions have resulted in challenging situations for yourself and others, you are asked to use reflexivity to reflect on how your perspectives, biases and assumptions drove your actions or lack of actions within the community.

Storytelling elements in narrative assessment

Narrative assessment involves a well-organized and unified account of events that happened during a specific timeline in a specific context. A narrative assessment is developed from the following five elements:

1. It contains an element of transformation (something important changed).
2. It presents this transformation as a movement over time.
3. It contains actions by which this transformation happens.
4. Characters (one of whom is the interviewee) carry it out.
5. These actions take place in specific well-described settings.

(Source: van Wessel et al., 2021, p.14)

These elements are brought together in a plot that includes both challenges and turning points. This plot leads to a key message you would like to communicate. Your narrative assessment will be considered plausible if you include enough detail—meaning that you are precise in your storytelling to avoid it sounding impersonal or too general. It is important to share enough about the story's context and to be consistent with the details.

While narrative assessment involves the use of the word 'story', it is critical to understand that this is not a fictionalized account of your CE work. Your story must be authentic and true, and it must reflect what you have experienced in and with the community. When compiling your story elements, there may be a risk of simplifying or exaggerating details so that they fit into your narrative. Avoid simplifying or exaggerating your story, and ground it in what you have genuinely experienced. Make sure that there is coherence, meaning, order and consistency. Be precise about the events and make sure you clearly describe the contexts for your actions, asking questions like:

- Why was it evident to me that …?
- Why was this strategy or approach the best fit for that specific situation?
- In retrospect, why was this strategy or approach not the best fit for that specific situation?
- What happened that made me think that my action or non-action was the key element of success?
- When, where, why and how did my thinking and actions change at specific points in my story?
- What values, assumptions, biases and perspectives shaped my thoughts and actions? How did this impact myself and the community?

The figure on the next page will help you to shape your understanding about narrative assessments. You can start at any point in the figure. Although your narrative assessment will be constructed across a timeline, you do not need to start at any particular point. For example, you can start by thinking about the main themes of your CE work and what message you would like to convey, or you can start with a consideration of your timeline or what important things have changed. The main point is to make sure that you connect all of these points in a clear and consistent way, providing details that support the story's context.

Themes and message

Which significant learning moments will you choose to focus on? How does this help you articulate your learning in relation to the LOs? What is the most important thing you learned about CE? What have you learned in relation to the three dimensions of community and the three principles of engagement? How would you like the insights you have gained to influence your future decisions, actions and behaviours?

How can you communicate transformation that has taken place? How have you grown in relation to the LOs? What are the (intended or unintended) impacts of your engagement on yourself and the community? How do you know?

What timeline are you discussing? When does this story start? How did this begin? Will this timeline allow for enough detail and to demonstrate learning and growth?

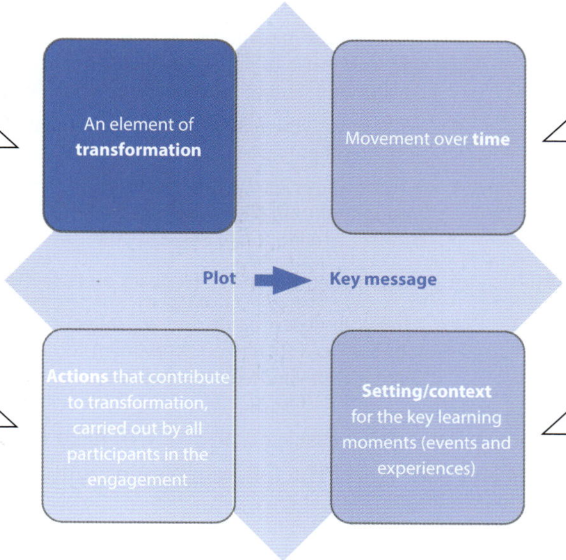

Which significant events are you choosing to focus on? Who was involved? What did they do that mattered? What actions did you and others take or not take? How did these make a difference (e.g. community impact, transformed views, etc.)? How do you know?

What is the context of your story? How was the reality different from what you expected when you started? Can you relate this story to other things unfolding in this context? Which systems and which local/global aspects are relevant (e.g. socioeconomic, political, ecological)?

Plausibility: Detail, contextualization, consistency

What details (examples, observations, analytical reflections) can you provide to support the different elements of your narration about your engagements, including your reflexive responses to interactions and experiences? Is your story consistent with what others understand as evolving within the same context? How can you include community voice in your story? What are your most important failures and achievements, challenges and successes?

How can you describe and explain how you became involved in a community experience? How can you describe how people responded to your actions? How can you explain why you think they responded in a certain way, and how your own and others' responses to the experience might have changed over time? Can you provide a useful example of when you chose a different strategy to fit a changing context?

■ Preparing for narrative assessment (Source: IBO, 2025a, p.2)

■ Key features of a narrative assessment

Narrative assessments offer an opportunity for you to communicate your most authentic and significant learning engagements. While they can be formatted in different ways, including one-to-one conversations with your teacher, group storytelling and even including community partners, there are four main parts to every narrative assessment: preparation (student), storytelling (student), discussion (student and teacher) and reflection (student).

■ **Table 1.32** The four main parts of a narrative assessment

Preparation	• Create your story in a way that is meaningful for you while meeting teacher and school requirements. • Be clear about your actions, inactions, challenges, successes and the details of your story. Create connections between events and larger themes. • Choose evidence from your learning journal that supports your story. • Make clear connections to the learning outcomes. Connect your active engagements to what you learned during your guided-learning time. Show how your guided-learning time influenced your active engagements.
Storytelling and discussion	• What matters to you in this story, and how does it matter to the people, community or world around you? • What are the motivations and values that cause you to engage in this learning and find your sense of purpose? Include important details from your family or cultural background, faith or spirituality, personal principles and societal influences. • What drives your learning and engagement? Connect your learning to your core beliefs and ethical principles. Discuss how they shape your worldview and decision-making. • Why does this learning matter to you and the community? What have you learned throughout both your successes and challenges? How does your own sense of purpose connect to community care?
Discussion	• Remain open-minded to feedback and use it in your future learning and engagements.
Reflection	• After your review point, you will reflect on and self-assess your narrative assessment rubric using a structured assessment tool. You may choose to develop your own and share it with your teacher in advance.

As you create your narrative assessment, you will need to consider the level of *detail*, *context* and *consistency* in your story. The following points will help you determine the plausibility of your story.

■ **Table 1.33** Providing detail, context and consistency in your narrative assessment story

Detail	• Provide details about what happened, how challenges were engaged with, and the impacts and outcomes of your engagements. • Include examples, observations, analytical reflections and creative contributions. • Be precise. Explain how you became involved in the community experience and describe how your (and perhaps others') responses to the experience changed over time.
Context	• Root your story in the context in which the engagements happened. • Focus on how your story aligns with what you and others know about the context and other developments taking place within that context. • Describe why, when and how you chose a different approach, strategy or way of thinking/acting to fit a changing context. • Describe why you think people (or non-humans and nature) responded to you in a certain way, given the context of a particular moment in time.
Consistent	• Make sure your story is personally consistent and also consistent with what others know about your engagements and developments within the community. • Include challenges or difficulties, particularly when there is a gap in your storyline. • Fill in as many details as you can to help integrate your knowledge and understanding and share new insights.

LEARNING ENGAGEMENT

Revisiting Kenji's story

Knowing what you now know about narrative assessment, revisit Kenji's three review points. With your teacher or a peer, discuss how Kenji's review points could have followed narrative assessment protocols. Discuss the following questions, perhaps adding some of your own. Your teacher may ask you to share with a larger group.

1. Referencing Kenji's systems iceberg diagram, what are the main themes in Kenji's story?
2. What was the timeline and element(s) of transformation?
3. What actions took place and in what settings/contexts?
4. What details could be expanded to support Kenji's story?
5. What details need to be added for consistency?
6. What are the key messages the listener/reader would take away from a revised narrative assessment version of Kenji's story?
7. Considering the themes, actions and key messages in Kenji's review points, what title would you give each of these three review points to show his growth over time?

Student narrative assessment rubric

Here is a suggested rubric that you can use when planning (and self-assessing) your narrative assessment, or which you can adapt as needed to your context. It focuses on what has gone well, transformations you feel happy about, the learning that has happened, as well as on those areas that you think might need fine-tuning through additional work and/or a different approach.

Table 1.34 A narrative assessment rubric

Areas for celebration	Learning outcomes	Areas for growth
	Foster reciprocal and dialogic engagement	
	Explore systems and develop awareness of their roles within these	
	Develop, articulate and enact ethical thinking and action	
	Engage in reflective and reflexive practice	

Your role and responsibilities in narrative assessments

You will play a role in every part of your narrative assessment. You are responsible for ensuring you clearly understand the requirements for the narrative assessment as outlined by your teacher. Your narrative assessment is not meant to be completely spontaneous. You are expected to prepare well for it and make it personal rather than based on the more generic aspects of CE. Your preparation will take place over time as you collect evidence and artefacts in your learning journal. It is your job to select and organize your learning journal evidence and artefacts and organize them well for your narrative assessment.

As you review your narrative assessment, looking for evidence of your learning, consider the following when contemplating your main theme or message. These questions are intended to guide your thinking, although you are encouraged to expand upon them as needed.

- Where are the reflexive responses to interactions and experiences?
- What were major moments of insight for me, and why did I care about those insights? What can this tell me about the theme for my story?

- How am I relaying the community voice in my learning journal? Would other people involved have the same story about what happened?
- What important failures, achievements, challenges and successes do I want to highlight in my story?
- What part of my community experience in and out of school marks the beginning of my involvement with the story I want to tell?
- Do I have any examples of using a different strategy to fit a changing context in my story?
- What examples of me and others showing reciprocity, commitment, care, compassion and inclusion can I give?
- Where have I highlighted my ATL skills and the learner profile, and how can their terminology and concepts help me tell my story?
- In what ways have I grown in my understanding and practice of international-mindedness?

REAL-WORLD EXAMPLE

Challenges with self-management

CE students are preparing for a review point. In their narrative assessments, they will need to reflect on their learning and growth throughout the term, including successes and challenges. The CE teacher, Ms Rodríguez, has devoted time to ensuring her students understand the importance of authenticity and significant learning engagements, relating these to the learning outcomes. Multiple times, she has reminded students to curate parts of their learning journal and select meaningful artefacts for their review points. Students have been given time for preparation and opportunities to meet with Ms Rodríguez outside of class time.

Ana, one of the students in the CE class, has challenges with her time-management skills. In the week before the assessment, she feels anxious and guilty that she has not kept her learning journal up to date. As she prepares for the assessment, she faces an ethical dilemma. Ana values honesty and transparency, but she is afraid to admit that she has not been keeping up with her learning journal work. She thinks that if she looks at her calendar, she can probably recall the general timeline of events, but she would have problems remembering the order in which things happened. She knows the context of her story, but is not clear on the theme or details. She is confused about what her key message would be.

She remembers Ms Rodríguez saying that it is okay for students to reflect on failure, including their own lack of action. Ana has always had a good relationship with Ms Rodríguez and she does not want to disappoint her. She also knows that Ms Rodríguez is aware of her challenges with self-management skills and she has not been honest with Ms Rodríguez during informal check-ins, often saying that the work has been done elsewhere and that she will transfer it to her learn ng journal.

LEARNING ENGAGEMENT

Challenges with self-management

Read the real-world example and answer the questions below. Your teacher may ask you to share with a peer or the whole group.

1. What ethical concepts and paradigms are useful/relevant to this situation?
2. Honesty and transparency are critical in narrative assessment. What might be lost by not being honest? What might be gained?
3. How is narrative assessment related to accountability? How does this differ from other types of assessments?
4. If you were the teacher, how would you create a narrative assessment space where students might feel more comfortable admitting their mistakes and failures?

5 What aspects of the learning outcomes can be authentically woven into Ana's assessment? Be specific.
6 Given that narrative assessment is based on one's perception of one's journey, how does this relate to academic integrity?
7 If you were Ana, what would you do and why?
8 What questions can you imagine Ms Rodríguez asking you?

Designing your narrative assessment resources

Your teacher will clarify acceptable presentation formats, which may include a PowerPoint or Google Slides presentation, and might feature:

- posters or infographics
- social-media posts
- videos or audio reflections
- journal entries
- artistic performances
- creative expressions (e.g. artworks, poetry, comic strips or zines)
- excerpts from advocacy letters
- mind maps
- growth-over-time maps
- stakeholder maps
- systems icebergs
- stock-and-flow diagrams
- causal-loop diagrams
- podcast segments
- annotated photos
- digital stories
- self-created simulations or games showing systems feedback loops or unintended consequences.

As you present your story, supported by learning journal evidence and artefacts, your teacher may ask you to expand on certain details with more clarity. They may ask questions like: 'So, what happened next?', 'Who did that?', 'Can you tell me a bit more?', 'What kind of event was that?', 'Where did that happen?', 'Why do you think this matters for your story?', 'Can you provide more clarity about how that happened?', 'What makes you think so?', etc.

The timing of your narrative assessment

Make sure that you understand how long you will have for your narrative assessment, budgeting both presentation time and discussion time with your teacher. You will coordinate the timing with your teacher and your teacher will listen to your story with as few interruptions as possible. Your teacher may ask for additional details or an extension of observations to further support your narrative, particularly if there is a gap in your storyline.

Your teacher may ask you to bring your presentation to a close if you have gone over your allotted time. Practising your presentation in advance will ensure you are well-prepared and give you the confidence you need to be spontaneous and be able to respond in the moment. Good preparation will also help you engage with your teacher about the learning outcomes, three stages, community dimensions and principles of engagement. Your teacher may also ask you to connect your work to the ATL skills and learner profile. Additionally, you may be asked to interpret and evaluate your ideas using a rubric. At the end of your narrative assessment, your teacher will help you determine your next steps, identify challenges and opportunities, and set goals around ongoing or new strategies.

After your review point, you will reflect on your narrative assessment. You may wish to revisit the structured assessment tool in Table 1.34 to consider how your thinking and approaches have changed, or you may choose to capture your reflection in a different way.

Featuring the learning outcomes

Once you have finished telling your story, you will transition to discussion time with your teacher. During this discussion, your teacher may ask you to connect to the learning outcomes in more detail. Table 1.35 may help you prepare for conversations around the learning outcomes.

Table 1.35 Questions around the learning outcomes

Learning outcomes	Questions to consider
Foster reciprocal and dialogic engagement	• How did you give something to others (time, care, ideas)? • What did you learn or receive from others? • When and how were your actions respectful or disrespectful of community members?
Explore systems and develop awareness of their roles within these	• What are the bigger systems and root causes of the issues you explored? • What events, patterns and trends, underlying structures and mental models affect the situation? • How has your compassion grown as you learned more about the systems around you?
Develop, articulate and enact ethical thinking and action	• What ethical decisions and dilemmas came up for you? • What values and ethics helped guide your decisions? • When did you feel unsure or conflicted and how did ethics support your decision-making?
Engage in reflective and reflexive practice	• What did you notice about your thoughts and actions in the community? • What assumptions and habits of thinking or doing have you noticed? • How are your thinking and actions changing over time? • How have you reflected on your challenges and made sense of your mistakes and failures?

Reflection and reflexivity

Preparing for narrative assessment

With your teacher or a peer, answer the questions below. Your teacher may ask you to share your ideas with others.

- What is exciting about narrative assessment?
- What questions do you have about narrative assessment?
- What key transformations do your narratives revolve around?
- What messages are you trying to convey through your narratives?
- How will you know which significant events to choose?
- What timeline are you discussing?
- What is your role, responsibility, understanding, purpose and voice within the context you are discussing?

Reflection and reflexivity

Post self-assessment/reflection

When reflecting on your CE journey, these prompts can help you move from simply noticing what you are thinking and feeling to expressing it meaningfully in your chosen reflection space.

- How do your engagements tell a story?
- Now that your CE review point/narrative assessment is complete, what are your first thoughts?
- What problems did you encounter before, during and after your review point/ narrative assessment and how did you address them?
- Which resources were especially helpful? Which ones would you use in the future?
- What were your most challenging moments and how did you learn from them?
- What were some of your most powerful learning moments and what made them so?
- What is the most important thing you have learned about yourself and the community between and throughout the review points?
- How have your community engagements made an impact on others, and how did this come through in the review points/narrative assessment?
- How will you take what you have learned into the future?
- What are some intentions you have for further engagement with the community?

1.5.4 Assessment and the learning journal

Your reflexive practice and your evidence of engagement need to be visible to your teachers. Everything must be kept in your learning journal so that your teachers can assess your growth and transformation during your CE journey. It is important that you establish a reliable learning journal routine and manage it in a way that allows you to meet CE requirements. Contributing to your learning journal meaningfully and consistently will help you with this goal. Putting the effort in along the way will make your review points much less stressful as you'll have the evidence you need to support you. As discussed in the CE section of this book, it is important to track your CE growth over time in relation to the four learning outcomes and explicitly show this in your learning journal.

The three review points are structured throughout your journey and they help track your growth over time. They are also opportunities to deepen your reflective and reflexive practice. Over time, your review points will reflect your cumulative work, which will inform final decisions on the completion of your CE programme.

Your learning journal is expected to contain meaningful and relevant material that can be used as stimuli for discussion. You will need to curate material specifically for each review point to reflect your ongoing learning and growth.

Completion of the CE requirements

Your school will determine whether you have satisfactorily completed the CE requirements based on an evaluation of evidence of the learning outcomes and sustained engagement with the CE Core component over the two years of the programme.

Evidence is collected by you through the learning journal and discussed in the review points. These three review points have equal value and will provide support for a final decision on your completion of the CE requirements.

And finally, in collaboration with your teacher and school, you will discuss the ways in which you will share your work with your school (and possibly broader) community. It is important to find meaningful ways to share and by sharing your work, you will:

- inspire others to engage ethically with their community
- inspire others to continue exploring your topic areas
- educate your community around best CE practices
- share your meaningful work with others in a community setting
- play a role in ensuring future CE classes have a meaningful sharing experience.

1.5.5 Summary

- The aim of CE assessment is to generate evidence of whether or not you have met the learning outcomes.
- Your progress will be evaluated in an ongoing manner, formally and informally, including observations and self-reflection.
- Your engagement will be assessed throughout the two years of the programme.
- The repeating, circular and continuous nature of assessment means that you can make real-time adjustments to your engagement.
- Your engagement will also be evaluated in a systematic manner through the three review points.
- The review points are approached through narrative assessment, which has its own protocols.
- Your reflective practice and evidence of your engagement need to be visible to your teachers in your learning journal.
- Your school will determine the completion of the CE requirements based on evidence of the learning outcomes and sustained engagement.

2 Language and cultural studies (LCS)

2.1 Understanding LCS

INQUIRY QUESTIONS

- How might your languages and cultures shape how you view the world?
- How can you engage with the possibilities in LCS in a way that is meaningful to you?

Learner profile

Open-minded

In LCS, you will 'be encouraged to appreciate the linguistic and cultural practices of others, and approach linguistic and cultural difference and diversity with openness and curiosity.' (Source: IB LCS guide, p.8)

2.1.1 What is LCS about?

LCS stands for 'language and cultural studies'. Another language course? Not at all! LCS is all about *you* and the languages and cultures *you* know and use, as well as the languages and cultures in your school, in your community and in the wider world. In LCS, you will have the opportunity to explore how *you* use your languages, your understandings of different cultures and how they all interact with one another.

You will learn from your peers, and your peers and teachers will learn from you, as everyone brings their own unique set of knowledge and experiences to the LCS course. During your LCS learning journey, you will hopefully gain a better understanding of yourself and others.

■ Get packing for your LCS learning journey

You will choose your own language and cultural learning goals in LCS and you (and your teachers) will assess your progress along the way. You will need to show that you can use the LCS key terms and concepts to talk about your LCS learning journey. You will design (and co-design with peers and teachers) your own learning engagements to help you reach your goals. Some of these learning engagements will be outside your school and your LCS classroom.

> LCS is about how our world, our languages and our cultures offer limitless possibilities to explore how we see and co-habit our world.

Key term

◆ **Repertoire:** The full range of linguistic resources and cultural tools that you possess, so you can effectively communicate and interact in different contexts. (Adapted from IB LCS guide, p.52)

Have a look at the LCS aims, which strive to create opportunities for you to:

- explore and expand your linguistic and cultural **repertoires**
- develop your curiosity, openness and empathy through your awareness and appreciation of linguistic and cultural diversity, locally and globally
- develop transferable knowledge, skills and attitudes for your present and future study, work and leisure.

(Source: IB LCS guide, p.9)

LEARNING ENGAGEMENT

Look closely at the LCS aims and create a visual representation (in the form of a Venn diagram, mind map or drawing) to show your understanding of them. Some of the key terms might be new to you and will become clearer as you continue on your LCS learning journey.

LEARNING ENGAGEMENT

Working alone, in a pair or small group, do *one* of the following suggested activities:

1. **LCS word cloud:**
   Thinking of the words 'language' and 'culture', brainstorm a series of related words to form a word cloud. You can create your word cloud by hand or using an online tool.
2. **School language profile:**
   Try to discover how many languages are present in your school and represent this as a mind map. Think about students, their parents, teachers and staff.
3. **There is no such thing as a monolingual:**
   Create a list of reasons to prove that there is no such thing as a monolingual (a person who identifies as 'only speaking one language'). Imagine using this list to help in a class debate/discussion.

Top tip!

Keep what you have produced in the learning engagements so far, as you will be adding these to your learning journal in the upcoming section.

The LCS learning journey

The visual below shows the stages you will go through during the LCS learning journey. Your school will already have done a school language profile to decide how they wish to set up LCS in your particular school. A school language profile is similar to what some of you might have done in the second task in the learning engagement above.

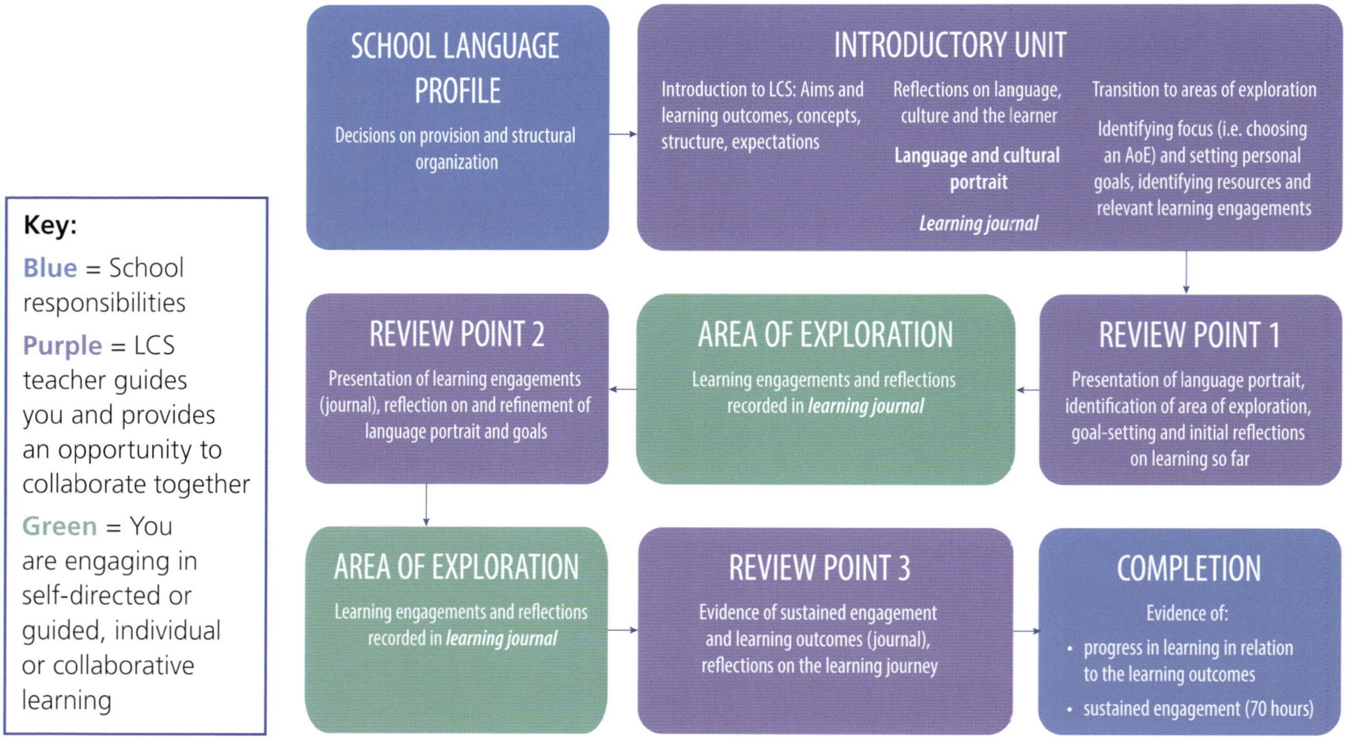

■ Linear representation of the two-year LCS learning journey (Source: IB LCS guide, p.30)

You are now doing the introductory unit, where you are building an understanding of what we mean by language and culture in LCS (and other key terms), as well as the LCS concepts, aims and learning outcomes. In the introductory unit, you will also start to think about your own language and cultural portrait (the languages and cultures you know), how this might have changed over time and how you imagine your portrait might look in your future. You will start to record your learning journey in a (multimodal) learning journal. By the end of the introductory unit, you will have chosen a language, a cultural learning focus and goal within a chosen area of exploration (career, community, or personal).

After the introductory unit, you'll continue to build on your learning journey. Depending on how LCS is taught in your school, this might look different for each student. In some cases, you'll have the chance to work more independently: setting your own goals and designing your own learning engagements, finding opportunities outside of the LCS classroom and your school. In other schools, your LCS learning might follow a more structured, teacher-guided course where learning engagements are planned and supported by your teacher. Your input will be very valuable and you are encouraged to share ideas and take initiatives.

There is no exam at the end of LCS as the whole of the two-year learning journey is assessed as a process. Your learning journal is where you will keep evidence of what you have done, as well as how this has led you to reflect and use reflexive practice. There are three review points where you will have the opportunity to share, celebrate and reflect on your progress, and how you are working towards the LCS learning outcomes. Feedback on your progress will come from yourself, your peers and your teachers. LCS completion is awarded by considering all three review points and the whole of your LCS learning journey.

■ LCS terminology

Table 2.1 (on the following spread) gives a brief explanation of the LCS terminology used in the visual, as well as where you will find out more later in this section of the book.

2.1.2 How is LCS assessed?

LCS learning outcomes

Understanding the four LCS learning outcomes is central to your success and completion in LCS, as you will use and refer to them when you:

- create your first language and cultural portrait
- decide on your focus, goals and area of exploration
- plan your learning engagements
- reflect on planned and unplanned learning engagements
- monitor and justify your progress in your learning journal and review points.

LCS learning outcomes drive us towards our learning goals

Table 2.2

With the goal of expanding your linguistic and cultural repertoires, you will be able to:	
LO1	Articulate how personal identity is shaped by engaging with languages and cultures and diverse perspectives.
LO2	Identify your own strengths and aspirations, set personally relevant goals and monitor your multilingual and intercultural learning through ongoing reflection.
LO3	Apply communication skills and understandings to various contexts.
LO4	Practise reflexivity and develop self-awareness as communicators within and across languages and cultures.

LEARNING ENGAGEMENT

Look closely at the LCS learning outcomes and make a list of the key terms and your understanding of them. Rephrase the learning outcomes in your own words to show your understanding of them.

Your learning journal

Your learning journal is a very important part of your LCS learning journey, as it is a centralized space where you can store evidence of your work from the introductory unit. Somewhere you can state, refine and justify your learning goals and area of exploration, plan and record your learning engagements and show evidence of reflexive practice. You will regularly share your learning journal with your LCS teacher and you will use it in your three review points.

Table 2.1 LCS terminology

Terms used in the diagram	Brief definition	Learn more later
Introductory unit	The purpose of the introductory unit is to understand the aims, learning outcomes and concepts in LCS. The introductory unit will lay the foundations for identifying an area of exploration and learning goals for your LCS learning journey.	You are currently doing the introductory unit with your LCS teacher.
LCS concepts	LCS concepts (communication, identities, perspectives, power) are embedded in the learning outcomes, and should be referred to when planning learning engagements, as well as in all reflections and review points.	Section 2.3
Areas of exploration	You will choose one of the three areas of exploration (career, community, personal) as a focus of your LCS learning journey, based on your interests, aspirations and language-learning goals.	Section 2.4
LCS aims and outcomes	You will plan your learning engagements and justify your progress in LCS against the aims and outcomes. You will keep evidence of this in your learning journal.	Section 2.5
Language and cultural portrait	A representation of all the languages and cultures you know and are curious about. This is unique to you at a particular point in time and will change in the future.	Section 2.2 Section 2.3
Multimodal learning journal	A centralized learning space and record of your LCS learning journey, which can be digital or physical or a combination thereof. You are encouraged to use multiple modes of expression (visual, aural/oral, written, linguistic, spatial, gestural). You will record every learning engagement (planning, justification and reflections) as well as your portrait here.	Section 2.1

Terms used in the diagram	Brief definition	Learn more later
Goals	You will set your own language and cultural learning goals in LCS. This might be an aspect of one of the languages in your repertoire or a new language. You might refine and reset your goals along the way.	Section 2.4
Learning engagements/ experience	This is any activity that you engage in as an individual, a pair, a group or a whole class towards your LCS outcomes and goals. Some learning engagements will be planned by your teacher and others will be planned by you alone or in collaboration with your peers.	Section 2.4
Reflection and reflexivity	An intentional, active and ongoing process of reviewing your thinking, practice and actions, examining views and assumptions, and being open to having your own perspectives challenged and changed.	Section 2.4
Review points	The purpose of the three review points is to monitor, review and celebrate your LCS learning journey. All three review points contribute to the decision of your LCS completion.	Section 2.5

What questions do you have at this point? What are you excited to learn about? What impact could LCS have on the way you see the world?

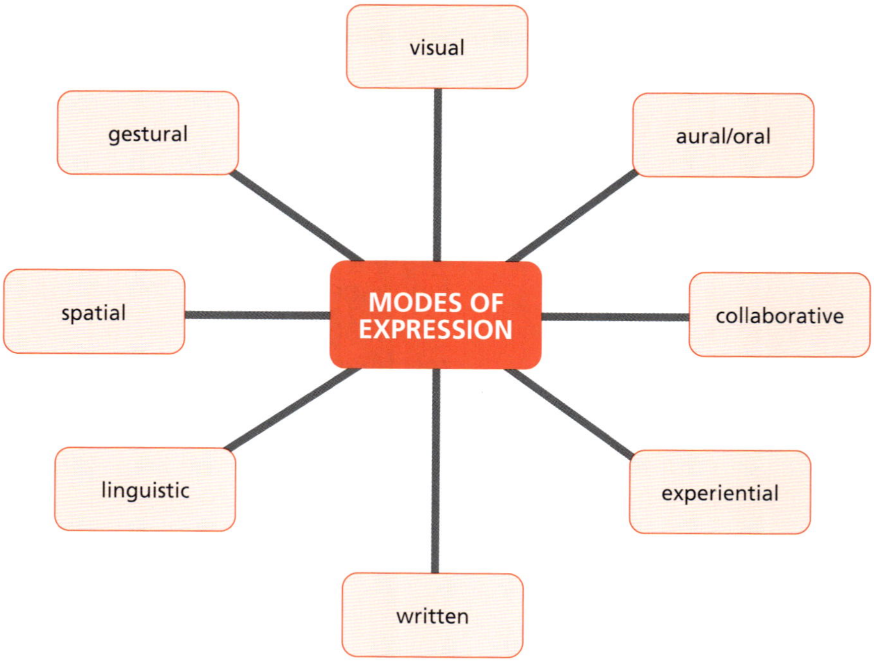

Modes of expression

Top tip!

When you create your learning journal in the next section, you should add some of the key elements such as the LCS learning outcomes at the start so that you can easily refer to them in future.

LCS is designed to include a range of modalities (visual, aural/oral, written, linguistic, spatial, gestural) in your learning engagements, as well as how you show evidence of your progress. Your learning journal should also reflect these multimodalities.

What do we mean by multimodalities? In LCS, the word *modality* simply means the different ways you can show evidence of your learning. When we say *multimodalities*, we mean using more than one mode of expression at a time. LCS encourages you to learn and show your learning in different ways: not just by writing essays or answering questions. This helps you think more deeply, reflect in different forms, and make your learning more engaged and personal.

Table 2.3 Examples of modalities in LCS

Modality	What it means	Examples in LCS
Visual	Using images, 3-D objects, colours, layout or graphics to understand or express ideas	Creating a poster, work of art, mood board, infographic, photo collage or mind map
Aural (Auditory)/ Oral (Spoken)	Using sound, speech or listening as a way to learn or express	Recording a voice note, doing an audio interview, reflecting through a podcast
Written	Using written words to think, reflect or explain	Writing a journal entry, a story, a paragraph, or creating subtitles or captions
Linguistic	Using language (spoken or written) to communicate ideas	Doing a speech, a bilingual project, or reflecting on how language shapes identity
Gestural	Using movement, body language, facial expressions	Acting out a scene, showing meaning through gesture in a video, analysing cultural gestures
Spatial	Using space, layout, or physical arrangement of things to organise thinking	Designing a room map to show cultural values, laying out a visual timeline of your identity
Collaborative	Learning through interaction with others	Group discussions, peer interviews, co-creating a visual project
Experiential	Learning through real-life or hands-on experiences	Going to a community event, interviewing someone, visiting a cultural space

Your learning journal can be a physical or digital space. You should choose the format (physical or digital) based on your personal preference after a discussion with your LCS teacher. Note that a digital learning journal can still have physical evidence in it, and vice versa. Have a look at Table 2.4 below for some suggestions of what multimodalities you can include and how you can include them in any learning journal format.

Top tip!

Your learning journal will show your sustained engagement with LCS over the two-year period, so remember to put a date next to each entry.

Table 2.4 Learning journal format ideas

Physical (e.g. exercise book)	Digital (e.g. website)
• Handwritten notes and visuals • Typed and printed out notes • Photos (learning engagements, artefacts, etc.) • Handwritten links or printed QR codes to audio and video files and resources	• Scans of handwritten notes and visuals • Typed notes • Images and photos • Audio and video files (reflections, performances, etc.) • Links to resources

Learning journal

Start your learning journal today:

- Decide on what form your learning journal will take—physical or digital.
- Create your first dated entry/entries by adding the learning engagements you have already taken part in.
- Add any additional thoughts and reflections to your learning journal.

Have a look below at the three examples of different learning journal entries.

Learning journal example 1

Exploring bilingualism through documentaries and discussion

3rd October

Last week, Jack and I decided to watch a documentary about bilingualism as part of our LCS course. I took some notes as there was a lot of technical language. The documentary showed both the benefits and challenges of being bilingual. It explained how bilingualism can help with 'cognitive flexibility' (you can adapt easily to new situations), improve communication skills and 'open doors to cultural understanding'. On the other hand, it also talked about the challenges of feeling that you are caught between two cultures or facing 'societal bias' against certain languages.

After watching, we talked about it. Jack thought that bilingualism might confuse the brain or cause difficulty in learning each language. I shared how research in the documentary showed that bilinguals often develop stronger problem-solving skills and adaptability. It was interesting to see how Jack changed his views and shared what he thought was true, and how he had been influenced by stereotypes.

Reflecting on the activity, I realized how bilingualism shapes identity by allowing individuals to 'navigate multiple cultural perspectives'. It also made me think about my own experiences with language learning and how it has helped me connect with others. This activity highlighted the importance of challenging biases and understanding the value of multilingualism. It also made me more aware of my role as a communicator in bridging cultural differences.

Learning journal example 2

Audio file: Accents tell a lot about the world

As part of our language and cultural studies course, we explored how language varies even within the same language and how accents can reveal so much about a person's background—like where they're from or their social class. We started by researching different accents and dialects, then debated how these variations shape perceptions and often lead to cultural stereotypes. To support our findings, we recorded samples of different accents, which helped us appreciate the richness and diversity of language. We really enjoyed the process! This activity made us reflect on our own biases and realize how important it is to celebrate linguistic diversity instead of judging it. It also deepened our understanding of how language connects to identity and culture. We decided to present our work to the rest of the LCS class with a mind map and, of course, the recording made about accents.

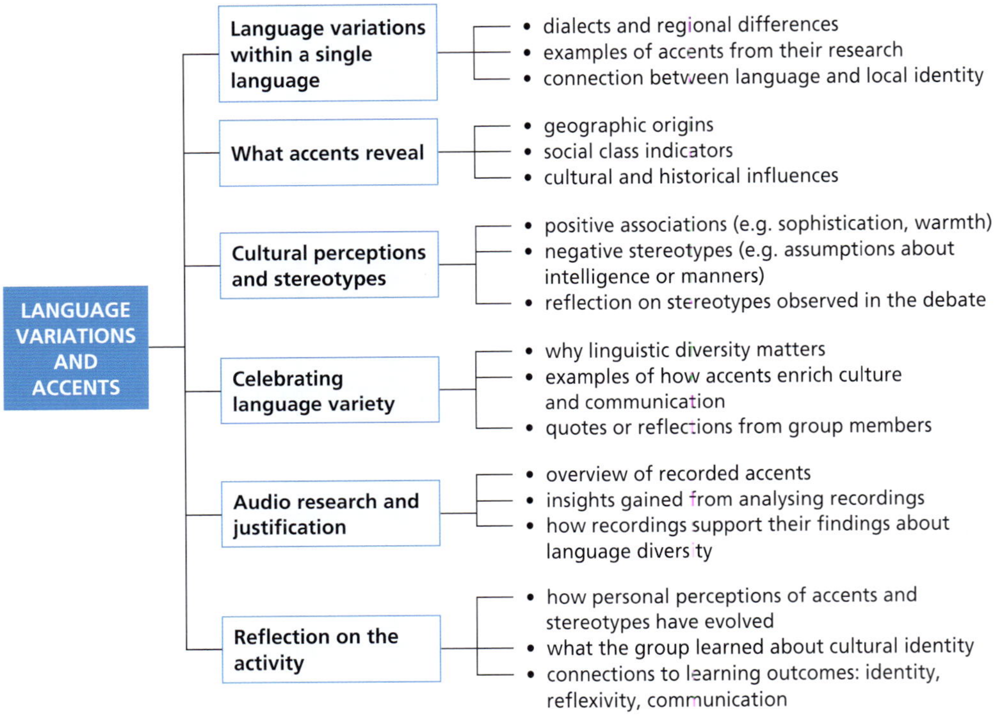

■ A mind map as a visual summary

Learning journal example 3

Transcription: LCS student and teacher discussion during review point 2 (oral)

Teacher: Thank you for coming to this second review point. Let's start by reflecting on your learning so far. Can you recount some of the activities you've done and what you've learned from them?

Student: Sure! One of the best activities was the group research and debate on language variety. We explored how accents and dialects differ within the same language and what they reveal about a person's background—like geography or social class. We also recorded different accents to provide evidence. I included my reflections in my learning journal, especially how stereotypes tied to accents can be harmful but also how celebrating language diversity can be empowering.

Teacher: That sounds insightful. How would you evaluate your progress towards your personal goals in this course?

Student: My initial goal was to better understand how language shapes identity and to improve my intercultural communication skills. I think I've made progress because I've become more aware of my own biases. For instance, during the debate, I realized I had assumptions about certain accents being more 'prestigious', which we discussed as a stereotype. I've also started to use more precise terminology, like 'sociolect' and 'linguistic prejudice', when reflecting in my journal.

Teacher: That's great progress. Have you faced any challenges in achieving your goals?

Student: Definitely. One challenge was stepping out of my comfort zone to actively listen and engage with perspectives I didn't initially agree with. For example, one group member felt that certain accents signalled a lack of education, which was frustrating to hear, but it pushed me to discuss stereotypes more constructively. Another challenge was analysing the recordings—we had to identify patterns without making assumptions.

Teacher: Those are valuable insights. How do you plan to address these challenges?

Student: I think I'll refine my goal to focus more on improving active listening during discussions. I also want to revisit the recordings with a clearer framework for analysis—maybe using some of the resources we've been given on sociolinguistics.

Teacher: That sounds like a solid plan. Have any of your understandings about language and culture evolved through this process?

Student: Yes, definitely. I used to think of language as just a tool for communication, but now I see it as a way for people to express identity and connect to their culture. I also understand more about the power dynamics in language—like how certain accents are valued more than others, which can reinforce inequality.

Teacher: You're demonstrating strong connections to the learning outcomes. Can you explain how your work reflects them?

Student: For LO1, I've reflected a lot on how accents relate to personal and cultural identity. For LO2, I've been setting goals in my journal and tracking progress, like improving my understanding of linguistic diversity. For LO3, the debate and group work have helped me apply communication skills in different contexts. And for LO4, I've definitely been practising reflexivity by questioning my assumptions and thinking critically about stereotypes.

Teacher: Excellent. Keep building on these reflections and don't hesitate to refine your approaches as you move forward. Let's set a time for the next review and I'll look forward to seeing how your understanding deepens.

Student: Thank you! I'll keep working on my goals and journaling regularly.

Key terms

◆ **Multilingualism:** The availability of two or more languages/language varieties in an individual's linguistic repertoire, regardless of stage of acquisition or degree of proficiency.

◆ **Interculturalism:** The reciprocal act of negotiating understanding of meaning in diverse situations within and across languages and cultures; coming to understand and appreciate the mediating role of languages and cultures in identity formation.

LEARNING ENGAGEMENT

Learning journal examples

Look at the three learning journal examples, then copy and complete the table below.

1 What modality has the student used for their learning journal?
2 What evidence has the student demonstrated for each of the four LCS learning outcomes?

■ **Table 2.5** Three learning journal examples

	Mode (visual, aural/oral, written, linguistic, spatial, gestural)	Learning outcome	Evidence
Exploring bilingualism through documentaries and discussion			
Audio file: Accents tell a lot about the world			
Transcription: LCS student and teacher discussion during second review point 2 (oral)			

2.1.3 LCS is all about you!

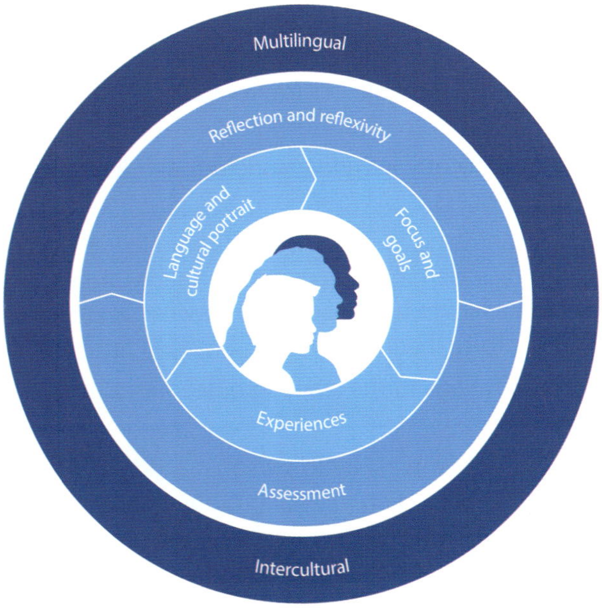

■ The student at the centre of LCS (Source: IB LCS guide, p.29)

The visual on the left demonstrates how *you*, the student, are at the centre of *your* LCS learning journey.

The inner circle shows how you will create your language and cultural portrait, choose your focus and goals and engage in learning engagements, and how this in turn will expand and/or cause you to refine your language and cultural portrait, and so on. This cycle will continue throughout the two-year LCS.

The outer circle shows the ongoing process of assessment and reflection and reflexivity, and how this will also interact with the inner circle. For example, you might engage in a learning engagement which will cause you to reflect and refine your goals, which will then lead to changes in your future engagements and how your linguistic and cultural repertoire will expand.

When the inner and outer circles interact together, we develop **multilingualism** and **interculturalism** as a result.

LEARNING ENGAGEMENT

Look at the LCS visual and:

1 Identify the key terms which you understand at this point and also what you do not (yet) understand.
2 Describe this visual in your own words, starting from the inner circle and working towards the outer circle.
3 Consider the relationship between this circular visual and the linear representation of LCS in Section 2.1.1.
4 Note how it feels to have you at the centre of your LCS.

Learning journal

Remember to record your thoughts in your learning journal.

LCS learning journeys

The following pages contain three examples of LCS learning journeys, which will show you some of the possibilities open to you in LCS.

REAL-WORLD EXAMPLE

A career-focused learning journey

Rowan was born in Canada but has lived in Dubai since he was three years old, as his mother is a senior vice-president of an oil company in the United Arab Emirates (UAE). As a student in an international school, Arabic has been part of Rowan's timetable since kindergarten. He is somewhat fluent but would like to improve his linguistic skills in business vocabulary. He is inspired by his mother and her business knowledge, so his career-related study is business with a focus on finance.

Rowan is interested in working with mentors who can help him improve his Arabic, as his chosen language. Rowan's goals are to improve and refine his business vocabulary in Arabic by conversing with mentors who work in the finance sectors and explore how he can implement these skills in his future career as a financial planner.

Rowan is currently in IB Arabic B SL class. He emails two financial advisors who work for a local financial institution in Dubai about their positions with the company and how they have increased their client base. He shadows one of these individuals for a day to experience their interactions with colleagues and clients. Rowan also has informal conversations with his mother about her professional interactions and uses his learning journal to note her input and comments about the business world using the Arabic language and how it relates to her current position. Rowan watches the financial news in Arabic once a week, initially with English subtitles and then later without. He notes down vocabulary and expressions that he might use himself in a professional setting. Rowan also listens to a podcast in Arabic about well-being in the workplace.

Through communication with these advisors and his mother, Rowan realizes that spoken Arabic has different versions, influenced by different regions, and that most locals speak a dialect known as Gulf Arabic or Khaleeji. The second most used dialect is Egyptian Arabic, known as Masri. He understands that English plays an equally important role in the global business world and that knowledge of both languages could be advantageous in his career. He decides to pursue this as the topic of his reflective project.

Rowan's learning journal is on an online platform which his teacher and some of his classmates also have access to so that they can give him regular feedback.

REAL-WORLD EXAMPLE

A community-focused learning journey

Otieno is Kenyan and belongs to the Luo community. In Kenya, there are 42 spoken languages but only two official languages: Kiswahili and English. Otieno speaks English and Kiswahili daily. The language of instruction in primary school was Kiswahili and it became English in secondary school. His parents talk to him in Kiswahili, but communicate with each other and other family members using Luo language. Otieno understands most of what he hears in Luo, but never speaks it, except for greetings and a few expressions which he uses when he goes to Kisumu, by Victoria Lake, to visit his grandmother. Otieno is passionate about music and knows many songs in Luo, which he sings without understanding most of them.

Otieno is interested in improving and expanding his Luo repertoire. He would like to be able to speak it with his family members. He also wants to better understand the songs he loves, and dreams of composing a song in Luo for his graduation ceremony.

Otieno decides to work with his mother once a week to translate a few songs that he loves and makes notes on the lyrics. He then contacts the Swahili teacher and the librarian to ask for recommendations on books and novels to learn about the Luo language and community. Otieno makes a conscious effort to communicate in Luo with his cousins at family gatherings, as well as more frequently with his mother. He meets with the music teacher every Wednesday during breaktime to discuss his composition of his Luo music. He also meets with the graduation ceremony committee to propose and plan his performance.

Through communication with the LCS teacher, the music teacher, the librarian and his mother, he has learnt more about the Luo culture, history and heritage. He became fascinated by a traditional musical instrument: nyatiti, a traditional Luo lyre. He started to learn how to play the nyatiti with the music teacher at their weekly meeting and embedded it in the song he composed. The lyrics of his song talk about the Luo culture and how it is important to connect to our roots. He rehearses every weekend in preparation for the graduation ceremony.

Otieno's learning journal is a shared document with the LCS teacher. He adds hyperlinks to videos and recordings of music sessions and gets comments from his teachers and peers.

REAL-WORLD EXAMPLE

A personal-focused learning journey

Noi is passionate about fashion and design. She lives in Bangkok and speaks Thai and English. She speaks Thai with her family and in her everyday life, and speaks English in school with the international teachers and with her best friends. She wants to study fashion in Milan and has already talked to her parents, who fully support her goals.

Noi is determined to learn Italian to prepare for moving to Milan when she begins university. Her course would be taught in English but she wants to immerse herself in the local language and everyday life. She wants to focus on basic situations/contexts such as *finding your way in town*, *ordering some food*, etc. Her approach will focus more on oral communication. She also wants to focus on Italian culture in order to better understand people, society, customs and history, which will help her to integrate smoothly when she settles down in Italy.

With the help of her LCS teacher, Noi found a useful website for students who are learning Italian as a foreign language. Noi also discovered a lot of resources to help her learn numbers, colours and days of the week. She is planning to work on it for an hour a week and record her progress in her learning journal. Noi also went to the Italian cultural centre with her mum to view a photography exhibition about Italian architecture. She inquired about the cultural programme and is planning to attend some cultural events (a European film festival, concerts, etc.). She was very enthusiastic about her first contact with Italian culture (a lot of young people, welcoming staff, speech from the artist). Noi asked one of her classmates who is Italian to assist her with conversation, pronunciation and reviewing her work (especially the role-play scenario she wants to write: *at the restaurant*). Her Italian friend suggested that Noi come for dinner at her house, where she would be immersed in Italian. Noi found some Italian TV shows and movies online and decided to watch them with the Italian subtitles to improve her repertoire, her pronunciation and to better understand Italian everyday culture.

Noi has been keen and has learned Italian following her action plan and goals. She has now reached an A2 level and registered for CILS certification. Noi also found very interesting information about Milan, and Lombardy history and culture. Noi discussed everyday Italian culture, such as greetings, with her classmate so that she could become more familiar and comfortable with this. She has been able to record six scenarios of everyday life situations, which she uploaded to her learning journal. She acted them out with some of her classmates and taught them how to have the Milanese accent.

Through her research, Noi discovered that there is 'Milan slang' used among young people and she thought it would be helpful to have some knowledge about it. She has had several opportunities to discuss it with her Italian classmates and people at the Italian cultural centre.

Noi started her learning journal with a notebook, but found that she needed a digital format to support the record of her online research. She decided to open an online blog divided into different sections: culture and history, vocabulary, daily life context, slang and communication, music and cinema. In each of the sections, she touched on the vibrant fashion world in Milan.

LEARNING ENGAGEMENT

Learning journey examples

Read the learning journeys of Rowan, Otieno and Noi, then answer the questions below.

1. Identify the following elements:
   - the student's portrait (languages, context)
   - the chosen language, as well as which aspect of the language (speaking, reading, writing)
   - the area of exploration
   - reflection and refined goals
   - multimodalities used (visual, aural/oral, written, linguistic, spatial, gestural)
   - learning engagements.
2. Think about the three learning journeys.
   - What did you think of each learning journey?
   - How did Rowan's professional focus drive him to expand his linguistic and cultural repertoires?
   - How did Otieno's passion for music and interest to connect with his community lead him to explore a different language and culture?
   - How did Noi's passion for fashion lead her to explore a different language and culture?
3. What would you have done differently and what inspired you?

2.1.4 Summary

- Language is central to all aspects of our lives, both personal and professional.
- We all belong to, or interact with, a range of linguistic and cultural groups.
- Studying languages and cultures is a unique opportunity to develop curiosity, appreciation, openness and empathy.
- To complete LCS, you will have to demonstrate sustained engagement and reflection around four learning outcomes.
- To complete LCS, you will create and use a personal learning journal that will include evidence of experiences, collaboration with peers and educators using a wide range of formats/modalities.
- To complete LCS, you will design your own personal journey: choose an area of exploration, set and refine personal goals, and take part in three review points to demonstrate your progress towards the learning outcomes.

2.2 What is language and culture?

INQUIRY QUESTIONS

- How does your way of communicating change depending on where you are and who you are communicating with?
- To what extent do the languages you speak, and your lived experiences, make you unique?

2.2.1 What is 'language'?

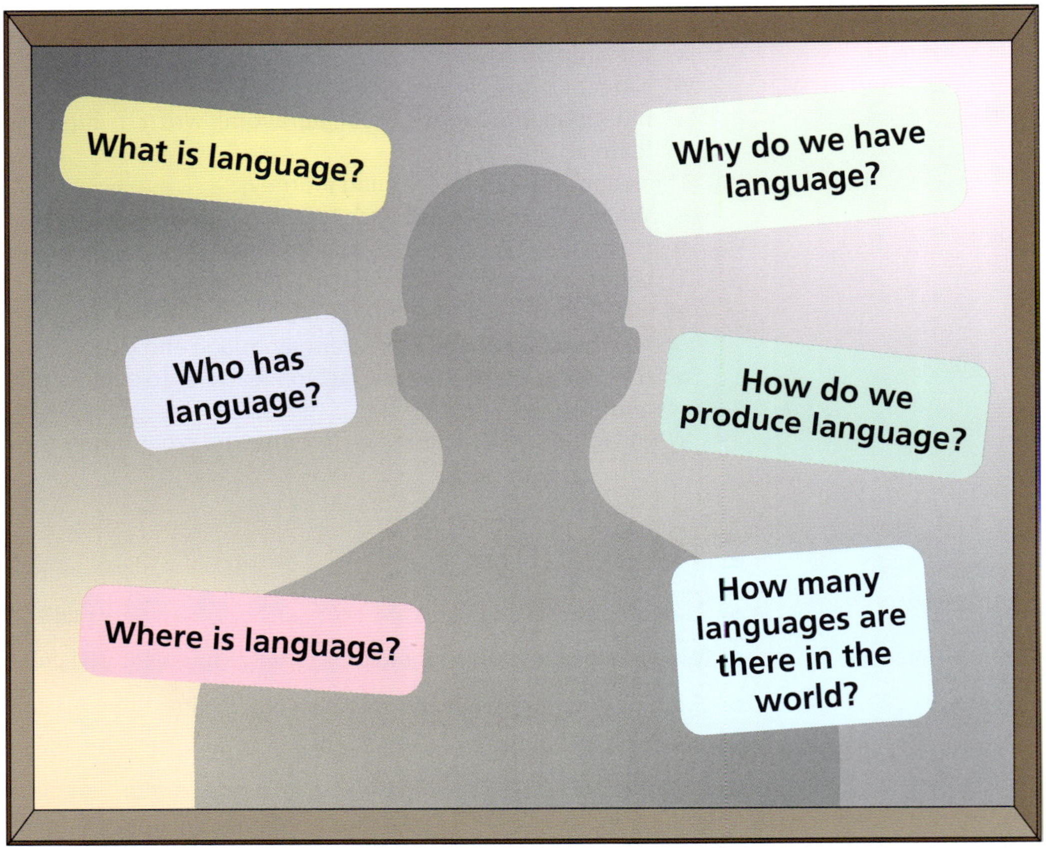

Questions around 'language'

Learning journal

Discuss the questions in the image above and record your thoughts and ideas in your learning journal.

In this section, we will be looking more closely at the word 'language' and how we will be using it in LCS. The word 'language' comes from Latin. The root word in Latin is 'lingua' meaning 'tongue' or 'language'.

Key terms

◆ **Named languages:** Such as Polish, Arabic, Zulu, Thai.

◆ **Language variety:** Different versions of a named language (e.g. American English, Gulf Arabic).

There are thousands of **named languages** in the world, such as Polish, Arabic, Zulu, Thai, American Sign Language (ASL) and Kenyan Sign Language (KSL). Some languages have millions (and even billions) of speakers, while others have only a few hundred speakers left and are at risk of dying out. Some languages are written and spoken, while other languages are mainly used for speaking. Many of these named languages also have different versions, which we call **language varieties**, such as American English, Gulf Arabic and Colombian Spanish.

All languages share common features, such as sounds, words and sentences. In sign languages, sounds are replaced with handshapes, body movements and facial expressions to produce the words and sentences. Many languages are written, some with alphabets (with consonants and vowels), or abjads (consonants and optional vowels), or logograms (each symbol represents a word), or syllabaries (each symbol is a syllable in a word). If you travel to some parts of the world, street signs might be written in two different scripts so that tourists can find their way around. Today, many of us use emojis to express ourselves, which could be seen as a sort of logogram. Look at the cave paintings below from Cerro Azul (Colombia) and try to imagine what story/information the painters were trying to convey.

■ Cave paintings

All of this is very technical, and you are not expected to know this in detail. LCS, however, is a space where you can find out more about your language(s) and culture(s) and those around you. You might have knowledge and understanding about languages that you can share with your peers and LCS teacher. The LCS classroom is also a space for curiosity!

LEARNING ENGAGEMENT

'Language' in many languages

What is the word 'language' in the other languages you know?

In a pair or small group, create a display for your LCS classroom or elsewhere in your school to show what the word 'language' is in as many different languages as you can. How could you make sure that you include all the languages and language varieties that are spoken by all the students and all the teachers at your school?

Linguistic diversity

Linguistic diversity refers to the range of different languages and language varieties spoken in a particular space (e.g. a school, community, town or country). You might go to a school where there is a high level of linguistic diversity or come from an area or country that has many different languages.

Some countries are very linguistically diverse and have multiple official languages, which are used for schooling, in government business and the legal system. Other countries might be very linguistically diverse, but only have one official language, which often enjoys a higher social status than the others. Indeed, many countries who only have one official language also have hundreds of languages that are spoken in families and in local communities.

Learner profile

Principled

As an LCS student, you should acknowledge and celebrate the linguistic and cultural diversity in your school, community and the wider world.

LEARNING ENGAGEMENT

Linguistically diverse countries

Look at the graph below, which shows the top ten countries with the most spoken languages.

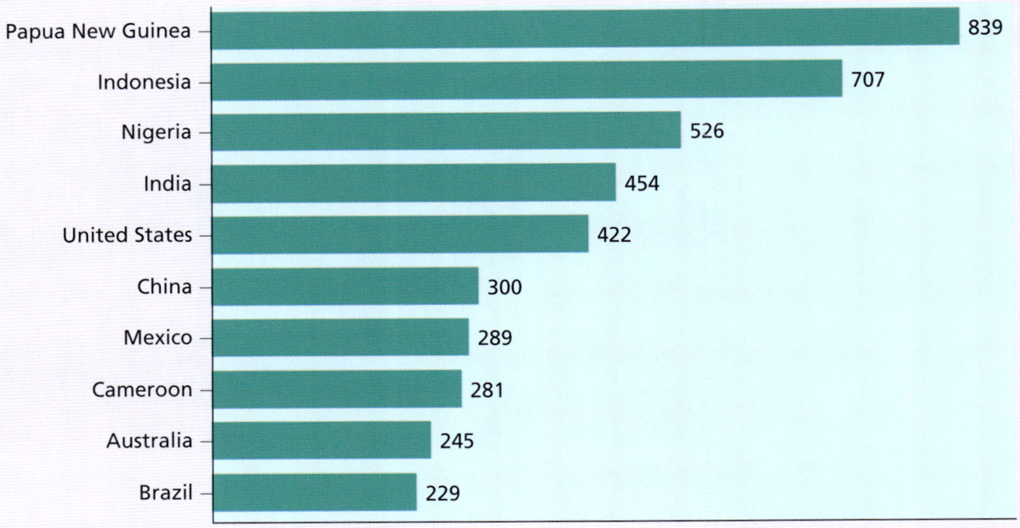

■ The countries with the most spoken languages

1. Choose *one* of the countries above and do some more research about *one* of its languages. Challenge yourself by choosing a language that you might not know anything about.
2. Create an infographic about the language you have chosen and include information such as the name of language, number of speakers, geographical location and five useful words in the language.

Learning journal

Thinking about the activity you have just done, use the sentence starters below to create a written or spoken reflection for your learning journal. You could choose to speak and record yourself.

- In the activity looking at linguistic diversity, I chose to research the language ...., which is spoken in .... by approximately .... speakers. The language uses the .... script.
- I found a place where you can hear what the language sounds like: .... *(source)*
- When I first discovered .... *(language)*, I felt .... because ....
- I was fascinated to learn that ....
- I selected these five words from the language: ....
- I found these words useful because ....
- I think that linguistic diversity should be acknowledged and celebrated because ....
- This made me think about .... *(an example from your own experiences)*.

Languages are constantly undergoing change. Some of these changes are noticeable, such as the new vocabulary we add to dictionaries as we invent new tools and technology. You might notice when you try to read literature from a few hundred years ago (such as Shakespeare in English) that the vocabulary and sentence structures are very different from what we use today. Languages also change when they come into contact with one another, as we 'borrow' words from one language to another. For example, words in English such as 'algebra', 'sofa' and 'sugar' have all been 'borrowed' from the Arabic language. It is fascinating to investigate the origins of words and then to look back into history to discover how languages have and continue to influence one another.

Languages can also be organized into language families. Languages which are part of the same language family might look or sound similar and share vocabulary and common language structures and features.

LEARNING ENGAGEMENT

My language family

Do some research about language families:

1. Which language family/families do your languages belong to?
2. Where are related languages (such as Germanic languages) located around the world?
3. Can you find out more about how these languages spread around the world? Have the languages become more varied (with more language varieties) over time and across geographical space? Why do you think this is?
4. Do you know anyone else who speaks a language in the same language family? Can you understand one another?

Key term

◆ **Language:** The primary means by which people construct, share and maintain understanding and meaning. Language is not understood only as code and system (words and grammar), but also as social practice; it includes language use in the contexts of situation and in the context of culture. (Source: IB LCS guide, p.50)

'Language' in LCS

In LCS, we use the term **language** to mean more than just named languages (such as Italian or Thai) and language varieties (such as South African English or Chilean Spanish).

As we saw in the previous section, we use code (sounds, words, sentences) and systems (grammar) to communicate using different named languages and language varieties. In order to communicate with someone, we need to construct, share and maintain understanding and meaning. Humour is often built on misunderstandings, where one person in the conversation misinterprets something, as they do not share the same understanding as the other person.

In LCS, we also look at the other elements that help us to communicate and understand one another—we need to have shared understandings. For example, if you live in the UK, a common way to start talking with someone you don't know very well is to make small talk about the weather. In contrast, with a good friend, you might immediately start talking about the football/soccer results from the weekend. In school, you might notice that teachers would ask you questions about yourself that you would never dream of asking them. This is what we call social practice: we all know and understand these contexts of situation and contexts of culture that make things acceptable.

Language in LCS

In 2024, one of the top Gen Z slang terms was 'salty' (meaning 'bitter', 'annoyed' or 'a little bit upset'). If you imagine the conversation between two football/soccer fans at school, you might hear one of them saying, 'I'm still feeling a bit salty about us losing the match in the last few minutes'. That same person might not use the word 'salty' when they are discussing the football/soccer match with their grandfather or a teacher. Have you noticed similar situations around you? Or have you noticed that you do the same?

Learning journal

Summarizing 'language' in LCS

Take a moment and go back to the definitions of the three key terms shared so far in this section. Use the structure below to define these keywords with your own words, vision or representation. You can write, draw, sketch or record yourself.

To me, language is ... while languages are ... and a language variety is ...

Reflection and reflexivity

Review this section. What new elements have you learnt about language in LCS by working on these learning engagements? Anything new? Anything intriguing?

2.2.2 What is culture?

■ Different groups we might belong to

In this section, we will be looking more closely at what we mean by the word **culture** in LCS.

Culture is all around us; it is vibrant, alive and can be very diverse. It also frames the way we and others see the world. We should embrace this diversity and get to understand as many cultures and cultural practices as we can when we get the opportunity: a trip, a movie, an interaction happening in front of us, a novel ... All of these are opportunities to explore cultures. In LCS, we view culture as *shared understandings* within different groups of people, and we all belong to a range of different groups.

Notice the range of groups in the image on the left; how some of them are larger than others, and how they overlap with each other. For example, you might have friends your age that share the same interests or nationality as you, just as you might have friends your age who might not share the same cultural background as you. Some of the bubbles are larger and are clearly more important than the others (to the person who created this), while others are smaller. This might change over time. What other groups would you add to this?

Key term

◆ **Culture:** Shared understandings within a group of people and the interpretive lenses that they bring to any interaction. Through these lenses, they interpret, create and exchange meanings. (Source: IB LCS guide, p.50)

REAL-WORLD EXAMPLE

Cultural groups

The visual below, created by LCS student Aidan, shows the different groups that he belongs to: his family, Ireland, his rugby club, Irish English speakers, Italian speakers, Chinese speakers, the Catholic Church and guitar players. Notice how Aidan represented some of his groups as larger (more important) than others, such as his family, being an Irish English speaker and being a guitar player. This might change over time, as Aidan joins more groups or starts to feel more connected to different groups.

■ Aidan's cultural groups

LEARNING ENGAGEMENT

Cultural groups

Think about the different groups you belong to: linguistic, geographical, religious, hobbies/interests, social, personal, age, political, etc.

1 Which groups do you feel at the centre of and which groups are you more on the periphery? Do you feel like you belong to some groups more than others?
2 Create a list or visual of these groups, showing which ones play a more important role to you (at this time).
3 What are some of the shared understandings that exist in your different groups?

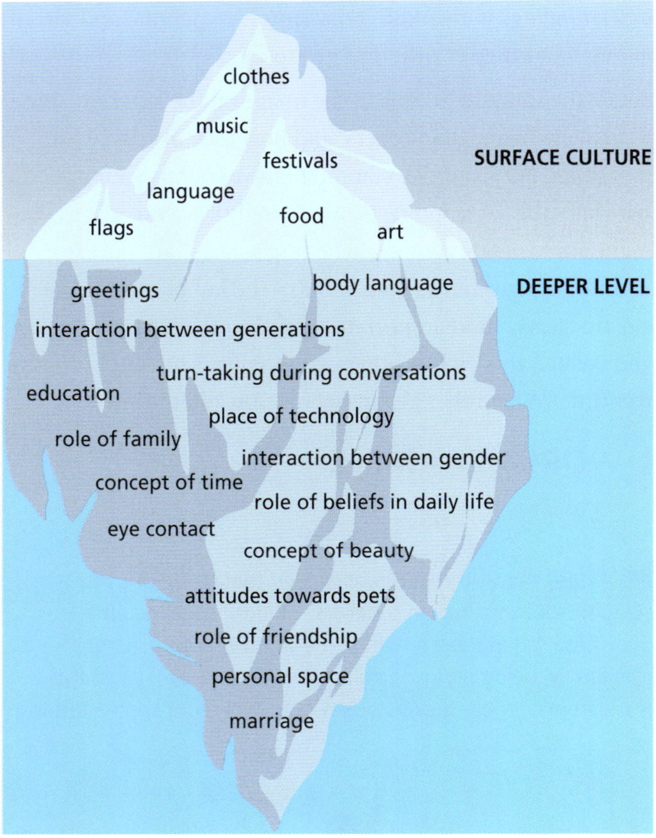

■ The cultural iceberg

■ The cultural iceberg

Look at the image on the left of a cultural iceberg, which shows the visible aspects of culture (at the 'surface') as well as the less visible aspects (at a 'deeper level'). When people talk about culture, they very often focus on the more visible aspects and ignore the more subtle elements that are at the deeper level. You might find more examples of cultural icebergs and it is interesting to compare what other aspects are included at the deeper level.

Reflection and reflexivity

Deep culture

The cultural iceberg (left) shows some of the parts of culture that are 'visible' on the surface. Look at the deeper level and think about more elements of culture that are less 'visible' that you could add. Which elements resonated the most for you? List them and give an example from your own life and experience.

Sometimes the word 'culture' is used to stereotype groups of people. What have you observed in your everyday life? This is often based on elements from the surface level of the iceberg. Sometimes these stereotypes are used in humour and other times they might be a form of discrimination. Part of being an IB student is to be aware of these stereotypes and to use these experiences to build your intercultural understanding.

Learning journal

Complete the sentence below:

Just because I am …, doesn't mean that …

You can use some of the key terms from the cultural iceberg to inspire you.

For example: *Just because I am 16 years old, doesn't mean that I like loud music.*

Using this format, create several sentences about yourself. You could also gather examples from your friends and family.

The 'lenses of culture'

Cultural practices are deeply rooted in traditions, beliefs and ways of life. It defines a common understanding that allows you to interpret what others mean, what it is okay to do in a certain context and what is not! For example, notice the way different groups of people greet each other, with a hug, a kiss, a bow, a handshake or a smile. In some communities, certain forms of greeting might be inappropriate or if you do not adopt a certain greeting, it might also cause confusion or offence. In some cultures, it is normal to remove your shoes when entering a house and failure to do so, or to offer to do so, might lead to an awkward exchange. Of course, the person inviting you might have an understanding of your cultural norms and will make allowances or might provide a suggestion on a compromised way of doing things. In some cultures, silence and listening is more valued than speaking, and there are also cultural rules around when it is appropriate to interrupt and how you would do this.

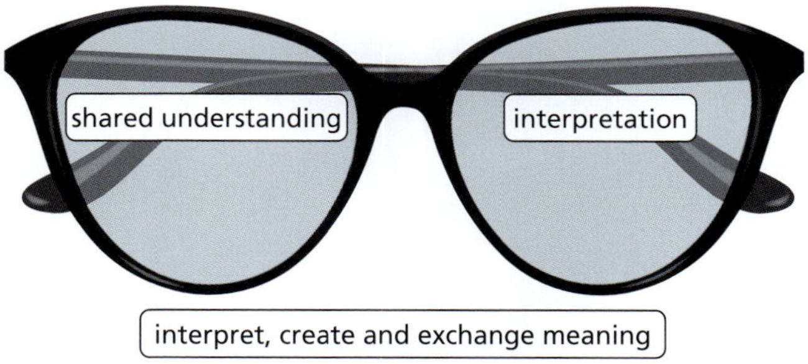

The 'lenses of culture'

The visual above illustrates how we are all wearing our 'cultural lenses' when we engage across and within different cultural settings.

How might others interpret some of your shared understandings? What would happen if someone didn't understand the view and cultural practices of someone else? How could that lead to misunderstandings? And how might learning more about these lenses create better connections between people and communities?

As a unique individual, you have a set of common and shared understandings within your different communities (local to global). Based on these shared understandings, people can accurately interpret what you say, what you do, what you sing, what you write and so on. But let's imagine you are in another context, where you do not have the same set of shared understandings. How would you interpret what is going on? In the next learning engagement, you will examine three pictures from different contexts and then analyse and explain what you 'see' based on your shared understandings and your skills of interpretation.

LEARNING ENGAGEMENT

What do you see?

Working initially on your own, then discussing in a pair and then with a larger group, discuss what you see in these three pictures.

1 List all the elements that you discussed and that helped you to refine your interpretation.
2 Identify how you arrived at your interpretation of the photo's context and perspective.
3 What caption would you give each photo?
4 Compare with your peers and analyse why some of you shared the same understandings and interpretations. Were your lenses of culture the same, similar or different?

2.2.3 Language and culture

You will have noticed that language and culture in LCS are not independent of one another, and that there is a lot of overlap in their definitions and how we use them in LCS. If you look closely at any example of communication, you can probably identify elements of language and elements of culture.

LEARNING ENGAGEMENT

Language or culture?

Look at the images below and discuss in a pair or small group whether you think these images represent 'language' or 'culture' or both.

Summarize the different perspectives you have heard and shared.

■ Language or culture or both?

What are 'multilingualism' and 'interculturalism'?

Multilingualism means being able to understand or use more than one language. It could mean speaking two languages at home, like French and Arabic, or learning a new one at school, like Spanish or Japanese for a language acquisition course. Some people grow up hearing different languages from family members, while others pick them up through travel, media or school. In LCS, we explore how multilingualism shapes our identity, affects how we see the world and helps us connect with people from different cultures. It's also a powerful way to think about communication: how language gives us access to ideas, cultures and even opportunities we might not have in just one language.

> What percentage, do you think, of the world's population is multilingual?

Interculturalism is about how people from different cultures interact, understand each other and live together with respect. It goes beyond just knowing that other cultures exist—it's about creating real connections, learning from each other and finding ways to work together despite our differences. In LCS, we look at how interculturalism helps build more open-minded, inclusive societies. It also helps us reflect on our own culture and how we can communicate across differences in respectful and meaningful ways.

'LCS forges a space for multilingualism and intercultural understanding, two cornerstones of international-mindedness.'

(Source: IB LCS guide, p.8)

Multilingualism and interculturalism are a key part of LCS, as well as the other three CP Core components:

- Intercultural understanding is one of the four domains of skills developed in personal and professional skills (PPS). It means being able to understand your own culture and other cultures, and recognizing both the similarities and the differences. It's about learning to respect different ways of thinking, communicating and living. To do this well, we need skills like empathy, ethical thinking, self-awareness and collaboration. In LCS, we explore how language and culture shape identity, behaviour and beliefs—which helps us to build the same intercultural skills that PPS encourages.
- Community engagement (CE) gives you the chance to get involved with different communities, gaining a deeper understanding of different cultures, values and perspectives. When you take part in CE, you're putting into action many of the skills you've developed in LCS, like understanding identity, power, perspectives, communication and different ways of seeing the world. LCS can also help you communicate more effectively with community members (especially if they speak different languages or come from different backgrounds). At the same time, your CE projects can make your LCS learning more meaningful, by giving you real-life examples of language and culture in action.
- The reflective project (RP) encourages you to explore an ethical issue linked to your career-related studies. To do this well, you'll need to understand different points of view. This is where LCS can really help when learning about intercultural understanding. You'll also develop skills like critical thinking, communication and awareness of different cultural perspectives. These tools can give your RP more depth and insight.

Links

Keep in mind that LCS can support your growth in PPS, and at the same time, PPS skills can help you think more deeply in LCS. They work hand in hand to help you become a more globally aware citizen.

Your learning in LCS can inspire your CE project, and what you experience in CE can deepen your intercultural understanding in LCS.

LCS can give you the ideas and thinking skills for your RP, and working on your RP can help you apply what you've learned in LCS in a real and thoughtful way.

Why multilingualism and cultural understanding matter to you

Let's be honest, languages aren't just what you learn in school to pass exams. They're alive, like people. They carry identity, history and the power to connect or divide us. So, what if I told you that understanding different languages and cultures isn't just nice to have—it's a right, a fact and one of the best resources you can use to thrive in a globalized world? Here's why it matters to you.

Languages are everywhere (and that's amazing!)

Think about it: over 7,000 languages exist globally. Even within one language, there are countless accents and dialects that tell unique stories. Take English, for example—someone speaking Cockney English in London sounds totally different from someone speaking English in New York or Jamaica. And those differences tell us a lot about where people come from, their history, and even their social circles.

But why stop at English? Maybe you've noticed how Spanish spoken in Spain differs from what you might hear in Mexico or Argentina. Each variation reflects the culture and values of the region. Seeing language in this way doesn't just make you a better communicator, it makes you curious about the world.

It's your right to speak and keep your language

Languages aren't just tools, they're 'a right'. You have the right to keep, use and share your language—and that's protected globally by agreements like the Universal Declaration of Linguistic Rights. Imagine how different the world would feel if languages continued to disappear. Losing a language is like losing a piece of history and identity.

Have you ever met someone whose family speaks a language that's different from the one they use at school? Keeping both languages alive is powerful—it gives people a connection to their roots and helps to bridge cultures. For example, in India, where hundreds of languages coexist, bilingualism isn't just common, it's necessary to function on a daily basis.

The power in multilingualism

Here's a cool fact: if you're bilingual or multilingual, your brain literally works differently. People who speak more than one language often find it easier to solve problems and adapt to new situations. Think of multilingualism like having a superpower in a world where global communication is everything. Knowing multiple languages can open up paths for making friends, working abroad or even tackling misconceptions about other cultures.

Take accents again. Someone speaking English with a strong French accent or a Southern American accent might face assumptions about their intelligence or background. But breaking through those assumptions helps to change the conversation about cultural stereotypes. Your understanding of these differences allows you to value the richness of language.

Why intercultural understanding matters

So, languages are more than words—they're a way of life. Intercultural understanding is about stepping into someone else's shoes. Think about the stereotypes people might associate with certain accents. For example, Scottish accents are sometimes stereotyped as 'charming but hard to understand', while American accents can be seen as 'confident but loud'. Interrogating these perceptions and learning about the people behind them helps you break down walls, build empathy and work better with others.

Here's another example: a student in your school might speak Arabic at home and English in class. Their Arabic might come with cultural traditions that are unfamiliar to you. What if, instead of assuming they're different, you learned a few words of their language? That small act shows respect and builds a connection, proving that languages bring us closer together rather than pushing us apart.

What you can do

Now, what does this mean for you? First, keep an open mind when you encounter other languages or accents—they're all unique and important. Second, practise a language you're learning with a new purpose: not just to speak it, but to understand the cultures it's tied to. Third, challenge stereotypes you might hear about how someone sounds or what language they use.

At the end of the day, multilingualism and intercultural understanding are skills that let you navigate the world with confidence. They show us that our differences make us stronger and that by respecting languages and cultures, we can connect with people in ways that truly matter.

So, the next time you hear an accent you've never encountered, don't judge—be curious. Ask questions, learn the stories behind the words and watch how much broader your world becomes.

LEARNING ENGAGEMENT

Analysing multilingualism and intercultural understanding

Using the information in the text above, copy and complete Table 2.6 by undertaking the following tasks.

1. **Identify key ideas:** Review the text and fill in the 'Key idea' column with the main concepts for each category.
2. **Provide examples:** Locate examples from the text or your own experience and record them in the 'Examples' column.
3. **Reflect:** For each idea and example, explain the broader implications for language, culture or personal growth in the 'Reflections/Implications' column.

Some answers have been provided to help you.

■ Table 2.6

Category	Key idea	Examples	Reflections/Implications
Languages as a fact	There are over 7,000 languages globally, with unique accents and dialects.		
Languages as a right			
Languages as a resource			Multilingualism is empowering and helps combat bias, fostering connection.
Intercultural understanding			
Actions to take		Learning words in a peer's home language Asking questions instead of making assumptions	

■ International-mindedness

■ Celebrating and protecting what connects us

The IB reminds us that 'multilingualism and intercultural understanding are cornerstones of international-mindedness' (IB LCS guide, p.9). In our globalized world, the variety of languages and cultures around us is something to celebrate—it's rich, vibrant and full of possibilities. But like any ecosystem, it's also delicate. Each time we make the effort to speak another language, listen to a different perspective or bridge cultural differences, we help keep this diversity alive. Multilingualism is not just a fact—it's a right and a resource that belongs to all of us. In LCS, and beyond, we each have a role to play in protecting and nurturing this diversity.

'Safeguarding the diversity of languages is crucial to protecting both cultural and biological diversity, as stated by the UNESCO 2001 Universal Declaration on Cultural Diversity, which raised cultural diversity to the level of 'the common heritage of humanity', 'as necessary for humankind as biodiversity is for nature'. It is through their language that people transmit cultural values to their children and fully exercise their rights and human dignity.'

(Source: https://unesco.org/en/articles/cutting-edge-indigenous-languages-gateways-worlds-cultural-diversity)

'It is multilingualism that has kept humanity, separated by so many languages, together.'

(Source: A. De Swaan, *Words of the World*, p.1)

Key terms

◆ **Linguistic repertoire:** The totality of linguistic resources (such as words, sounds, structures, styles, genres, registers and their respective norms) that individuals have at their disposal in all of their languages/language varieties (irrespective of their level of linguistic competence) and which they can select from, and deploy, in order to create and communicate meaning in various contexts. (Source: IB LCS guide, p.52)

◆ **Cultural repertoire:** The full range of resources and tools (such as skills, styles, ways of understanding the world) that individuals have at their disposal and which they can select from, and deploy, in order to act and interact adaptively and responsively in various social and cultural contexts. (Source: IB LCS guide, p.52)

LEARNING ENGAGEMENT

1 Reread the quotes above.
2 Reflect on their meaning using the different categories in Table 2.6 from the previous learning engagement, namely:
   - languages as a fact
   - languages as a right
   - languages as a resource
   - intercultural understanding
   - actions to take.
3 Discuss how the different categories can overlap and be interconnected.

Learning journal

Make a page in your learning journal where you summarize what you have understood about 'multilingualism' and 'interculturalism'.

2.2.4 Linguistic and cultural repertoire

In LCS, one of the most important things you'll be working on is expanding your **linguistic repertoire** and **cultural repertoire**. This means all the language and cultural knowledge you already have, as well as what you are continuing to build, like words and phrases you know in different languages, your ability to switch between formal and informal speech, and your understanding of different ways people communicate, think and behave in various cultures. Everyone's repertoire is unique, because it reflects your personal experiences and backgrounds. You choose, consciously or unconsciously, what aspects of your repertoire to use depending on where you are and who you are with.

Throughout the course, you'll explore, reflect on and expand your repertoire by engaging with new languages, ideas and cultures. How would you define the word 'repertoire'? Have you heard or used this word before? If you are a music-lover, how have you used the word repertoire? What synonyms could you use?

The word 'repertoire' is also in the LCS learning outcomes:

Table 2.7

With the goal of expanding your linguistic and cultural repertoires, you will be able to:	
LO1	Articulate how personal identity is shaped by engaging with languages and cultures and diverse perspectives.
LO2	Identify your own strengths and aspirations, set personally relevant goals and monitor your multilingual and intercultural learning through ongoing reflection.
LO3	Apply communication skills and understandings to various contexts.
LO4	Practise reflexivity and develop self-awareness as communicators within and across languages and cultures.

Learning journal

LCS learning outcomes and the repertoires

Look closely at the definitions of linguistic and cultural repertoire as well as how these terms are used in the LCS learning outcomes.

Create a visual, a mind map, a (recorded) spoken explanation or annotate the definitions to show that you fully understand these key terms, as well as how they link to the LCS learning outcomes.

Unique and dynamic repertoires

Your linguistic and cultural repertoire includes all of the languages/language varieties you know, as well as your cultural understandings and skills. Your repertoire is always available to you and you can choose exactly what to use depending on the context (where you are and who you are with).

Everyone has a linguistic and cultural repertoire and no two are exactly the same. If you have a sibling, observe how (even though you live in the same house and have had similar experiences) you are still not identical. Your repertoire is unique because it includes your personality, your interests, your preferences and is also possibly influenced by the age at which you were exposed to the languages and cultural experiences. Your repertoire is also dynamic as it will grow, develop and shift over time. For example, you might speak differently in school than you do with family, or you might acquire new expressions and cultural habits after travelling or meeting people from other backgrounds.

A person's linguistic and cultural repertoire is:

- unique—every person brings unique attitudes and aptitudes to multilingual and intercultural exchanges
- dynamic—repertoires change over time, and language use and cultural practices are also manifested differently depending on the particular contexts of situation and culture. (IB LCS guide, p.31)

Look at the timeline on the next page, which shows how a linguistic and cultural repertoire changes over time and is influenced by exposure to different contexts and opportunities, as well as plans for the future.

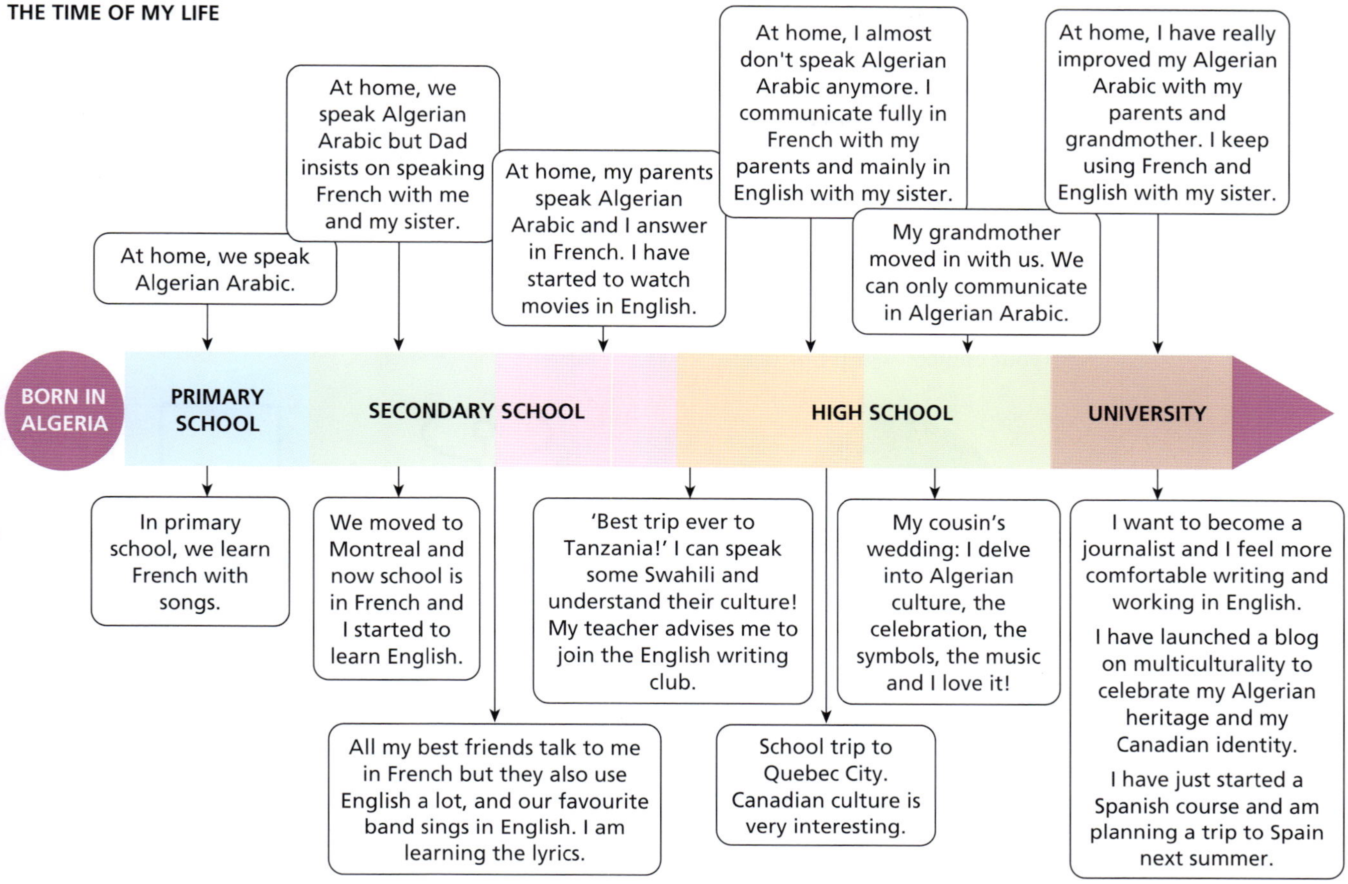

■ A repertoire timeline

Key term

◆ **Language and cultural portrait:** A way to represent your linguistic and cultural repertoire. Your portrait can be represented as a diagram, a mind map, a timeline, a piece of writing, a spoken reflection or presentation, a performance, a video, a blog or any combination of any modality. Your portrait *changes over time* as your repertoires expand and develop, as well as when you gain new insights into your portrait. Your portrait has a key role in your learning journal and should be regularly updated, annotated and referred to.

LEARNING ENGAGEMENT

Your own timeline

1 Create a timeline of your life (or for someone you know, such as a friend, parent or teacher).
2 Highlight times where experiences impacted your/their linguistic repertoire.
3 Highlight moments where experiences impacted your/their cultural repertoire.

Reflection and reflexivity

How do you feel knowing that you are linguistically and culturally unique? Add your thoughts to your learning journal.

2.2.5 Language and cultural portraits

Your **language and cultural portrait** is the starting point of your LCS learning journey. You will have the freedom to represent your unique and dynamic linguistic and cultural repertoire using the modality/modalities of your choice. You will review and refine your portrait throughout the two years as it evolves over time, and to capture and reflect the impact of your LCS learning engagements. The portrait is kept in a central place in your learning journal so that you can regularly refer to it.

Top tip!

Consider how your learning engagements in the rest of the CP Core might also contribute to your portrait.

In this section, we will help you to understand the important elements to take into consideration to create a detailed portrait. You are going to see different example portraits that showcase the languages and language varieties that are used or known, the lived experiences, and some language and cultural goals of different students. You can also look at your future aspirations and your passions and interests related to language and culture. In the examples, you will also see some feedback from the LCS teacher, which will lead naturally to follow-up questions that will help to review and refine the portraits.

The visual below provides a summary of what you will include in your language and cultural portrait, as well as suggestions for how you can represent it using a modality or modalities of your choice.

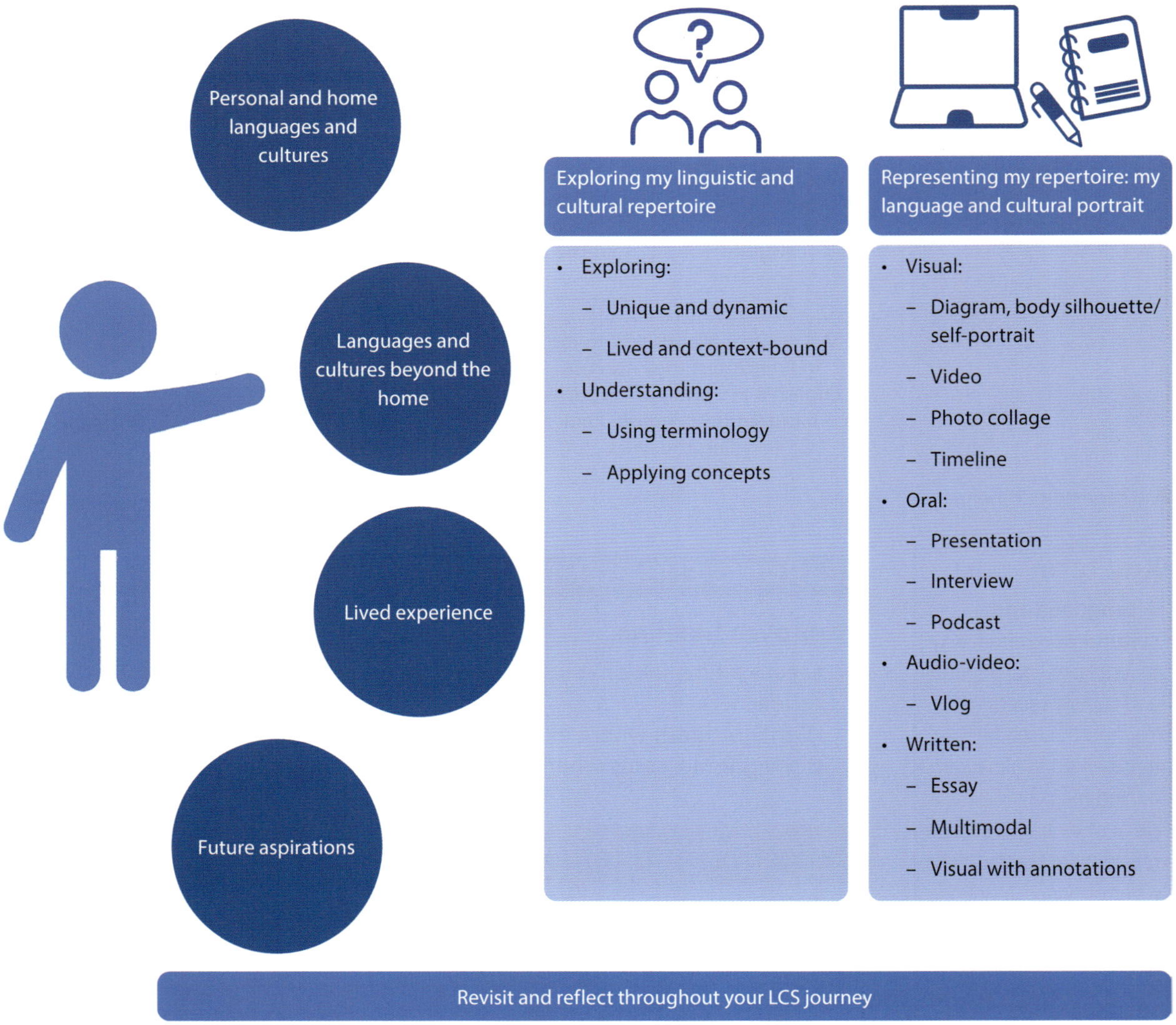

■ Language and cultural portrait tool (Source: IB LCS toolkit)

Language and cultural portrait examples

On the next few pages, you can see examples of language and cultural portraits. Each portrait is followed by some (example) LCS teacher feedback and/or follow-up questions that could be raised by the teacher, but also by your peers.

Take this opportunity to identify the:

- context where languages/language varieties are used
- modality or modalities the student has chosen to use in their portrait

- language and cultural goals of the student
- nature of the teacher feedback
- role of the follow-up questions.

REAL-WORLD EXAMPLE

Todd's language and cultural portrait

■ Todd's portrait

Hi, my name is Todd! I am proficient in English but am also familiar with spoken French as my maternal grandparents live in Québec. One of my close childhood friends is deaf and I understand some American Sign Language (ASL).

Contexts where I use my languages/language varieties:

- English to write song lyrics, but I am also very interested in finding out how international rappers develop their lyrics/songs
- French to interact with family members
- American Sign Language to interact with my childhood friend.

Some of my language and cultural goals:

- I am interested in learning how to read French as I only know how to speak it. I want to investigate ways in which I can learn to do this without taking a formal class, such as:
  - spending my summers with my grandparents in Québec to interact with them
  - using French subtitles when streaming videos.
- I am interested in learning to become proficient in American Sign Language so that I can understand my childhood friend more.

Feedback from Todd's teacher

- You have explained your exposure to different languages and the contexts where you encounter these.
- You have noted an awareness of sign language.
- You have included examples of some of your goals.
- There is a sense of community (e.g. grandparents, deaf friend) in your portrait.
- Your personal interests are included (e.g. rap lyrics, writing lyrics).
- How do your different cultures and identities overlap in your different contexts?

Follow-up questions from Todd's LCS peers

- How often do you speak French? Can you interact with ease?
- What is your favourite rap song and why? Who is your favourite artist and why?
- What would you like to write about in your own song lyrics?
- Is there a difference between ASL and other sign languages?
- How do you plan to develop your ASL?
- How would you describe your level in ASL? Can you tell jokes? Can you argue with this language?

REAL-WORLD EXAMPLE

Zara's language and cultural portrait

Name: Zara Khan

Age: 16

Nationality: British-Pakistani

Languages I have been exposed to:

- Punjabi (spoken at home with family; expressive and connects me to my heritage)
- Urdu (understood but not spoken fluently, often heard at family gatherings)
- English (used in school, with friends and for academic purposes)
- Spanish (studying at school; fascinated by its rhythm and cultural richness).

Contexts where I use my languages:

- Punjabi: Talking to family
- Urdu: Listening during weddings, celebrations and while watching films with family
- English: Engaging with diverse classmates, social media and debates at school
- Spanish: Role-plays in Spanish class, discussing hobbies and daily activities.

Some of my language goals:

- Improve my fluency in Urdu, especially in writing, so I can communicate with relatives in Pakistan.
- Become more confident in using Spanish in 'real' situations.

Centre of interest linked to culture:

I'm passionate about Pakistani cuisine and traditions, especially the meaning behind cultural attire and celebrations. Recently, I've started exploring Flamenco music and how it reflects Spanish culture's vibrance and history.

Language and culture reflection:

I've realized that each language offers a unique window into understanding people's lives. For example, Urdu poetry feels incredibly emotional and reflective, while Flamenco lyrics I've heard in Spanish evoke a fiery spirit. Being bilingual has taught me to see the beauty in navigating multiple cultural identities.

Future aspirations:

I hope to bridge cultural gaps through storytelling and perhaps work in media or translation. Learning about different dialects and non-verbal expressions motivates me to embrace cultural diversity while helping others connect across languages.

Feedback from Zara's LCS teacher

- You define some elements of culture but you could go back to the cultural iceberg (in Section 2.2.2) to review your cultural portrait at the deeper level.
- What is the relationship between Urdu and Punjabi? Could you research this and share it with the class?

REAL-WORLD EXAMPLE

Will's multimodal language and cultural portrait

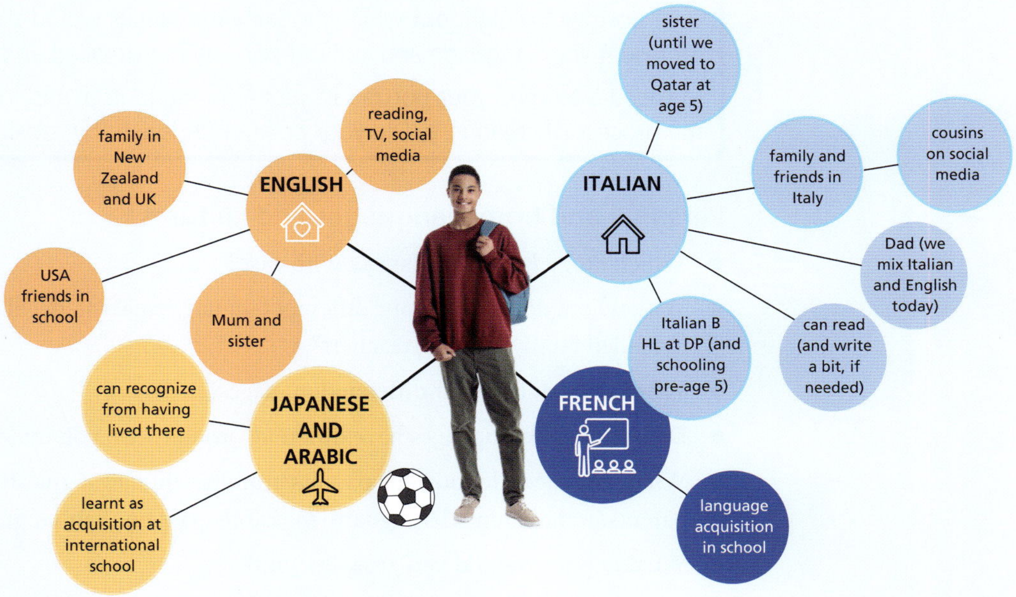

■ Will's portrait

Notes to explain my portrait:

- Italian used to be my dominant language.
- English is my dominant language today (home, academic, social).
- Not very confident today in Italian, but I realize it will be an advantage later (workplace, socially).
- I am used to hearing or using a lot of varieties of English (US, UK, New Zealand, South African, Indian).
- I did not enjoy studying French, but I was good at it (maybe because I was bilingual?!).
- I 'get better' at Italian when I am in Italy with my family.
- I follow the Italian football and support Juventus.
- I feel most at home in West London.
- Rather than adding more languages, I would like to improve my Italian.
- I have friends from all over the world and enjoy that more than being immersed in 'one culture'.
- I was born in the Middle East, Qatar, and have lived in Italy, Oman, Qatar, Japan, UK.
- I visit New Zealand almost every year.

Feedback from Will's LCS teacher

- Your portrait is very detailed and full of insights about how you use your languages.
- I like your positive attitude towards all of the cultures you have been exposed to.
- You have also shown how your portrait has evolved over time and also your future aspirations.
- I would be interested to know which variety of English you (think) you use.

Creating your language and cultural portrait

Here is a set of questions which are organized into categories. They have been designed to guide you and help you think about your linguistic and cultural repertoires so that you can create your first language and cultural portrait.

Learning journal

My language and cultural portrait

Select guiding questions from each category below to support you in creating your own portrait. Think about which modality/modalities would suit you and allow you to represent your language and cultural portrait in a detailed and meaningful way.

Make sure to keep your portrait in your learning journal and include your reflections on the process of creating it. Did your portrait undergo any revisions along the way?

Personal and home languages and cultures

- Which languages do you speak with ease?
- With whom do you use your different languages: parents/legal guardians/carers, siblings, extended family, friends, teachers?
- Where do you use your different languages?
- Do any of your languages have different varieties? Do you understand/speak (any of) them?
- What languages do/did your parents/grandparents/legal guardians/carers use? Did your parents/grandparents/legal guardians/carers pass on their languages to you? If not, why not?
- What language(s) did you grow up with?
- Do you use more than one language at home? Why?
- In which language(s) do you feel most at ease? Has this changed over time?
- Do you speak a language with ease, without reading/writing it?
- In which language(s) can you understand just enough to have a simple conversation?
- When you are playing chess, or deliberating a tough decision and debating with yourself in your head, do you speak to yourself in any language? Which one(s)?
- Which traditions do you have in your family? How are they celebrated? How meaningful are they to you? Do you know their origins? Have they changed over time, in your family or in the wider community? Have the names of celebrations or other language(s) used in the celebration (e.g. names of figures celebrated, greetings, etc.) changed? If so, why?

Languages and cultures beyond the home

- In which languages have you attended school? In which languages are you able to do academic work?
- Do you use more than one language in school? Why? Where, when and with whom do you use these languages?
- What languages do you use with friends and/or in activities outside of school (e.g. sports, clubs, etc.)?
- What languages are spoken in your local community? Are some languages valued more than others? Why do you think that might be?
- Do you speak the language(s) or language variety/varieties of the country in which you are currently living?
- Have you ever been inspired to learn a language/language variety by music, films, etc.?
- Do you celebrate traditions that you have adopted from your local community? Have you/your family also adopted new language expressions or uses related to such celebrations?

Lived experiences

- Where have you lived? What took you to these places?
- Are there any languages you used to use regularly, but no longer do? Why not?
- Do you sometimes use multiple languages in the same conversation? Describe how this occurs—with whom, where, when, what?
- Which languages have you learnt with pleasure? What was particularly important and enriching?
- In your experience of language learning so far, what has (de)motivated you?
- If I were to ask you to think of home, where would it be?
- What stereotypes do you think people have about speakers of your language(s)? How do you feel about these stereotypes? Why? How do you respond when you hear someone uttering such a stereotype?
- What stereotypes do you think you have about speakers of other languages/language varieties? How can you learn more and form a more informed and nuanced picture?
- Have you ever felt uncomfortable when speaking a particular language/language variety in public? Why?
- Which group of people do you share the most values in common with? In this group, who shares your values completely? Are there variants? Does the group belong to a larger community, or does it run counter to the larger community (culture, subculture, anti-culture)?
- What did you learn about where you belong and from whom did you learn that?
- Which roles do you identify with yourself?
- If people were to label you with an ethnic group and race, which do you think you'd agree with? Which cultural/social groups do you feel you belong to?
- Have you ever experienced a 'breakdown' in communication although you/participants in the conversation spoke the same language (relatively well)? What happened? What else is needed to be able to understand one another and communicate well (besides vocabulary and grammar)?

Future aspirations

- Is there a language/language variety you wish you could speak or speak better?
- What language(s)/language varieties do you think will be useful to you in the future, for studying, work, internships, community engagement projects, socializing, travelling, connecting with family, etc.?
- Imagine you do not have fluency/literacy in one of your languages/dialects. How would your life be different to how it is now?
- Imagine that you have fluency/literacy in another language or that you could enhance your fluency/literacy in one of your current languages. How would that change your everyday life?

(Source: IB LCS toolkit)

Top tip!

Review, revisit and refine your portrait to adjust it regularly. It will capture your unique and dynamic repertoires and will be an important piece of evidence in your review points.

2.2.6 Summary

- Languages reflect the rich diversity of our world and language is our primary way to construct, share and maintain understanding and meaning.
- Cultures reflect the rich diversity of ways of seeing our world. Knowledge of and exposure to cultures allow you to appreciate and understand different perspectives.
- Intercultural understanding is a skill for you to become an ethical global citizen across local and global contexts.
- Exploring and expanding your unique and dynamic linguistic and cultural repertoire is part of your LCS journey.
- The language and cultural portrait is the starting point of your LCS learning journey and you will review and refine it regularly.

2.3 LCS concepts

INQUIRY QUESTIONS

- How do your linguistic and cultural repertoires shape your identity and communication styles, influencing your perspectives and your understanding of power dynamics?
- How can the LCS concepts open ways of reflection to refine your language and cultural portrait and learning journey?
- What is the relationship between the four LCS concepts?

You will now start to explore the four LCS concepts: communication, identities, perspectives and power. These concepts play an important role in helping us to better understand how language(s) and culture(s) are connected. You'll explore each concept individually to see how it shapes language and culture, and begin to see where these concepts fit in your own experience, helping you uncover new layers of your language and cultural portrait. You'll also look at real-life examples where all four concepts appear together, so you can apply what you've learned, make meaningful connections and reflect on how language and culture shape your own experiences and the world around you.

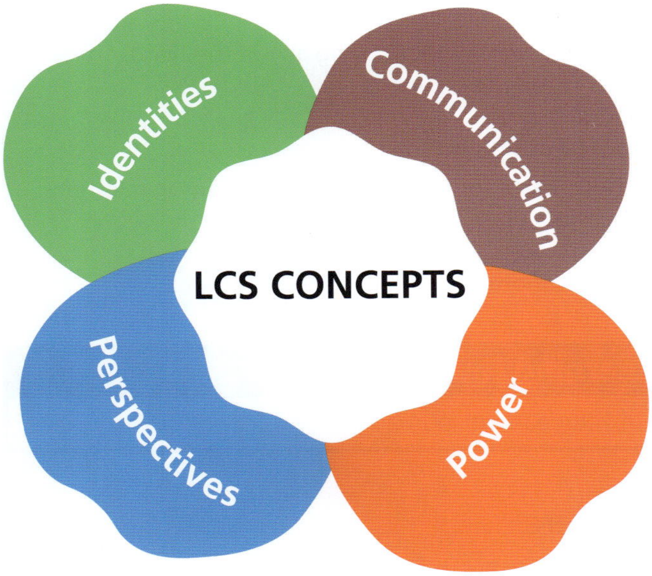

■ LCS concepts

The LCS concepts will help you to:

- deepen your understanding of the key terms 'language' and 'culture'
- further refine your language and cultural portrait
- plan your learning engagements
- choose your goals and areas of exploration
- reflect on your learning journey and progress towards the LCS learning outcomes in your learning journal, as well as in the review points.

2.3.1 Communication

What is **communication** in LCS? In LCS, communication means more than just speaking or writing—it's about *how* we share meaning with others. This can happen through words, but also through things like tone of voice, facial expressions, gestures, images or even silence. We often use many of these at once. This is called multimodal communication. What we say and how we say it can change depending on who we're talking to, where we are and what's happening around us. Let's discover how communication works, how meaning is created and interpreted in different situations, and how things can sometimes be misunderstood across cultures or languages.

Key term

◆ **Communication:** The expression and exchange of meaning through language or any other mode. Communication is often multimodal, including non-linguistic elements such as body language, gestures and images. The success of communication depends on the negotiation of meaning and cooperation between individuals within a given sociocultural and situational context. (Source: IB LCS guide, p.17)

Communicating and miscommunicating

LEARNING ENGAGEMENT

Let's play 'Guess what?'

Create a set of blank cards and distribute one to each person in the group. Each person writes one short expression on the card. See below for examples.

There is a fire!	I am in pain.	I'm broke.	I'm going to university next year.

Cards with clues

Each person folds their card in two and adds it to a pile at the centre of the group. Taking turns, each person picks up a card (keeping it hidden from the others). They then have one minute to describe what is on their card, with classmates guessing the answers. You get one point per correct answer.

Play the game in three rounds:

- **Round 1:** You can speak as much as you want *without* using any of the words from the card.
- **Round 2:** You can only use *one* word.
- **Round 3:** You may not use any spoken or sign language, only *mime*.

After playing the game, reflect either individually or as a group on the following questions:

- What did you notice when playing the game?
- What did you use to communicate?
- What led to any form of miscommunication?

Learning journal

Remember to add your thoughts to your learning journal.

Communication is everywhere!

On the next page is a poem in French that highlights the complexity of communication. Do you understand it? If not, how could you discover the meaning of the poem? Do you know someone who could translate this for you?

Entre

Ce que je pense
Ce que je veux dire
Ce que je crois dire
Ce que je dis
Ce que vous avez envie d'entendre
Ce que vous croyez entendre
Ce que vous entendez
Ce que vous avez envie de comprendre
Ce que vous croyez comprendre
Ce que vous comprenez ...
Il y a dix possibilités qu'on ait des difficultés à communiquer.
Mais essayons quand même ...

(Source: *L'Encyclopédie du Savoir Relatif et Absolu* by Bernard Werber)

Top tip!

Use technology, in class or at home, to translate this poem into one of your languages.

LEARNING ENGAGEMENT

A social-media post

1 Look carefully at the poem above and think of examples in your everyday life where you might have experienced difficulties in communicating.
2 Create a list of 'communication tips' and turn this into a social-media post which you could imagine posting online.

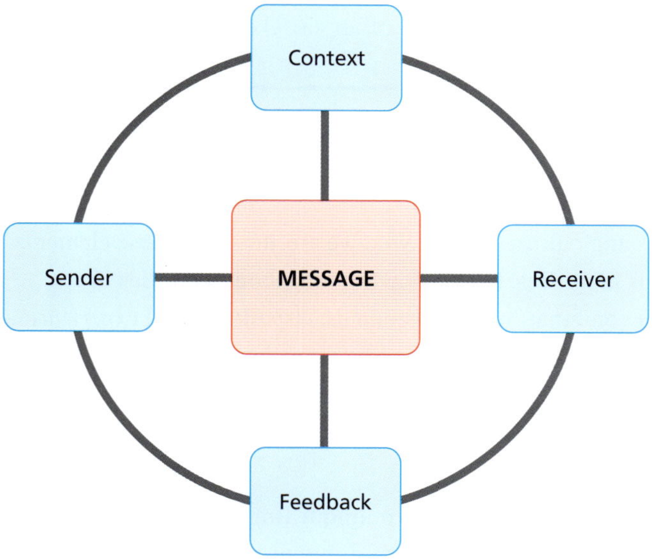

The communication process

Effective communication

Look at the visual on the left which shows the different elements of the communication process. Every act of communication involves:

- **a sender:** the person who communicates the message
- **a receiver:** the person who receives and interprets the message
- **the message:** what is being shared
- **a context:** a situation, place or cultural background
- **feedback:** the response from the receiver.

By learning to notice each part of this process, we can become more thoughtful and effective communicators.

Top tip!

Use your LCS knowledge in PPS!

Links

Communication is one the interpersonal skills explored in PPS to understand how to interact in an effective way.

Learner profile

Thinkers use critical-thinking skills to be able to understand the complex ways in which language and culture relate to each other.

LEARNING ENGAGEMENT

The missing part

Think about the communication process above. What would happen if one part were missing? Consider every element of the communication process, then copy and complete the table below:

■ **Table 2.8**

Element	If this element were missing ...
Sender	
Receiver	
Message	
Context	
Feedback	

Key term

◆ **Identities:** This refers to the particular combinations of backgrounds, dispositions and experiences that define individuals, groups, communities, organizations, objects, eras and places. Identities are complex and dynamic. They can be shaped through internal and external, present and past influences. Individual and collective identities are manifested in both tangible and intangible ways, and these identities influence our view of the world and how others view us. (Source: IB LCS guide, pp.17–18)

Learning journal

Look again carefully at the definition of communication at the start of Section 2.3.1, the connections to PPS and the IB learner profile, as well as reflecting on what you have seen and done in this section. Then rewrite the definition in your own words to ensure you understand all of its key elements, and include any other visual elements if you wish. Add this to your learning journal.

2.3.2 Identities

In LCS, you'll explore how languages and cultures reflect who we are, and how these elements work together to form and shape your **identities**. Notice how we talk about identities in the plural because we all have a different combination of *backgrounds, dispositions* and *experiences*. You might be a student, a sibling, a gamer, a speaker of more than one language, a music lover, a holder of a passport and a member of an ethnic, national, regional, social, cultural or sports community. You might see yourself as being 'at the centre' of some of these groups and more on the 'edges' of other groups.

In this section, you'll have the chance to reflect on your own unique linguistic and cultural journey, how it changes over time and how it connects you to different communities. You'll also explore the idea of collective identity and how belonging to a group is often shaped and expressed through shared language and culture. This will help you understand not only yourself better, but also how others see and express who they are in a diverse world.

LEARNING ENGAGEMENT

Unpuzzling identity

The blue puzzle pieces below are all key terms from the definition of the LCS concept of identities. Match each blue puzzle piece with a corresponding green puzzle piece which describes the key term in everyday language. As you are working through this learning engagement, consider these questions:

- How do you express your different identities?
- What makes you unique?

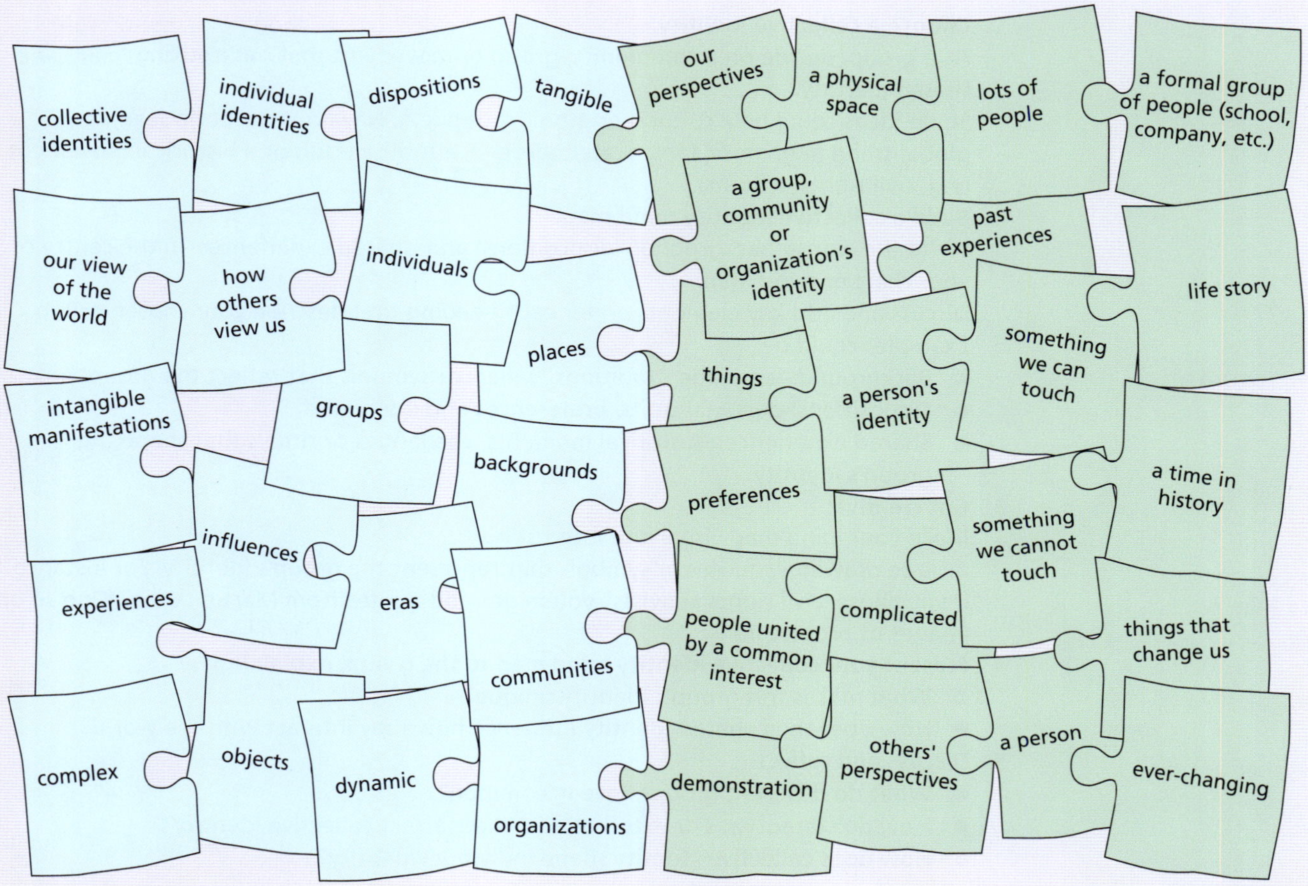

Collective identities

Learner profile

Inquirers

Nurture curiosity in connection with varied linguistic and cultural practices.

In LCS, we use the term 'collective identity' to describe the part of our identity that comes from belonging to a group. This could be a cultural or ethnic group, a sports team, a music community, an activist movement or even an online fan group. Being part of a group can give us a shared sense of meaning, values, traditions or ways of expressing ourselves. It is important to remember that a group's identity can overlap with other groups and that the way people inside a group see themselves can be very different from how others outside the group might see them. In this section, we'll explore collective identities and reflect on the different groups we feel connected to, and how they shape the way we see ourselves and the way others might see us.

LEARNING ENGAGEMENT

What makes communities and groups unique?

Follow these steps to create a mind map or chart exploring a collective identity.

1 **Choose a collective identity:**
As a group, decide on a community, group or movement that has a strong shared identity.
Some ideas could be a cultural or ethnic group (e.g. Navajo, Afro-Caribbean), a global trend (e.g. music fans, skateboarders), a football club or a historical movement (e.g. civil rights activists).

2 **Build a collective identity mind map:**
Write the words 'background', 'dispositions' and 'shared experiences' in the centre of your chart or mind map.
Discuss and add key elements under each heading that describe your chosen group. Examples could be:
- Background: language, traditions, beliefs or symbols that reflect the group.
- Dispositions: personal traits, preferences and interests.
- Shared experiences: historical moments, challenges or rituals that shape the group's identity.

3 **Get creative:**
Make your mind map visual and interesting!
Include drawings, quotes or symbols that represent the group's identity. For instance, if you chose 'civil rights activists', you might add quotes from Martin Luther King Jr. or images of protest signs.

4 **Present your collective identity mind map to the group, explaining:**
- What makes this group's identity unique?
- How does their shared identity influence how they interact with the world?

5 **Discuss and reflect:**
- What do different groups have in common?
- How do stereotypes or external influences affect collective identity?
- How does collective identity shape individual identity?

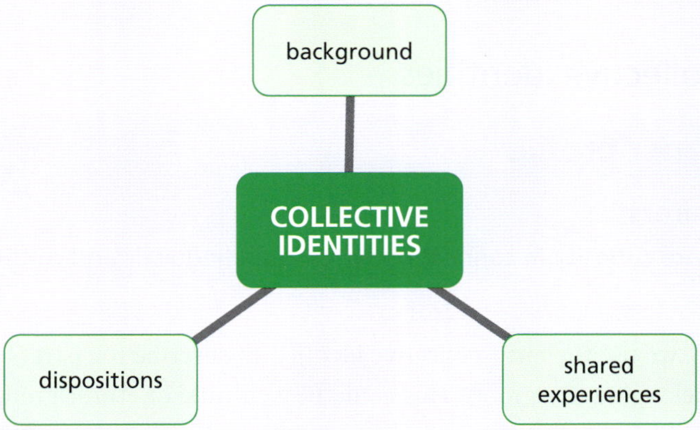

A collective identities mind map

■ Dynamic identities

What do we mean by 'dynamic identities'? The word 'dynamic' implies that our personal, cultural and collective identities are undergoing constant change. These changes might be visible:

- over time, for example, if you move to a new location and you add a new language to your repertoire, or if you come into contact with new languages and cultures
- from moment to moment, as you interact in different contexts (such as school, family, friends, personal interests and hobbies). You might notice that you subtly change the variety of language you use (slang or words/expressions) so that you 'fit in' better in each different context.

You can visualize your dynamic identity in different ways, for example:

- in the form of a timeline, where you identify key events in your life that have caused your identity to change
- as a circle, where some aspects of your identity are at the centre, whereas others might be closer to the periphery.

Learning journal

Look again carefully at the definition of identities at the start of Section 2.3.2, as well as reflecting on what you have seen and done in this section. Then rewrite the definition in your own words to ensure you understand all of its key elements, and include any other visual elements if you wish. Add this to your learning journal.

2.3.3 Perspectives

Key term

◆ **Perspectives:** This refers to the positions from which we view situations, objects, facts, ideas and opinions. Perspectives may be associated with individuals or groups, and they may be influenced by social, cultural, disciplinary, political or historical contexts. Different perspectives often lead to multiple representations and interpretations. (Source: IB LCS guide, p.18)

LCS offers students a lens to explore ethics and ethical practices within the context of language and culture. By evaluating how language and culture influence and impact the perspectives of different community members within societal systems, students gain insight into the intricate interplay between ethics, language and culture. (Source: IB LCS TSM, p.5)

In LCS, we use the word **perspectives** to talk about the different ways people see and understand the world around them. Our perspectives are shaped by many things, such as our cultures, languages, history, beliefs and the communities we are part of. This means that the same situation or idea can be seen in completely different ways depending on who you are, where you're coming from and what previous experiences you've had. In this section, you'll explore how language and culture act like lenses that influence how people think, communicate and make sense of the world. You'll also think about your own positionality (how your background and your identity affects your own point of view) and how we can try to understand perspectives that are different from our own.

LEARNING ENGAGEMENT

How do you see the world?

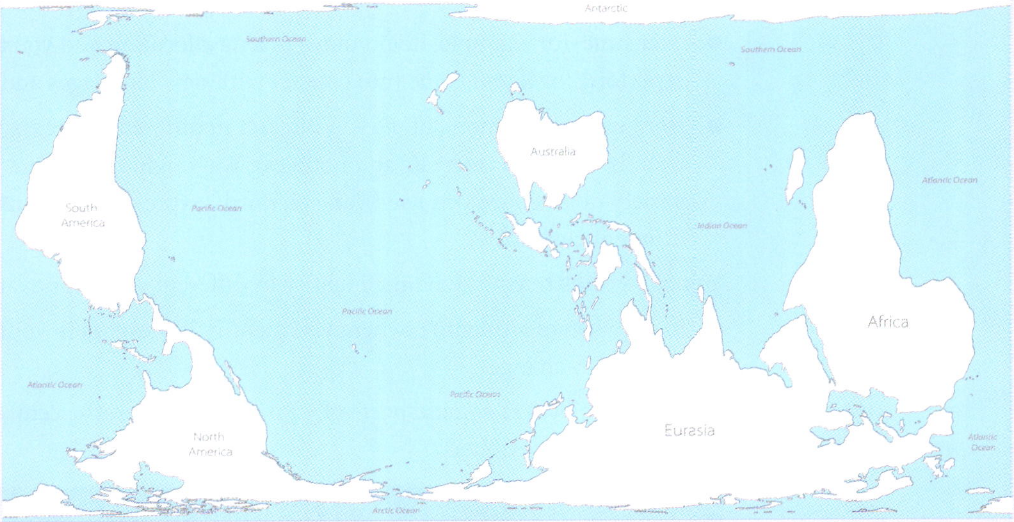

■ A world map

Look at this map of the world and respond to the questions below. You can record your thoughts in a modality of your choice (such as a voice note, word cloud, bullet-point list, paragraph, etc.).

1. Why do we usually see world maps only one way up, and what does that say about who gets to decide on the perspectives we use?
2. How does flipping the map change the way you think about the world?
3. Are world maps to scale? Can you find other versions of the world map to compare?
4. How would you draw the world map if you had the choice?

Same action, different meaning

In everyday life, we do things like greet people, make eye contact, eat together or stay silent during conversations and we don't always think twice about them. But in LCS, we learn that these simple actions can mean very different things depending on your perspective. For example, in the United States, making eye contact is often seen as a sign of confidence and honesty, but in Japan or Nigeria, avoiding direct eye contact can be a sign of respect, especially when speaking to someone older. Greeting practices also vary: in France, it's common to greet friends with kisses on the cheek (*la bise*), while in Thailand, many people greet each other with a respectful bow called the *wai*. When it comes to eating, in India or Ethiopia, using your hands is generally a normal and respectful way to share food, while in South Korea, it can be considered polite to wait for the oldest person to start eating before you do. Silence, too, can mean different things: in Finland, it's often seen as thoughtful and respectful, while in Italy or Brazil, silence during conversation might feel uncomfortable. Even colours can carry different meanings: in China, red symbolizes good luck and celebration, but in some parts of South Africa, it can be associated with mourning.

By exploring these examples, we start to see that culture shapes different perspectives and that understanding them helps us become more open, respectful and curious global citizens.

LEARNING ENGAGEMENT

Cultural practices from around the world

1 Select three different cultural communities, ideally spread across the world. Do some research (online or by asking members of your LCS team, your teacher or other students) to learn about the unique cultural practices within these groups. Then copy and complete the table below.

Table 2.9 Research into different cultural communities

Cultural community	Greeting practices	Eye contact	Eating practices	Silence in communication	Concept of time	Colour symbolism	Verbal expressions of agreement

2 Choose one of the categories below and showcase the wide range of practices from all around the world:

- greeting practices
- eye contact
- eating practices
- silence in communication
- concept of time
- colour symbolism
- verbal expressions of agreement

Represent your findings in a modality of your choice. See below how Maddie, an LCS student, shared her findings.

Eye contact as a cultural practice

The perspectives we have at any given time in our lives are often rooted in our own cultural practices and our understandings and misunderstandings about other cultural practices.

Reflection and reflexivity

- How might someone from a different cultural background experience these cultural practices differently than you do?
- What does your reaction to a cultural practice say about your own values, habits or assumptions?

Top tip!

'Switching positions' can help you to build empathy, challenge stereotypes and become a more thoughtful world citizen within different communities.

Switching positions

How would you feel about stepping into someone else's shoes and taking part in their cultural practices?

What happens when you view a situation through someone else's cultural lens?

How might their perspectives challenge or change your own understanding?

How do your assumptions and biases influence your actions?

How do your assumptions and biases impact others?

In LCS, one of the most powerful things you can do is to 'switch positions' so that you see things from someone else's cultural point of view, while also reflecting on your own. When you do this, you start to realize that what feels 'normal' to you might feel unfamiliar to someone else and vice versa. You become more aware of your own habits, values and assumptions, and you also begin to appreciate that there are many different ways of seeing and doing things! This doesn't mean agreeing with everything, but it does mean listening, questioning your first impressions and recognizing that your perspectives are shaped by your identity and experiences, just like everyone else's.

Our language(s) and culture(s) shape our perspectives. Through reflexive practice, we can examine and interrogate our positionality and understand its impact on our own views of our world.

How can shifting your position change your perspective?

Learner profile

Communicators

Listen carefully to the perspectives of other individuals and groups, be able to understand and express your own perspectives, and communicate in various contexts. (Source: IB LCS guide, p.8)

Key terms

◆ **Positionality:** This refers to the stance or positioning of individuals or groups in relation to overlapping cultural, social, historical and political contexts and relations of power, and how identities (including the perspectives, biases, assumptions, values and experiences we hold) shape frames of reference and, therefore, the way we understand and engage with the world. It also aims to highlight both how individual identities are created by social constructs and how they are malleable. (Source: IB LCS guide, p.51)

◆ **Power:** This refers to the hierarchical structures, relations and processes that are formed by social, cultural, political, economic and historical factors, and that involve a person's or group's capacity to exert influence, domination or control over other individuals and groups. Power is not equally distributed in all contexts. Individuals' and communities' choices and actions can influence, or be influenced by, power structures and relations. (Source: IB LCS guide, p.18)

LEARNING ENGAGEMENT

Let's switch positions!

1 Look at the definition of **positionality**. Make sure that you understand all of the key terms in the definition. Rewrite the definition in your own words and add any other visual elements if you wish.

2 Look at different cultural practices around the world from your previous learning engagements (e.g. eye contact, eating practices, silence in communication, etc.). Complete the following sentences and answer the questions:
- *Before I used to think ... Why?*
- *Then I found out that ... How?*
- *Now I think ... Why?*

3 Respond to the following question and record your thoughts in your learning journal: *How does our positionality influence the way we see the world?*

2.3.4 Power

Language hierarchies

In LCS, the concept of **power** isn't just about who is in charge. It's also about who gets to speak and whose voices are heard or ignored. Power often creates hierarchies, where some people, languages or cultures are given more importance than others. For example, many countries have an official language, which is used in schools, government and media, but there are often many other languages and language varieties spoken by communities that aren't officially and equally recognized or valued. These hierarchies come from history, politics, economics and culture and they don't affect everyone the same way. Power structures are not fixed, as people and communities can question them, resist them and even help change them. In LCS, we look at how language(s) and culture(s) are deeply connected to power and we ask important questions like, 'Who gets to decide what counts as "normal"?', 'Whose voices are missing?' and 'How can we use what we learn to create more inclusive spaces?'

Key terms

◆ **Language ideologies:** The beliefs, opinions, biases and feelings (conscious or unconscious) that people have about different languages and ways of speaking. These ideas influence how we use language and how we view others based on their speech. (Adapted from IB LCS guide, p.51)

◆ **Criticality:** The ability to analyse, assess and evaluate information, ideas or situations in a thoughtful and objective manner. It involves examining different perspectives, questioning assumptions and evaluating evidence and arguments in order to form well-reasoned judgements and conclusions. In essence, criticality encompasses the process of thinking critically and applying critical-thinking skills.

LEARNING ENGAGEMENT

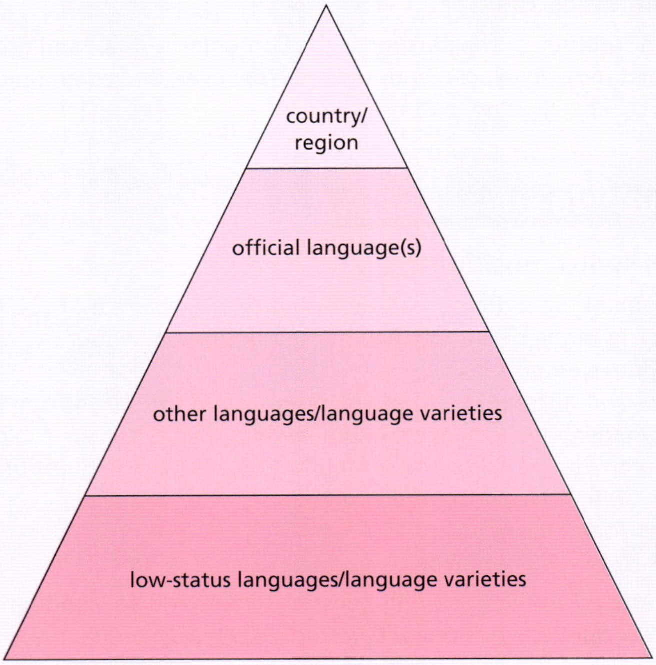

■ Language pyramid

Language hierarchies

Create a language pyramid to show a language hierarchy in a specific context.

1. Think of a country or region you are familiar with.
2. What is (are) the official language(s) which are typically used in media and education?
3. What other languages/language varieties are used in homes and communities?
4. Which languages/language varieties have a lower status? (They are often not present in media and education and might be used in popular humour.)
5. Verify your language pyramid using a reliable source of information.

Language ideologies

Understanding language ideologies helps us see that our perceptions of different ways of speaking are shaped by society and personal experiences. By being aware of these biases, we can work towards more inclusive and fair communication and we can analyse the diversity around us with criticality.

LEARNING ENGAGEMENT

The elements of language ideologies

The table below shows us the different aspects of language ideologies.

Table 2.10 The different aspects of language ideologies

Language ideologies			
Perceptions of language varieties	**Influence of media**	**Constructed language categories**	**Impact on social interactions**
People often have strong opinions about different accents or dialects. These judgements are based on personal experiences and societal influences, not on any inherent qualities of the language itself.	Media representations can shape our views on language and is not always an accurate representation of the vast diversity of a language variety.	Terms like 'Indian English' or 'American English' are broad labels that group together many ways of speaking. Within this labelled group, there's a wide range of accents and styles influenced by factors like education and other languages spoken. These labels can oversimplify and create imaginary boundaries between language varieties.	Our beliefs about language can affect how we interact with others. If someone views a particular accent as less intelligent or funny, they might treat speakers of that accent differently. Recognizing that these beliefs are subjective can help us become more open-minded and reduce unfair judgements.

How do each of these categories connect to your own world and experiences? Look at the different guiding questions for each category and create a written, oral or visual presentation.

Perceptions of language varieties:

- Can you think of any language varieties or accents that are considered 'better' or 'worse' in your community or culture? Why?
- How do you feel when you hear someone speak with an accent or language variety that's different from yours?

Influence of media:

- How are different accents or languages portrayed in films, TV shows or music?
- Have you ever seen a stereotype about a language or accent in the media? How did it make you feel?

Constructed language categories:

- Think about labels like 'American English' or 'African French'. How do these categories group together very different ways of speaking?
- What are some examples of language varieties in your community or culture that might not fit neatly into a 'label' or 'category'?

Impact on social interactions:

- Have you ever been in a situation where language affected how people treated each other?
- How might someone's accent influence the way they are perceived by others in school or at work?

What's behind the name?

Languages are constantly changing, as they come into contact with each other or as new concepts or inventions require new languages and ways of talking. Because of this close contact, speakers can often understand other languages within the same 'language family' (e.g. Spanish and Portuguese).

In some places in the world, people in different countries or regions use closely related languages that are mutually intelligible (they can be understood by each other to some extent because of shared vocabulary, etc.). Despite these similarities, they have evolved as distinct languages or language varieties with their own names.

LEARNING ENGAGEMENT

A look into how languages are named

Look at the examples below and try to find out what is similar and different about each of the named languages/language varieties within a set. Can you find out why they are so closely related? Can you find out why they have developed as separate named languages/language varieties?

1 Explore the table below, which shows how some shared languages have different names depending on their geographical location.
   - Take a close look at the example provided.
   - Investigate the 'why' behind it. Why do these different names exist? For what reasons? Put on your critical thinking cap and uncover the stories behind these names.
   - Copy and complete the table, adding any other examples you are knowledgeable about.

Table 2.11 Various names of languages

Name of language/ language variety	Country	Why different names?
Serbian	Serbia	Reflects Serbian identity, emphasizing the Cyrillic script and historical connections to the Serbian Orthodox Church.
Bosnian	Bosnia and Herzegovina	Associated with Bosnian identity, including influences from Turkish, Arabic and Persian during the Ottoman period.
Croatian	Croatia	Represents Croatian identity, with preference for Latin script and particular vocabulary choices.
Hindi	India	
Urdu	Pakistan	
Farsi	Iran	
Dari	Afghanistan	
Tajik	Tajikistan	
Indonesian	Indonesia	
Malaysian	Malaysia	
Flemish	Belgium	
Dutch	Netherlands	

2 Why do shared languages sometimes have different names depending on their geographical location? Sort the information you have gathered into these different categories and summarize it in a visual representation, such as a mind map.
- **National identity:** Countries often rename a shared language to reflect independence or uniqueness.
- **Regional differences:** Different varieties of a language can develop over time and can adopt their own identity based on geography or culture.
- **Political or historical events:** Colonization or decolonization, wars and conflict, and shifts in government often lead to rebranding languages to emphasize identity.

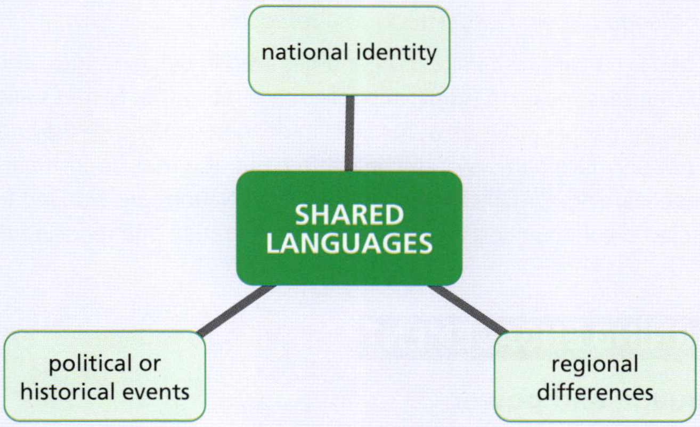

A mind map template

The naming and renaming of languages, as well as the recognition of a language as an official language in a particular region or country, is often linked to shifts in power between the speakers of languages.

REAL-WORLD EXAMPLE

Voices of exclusion: Stories of language and power

Lena, 18, Australia

Losing the voice of her ancestors

Lena grew up in a remote Aboriginal community in Northern Australia. She has heard stories from her grandmother about the days when speaking her native Yolŋu Matha ('Yolŋu tongue') in school was punishable. Although official attitudes have shifted, Lena says her cultural identity is still marginalized. 'My classmates laugh when I use Yolŋu words. I feel like I have to be someone else to fit in.' Modern initiatives, such as Indigenous language classes in Australian schools, are striving to change this, but only 13% of Indigenous children today speak their ancestral languages at home, highlighting the challenge.

Jason, 23, Liverpool, UK

Judged by his Scouse accent

Jason recently graduated from university and is looking for his first job in London. Despite having a first-class degree, he feels his Liverpool accent puts him at a disadvantage. 'Every time I open my mouth in interviews, I can see the judgements. They hear my accent and assume I'm not professional enough.' Jason's experience echoes research that shows how certain regional accents in the UK—like Scouse, Cockney or Geordie—are perceived as 'less prestigious', reinforcing socio-economic divisions.

Keisha, 21, Chicago, USA

The stigma of AAVE in higher education

Keisha speaks fluently in African American Vernacular English (AAVE) at home but switches to standard American English on campus. She explains, 'Using AAVE in class is frowned upon—it's like they think I'm not smart if I don't talk the way they do.' Yet AAVE is a recognized linguistic form with its own grammatical structure and rules. Movements like Black Lives Matter are pushing educators to see AAVE not as 'broken English', but as a legitimate and vibrant language variety that reflects the culture of black communities.

Salim, 19, Damascus/Brussels

The challenge of being understood as a refugee

Salim fled Syria with his family at 14 and has lived in Belgium since. Though he now speaks French fluently, he says speaking Arabic in public spaces still attracts stares and occasional hostility. 'Sometimes, people just look at me like I'm dangerous because they hear Arabic.' Refugees like Salim not only face barriers of discrimination, but also miss opportunities without access to proper language learning. Organizations like the United Nations are working to ensure language accessibility for displaced communities, which is vital for integration and reducing marginalization.

LEARNING ENGAGEMENT

Language and power

These four stories highlight the invisible barriers that people who use particular languages might face. Whether through direct prejudice, unconscious bias or systemic inequalities, language is often a tool of both inclusion and exclusion. As you think about Lena, Jason, Keisha and Salim:

- Identify the form of power present in each story.
- Reflect on the power of language to shape people's lives.

Reflection and reflexivity

Considering the key term 'criticality' (see p.182), create a reflection in a mode of your choice on these stories in your learning journal.

Learning journal

Look carefully at the definition of power at the start of this section, as well as reflecting on what you have seen and done in this section. Then rewrite the definition in your own words to ensure you understand all of its key elements, and include any other visual elements if you wish. Add this to your learning journal.

2.3.5 LCS concepts beyond the classroom

You are now an LCS expert at being able to identify, analyse and reflect on the four concepts. In this section, you will explore real-world examples for you to apply your knowledge and understanding of the LCS concepts. For each example, you will be able to look at different questions related to the concepts and choose your own pathway: you can research, create, reflect or take action.

REAL-WORLD EXAMPLE

Exploring social media as a space for multilingualism

In today's digital world, social media has become a vibrant space where languages and cultures interact. But have you ever wondered how social media platforms foster multilingualism, or how your own online language use reflects your identity? In this activity, you will delve into the power of language on social media and explore its impact on communication, identities, perspectives and power dynamics.

Read the following blog post:

THE DIGITAL VOICES

The power of multilingualism on social media: A window into our identities

Social media is a space where **languages** and **cultures** intersect, and your online language use can say a lot about who you are. In this post, we'll explore how multilingualism shapes **communication**, **identities**, **perspectives** and **power** dynamics in the digital world.

A digital linguistic repertoire

On social media, we often mix languages—whether to connect with friends or reach a global audience. This is also part of our **language and cultural portrait** that reflects both our **personal** and **cultural identities**. Multilingual users adapt to different platforms, using strategies like switching languages or incorporating emojis to communicate effectively with diverse audiences.

Communication and identity

Our **language choices** on social media reveal our identities. A post in your home language may showcase pride in your culture, while using English could help you connect with others worldwide. What does your online language say about you? It's more than just words—it's an expression of who you are.

Embracing perspectives

Multilingual content on social media allows us to see the world through different lenses. By interacting in multiple languages, we can break cultural barriers and foster **mutual understanding**. This creates a rich environment where diverse perspectives can thrive.

Power dynamics on social media

Not all languages hold the same power online. Some languages often dominate, leaving smaller linguistic communities unheard. But who holds the power in these digital conversations? Is it the **users**, the **platforms** or specific **language groups**? The answer shapes how we engage with global discussions.

In short ...

In today's world, our **linguistic repertoire** and **cultural repertoire** are constantly evolving through social media. Your language(s) reflect your identity and provide a platform to share your perspective, challenge power structures and engage in meaningful dialogue. What does your online language say about you? Let's keep exploring and understanding the power of multilingualism in our digital lives.

LEARNING ENGAGEMENT

Exploring social media as a space for multilingualism

Exploration questions

1 Think about these questions, linked to the LCS concepts, as you explore the idea of multilingualism on social media.

a Communication:

- How do multilingual individuals navigate and mix languages online?
- What strategies do people use to communicate effectively with diverse audiences?

b Identities:

- How does language choice on social media reveal or hide cultural and personal identities?
- What does your own online language say about you?

c Perspectives:

- How does multilingual content create opportunities for mutual understanding?
- What can multilingual posts teach us about embracing diverse perspectives?

d Power:

- How does the dominance of some languages affect smaller linguistic communities online?
- Who has the power in multilingual digital conversations—users, platforms or specific language groups?

Choose your pathway

2 Choose *one* of the activities below to complete.

- **Research it!** Investigate multilingual social media accounts. Look for patterns in language use. When do they switch between languages? Why? How do followers interact with multilingual content? Create a report or multimedia presentation that showcases your findings, with real examples.
- **Create your own!** Create your own multilingual social-media posts (real or simulated). Design posts in at least two languages. Think about how tone, visuals and captions cater to different audiences. Present your posts and explain your language choices, the audience you targeted and what impact you aimed to achieve.
- **Reflect on it!** Consider your personal experience with language online. When do you use different languages on social media and why? How do your language choices reflect your identity? Write a journal entry or record a spoken reflection on what your social media use reveals about your multilingual journey.
- **Take action!** Design a feature for a social media app that promotes multilingual inclusivity. Could it auto-translate comments? Encourage multilingual content creation? How does your feature promote fair and meaningful communication? Create a visual mock-up or pitch for your feature and explain how it works.

Reflect and connect

3 What did you discover about the role of social media in multilingualism?

4 How do the four concepts (communication, identities, perspectives, power) come to life on these platforms?

5 How has this activity changed your view of social media and multilingualism?

6 What role do you think you can play in creating inclusive online spaces?

Why does this matter?

Social media isn't just a way to connect—it's a space where languages and cultures interact in dynamic ways. By understanding how language is used online, you can appreciate the richness of multilingualism and learn to use social media as a tool for connecting, learning and including.

REAL-WORLD EXAMPLE

The world of slang

Slang is everywhere! Every language has it, even if it shows up in different ways or with different levels of importance. Whether you're swapping memes, chatting with friends or expressing frustration, slang gives language a playful, creative edge. Slang is much more than just casual words—it reflects who we are, where we come from and how we interact with the world.

So, what is slang exactly? It's an informal, often group-specific way of speaking. Think of it like secret code words for a club—whether it's a social group, an online community or even a generation. Slang helps define in-group identity and strengthen bonds.

Read the following article:

DOES SLANG EXIST IN EVERY LANGUAGE?

Yes, slang exists in every language, though its form, usage and prevalence can vary greatly across cultures and regions. Slang is a type of informal, often playful language used by specific groups of people. It typically emerges as a way to create in-group identity, differentiate social groups, or express certain attitudes or emotions in a more casual or creative manner.

A key element of communication and cultural identity

Language isn't just about words—it's a tool for **communication**. Communication refers to the exchange of meaning through language, gestures, images and other modes. It's often **multimodal**, involving both verbal and non-verbal elements, which make messages more dynamic.

One important aspect of communication is **slang**—informal language used by specific groups. Slang is part of your **linguistic repertoire**, which includes all the language tools you have for expressing yourself. It allows you to bond with friends, share humour and express cultural identity. Slang constantly evolves, reflecting **cultural changes** and trends. For example, phrases like 'ghosting' or 'lit' represent new ways of talking that emerge with time and context.

Understanding slang is essential because it helps you navigate your **cultural repertoire**—the set of experiences, symbols and values that define a group's identity. Slang not only communicates meaning, but also signals which group you belong to. It's a key element of your **language and cultural portrait**, reflecting where you come from, what you value and how you interact with others.

In communication, the success of conveying meaning depends on the shared understanding of language. Using slang in the right context helps ensure that communication is effective and meaningful, especially within specific groups. So, slang is not just a casual way of speaking—it's a crucial part of how you express and negotiate identity and culture.

LEARNING ENGAGEMENT

The world of slang

Exploration questions

1 Dive deeper into slang through the lens of the four LCS concepts: communication, identities, perspectives and power. The following are some guiding questions to think about as you explore.

- a Communication:
  - How does slang create its own special kind of communication?
  - In what ways can slang be misunderstood across groups or generations?
- b Identities:
  - How does the slang you use reflect who you are?
  - What does slang say about your community, age group or culture?
- c Perspectives:
  - How might people's views on slang differ across cultures or generations?
  - What does the slang from another culture teach us about their way of life?
- d Power:
  - Who decides which slang becomes popular and which fades away?
  - Can slang be a tool for social power or exclusion?

Choose your pathway

2 Choose *one* of the activities below:

- **Research it!** Investigate the origins of your favourite slang word or phrase. Where did it come from? Who started using it first? Use a timeline or digital map to trace its evolution.
- **Create your own!** What could your own personal or community slang look like? Think of 5–10 existing slang words and phrases. Then create some new relevant slang words and phrases. Create a visual dictionary or memes to help others learn them.
- **Reflect on it!** Consider your personal experience with slang. Think about a time when you used slang but weren't understood (or when someone used slang that you didn't understand). What was the result? How did it make you feel about communication and identity? Write a journal entry or record a spoken reflection on how your understanding about slang impacts your multilingual journey.
- **Take action!** Host a 'slang showcase'. Choose slang words from different languages or regions and present their meaning. Discuss how they capture unique cultural aspects. Combine it with a creative project, like creating a short skit or dialogue using these words.

Reflect and connect

3 What did you discover about the role of slang?

4 How do the four concepts (communication, identities, perspectives, power) come to life on this topic?

5 How has this activity changed your view on this topic?

6 How would you integrate slang into your language and cultural portrait?

Why does this matter?

Slang is more than just words—it's culture in action. Whether you're reflecting on your own language use or exploring the slang of others, there's a whole world of identity and expression waiting to be discovered.

- **It's dynamic:** Slang evolves constantly as cultures and technologies change. Phrases like 'cringe', 'cap' or 'vibe' didn't exist (in the same way) a decade ago. What's next?
- **It's multimodal:** Slang doesn't just show up in words. Emojis, memes and GIFs are today's slang too! They're tools for multimodal communication, combining text and visuals for extra flavour.
- **It's personal:** What's your favourite slang word? The slang you use says something about your personality, your culture and your experiences.
- **It's cultural:** Slang captures a community's ideas, humour and values. It's your language's reflection of what's trending and what people care about.

2.3.6 Bringing the LCS concepts and portrait together

Look again at the four LCS concepts and their definitions below. In LCS, you have the opportunity to make connections between:

- your experiences and ideas
- your future goals
- LCS concepts.

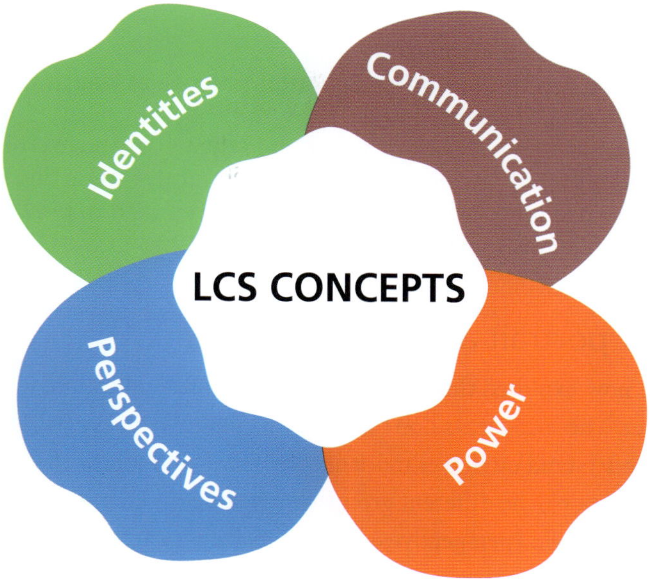

■ LCS concepts

Recapping the four LCS concepts:

Communication is the expression and exchange of meaning through language or any other mode. Communication is often multimodal, including non-linguistic elements such as body language, gestures and images. The success of communication depends on the negotiation of meaning and cooperation between individuals within a given sociocultural and situational context.

Identities refers to the particular combinations of backgrounds, dispositions and experiences that define individuals, groups, communities, organizations, objects, eras and places. Identities are complex and dynamic. They can be shaped through internal and external, present and past influences. Individual and collective identities are manifested in both tangible and intangible ways, and these identities influence our view of the world and how others view us.

Perspectives refers to the positions from which we view situations, objects, facts, ideas and opinions. Perspectives may be associated with individuals or groups, and they may be influenced by social, cultural, disciplinary, political or historical contexts. Different perspectives often lead to multiple representations and interpretations.

Power refers to the hierarchical structures, relations and processes that are formed by social, cultural, political, economic and historical factors, and that involve a person's or group's capacity to exert influence, domination or control over other individuals and groups. Power is not equally distributed in all contexts. Individuals' and communities' choices and actions can influence, or be influenced by, power structures and relations.

(Source: IB LCS guide, pp.17–18)

LEARNING ENGAGEMENT

Overlapping LCS concepts

- Read the definitions of the LCS concepts above as well as returning to your previous learning engagements.
- Notice how the LCS concepts overlap in the visual above. The LCS concepts are not independent of one another, but are constantly interacting with one another.
- List 4–6 examples from your own experiences or from previous learning engagements which show the connections and overlaps between the LCS concepts.

Your portrait and the LCS concepts

You have now explored the four LCS concepts: communication, identities, perspectives and power. These concepts don't just help us understand the world around us—they also help us understand ourselves more deeply. Think about how the way you express yourself (communication), the different groups you belong to (identities), the way you see and interpret the world (perspectives) and the influences around you (power) have shaped your personal story.

Learning journal

Refining your language and cultural portrait

Here is an opportunity to look at your language and cultural portrait again with fresh eyes.

Using the LCS concepts and key terms in the word bank below, as well as insights from the different learning engagements, add more detail and reflection to your portrait. Challenge yourself and think about your own lived experiences, future aspirations, biases and concerns, interests and objectives.

Table 2.12 Word bank

accent	culture	interdependence	perspectives
affinity	discrimination	language	positionality
belonging	dynamic	language variety	portrait
bias	empowerment	lens	power
channel	empathy	marginalization	repertoire
code	exclusion	meaning	reflection
collective	expression	medium	reflexivity
communication	heritage	modality	relationship
context	identities	multilingualism	stereotypes
cooperation	inclusion	non-verbal	symbols
criticality	interaction	participation	perspectives

Top tip!

Using the LCS concepts and the key terms introduced so far will enhance your work and allow you to demonstrate deeper understanding and reflection. Include them in your learning journal, your work in class and during the LCS review points.

2.3.7 Summary

- The four LCS concepts help you to make connections between 'language' and 'culture'.
- Using the LCS concepts across all learning engagements will support and enhance your LCS journey.
- Communication is multimodal and includes contextual elements that allow you to construct, interpret and exchange meaning effectively.
- Identities are a sum of individual and collective linguistic and cultural repertoires, which evolve over time and in interaction with new experiences.
- Perspectives enable you to explore the world through different lenses, and allow you to reflect on how your linguistic and cultural repertoires might contribute to your positionality.
- Power enables you to recognize linguistic and cultural inequalities, and the role of individual and community agency in making positive changes.

2.4 Designing your learning journey

INQUIRY QUESTIONS

- How can you choose a language/language variety and an area of exploration that aligns with your passions, aspirations and values?
- How can you take ownership of your learning to ensure it is meaningful and relevant to you?
- How can you set challenging yet achievable goals that reflect your interests and needs?
- How might your goals evolve as you gain new insights or experiences?
- How can you use different modalities to enrich your learning and your reflective and reflexive practices?
- In what ways can reflective and reflexive practices deepen the relevance of your learning engagements?
- How can your learning journey contribute to your growth as a global citizen?

Look again at the visual below, which shows the different stages of your two-year LCS learning journey. You are most probably currently engaged in the introductory unit, where you are building up an understanding of your unique and dynamic language and cultural portrait, as well as the LCS aims, outcomes and concepts. By the end of the introductory unit, you will choose one of the areas of exploration, set your goals and design your own learning engagements. In some schools, the LCS teacher might take on more responsibility for planning some learning engagements, and in other schools, the students will design all their own learning engagements. Whatever approach your school takes, it's important to remember that the LCS learning journey is *your* learning journey.

Key:
Blue = School responsibilities
Purple = LCS teacher guides you and provides an opportunity to collaborate together
Green = You are engaging in self-directed or guided, individual or collaborative learning

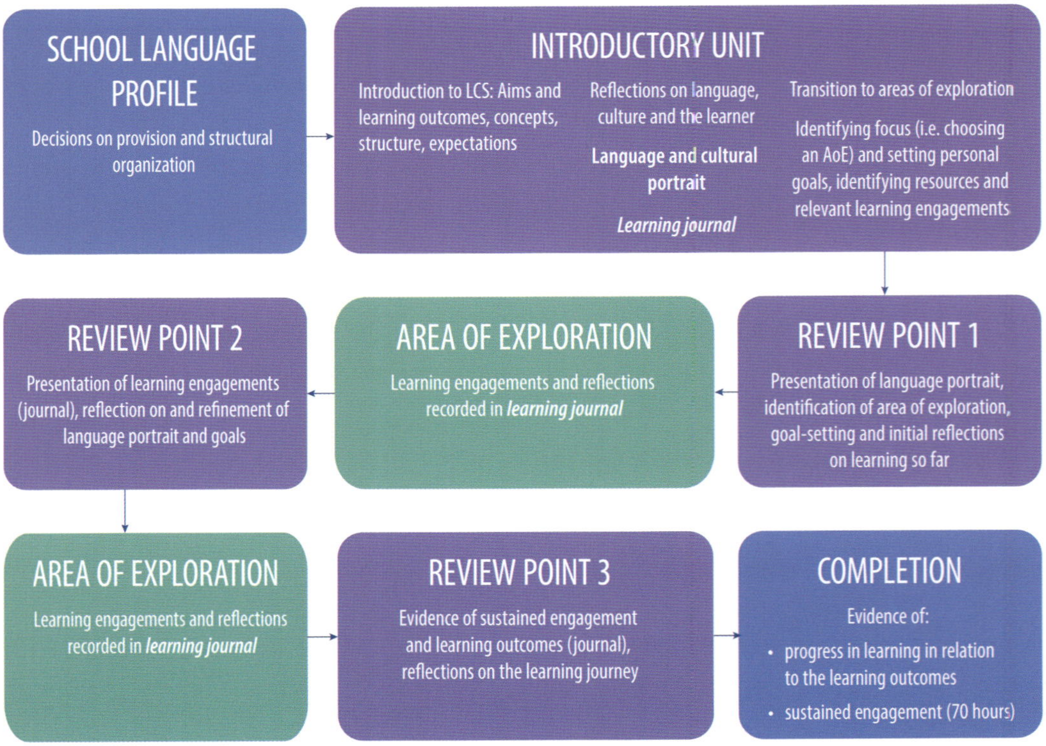

■ Linear representation of the two-year LCS learning journey (Source: IB LCS guide, p.30)

2.4.1 Areas of exploration

LEARNING ENGAGEMENT

What's your focus?

Answer each question below by choosing the option that resonates most with you. Add up how many of each shape you have chosen at the end to help you consider which areas of exploration might interest you the most.

1 What inspires you to study a new language?
- ● I'm fascinated by how it opens doors to different cultures and ways of thinking.
- ◆ It's a useful skill for professional or academic growth.
- ▲ It helps me form deeper ties with people or groups important in my life.

2 How do you prefer to use language in your life?
- ◆ To communicate effectively in formal or specialized settings.
- ● To explore personal interests, like art, history or new ways of expression.
- ▲ To celebrate traditions, share stories or collaborate with others.

3 If you could design a language project, what would it look like?
- ▲ Researching and documenting the cultural roots of a local dialect or language.
- ● Diving into a rare language to understand its unique structure and heritage.
- ◆ Creating a training module for an international work team.

4 Which situation sounds most exciting to you?
- ● Watching foreign films or reading books in another language to broaden my horizons.
- ▲ Learning traditional expressions that strengthen connections within a group.
- ◆ Preparing a multilingual pitch or presentation for an international audience.

5 What role does cultural context play in your language journey?
- ● It's fascinating to see how language reflects cultural identity.
- ▲ It's essential for maintaining or building relationships with others.
- ◆ It's important for adapting communication in professional environments.

6 If asked why you're learning languages, what would you say?
- ◆ 'It's a skill that can help me achieve my goals in education or work.'
- ▲ 'It helps me connect with people and understand their stories better.'
- ● 'It's a way to explore ideas, cultures and my own identity.'

7 What's your biggest motivation to improve your language skills?
- ● Personal growth and curiosity about diversity.
- ▲ Strengthening my sense of belonging to a particular group or community.
- ◆ The ability to handle practical tasks, like reports or formal conversations.

8 Imagine an opportunity involving language. What would you do?
- ▲ Organize a cultural event to celebrate linguistic diversity.
- ◆ Take part in an exchange program to improve industry-specific communication skills.
- ● Learn a new language purely for the intellectual challenge.

Scoring guide

Mostly ●: Personal focus

For you, language learning is about exploration and personal enrichment. You find joy in understanding different ways of thinking and expanding your cultural perspective through language.

Mostly ▲: Community focus

You value language as a way to connect deeply with others. Whether exploring cultural traditions or strengthening ties within a group, your journey is all about fostering connections and honouring stories.

Mostly ◆: Career focus

Your strength lies in structured and purposeful tasks. You view language as a tool for success in professional or academic contexts, whether it's presentations, networking or written communication.

The LCS areas of exploration offer you three possible pathways through your learning journey:

- personal
- community
- career.

Choosing one of these areas of exploration will help you to structure and focus your learning journey in a way that is meaningful to you.

Look again at the results of the quiz you took on the previous page. Did you have a clear tendency towards one or more of the areas of exploration? See the visual below for more details about each area of exploration.

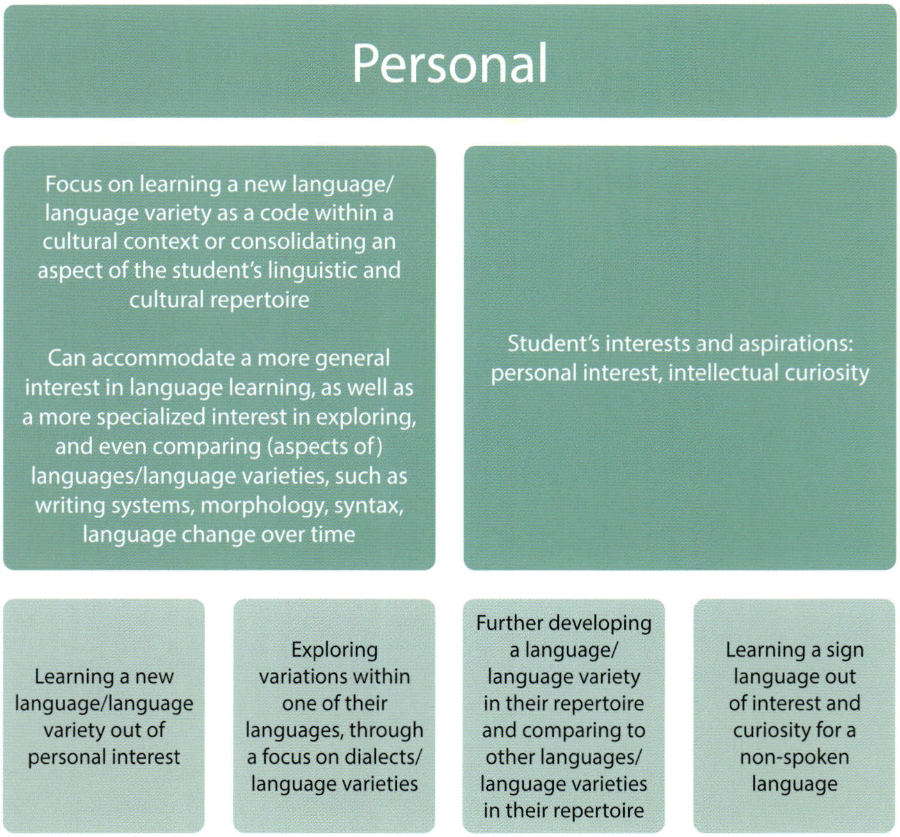

■ Area of exploration: Personal (Source: IB LCS TSM, p.32)

Key term

◆ **Heritage languages:** There are languages with which one has historical, cultural and/or personal connections. Heritage languages often exist alongside the dominant/official languages in your context. Heritage language speakers might also be able to read and write in the language, or they might speak and understand the language to varying degrees. Alternative terms include 'community language', 'home language', 'home background language' and 'minority language'.

Community

Focus on a language/language variety within the context of a local or global community or linked to personal/family, cultural or historical connections with a community

Student's interests and aspirations: create, consolidate or renew connections

- Learning or extending a personally or culturally significant language, such as a heritage language
- Learning or further developing host country/community language
- Exploring an Indigenous language (including endangered or revitalized languages) or a minority-spoken or -signed languages in the local or wider community
- Learning a signed language to engage with deaf and hard of hearing community in the area

■ Area of exploration: Community (Source: IB LCS TSM, p.31)

Career

Focus on language and intercultural capabilities for specific purposes, either professional (related to a career field) or academic (language of instruction)

Student's interests and aspirations: practical, applied

- Expand use of a language for professional purposes (e.g. healthcare, engineering)
- Consolidating the language of instruction
- Using an internship to create authentic, immersive learning opportunities
- Learning a new spoken or signed language to support engagement in a career field (e.g. healthcare, education, the arts)

■ Area of exploration: Career (Source: IB LCS TSM, p.31)

Learning journal

What if?

You will need to choose one area of exploration in LCS. In this learning engagement, you will think about what possibilities would be open to you if you were to choose either career, community or personal. This will be influenced by your unique language and cultural portrait, your passions and interests, as well as your career-related study and the rest of the CP Core.

Complete the brainstorm boards in the following visual and add them to your learning journal.

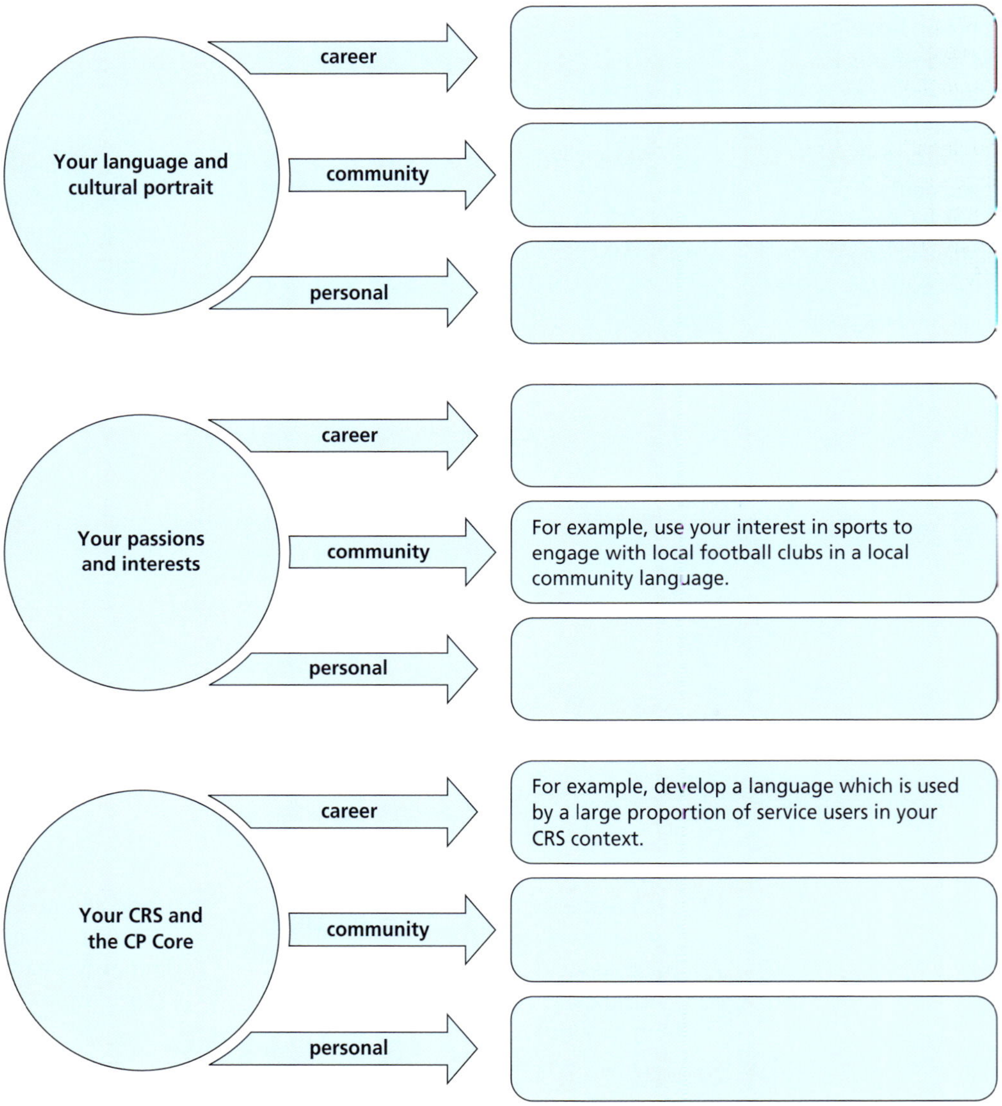

■ Areas of exploration brainstorm

It's almost decision time!

At this point, which area of exploration do you think will be the best option for you in LCS? Why do you think this?

Choice of language/language variety

In LCS, in order to set relevant goals you will choose a language/language variety that connects to your area of exploration (career, community, personal). This choice helps guide and refine your LCS goals and drive your LCS learning journey, as well as meeting the LCS aims of expanding your linguistic and cultural repertoires to new domains of use.

But how can you choose your language/language variety?

If you speak or know more than one language (you identify as multilingual), you can:

- further develop a language/language variety you already know
- choose a new language/language variety that interests you.

If you speak or know one language (you identify as monolingual), you can:

- choose a new language/language variety to explore.

You do not need to develop all four language skills as you would normally do in a language course. You can also choose to focus on just one aspect of your language/language variety, such as speaking or reading.

The language/language variety you choose must be a natural language, which includes spoken and signed languages, and does not include 'dead', classical or computer-programming languages.

Top tip!

When you make your choice of language/language variety, remember that in LCS you need to use the language/language variety for authentic communication in different contexts.

2.4.2 LCS goal(s)

Setting, monitoring and refining your LCS goals is stated explicitly in the second LCS learning outcome.

> ***Learning outcome 2:*** *Identify your own strengths and aspirations, set personally relevant goals, and monitor your multilingual and intercultural learning through ongoing reflection.*

(Source: IB LCS guide, p.10)

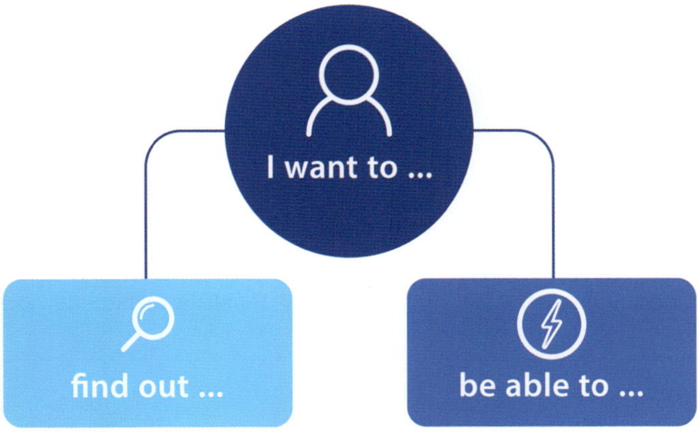

Goal-setting (Source: IB LCS guide, p.33)

Look at the visual and the learning engagement below to think about your own linguistic and cultural goal(s).

Learning journal

3P goal setting

The three 'P's are precision, purpose and progress!

Use the questions below to start to formulate your LCS goal. Add your notes to your learning journal.

Table 2.13 3P goal setting

Precision	**Purpose**	**Progress**
What do I want to *find out*?	*Why* do I want to achieve this goal/these goals?	How will I *measure* my progress? What will you track to see if you are improving? Set checkpoints for tracking your progress.
What do I want to be able *to do*?	*Where* and *with whom* do I want to be able to engage with this language/language variety?	What *specific actions* will I take and by when? Break the goals down into small, clear steps you can take daily or weekly. Set deadlines.
What *language/language variety* am I considering? What *aspect* of the language/language variety will be my focus (understanding/speaking/literacy)?	What *aspects of culture* will help me achieve this? Explain the motivation or reason behind your goals.	

2.4.3 Combining your area of exploration and goals

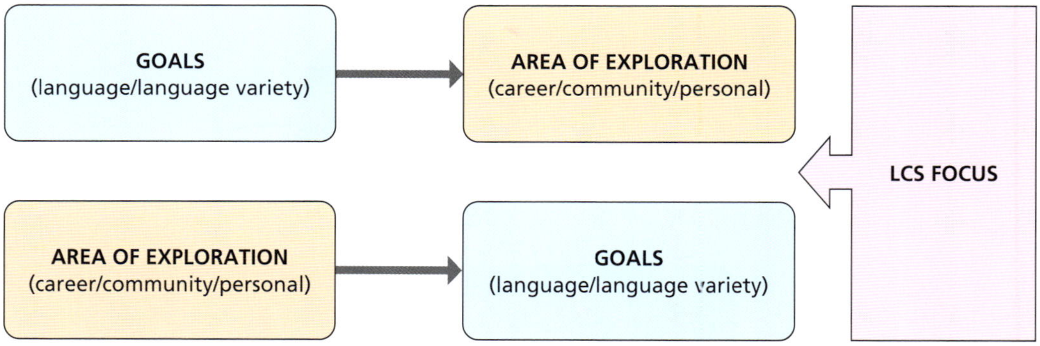

Arriving at your LCS focus

It is now time to choose your area of exploration and state your LCS goals. Some students choose their area of exploration first and then their language/language goals, while other students might have clear goals in mind and then choose which area of exploration will give them a specific focus. Your goals also include stating which language/language variety and which aspect(s) of language (listening, speaking, reading and/or writing) will be your focus.

Your LCS focus will guide you throughout your LCS learning journey and, as a result, might need to be refined over time as your linguistic and cultural repertoire and your own understandings evolve.

Learning journal

My LCS focus and goals

1 Look at the examples of some LCS goals below:
- I want to develop my ability to speak Thai, my heritage language, so that I can communicate with my grandmother and cousins when I visit Thailand.
- I want to develop my ability to communicate with the deaf/deaf community using Danish Sign Language so that I can apply this to my interest in inclusive performing arts.
- I want to improve my formal, written Arabic so that I can prepare myself to engage in a wider professional network in the Middle East.

2 Write down your LCS area of exploration and LCS goals in a central position in your learning journal.

3 Use the check list below to check your decisions and then arrange to meet with your LCS teacher to discuss them. Refine your goals if needed.

My area of exploration and goals:

☐ link to my current linguistic and cultural repertoire
☐ connect to LCS learning outcomes
☐ are underpinned by LCS concepts
☐ show how language and culture are intertwined
☐ will be challenging enough for me over the two-year LCS course.

Top tip!

Check carefully that your LCS focus and goals take into account all of these elements.

2.4.4 Authentic learning experiences

In LCS, you have the opportunity to design your own learning engagements outside of the classroom in authentic settings. This might be at a friend's house, in a professional setting, in your sports club or even in your local shopping centre.

LEARNING ENGAGEMENT

Poetry

Read the acrostic poem below:

AUTHENTIC

Actively explore, question and engage,
Uncovering truths from the past to the present.
Transform ideas through a lens of inquiry,
How language and culture shape us again and again.
Engage with concepts that challenge and expand,
Nurturing connections that help us understand.
Think deeply and let perspectives grow,
Integrate knowledge, make meanings flow.
Culture, identity, society in play—
Authentic learning opens the way.

1 Create an acrostic poem with your LCS team, your teacher or other students, using one or many languages, for the word 'experiences'.

2 Reflect on the difference between 'authentic learning experiences' and 'traditional school learning' by copying and completing the following table. It might help you to use the question words: who, why, where, what, when, how.

Table 2.14 Authentic learning experience versus traditional school learning

Authentic learning experiences	Traditional school learning

3 Why do you think you need to engage in 'authentic learning experiences' in order to meet the LCS learning outcomes? Write your answer in the form of an advertising slogan or a social-media post which could be used to promote LCS.

Top tip!

Share this with your LCS teacher or CP co-ordinator, who might like to share it with the wider school community.

Some authentic examples

Read the stories below from students around the world who have engaged in authentic learning experiences as part of their LCS learning journeys. Many of these learning engagements took place before the students had set their LCS goals and chosen their language/language variety and area of exploration.

REAL-WORLD EXAMPLE

Gloria: A survey of the languages and cultures in my school community

'When we started the LCS introductory unit, I started to notice the different languages present in my international school in Vietnam. I speak Italian at home with my parents, but tend to use English with my siblings and always English at school. I contacted the school's admissions department to ask about the data they had on student home languages and realized that they based all of their data on student passports, which does not always give a good indication of the languages students know and use on a daily basis. With the permission of the senior leadership team, I put together a survey which asked more in-depth questions about students' languages, as well as their previous schooling histories. I also included a more open question about how they felt about their different languages. My LCS teacher shared the 'school orientation tool' to help me. The digital survey was sent to all secondary students and time was given during tutor time to complete it. The data was anonymous and I was able to use my skills with spreadsheets to produce some interesting data. I was invited to share my findings with the admission department and the senior leadership team, and they have decided to do this on an annual basis as this will help them to better understand the school community and possibly make some decisions on curriculum too.'

Top tip!

The school language portrait tool is the first step your school took to set up the LCS programme.

REAL-WORLD EXAMPLE

Thandiwe: Interviewing my grandmother

'I was born in Zimbabwe, but have been living in the UK since I was five. I speak English at home with my family, but have grown up hearing my parents speak to their siblings and parents in Shona. Since starting LCS, I have been thinking about how it is a shame that my parents did not pass on Shona to me and my brother. I have only gone back to Zimbabwe twice since we left and so my aunts, uncles, cousins and grandparents will use English with me, although between themselves they tend to switch between Shona and English. When I discussed it with my parents, they said that they were worried about us 'fitting in' in the UK and switched to using English with us at home.

My grandmother is now living at my auntie's house in Harare and I felt the need to know more about her life and 'where I come from'. I prepared a set of questions, knowing that they would help me to ask everything I wanted to know. My cousin helped my grandmother use a laptop and we had a wonderful chat over a video call. She told me about her childhood and how she noticed English becoming more and more present in daily life. She seemed so pleased that I was interested in knowing more about her life! I have decided that I am going to have Shona as my language for LCS and plan to have regular calls with my grandmother where I will ask her to help me practise some basic Shona so that next time I visit Zimbabwe, I can feel more confident to speak.'

REAL-WORLD EXAMPLE

Manon: Planning my next trip to France (living in Oman)

'I have been living in Oman for the past eight years and before that I was in Ghana, where I had most of my primary school education. I speak French at home with my mother and also, weirdly, use it with my new kitten! Sometimes, when I am telling my mom about my day at school, I switch a bit to English too. When I go back to France in the summer break every year, it always takes me a few days to get back into the habit of using French all the time—my cousins, grandparents and aunts and uncles don't speak any English. This year, for the very first time, I am going to France to stay with family in Bordeaux all by myself. I am quite nervous about it, but also really excited! My cousin has gotten us concert tickets for her favourite French rap artist and I have been listening to the music and trying to understand the lyrics. I am learning words that I would never use at home with my mom! My aunt and grandparents know that I love going to see plays, and have asked me what I would like to see, so I have been researching what is on at the theatre over the summer. My LCS goal is to further develop my home language, French, by expanding the contexts I use it in (which is currently limited to my home). I am using this summer break as a series of learning engagements and will keep a record of them in my learning journal.'

REAL-WORLD EXAMPLE

Joep: Collaborating with my school's marketing department

'I am a Dutch national and have always lived in Den Haag, the Netherlands. My parents decided to put me in a CP programme as I wanted to have more choice and freedom in what and how I learn. I also liked the fact that CP could already prepare me for a career in business, which is what I have always been interested in. My father started the family business when he was in his twenties and I imagine that I will also do something similar. Switching from a Dutch secondary school to the IB school, which is taught in English, two years ago was a bit of a challenge for me, but I am now quite comfortable doing academic work in both languages. I am quite active on social media (using a mix of Dutch and English) and was interested in how the school markets itself to international students, as well as local students such as myself. I asked for an appointment with the head of marketing, where I explained my interest in business and marketing, as well as my LCS goal, which is to develop my business English. Initially, I was just hoping to do an interview and record this in my learning journal, however, this conversation led to something greater! I will be spending an afternoon a week as an intern in the school's marketing department, helping them to post on a new social media platform. We have also had conversations about possibly doing some posting in Dutch to attract local families, such as myself, to the school.'

LEARNING ENGAGEMENT

Approaches to learning

In LCS, you are encouraged to actively develop your thinking, research, communication, social and self-management skills as a learner.

Look at the table below and find examples for each of the skills from Gloria, Thadiwe, Manon and Joep's stories.

Table 2.15

Thinking skills	• Critically examining attitudes to linguistic and cultural practices • Transferring understandings from other areas of learning • Using new knowledge and insights to reformulate goals and perspectives
Research skills	• Formulating intriguing questions which will support 'doing' and 'knowing' • Selecting resources (including human) to reach your goals
Communication skills	• Using communication skills in new contexts • Evaluating effective communication
Social skills	• Developing active listening abilities to better understand diverse perspectives in a respectful manner • Collaborating with others to develop further reflections
Self-management skills	• Taking advantage of the opportunities in LCS to explore your own unique learning journey • Developing perseverance and independence in your own learning journey

Your first learning engagements

When you plan and take part in learning engagements, you need to be sure that you are working towards the LCS learning outcomes, as well as making connections to the LCS concepts. You will need evidence of this in your learning journal. Look below at how Farid planned his learning engagement.

REAL-WORLD EXAMPLE

Farid: Exploring my heritage language through storytelling

'When I started LCS, I realized I hadn't really thought deeply about how connected I was (or wasn't) to my heritage language, Dari from Afghanistan. I was born in Canada, and I mostly speak English and French. At home, my grandparents sometimes speak Dari with me, but I usually respond in English. I had always thought of Dari as something that belonged to my grandparents' world, not mine.

During the introductory unit, we were asked to reflect on our language and cultural portrait, and it made me curious: What would it feel like to speak Dari more confidently? I decided to focus on my heritage language for my first learning engagement and explore how language carries culture—especially through storytelling.

I asked my grandmother to tell me a few traditional Afghan stories that she remembered from her childhood. I recorded the conversations with her permission and then worked with her to transcribe and translate them into English. I was surprised by the richness of the imagery and cultural references—some things I had never heard before.

As part of the project, I made a bilingual picture book using the stories, with text in both Dari and English. I shared it with my younger cousins who don't speak much Dari, and it sparked a really interesting conversation about how we relate to our culture in different ways.

This learning engagement helped me understand how much identity, memory and emotion are wrapped up in language. It also made me reflect on the role I can play in keeping my heritage language alive—not just for me, but for others in my family too.'

■ **Table 2.16**

Authentic learning experiences planner	
My area of exploration:	Community
My LCS goals:	To explore and strengthen my connection with my heritage language, Dari, through storytelling with my grandmother.
Guiding questions:	What role does my heritage language play in shaping who I am? How does storytelling carry cultural meaning across generations? How can I use my language skills to connect with younger members of my family?
Links to LCS concepts:	
Communication: Exploring bilingual storytelling in Dari and English, and how language can convey emotion, tradition and identity.	**Identities:** Reflecting on my multilingual identity and discovering a stronger connection to my Afghan heritage through language.
Perspectives: Gaining insight into the lived experiences of older generations in my family and the cultural values embedded in their stories.	**Power:** Recognizing how language shift can marginalize heritage languages over time and how individuals can reclaim space for their languages within families and communities.
Learning outcome links: LO1: Articulated how my identity is shaped by reconnecting with my heritage language, expand my linguistic and cultural repertoire and engaging with the cultural values in family storytelling LO2: Set a personal goal to strengthen my connection with Dari and documented my journey through reflections and the creation of a bilingual book LO3: Applied communication skills by recording, transcribing, translating, and presenting the stories in a format accessible to younger family members LO4: Practised reflexivity by questioning my assumptions about my own language use, examining emotional responses, and exploring my position in keeping the language alive	
Practical steps/resources: • Reflected on my language and cultural portrait • Set a goal around Dari and storytelling • Interviewed my grandmother and recorded stories • Transcribed and translated stories with her support • Created a bilingual picture book • Shared the book with family and reflected on their responses	**Feedback/ideas:** • Consider sharing the picture book more widely (e.g. community centre or school library) • Could explore storytelling from other relatives for different perspectives • Reflect on how this experience might influence future language use in the family • Think about using more modalities: audio recordings, illustrations, or voiceovers in both languages

Top tip!

You can use or adapt this planner to design your own LCS learning engagements throughout your LCS journey, or your teacher might provide an alternative planner for you to use.

LEARNING ENGAGEMENT

A learning engagement planner

Look at the authentic learning experiences planner below. Choose one of the examples from the previous pages (Gloria, Thandiwe, Manon or Joep), then copy and fill in the planner as if you were that student.

Table 2.17 Authentic learning experiences planner

My area of exploration:	
My LCS goals:	
Guiding questions:	
Links to LCS concepts:	
Communication:	**Identities:**
Perspectives:	**Power:**
Learning outcome links: LO1: LO2: LO3: LO4:	
Practical steps/resources:	**Feedback/ideas:**

You will now start to plan one of your own learning engagements. This is a skill which is not only important to develop for LCS, but also for other parts of the Core, such as in personal and professional skills (PPS). You will notice that some of the suggested PPS activities could also be used as an authentic LCS learning experience.

Links

In PPS, the learning process considers 'act' as one of the stages of inquiry.

Act: apply new skills and understandings in a personal or professional context.

Depending on the nature of the inquiry, students might engage in a range of activities that are relevant to the specific concept, context, content or skill being explored. For example, students might:

- engage in peer discussions
- create a project
- visit a museum
- take part in an event
- develop and implement strategies
- take an active role within the school or community
- organize or host an event
- design and implement solutions. (Source: IB PPS guide, p.32)

Top tip!

You might choose at this point to collaborate with another LCS learner and create a learning engagement together, in particular if you have similar areas of exploration or goals.

Learning journal

Designing your own learning engagement

You have just read some examples of authentic learning experiences, which should show you the unlimited possibilities open to you.

- Look at your LCS focus (area of exploration and language goal(s)) and use the planner on the previous page to outline an authentic learning experience of your own.
- Share your planner with three different people (e.g. an LCS co-learner, a teacher, a friend, a family member).
- Record their ideas and feedback on your planner and make any necessary adjustments to your planned learning engagement.

What is student agency?

Student agency means you are in the driver's seat of your own learning. It's about having a *voice* in what and how you learn, making *choices* that reflect your interests and taking action to explore real questions that matter to you. With agency, you're not just following instructions! You are *solving problems, making decisions* and taking *ownership* of your learning journey. It's about being curious, reflective and confident in shaping your path as a multilingual and intercultural communicator.

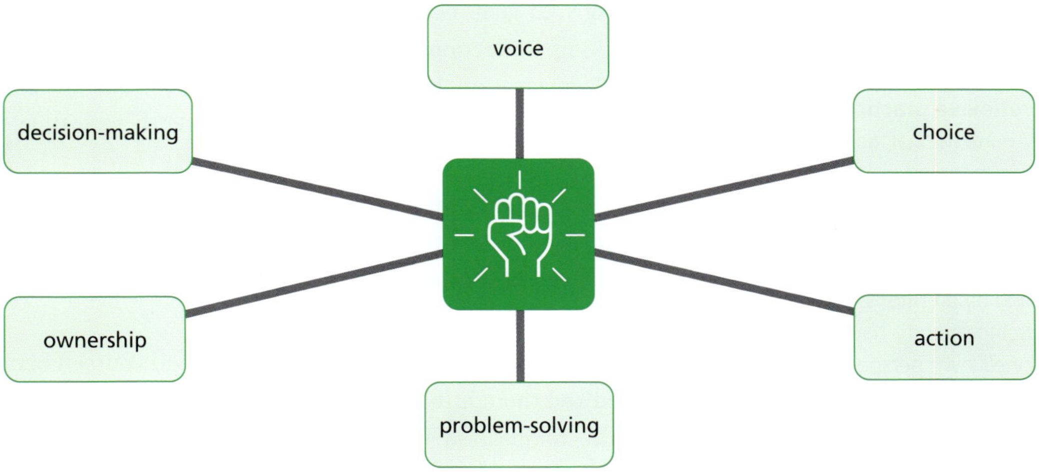

Agency

2.4.5 Reflection and reflexivity

Learner profile

Thinkers use critical-thinking skills to be able to understand the complex ways in which language and culture interrelate.

Reflective learners examine and question their own views about language and culture. (Source: IB LCS guide, p.8)

REAL-WORLD EXAMPLE

To tip or not to tip? That is the question

During a trip to Japan, Alice, a traveller from the United States, visits a local restaurant known for its traditional meals. The food and service are exceptional and Alice feels deeply impressed. Out of gratitude, she decides to leave a generous tip on the table. As she gets up to leave, she notices that the server, Hiro, seems uncomfortable and hesitant.

Hiro glances at the money but does not take it. Feeling self-conscious, Alice wonders if she may have offended him. She smiles awkwardly and prepares to leave, but inside, she feels hurt. 'I was just trying to show my appreciation,' she thinks to herself.

Hiro confides in the manager, who understands that tipping is not a common practice in Japan. For many, it could even be seen as implying that the server needs financial help, which might come across as patronizing. Hiro feels conflicted—on one hand, he appreciates Alice's kindness; on the other, he feels unsure how to respond without causing discomfort.

Afterwards, the manager kindly approaches Alice and explains the cultural context. She listens attentively and feels a mix of emotions—embarrassment for her *faux pas* (unintentional mistake) and relief at understanding the situation. She reflects, 'I thought tipping was always a good gesture, but now I realize it's not universal.'

■ A closer look at reflection and reflexivity

In LCS, one of your goals is to develop the ability to reflect on your own experiences, ideas and ways of thinking. **Reflection** means taking time to look back on what you've done or thought, whether in a conversation, an activity, or even in your daily life, and asking yourself what you learned, how you felt and what you might do differently next time. It is about analysing actions and their outcomes.

We also go a step further with **reflexivity**. This is when you think more deeply about why you reacted a certain way, how your background, assumptions, values or beliefs may have shaped your response, and how others might experience things differently. Reflexivity aims to answer the question, 'What does this mean for me now?'

Being reflective and reflexive helps you to understand yourself better and become more open-minded and thoughtful when interacting with others. This is a big part of what LCS is about: learning to question, understand and grow from your own experiences and from what you learn about language and culture.

Key term

◆ **Reflective and reflexive practice:** An intentional, active and ongoing process of reviewing one's thinking, practice and actions, examining views and assumptions, and being open to having one's own perspectives challenged and changed. (Source: IB LCS guide, p.52)

LEARNING ENGAGEMENT

A story of cultural misunderstanding

Thinking of the story about Alice and Hiro, read and discuss the questions below in pairs or small groups.

Understanding the story

What happened in the story?

Why might there have been a misunderstanding?

How did each character respond to the situation?

What specific actions contributed to the misunderstanding?

Evaluating actions and impact

How did Alice's action of leaving a tip impact Hiro?

How did Hiro's reaction impact Alice?

Could the misunderstanding in the story have been avoided? How?

What strategies could the tourist use to engage positively and adapt to cultural norms?

Connecting actions to a broader context

What role did cultural norms around hospitality and tipping play in this exchange?

How can this situation help us understand the challenges of navigating cultural differences?

Exploring personal beliefs

What assumptions did Alice or Hiro hold that led to the miscommunication?

Where do their viewpoints about tipping or hospitality come from?

What biases might Alice or Hiro have brought into the interaction?

Have you ever found yourself holding assumptions in a cultural exchange? What was the impact?

Examining collective beliefs

How do different cultures assign value to actions like tipping or showing gratitude?

Why might tipping be perceived differently in Hiro's community compared to Alice's?

How do collective beliefs shape our expectations of others in intercultural settings?

Questioning positionality

How might your own cultural background and experiences shape your interpretation of this story?

What did this activity teach you about your own assumptions or biases?

How can reflecting on this scenario influence the way you approach future cross-cultural interactions?

Look at each question and consider whether it focuses more on analysing actions and their outcomes, or on examining beliefs, assumptions and values. Sort the questions into the two categories on the right: reflection or reflexivity.

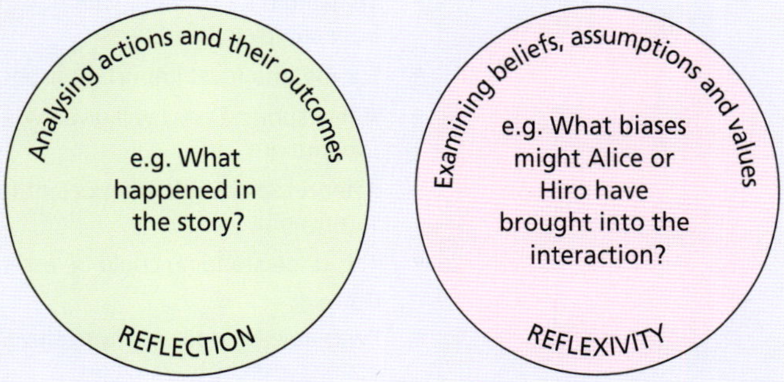

Learning journal

What did this activity teach you about your own biases or assumptions? Think of similar experiences you have lived or observed, and record your reflection and reflexive thoughts in your learning journal. Use the questions above to guide you.

Top tip!

Reflexivity is one of the four LCS learning outcomes, and so it is important to understand what it is and how to do it. Remember to record your reflexive practice in your learning journal!

Through reflection and reflexivity, you develop a deeper understanding of linguistic and cultural experiences, uncovering the layers of assumptions and biases that shape your perspectives. This critical self-awareness serves as a bridge between your personal identity and intercultural understanding, fostering a continuous journey of inquiry (adapted from IB LCS TSM, p.38).

You can choose how you practise reflection and reflexivity in ways that match your learning preferences, styles and interests. By exploring different modalities and settings, you can make these activities more meaningful and challenging for yourself. Having a say in how you engage helps make the process more authentic and personal. Your choice, your voice—the possibilities are endless!

2.4.6 Revisiting your language and cultural portrait

Your language and cultural portrait is constantly undergoing change as you expand your linguistic and cultural repertoires, as well as when you gain new insights into your portrait with reflexive practice.

Reflection and reflexivity

Mirror, mirror: A reflective and reflexive look at my portrait

Go back to your language and cultural portrait in your learning journal and refine it using reflective and reflexive practices.

Then choose one of your LCS learning engagements and review it using reflective and reflexive practices.

You could use the following sentence starters to guide you:

Table 2.18 Sentence starters (Selection taken from IB LCS TSM, p.28)

Reflection (action-oriented)	Reflexivity (beliefs and values)
• Today/recently I discovered … • The most significant issue arising from this experience was … • At the time I felt that … • This experience has highlighted that I need to develop my skills … • Thinking back to then, I am now able to see how complex the issue is … • For me, the most important aspect was … • A few suggestions I will give myself moving forward are … • After researching the important facts, I was surprised by … • This understanding could be essential for me in my … • I was able to see how my positive/negative actions affect others when …	• Initially, I never questioned … • I now realize that I was assuming that … • This experience has led me to question … • My comprehension/understanding/knowledge was expanded after/when I … • I slowly changed my mind about … • One way for me to challenge collective assumptions could be … • I now realize how my perceptions are shaped by … • I was able to see that my assumptions and attitudes come from … • This new insight/knowledge/understanding is essential for me because … • If we really want to make a difference, then …

2.4.7 Summary

- LCS promotes agency for you to take a lead in designing your own learning.
- Take ownership of your learning by choosing an area of exploration, setting personal goals and actively engaging in your learning journey to ensure it is authentic, relevant and meaningful to you.
- Revise your goals and refine your language and cultural portrait as your understanding deepens and your experiences evolve.
- Enrich your learning, your reflective and reflexive practices through diverse modalities by using different methods or settings (visual, auditory, experiential, collaborative) to enhance your learning.
- Use reflective and reflexive practices to ensure your learning journey is meaningful and contributes to your growth as a global citizen.
- Reflections allow you to:
  - enhance your awareness of your learning process
  - appreciate new, changed understanding or insight and critically analyse impacts and actions.
- Reflexivity allows you to:
  - consider your positionality and identify and question your own assumptions, biases and their impact
  - critically examine and challenge collective assumptions, values and frames of reference and understand their contexts.

2.5 Assessment in LCS

INQUIRY QUESTIONS

- How can being knowledgeable about assessment in LCS help you work more efficiently?
- How can you make good use of assessment tools to articulate your understanding and progress?
- How can you integrate and showcase your understanding of the learning outcomes to demonstrate a successful LCS learning journey?
- How can feedback help you to understand where you are and what the next steps are in your LCS learning journey?
- How can you prepare for review points?

In this section, we'll take a closer look at how your learning in LCS is assessed. We will explore how you can show progress towards the four LCS learning outcomes by reviewing the work you've done so far. You will also look at how to use your learning journal—your centralized learning space—to record evidence of your learning engagements and experiences, and to demonstrate that you have engaged in LCS regularly throughout the two years. Your journal entries help you and your teacher to see your learning journey and growth over time.

At three key moments of your journey, you will pause for a review point where you'll share, evaluate and discuss your learning so far. Each review point will be followed by a reflection in your progress and reflection form. The purpose of this section is to make sure you understand all the different elements of the assessment process, so that you can confidently and successfully complete your LCS journey.

LEARNING ENGAGEMENT

Evidence your progress

Examine the three pieces of information below and answer the questions that follow.

> *'Assessment in language and cultural studies (LCS) will consider whether or not there is evidence of the learning outcomes. Some of the outcomes may be demonstrated many times in a variety of activities/learning engagements, and others occasionally, but there must be some evidence of every outcome. [...] Schools make a summative decision about the completion of the component by each student based on a holistic evaluation of the evidence.'*

(Source: IB LCS guide, p.38)

> *'The learning outcomes are central to the evidencing and completion of LCS.'*

(Source: IB LCS guide, p.40)

> *'Evidence recorded in the learning journal could include reflections that leverage multimodality, and a range of evidence of authentic learning engagements.'*

(Source: IB LCS TSM, p.41)

1. What is the place of the four LCS learning outcomes in your learning journey?
2. What is the importance of recording evidence?
3. What is the role of the learning journal?

Top tip!

Evidence in your learning journal must always be dated to show your 'sustained engagement'.

Top tip!

Get into the habit of annotating your learning journal entries with the learning outcomes to gather evidence of your progress towards meeting them.

2.5.1 LCS learning outcomes

To demonstrate progress in LCS, you will have to link your learning engagements and your reflections to the learning outcomes. You will need to have an in-depth understanding of each of the four LCS learning outcomes, as these will guide you in your LCS learning journey.

LEARNING ENGAGEMENT

LCS learning outcomes in detail

Let's break down each learning outcome into smaller, more understandable parts. This will help you really make sense of what each one means, how it connects to your learning and how you can show evidence of it in your own way. The purpose is to help you truly take ownership of these outcomes, so they become part of how you think, learn and reflect throughout the course.

On the following pages, you will find a summary of each learning outcome. Have a close look at each one and check your understanding of every word. Think about how each of the learning outcomes make links to your:

- language and cultural portrait
- area of exploration
- past and future learning engagements.

Create a summary in a modality of your choice of each of the LCS learning outcomes in your learning journal. You can then refer back to this as you plan your learning journey.

Table 2.19 Details of LCS learning outcome 1

With the goal of expanding their linguistic and cultural repertoires, students will be able to: **LEARNING OUTCOME 1: Articulate how personal identity is shaped by engaging with languages and cultures and diverse perspectives.**	
Key terms	• articulate • personal identity • engaging with languages • engaging with cultures • perspectives
LCS concepts	• identity • perspectives
Guiding questions	
My language and cultural portrait **+** **My learning engagements**	• How does my language and cultural portrait reveal the variety of languages and cultures I engage with? • What does my portrait say about my identity and how it has been shaped by my language experiences? • How well can I articulate the relationship between my identity and the languages and cultures I engage with? • What aspects of my linguistic and cultural repertoires can I analyse more critically to better understand my identity? • How can reflecting on my portrait help me recognize the connections between my personal journey and my interactions with diverse cultures? • What complexities of language and culture can I explore further through analysis and discussion? • In what ways do my interactions with diverse perspectives challenge or enrich my understanding of my identity?
What's your evidence?	• Use LCS terminology. • Link your evidence to LCS concepts.
How does LO1 help you to expand your linguistic and cultural repertoires?	

Table 2.20 Details of LCS learning outcome 2

With the goal of expanding their linguistic and cultural repertoires, students will be able to: **LEARNING OUTCOME 2: Identify their own strengths and aspirations, set personally relevant goals and monitor their multilingual and intercultural learning through ongoing reflection.**	
Key terms	• strengths • aspirations • personally relevant goals • monitor • learning • ongoing reflection
LCS concepts	• communication • perspectives
Guiding questions	
My language and cultural portrait **+** **My learning engagements**	• How does my chosen area of exploration connect to my portrait, and why will it challenge and enrich my understanding of myself? • How does my chosen area of exploration reflect my strengths and aspirations, and why is it personally meaningful to me? • What specific resources (human, technological or physical) will support me in achieving my multilingual and intercultural learning goals? • How can I use ongoing reflection and feedback to monitor my progress and adapt my goals to ensure they remain relevant? • In what ways do I celebrate milestones and reflect on challenges to deepen my understanding of my strengths and growth areas? • How can my reflections help me adjust my approach to stay aligned with my personal and intercultural aspirations?
What's your evidence?	• Use LCS terminology. • Link your evidence to LCS concepts.
How does LO2 help you to expand your linguistic and cultural repertoires?	

Table 2.21 Details of LCS learning outcome 3

With the goal of expanding their linguistic and cultural repertoires, students will be able to: **LEARNING OUTCOME 3: Apply new communicative skills and understandings to various contexts.**	
Key terms	• apply • communicative skills • communicative understandings • contexts
LCS concepts	• communication • power
Guiding questions	
My language and cultural portrait **+** **My learning engagements**	• What specific communicative skills do I aim to improve through the LCS course, and how will I prioritize these during my initial learning engagements? • How have I planned and implemented strategies to develop and apply these skills in authentic, hands-on contexts? • How do I adapt my communication methods based on feedback or when communicating in different contexts? Can I give an example? • What examples can I provide that demonstrate how I have effectively applied my communicative skills in diverse situations? • How would I analyse my communication experiences critically? What insights have I gained from both successes and challenges? • How would I describe my ability to communicate effectively as a multilingual and intercultural speaker across multiple settings? Can I reflect on ways to enhance this ability?

With the goal of expanding their linguistic and cultural repertoires, students will be able to: LEARNING OUTCOME 3: Apply new communicative skills and understandings to various contexts.	
What's your evidence?	• Use LCS terminology. • Link your evidence to LCS concepts.
How does LO3 help you to expand your linguistic and cultural repertoires?	

Table 2.22 Details of LCS learning outcome 4

With the goal of expanding their linguistic and cultural repertoires, students will be able to: LEARNING OUTCOME 4: Practice reflexivity and develop their self-awareness as communicators within and across languages and cultures.	
Key terms	• reflexivity • self-awareness • communicators within languages and cultures • communicators across languages and cultures
LCS concepts	• communication • identities • perspectives • power
Guiding questions	
My language and cultural portrait + **My learning engagements**	• Can I share a specific story where my cultural or historical background shaped the way I view the world? How does this influence how I communicate and interact with others? • How have my experiences and reflections helped me identify and question any biases in my own perspective? How might these biases change over time? • How will my learning engagements help me demonstrate critical thinking about myself and my ability to make intentional communication choices in cross-cultural settings? • Can I provide an example of how I've critically reflected on a learning engagement to better understand myself as a multilingual and intercultural communicator? • How have I demonstrated reflexivity by examining and challenging assumptions or perspectives, either my own or others'? • How do my reflections on personal identity and diverse perspectives help me build bridges of understanding and communicate effectively across cultures?
What's your evidence?	• Use LCS terminology. • Link your evidence to LCS concepts.
How does LO4 help you to expand your linguistic and cultural repertoires?	

Connecting the learning outcomes

REAL-WORLD EXAMPLE

Meet Nour

Nour is a 16-year-old CP student living in Casablanca, Morocco. She speaks Darija (Moroccan Arabic) at home, French at school, and has been learning English since she was eight. She also understands some Tamazight, spoken by her grandparents. She often moves between these languages depending on context—chatting in Darija with friends, switching to French in class, or using English online and in formal situations.

Nour has always dreamed of working in the tourism industry. For her area of exploration, she chose the 'career' path because she wants to improve her professional English and better understand how language and culture affect communication with people from around the world.

A learning engagement

As part of her LCS learning journey, Nour created a mini travel guide video in English, introducing tourists to local customs in Morocco. She focused on things international travellers might not know, like the importance of greeting people politely or how bargaining works in markets. She interviewed her uncle, who works in a hotel, to better understand how cultural knowledge matters in real workplace settings. She used this project to practise clear and respectful communication in English, especially across cultural boundaries, to explain why being culturally sensitive is important in customer service.

Nour's reflective and reflexive thoughts

'When I first thought about my identity, I just listed the languages I speak. But now I realize it's also about how I use those languages, how they connect me to different people and even how others see me. Making the travel guide helped me to develop my English language, using specific and professional vocabulary, but it also helped me to understand that every choice I make in communication (what I include and how I speak) reflects part of who I am, and that I can make sure my message is clearly understood in order to build bridges between my own and other cultures.'

How Nour's language and cultural portrait links to the LCS learning outcomes

Table 2.23

LO1: Personal identity	Nour's multilingual and multicultural background plays a central role in how she sees herself. Navigating between Arabic, French, English and Tamazight has made her more aware of the layers of her identity and how culture shapes communication and behaviour.
LO2: Strengths and aspirations	Nour recognizes that her linguistic flexibility is a strength, and that improving her English for professional communication aligns with her personal goals. She is learning to reflect on how her cultural background adds value in international settings.
LO3: Communication skills	Her repertoire allows her to adapt to different audiences and contexts. She already knows how to code-switch and adjust her tone when needed, which helps her navigate multilingual environments effectively.
LO4: Reflexivity and self-awareness	Through her multiple identities and cultural influences, Nour has begun to reflect on how her own assumptions and ways of seeing the world are shaped by her context, and how this can affect how she interacts with others.

How Nour's learning engagement links to the LCS learning outcomes

Table 2.24

LO1: Personal identity	By presenting Moroccan culture to outsiders, Nour deepened her understanding of her own cultural identity and how others might perceive it differently.
LO2: Strengths and aspirations	She set clear, personal goals to improve English for professional use, and tracked her progress through reflections and peer feedback.
LO3: Communication skills	She applied intercultural communication skills by adjusting tone, content and style depending on her audience, and thought carefully about what needed to be explained.
LO4: Reflexivity and self-awareness	Nour reflected critically on how she represents her culture. She asked herself: 'What assumptions do I have about tourists? What assumptions might they have about me?' This helped her to challenge stereotypes and broaden her perspective.

Learning journal

Use the outlines below to show how your work links to the LCS learning outcomes. Redraw the diagrams and fill in the boxes with examples that link to each LO. You can then use this as evidence in your upcoming review points.

1 How can you find evidence for each learning outcome in your language and cultural portrait?

2 How can you find evidence for each learning outcome among your learning engagements?

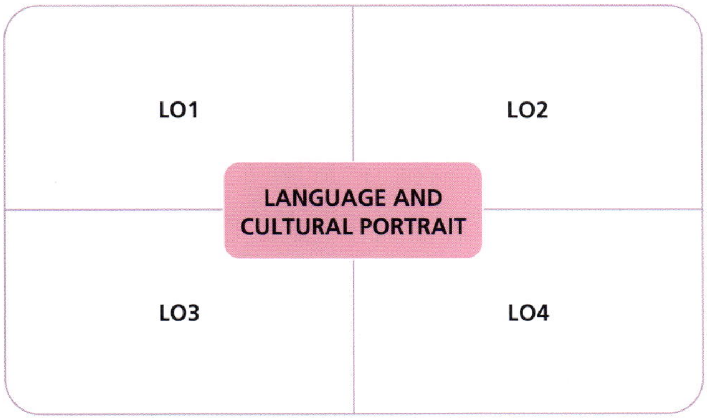

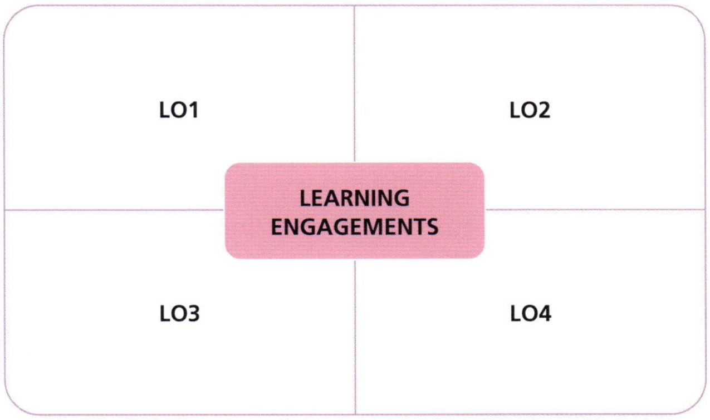

2.5.2 Review points

Top tip!

Review points are student-centred, supportive and celebratory. (Source: IB LCS guide, p.43)

In LCS, you will have three review points. The purpose of the review points is to pause, look back and celebrate your progress, as well as to discuss how things are going and help you keep moving forward with confidence. You will share evidence from your learning journal and demonstrate your understanding of the LCS concepts and learning outcomes using LCS terminology. You might talk one-to-one with your teacher, in small groups or with the whole class. These conversations are supportive, student-centred and focused on growth and not about getting things perfect. You will get feedback from your teacher and classmates, and have the chance to share your ideas, ask questions and learn from different perspectives. Think of each review point as a snapshot of your journey and a moment to check in, connect and keep growing.

Reflection and reflexivity

Look again at the linear representation of the two-year LCS learning journey in the image below and reflect on the questions that follow.

Key:
Blue = School responsibilities
Purple = LCS teacher guides you and provides an opportunity to collaborate together
Green = You are engaging in self-directed or guided, individual or collaborative learning

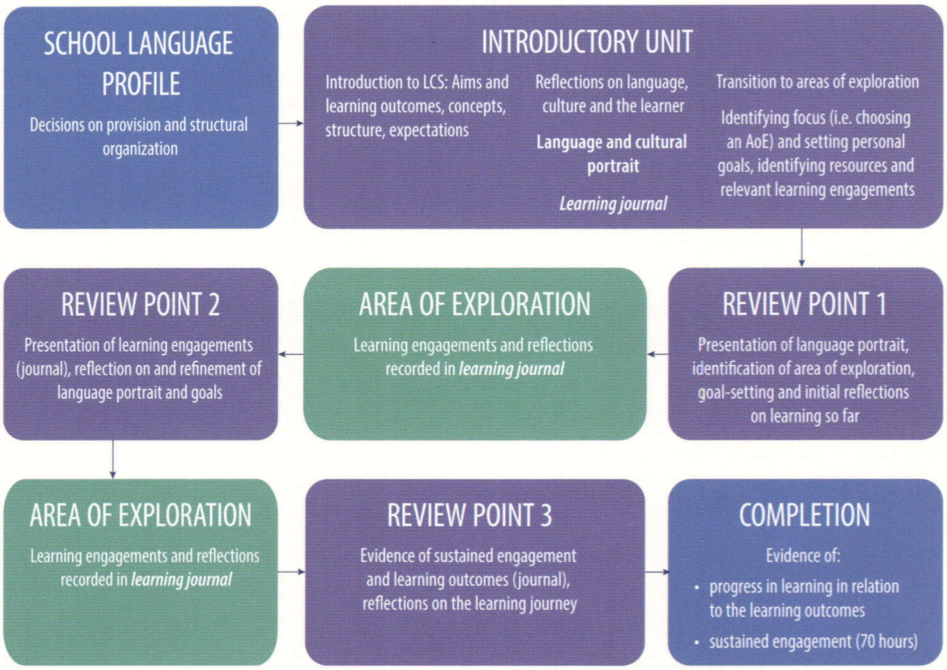

■ Linear representation of the two-year LCS learning journey (Source: IB LCS guide, p.30)

- Where are you currently on this linear learning journey?
- Where are the review points in the learning journey?
- What is the purpose of the review points?
- Where are the review points heading to?

Each review point has a specific focus and purpose, and these are outlined in the visual below.

REVIEW POINT 1	REVIEW POINT 2	REVIEW POINT 3
• Talking about the language and cultural portrait using key terminology • Articulating and justifying the chosen area of exploration • Setting challenging goals that are relevant to the LCS aims and LOs • Identifying resources for achieving goals • Describing the first planned learning engagement in line with the LOs	• Recounting and evaluating learning engagements using evidence from the learning journal • Describing achievements/progress towards the goals using key terminology • Identifying challenges to achieving goals and subsequently refining goals or revising approaches • Reflecting on any new, evolving understandings of language and culture • Demonstrating LOs	• Recounting and reflecting on learning engagements using evidence from the learning journal • Celebrating achievements/progress towards the goals using key terminology • Looking towards the future as a multilingual user and intercultural communicator • Demonstrating LOs

■ Purpose of the review points (Source: IB LCS TSM, p.47)

Review points can adopt a variety of modes, configurations and settings. You and your LCS teacher will agree on the combination which will best support your reflective and reflexive practice.

■ **Table 2.25** Modalities, configurations and settings for reflective and reflexive practice (Source: IB LCS TSM, p.37)

Modes/modalities	Configurations	Settings
• Written: paragraph (with/without guided template), annotated interview, transcribed and annotated discussion/interview • Aural/oral: guided interview, speech, informal conversation, discussions, performance • Visual: artwork, mind map • Digital: video, digital artwork, podcast • **Note:** Modalities naturally overlap; therefore, in the spirit of multimodality, a reflection could be a combination of some or all of the above (e.g. annotated photos). Students could choose to present their reflections **in any language**.	• Individual: private or shared • Small groups/pairs: interviewing one another, discussion, feedback on chosen modality, preparation for formal review points/meetings • Large group discussions: classroom, public/larger community • Digital forum: comments from peers/experts/wider community • **Note:** The configuration depends on the purpose of the reflection/ reflexive practice. Using feedback from a larger group can serve as a springboard for further reflection. There should be value in bringing thoughts to a larger group, either for yourself or for others.	• In class: formal (review points)/informal (discussions) • School community: performance, using expertise (teachers, parents), campaign, events, exhibitions • Local and/or global community: host country/countries and regions (territories), digital platforms, professional communities • **Note:** The setting/context depends on the purpose of the reflection/reflexive practice. Using feedback from experts can serve as a springboard for further reflection. There should be value in bringing thoughts to a wider audience.

LEARNING ENGAGEMENT

Reread the information above, then copy and complete the table below:

■ **Table 2.26** A closer look into the three review points

	Review point 1	Review point 2	Review point 3
Key terms			
What do you need to do?			
How are you going to present it? • Modalities • Configurations • Settings			

2.5.3 Assessment tools

The IB has prepared a number of tools that are designed to support you and your LCS teacher in assessing your progress in your LCS learning journey. These can be used to prepare and present your progress in the review points, as well as at any point along the way.

Review point questions

The purpose of these questions is to help you ensure that you are meeting the required focus of each review point, as well as touching upon each of the four LCS learning outcomes.

Table 2.27 Guiding questions: Review point 1 (Source: IB LCS toolkit)

Guiding questions: REVIEW POINT 1 ***How am I embarking on my LCS learning journey?***	
Focus: • Talking about language and cultural portrait using key terminology • Articulating and justifying the chosen area of exploration • Setting challenging goals that are relevant to the LCS aims and learning outcomes • Identifying resources for achieving goals • Describing first planned learning engagement in line with the learning outcomes	
LO1	• Could you describe yourself in terms of the languages you use and the cultures you have been exposed to? • How would you define your understanding of culture and language? Can you explain why you currently understand it in this way? Where and how do you see this in your community and in your own life? • How do you think that culture and language have influenced your experience of your own self/social identity? • What are the different linguistic/cultural groups that you belong to/identify with?
LO2	• What are your goals for LCS? • Why did you select this area of exploration? • Do you feel LCS and your area of exploration and associated goals will take you out of your comfort zone? • What resources (people, IT-based, books, courses) will you need to work towards your goals? How will you access them? • Explain in detail what you have planned for your first learning engagement.
LO3	• Explain in detail which communication skills (written/spoken) you are hoping to improve. • How will you get feedback to help you improve? • How will you measure your progress? • How and where do you plan to use your language/cultural understanding in authentic/real settings? • What have you found challenging when you find yourself in a new communicative context?
LO4	• What have you learned about yourself and other people in your class/group/school? • Can you give some examples of how your perspectives have been influenced by cultural, societal and/or historical experiences? • How have these learning engagements influenced your own understanding and attitudes towards cultural and linguistic diversity? • Can you give an example of how your assumptions and perspectives are very personal to you and how engaging with alternate perspectives has led you to new insights?

■ **Table 2.28** Guiding questions: Review point 2 (Source: IB LCS toolkit)

Guiding questions: REVIEW POINT 2 ***Where am I on my LCS learning journey?***	
Focus: • Recounting learning engagements using evidence from learning journal • Describing progress towards the goal using key terminology • Identifying challenges to achieving goals, and subsequent refining of goals • Reflecting on any new, evolving understandings of language and culture • Demonstrating learning outcomes	
LO1	• Keeping in mind your own previous definitions of language and culture, what is the purpose of language and culture in your life? In the lives of others? In other words, what do language and culture 'do' and 'represent' for you? • Do you find yourself using language and behaving differently in different contexts? Give an example and try to find reasons for this. • Do you think that some languages/cultural groups are valued more than others? How do you know and why do you think this is so? • Have your experiences so far altered your understanding of your portrait? If so, how?
LO2	• Can you take me through your learning journal? Have you found it easy/challenging to regularly engage with your chosen area of exploration and associated goals, as well as recording your progress? • Do you think that your goals are achievable within the time limit of the LCS? How will you know if you have achieved your goals? • Have you broken down your goals into smaller steps? • What is your biggest challenge to achieving your goals? • Have you discovered new strengths/skills along the way? • Have you had any unexpected discoveries along the way? • What is your next planned learning engagement and how is this contributing to you achieving your goals?
LO3	• Explain in detail a situation where you were able to use your communication skills (in a new context/with a new person). • What are the main issues/challenges you experience in using your language in new situations? • Analyse what language (structures) you still need to work on to improve your ability to communicate more confidently.
LO4	• In your learning engagements so far, what different perspectives have you encountered? Have you experienced the same event/message/etc. being interpreted differently by different people? Why did this happen? • To what extent has your learning so far helped you develop empathy, openness and an appreciation of linguistic and cultural diversity? • Can you give an example of an occasion when your use of language had an impact, positive or negative, on others? • Can you give an example of how one of your beliefs/perspectives has been changed following an exchange?

■ **Table 2.29** Guiding questions: Review point 3 (Source: IB LCS toolkit)

Guiding questions: REVIEW POINT 3 ***How am I rounding off my LCS learning journey? What will I take from it into the future?***	
Focus: • Recounting and reflecting on learning engagements using evidence from learning journal • Celebrating achievements/progress towards your goals using key terminology • Looking towards the future as a multilingual user and intercultural communicator (future portrait) • Demonstrating learning outcomes	
LO1	• If you were to present/talk about your language and cultural portrait today, would it look any different to how you talked about it at the start of the LCS? If so/if not, can you explain why? • Can you give an example of an occasion where you were able to use a language or an understanding of a particular culture to bring about something positive? • Explain how your portrait has changed over time and how you imagine/hope that your portrait will look in the future. • Are there any attitudes, perspectives or behaviours that you can now understand (better)? How have you noticed this? How does this help you be a better communicator?
LO2	• Looking at your learning journal, which learning engagements are you most proud of/excited by/ disappointed by? • Do you feel that you have mostly achieved your goals? Give concrete examples from your learning journal as evidence. • Which resources (people, IT, books, media, etc.) were the most valuable in helping you achieve your goals? Why? • Were there any unexpected achievements along the way? How/why did that surprise you? • If you were to redo the LCS, would you approach/do things differently? Why? • What would be your advice for a CP year one student starting their LCS course?
LO3	• Describe in detail one of your learning engagements, explaining the successes and challenges, and how these connected with your goals. • Has your learning helped you expand your multilingual and intercultural capabilities? • Did you find yourself using your language(s) in an unplanned/spontaneous situation? How and why did that happen? • Using your learning journal, show evidence of how you analysed language use/intercultural understanding in a particular situation.
LO4	• How does a more in-depth understanding of what language and culture are help you better understand yourself and the world around you? • Tell me the story of an experience you have had where your interpretation and understanding of someone else's point of view or perspective helped you change your own response and behaviour. This experience can be positive, negative or neutral. • Thinking of yourself as a 'lifelong learner', what do you see as your next goal in terms of language/ cultural learning?

Top tip!

The rubric can be placed in a central part of your learning journal and can be discussed during your review points, as well as at any point along your LCS learning journey.

Developmental rubric

The developmental rubric can be used by you and your teacher to assess where you are and what you need to do to continue to make progress. The rubric is organized into the three review points, and it allows you to assess yourself against each of the LCS learning outcomes.

■ **Table 2.30** Developmental rubric: Review point 1 (Source: IB LCS toolkit)

Developmental rubric: REVIEW POINT 1 ***How am I embarking on my LCS learning journey?***				
Levels of engagement	**LO1: Articulate how personal identity is shaped by engaging with languages and cultures and diverse perspectives.**	**LO2: Identify their own strengths and aspirations, set personally relevant goals, and monitor their multilingual and intercultural learning through ongoing reflection.**	**LO3: Apply communicative skills and understandings to various contexts.**	**LO4: Practise reflexivity and develop self-awareness as communicators within and across languages and cultures.**
Emerging	As I engage with my language and cultural portrait, I can mention languages I use and cultures I have encountered.	I am demonstrating limited self-regulated learning. I have identified an area of exploration and associated goals; however, the links to my language and cultural portrait need further development. I have some ideas about a first learning engagement, but still have several practical issues to consider.	I can identify a few communicative skills I am familiar with. I have not yet identified new (authentic) contexts in which to use or develop my language and intercultural skills.	I can make limited observations on my own perspectives and biases.
	I can make limited use of LCS terminology and concepts. The evidence in my learning journal is ineffective or superficial.			
Developing	With reference to my portrait, I can talk about the languages I use and the cultures I have encountered, or I feel I belong to, and describe how my linguistic and cultural repertoire interacts in different contexts.	I am starting to demonstrate self-regulated learning. I have identified an area of exploration and associated goals and can explain how this links to my language and cultural portrait. I have planned my first learning engagement, but still have some practical issues to consider.	I can talk about the communicative skills that I am hoping to improve over the course of the LCS. I can outline how I will put these skills to use in new (authentic) contexts.	I can share some examples of how my way of thinking is shaped by my culture, the society I live in and history. I can recognize some of my own biases and talk about my point of view. I can talk about how my first learning engagement will help me become more aware of how I communicate with others.
	I am starting to understand some of the LCS terminology and concepts and to use some of them in my descriptions and explanations. My learning journal shows some progress and reflection, but the evidence is underdeveloped or inconsistently balanced.			
Capable	Through engaging with my portrait, I can talk about the languages I use and the cultures I have encountered, or I feel I belong to, and how this shapes who I am. I can explain how my linguistic and cultural repertoire interacts and adapts in different contexts.	I am demonstrating self-regulated learning. I have identified an area of exploration and associated goals and can explain how this links to my portrait, as well as justifying why this will be challenging and enriching for me. I have planned my first learning engagement, and have identified some appropriate (human, technological, physical, etc.) resources.	I can talk about the communicative skills that I am hoping to improve over the course of my LCS journey as well as those I would like to focus on in the initial learning engagements. I can describe in detail how I will put these skills to use in new (authentic) contexts. I have the ability to adapt my communicative skills based on feedback or different contexts.	I can share some ways that my views are shaped by my culture, the community I live in and the past. I can think about my own views and any unfair biases I might have and see how they've changed as time goes on. I can explain how my first learning engagement is a chance for me to get better at talking and connecting with others.
	I can integrate relevant LCS terminology and concepts in my explanations of ideas and experiences. The evidence in my journal is relevant and focused, and showcases meaningful reflections.			

Developmental rubric: REVIEW POINT 1 ***How am I embarking on my LCS learning journey?***				
Levels of engagement	**LO1: Articulate how personal identity is shaped by engaging with languages and cultures and diverse perspectives.**	**LO2: Identify their own strengths and aspirations, set personally relevant goals, and monitor their multilingual and intercultural learning through ongoing reflection.**	**LO3: Apply communicative skills and understandings to various contexts.**	**LO4: Practise reflexivity and develop self-awareness as communicators within and across languages and cultures.**
Exemplary	As I engage with my portrait, I can critically analyse my linguistic and cultural repertoire. I can reflect on my personal identity and on my encounters with different languages and cultures.	I am demonstrating strong self-regulated learning and reflection. I have identified an area of exploration and associated goals and can explain in detail how this links to my portrait, as well as justifying why this will be challenging and enriching for me. I have planned my first learning engagement in detail and have identified relevant (human, technological, physical, etc.) resources. I have the ability to modify or adapt goals based on reflection and feedback.	I can explain in detail the communicative skills that I am hoping to improve over the course of the LCS as well as during the initial learning engagements. I can explain how I am planning to develop and apply these skills in new (authentic) contexts. I can show, with examples, how I can adapt my communicative skills based on feedback or different contexts.	I can share specific stories of how my views are shaped by my culture, society and history. I can think deeply about my own views and biases, question them and understand how they might have changed as time passed. I can also think about how my experiences form these views and affect the way I communicate and interact with other people. I can explain how my first learning engagement is a chance for me to show that I can think critically about myself and make my own choices in how I communicate with people from different cultures.
	I can make connections across ideas and perspectives, and analyse experiences, using LCS terminology and concepts in insightful ways. The evidence in my learning journal is thorough and purposefully balanced, showcases rich reflections and effectively captures my insights.			

■ **Table 2.31** Developmental rubric: Review point 2 (Source: IB LCS toolkit)

<table>
<tr><td colspan="5">Developmental rubric: REVIEW POINT 2
Where am I on my LCS learning journey?</td></tr>
<tr><th>Levels of engagement</th><th>LO1: Articulate how personal identity is shaped by engaging with languages and cultures and diverse perspectives.</th><th>LO2: Identify their own strengths and aspirations, set personally relevant goals, and monitor their multilingual and intercultural learning through ongoing reflection.</th><th>LO3: Apply communicative skills and understandings to various contexts.</th><th>LO4: Practise reflexivity and develop self-awareness as communicators within and across languages and cultures.</th></tr>
<tr><td rowspan="2">Emerging</td><td>I can mention basic aspects of language and culture, drawing from a few personal experiences.</td><td>I can describe my learning progress and recognize some challenges in reaching my goals.</td><td>I can recall instances where I tried using new communicative skills in different situations.</td><td>I can talk about some of my understandings, drawing on my learning engagements and learning journey as a multilingual and intercultural communicator.</td></tr>
<tr><td colspan="4">I can make limited use of LCS terminology and concepts.
The evidence in my learning journal is ineffective or superficial.</td></tr>
<tr><td rowspan="2">Developing</td><td>I can provide more detailed examples about language and culture, and their effects on my identity and my perspectives.</td><td>I can discuss my progress, identify specific challenges and consider ways to adjust my goals.</td><td>I can describe instances where I used my communicative skills in a new context.</td><td>I can talk about new, evolving understandings about my learning engagements and learning journey as a multilingual and intercultural communicator.</td></tr>
<tr><td colspan="4">I am starting to understand some of the LCS terminology and concepts and use some of them in my descriptions and explanations.
My learning journal shows some progress and reflection, but the evidence is underdeveloped or inconsistently balanced.</td></tr>
<tr><td rowspan="2">Capable</td><td>I can discuss language and culture, and how they influence identity and perspective, with increasing depth.</td><td>I can justify how I am progressing towards my goals, explain specific challenges and consider ways of overcoming them. I can adjust my goals based on feedback and reflection.</td><td>I can provide convincing examples to show how I have applied communicative skills in new contexts.
I can describe in detail how I have adjusted my communicative approach based on different contexts, and how the new contexts helped me develop new skills and understanding.</td><td>I can provide a critical reflection on my learning engagements and learning journey as a multilingual and intercultural communicator.</td></tr>
<tr><td colspan="4">I can integrate relevant LCS terminology and concepts in my explanations of ideas and experiences.
The evidence in my journal is relevant and focused and showcases meaningful reflections.</td></tr>
<tr><td rowspan="2">Exemplary</td><td>I can deeply analyse and discuss the intricacies of language and culture.</td><td>I can critically evaluate my learning journey, anticipate challenges and strategically refine my goals.</td><td>I can provide convincing examples of how I have applied my communicative skills in different contexts.
I can critically analyse and discuss my communicative experiences.</td><td>I can provide a detailed critical reflection on my learning engagements and learning journey as a multilingual and intercultural communicator.</td></tr>
<tr><td colspan="4">I can make connections across ideas and perspectives, and analyse experiences, using LCS terminology and concepts in insightful ways.
The evidence in my learning journal is thorough and purposefully balanced, showcases rich reflections and effectively captures my insights.</td></tr>
</table>

■ **Table 2.32** Developmental rubric: Review point 3 (Source: IB LCS toolkit)

Developmental rubric: REVIEW POINT 3 ***How am I rounding off my LCS learning journey? What will I take from it into the future?***				
Levels of engagement	**LO1: Articulate how personal identity is shaped by engaging with languages and cultures and diverse perspectives.**	**LO2: Identify their own strengths and aspirations, set personally relevant goals, and monitor their multilingual and intercultural learning through ongoing reflection.**	**LO3: Apply communicative skills and understandings to various contexts.**	**LO4: Practise reflexivity and develop self-awareness as communicators within and across languages and cultures.**
Emerging	I can talk about my own identity in relation to language and culture, and have some awareness of other perspectives.	I acknowledge my progress and recognize the milestones achieved towards my goals.	I can describe how I am able to be a multilingual and intercultural communicator across multiple contexts. I can envision potential scenarios where I might use the multilingual skills and intercultural understanding that I have been developing.	I have limited awareness of reflection and reflexivity when considering individual and collective assumptions, perspectives and perceptions. I have limited awareness of how personal identity can interact with multiple perspectives to bridge understanding between myself and others.
	I can make limited use of LCS terminology and concepts. The evidence in my learning journal is ineffective or superficial.			
Developing	I can talk about my understanding of my own identity in relation to language and culture, and can explain how I interact with diverse perspectives.	I can discuss my progress, identifying some achievements and areas of improvement, and make some connections to my multilingual and intercultural learning.	I can describe and explain how I am able to be a multilingual and intercultural communicator across multiple contexts.	I am increasingly aware of reflection and reflexivity by examining and challenging individual and collective assumptions, perspectives and perceptions. I can occasionally use my understanding of personal identity and multiple perspectives to bridge understanding and communication between myself and others.
	I can use some LCS terminology and concepts in my descriptions and explanations. My learning journal shows some progress and reflection, but the evidence is underdeveloped or inconsistently balanced.			
Capable	I can articulate my understanding of my own identity in relation to language and culture, and can reflect on how I interact with diverse perspectives.	I can thoroughly discuss my progress, analysing both achievements and areas of improvement, and make detailed connections to my multilingual and intercultural learning.	I can articulate and reflect on how I am able to be an effective multilingual and intercultural communicator across multiple contexts. I can describe specific future scenarios, integrating LCS concepts, where I utilize my multilingual and intercultural competencies.	I demonstrate, at times, reflection and reflexivity by examining and challenging individual and collective assumptions, perspectives and perceptions. I can generally use my understanding of personal identity and multiple perspectives to bridge understanding between myself and others, and manage communication with people from other cultures.
	I can integrate relevant LCS terminology and concepts in my explanations of ideas and experiences, and in my reflections. The evidence in my journal is relevant and focused and showcases meaningful reflections.			

<table>
<tr><th colspan="5">Developmental rubric: REVIEW POINT 3
How am I rounding off my LCS learning journey? What will I take from it into the future?</th></tr>
<tr><th>Levels of engagement</th><th>LO1: Articulate how personal identity is shaped by engaging with languages and cultures and diverse perspectives.</th><th>LO2: Identify their own strengths and aspirations, set personally relevant goals, and monitor their multilingual and intercultural learning through ongoing reflection.</th><th>LO3: Apply communicative skills and understandings to various contexts.</th><th>LO4: Practise reflexivity and develop self-awareness as communicators within and across languages and cultures.</th></tr>
<tr><td rowspan="2">**Exemplary**</td><td>I can clearly articulate my understanding of my own identity in relation to language and culture, and can critically analyse how I interact with diverse perspectives.</td><td>I critically analyse my learning journey, celebrate accomplishments, articulate what I have learned from challenges and provide insights on my multilingual and intercultural learning.</td><td>I can clearly articulate and critically reflect on how I am able to be an effective multilingual and intercultural communicator across multiple contexts.</td><td>I demonstrate reflexivity by examining and challenging individual and collective assumptions, perspectives and perceptions.
I can use my insights into personal identity and multiple perspectives to bridge understanding between myself and others, and communicate effectively with people from other cultures.</td></tr>
<tr><td colspan="4">I can make connections across ideas and perspectives, and analyse experiences, using LCS terminology and concepts in insightful ways.
The evidence in my learning journal is thorough and purposefully balanced, showcases rich reflections and effectively captures my insights.</td></tr>
</table>

Levels of engagement

The levels of engagement used in the developmental rubric can help you to assess your progress, as well as to guide you in how to better design your learning engagements and reflections.

Table 2.33 Source: IB LCS guide, p.53

Level of engagement	Generic level descriptor
Emerging engagement	Students at this stage are beginning to understand the core concepts of the course. Their knowledge is basic, and they often rely on personal experiences without delving into deeper analysis or reflection. They recognize some languages and cultures they have encountered but might not yet see the broader implications or connections. Their goals are identified but might lack depth or clarity, and they may struggle to apply their learning in diverse contexts.
Developing engagement	Students show a growing awareness of how languages and cultures influence identity and perspectives. They can relate their personal experiences to the LCS content, concepts and contexts, and are starting to plan and organize their learning. Their goals are more clearly articulated and connected to their personal experiences. They demonstrate some ability to apply their learning in new contexts, although they might still need guidance and support.
Capable engagement	Students demonstrate a solid understanding of the LCS content, concepts and contexts and can effectively use terminology and concepts. They can analyse how languages and cultures shape identity and perspectives, drawing on both personal experiences and broader contexts. Their goals are well defined, challenging and linked to a range of resources. They can independently apply their learning in diverse contexts and are beginning to reflect on their experiences, showing evidence of self-regulated learning. They recognize their own and others' situatedness in their languages and cultures.
Exemplary engagement	Students exhibit a deep and thorough understanding of how languages and cultures influence identity and perspectives. They critically analyse and reflect on their experiences, demonstrating a mature understanding of LCS terminology and concepts. Their goals are comprehensive, well reasoned, and show anticipation of challenges. They adeptly apply their learning in diverse contexts, justifying their choices, and their reflections are detailed and insightful. They recognize their own and others' situatedness in their languages and cultures, and often challenge their own and others' assumptions and preconceptions.

Progress and reflection form

You will complete a progress and reflection form before and/or after each review point. This form must be kept in a central position in your learning journal, as this will support your LCS teacher's decision for LCS completion.

Table 2.34 Source: IB LCS guide, p.54

Language and cultural studies **Progress and reflection form**			
Student name:		**Session:**	
Review point 1	**Student reflection** *Can be written (by hand/typed) or spoken (recorded voice/video with a link pasted here)*	**Date**	**Teacher signature**
Review point 2	**Student reflection** *Can be written (by hand/typed) or spoken (recorded voice/video with a link pasted here)*	**Date**	**Teacher signature**
Review point 3	**Student reflection** *Can be written (by hand/typed) or spoken (recorded voice/video with a link pasted here)*	**Date**	**Teacher signature**
	Teacher comments		

2.5.4 Tips for a successful LCS learning journey

LEARNING ENGAGEMENT

Refining your language and cultural portrait

Read these different attempts by one of your co-learners to present their language and cultural portrait. Look at the assigned level of engagement (in Table 2.35).

Suggest a set of questions for each level of engagement that you could ask this co-learner to help them further develop their portrait. Think, for example, about how to help them make more connections to the LCS concepts.

Table 2.35

Level of engagement	Language and cultural portrait
Emerging engagement	I speak French and English.
Developing engagement	I speak French and English. French is my first language and I have learned English in school and travelling abroad. I have been living in the UK for the past three years. British English is very interesting and represents a challenge for me, especially the pronunciation. Some of my friends tease me because of my French way of saying it. And my friends back in France tease me with my English way of saying it!
Capable engagement	I speak French and English. French is my first language and it is the language we are all using at home. My family is from the west side of France, Bretagne, and there is the Breton language there but no one in my family speaks it, just a few words here and there. I have learned English in school and while travelling abroad. I have been living in the UK for the past three years. At first, I was very shy interacting in English; British English is very interesting and represents a challenge for me, especially the pronunciation. I had to listen to the radio every morning in the car going to school and repeat loudly what I was hearing to figure out how to pronounce better. Some of my friends tease me because of my French way of saying it. And my friends back in France tease me with my English way of saying it!
Exemplary engagement	I speak French and English. French is my first language and it is the language we are all using at home. My family is from the west side of France, Bretagne, and there is the Breton language there but no one in my family speaks it, just a few words here and there. I know how to say 'hello': 'demat', 'bye': 'kenavo'. I also know how to say 'head' and 'wind'! Because our family house has a name, 'wind to head': 'avel a ben'. I wish my grandparents could have transmitted the Breton language but when they were young, they were not allowed to speak it in school. I have done research and found out that if they were using Breton, they were punished. That is how French has become the official language of France! It is interesting to look at 'the love language' with a different perspective and see how it is a language of power. I have learned English in school and while travelling abroad. I have been living in the UK for the past three years. At first, I was very shy interacting in English; British English is very interesting and represents a challenge for me, especially the pronunciation. I had to listen to the radio every morning in the car going to school and repeat loudly what I was hearing to figure out how to pronounce better. Some of my friends tease me because of my French way of saying it. And my friends back in France tease me with my English way of saying it! And this is who I am!

The three review points are an opportunity for you to share and reflect on your progress, as well as looking towards the rest of your LCS learning journey and beyond. Each review point carries equal weight with regards to the decision of you achieving 'completion' in LCS. Look at the table below for some reminders on how to make sure you make the best use of each review point.

Table 2.36 Making the best of each review point

Get started	• Revisit your language and cultural portrait. • Review your learning engagements. • Recall LCS keywords and terminology.
Get ready	• Choose questions from the review point questions. • Examine the developmental rubric. • Remind yourself of the focus of the particular review point. • Select evidence from your learning journal to support the discussion. • Refer to LCS concepts and learning outcomes.
Keep moving	• Reflect on the review point session. • Record your reflection (written or oral) into the progress and reflection form. • Refine your portrait, your goals. • Define your next steps in your LCS learning journey.

Completion of LCS

In order to achieve completion of LCS, which is a requirement for the CP, you will need to show evidence (in your learning journal and review points) that you have:

- made progress in relation to the LCS learning outcomes
- engaged in a sustained manner with LCS over the two years of the CP, with at least 70 learning hours.

2.5.5 Summary

- Your LCS learning journey is assessed by yourself, your co-learners and your LCS teacher.
- LCS is assessed against the four LCS learning outcomes.
- Assessment is an ongoing process.
- Review points are a moment where you share and reflect on your learning journey.
- Each review point counts equally towards LCS completion.
- Reflections can be multimodal.

3 Personal and professional skills (PPS)

3.1 Setting the stage

INQUIRY QUESTIONS

- What is PPS?
- Why does developing personal and professional skills matter for *your* future?
- What will you learn in PPS?
- What is inquiry?
- How do inquiries help you develop foundational skills?
- How will you showcase your learning in PPS?

3.1.1 PPS: A two-year journey

Personal and professional skills (PPS) is one of the four essential components of the IB Career-related Programme (CP) Core, designed to help you develop skills and attitudes that are crucial for personal and professional growth.

The focus of PPS is to equip you with **transversal skills**—skills that are valuable across a wide range of contexts and disciplines. These include critical thinking, ethical decision-making, collaboration and intercultural understanding, as well as empathy, social awareness and the ability to reflect and engage in reflexive thinking. For example, developing empathy helps you understand diverse perspectives and build respectful relationships, while reflection and reflexivity support personal growth and responsible action. PPS is not just about gaining knowledge—it's about applying what you learn in meaningful ways to grow as a learner and as a global citizen.

Key term

◆ **Transversal skills:** These are not specifically related to a particular job, task, academic discipline or area of knowledge, but can be used in a wide variety of situations and work settings. These skills can be transferred and applied to different contexts.

Building the foundations

The start of the PPS course is structured to develop essential transferable skills that prepare students for their future careers, studies and life challenges. The year is designed around three key elements:

1. **Skill development:** Engaging in activities that enhance communication, critical thinking, collaboration and self-management.
2. **Personal reflection:** Understanding personal strengths, areas for growth and setting meaningful goals.
3. **Portfolio creation:** Compiling evidence of learning, reflections and skill development throughout the year.

While the course progressively becomes more student-led, the initial stages provide structured learning engagements that help you develop the skills and mindset necessary for independent inquiry.

By the time you are ready to begin your independent inquiries, you should have developed a strong foundation in the core skills outlined in the IB guide. These skills will be built through a variety of learning engagements designed to support your growth as a reflective, ethical and self-directed learner.

- **Classroom activities:** Weekly sessions focus on interactive activities such as debates, problem-solving challenges, ethical dilemmas and team-based projects.

- **Connections beyond the classroom:** You will analyse case studies, reflect on workplace scenarios and engage with guest speakers from various industries.
- **Out-of-school learning:** Assignments and reflections allow you to apply your learning in real-life contexts, whether through work experience, personal projects or career exploration tasks.
- **Portfolio development:** You will gradually build your PPS portfolio, recording insights, challenges and skill development milestones. The portfolio is not simply a collection of work, but a narrative of growth, showcasing personal and professional progress.

Independent inquiry and application

As the course progresses, you will transition from structured learning to self-directed inquiry, selecting and exploring a topic of personal and professional interest. This phase encourages the application of previously developed skills to a real-world issue, challenge or area of professional focus. Your portfolio continues to evolve, capturing insights from your inquiry process and demonstrating your ability to apply personal and professional skills in a meaningful way.

3.1.2 What will you actually do in PPS?

Foundational phase activities

You'll take part in a mix of structured learning engagements—classroom discussions, guided inquiries, reflections and skill-building exercises. Expect to complete targeted tasks and engage in regular reflections that help you connect PPS skills to your everyday life, studies and career interests.

Independent phase activities

As you gain confidence and skills, you'll take more ownership of your learning. You'll design and carry out a self-directed inquiry into a topic that matters to you personally, professionally or both. This could include research, interviews with mentors or professionals, internships or independent projects. You'll document your progress and make connections between theory and practical application through your portfolio.

Expectations during your independent inquiry

- Define a focus area based on your personal and career-related interests.
- Conduct meaningful research and engage with mentors or industry professionals.
- Reflect regularly on your learning and development.
- Document your insights, experiences and skill growth in your PPS portfolio.

PPS is more than just a course—it's a foundation for lifelong learning and success. Through PPS, you'll develop the skills and attitudes needed to thrive in a rapidly changing world, from self-management and resilience to collaboration and innovation; skills that will serve you not only in school, but in your future career and everyday life. From communication to critical thinking and intercultural understanding, these skills will help you become a well-rounded individual and a capable professional. Whether you're reflecting on your own growth, collaborating with others or applying what you've learned to situations beyond the classroom, the goal is to prepare you to thrive in a dynamic and interconnected world.

By the end of the course, you will have gained the tools necessary to navigate challenges, adapt to change and lead with integrity. These are the skills that will set you up for success, no matter where life takes you.

The five learning outcomes of PPS

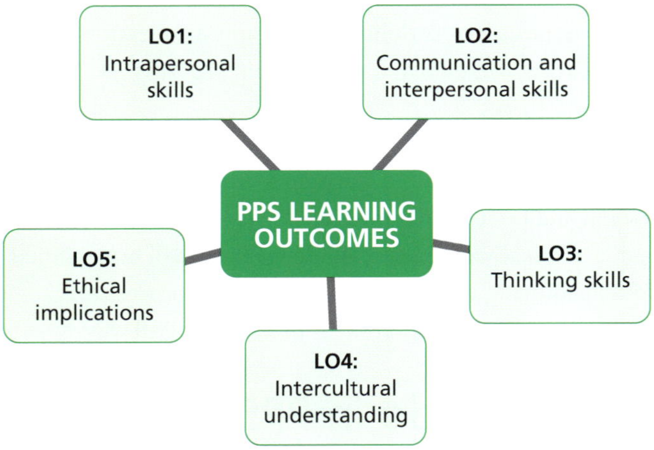

What are the five PPS learning outcomes?

In PPS, you'll have the chance to go beyond being a passive consumer of knowledge. Instead, you'll be challenged to take this content and become ignitors, activators and creators—individuals who take initiative and inspire others. Through reflective practices, experiential learning and inquiry-based projects, you'll discover how these skills matter to your future.

There are five learning outcomes in PPS. Remember that a learning outcome identifies what you should be able to do at the end of your course. These are key goals that guide your growth in various contexts. These outcomes focus on developing skills in self-awareness, communication, thinking and intercultural understanding—all essential for success in the CP—and are summarized in Table 3.1.

Key terms

◆ **Intrapersonal skills:** Intrapersonal skills involve self-awareness and the understanding of our own emotions.

◆ **Interpersonal skills:** The behaviours and strategies we use to interact effectively with others.

Table 3.1 PPS learning outcomes

Learning outcome		Explanation	Application
LO1	**Develop and apply intrapersonal skills in a variety of contexts.**	These are the skills you develop within yourself. They include self-awareness, emotional regulation, resilience and personal responsibility. Essentially, **intrapersonal skills** are about how you understand and manage your thoughts, feelings and actions.	In this outcome, you'll learn how to reflect on your experiences, understand your strengths and areas for growth, and manage stress or difficult situations. This might involve practices like journaling, self-reflection and setting personal goals.
LO2	**Develop and apply communication and interpersonal skills in a variety of contexts.**	These skills are focused on how you interact with others. Effective communication isn't just about speaking clearly but also about listening, understanding and empathizing. **Interpersonal skills** include teamwork, collaboration and conflict resolution.	You'll practise active listening, giving and receiving feedback, and expressing your ideas clearly. Whether you're working in a group, leading a project or engaging with a mentor, these skills will help you build positive and productive relationships.
LO3	**Develop and apply thinking skills in a variety of contexts.**	Thinking skills refer to critical thinking, creative problem-solving and decision-making. These skills enable you to analyse information, consider different perspectives and make well-informed choices.	You'll practise thinking processes that can be applied to many different situations in your life. This practice will support your ability to make decisions, prioritize and problem solve when challenges or conflicts arise.
LO4	**Develop and apply intercultural understanding in a variety of contexts.**	Intercultural understanding refers to the knowledge and understanding of your culture, other cultures and the similarities and differences between them.	You'll practise reflection, ethical thinking and collaboration, as well as social awareness and social responsibility. Through learning, sharing and reflecting on your and others' cultures, you'll gain skills to become a global citizen.

Learning outcome		Explanation	Application
LO5	**Demonstrate an awareness of the ethical implications of one's choices and actions on self and others.**	This outcome focuses on understanding how your decisions and behaviours affect not just yourself, but also others, both locally and globally. It involves developing a sense of ethics, integrity and responsibility when navigating complex situations. Ethical awareness means considering fairness, justice, consequences and the impact of your actions on individuals, communities and the environment.	You'll explore ethical issues through real-world scenarios and personal experiences. This might involve reflecting on dilemmas in your career-related studies, analysing the consequences of different actions, or considering multiple perspectives before making a decision. You'll learn to ask questions like: Is this fair? Who is affected? What are the short- and long-term impacts? Over time, you'll build the capacity to act thoughtfully and ethically in personal, academic and professional contexts.

To support you in meeting the learning outcomes, there are key PPS concepts, contexts, content and skills that you will explore. You will learn more about these building blocks of PPS in Section 3.2.

Reflection and reflexivity

Which learning outcome are you most excited to develop?

3.1.3 The PPS learning process

The types of inquiry

Key term

◆ **Inquiry:** The process of exploring a topic by asking questions to deepen understanding.

Inquiry is the process of exploring a topic by asking questions to deepen understanding. In PPS, it helps you engage actively with content, develop skills and apply your learning to real-world situations.

There are three types of inquiry in PPS: directed, guided and open inquiry. Through these you build essential skills like problem-solving and self-reflection, fostering a mindset of continuous learning and growth. The three types of inquiry are summarized in Table 3.2.

Table 3.2 The three types of inquiry

Type of inquiry	Description
Directed inquiry	Students investigate a teacher-presented inquiry. The inquiry focus question and learning outcomes are predetermined for students by the teacher.
Guided inquiry	Students investigate a teacher-presented inquiry focus question and concept using student-designed and student-selected activities. Teachers and students co-construct and develop key elements of the inquiry, but the teacher sets some non-negotiable elements.
Open inquiry	The inquiry focus questions are designed and created solely by the students. Students design the activities to explore a topic of their choosing. While teachers might provide support or guidance, these inquiries are student-led.

Reflection and reflexivity

Considering the different types of inquiries in PPS, which presents the most challenge for you personally, and why?

Right now, you may not feel completely confident in building your own inquiry from scratch, and that's okay. Through PPS, you will learn tools to support you in developing your own inquiries, enabling you to become lifelong learners.

Here's a glimpse of how you will develop your inquiry skills:

- learning what is most important and relevant for your growth and development
- discovering how to ask better questions—because good questions lead to deeper answers
- seeking out resources, knowledge, activities and assignments that will support your learning
- practising reflection to connect what you're learning in school, at home or in the world around you
- learning how to turn knowledge into action, from crafting a presentation to solving a community problem.

The PPS portfolio

There are two main purposes for your PPS portfolio:

- **Progress tracker:** Throughout the course, your portfolio is like your progress bar. It shows how you're getting stronger, smarter and more skilled. Through your portfolio, you will reflect on your progress in all of your learning.
- **Final showcase:** Your portfolio is your way to showcase everything you've learned at the end of the course. It proves you've met the learning outcomes and developed both your personal and professional skills.

You'll learn many strategies on ways to build and present your portfolio later in this section. For now, know that the portfolio is the way you will demonstrate what you have done. It is your chance to tell your learning story in your own way.

Transitioning from the learning journal

In earlier Core components, you have used learning journals to capture reflections, track progress and deepen your understanding of key concepts. These journals helped you think critically about your experiences and document your learning journey. Now, in the PPS course, you'll build upon that foundation by transitioning from learning journals to a portfolio—a structured collection of evidence showcasing your growth, skills and insights.

A portfolio is more than just a collection of assignments; it's a dynamic representation of your learning and personal development. While learning journals helped you reflect informally, a portfolio allows you to **curate** and organize your best work, demonstrating how your skills and knowledge have evolved. This transition helps you:

- take ownership of your learning by selecting meaningful artefacts
- connect your experiences to practical applications and career aspirations
- showcase key competencies, such as critical thinking, communication and problem-solving
- prepare for university, internships or job applications by building a professional record of your achievements.

As you begin to build your PPS portfolio, you might consider the following approaches to help you document and reflect on your learning journey:

- **Review past learning journals:** Identify key insights, reflections and experiences that are meaningful to your personal and professional growth.

Key term

◆ **Curate:** To prepare materials for an audience to communicate meaning. In the context of PPS, this refers to the collection of evidence for students' portfolios in a way that communicates students' learning.

- **Select and organize artefacts:** Choose work samples, reflections, projects and evidence of skills that best represent your learning journey.
- **Use the inquiry tracker matrix:** This tool helps you categorize and track your inquiries, projects and reflections in an organized way.
- **Engage in continuous reflection:** Like your learning journal, your portfolio will include reflections that analyse challenges, successes and areas for growth.
- **Curate for impact:** Think about how your portfolio tells a story about who you are as a learner, professional and individual.

This transition encourages intentional learning—moving beyond passive documentation to actively curating a record that highlights your unique skills, strengths and goals. The portfolio is your space to showcase who you are becoming, making learning not just visible, but impactful.

Every challenge is a chance to build resilience. Remember, growth happens when you step out of your comfort zone.

Top tip!

Remember, PPS is about discovering your potential and developing skills that will serve you for a lifetime. Take initiative, ask questions and don't be afraid to make mistakes!

LEARNING ENGAGEMENT

Thinking about outcomes and inquiry

Now that you've explored the core elements of PPS, it's time to put what you've learned into action. Answer these questions individually.

1. Reflect on the PPS learning outcomes and identify which one excites you the most. Write a short paragraph explaining why that outcome matters to your future and how you think you can develop it.
2. Choose one type of inquiry (directed, guided or open) and think about how you would approach an inquiry question related to your interests. Write down your inquiry question and outline the steps you would take to explore it.

3.1.4 Summary

- PPS is one of the four essential components of the CP Core that focuses on helping you develop skills and attitudes that are crucial for personal and professional growth.
- You will engage in direct, guided and open inquiries throughout your time in PPS to explore content and contexts that are most relevant and interesting to you.
- In order to showcase your learning and growth, you will create a PPS portfolio that can be used to support you in your future goals and endeavours.

3.2 Concepts, contexts and content in action

INQUIRY QUESTIONS

- What are the building blocks of PPS and how do you use them to develop meaningful inquiries?
- How do you build skills through the exploration of PPS concepts in different settings or contexts?
- Besides the classroom, what are other settings and environments where you can build your skills and explore the PPS concepts?
- Which PPS skills do you need to develop the most?
- What content or information will you explore in PPS?

3.2.1 Your PPS journey

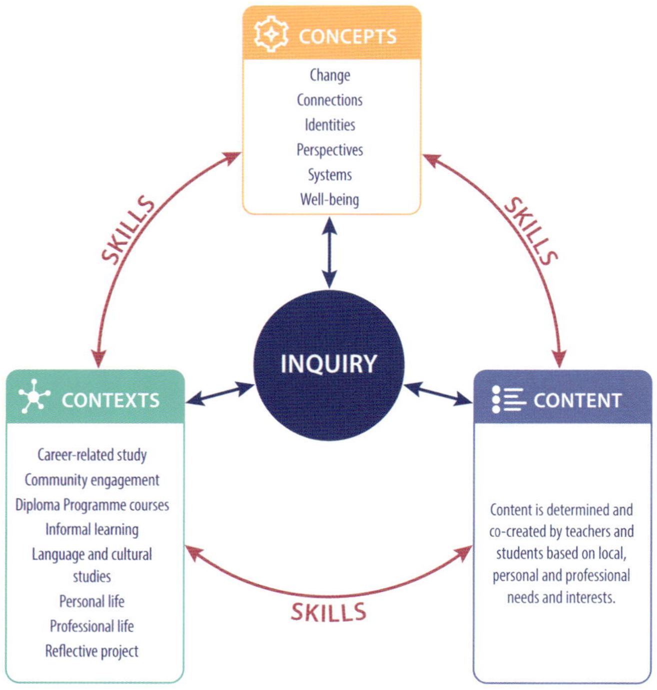

■ The PPS course is built from concepts, contexts and content, linked by skills and inquiry. (Source: IB PPS guide, p.13)

This section outlines the foundational concepts, contexts and skills necessary for success in the PPS course. It introduces these core elements and shows how they are relevant in both personal and professional contexts. Understanding these building blocks is essential because they form the backbone of the PPS course, equipping you with transferable skills that prepare you for career-related studies and life beyond school. By mastering these skills, you can navigate complex situations, enhance your employability, and develop a strong ethical and reflective mindset. The section provides an introduction to structured activities and reflective exercises that help you apply these foundational skills in meaningful ways. It encourages experiential learning through real-life scenarios, discussion prompts and self-assessments, allowing you to actively engage with the material and track your personal growth.

This section will establish the foundational skills and concepts that you will develop throughout your PPS journey. To start with, you will engage in structured inquiry, reflection and skill-building exercises that will prepare you for the more independent inquiry process as you progress through the course. The portfolio serves as a central component of this process, capturing learning engagements, personal growth and skill development.

Imagine that you're building a house. The foundation is laid first and, from there, you will slowly add the bricks on top of another until your structure begins to form. The PPS course is similar. Its building blocks—concepts, contexts, content and skills—help you create meaningful inquiries and explore personal and professional growth. In this section, you will explore these building blocks and begin to reflect on the ways to use them to build your PPS experience.

- **Concepts:** Concepts organize and connect learning and information. Concepts are transferred and applied across multiple contexts.
- **Contexts:** Circumstances, events and settings that give relevance to learning and information. Concepts are tested and expanded through contexts.
- **Content:** Information learned and retained for understanding and communication. Contexts make content relevant and concepts organize it.

You will also delve into these building blocks to look at the way one concept is an essential thread through your whole CP experience: **well-being**.

Well-being is an integral part of self-management skills. It involves taking time to reflect on your mental, emotional and physical state. Throughout this section, you will find opportunities for well-being checks, encouraging you to reflect on your learning and maintain balance as you grow personally and develop career-related skills.

Key term

◆ **Well-being:** Well-being generally refers to one's physical, emotional and mental state of being, which influences overall quality of life. Individual well-being exists in conjunction with the well-being of communities, as well as with ecological and planetary well-being.

3.2.2 PPS concepts

Sometimes inquiry can seem like a daunting task. You might ask yourself questions like 'Where do I start?' or 'What should I focus on?' The building blocks of the PPS course also enable you to organize your thinking and maximize your agency. The simple question, 'What do I care about?' can sometimes be very challenging to answer. In PPS, agency is the ability to take ownership of your learning, make independent choices and actively shape your personal and professional growth. It means recognizing your capacity to set meaningful goals, explore inquiries that matter to you, and apply your skills across different contexts to create impact in your life and community.

What are PPS concepts and why are they important?

There are six overarching **concepts** that you can explore to build your skills in various **contexts** in your life around **content** that interests you. Thinking in these terms will help you in developing meaningful, varied inquiries that will support your personal and professional growth.

The six overarching PPS concepts are: change, connections, identities, perspectives, systems and well-being. These concepts encourage you to develop meaningful inquiries while growing personally and professionally.

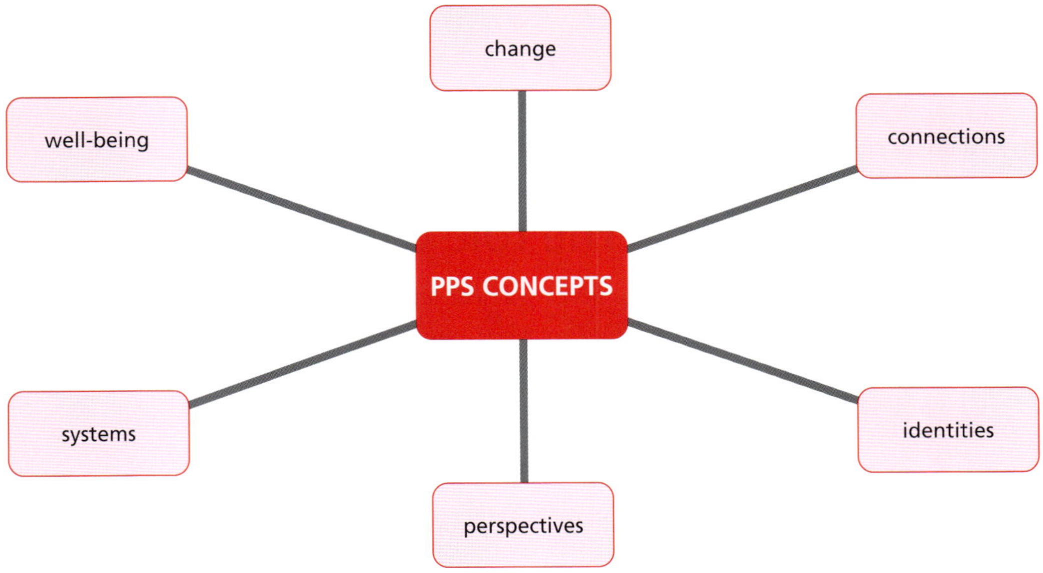

The six concepts in PPS

PPS concepts are broad, fundamental ideas that span a wide range of subjects, topics and experiences. They help you to find connections and similarities in different contexts and environments. Since they apply to so many different situations, you can use them in many ways to help guide your inquiries.

PPS concepts typically answer the question, 'What is this inquiry generally about?'

Reflection and reflexivity

Which concepts do you most want to explore and in what contexts might you explore them?

LEARNING ENGAGEMENT

Create a mind map in your learning journal of the first words that come to mind with each concept. This will be a snapshot of your starting point in the PPS course and will make for an interesting reflection as you progress through the course.

By incorporating the concept of well-being into this framework, you're invited to examine how your mental, emotional and physical health are impacted.

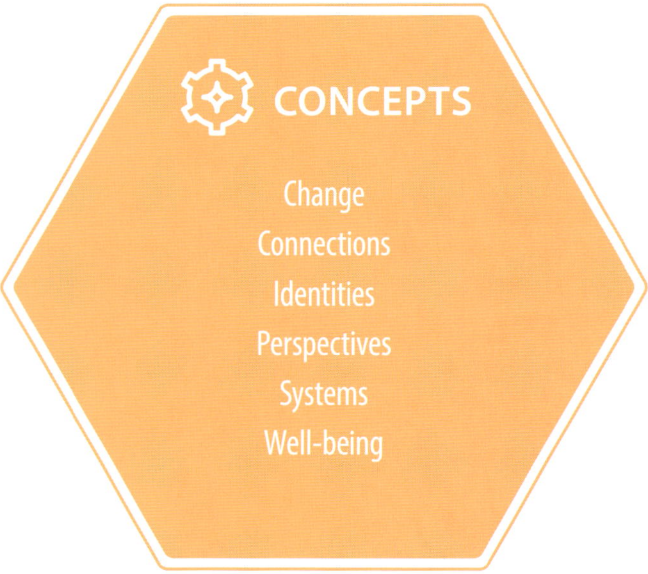

■ PPS concepts (Source: IB PPS guide, p.15)

Table 3.3 (on the following spread) explores the PPS concepts, explaining what each one is about and outlining some potential inquiry questions related to the concepts.

Reflection and reflexivity

Consider the concepts of PPS. Which concept do you feel you most need to explore to grow and develop? What questions might you begin to ask that would support your exploration of that concept? (Consider some of the examples that are outlined in Table 3.3.)

3.2.3 The role of inquiry in PPS

To help you develop a deep and meaningful understanding of PPS, structured inquiries are woven into your learning engagements. These inquiries are designed to guide your exploration of key themes while building essential skills such as critical thinking, research, communication and self-management.

As you progress, you'll engage in different types of inquiry—some guided by your teacher, others shaped by your own interests. For example, you might investigate the ethical challenges of social media use in your future profession, or explore how intercultural communication impacts collaboration in global teams.

These inquiries are opportunities to not only apply what you're learning, but also to reflect on your values, interests and goals as a learner and a professional.

Throughout this chapter, there will be several examples of inquiries that you could explore. These are meant to provide you with practice in the inquiry process and eventually inspire you to build and develop your own inquiries. As you engage in them, consider how they might influence your own inquiry development.

INQUIRY EXAMPLE 1: CONCEPT DRIVEN

Exploring personal and professional identity

In PPS, you'll be required to explore these concepts in your life. This inquiry invites you to investigate your personal identity and how your values, interests and skills shape it.

Focus question:

How do my values, interests, and skills shape my personal and professional identity?

List the concepts, contexts and skills that will be explored and developed in this inquiry:

Identities, career-related study, intrapersonal skills

Why am I undertaking this inquiry? What are my learning outcomes?

Learning outcomes:

- Reflect on personal strengths, weaknesses and aspirations.
- Identify how individual identity influences career and academic choices.
- Develop goal-setting strategies to align personal identity with future pathways.

How will I explore these topics?

Activities:

1. Self-reflection journal: Students write about their strengths, interests and skills, drawing connections to potential career paths.
2. Values and strengths mapping: Using a visual organizer, students map out their core values and how these relate to different professions.
3. Case study analysis: Students examine real-life examples of professionals who have built careers aligning with their identities.

How will I reflect on my learning?

- Personal reflections on strengths and interests.
- A completed values and strengths map.
- Summaries of case study findings with personal takeaways.

How will I share my learning?

- Add artefacts to my portfolio to illustrate my learning.
- Share with friends, family members, teachers and mentors.

Portfolio integration (artefacts to include):

- Reflections on strengths and interests.
- Strength map.
- Summaries of case study findings.

Table 3.3 PPS concepts and inquiry questions related to them

Concept	Explanation	Questions
Change	Change refers to the evolution, adaptation, movement or transformation of an idea, person, groups of people or state of being. Change can occur in social, cultural, economic, technological or ecological contexts in your life. It can have large or small intended or unintended consequences.	How can you embrace change more effectively? What are common drivers of change? How can individuals contribute to positive social change?
Connections	Connections are links, bonds and relationships between people, groups of people, objects and/or ideas. Connections have a tremendous amount of influence and can be influenced by identities, interactions and perspectives.	What are barriers to feeling connected to others? How does empathy play a role in connecting with others? In what way does the world classify or organize connections?
Identities	Identities refer to the combination of backgrounds, dispositions and experiences that define a person, groups, organizations and communities. They shape the way you define and describe yourself or others and they can be very complex and change overtime.	How does a person's identity change over time? How do societal expectations and social structures shape individual identities? How can we promote inclusivity and respect for diverse identities in society?

Concept	Explanation	Questions
Perspectives	Perspectives are the positions from which we view situations, objects, facts, ideas and opinions.	How does your perspective influence your understanding of the world? How can you resolve conflicts by considering and valuing different perspectives? What are the ethical implications of imposing our own perspectives on others?
Systems	Systems are sets of interacting elements that use processes or procedures to work towards a common goal. Systems are the way in which information, actions, thoughts or people are organized and classified.	What are the key elements of a successful system? How do you define the boundaries of a system? What systems are present in your world and how do they impact you?
Well-being	Well-being refers to a person's physical and mental state of being and it can fluctuate at different times in life. Factors such as physical health, emotional resilience, personal fulfilment, financial stability and work–life balance.	What factors contribute most significantly to your well-being? How do you cope with stress and maintain your personal well-being? How do you express and manage your emotions to better your well-being?

3.2.4 PPS contexts

In many classes or subjects, the learning opportunities offered stay in the classroom; that is, the skills you develop and the content you learn are used to complete activities, assignments or tests for the course. PPS is different.

> This course not only encourages you to apply your knowledge and skills in various settings outside of the classroom, it requires you to do so.

By outlining various contexts—or settings—the PPS course invites you to think outside of the classroom and ask yourself, 'Where in my life can I apply this skill and leverage this knowledge?' The practice of leveraging skills, or using them to your advantage and maximizing them in different situations, will provide you with an authentic experience that will be useful in developing your personal and professional skills.

The eight PPS contexts (Source: IB PPS guide, p.17)

What are PPS contexts and why are they important?

'Context' is a word that simply means the settings in which you explore the concepts and develop various skills in this course. Think about contexts as the place in which you're engaging in your inquiry. We all move through different contexts, probably several times every day. The context is important because you might be exploring the same concept and skills, but if you change the context, even slightly, you will have a totally different experience.

To help name and navigate these different contexts, the PPS course offers a way to organize them. The contexts in PPS could include the following:

- **Academic:** An academic context refers to all the elements that make up your CP course. You can draw upon your experiences in other CP Core elements (CE, LCS or the RP) as well as diploma courses, career-related studies, or other academic courses or experiences.
- **Professional:** A professional context includes settings in which you are required to engage in a professional manner. These can include work, internships, leadership or mentoring opportunities, job fairs or other instances in which you engage with employers.
- **Personal:** A personal context is anything that you experience in your personal life, such as relationships with family, friends and/or community members.
- **Informal:** Informal contexts are settings in which you are learning and growing in informal ways and might include extracurricular activities, athletics, music, arts and clubs.

> This course is all about you. Determining what you want to explore can sometimes be hard, so consider thinking about the different experiences you have in different contexts of your life.

In PPS, you'll use real-life contexts to explore key concepts and develop transferable skills. One way to do this is by identifying situations in your own life that challenge you and using them as a starting point for inquiry.

Reflection and reflexivity

Think of a context in your life that you find challenging—this could be personal, academic, professional or community-related.

- What makes this context challenging for you?
- How might you explore a PPS concept (such as resilience, ethical thinking or intercultural understanding) within this context?
- What skills could you build through this inquiry to help you navigate similar challenges in the future?

INQUIRY EXAMPLE 2: CONTEXT DRIVEN

Navigating ethical dilemmas in professional and academic settings

In PPS, you'll explore how different contexts (such as personal, academic and professional environments) can shape the way you apply concepts and develop skills. This inquiry invites you to investigate how ethical decision-making plays out across settings, helping you make deeper connections between your learning and real-world challenges.

Focus question:

How do ethical considerations impact decision-making in different contexts?

List the concepts, contexts and skills that will be explored and developed in this inquiry:

Perspectives, career-related study, interpersonal skills

Why am I undertaking this inquiry? What are my learning outcomes?

Learning outcomes:

- Define ethics and its role in academic and professional settings.
- Analyse ethical dilemmas and evaluate possible responses.
- Develop strategies for ethical decision-making.

How will I explore these topics?

Activities:

1. Ethical scenario role-play: Students engage in role-play exercises based on local or global ethical dilemmas.
2. Debate on ethical issues: Groups research and present arguments on different sides of an ethical issue.
3. Ethical decision-making framework: Students create a step-by-step framework for addressing ethical challenges.

How will I reflect on my learning?

- Reflect on a role-play experience and personal decision-making process.
- Notes and key takeaways from the debate.
- A personalized ethical decision-making framework.

How will I share my learning?

- Add artefacts to my portfolio to illustrate my learning.
- Share with friends, family members, teachers and mentors.

Portfolio integration (artefacts to include):

- Reflections on role playing and personal decision-making process.
- Notes from debate.
- Personalized ethical decision-making framework.

3.2.5 PPS skills

Building skills that you can use throughout the rest of your life is central to the PPS course. After all, the course is called personal and professional *skills*. It is critical to both develop your skills and think about their benefits in various contexts. We call this idea transversal skills.

Have you ever learned a skill in one class, and then realized later that the same skill has helped you in another class? For example, perhaps you needed to evaluate the pros and cons of a historical figure's decision in your history class, and then used the same skill to determine the validity of an author's claim in literacy class. This skill is transversal; that is, it's a skill that you can use in a particular context and then apply the same skill to a different context. All skills outlined in the PPS course are transversal and can be used in many different settings.

The image below shows the transversal skill of collaboration. Let's say you develop the skill of collaboration in your literature class during a group presentation. How might you apply that same skill on your sports team? When planning an outing or trip with friends? At your job as a server? When your family is making a difficult decision?

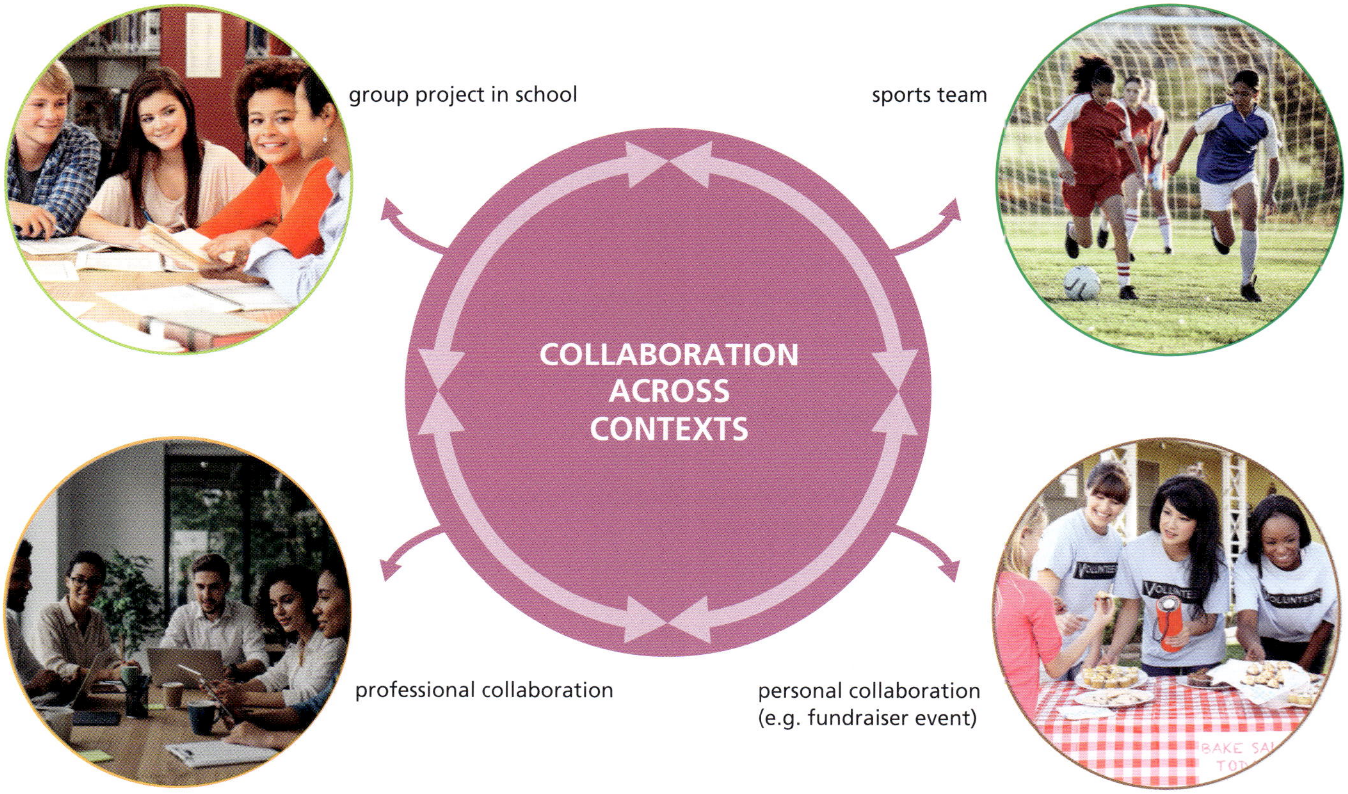

■ The transversal skill of collaboration: How does it support your learning, relationships and professional growth across contexts?

Building and strengthening PPS skills will enable you to adapt to a rapidly changing world and provide you with the ability to become a lifelong learner. Furthermore, these skills aren't only for you to improve in school; they are the skills that will support you in all of the contexts in both your personal and professional lives, including those outside of school. This will empower you to live meaningful, contributive lives.

What are PPS skills and why are they important?

The PPS course has outlined specific skills that are transversal in nature and that will support you in developing your own inquiries. Identifying the skill is just the start. As you engage in activities to build your skills, you will want to reflect on your growth in these skills and the multiple ways that you've used them. Your portfolio is a great place for this reflection!

The PPS skills have been organized into the following four domains:

- intrapersonal skills
- interpersonal skills
- thinking skills
- intercultural understanding.

Intrapersonal skills

Intrapersonal skills involve your self-awareness and the understanding of your own emotions. Exploration of intrapersonal skills requires that you understand and evaluate your traits, behaviours, emotions and abilities to develop an awareness of your interests, goals, strengths and areas for improvement. Simply put, intrapersonal skills are all about the way you manage and know yourself.

Table 3.4 Skills in the intrapersonal domain

Skill	Definition	Question(s)
Adaptability	The ability for you to adjust to new conditions, which means being flexible and proactive in your thinking.	How well do you adjust to changes in your life? Do you have strategies to navigate change or does change cause you stress and anguish?
Reflection and reflexivity	Reflection is a process of determining the what, how, why and with what effect we and others do what we do. Reflexivity is a process relating to our beliefs and values—what, how, why and with what effect we and others think what we think.	Do you take time and know how to meaningfully reflect on actions, situations and decisions you made? Are you able to understand the impact of your actions and consider ways to apply the outcome of this reflection to future situations?
Resilience	The ability to thrive in the face of adversity by developing coping skills to lessen stress and improve emotional wellness.	Do you have coping strategies and confidence to overcome challenges in your life, or do you find it hard to keep going when adversity hits?
Self-advocacy	The ability to communicate our needs comfortably and with confidence. This involves learning about our strengths and challenges, the different tools and resources that can support personal and professional growth, and how to ask for help.	Are you reluctant or shy when you need to ask for help or guidance? Do you know what you need help with and how to access it?
Self-awareness	The ability to be aware of different aspects of ourselves, including traits, behaviours and feelings.	Do you know what you feel and why you feel that way? Do you understand why you do what you do in situations or in relationships?

Interpersonal skills

Interpersonal skills are the behaviours and strategies we use to interact effectively with others. These skills include communication, collaboration and teamwork, and help you to build confidence in relating to others. Development of them will enable you to influence, manage and respond to change in a complex world.

Top tip!

Intrapersonal and interpersonal skills sound very similar, and can be easily confused. An easy way to remember the difference is to note that the prefix 'inter' means 'between' or 'among', while 'intra' means 'within'. **Inter**personal skills refer to skills necessary to work between or among people or groups of people, while **intra**personal skills refer to skills necessary to understanding and empowering yourself.

Table 3.5 Skills in the interpersonal domain

Skill	Definition	Question(s)
Change management and conflict mediation	Change management is your ability to build a systematic approach to managing significant changes that occur in your life. Conflict mediation is your ability to handle and resolve perceived disagreements or conflicts within organizations, between individuals or in any social or interpersonal context.	Do you have a system and/or strategies to use when significant change occurs in your life? Are you able to successfully handle conflicts with others by finding constructive ways to address and resolve issues?
Collaboration and networking	Collaboration refers to your capacity to work with others in a genuine joint activity to reach a common goal. Networking is your ability to build and maintain a relationship with other people from a point of common interest.	When working with others, how easy is it for you to give up control, hear others' ideas and work together to meet a goal? Are you able to seek out and maintain relationships with others based on a common interest?
Communication	The ability to express and exchange meaning through language or any other mode, including non-verbal and/or body language.	Are you able to communicate effectively to others and also successfully understand other people when they are communicating to you, or do you find that there are breakdowns in your communication with others?
Leadership	The ability to influence or guide others towards a goal or aim.	Do you see yourself as a leader or do you wait for others to take the lead?

Thinking skills

Thinking skills involve cognitive processes that we use to solve problems, make decisions, ask questions, plan, organize and create. Critical and creative thinking, problem-solving and information literacy skills consistently top the list of skills necessary to successfully navigate our ever-changing world in a variety of contexts.

Table 3.6 Skills in the thinking domain

Skill	Definition	Question(s)
Critical thinking	The ability to explore assumptions, evaluate claims and critique solutions based on evidence. It is a purposeful process that uses analysis, synthesis, interpretation and inference to arrive at a judgement.	Can you break down ideas into smaller parts to understand their relationship with each other?
Creative thinking	The ability to look at things differently and find new ways of solving problems or developing something novel or original.	Do you have ideas that are unique or different from what's already been presented?
Ethical decision-making	Your ability to identify and describe ethical issues in a variety of contexts, including understanding the impacts on various perspectives.	When making a decision, are you able to see the perspectives of all stakeholders involved, or do you often focus solely on the impact from your own perspective?
Information literacy	The ability to effectively find, evaluate, use and communicate information from various sources in a critical and responsible manner.	When you need to learn something new or answer a question, do you know how to access credible sources and apply that information?

Skill	Definition	Question(s)
Problem-solving	The ability to find solutions to problems in an effective and timely manner through defining a problem, determining the cause of the problem, and identifying, prioritizing and selecting potential solutions.	Are you able to identify and offer potential solutions when problems arise or do problems cause you stress and uncertainty?
Reflection and reflexivity	Reflection is a process of determining the what, how, why and with what effect we and others do what we do. Reflexivity is a process relating to our beliefs and values—what, how, why and with what effect we and others think what we think.	Do you take time and know how to meaningfully reflect on actions, situations and decisions you made? Are you able to apply the outcome of this reflection to future situations?
Systems thinking	Your ability to problem-solve and understand complex situations, ideas or systems. It is your ability to understand the various parts that make up a system and then identify how they interact with each other or how they are connected.	Are you able to see how things connect and work together in a large organization like schools, governments or agencies?

Intercultural understanding

Intercultural understanding involves knowledge and understanding of our own culture, other cultures and the similarities and differences between cultures. It relies on a variety of interpersonal and intrapersonal skills, such as ethics, values and collaboration across cultures, as well as the social awareness and responsibility required to be an effective global citizen. These skills enable you to be effective and ethical participants in diverse settings.

■ **Table 3.7** Skills in the intercultural understanding domain

Skill	Definition	Question(s)
Change management and conflict mediation	Change management is your ability to build a systematic approach to managing significant changes that occur in your life. Conflict mediation is your ability to handle and resolve perceived disagreements or conflicts within organizations, between individuals or in any social or interpersonal context.	Do you have a system and/or strategies to use when significant change occurs in your life? Are you able to successfully handle conflicts with others by finding constructive ways to address and resolve issues?
Civic and social responsibility	Your ability to identify and understand behaviours, attitudes and actions that support active participation within a community in an informed, committed and constructive manner.	Are you aware of the current issues and solutions that exist within your community? Have you actively participated in supporting the work to resolve these issues?
Empathy	Your ability to emotionally understand what other people may be feeling and to see things from others' points of view.	Are you consistently able to put yourself in another person's shoes to understand their feelings and perspective?
Ethics and personal values	Ethics is your ability to study what's right from wrong, including evaluating and analysing morals, rules, principles or values. Personal values are your principles that influence your choices, shape your behaviours and provide a framework for understanding your place in the world.	Do you have a firm understanding of what is right and wrong? Are you able to make informed decisions when there is more than one right solution or the solution is complicated?
Reflection and reflexivity	Reflection is a process of determining the what, how, why and with what effect we and others do what we do. Reflexivity is a process relating to our beliefs and values—what, how, why and with what effect we and others think what we think.	Do you take time and know how to meaningfully reflect on actions, situations and decisions you made? Are you able to apply the outcome of this reflection to future situations?

Skill	Definition	Question(s)
Self-efficacy	The belief you have in your own abilities—specifically your ability to meet challenges and complete tasks successfully.	When things get hard for you, do you have confidence in yourself to work through the issue, or do you find yourself being discouraged or unable to act?
Social awareness	Your ability to consider the perspectives of individuals, groups or communities, and to apply that understanding to interactions with them.	When you move through different contexts in your day, are you able to easily understand and adapt to the social norms and the way you should act in that context?

Reflection and reflexivity

Which three skills in the table above do you feel are most important for you to develop?

INQUIRY EXAMPLE 3: SKILLS DRIVEN

In PPS, you'll engage in inquiries that allow you to explore key concepts, apply skills and reflect on your experiences across different contexts. This inquiry focuses on how interpersonal skills (like communication, empathy and active listening) can support your sense of connection and well-being in your personal life. By examining barriers to connection, you'll consider how developing these skills can positively impact your relationships and overall well-being.

Focus question:

What are some barriers to feeling connected to others?

List the concepts, contexts and skills that will be explored and developed in this inquiry:

Connections, well-being, personal life, interpersonal skills

Why am I undertaking this inquiry? What are my learning outcomes?

Learning outcomes:

- Identify barriers that impede teens from connecting with others.
- Research possible strategies and solutions to build connectivity.
- Reflect on my personal relationship skills.

How will I explore these topics?

Activities:

1. Create a questionnaire to survey peers on when they most feel connected to others and when they least feel connected to others.
2. Research digital tools and social media apps that impede/improve connectivity.
3. Develop an infographic to communicate suggestions on building connectivity for teens.

How will I reflect on my learning?

- Reflect on my learning on connection and how I will apply it to my personal and professional life.
- Create a presentation to share key takeaways from my research.
- Summarize suggestions on building stronger relationships for teens.

How will I share my learning?

- Add artefacts to my portfolio to illustrate my learning.
- Share with peers and friends.

Portfolio integration (artefacts to include):

- Survey results and infographic communicating key takeaways.
- Presentation of key takeaways from my research.

3.2.6 PPS content

Content refers to the information that you explore in your inquiries. Since this course is all about you, the content will come from the ideas you are most interested in or items you would like to learn more about. For example, you may want to learn more about artificial intelligence, your value system or ethics in your community. When you begin to build your inquiries, you will do so by identifying the concepts, content, contexts and skills. Often, the content will be inspired by what is most interesting or exciting to you at the time. This will help you capture and reflect on your learning and present it in your portfolio.

■ Pulling it all together

Now that you have an understanding of the building blocks of the PPS course, you can begin to take a systematic approach in exploring anything you're interested in through inquiry. The inspiration for a new inquiry can come from anywhere—a *concept* you're interested in, a new *context* that perhaps has raised questions for you, a *skill* that you realize you need to hone or *content*/information you'd like to learn more about. Vary your entry points and you will create a richer experience for yourself. For example, if your first inquiry is inspired by a concept, maybe have the next be inspired by a skill or context you'd like to explore.

■ Connections to the other Core components

The PPS building blocks provide an excellent opportunity for you to make explicit connections to the other CP Core components, and continue to develop skills across the CP. There are countless ways to explore the concepts, context, content and skills in PPS in the other Core components. Some examples are:

- **Community engagement:** You could directly apply communication skills learned in PPS to write emails, conduct meetings in a professional manner or speak in a public setting as you engage with the community to meet CE aims and learning outcomes.
- **Reflective project:** You can develop ethical thinking in PPS which will support you in identifying an ethical dilemma for your RP. Furthermore, your ability to critically think and reflect will support you in developing a personal position on the dilemma.
- **Language and cultural studies:** You might explore your own personal identities, values and cultural backgrounds in PPS, which would support you in your language and cultural portrait. This work can support your ability to set personally relevant goals for yourself in LCS.

As you move through the rest of Section 3 and engage in different experiences, each subsection will highlight a key skill that you will develop, understand and apply. These skills will help you grow personally and professionally, equipping you with the tools needed to navigate real-world challenges. Pay attention to the skills focus at the start of each subsection, as it will guide you in understanding which competencies you are strengthening and how they connect to your overall learning journey.

Common pitfalls

Keep in mind that these course building blocks can be used in a myriad of ways to develop a variety of inquiries. It is important to begin to think about what excites you and what you feel is most important for you to explore at this time. Avoid narrow thinking about just a small number of options.

One of the biggest pitfalls is not taking ownership of your own learning, and waiting for someone else to prescribe your experiences for you. You may be used to a teacher, mentor, parent or other authority figure dictating what and how you learn. This is an invitation to shift your thinking to the idea that *you* take ownership of your learning, so what is it that *you* want to learn about? You have the context, concepts and skills to help you figure it out. You will find that it can be highly motivating and exhilarating to find a passion to explore. Only *you* can determine that and find it.

Voices from fellow students

I love learning about myself. Like I took a personality inventory, explored my values and created goals for myself as one of my inquiries. It didn't feel like work because it was something I was very interested in!

Noam, PPS student

At first it was really hard to come up with ideas of what to explore because I never had to do that before in other classes. Once I started learning more about structuring inquiries, it got a lot easier.

Priya, PPS student

Reflection and reflexivity

Now that you have an idea of the building blocks of the PPS course, where would you like to begin? What concepts, context, content or skills most excite you? How will you explore them?

Learner profile

This chapter helped you develop the following learner profile traits:

Reflection, self-awareness, critical thinking, self-management

Learning journal

Portfolio work: Evidence of learning

Throughout this section, you will have documented your learning through:

- written reflections and self-assessments
- visual organizers and planning tools
- case study analyses and debate notes
- personal ethical decision-making frameworks.

By engaging with these inquiries and actively contributing to your portfolios, you will lay a strong foundation for your PPS journey, equipping yourself with the skills and knowledge necessary for an increasingly independent inquiry process.

3.2.7 Summary

- PPS is a unique course that develops your skills and dispositions in your personal and professional life.
- The building blocks of the course include concepts, contexts and skills.
- You will engage in inquiries to practise applying the building blocks in your life.
- It is critical that you showcase your learning in your PPS portfolio.

3.3 Keeping track: Your portfolio

INQUIRY QUESTIONS

- What is the PPS portfolio?
- What are the requirements for the PPS portfolio?
- What are some practical strategies you can implement over your time in PPS to develop and produce a robust PPS portfolio?
- How can you best represent your growth and learning in your PPS portfolio?

3.3.1 The PPS portfolio

This section explores the importance of maintaining a personal and professional skills (PPS) portfolio as a reflective and developmental tool. It explains how a portfolio is more than a collection of assignments—it is a curated record of learning, growth and skills development that connects experiences to the core concepts of PPS. You will find strategies here for building, organizing and using a portfolio effectively.

Keeping a portfolio is essential for tracking your progress, making connections between learning engagements and showcasing skills in wider contexts. It helps you to develop self-awareness, build confidence and prepare for future career opportunities, internships or further education. By curating artefacts and reflecting on them, you will gain a deeper understanding of your personal and professional growth.

You will discover practical steps for building a portfolio, including starting a 'dumping folder' to collect potential artefacts, using an inquiry tracker matrix to organize learning, and annotating artefacts to highlight key takeaways. There are various portfolio formats (digital, physical or hybrid) you can use and we will explore real-world student examples to demonstrate how portfolios can be leveraged for career and academic success. Through structured reflection and intentional curation, you can transform your portfolio into meaningful narratives of your learning journeys.

Your portfolio is more than just a collection of assignments; it's your story—a living record of what you've tried, what worked, what didn't and, most importantly, what you've learned along the way. It's a personal archive of growth, reflecting your journey through PPS as you develop new skills, face challenges and discover your potential.

Think of your portfolio as a mirror, capturing moments that show who you are now and who you're becoming. By curating your experiences and insights, you'll create a meaningful tool that not only demonstrates your learning, but also helps you make connections between what you've done and where you want to go.

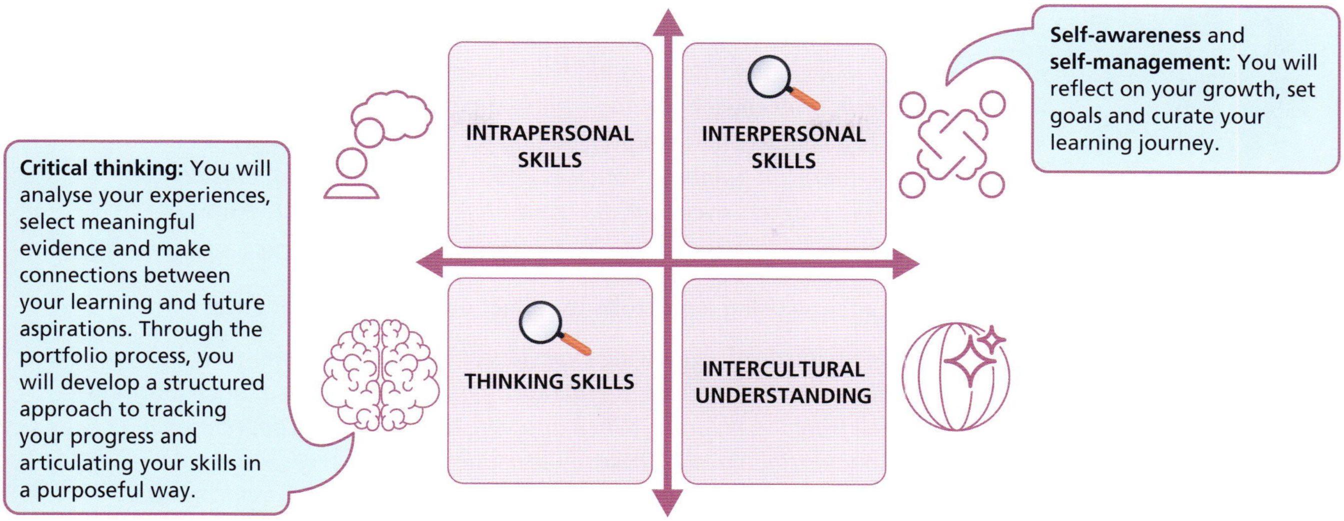

■ PPS skills focused on in Section 3.3

Throughout Section 3, you will hear directly from students who have already experienced the CP. Take it from them—they know! However, you will notice they all have very different experiences.

Top tip!

Remember that 'curate' means to select, organize and prepare the items in your portfolio for presentation.

REAL-WORLD EXAMPLE

The value of the PPS portfolio

'At first, I wasn't sure about keeping a portfolio. It just felt like extra work. But as I started adding reflections, projects and feedback, I realized it was actually a way to see how much I had grown. Now I use it to track my progress and even showcase my work in college applications.'

(Liam, CP student)

'The portfolio helped me connect the dots between different projects and skills. I used to think of assignments as separate tasks, but now I see how everything ties together. It made me more confident when explaining my learning journey during an internship interview.'

(Sofia, PPS student)

Aspiring graphic designer—Showcasing growth through a digital portfolio

'When I applied for an internship at a design studio, my PPS portfolio became my biggest asset. Instead of just listing my skills, I showed my creative process—initial sketches, client feedback and final designs. The interviewer said my ability to reflect on my work and explain my growth set me apart from other applicants.'

(Ava, CP student in CRS visual arts)

Future business analyst—Making connections between skills and career goals

> *'I never thought a portfolio would help in business, but tracking my teamwork, problem-solving and leadership experiences helped me land a spot in a competitive entrepreneurship program. I included project reports, financial planning exercises and reflections on collaboration. Seeing my progress over time made me more confident in interviews.'*

(Daniel, CP student in CRS business management)

Healthcare student—Using a portfolio to reflect on practical experiences

> *'During my medical shadowing experience, I documented everything in my portfolio—notes on patient interactions, reflections on ethical dilemmas and feedback from my mentors. When applying to a healthcare apprenticeship, I used my portfolio to showcase my learning. The panel was impressed by my ability to connect classroom knowledge with real-world applications.'*

(Emma, CP student in CRS health sciences)

3.3.2 Building your portfolio

Top tip!

Think of your artefact annotations as the voiceover to your story, providing context, showing your thinking and highlighting your learning

To make your portfolio meaningful, start by including artefacts—pieces of evidence that tell the story of your learning. These might be projects you're proud of, reflections on moments of growth, or even feedback from teachers, mentors or peers. Each artefact should represent a step in your journey, whether it's a success, a lesson learned from failure or a new skill you've developed.

But a portfolio isn't just about collecting artefacts. To truly bring them to life, you'll need to include a brief annotation with each one. Write a short explanation that identifies the artefact and explain why you selected it. For example, if you include a reflection on a group project, you might note how it helped you build communication skills or taught you the value of listening to diverse perspectives.

There is no prescribed format for the PPS portfolio. You may choose to keep a physical, digital or hybrid portfolio. Each format has its benefits; think about your preference, personal style and goals for the portfolio to help determine which format you want to use.

Your portfolio can include an array of different media—physical, digital or both.

Some examples of portfolio formats include:

- a website that includes pictures, audio files, videos, documents and summaries in your own style and branding
- a cloud-based folder with sub-folders containing documents, pictures, audio files and/or presentations that you and your teacher both can access and explore together
- an online classroom interface that logs assignments, activities, pictures, presentations, assessments and feedback
- a file to organize physical copies of your work
- a binder that houses your artefacts, reflections and growth.

Regardless of your format, it is critical that your portfolio highlights connections—how your artefacts tie back to the skills, concepts, contexts and content you're exploring in PPS. These connections are what turn your portfolio into more than just a scrapbook. They show how your experiences relate to the broader themes of the course and how the skills you're building can be applied in different areas of your life.

PPS portfolio requirements

Your portfolio is a record of your growth throughout the PPS course. It must meet the following IB requirements:

- Evidence from the exploration of a minimum of four concepts from the PPS course.
- Artefacts from a range of contexts (such as personal life, community engagement, academic work or career-related experiences).
- Evidence of skill development related to each of the five learning outcomes.
- Brief annotations that identify each artefact and explain why it was selected and how it reflects your learning.
- Each skill developed must be applied in at least two different contexts to show how your skills transfer across settings.
- A minimum of two skills must be developed from each of the four skill domains, resulting in a total of at least eight distinct skills.
- The portfolio must be curated and developed across the two years of the course as ongoing evidence of your progress.

By reflecting on your experiences using the PPS building blocks (skills, concepts, contexts and learning outcomes), your portfolio will show how your learning connects and how you've grown personally and professionally.

Building your portfolio over time

Once you've started collecting your artefacts, you can then start to curate them. This requires you to think about what you want to showcase about yourself. You can also begin to think about the experiences that were most impactful to your growth, and how you want to share them with your audience.

One way to curate your artefacts and experiences is through using the PPS inquiry tracker matrix provided by the IB. This tool will allow you to colour-code each inquiry, experience or learning engagement and determine which learning outcome, concepts, contexts and skills you have developed. You can also generate some reflection notes to include in your portfolio for the artefacts you choose. This will ensure that your portfolio includes all necessary components and has a variety of experiences and content. Think of this as your ongoing brainstorming guide for your portfolio!

■ **Table 3.8** PPS inquiry tracker matrix template (Source: IB PPS TSM, p.40)

Learning engagement/ inquiry	Learning outcomes	Concepts	Contexts	Skill domain	Notes, activities, artefacts, content
Details	Learning outcome	Concept	Context	Skill domain	
	Learning outcome	Concept	Context	Skill domain	
Details	Learning outcome	Concept	Context	Skill domain	
	Learning outcome	Concept	Context	Skill domain	
Details	Learning outcome	Concept	Context	Skill domain	
	Learning outcome	Concept	Context	Skill domain	

3.3.3 Where to start?

■ The dumping folder

Often, the hardest part of building a portfolio is getting started. You may be thinking, 'Where do I start?', 'What do I include?', 'How do I know what's a good artefact?', 'Where might it fit in my portfolio?', etc. These questions can paralyse your thinking and stop you from making any progress. One easy solution to combat this is to simply start saving items that might be useful for your portfolio.

Here's how: Create an electronic or physical folder and call it the 'dumping folder' and then, just start dumping! Dump in assignments, activities, presentations, email correspondences, pictures, videos, etc.—anything that could be an artefact for your portfolio! Don't worry about if, how or where it might fit into your portfolio. The only rule about the 'dumping folder' is that you simply 'dump' items into it. Instead of losing track of valuable artefacts, you can dump them into this folder and later revisit them to organize, reflect and repurpose them when needed.

After just a little bit of time, you'll start to see a collection of your work and you can begin curating (or critically selecting and organizing your items) into a meaningful, robust portfolio! Go ahead! Get dumping!

REAL-WORLD EXAMPLE

From dumping folder to PPS inquiry tracker matrix

Jaden participated in a sustainability initiative at his school, where students created an upcycling station to turn old clothes into reusable tote bags. In preparation, he attended meetings, collaborated with peers, reached out to local environmental organizations and documented the process. Throughout this experience, Jaden added materials to his dumping folder, including:

- meeting notes and planning agendas
- email exchanges with local sustainability groups
- photos of the upcycling station in action
- personal reflections on the event.

Months later, when curating his PPS portfolio, Jaden used the inquiry tracker matrix to categorize and analyse his experience. He identified the learning outcomes, key concepts, global contexts and professional skills he developed. From his dumping folder, he selected artefacts to include in his portfolio, such as email correspondence, event photos and a reflection on teamwork and problem-solving.

Top tip!

Keep your dumping folder organized by labelling files with dates and brief descriptions, so it's easy to find what you need later!

As you begin to populate your inquiry tracker matrix, you may start to notice that there are contexts, concepts or skills you have not yet explored. This would be a great opportunity to stretch yourself to develop inquiries to explore some of those items.

Table 3.9 An example of a completed PPS inquiry tracker matrix. Notice the different experiences that are included. (Source: IB PPS TSM, p.40)

Learning engagement/ inquiry	Learning outcomes	Concepts	Contexts	Skill domain	Notes, activities, artefacts, content
CV creation	LO1: Intrapersonal skills	Identities	Community engagement	Intrapersonal skills	Personality and career interest profile; curriculum vitae (CV)
	LO3: Thinking skills		Personal life	Thinking skills	
		Focus question: How do my skills align to my career interests?		Self-awareness; analysis and synthesis	
Interviewing for an internship	LO2: Interpersonal skills	Connections	Career-related study	Intrapersonal skills	CV/résumé; cover letter for application; feedback from interviewer
		Identities	Professional life	Interpersonal skills	
			Practise interviews in class; practise networking with peers	Communication; collaboration and networking; self-awareness; self-advocacy	

Learning engagement/ inquiry	Learning outcomes	Concepts	Contexts	Skill domain	Notes, activities, artefacts, content
Gender neutrality in language—Socratic seminar	LO5: Ethical awareness	Perspectives	Language and cultural studies	Intercultural understanding	Notes from research/ preparation and reflections on the in-class, student-facilitated Socratic seminar
	LO4: Intercultural understanding	Change		Thinking skills	
			Research different perspectives to arrive at a personal opinion on the issue of gender neutrality in language; peer discussions	Ethics and personal values; change management and conflict mediation; social awareness; critical thinking (analysis of differing perspectives to draw conclusions and evaluate choices); reflection on learning	

Reflection and reflexivity

What inquiries and learning engagements would you like to include in your PPS inquiry tracker matrix and, eventually, in your portfolio?

3.3.4 Why your portfolio matters

Keeping a portfolio isn't just about documenting what you've done—it's about understanding your own growth and well-being. As you look back over your artefacts and annotations, you'll see patterns emerge: strengths you've developed, challenges you've overcome and areas where you still want to grow. This self-awareness is a crucial part of the PPS journey, helping you take ownership of your learning and chart a course for your future.

Your portfolio will be a powerful tool for sharing your story with others. Whether you're applying for a job, an internship, admission to a program or simply reflecting with a mentor, your portfolio gives you a way to showcase your skills, values and accomplishments. It's a tangible representation of your effort and growth—a testament to the work you've put in and the person you're becoming.

Remember, your portfolio is a work in progress, just like you. Keep it updated, revisit it often and use it as a space to celebrate your growth. Every artefact you add, every connection you make and every insight you annotate brings you closer to understanding the incredible potential you hold. This is your story—own it, shape it and share it.

LEARNING ENGAGEMENT

Getting started

Choose one artefact to include in your portfolio—a project, a reflection or even a piece of feedback that stood out to you.

1. Annotate it, explaining why it's important and what it taught you.
2. Think about how it connects to the PPS skills and concepts you're exploring.
3. Consider accessing the PPS inquiry tracker in the PPS toolkit to help organize your thinking and keep it in one space.

As you add more pieces, your portfolio will begin to take shape, becoming a rich and layered story of your learning journey.

REAL-WORLD EXAMPLE

A student has a leadership role in a community project and links these to the PPS concepts of 'systems' or 'connections' so they can demonstrate what they learned about those concepts when working with multiple people in the community and within a unique organization. The student found they could highlight specific skills such as collaboration, communication and creative thinking to illustrate the ways they developed them while working in this context.

> *'At first, I wasn't really sure about keeping a portfolio. Once I was finished, though, I was really proud because everything that I worked on was all in one place and I could use it to show others everything that I did.'*

> *'I show my PPS portfolio to everyone—my family, teachers, my boss and I recently used it in a college interview. People are always very impressed to see all of the different things I did while in high school.'*

Reflection and reflexivity

What's next?

By the end of this year, you'll reflect on this question:

- Which foundational skills do you want to strengthen, and why?

But for now, start with this:

- What's one skill you'd like to develop this year, and how can you take the first step today?

3.3.5 Summary

- Your portfolio is an ongoing work that highlights your journey in PPS including your development, learning and even setbacks (which you can learn from).
- Having a system to collect artefacts over the course of two years is critical to fully develop your portfolio.
- Having a variety of experiences, artefacts and inquiries in your portfolio is an essential way to showcase your full PPS experience.

3.4 How PPS connects to the Core

INQUIRY QUESTION

- How does PPS fit into the CP Core?

3.4.1 How PPS links everything together

This section examines how personal and professional skills (PPS) connects to the other components of the IB Career-related Programme (CP) Core—language and cultural studies (LCS), community engagement (CE) and the reflective project (RP). It highlights how PPS acts as a unifying thread, reinforcing key skills such as critical thinking, ethical reasoning, communication and intercultural understanding. The section also emphasizes the role of ethics in tying together all elements of the CP Core.

Understanding the connections between PPS and the CP Core is essential because it helps you to apply your learning in meaningful contexts. PPS skills are not isolated; they enhance your ability to navigate cultural perspectives in LCS, engage effectively with communities in CE and conduct ethical inquiry in the RP. By making these connections, students develop a more integrated, reflective and purposeful approach to their education and career aspirations.

The section provides concrete strategies for applying PPS skills across the CP Core:

- **LCS:** Encourages you to use PPS skills like intercultural understanding and ethical reasoning to analyse cultural perspectives, identities and communication styles.
- **CE:** Guides you in applying PPS skills such as collaboration, ethical decision-making and critical thinking to service projects and real-world problem-solving.
- **RP:** Supports you in using PPS inquiry skills, ethical reasoning and research techniques to explore and articulate a well-reasoned perspective on an ethical dilemma.
- **Ethics as a unifying theme:** Demonstrates how ethical considerations run through all CP Core components, urging you to reflect on your values and the impact of your actions.

Additionally, the section emphasizes portfolio-building as a way for you to document and reflect on your growth across all CP Core experiences, ensuring you can carry these skills into future academic and professional settings.

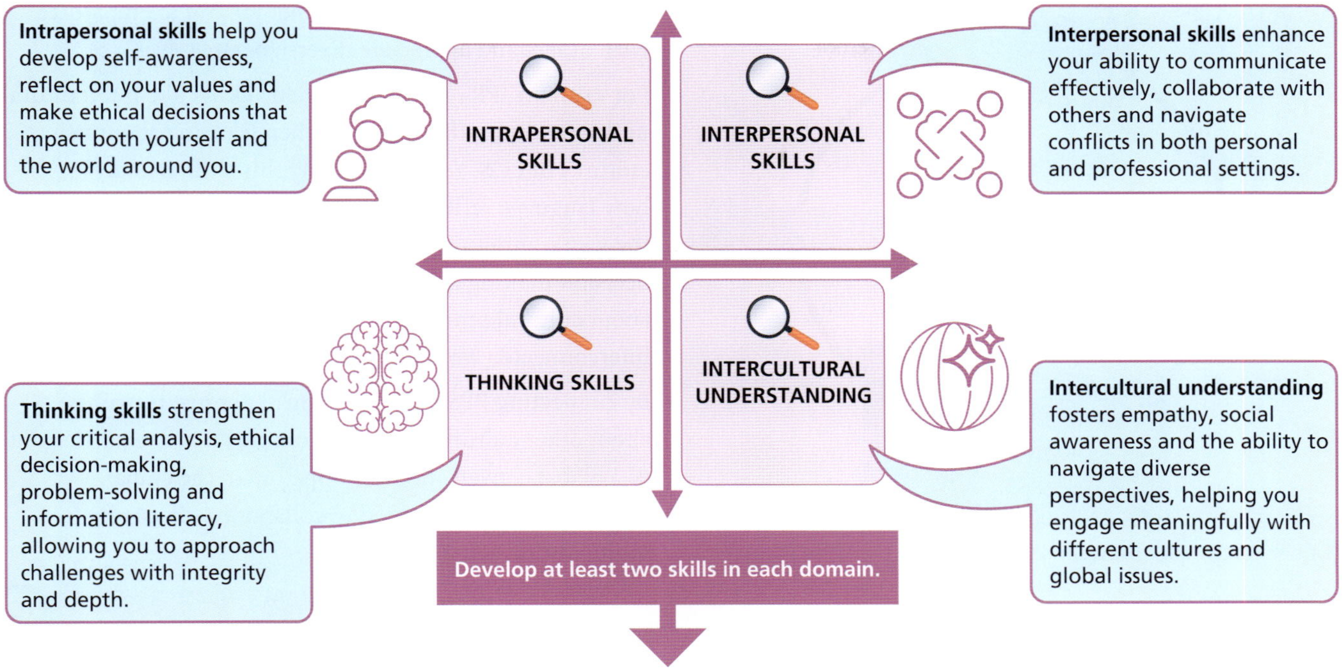

■ PPS skills focused on in Section 3.4

3.4.2 Bridging skills across the Core

One of the most powerful aspects of PPS is its ability to connect your learning in one part of the CP Core with your learning in other areas. Three of the suggested contexts to explore in PPS are CE, LCS and the RP, allowing you to apply the PPS skills, concepts and content in those experiences. As you begin to work in the other Core components, reflect on how you are developing both personal and career-related skills.

In PPS, you explore six key concepts—change, connections, identities, perspectives, systems and well-being—and these act as the building blocks for linking your learning engagements. For instance, when you explore *connections* in PPS, you might examine how relationships between people, ideas or systems impact your life and your studies. This could lead to insights that enhance your work in CE projects, where understanding relationships is key to fostering collaboration. Exploring *perspectives* in PPS could deepen your RP by encouraging you to consider multiple viewpoints on an ethical dilemma, helping you craft a balanced and thoughtful argument.

The skills you practise in PPS, such as self-management, collaboration and ethical reasoning, are also essential across the CP Core. Whether you're participating in a community service initiative, working on your RP or engaging with a new language in LCS, these skills will help you approach challenges with confidence and purpose. Let's take a look at some examples of ways that PPS skills connect to the other CP Core components.

■ LCS: Seeing the world from different angles

Language and cultural studies is your opportunity to explore the power of language and culture in shaping identity and communication. In PPS, you delve into concepts like *identities* and *connections*, which directly relate to LCS.

Through LCS, you study how cultural values, traditions and histories influence the way people interact and view the world. PPS strengthens this by encouraging you to reflect on your own identity and how it is shaped by your culture, personal experiences and community.

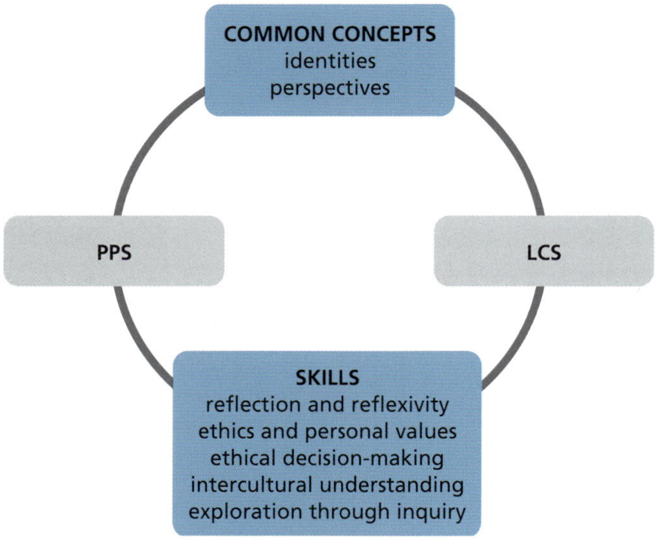

■ Common threads between LCS and PPS

This self-awareness makes it easier for you to empathize with others and appreciate diverse perspectives.

For example, PPS helps you develop skills like intercultural understanding, which is vital when learning about new cultures in LCS. You might apply this skill to analyse how language reflects societal values or influences the way communities communicate. Similarly, ethical decision-making in PPS can guide you to think critically about cultural representation and its implications in today's interconnected world.

By connecting PPS with LCS, you're not just learning about other cultures; you're becoming an active participant in a global conversation, equipped with the empathy and understanding needed to collaborate effectively in multicultural settings.

Reflection and reflexivity

Part of being a reflexive person is being able to identify what your values are, how they are developing and what impacts their development. You also can consider how your values impact the wider world as well. Here are some reflection suggestions that can help you make connections between PPS and LCS throughout the course.

- How do you see the identity as a shared concept between PPS and LCS? By exploring your identity in PPS, this can help you develop your language and cultural portrait and your personal goals for your work in LCS.
- Can you connect ethical thinking in PPS with LCS? It's interesting to see how exploring ethics and ethical practices within the context of PPS can support similar explorations in LCS. In LCS, you might explore how language and culture influence and impact the perspectives of different community members within societal systems.

CE: Turning learning into action

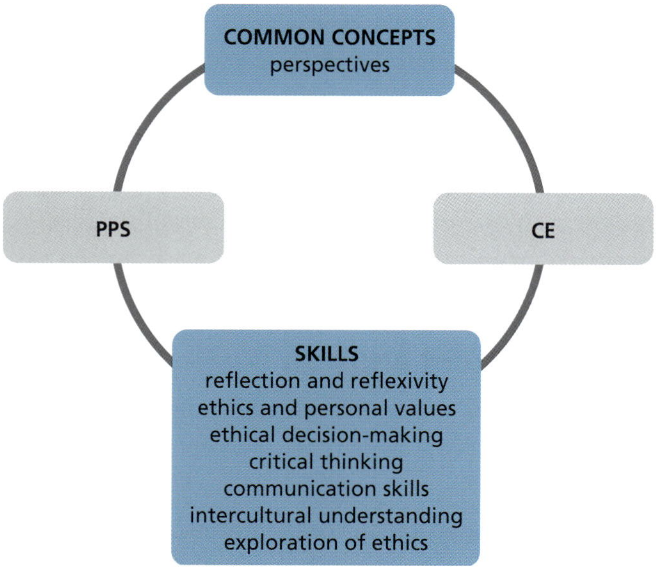

■ How do PPS and CE connect?

Community engagement is where you take the skills and concepts from PPS and apply them to real-world challenges. In CE, you work with communities to address local or global issues, and PPS gives you the tools to navigate these experiences thoughtfully and effectively.

One key connection between PPS and CE is the focus on *systems* and *connections*. In PPS, you learn how systems—whether social, economic or ecological—shape the world around us. This understanding helps you identify your role within these systems during CE projects, whether you're volunteering, leading a service initiative or advocating for change.

PPS also emphasizes collaboration and communication skills, which are critical for successful CE. For example, when working with a team or engaging with community stakeholders, you'll need to listen actively, respect diverse viewpoints and work toward shared goals. By applying the reflective practices you learn in PPS, you can assess the impact of your actions and continuously improve your approach to community involvement.

Additionally, PPS introduces you to ethical thinking, encouraging you to consider the long-term effects of your actions on the community. This means asking important questions like, 'Is this solution sustainable?' or 'How does this action impact the people it's meant to help?' By integrating PPS and CE, you develop the mindset and skills to create meaningful, lasting change in the world around you.

Reflection and reflexivity

Community engagement takes place beyond the classroom and is a chance to develop some very useful transversal skills. Reflect on the following questions throughout your course on the connections between PPS and CE, recording any thoughts in your portfolio:

1. How might you apply communication skills learned in PPS to write emails, conduct meetings in a professional manner or speak in a public setting? These are all activities you might take part in as you work in your community to meet the CE aims and learning outcomes.
2. In what ways did you network with others to make this experience a success?
3. Did you take on any leadership roles while taking part in this learning engagement and what did you learn? What worked and why might you change in the future?
4. What types of problem-solving skills did you employ?

Links

CE is a great context to develop and apply critical- and self-reflexivity as you work with community partners to build and improve relationships. You can use this experience within your PPS course as you consider other contexts.

RP: Deepening ethical understanding

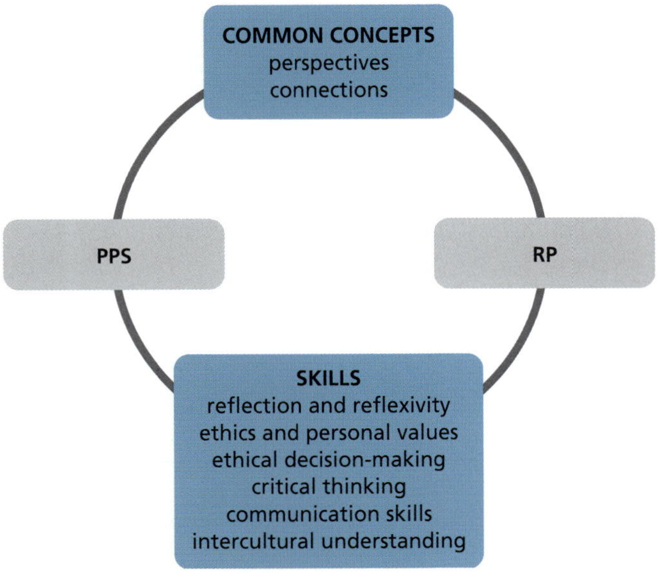

■ How do PPS and the RP connect?

The reflective project is your chance to showcase the critical thinking and ethical reasoning skills you've developed in PPS. It challenges you to investigate an ethical dilemma related to your career interests, requiring you to consider multiple perspectives and use evidence-based reasoning.

PPS provides a foundation for this process by teaching you how to approach complex issues with clarity and confidence. Through activities in PPS, you practise research skills, critical thinking and communication, all of which are essential for developing a well-rounded reflective project.

For example, in PPS, you might analyse case studies or discuss ethical dilemmas to learn how to evaluate arguments and form your own opinions. These experiences prepare you to tackle the RP with a structured approach:

- **Identifying an ethical dilemma:** Use the reflective skills you've honed in PPS to select a topic that resonates with you and aligns with a career-related study.
- **Researching and analysing perspectives:** Apply your critical thinking skills to explore diverse viewpoints, considering the historical, cultural and societal contexts of the dilemma.
- **Communicating your findings:** Use the communication strategies from PPS to present your arguments clearly and persuasively, whether through a written essay or an oral presentation.

By the time you complete your RP, you'll have not only a deeper understanding of the ethical issue you've explored, but also a portfolio of skills that will serve you in higher education and beyond.

Reflection and reflexivity

Being a reflective and ethical member of any community—be that personal, professional or school—means you are someone committed to developing both self- and social awareness. The more you reflect to understand, not just about the impact of your actions, but also your values, the more you will be willing to advocate for yourself. And the RP asks you to do just that.

- Which aspects of ethical thinking that you will explore through PPS inquiries might support you in identifying an ethical dilemma to explore in your RP?
- What reflective and reflexive tools have you used in PPS that might support you in the RP?

As you regularly engage in reflective practice throughout the PPS course, you can apply the skills of reflection and reflexivity to investigate an ethical dilemma, to support the selection and evaluation of resources, and to explore various perspectives on the ethical dilemma for your RP.

Ethics and the Core

Ethics is the thread that ties all CP Core components together, and PPS serves as the foundation for developing your ethical thinking. Whether you're examining cultural norms in LCS, collaborating with a community in CE or analysing an ethical dilemma in your RP, PPS helps you approach these challenges with integrity and thoughtfulness.

In PPS, you explore topics like social justice, equity and sustainability, considering how your actions and decisions impact others. These discussions encourage you to think beyond yourself and reflect on your role in creating a fairer, more compassionate world. By embedding ethics across the CP Core, PPS ensures that you're not only learning, but also growing as a responsible global citizen.

For an immediate and impactful way of understanding what these sorts of topics might stem from and their impact on the world, look at the UN's sustainable development goals and consider which goals are most relevant to your immediate community.

Links

In CE, you might use PPS to evaluate the ethics of a community project, asking questions like, 'Are we listening to the community's needs, or imposing our own solutions?' or 'How can we ensure that our actions are inclusive and respectful of cultural differences?'

Similarly, in the RP, PPS helps you navigate the complexities of ethical dilemmas by teaching you to balance competing values and make reasoned decisions.

PPS and the Core: Portfolio connection

As you complete the CP Core, think about how PPS has shaped your journey. How has it helped you connect your learning across LCS, CE and the RP? How have you applied PPS skills to a career-related study or personal project? Consider which items you would like to include in your portfolio. By reflecting on these experiences, you can carry the lessons of PPS with you into higher education, your career, and beyond.

Reflection and reflexivity

Think about your experiences in the CP Core. How are the skills and concepts in PPS supporting your growth and development? How will you take what you've learned and apply it in the future?

3.4.3 Student sample inquiries

Below are inquiries that students like you have developed and explored in PPS in context to the Core components. As you read through them, consider if any of them are inspiring your own independent inquiry that might connect PPS to other CP Core components.

INQUIRY 1

Breaking language barriers in healthcare

Link: Language and cultural studies

Scenario: Tonya is a CP student interested in a career in healthcare. During her internship at a local clinic, she notices that some patients struggle to communicate with doctors because they don't speak the local language fluently. She wonders how language and cultural barriers impact patient care and how healthcare professionals can bridge this gap.

Focus question: How do language and cultural barriers impact patient care, and how can healthcare professionals bridge this gap?

List the concepts, contexts and skills that will be explored and developed in this inquiry:

- Concepts: Identities and connections
- Context: Language and cultural studies; career-related (healthcare and medical professions)
- Skill development: Intercultural understanding, communication, ethical thinking

Why am I undertaking this inquiry? What are my learning outcomes?

Aligned with PPS learning outcomes:

- **LO2:** Develop and apply communication and collaboration skills.
- **LO5:** Apply ethical reasoning to context-based issues.

How will I explore these topics?

Activities:

- Explore:
  - Research how language barriers affect healthcare outcomes in different countries.
  - Interview medical professionals or interpreters about their experiences.
- Act:
  - Create a multilingual patient guide explaining common medical terms.
  - Organize a language workshop for healthcare students to practise basic medical phrases in different languages.

How will I reflect on my learning?

- What were some of the intercultural challenges encountered in medicine?
- What are some measures healthcare professionals are taking to mitigate these challenges?
- Are there any ethical implications that need to be considered with some of these strategies?

How will I share my learning?

- By presenting findings in a simulated hospital training session.
- By writing an article on the importance of cultural competency in healthcare.

Portfolio integration (artefacts to include):

- Journal reflections on intercultural challenges in medicine.
- Research report on best practices for overcoming language barriers in healthcare.
- The multilingual patient guide.
- Potentially, materials or a reflection on the language workshop I organized.
- The presentation materials from the simulated hospital training session.
- The written article on cultural competency in healthcare.

INQUIRY 2

Ethical volunteering—who really benefits?

Link: Community engagement

Scenario: Raj is passionate about social impact and joins a volunteer program to build houses in a low-income community. While working, he overhears locals saying they weren't consulted about the project and they feel like outsiders are making decisions for them. Raj begins to question whether international volunteering always helps communities or sometimes causes harm.

Focus question: Does international volunteering always help communities or can it sometimes cause harm, and how can we ensure volunteering is ethical and truly beneficial?

List the concepts, contexts and skills that will be explored and developed in this inquiry:

- Concepts: Perspectives and systems
- Context: Community engagement, informal learning
- Skill development: Empathy, social awareness, civic and social responsibility

Why am I undertaking this inquiry? What are my learning outcomes?

Aligned with PPS learning outcomes:

- **LO3:** Apply thinking skills to analyse context-based challenges.
- **LO5:** Demonstrate awareness of ethical implications of one's choices and actions.

How will I explore these topics?

Activities:

- Explore:
  - Read case studies of international aid projects that had unintended negative consequences.
  - Conduct surveys or interviews with community members on their perceptions of volunteering.
- Act:
  - Design a checklist for ethical volunteering, ensuring local communities have a voice.
  - Organize a debate on whether certain volunteer programmes do more harm than good.

How will I reflect on my learning?

- How do power dynamics shape volunteer projects?
- What strategies ensure that community engagement is ethical and sustainable?

How will I share my learning?

- Create an awareness campaign on responsible volunteering.
- Write a reflection piece for a student newspaper about ethical dilemmas in community engagement.

Portfolio integration (artefacts to include):

- Ethical decision-making journal.
- Case study analysis notes.
- Potentially, transcripts or summaries of surveys/interviews with community members.
- The designed checklist for ethical volunteering.
- Materials related to the organized debate (e.g. arguments prepared, reflections on the debate).
- The awareness campaign materials.
- The reflection piece written for the student newspaper.
- The policy proposal for improving ethical standards in volunteer work.

INQUIRY 3

The ethics of artificial intelligence in hiring

Link: Reflective project

Scenario: Sofia is preparing for her RP and wants to investigate the ethical implications of AI in job recruitment. She reads about companies using AI-driven hiring systems to scan résumés and conduct video interviews. While AI promises efficiency, she learns that some systems have been accused of bias—rejecting qualified candidates based on race, gender or socio-economic status. She wonders: Can AI truly be fair or does it reinforce existing biases?

Focus question: Can AI be truly fair in hiring processes or does it risk reinforcing existing biases based on factors like race, gender or socio-economic status?

List the concepts, contexts and skills that will be explored and developed in this inquiry:

- Concepts: Change and systems
- Context: Reflective project, career-related study
- Skill development: Information literacy, critical thinking, ethical reasoning

Why am I undertaking this inquiry? What are my learning outcomes?

Aligned with PPS learning outcomes:

- **LO1:** Develop and apply intrapersonal skills in a variety of contexts.
- **LO5:** Apply ethical reasoning to context-based issues.

How will I explore these topics?

Activities:

- Explore:
  - Research real-world cases of AI bias in hiring.
  - Interview HR professionals about their experiences with AI recruitment tools.
- Act:
  - Conduct a small experiment: Submit identical résumés with different names to AI screening tools and analyse the results.
  - Develop recommendations for ethical AI hiring practices.

How will I reflect on my learning?

- Who is responsible when AI systems discriminate? The company, the programmers or the AI itself?
- How can businesses balance efficiency with fairness in hiring?

How will I share my learning?

- Write a blog post summarizing research findings.
- Present recommendations to a local business association or ethics committee.

Portfolio integration (artefacts to include):

- Ethical dilemma case study analysis.
- Notes and analysis from research on real-world cases of AI bias.
- Transcripts or summaries of interviews with HR professionals.
- Data and analysis from the résumé experiment.
- The developed recommendations for ethical AI hiring practices.
- The blog post summarizing research findings.
- Materials from the presentation to the local business association or ethics committee.
- The RP research paper on AI bias in hiring.

As you build your PPS portfolio, you're not just collecting artefacts, you're telling the story of who you are becoming as a learner and as a person. To help you reflect more deeply on your growth, we can look to the IB learner profile. These ten traits describe the qualities IB learners strive to develop, and offer a powerful lens through which to reflect on your skills, values and actions throughout the PPS course and the CP Core.

This chapter highlights two of these traits—inquirer and principled—and how they relate to your learning journey and your portfolio.

Learner profile

Inquirer

Why it connects: This is all about developing curiosity and the ability to ask meaningful questions. Your portfolio gives you the chance to track your learning journey by reflecting on the questions you've asked and how they've shaped your understanding. By being an inquirer, you're not just passively absorbing information, but actively seeking to explore and make connections.

Learner profile quote: 'You nurture your curiosity, developing skills for inquiry and research. You actively enjoy learning and this love of learning will be a lifelong pursuit.'

In action:

- Reflect on the questions you've asked during a project or lesson and show how your curiosity led to deeper understanding.
- Add research projects or inquiry-based activities to your portfolio and explain what you learned from investigating a topic.
- Ask yourself how your learning connects with other areas and track your personal growth through exploration.

Learner profile

Principled

Why it connects: This encourages you to not only focus on your academic growth, but also to think about your values, ethics and how you make decisions. By being principled, you're making sure that your work in your portfolio reflects your integrity and the decisions you've made in the learning process. This ensures that everything you add is a true reflection of your learning journey.

Learner profile quote: 'You act with integrity and honesty, with a strong sense of fairness and justice. You take responsibility for your actions and the consequences that accompany them.'

In action:

- Reflect on moments when you made ethical decisions during a project and how those decisions shaped the outcome.
- Include examples of work that show how you held yourself accountable for your learning, even when faced with challenges.
- Share how your values influenced your approach to problem-solving or collaboration in group activities.

3.4.4 Summary of skills, contexts and concepts

Table 3.10 What have we explored in this section?

Skills developed	Contexts explored	Key concepts
• Ethical thinking • Reflection • Critical thinking	• Reflective project • Community engagement • Language and cultural studies	• Change • Systems • Connections

Learning journal

Portfolio work: Evidence of learning

Throughout this section, you have documented your learning by exploring how PPS connects to the CP Core components, reflecting on ethical thinking, and curating artefacts that demonstrate your growth as both a learner and a professional.

3.4.5 Summary

- PPS serves as a unifying thread across the CP Core components (LCS, CE, RP), reinforcing the development of intrapersonal skills, interpersonal skills, thinking skills and intercultural understanding.
- Understanding the interconnectedness of PPS and the CP Core enables you to apply your learning in relevant, context-based scenarios, fostering a more integrated and purposeful educational experience aligned with your career aspirations.
- Ethics is a unifying theme throughout the CP Core, meaning that you should consistently reflect on your values and the consequences of your actions in all learning engagements.
- Portfolio-building is highlighted as a crucial method for you to document and reflect on your skill development across the CP Core, helping you to transfer these skills to future academic and professional endeavours.

3.5 Your personal and professional well-being

INQUIRY QUESTIONS

- What is meant by 'well-being' and how does PPS support your overall well-being?
- How can you make decisions that align with your values and impact others positively to support your well-being?
- Why is it important to understand different perspectives from your own and how does that contribute to your own well-being?
- How will practising transversal skills support your well-being and help you succeed in a complex and changing world?

3.5.1 Connecting PPS and well-being

This section explores the connection between well-being and essential personal and professional skills. It introduces key concepts such as self-awareness, ethical decision-making, international-mindedness and transversal skills. Through self-reflection and inquiry-based activities, students assess their well-being and develop strategies to enhance their mental and physical health.

Understanding and actively improving well-being is critical for success in both personal and professional life. In the PPS course, you'll develop skills that help you manage stress, respond to challenges and stay focused on your goals. This includes building resilience—the ability to bounce back from setbacks, adapt to change and keep moving forward even when things get tough.

You'll also learn how to make thoughtful, ethical decisions and understand multiple perspectives, especially when engaging with complex global issues. These experiences will help you grow in empathy and adaptability—qualities that not only support your well-being, but also prepare you for long-term success and fulfillment in a rapidly changing world.

The section includes structured activities such as personal well-being inventories, case studies and reflective exercises. You will engage in ethical dilemmas, analyse different viewpoints and apply transversal skills to real-world challenges. The learning engagements guide you in developing self-awareness, problem-solving abilities and a growth mindset, ultimately strengthening your overall well-being and preparing them for future challenges.

Skills focused on in this chapter are outlined in the following visual.

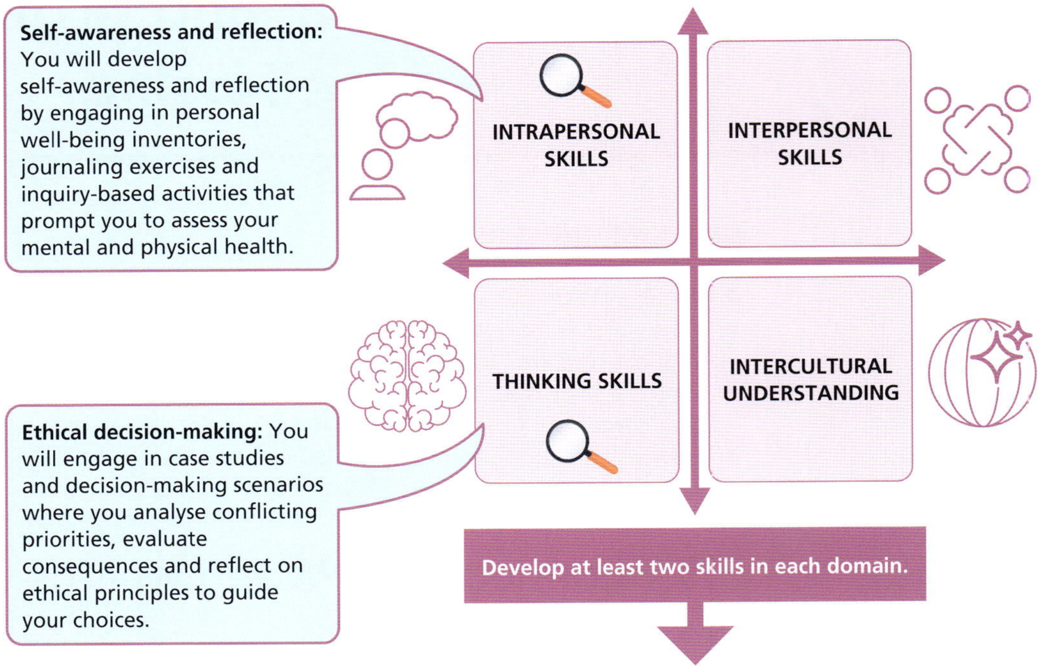

■ PPS skills focused on in Section 3.5

3.5.2 What is well-being?

'Well-being' refers to your physical, emotional and mental state of being, which influences everything in your life—your relationships, productivity, sense of self and ability to overcome challenges and obstacles.

PPS offers a wonderful opportunity for you to get really good at developing a positive well-being. By exploring skills in PPS, you will become very adept at first determining the state of your well-being at any point in life and, second, developing your own strategies to cope with stress and setbacks when they occur.

It is important to recognize that well-being is an individual experience. What works for one person may not work for another, and it is essential to be mindful and avoid judging others based on their approaches to well-being.

This section will outline some of the essential skills that will contribute to your own well-being and the ways you can leverage them to be more successful, balanced, content and productive, so you're able to meet your personal and professional goals now and in the future!

■ Why is understanding and evaluating your well-being so important?

Life can be challenging at times. Our individual well-being can fluctuate based on a variety of factors, such as physical health, emotional resilience, social support, financial stability, work–life balance and personal fulfilment. Successful people are always reflecting on and determining strategies to improve their well-being. The PPS skills outlined in this section will help you to develop a positive mental, emotional and physical well-being.

However, personal well-being is not a one-size-fits-all approach. Some strategies may work well for you but not for others. Being open to different perspectives and approaches is key to maintaining a healthy and respectful mindset regarding well-being.

Reflection and reflexivity

Well-being personal inventory quiz

Take a moment to reflect on your personal well-being. Use the scale below to rate how true each statement feels for you right now. This activity may help you identify areas of strength and areas where you might develop new skills or focus an inquiry.

Scale:

1 = Not at all true

2 = Rarely true

3 = Sometimes true

4 = Often true

5 = Always true

Physical well-being

- ☐ I get enough sleep and have a consistent sleep routine.
- ☐ I eat a balanced diet and drink enough water each day.
- ☐ I get regular physical activity or movement.

Mental and emotional well-being

- ☐ I am aware of my biggest stressors and have healthy coping strategies.
- ☐ I can identify and communicate my emotions in a healthy way.
- ☐ I feel connected to friends, family or my community.

Context and relationships

- ☐ My well-being stays steady in different environments or social situations.
- ☐ I set healthy boundaries in my relationships.
- ☐ I have a balanced relationship with social media and digital content.
- ☐ I communicate with others in healthy and productive ways.

Balance and self-care

- ☐ I maintain a healthy balance between school, relationships and personal time.
- ☐ I make time for hobbies or activities that help me relax and recharge.
- ☐ I stay committed to responsibilities without neglecting personal well-being.

Reflection: What do your results suggest?

- Mostly 4s and 5s: You have strong habits that support your well-being. Keep reflecting and exploring new ways to grow.
- Mostly 2s and 3s: You're developing awareness of your well-being. Consider focusing your next inquiry on building specific skills like stress management, time balance or communication.
- Mostly 1s and 2s: This may be a signal to prioritize self-care. You might want to explore support systems, reflect on boundaries or seek guidance in areas that feel overwhelming.

In your PPS portfolio, jot down any patterns you noticed and highlight one or two skills you'd like to explore further (e.g. emotional regulation, resilience, self-management). These could become the focus of a personal inquiry to strengthen your well-being.

3.5.3 Key skills in PPS that contribute to your well-being

Ethical thinking

'Emotions aren't the enemy in the workplace; they are data.'

(Liz Fosslien and Mollie Duffy (2022), *Big feelings: How to be okay when things are not okay*)

Ethical thinking is a cornerstone of navigating the complexities of both personal and professional life. It involves making decisions that not only reflect your values but also consider the well-being of others and the broader community.

Ethical decision-making requires recognizing how our emotions inform our values and actions. When you have strong ethical thinking, you make decisions you can feel good about, reducing stress and enhancing well-being. Conversely, when you do not engage in ethical thinking, you may make decisions that are misaligned with your values, leading to stress, regret and diminished well-being.

Let's take a look at an example that required students to draw on several PPS skills to be successful.

REAL-WORLD EXAMPLE

Local history documentary

A team of students are tasked with creating a documentary film about the history of their local community for an upcoming school event. All of the students are excited and each brings a specific skillset to the team. These are the members of the crew and what they are most passionate about for this project:

- **Saige:** Passionate about preserving local history. Wants the documentary to focus on in-depth interviews with elderly residents and the collection of historical artefacts.
- **Will:** Skilled in filmmaking. Prioritizes a visually appealing and engaging documentary with professional-quality filming, editing and sound design.
- **Gabe:** Concerned about the accuracy and authenticity of the historical information presented. Wants to ensure all information is thoroughly researched and properly cited.
- **Sierra:** Believes the documentary should be accessible and engaging for a wide audience, including younger students. Wants to incorporate interactive elements and use modern storytelling techniques.
- **Josh:** Focuses on community involvement. Wants to involve local residents in the filmmaking process, such as conducting interviews, providing historical insights and participating in the film's premiere.

As the students work together, they realize that their passions and different areas of focus created some conflicting priorities and tension within the group. They find it difficult to manage these conflicts.

Here are some of the issues the group face:

- **Historical accuracy versus entertainment:** Gabe's focus on historical accuracy clashes with Will's desire for a visually engaging and potentially more dramatic presentation.
- **Community involvement versus professionalism:** Josh's emphasis on community involvement conflicts with Will's vision for a professionally produced and edited film.
- **Accessibility versus historical depth:** Sierra's focus on accessibility requires simplifying the historical narrative, potentially compromising the depth and complexity of the historical information, which is frustrating to Gabe.
- **Resources versus scope:** The team faces limitations in terms of budget, time and resources from the outside, which constrains their ability to fulfil all their goals, such as extensive interviews, hiring professional equipment and community outreach events. This is upsetting for Saige.

Recognizing that compromise and teamwork are necessary components to this work, the team needs to draw on a variety of PPS skills to think through these conflicting priorities and make decisions that will produce the best outcomes, honour each other's priorities, maintain amicable working relationships and finish on time and within budget.

Working through challenges as a team

When teams face conflicting priorities, they must draw on a variety of PPS skills to navigate differences, make effective decisions and maintain strong working relationships—all while meeting deadlines and staying within budget.

Here are some key PPS skills that are especially useful in this situation:

- adaptability
- collaboration
- ethical thinking
- communication
- emotional regulation
- problem-solving

Using PPS skills to overcome conflict and adversity, the team works together to develop a clear plan. After a lot of discussion, time to process and reflect, the team compromise by shortening the documentary, so that they will make the deadline and come in under budget. This helps them to maintain historical accuracy and make it accessible, but they are unable to cover as much content in their documentary. Knowing this limits the documentary's artistic style, they all work to find another opportunity in the future to work together on another documentary. Overall, it isn't exactly what they have set out to do but, in the end, they feel proud of the product they have produced.

LEARNING ENGAGEMENT

Your turn: Skills in action

Choose three skills from the PPS list in the real-world example above. For each, complete the following sentence frame to show how the team might apply that skill in this scenario:

The group needs to develop (specific skill) when ... since ...

Example: The group needs to develop adaptability when a team member's priority conflicts with the project timeline, since sticking to one plan without adjusting could delay progress.

Optional examples for inspiration:

- The group needs to develop collaboration when balancing different ideas about how to allocate the budget, since all members bring unique perspectives that need to be heard.
- The group needs to develop ethical thinking when deciding whose priorities take precedence, since fairness and transparency are key to team trust.
- The group needs to develop emotional regulation when tensions rise during disagreements, since reacting impulsively could harm team dynamics.

Top tip!

It is said that the biggest issue with communication is the illusion that it has taken place. When working in groups, it is important to communicate in a variety of ways (i.e. follow up a conversation with a team member by sending them an email summarizing the main points discussed) to ensure that your message is clear, effective and, most importantly, received.

Reflection and reflexivity

Local history documentary

1 Take a minute to imagine you are on this team. Are there additional skills that you feel would have supported this team? Of those skills, which do you find more challenging to implement? How could this situation help develop those skills for you?

2 Consider the skills required to best work on this team, then think about the following questions. Which skills would you most likely employ to help answer these questions?
- How would you balance fairness, transparency and effectiveness in your decision-making?
- How will you ensure you act with integrity while managing the realistic limitations in this situation?
- How will you evaluate the potential consequences of your decisions?
- What actions might you take to ensure a healthy working relationship between you and your team members?

Ethical thinking requires reflection on your principles and actions. As Fosslien and Duffy (2022) note, 'We do our best work when we feel like we belong and our contributions matter.' Ethical decision-making fosters a sense of purpose and belonging, reinforcing well-being for yourself and others.

As you practise ethical thinking, you build a foundation for making thoughtful, impactful choices in a rapidly changing world that align with your values and increase your well-being.

LEARNING ENGAGEMENT

Consider one ethical principle you want to embody, and how you can ensure it becomes a part of your ethical thinking.

1 Think about a time you witnessed someone acting in a way that strongly impressed you ethically, or a time you felt proud (or regretful) about an ethical decision. What principle was at play? How did it make you feel? Create a visual that illustrates the experience, the principle at play and the feelings you had associated with it.
2 Write a short personal pledge or manifesto outlining a principle that is important to you and 2–3 concrete actions you will take to embody it in your daily life. Post it somewhere visible, so you can see it often.

International-mindedness and multiple perspectives

In our interconnected world, understanding diverse perspectives is more critical than ever. Fosslien and Duffy (2022) emphasize, 'Empathy isn't about fixing someone's problems; it's about showing them they aren't alone.' When you develop international-mindedness, you strengthen your ability to connect with others, reducing feelings of isolation and increasing well-being. International-mindedness involves recognizing and valuing the experiences, beliefs and cultures of others. It requires empathy and a willingness to step outside your own viewpoint.

LEARNING ENGAGEMENT

Mapping our worldview

Draw a map of the world as you perceive it, labelling countries and regions based on your existing knowledge and understanding. Then reflect on your map, considering the information you added.

1 What did you include?
2 What is missing?
3 What might be inaccurate?

Reflection and reflexivity

Mapping our worldview

In your journal or with peer, reflect:

- How do you think your personal experiences, media exposure and cultural background shape your mental maps of the world?
- What biases might have entered into your world map?
- How does your worldview influence your interactions with people from different backgrounds?
- How can you develop a more accurate and nuanced understanding of the world?
- How might this work improve your well-being and the well-being of others?

Engaging with multiple perspectives deepens your understanding of the world and your place in it. It enables you to appreciate complexity, resolve conflicts and collaborate effectively in diverse environments, all of which increase your well-being.

Now consider the following global issue.

LEARNING ENGAGEMENT

Inequity in technology access

Across the world, there is unequal access to and use of information and communication technology (ICT) like computers, the internet and mobile phones across different groups within a country and between countries.

In a small group, research the countries that have the least access to ICT and then analyse this situation by considering how culture, history and social context shape the perspectives of people from different countries and cultures. You may find www.amnestyusa.org a useful resource in your research. Discuss the following points:

1. How do new technologies amplify existing inequalities and biases?
2. How can inequality in access to technologies amplify existing disparities in health, education and employment?
3. To what extent can 'digital borders' impact the most at risk around the world?

By actively seeking out and reflecting on other viewpoints, you enhance your ability to connect and contribute meaningfully to a global community.

Reflection and reflexivity

What steps can you take to appreciate and engage with diverse, global communities?

Transversal skills and well-being

Using skills such as self-awareness, self-management and reflection will enable you to evaluate your well-being and take action if you need to change or adapt. As Fosslien and Duffy (2022) state, 'Tiny changes, over time, make a huge difference.' Small, consistent efforts to reflect and adjust your habits can greatly impact your overall well-being.

You can then employ skills such as critical and creative thinking, resiliency, collaboration, adaptability and problem solving to pivot gracefully when faced with unexpected changes or challenges. For example, adaptability allows you to navigate uncertainty with resilience, while critical thinking helps you analyse situations and solve problems creatively. Collaboration enables you to work effectively with others, leveraging diverse strengths to support your growth and development. Being able to apply these skills when challenges arise will increase your ability to maintain a positive well-being.

Developing transversal skills is an ongoing process. Reflect on your experiences, seek feedback and set goals for continuous improvement. These skills are your toolkit for success in a world that is constantly evolving.

LEARNING ENGAGEMENT

Transversal skills and well-being

Life is full of challenges—big and small. The way you respond to these challenges can impact your well-being. In this activity, you will reflect on your own well-being, explore different situations where transversal skills can help, and create a personal action plan to strengthen your ability to adapt, problem-solve and thrive.

Step 1: Check-in

Take a moment to reflect:

- On a scale from 1 to 10, how is your well-being today?
- What is one challenge you are currently facing that affects your well-being?
- Write a few thoughts in your journal or a note on your device.

Step 2: Apply transversal skills

Read the following real-life situations. Choose one and think about how transversal skills (such as adaptability, problem-solving, self-awareness, collaboration and resilience) could help.

- You have a big project due but you're feeling stuck and unmotivated.
- You had a disagreement with a friend and it's been on your mind all day.
- You have several commitments (school, sports, family, etc.) and you're feeling overwhelmed.
- You're in a group project but you feel like no one is listening to your ideas.

Step 3: Reflect

Ask yourself:

- What transversal skills could help in this situation?
- How developed are these skills and what skills might you need to continue to develop?
- How could you apply those skills to improve the outcome and your well-being?
- Write down your thoughts or discuss them with a partner.

Step 4: Take action

Now apply this to your own life.

- What is one small action you can take this week to improve your well-being using transversal skills?
- How will this action help you navigate challenges and grow?
- Write your action plan and share it with a classmate or reflect on it privately.

Reflection and reflexivity

Stop to reflect

Take time to reflect on the skills and concepts explored in this section. Consider these questions:

- Are you aware of your current well-being and do you have strategies to develop a positive well-being?
- What ethical dilemmas have you faced and how did you navigate them?

- How have you engaged with perspectives different from your own and what did you learn?
- Which transversal skills have you strengthened and how can you continue to develop them?
- How will these skills and understandings support your well-being and growth for the future?
- How can you improve your well-being by developing these skills?

Reflection is a powerful tool for growth. Use these questions to deepen your understanding and chart your path forward, building the skills and mindset needed for a future full of possibilities.

3.5.4 Student sample inquiries

Below are inquiries developed by students who wanted to further explore the idea of well-being. As you read through them, consider if any of them are inspiring your own independent inquiry on well-being.

INQUIRY 1

Developing adaptability in a changing world

Throughout my inquiry, I aim to explore the concept of change and systems, focusing on how adaptability plays a crucial role in both personal and professional life. This inquiry will take place in career-related study, professional life and personal life contexts, as I seek to navigate uncertainties and transitions with confidence. I will develop intrapersonal, interpersonal and thinking skills to enhance my ability to embrace change, problem-solve effectively and adjust to new situations.

I am undertaking this inquiry because adaptability is essential for success in a fast-changing world. By improving my ability to respond to unexpected challenges and shifts, I hope to become more resilient and proactive in my personal and professional endeavours. The specific skills I will develop include flexibility in decision-making, openness to new perspectives and the ability to manage uncertainty with confidence.

To explore the concepts of change and systems, I will assess what I already know about adaptability and identify areas where I need growth. I recognize that being open to change is important, but I want to strengthen my ability to embrace uncertainty without feeling overwhelmed. To do this, I will engage in problem-solving exercises, read case studies on successful adaptability and seek mentorship from professionals who have navigated change effectively. I will also refine my ability to remain composed and analytical when faced with unexpected challenges.

To take action, I will document instances where I encounter change, analyse my reactions and identify ways to improve my adaptability. I will engage in role-playing exercises, take on new challenges that push me out of my comfort zone and reflect on how I handle transitions. I will track my progress through journaling, gather feedback from peers and mentors, and refine my approach based on real-world experiences. I will share my insights by writing a reflection, giving a presentation or facilitating a discussion on the importance of adaptability in personal and professional life.

Through this inquiry, my refined focus is to develop strategies for maintaining a growth mindset and handling change with confidence. By the end of this process, I aim to be more adaptable in both planned and unexpected situations, improve my problem-solving skills and develop a stronger sense of resilience when faced with uncertainty.

INQUIRY 2

Building resilience in professional and personal life

Throughout my inquiry, I aim to explore the concept of change and well-being, focusing on how resilience can help me navigate challenges in both personal and professional life. This inquiry will take place in informal learning, personal life and professional life contexts, as I seek to apply practical strategies to real-world situations. I will develop intrapersonal, interpersonal and thinking skills to enhance my ability to recover from setbacks and manage stress effectively.

I am undertaking this inquiry because resilience is essential for maintaining well-being and achieving long-term success. By developing emotional resilience and stress-management techniques, I hope to cultivate a growth mindset and improve my self-awareness. The specific skills I will develop include identifying personal triggers, applying resilience-building strategies such as mindfulness, and enhancing my emotional intelligence to manage challenges more effectively.

To explore the concept of resilience, I will reflect on what I already know about resilience and identify areas where I need to grow. I understand that resilience is key to handling setbacks, but I need to learn more about practical techniques for building it. I will read self-help books, attend workshops and participate in guided mindfulness sessions. I will also explore my skills in this context by journaling, attending resilience-building webinars and engaging in discussions with peers.

To take action, I will maintain a journal documenting stressful situations and coping strategies, read books and articles on resilience and join a discussion group focused on personal development. I will reflect on my learning by writing weekly reflections, tracking my stress-management progress and seeking feedback from mentors or peers. I will share my experience by writing a blog post, discussing key takeaways with a mentor or creating a short presentation on building resilience.

Based on my planning, my refined focus is to make resilience a daily habit and develop longer-term strategies for maintaining well-being and motivation. Through this process, I hope to learn effective stress-management techniques, understand how mindset influences resilience and develop practical strategies to navigate setbacks with confidence.

INQUIRY 3

Enhancing communication skills for leadership

For this inquiry, I will explore the concept of connections and perspectives by focusing on how I can improve my communication skills to become a more effective leader. This inquiry will take place in career-related study, personal life and professional life contexts, as communication plays a critical role in leadership across different areas. I will develop intrapersonal, interpersonal and thinking skills to enhance my ability to articulate ideas clearly, inspire others and foster collaboration.

I am undertaking this inquiry because strong communication skills are essential for leadership, teamwork and professional success. By developing clarity and confidence in verbal and written communication, I hope to improve my active listening, conflict-resolution and persuasive-speaking abilities. The specific skills I will develop include public speaking, structuring messages clearly and using emotional intelligence to navigate difficult conversations.

To explore these concepts, I will assess what I already know about communication and identify areas for improvement. While I understand that effective communication is key to leadership, I sometimes struggle with nervousness and unclear messaging. To address this, I will practise public speaking, attend leadership workshops and seek feedback from mentors and peers. I will also explore my communication skills by engaging in structured debates, participating in discussions and refining my articulation through reflective practice.

To take action, I will practise delivering short speeches, engage in discussions to refine my articulation and seek constructive feedback from others. I will reflect on my progress by recording and analysing my speeches, keeping a log of communication experiences and tracking improvements in confidence and clarity over time. I will share my experience by writing a reflection on my communication growth, participating in a panel discussion or debate, and mentoring someone who struggles with communication.

Through this inquiry, I hope to refine my focus on adjusting my communication style to different audiences and inspiring others through my words. By the end of this process, I aim to improve my confidence in public speaking, gain insights into persuasive and motivational communication, and develop strategies to manage nervousness and enhance clarity in leadership situations.

Learner profile

Risk-taker

Why it connects: This challenges you to try new ideas when it comes to improving your well-being. Trying new strategies to manage stress, setting boundaries or experimenting with new coping mechanisms can feel intimidating, but it's essential to push yourself out of your comfort zone. By being a risk-taker, you're embracing the possibility of growth and change, which can ultimately enhance your overall well-being.

Learner profile quote: 'You approach unfamiliar situations and uncertainty with courage and forethought. You are not afraid to explore new roles, ideas and strategies.'

In action:

- Experiment with a new stress-management technique and reflect on how it impacts your emotional and physical state.
- Take the risk of expressing your feelings to others in a healthy way, even if it feels vulnerable.
- Challenge yourself to try a new self-care activity or routine to see how it affects your sense of well-being.

Learner profile

Thinker

Why it connects: This emphasizes the importance of thoughtful reflection and critical thinking when evaluating your well-being. As a thinker, you can analyse the strategies that work for you, consider the impact of your decision and adjust your habits accordingly. Reflecting on your well-being is an essential skill in recognizing what's helping or hindering your personal growth and mental health.

Learner profile quote: 'You apply thinking skills critically and creatively to recognize and approach complex problems and make reasoned, ethical decisions.'

In action:

- Reflect on your personal well-being by analysing what's currently working and what might need improvement.
- Use critical thinking to examine your emotional responses and how they influence your well-being, and make adjustments as needed.
- Set specific, measurable goals to enhance your well-being and track your progress using the skills you've learned.

3.5.5 Summary of skills, contexts and concepts

■ **Table 3.11** What have we explored in this section?

Skills developed	Contexts explored	Key concepts
• Reflection • Self-awareness • Adaptability	• Personal • Professional • Informal learning	• Well-being • Perspectives • Connections

Learning journal

Portfolio work: Evidence of learning

Throughout this section, you have documented your learning through:

- well-being inventory
- reflective exercises
- analysis on case studies.

3.5.6 Summary

- Understanding and actively improving well-being is vital for personal and professional success, enabling you to navigate challenges, make ethical choices and build resilience.
- Developing skills such as recognizing different perspectives and engaging with global issues fosters empathy and adaptability, contributing to long-term success and personal fulfilment.
- Exploring case studies, well-being inventories and reflective exercises can help you assess and enhance your mental, emotional and physical health.
- The development of skills such as self-awareness, problem-solving abilities and a growth mindset will strengthen your overall well-being and preparedness for future challenges.

3.6 Independent inquiry and agency

INQUIRY QUESTIONS

- How can you take ownership of your learning?
- What does it mean to be in charge of your own learning?
- How do you design and manage a meaningful inquiry?

3.6.1 The independent inquiry

This section is likely to be most relevant to you in the second year of your personal and professional skills (PPS) studies. It focuses on the concept of independent inquiry, emphasizing the development of curiosity, critical thinking and self-directed learning. It introduces strategies for formulating meaningful questions, conducting research and reflecting on the learning process. You will also explore how independent inquiry connects to the broader PPS framework.

Independent inquiry is a fundamental skill for lifelong learning, career development and personal growth. It empowers you to take ownership of your learning, think critically about complex issues and develop problem-solving skills. By engaging in independent inquiry, you will cultivate intellectual curiosity, resilience and the ability to navigate uncertainty—key attributes for success in both academic and professional settings.

The section provides practical tools and strategies, including:

- **Question development:** Techniques for crafting effective research questions.
- **Research skills:** Methods for gathering, evaluating and synthesizing information.
- **Critical reflection:** Approaches to analysing learning engagements and identifying areas for growth.
- **Application in PPS and beyond:** Guidance on integrating inquiry-based learning into projects, portfolios and career-related experiences.

Through structured activities and real-world examples, you will learn how to apply independent inquiry to personal interests, academic projects and professional aspirations, making learning more meaningful and impactful.

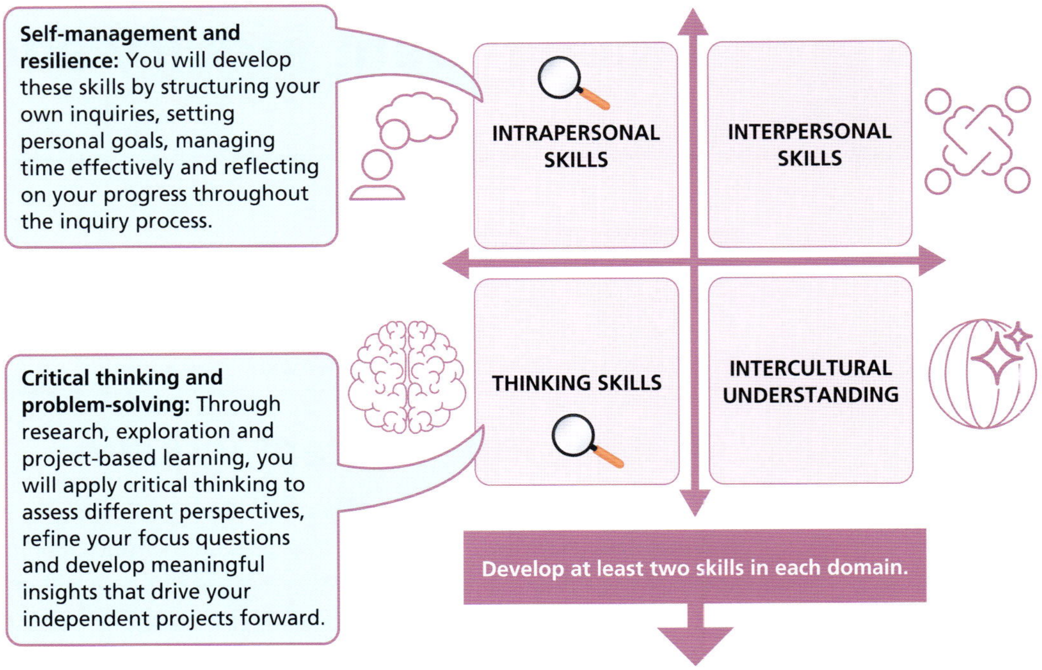

■ PPS skills focused on in Section 3.6

3.6.2 Taking the lead

Congratulations on progressing in your PPS journey! This stage marks an exciting shift toward focusing more on you as a learner. Think of this as an opportunity to step into the role of a researcher, creator and leader.

Earlier in the course, you may have engaged with more guided inquiries designed to help you build foundational skills. As you advance, ideally by the second year, you will begin to take greater ownership of your learning—exploring questions that spark your curiosity, identifying challenges that inspire you and discovering solutions that make an impact.

Consider this phase as your personal lab for testing ideas, pursuing your passions and sharpening the skills that align with your goals.

■ What does this look like in action?

You'll design your own projects, create meaningful connections between your interests and the world around you, and reflect deeply on how your learning shapes who you are and who you want to become. This is about more than academics—this is about finding your voice, honing your agency and building a toolkit for success in life.

So here's the challenge: What excites you? What problems do you want to solve? What ideas do you want to explore?

> What is your initial response to the questions above? As you develop your thoughts, you will find the answers to these questions are your starting point.

Top tip!

Remember that agency is an individual's ability to initiate and influence their own actions.

3.6.3 Why talk about agency?

Imagine you're the captain of a ship, navigating a vast, open sea. Agency is the compass that points you in the direction you want to go. It's the wind in your sails that propels you forward. Being in charge of your learning means setting your own course, charting your own maps and adjusting as you go.

Agency is about more than just independence—it's about ownership. When you take charge of your learning, you're no longer waiting for someone else to tell you what to do. Instead, you're asking the big questions:

- What matters to me?
- How can I explore it?
- What's the best way to reach my goals?

But agency isn't always easy. Sometimes, it means facing hard questions about what's working and what's not. Sometimes you're not feeling inspired, motivated or determined. That's normal, but successful people are the ones who are able to find a way through difficulties and continue making progress, no matter what.

Agency is about making decisions that reflect your values and being willing to pivot when things don't go as planned. When you develop agency, you're building transversal skills that go far beyond the classroom—skills like resilience, critical thinking and self-direction. These are the same skills that will serve you in your career, relationships and personal growth.

As you step into this year, think about what agency looks like for you. What does it mean to truly take ownership of your learning? And how can you make choices that align with the person you want to be?

Structuring your own inquiries

Key term

◆ **Independent inquiry:** An inquiry that you initiate, develop and execute on your own based on something you want to explore or learn about. You can use the tools provided by your teacher or the PPS toolkit to guide you in developing independent inquiries.

Creating your own inquiry (or **independent inquiry**) might feel overwhelming at first, but don't worry—you have a roadmap. The inquiry cycle is your guide to breaking down the process into manageable, meaningful steps.

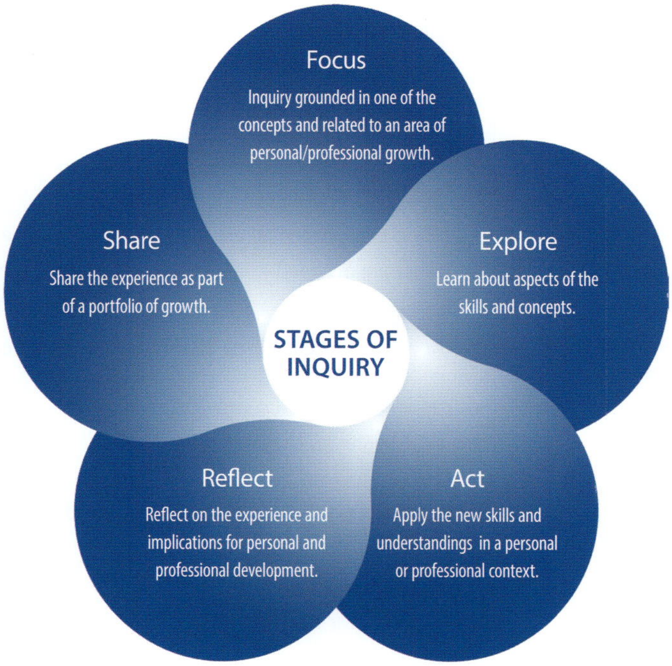

■ The PPS inquiry cycle (Source: IB PPS guide, p.29)

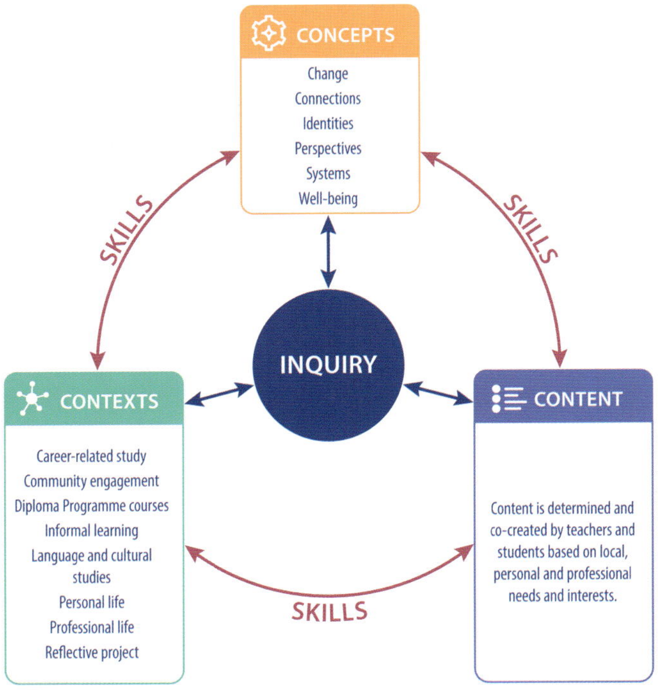

■ PPS course design (Source: IB PPS guide, p.13)

Focus

Start by identifying a big, open-ended question that excites you. This question is your north star—it will guide everything you do. Remember the building blocks of PPS: concepts, contexts, content, skills and learning outcomes. These can help give you inspiration for a starting point from which to expand.

Top tip!

Pay attention to your day-to-day interactions and experiences. Is there something that is bothering you or an issue that seems to challenge your thinking in some way? Make a note of it. This might be inspiration for a fantastic focus question for an independent inquiry!

Using the PPS building blocks

■ **Table 3.12** Examples of using the PPS building blocks to build meaningful inquiry questions

PPS building block	Potential focus questions
Concept: Change	• Why do some people embrace change while others resist it? • What factors influence our responses? • What are the psychological and emotional impacts of change? • How do individuals and communities cope with change?
Context: Career-related study—artist	• Can art help to improve one's well-being? • How might technology improve art and in what ways might it impede creativity? • How can art be a tool for self-discovery and understanding one's own identity?
Content: Social media and one's well-being	• What is the relationship between social media use and anxiety, depression and loneliness? • How does the constant exposure to others' 'highlight reels' impact our perception of our own lives and accomplishments?
Skills: Self-management and self-awareness	• What are my core values and how do they guide my decisions and actions? • What are my deeply held beliefs and how do they shape my worldview? • How effectively do I manage my time? Where do I tend to 'waste' time?
LO5: Demonstrate an awareness of the ethical implications of one's choices and actions on self and others.	• How do I navigate ethical dilemmas when there is no clear right or wrong answer? • How do I prioritize competing values and make difficult decisions? • How might my choices impact future generations?

Be sure to choose a question that feels personal and important to you!

Explore

Once you've chosen your focus, dive into the research. This is where you gather information, explore different perspectives and build a foundation of knowledge. Here are some places to start:

Research your topic

- What do experts say?
- What can you learn from case studies, videos, blogs, books or articles?
- Who might you be able to interview or talk to that may provide a helpful perspective?
- Can you create a survey and collect data from different people?

Locate and plan for experiences

- Is there an activity you can do to help you explore your question?
- What events or experiences might provide you with insight into answering your question?

Explore

Exploration is all about uncovering the 'why' behind your question. Collect as much information as possible to help answer your focus question. Think of research as asking and answering questions carefully. There are so many ways to do this (beyond simply using a search engine or AI).

Qualitative research

Key terms

◆ **Qualitative:** Measuring by the quality of something, rather than its quantity (the size or number).

◆ **Quantitative:** Measuring by the size or number of something.

Qualitative research is when you ask or observe people directly about your topic. Some ways to conduct qualitative research include:

- **Talking to people (interviews):** Having conversations with people to get their detailed opinions and stories.
- **Group discussions (focus groups):** Talking to a small group to see what they think and how they react to each other's ideas.
- **Watching people (observations):** Carefully watching what people do in real life.
- **Reading, watching or listening to stories (case studies, movies, TEDx talks, biopics, etc.):** Deeply studying one person, group or event to understand it well.

Quantitative research

Quantitative research occurs when you count, read or measure information.. Some ways to research quantitatively include:

- **Surveys (with specific answers):** Asking lots of people the same questions with set answer choices so you can count the results.
- **Experiments:** Setting up a test to see if changing one thing causes something else to happen.
- **Looking at numbers (data analysis):** Studying existing numbers and statistics to find patterns.

While using a search engine to investigate your topic is a good place to start, you should be using other methods such as those decribed above to fully explore your topic.

Act

Now it's time to roll up your sleeves and get to work! Use what you've learned to create something meaningful. Here are some potential ideas of ways you could act:

- Create an activity or experience to showcase your learning.
- Create a project, a presentation or a campaign.
- Develop and execute an experiment.
- Organize or plan a community initiative.
- Join an organization and take an active role in their work.

Whatever you choose to do, make it count. Make it meaningful to you!

Reflect

Pause and think about what you've learned—not just about your topic, but about yourself. Here are some questions to think about in your reflection:

- What new learning did you acquire and how can it apply to your future, both personally and professionally?
- What worked well and what challenges did you face?
- What would you do differently next time?

Reflection is where growth happens. Your reflection can come in a variety of ways, including written, visual or multi-modal (blogs, vlogs or videos). You might consider reflecting with a peer or your teacher. The most important thing is that you take time to think about how this work has impacted you now and in the future.

Top tip!

The inquiry cycle is flexible—it's okay to revisit earlier steps or change your focus as you go. Inquiries can also be different sizes; that is, some may take days while others may take months, depending on your content and context. It is helpful to consult with your teacher if you need guidance on the time length of your inquiry. The important thing is to stay curious and keep moving forward.

Share

Don't keep your learning to yourself! Sharing your work is a chance to celebrate your growth and inspire others. Here are some examples of ways to share your learning:

- Present your findings to classmates.
- Write an article to publish or share with others.
- Create a video on your learning.
- Craft something visual to share with others.

Sharing makes your learning real and connects it to the wider world.

The sky's the limit when it comes to how to develop and plan your inquiry! Be creative, use your resources and think outside of the box. Consider asking friends, family members, teachers or mentors to support you in developing ideas for your inquiry.

3.6.4 Brainstorming inquiries using the focus question flow chart

By now, you've had some practice moving through structured inquiries that were designed for you. Now it's time to flip the script. You get to develop your own inquiry from scratch! This is *your* learning journey and the most important thing is that your inquiry is authentic to *you*. It must answer the big question: 'What do I want to learn and explore?'

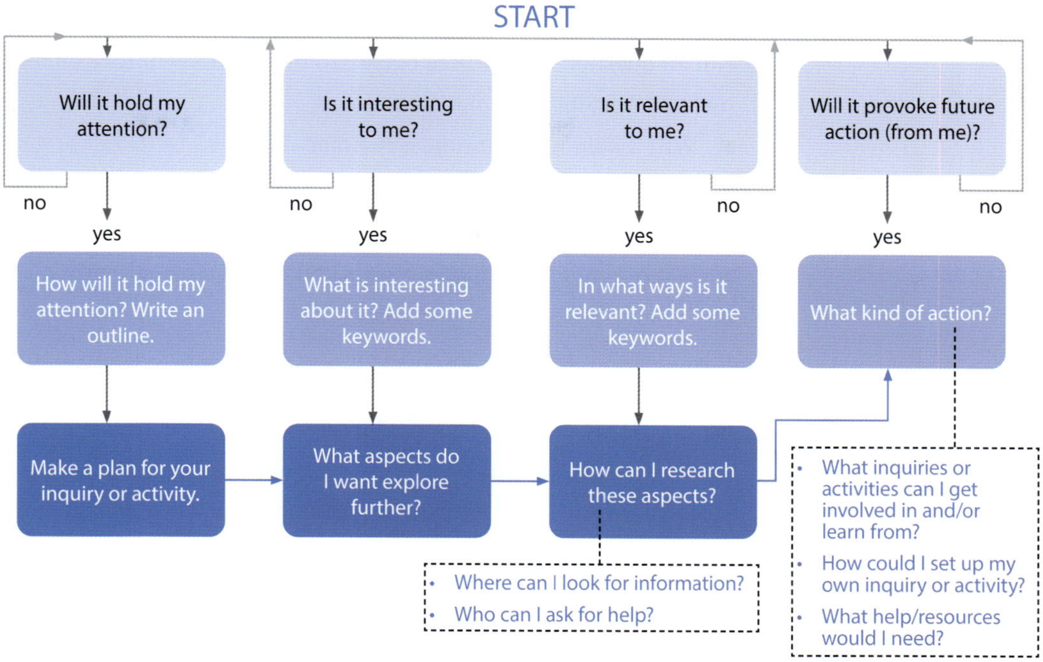

■ Focus question student flow chart (Source: IB PPS toolkit)

Step 1: Crafting your focus question

Think of this as setting the coordinates for your journey. Your focus question is the guiding light that will shape your inquiry. Here are some prompts to help you create one:

- What do you really want to learn about?
- Has there been an issue or challenge that you would like to learn to solve?
- What do you enjoy learning about?
- Are there any PPS concepts, contexts, skills or learning outcomes that inspire you?
- What excites your curiosity? What makes you want to dig deeper?

Write down your ideas. If a question doesn't excite you, keep refining!

Step 2: Evaluating your focus question

Not all questions are created equal! To make sure your focus question will sustain your interest, ask yourself:

- Will it hold my attention over time?
- Is this something I am truly passionate about and not just something I think my teacher wants me to study?
- Is it relevant to my life, my goals and my personal growth?
- Will it lead to meaningful action?

If you answered 'yes' to all, great! If not, tweak your question until it feels just right.

Step 3: Breaking it down with the flow chart

Now it's time to brainstorm! The focus question flow chart will guide you through the details of your inquiry. Use the following guiding prompts to deepen your thinking:

- How will it hold my attention? List activities, experiments or projects that excite you.
- What is interesting about it? Jot down key themes, ideas and connections.
- In what ways is it relevant? Identify how this topic connects to your life and future goals.
- What kind of actions could it provoke? Think about how you could apply what you learn.

Now that you've considered the above, are there any PPS concepts, contexts, skills or learning outcomes that are inspiring a question for you to explore?

Think about what is most interesting to you and use the PPS building blocks to support in crafting your focus question. Take a minute to look at your plan and evaluate. Is this something that you really want to explore? Will it hold your attention, be relevant and support your growth in the future? If yes, then you are on your way!

3.6.5 Building your inquiry plan

Now that you've got your focus question and brainstorming notes, it's time to map out your plan. Think of this as your personalized GPS for learning. Use the PPS student inquiry planner to connect your inquiry to the PPS building blocks.

Table 3.13 PPS student inquiry planner (Source: IB PPS toolkit)

Focus question(s) for my inquiry		
What concept will I explore?	**In what context will I explore it?**	**Which skill area(s) will I develop?**
☐ Change ☐ Connections ☐ Identities ☐ Perspectives ☐ Systems ☐ Well-being	☐ Career-related study ☐ Community engagement (CE) ☐ Diploma programme (DP) courses ☐ Informal learning ☐ Language and cultural studies (LCS) ☐ Personal life ☐ Professional life ☐ Reflective project (RP)	☐ Intrapersonal skills ☐ Interpersonal skills ☐ Thinking skills ☐ Intercultural understanding

Key questions to guide your planning

- What concepts, contexts and skills will this inquiry help you explore?
- Why is this inquiry important to you?
- How is it relevant to your life?
- What PPS learning outcomes will it support?
- What do you already know?
- What do you need to find out?
- What resources, time or collaboration will be required?
- What actions will you take? In what order?
- How will you reflect and share your learning?

Top tip!

Portfolio building

As you build inquiries, remember to add any of your activities, experiences or assignments to your portfolio dumping folder and/or add it to your inquiry tracker matrix. Before long, you'll have plenty of wonderful items to highlight in your portfolio!

Final check-in: Are you ready?

Take a step back and ask yourself:

- Does this inquiry excite me?
- Will it challenge and grow my skills?
- Can I see myself following through on this?

If the answer is 'yes', congratulations! You've built a meaningful inquiry. Now it's time to dive in, explore and discover. Your learning, your way!

Voices from fellow students

Here's what other students who have been in your shoes have to say:

I was terrified of picking the wrong question at first. But I learned that no question is 'wrong'—every path teaches you something valuable.
Maya, Grade 12

Time management was my biggest challenge. I started using a planner and it really helped me stay on top of everything. Plus, it feels great to check things off my list!
Jordan, Grade 11

Don't be afraid to ask for help. I thought doing it on my own was part of 'ownership', but reaching out to my teacher for guidance made my project so much better.
Samira, Grade 12

When I hit a dead end, I thought I failed. But reflecting on what went wrong helped me come up with an even better idea. Don't give up!
Alex, Grade 11

Common pitfalls

Taking ownership of your learning is exciting, but it also comes with its own set of challenges. One common hurdle is *overwhelm*. When the possibilities feel endless, it can be difficult to know where to start. The key is to narrow your focus to a single question or topic that feels meaningful to you. Break your inquiry into small, manageable steps and suddenly, the journey will feel more achievable.

Another challenge is the *fear of failure*. What if your project doesn't turn out the way you hoped? It's important to remember that failure is part of the process. Reflect on what didn't work and use those lessons to improve. Often, the greatest growth comes from overcoming challenges and learning from mistakes.

Time management can also be tricky, especially when balancing your inquiry with other responsibilities. To stay on track, set clear deadlines for yourself and stick to them. Tools like planners or apps can help you organize your time effectively and keep you accountable.

Finally, there's the experience of *feeling stuck*. It's completely normal to hit a roadblock or feel like you're not making progress. When this happens, take a step back and revisit your original goals. Talking to a teacher, peer or mentor can provide a fresh perspective and help you find your way forward. Remember, every challenge you face is an opportunity to grow and refine your approach.

Reflection and reflexivity

Reflection is one of the most powerful tools you have as a learner. Take a moment to think about what this part of the course means for you. Here are some questions to guide your reflection:

- What does 'taking ownership of my learning' mean to you personally?
- What excites you about open inquiries? What feels challenging?
- How can you use the inquiry cycle to explore the ideas and questions that matter most to you?
- What skills do you want to focus on developing this year, and why?

Your reflections are the key to unlocking the potential of this year. Use them to set your goals, plan your next steps and remind yourself why this journey matters. You have the power to shape your learning and create something extraordinary—now's the time to begin!

Independent inquiry checklist

Owning your learning starts with action. Use this checklist to guide your journey.

- **Identify your passion:** What excites you? Is it a problem to solve, a skill to master or a topic to explore? Write it down.
- **Ask big questions:** What do you want to understand or create? Make it personal and meaningful. Use the focus question flow chart if you need help.
- **Set clear goals:** Break your inquiry into smaller steps. What can you achieve this week? This month? Use the student PPS inquiry planner to stay on track.
- **Gather your tools:** What resources do you need? Books, interviews, mentors or creative supplies? Prepare your toolkit.
- **Get started:** Take that first step—write your question, start some research or brainstorm ideas.
- **Stay reflective:** Pause regularly to check your progress. Are you moving toward your goals? What might you adjust?

Remember, this journey is yours. Every choice you make, every challenge you face and every success you achieve is a step toward becoming the best version of yourself. So take a deep breath, trust your instincts and dive in. Your learning belongs to you and no one else—make it extraordinary!

3.6.6 Student sample inquiries

Below are inquiries that students like you have developed and explored in PPS. As you read through them, consider if any of them are inspiring your own independent inquiry.

INQUIRY 1

Cultivating a curious mind

Scenario: Mohammed had always been fascinated by the world around him, constantly asking 'why?'. However, as he progressed through school, the structured curriculum and emphasis on right answers seemed to stifle that natural inquisitiveness. He noticed that while he could learn what was required for tests, his genuine excitement for discovery had waned. He wanted to reignite his innate desire to explore, question and continuously learn throughout his life, both within and beyond the classroom.

Focus question: How can I develop a mindset of curiosity and lifelong learning?

List the concepts, contexts and skills that will be explored and developed in this inquiry:

- Concepts: Systems, well-being
- Context: Personal life, informal learning
- Skill development: Self-management, reflection, adaptability

Why am I undertaking this inquiry? What are my learning outcomes?

Aligned with PPS learning outcomes:

- **LO1:** Develop techniques for cultivating curiosity (e.g. active questioning, pattern recognition, exploring diverse viewpoints).
- **LO2:** Understand how curiosity influences the learning process.
- **LO3:** Reflect on the role of curiosity in achieving future goals.
- **LO4:** Strengthen the ability to ask thought-provoking questions.
- **LO5:** Develop an open and adaptable mindset towards learning and uncertainty.

How will I explore these topics?

Activities:

- Practise techniques for cultivating curiosity, such as active questioning.
- Engage in pattern recognition exercises.
- Explore and consider diverse viewpoints on various topics.
- Reflect on personal experiences of curiosity and their outcomes.
- Regularly ask self-reflective questions about personal curiosity and reactions to uncertainty.

How will I reflect on my learning?

- What strategies allowed me to maintain curiosity?
- How does reflection play a role in maintaining curiosity?

How will I share my learning?

- Share a tool to support curiosity with my peers.
- Develop an infographic that can be shared informally with classmates.

Portfolio integration (artefacts to include):

- Reflections on moments when curiosity led to unexpected discoveries, including what was learned and how that mindset can be applied to future inquiries.
- Potentially, examples of thought-provoking questions developed and explored.
- Records of pattern-recognition exercises or explorations of diverse viewpoints, along with reflections on the process.

INQUIRY 2

The power of self direction

Scenario: Judy had always been a good student, diligently completing assignments and studying for tests. However, as she entered a more project-based learning environment, she began to feel a disconnect. Feeling a lack of ownership over her academic journey and realizing this might hinder her in future endeavours, Judy decided to explore how she might be able to take more ownership of her learning.

Focus question: What does it mean to take full responsibility for my learning?

List the concepts, contexts and skills that will be explored and developed in this inquiry:

- Concepts: Well-being, connections
- Context: Personal life, professional life
- Skill development: Self-management, self-awareness, self-advocacy

Why am I undertaking this inquiry? What are my learning outcomes?

Aligned with PPS learning outcomes:

- Understand the meaning of taking ownership of learning. (**LO1:** Take responsibility for your learning and personal development.)
- Develop clear learning goals and track progress effectively. (**LO2:** Set achievable goals and monitor your progress towards them.)
- Improve time and resource management skills for learning. (**LO3:** Manage time and resources effectively to support your learning.)
- Enhance self-motivation and discipline in learning. (**LO4:** Demonstrate motivation, discipline, and perseverance in your learning journey.)
- Learn to seek feedback and adjust learning strategies based on it. (**LO5:** Use feedback constructively to adapt and improve learning strategies.)
- Create a personal learning roadmap. (**LO2 and LO3:** Plan your learning path by setting goals and organizing resources.)
- Experiment with different approaches to maintain engagement and accountability in learning. (**LO4:** Apply different strategies to stay motivated and accountable.)
- Identify key resources and mentors to support learning growth. (**LO3 and LO5:** Seek and utilize resources and feedback from mentors to enhance learning.)

How will I explore these topics?

Activities:

- Develop strategies to become a self-directed learner.
- Create a personal learning roadmap.
- Experiment with different learning approaches to stay engaged and accountable.
- Identify and utilize key learning resources.
- Seek out and engage with potential mentors.
- Reflect on current levels of ownership in learning.
- Analyse barriers to self-direction and brainstorm solutions.
- Identify strategies that support motivation and staying on track.

How will I reflect on my learning?

- What are the best strategies to become a self-directed learner?
- What barriers exist for people when attempting to take responsibility for their own learning?
- How can I improve my autonomy and agency within my own learning?

How will I share my learning?

- Present findings to peers at a meeting or student leadership conference.
- Create a list of practical strategies for self-directed learning and publish it on the school's website or social-media page.

Portfolio integration (artefacts to include):

- Documentation of personal learning goals.
- Records of progress made towards learning goals.
- Reflections on the learning process, including challenges and successes.
- Potentially, the personal learning roadmap.
- Examples of different learning approaches experimented with.
- Notes on identified resources and interactions with mentors.

Learner profile

Risk-taker

Why it connects: In PPS, you're encouraged to take ownership of your learning and being a risk-taker is key to this journey. This encourages you to embrace discomfort, challenge the status quo and venture into the unknown. Risk-taking allows you to experiment, learn from failure and grow in ways you can't predict. It's about stepping outside your comfort zone and learning from those experiences, both successes and setbacks.

Learner profile quote: 'You approach uncertainty with courage and determination, exploring new ideas and strategies, and learning from mistakes and failures.'

In action:

- Choose projects or questions that push you outside of your comfort zone and challenge your current thinking.
- Take ownership of your learning by experimenting with new ideas, even if they might fail—failure is part of the process and can lead to valuable growth.
- Reflect on how stepping outside your comfort zone has helped you grow, and think about how you can apply this to future inquiries and learning engagements.

Learner profile

Balanced

Why it connects: This emphasizes the importance of balancing independence with reflection and well-being as you take ownership of your learning. As a balanced learner, you can manage both your intellectual and personal growth by recognizing when to push yourself and when to pause and reassess. Balance is crucial for maintaining focus, energy and well-being while navigating your inquiry journey.

Learner profile quote: 'You understand the importance of balancing different aspects of your life—intellectual, physical and emotional—so you can learn effectively and achieve your goals.'

In action:

- Regularly check in with yourself to assess if your work–life balance is sustainable, especially as you take on independent projects.
- Use reflection to manage your time and energy, ensuring you're dedicating effort not only to your academic growth but also to your well-being.
- Set personal boundaries and goals that allow for both challenge and self-care, ensuring you're thriving as a whole person, not just as a learner.

3.6.7 Summary of skills, contexts and concepts

Table 3.14 What have we explored in this section?

Skills developed	Contexts explored	Key concepts
• Self-management • Self-advocacy • Adaptability	• Personal • Professional • Informal learning	• Systems • Well-being • Connections

Learning journal

Portfolio work: Evidence of learning

Throughout this section, you have documented your learning through:

- notes and reflections on independent inquiries
- artefacts from independent inquiries you've explored.

3.6.8 Summary

- Independent inquiry requires you to be curious, think critically and engage in self-directed learning.
- Independent inquiry is a vital skill for lifelong learning, career development and personal growth, empowering you to own your learning and solve complex problems.
- Practical strategies for effective independent inquiry include techniques for formulating meaningful questions, conducting thorough research and engaging in critical reflection.
- Through structured activities and real-world examples, you can apply independent inquiry to personal interests, academic projects and professional aspirations, making learning more relevant and impactful.

3.7 Independent student inquiry example

INQUIRY QUESTION

▶ What can you learn from a student inquiry example?

3.7.1 The independent inquiry

The independent inquiry is a cornerstone of the PPS course. It is an opportunity for you to explore something meaningful to you, connect it to your career goals and develop important skills such as self-awareness, ethical reasoning, communication and intercultural understanding. But more than that, it's a space to learn about the world and yourself—through your own lens, in your own voice. In this section we will look at examples to help you plan your own inquiry.

The independent inquiry is a self-directed project that allows you to ask big questions, investigate topics that matter to you and share your insights. Learning how to lead your own inquiry—guided by curiosity, research and reflection—is a vital life skill that supports your career, academic and personal development.

An inquiry starts with a question. Then, using the tools from earlier sections—concepts, contexts, content and skills—you explore, take action, reflect and share your learning. Your portfolio is where you can record this journey.

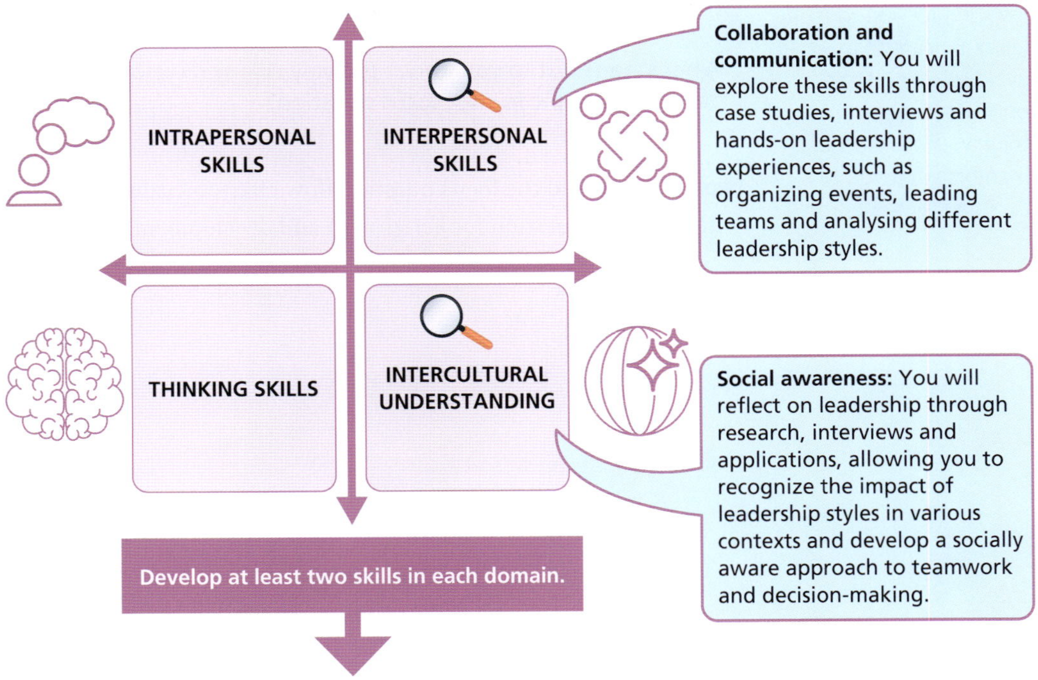

■ PPS skills focused on in Section 3.7

We are now going to explore some examples of one student's independent inquiry development. As you review, take time to think about your own process.

3.7.2 Case study 1: Ailany

Meet Ailany. She's a twelfth-grade student who is interested in business marketing. Recently, she led a team of students in a state-wide business competition and, after reflecting on the experience, Ailany was disappointed in the way her team worked together. Some group members didn't seem motivated and she felt like she could have done a better job as the group leader.

Ailany started to think about the idea of leadership as a possible independent inquiry. Using the tools provided in the previous sections, she began to consider the answers to these questions:

Table 3.15

Prompting questions	Ailany's responses
What do you really want to learn about?	I want to become a better leader, but I am not sure how.
Has there been an issue or challenge that you would like to learn to solve?	Yes, my team did not perform well at our competition, and I feel like I could have done a better job leading them.
What do you enjoy learning about?	I enjoy learning about how people work best together and ways that a leader can motivate others.
Are there any PPS concepts, contexts, skills or learning outcomes that are inspiring a question for you to explore?	Yes, leadership, developing communication and interpersonal skills (LO2). I am also using my career-related study as the context for this inquiry.

Top tip!

It is critical that your independent inquiries are developed from something you are interested in and motivated to learn. Following the flow chart will help guide you into discovering what is most valuable, important and inspiring for you to learn. Be careful to avoid selecting topics only because you think your teachers or mentors want you to explore them.

Creating a focus question

Now, Ailany can create a focus question:

'What are the core qualities and characteristics of a leader?'

Reflection and reflexivity

What stands out to you about the way Ailany developed a focus question? How did she decide on a topic for her focus question?

Next, Ailany used the focus question flow chart to evaluate her question to make sure that it will be a good question for *her* growth and development.

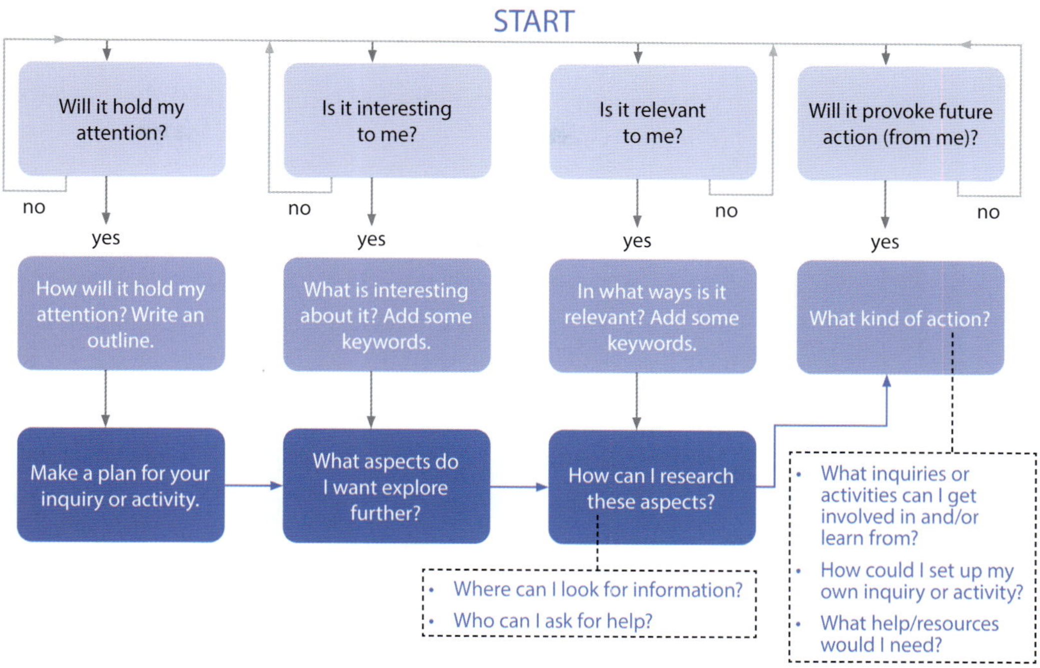

■ Focus question flow chart (Source: IB PPS toolkit)

Ailany starts by answering the first row of questions to see if this would be a good inquiry for her to explore.

■ **Table 3.16** (Source of questions: IB PPS toolkit)

Prompting questions	Suggestions to consider	Ailany's responses
Will it hold my attention?	To answer this question, consider whether this is a question that you will stay interested in over time.	Yes, I really want to become a better leader.
Is it interesting to me?	In other words, is this truly something that you want to learn more about?	Yes, I really like being in charge and taking the lead, but sometimes my team members do not respond to me. I want to find a way to better lead, so that next time is more successful.
Is it relevant to me?	Consider whether this is something that will support your growth and development, and help you in achieving your goals.	Yes, it is very relevant to me as I want to own my own business some day. I will need to have good leadership skills.
Will it provoke future action (from me)?	Think about whether you will be able to take what you learn from this inquiry and apply it in the future.	It is and isn't. It will be helpful to know good leadership qualities, but I also want to learn ways to improve my own leadership skills. There is another business competition coming up later this year, and I would like to form another team and take what I learned in this inquiry and apply it there. I think I need to add to my focus question.

Ailany decided to refine her question, so that she answered 'yes' to all of the questions. She edited her question from 'What are the core qualities and characteristics of a leader?' to 'What are the core qualities and characteristics of a leader, and how can leadership skills be developed and improved? This creates a better and more focused question for what she is aiming to learn.

After her changes, Ailany was confident that her focus question was one that would help her develop and grow.

Top tip!

Developing a solid, well-thought-out focus question will lead to a successful inquiry. Take time to think through your focus question and make sure it is specific, clear and focused.

Reflection and reflexivity

What caused Ailany to refine her focus question? How might this help you in developing your focus question?

Outlining an inquiry

Ailany continued using the flow chart to form her inquiry, following the second row of questions. This allowed her to build an outline and expand on how she was going to carry it out.

Table 3.17

Prompting questions	Suggestions to consider	Ailany's responses
How will it hold my attention?	Build an outline that communicates the ways you will explore this inquiry. Consider what kinds of activities, experiences and events you will engage in.	• **Brainstorming:** I will generate a list of individuals considered 'leaders' (historical figures, community members, politicians, business people, religious leaders). I can ask others why these individuals are perceived as leaders and discuss their responses with them. Record my findings. • **Image analysis:** I can analyse images or videos depicting leadership in action. What behaviours and characteristics are observed? What emotions are evoked? • **Case study analysis (mini-cases):** Briefly examine short case studies of leadership successes and failures. Identify contributing factors to the outcomes (e.g. a team that achieved an impossible deadline, a company that experienced a major ethical lapse, etc.). • **Reflection:** Think about times when I was a leader. What went well? What didn't go well? How might I consider changing or improving my actions for the future?
What is interesting about it?	Consider the key words, topics or ideas are associated in exploring this inquiry. Make a list.	Leadership styles, authority, control, power, emotional intelligence, organization, confidence
In what ways is it relevant?	Determine how this inquiry relates to you personally and professionally. Generate a list.	It will personally help me to become a more confident leader. It will also help me to better understand my own leadership style. I will be able to apply this to my professional life, as I want to own my own business some day.
What kind of actions could it provoke?	Think about how you can use what's learned in this inquiry in the future. Create a list.	I will use what I learn in this inquiry in the next business competition, but also in any area of my life when I take the lead, like at work, with my friends or in the other clubs that I am involved in at school.

Top tip!

If you're struggling with activities, experiences or events to support the exploration of your inquiry, check out the tools on how to use AI as an ethical tool for research in Section 4.3.2.

Reflection and reflexivity

- What type of activities does Ailany brainstorm for her inquiry?
- What other activities might have been good for her to include?
- Where might you go to help you build your list of activities for exploration?

Solidifying the plan

Next, Ailany used the PPS student inquiry planner, which is found in the PPS toolkit (and you saw earlier in Section 3.6.5), to solidify her plan.

Table 3.18 Ailany's PPS student inquiry planner

Focus question(s) for my inquiry		
What concept will I explore?	**In what context will I explore it?**	**Which skill area(s) will I develop?**
☐ Change ☐ Connections ☑ Identities ☐ Perspectives ☐ Systems ☐ Well-being	☑ Career-related study ☐ Community engagement (CE) ☐ Diploma programme (DP) courses ☐ Informal learning ☐ Language and cultural studies (LCS) ☐ Personal life ☐ Professional life ☐ Reflective project (RP)	☑ Intrapersonal skills ☑ Interpersonal skills ☑ Thinking skills ☐ Intercultural understanding

Table 3.19

Prompting questions	Ailany's responses
What concept(s), context(s) and skill(s) will this inquiry help you explore?	• **Concept:** Identity • **Context:** Career-related study (business leadership) • **Skills:** Intrapersonal skills (self awareness, reflection); interpersonal skills (leadership, collaboration, communication); thinking skills (problem solving)
Why are you exploring this inquiry?	To become a better leader.
Which PPS learning outcome(s) will this inquiry support you in developing?	Develop and apply communication and interpersonal skills in a variety of contexts.
Which specific skills will you develop in this inquiry?	• **Intrapersonal skills:** Self-awareness, reflection • **Interpersonal skills:** Leadership, collaboration, communication • **Thinking skills:** Problem solving

How do I plan to explore concepts in the selected contexts?	• **What do I already know?**
	Leadership is hard. Good leaders are confident, organized and smart.
	• **What do I need to know?**
	What happens when your team isn't responding to you? How do you motivate a team? What strategies make for a good team and how does the leader employ those strategies?
	• **What time, resources or collaboration are required?**
	  • Research articles, TEDx talks, videos, blogs, etc. on leadership styles.
	  • Research and reflect on case studies involving leadership.
	  • Talk to people who I feel are strong leaders.
	  • Reflect on my own leadership experiences.
	  • I will need a few weeks to complete this inquiry.

Top tip!

Portfolio building

Remember to keep adding all of your activities, experiences or assignments to your portfolio dumping folder and/or adding them to your inquiry tracker matrix. By now, you may already have plenty of wonderful items to highlight in your portfolio!

Reflection and portfolio building

Ailany added the following to her dumping folder, and added this inquiry to her inquiry tracker matrix:

- notes from interviews with leaders in her field
- reflections on leadership opportunities in her own life
- leadership case-study analysis.

Ailany took time to explore effective leadership and reflected on ways that she could apply these ideas to her own leadership style. She learned tangible strategies that she could use the next time she finds herself in a leadership position. It is important and relevant to her and she can showcase this learning in her PPS portfolio.

Reflection and reflexivity

What takeaways do you have from Ailany's process? How might you use these takeaways to support your own independent inquiry development?

Let's take a look at another example. As you do, consider the similarities and differences between Ailany's and Jamie's processes to help you to see the various ways different inquiries can be developed from a similar inspiration.

3.7.3 Case study 2: Jamie

Meet Jamie, a 17-year-old with a passion for event planning and community outreach. Jamie recently volunteered to organize a local charity concert, bringing together bands from their school to raise money for a food bank. While the event raised significant funds and drew a big crowd, Jamie noticed some problems with their approach. Deadlines were missed, communication with band members fell through and Jamie felt overwhelmed by the lack of teamwork.

One night, as Jamie replayed the challenges of the concert, a question popped into their head: 'Why didn't my team work as smoothly as I expected?' This sparked curiosity about leadership and how Jamie could improve their skills.

Jamie grabbed a notebook and started brainstorming, using some of the same prompting questions that Ailany used:

Table 3.20

Prompting questions	Jamie's responses
What do you really want to learn about?	How can I become a better leader who motivates people and ensures everything gets done?
Has there been an issue or challenge that you would like to learn to solve?	Yes, the concert planning was chaotic and I struggled to get everyone on the same page.
What do you enjoy learning about?	I love understanding how teams succeed and how people's strengths can shine in group settings.
Are there any PPS concepts, contexts, skills or learning outcomes that are inspiring a question for you to explore?	Definitely leadership and teamwork, along with communication and adaptability skills (LO2).

Creating a focus question

Jamie crafted their initial focus question:

'What makes a great leader?'

However, as they worked through the focus question flow chart, Jamie realized the question could be refined:

Table 3.21

Prompting questions	Jamie's responses
Will it hold my attention?	Yes, because I want to improve for future events.
Is it interesting to me?	Absolutely. Leadership and teamwork are challenges I face all the time.
Is it relevant to me?	Very relevant—I want to lead more events and eventually manage larger projects in my career.
Will it provoke future action?	Not quite. I also want to know how to improve my leadership, not just understand it.

So Jamie refined their question:

'What makes a great leader, and how can I improve my leadership skills?'

Mapping out an inquiry

Jamie developed the following system to organize their approach for engaging in this inquiry:

Table 3.22

Brainstorming	• Interview leaders from different fields, like a coach, a student council president and a local entrepreneur, to understand their methods. • Research examples of successful and unsuccessful leadership in history. What worked and what didn't?
Observation	• Watch videos of leaders in action—TEDx talks, debates or behind-the-scenes documentaries. Take notes on their communication styles and problem-solving approaches.

Action plan

Jamie planned to organize another event: a school-wide volunteer day. This time, they would implement specific leadership techniques, such as setting clearer goals, assigning roles based on strengths and holding weekly check-ins.

Jamie defined the following key ideas to explore:

- leadership styles
- communication
- motivation
- team dynamics.

Personal relevance

Jamie reflected on how better leadership could reduce their stress and build stronger relationships. They also saw how these skills would be critical in their dream of running a nonprofit one day.

Taking action

Jamie created a detailed timeline for their inquiry, breaking it into steps:

■ Table 3.23

1	**Learn**	Conduct interviews, watch videos and read articles about leadership.
2	**Reflect**	Analyse findings and identify strategies they could apply.
3	**Experiment**	Use these strategies while leading the volunteer day.
4	**Evaluate**	Gather feedback from participants and assess what worked and what didn't.

Sharing the journey

Jamie decided to document their progress in a blog. Each post would include reflections, challenges and lessons learned. At the end of the project, they planned to present their findings to their class, highlighting how their leadership evolved.

Reflection and portfolio building

Jamie kept a 'dumping folder' where they stored:

- notes from interviews
- leadership case studies
- feedback from team members
- photos and videos from the volunteer day.

Using the PPS inquiry tracker matrix, Jamie categorized each artefact, linking it to skills, concepts and learning outcomes. This process helped Jamie see their growth and identify areas to explore further.

Jamie's journey wasn't just about becoming a better leader—it was about discovering their potential to inspire and motivate others. Their inquiry didn't just answer a question; it transformed the way Jamie approached challenges.

Reflection and reflexivity

How did Ailany's and Jaime's processes differ? What about each approach might inspire your independent inquiry development?

Top tip!

Start small! Pick one question or challenge that excites you. Use your PPS tools to dive in and let your curiosity guide the way!

LEARNING ENGAGEMENT

1. Create a mind map of similarities and differences between Ailany's and Jamie's processes and add it to your portfolio.
2. Look back on your portfolio observations about the similarities and differences between Ailany and Jamie in their inquiries. Pick out up to five examples of something you found appealing about these inquiries.
3. What inspires you to take action? How could you use a personal experience to spark your own inquiry? How might you use these examples to inspire an independent inquiry? Respond to this in your portfolio and make your thinking visible.

3.7.4 Student sample inquiries

Below are inquiries that students like you have developed and explored in PPS. These show how you can use the same ideas and supporting resources to approach your inquiry in different ways. As you read through them, consider if any of them are inspiring your own independent inquiry.

INQUIRY 1

Building resilient communities through environmental action

Scenario: Luis is passionate about environmental justice. After learning about the effects of pollution on underserved neighbourhoods, he decided to focus his inquiry on how youth can lead environmental action in their communities.

Focus question: How can I lead environmental action in my community?

List the concepts, contexts and skills that will be explored and developed in this inquiry:

- Concepts: Change, systems
- Contexts: Community engagement, career-related study
- Skills: Interpersonal (leadership, collaboration), thinking skills (critical thinking), intercultural understanding (civic and social responsibility)

Why am I undertaking this inquiry? What are my learning outcomes?

Aligned with PPS learning outcomes:

- Determine existing opportunities and organizations in my community that work towards bettering our environment. (**LO1:** Take responsibility for researching and gathering relevant information independently.)
- Interview and network with environmental leaders in my community. (**LO2:** Communicate effectively and collaborate with others to gather perspectives.)
- Develop or join efforts to create opportunities for environmental events or action within my community. (**LO4:** Demonstrate active, effective and ethical participation in diverse contexts.)

How will I explore these topics?

Activities:

- Research local and global environmental justice movements.
- Interview youth leaders from grassroots environmental campaigns.
- Encourage peers to support and/or attend local environmental organizations.
- Organize a community clean-up and awareness campaign.
- Create a social-media toolkit for peers to advocate for greener policies.

How will I reflect on my learning?

- How did I meet the responsibilities we have to our communities when it comes to the environment?
- Were there ethical dilemmas that arose in balancing development with environmental preservation?
- What did I learn about the ways that community organizations work?

How will I share my learning?

- Deliver a public presentation at a local youth forum.
- Submit a proposal for an environmental grant to support future projects.

Portfolio integration (artefacts to include):

- Photos and documentation from the community clean-up.
- Journal reflections on ethical questions and leadership experiences.
- Slides and feedback from the public presentation.

INQUIRY 2

Creativity and identity in the digital age

Scenario: Sam is an aspiring digital artist who noticed how online platforms shape—and sometimes distort—personal identity. Sam is considering this topic for the RP. Curious about how social media influences the way we express ourselves, Sam decided to explore the impact of digital creativity on identity formation.

Focus question: How does social media influence, impact and change our personal identities?

List the concepts, contexts and skills that will be explored and developed in this inquiry:

- Concepts: Identity, perspectives
- Contexts: Personal life, reflective project
- Skills: Intrapersonal skills (reflection, adaptability), thinking skills (information literacy, systems thinking)

Why am I undertaking this inquiry? What are my learning outcomes?

Aligned with PPS learning outcomes:

- Research studies, TEDx talks and other sources that explore the impact of social media on personal identity. (**LO1:** Take responsibility for researching and gathering relevant information independently.)
- Explore various social-media platforms to determine their impact on personal identity. (**LO3:** Analyse information from diverse sources to understand complex issues.)
- Interview and/or survey peers on the impact they believe social media has on their mental health and identity. (**LO2:** Communicate effectively and collaborate with others to gather perspectives.)
- Develop literature to inform peers on the ways social media impacts personal identity. (**LO4:** Create and share meaningful content that reflects understanding and informs others.)

How will I explore these topics?

Activities:

- Study academic articles and interviews with digital artists.
- Analyse popular platforms (e.g. Instagram, TikTok) for trends in identity portrayal.
- Create a visual portfolio of self-portraits exploring different aspects of identity.
- Facilitate a discussion at school about media and mental health.

How will I reflect on my learning?

- How do digital platforms both empower and limit creativity?
- What part of identity is truly 'you' and what is shaped by your audience?

How will I share my learning?

- Curate a digital exhibition on identity and art.
- Write a reflective essay connecting this inquiry to ethical dilemmas around authenticity online.

Portfolio integration (artefacts to include):

- Screenshots and analysis of digital artworks.
- Reflection journal entries on emotional responses and growth.
- Excerpts from artist statements.

Reflection and reflexivity

Now that you've explored various independent inquiries, reflect:

- What topics do you care deeply about?
- What context—personal, professional, informal, academic—could you explore it in?
- What artefacts could demonstrate your growth in your portfolio?

Inquiry, growth and the portfolio

As you've seen from Luis and Sam, strong inquiries:

- are rooted in personal passions or hands-on experiences
- connect meaningfully to concepts, contexts and skills
- produce *evidence of action*—from presentations to reflections
- show growth through *documented reflection* and goal setting.

Learner profile

Thinker

Why it connects: This emphasizes the importance of thoughtful reflection and critical thinking when evaluating your well-being. As a thinker, you can analyse the strategies that work for you, consider the impact of your decisions, and adjust your habits accordingly. Reflecting on your well-being is an essential skill in recognizing what's helping or hindering your personal growth and mental health.

Learner profile quote: 'You apply thinking skills critically and creatively to recognize and approach complex problems and make reasoned, ethical decisions.'

In action:

- Reflect on your personal well-being by analysing what's currently working and what might need improvement.
- Use critical thinking to examine your emotional responses and how they influence your well-being, and make adjustments as needed.
- Set specific, measurable goals to enhance your well-being and track your progress using the skills you've learned.

Learner profile

Balanced

Why it connects: This highlights the importance of achieving balance in all aspects of life, particularly when it comes to well-being. As a balanced individual, you recognize the need to nurture different areas of your life—emotional, social, physical and mental. Striving for balance helps ensure that no single aspect of life dominates at the expense of others, which supports overall health and personal growth.

Learner profile quote: 'You understand the importance of intellectual, physical and emotional balance to achieve personal well-being and success.'

In action:

- Prioritize self-care activities that support a balanced lifestyle, such as exercise, rest and mental-health practices.
- Reflect on areas of your life that may need more attention, whether it's work, relationships or personal interests, and adjust to create more equilibrium.
- Set boundaries to maintain a healthy balance between work and personal life, ensuring time for rest and rejuvenation.

3.7.5 Summary of skills, contexts and concepts

Table 3.24 What have we explored in this section?

Skills developed	Contexts explored	Key concepts
• Reflection • Self-awareness • Critical thinking	• Personal • Reflective project • Professional	• Identities • Well-being • Connections

Learning journal

Portfolio work: Evidence of learning

Throughout this section, you have documented your learning through:

- the inspiration from the sample inquiries in this section
- identifying two skills you'd like to develop through a similar inquiry and considering how your inquiry might change if you altered the focus (such as changing the concept, the skill or the related learning outcome)
- drafting your first version of a focus question using the PPS flow chart.

By engaging with these inquiries and actively contributing to your portfolios, you will lay a strong foundation for your PPS journey, equipping yourself with the skills and knowledge necessary for progressing to an independent inquiry process.

3.7.6 Summary

- Independent inquiries are student driven and should be inspired by your interests, passions or hands-on experiences.
- Using the PPS student inquiry templates can provide helpful guidance when building an independent inquiry.
- Exploring independent inquiries will provide you with a meaningful experience that will develop your personal and professional skills.

3.8 Beyond the classroom

INQUIRY QUESTIONS

- How can you communicate and apply what you've learned beyond the classroom?
- How do you handle setbacks and learn from failure when reaching beyond the classroom?

3.8.1 Applying PPS beyond school

Beyond-the-classroom learning is when you take the skills you have developed in PPS and apply them in authentic, context-based situations. This stage of your journey challenges you to move from theoretical learning to practical application, developing not only knowledge, but also experience and wisdom.

Learning does not reach its full potential until it is applied. When you seek opportunities beyond the classroom, you begin to solidify your transversal skills. You gain firsthand experience, strengthen your resilience and adaptability, and build the confidence necessary for your future personal and professional lives.

In this section, you will explore student inquiries that show how learning can bridge the gap between academic theory and the demands of the wider world. You will see how concepts, contexts, content and skills combine to create powerful opportunities for growth. You will also learn ways to capture your experiences as portfolio evidence.

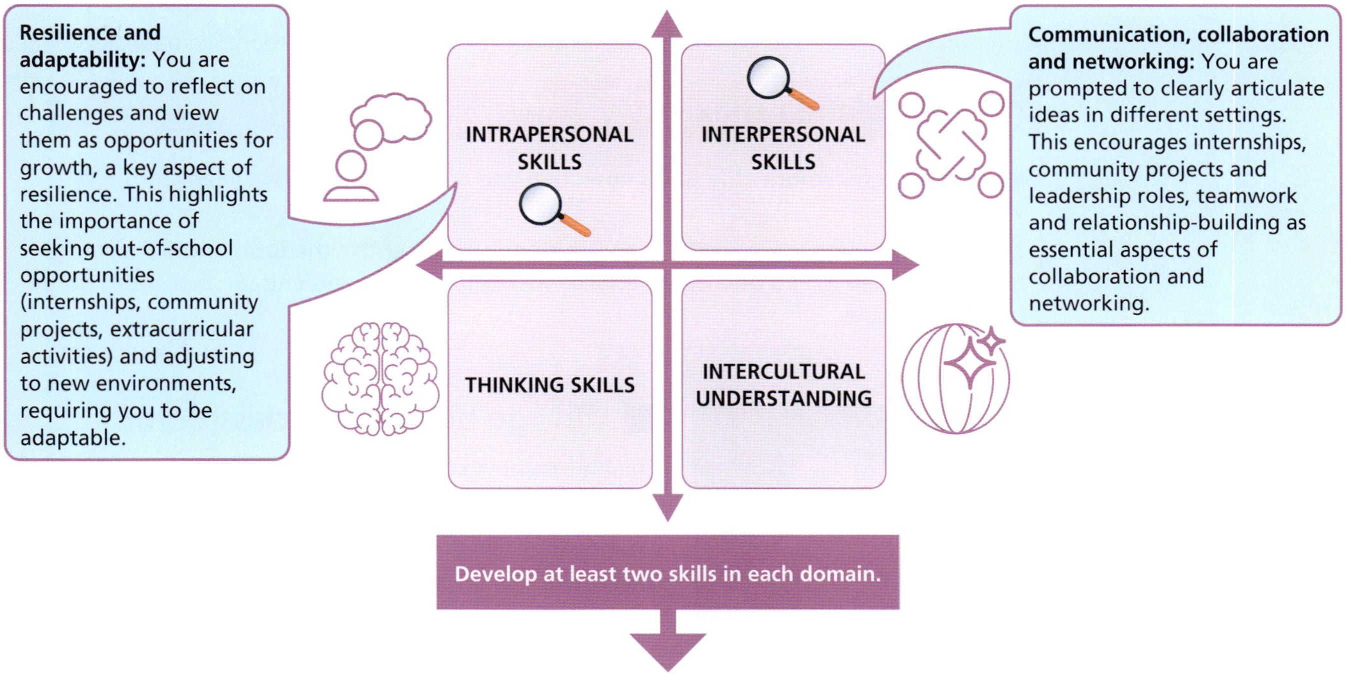

■ PPS skills focused on in Section 3.8

3.8.2 Creating opportunities outside the classroom

Learning extends far beyond the walls of the classroom, and this part of the course focuses on helping you bridge the gap between academic skills and practical applications. Remember the PPS contexts? Many of the contexts require you to consider settings outside of school to practise and apply your skills.

> Once you are able to take what you've learned in class and apply it to out-of-school situations, you have truly mastered transversal skills.

What does this stage involve?

You are going to seek out opportunities that not only enhance your understanding of the world, but also help you develop a sense of purpose and connection to your community. Therefore, this stage challenges you to seek out internships, community projects and extracurricular activities that align with your interests and passions. Perhaps you might use your communication skills to organize a local event, apply your problem-solving abilities in a volunteer initiative, or you might seek out an internship with a company to gain hands-on experience in a field that excites you.

Articulate your goals

Taking this step means exploring options that *resonate with your goals*. Whether you're creating a campaign to address a local issue or collaborating with peers on a CE project, these experiences provide invaluable lessons in collaboration, resilience and adaptability. As you venture into the wider world, think about how your classroom learning connects to the skills required in these settings and consider how you can communicate your ideas effectively to make an impact.

Reflection and reflexivity

What do you feel more able to do now than you did a year ago? Two years ago? Five years ago?

Look back through your portfolio and this book and identify the tools and skills you have developed in PPS that might enable you to take a risk and engage in a wider range of opportunities.

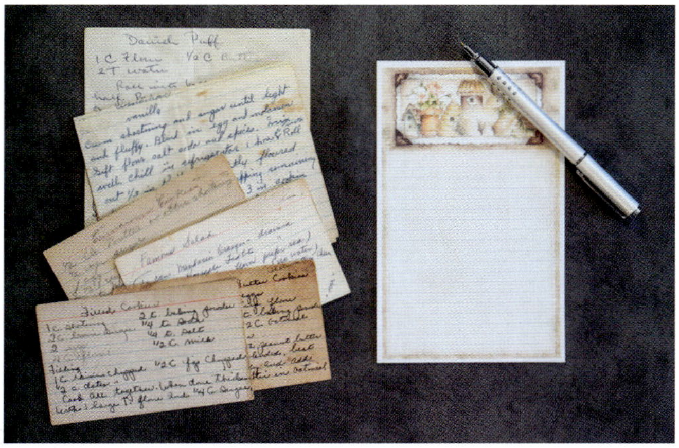

It's all theory until you put it into practice.

Why go beyond the classroom?

Imagine trying to learn to cook solely from a cookbook, never stepping into the kitchen. How would you know what to do when something was overcooked or if an ingredient was unavailable? That's what learning without practical application feels like—incomplete. Engaging with opportunities outside the classroom brings your education to life, allowing you to enhance your skills by practising what you've learned in hands-on settings. It helps you to see how the skills will be applied to your life. It's also a chance to build your network, connecting with mentors, peers and professionals who can support your growth.

CONTEXTS

Career-related study
Community engagement
Diploma Programme courses
Informal learning
Language and cultural studies
Personal life
Professional life
Reflective project

■ Use the PPS contexts to help inspire meaningful experiences. (Source: IB PPS guide, p.17)

These experiences can help you discover your passions as you explore different fields and uncover what excites you. Most importantly, they give you the opportunity to make an impact, using your skills to solve real problems and contribute meaningfully to your community, and that is more rewarding than anything!

3.8.3 Suggestions for real-world opportunities

As students who have spent a lot of time in the classroom, it may be difficult to think of, seek out or engage in outside opportunities. Where do you start? How do you find these opportunities?

Out-of-school opportunities are a vital part of transforming what you learn into practical experience, and there are many ways to get involved. Using the PPS contexts is an excellent place to start.

■ Career-related study

Internships are an excellent starting point, offering hands-on experience in fields that align with your career goals or spark your curiosity. For instance, if environmental sustainability inspires you, consider applying for an internship with a local conservation organization. Through this experience, you can reflect on how your efforts contribute to global initiatives to protect the planet.

Consider talking to your counsellors, mentors or career-related studies teachers to help identify internship opportunities in your area.

■ Community engagement

Community projects provide another meaningful avenue, allowing you to give back while developing essential skills. Collaborate with peers, local organizations or schools to address challenges in your community. Imagine organizing a neighbourhood clean-up or leading a mental-health awareness campaign at your school. Projects like these not only make a difference, but also help you practise leadership and teamwork.

Using the skills learned in CE, work with local organizations, your school or agencies to seek out opportunities for community projects. Often local libraries, community blogs or websites will advertise events and upcoming projects.

■ Reflective project

Your RP gives you the freedom to explore an ethical dilemma connected to a career-related study that resonates deeply with you. This project not only showcases your initiative, research skills and knowledge, but also provides opportunities to apply your skills in unique and impactful ways. You can reflect deeply on a real issue that impacts our world.

Work with your RP supervisor to help you in this process. Use your network of career-related teachers to provide insights and information on your topic and make connections to your own life and goals.

Diploma Programme courses

Diploma Programme courses provide opportunities for you to explore content and construct your own meaning from it. Taking inspiration from your courses, you may develop new understandings that will lead you to opportunities for growth. For example, through fieldwork in a DP course, you may learn new ways of viewing the world. You can apply these concepts to your everyday life and reflect on their significance.

While engaging in your DP courses, consider what skills and content are relevant to your life. Talk to your DP teachers to help you make connections between what you are learning and the rest of your life.

Informal learning

Extracurricular activities are equally valuable, offering school-based platforms like clubs or sports teams to explore your interests. They help you strengthen skills such as collaboration, leadership and problem-solving. Joining a debate team, for example, can enhance your communication abilities, while joining a coding club can allow you to refine your technical expertise.

Schools often offer a variety of extracurricular activities. Ask your teachers, mentors and coaches about the types of activities that are available at your school or in your local community.

Personal life

Your personal life is a wonderful place to apply the PPS skills and take your learning outside of the classroom. Developing and maintaining relationships, engaging in courageous conversations or organizing a night out with friends will require the same skills that you're learning in PPS. For example, you may take the initiative to organize a surprise birthday party for a relative, giving you the opportunity to apply your leadership, communication and problem-solving skills.

Be reflective in your personal life and identify areas where you can apply the skills from PPS. Talking with friends and family members is a great way to identify areas to apply these skills.

Top tip!

Seeking opportunities to extend your learning outside of the classroom is a critical way to develop your skills; however, you will not work in all of these contexts all of the time. Remember to aim to be balanced in life, and make decisions about which are most aligned with your goals.

Professional life

Work life is a wonderful opportunity to apply PPS skills in different situations. For example, you may be a server at a local restaurant and will need to apply skills like adaptability, communication, problem solving and self-awareness each day at work.

Look for opportunities for work through your counsellor's office, local establishments and community websites.

Learner profile

Balanced

We understand the importance of balancing different aspects of our lives—intellectual, physical and emotional—to achieve well-being for ourselves and others. We recognize our interdependence with other people and with the world in which we live.

Reflection and reflexivity

- What real-world applications do you currently have in your life?
- Where might you seek other opportunities?

LEARNING ENGAGEMENT

Pursue growth beyond academics

Reflect on your interests and goals by looking back over your PPS portfolio, other Core learning journals and your course files. Be honest with yourself.

1 What opportunities have excited you? Think about the kinds of activities that have challenged you to grow.
2 What has challenged you or pushed you outside of your comfort zone?
3 Is there an experience that you haven't tried yet that would help you to grow personally and professionally?

Whether it's joining a club, taking on a leadership role or seeking an internship, the opportunities are endless. Start by identifying areas where you want to make a difference or skills you want to strengthen, and take proactive steps to explore these avenues.

Voices from fellow students

Hearing from peers who have ventured beyond the classroom can inspire your own journey. Many students have shared stories of how internships, volunteering or leadership roles shaped their perspectives and opened doors to new possibilities. For instance, one student recounted organizing a community clean-up event that taught them valuable project-management skills. Another shared their experience of interning at a local tech company, which not only deepened their understanding of their field, but also expanded their professional network. These voices remind us of the transformative power of stepping outside our comfort zones and embracing real-world challenges.

Building my portfolio was like creating a map of my journey. Every project I worked on, every skill I developed—whether it was through an internship, a community project or extracurricular activity—was captured. It wasn't just about the end result; it was about showing my growth along the way.

Sam, PPS student

I used to think that the stuff we learned in class wasn't really relevant. But when I started working with a local start-up, I realized that everything from marketing strategies to problem-solving in class applied directly to my tasks there. It helped me connect the dots between theory and practice.

Sonia, PPS student

I had to organize an event for a school-wide awareness campaign. I was nervous at first, but communicating my ideas clearly to my team helped us stay on track and accomplish our goal. It showed me the power of clear, direct communication and how it can lead to success.

Anabelle, PPS student

When I look back at my portfolio, I can see how far I've come. It's not just about the projects or grades, but the challenges I overcame and how I developed new skills. My portfolio has become a reminder that every experience counts and contributes to my journey.

Sean, PPS student

3.8.4 Student sample inquiries

Below are inquiries that students like you have developed and explored in PPS to extend their learning beyond the classroom. As you read through them, consider if any of them are inspiring your own independent inquiry that would extend your learning beyond the classroom.

INQUIRY 1

Connecting environmental action to career goals

Scenario: Emma wanted to combine her passion for the environment with her interest in marketing. She noticed that many environmental campaigns struggled to connect with young people. Curious about how communication strategies could support environmental causes, Emma decided to explore the intersection of marketing and environmental action.

Focus question: How might I be able to use marketing strategies to support environmental action in my community?

List the concepts, contexts and skills that will be explored and developed in this inquiry:

- Concepts: Systems, change
- Contexts: Career-related study, professional life
- Skills: Communication, ethical decision-making, collaboration

Why am I undertaking this inquiry? What are my learning outcomes?

Aligned with PPS learning outcomes:

- Research marketing techniques utilized to develop a strong environmental campaign. (**LO1:** Take initiative and responsibility for independently researching and gathering relevant information.)
- Develop and execute a marketing plan that will create awareness around environmental issues. (**LO3:** Plan and organize complex tasks effectively to achieve specific goals.)
- Market and host an event to encourage environmental awareness. (**LO2:** Communicate and collaborate effectively with others to implement ideas and actions.)

How will I explore these topics?

Activities:

- Research successful and unsuccessful environmental marketing strategies.
- Interview professionals working in sustainability marketing.
- Create a mini-campaign promoting the reduction of single-use plastics at school.
- Host a workshop for peers on green communication techniques.

How will I reflect on my learning?

- How can marketing influence sustainable behaviour change?
- What ethical responsibilities do marketers have when promoting environmental causes?

How will I share my learning?

- Launch the mini-campaign on school social media and in the local community.
- Present findings to a student leadership group on using communication for advocacy.

Portfolio integration (artefacts to include):

- Campaign flyers and social-media posts.
- Workshop outline and peer feedback.
- Reflective journal entries about ethical dilemmas in marketing.
- Entries in the inquiry tracker matrix linked to communication and systems thinking.

INQUIRY 2

Empowering youth voices through community engagement

Scenario: James noticed that many young people in his town felt disconnected from community decision-making. Determined to change this, he designed an inquiry into how youth can be empowered to influence local government decisions and create positive change.

Focus question: How can young people be empowered to influence local government decisions and create positive change?

List the concepts, contexts and skills that will be explored and developed in this inquiry:

- Concepts: Connections, perspectives
- Contexts: Community engagement, personal life
- Skills: Leadership, Social awareness, collaboration, critical thinking

Why am I undertaking this inquiry? What are my learning outcomes?

Aligned with PPS learning outcomes:

- Research possible ways for young people to become more involved with community organizations and leadership. (**LO1:** Take responsibility for researching and gathering relevant information independently.)
- Develop opportunities to empower young people to share their ideas and connect them with community leaders. (**LO2:** Communicate and collaborate effectively with others to implement ideas and actions.)
- Create a proposal to connect young people to community leaders. (**LO3:** Plan and organize complex tasks effectively to achieve specific goals.)

How will I explore these topics?

Activities:

- Research youth councils and case studies of young civic leaders.
- Interview local government officials about youth participation.
- Organize a youth forum to discuss community issues.
- Create a proposal for a youth advisory board to present to local leadership.

How will I reflect on my learning?

- What barriers prevent young people from participating in decision-making?
- How can communication strategies bridge the gap between youth and government?

How will I share my learning?

- Present the youth engagement proposal to local council members.
- Publish a reflective article about empowering youth voices in civic life.

Portfolio integration (artefacts to include):

- Event flyers, agenda and participant feedback.
- Reflection essays connecting leadership concepts to civic action.
- Interview transcripts and analysis.
- Inquiry tracker matrix entries linking activities to collaboration and advocacy skills.

Reflection and reflexivity

Consider the following questions to help you apply your classroom skills:

- What opportunities outside the classroom resonate with your goals and interests?
- How can you effectively communicate what you've learned in different settings?
- What setbacks have you faced and how have you grown from them?
- How can you use resilience and adaptability to navigate future challenges?

Take time to think about these questions and write down your insights. Reflection will not only solidify your learning, but also prepare you for the next steps in your journey. This phase is about taking ownership of your experiences, embracing challenges and finding opportunities to thrive beyond academics.

Learner profile

Knowledgeable

Why it connects: This emphasizes the importance of applying the knowledge you have gained in the classroom to practical contexts. As a knowledgeable individual, you understand the value of using your academic skills to solve problems, create new opportunities and make informed decisions in practical situations. Beyond the classroom, knowledge becomes more than just theory; it becomes a tool for action, personal growth and societal impact.

Learner profile quote: 'You explore concepts, ideas and issues that have local and global significance. You understand and apply knowledge to understand the world around you.'

In action:

- Take what you've learned in your courses and apply it to real-world challenges or situations.
- Seek opportunities, such as internships or community engagement projects, where you can use your knowledge to solve problems or create positive change.
- Document and reflect on these experiences to deepen your understanding and track how your knowledge is evolving in different contexts.

Learner profile

Caring

Why it connects: This encourages you to bridge the gap between academic learning and practical applications through community engagement and social impact. As a caring individual, you recognize the importance of using your skills and knowledge not just for personal growth, but also to make a positive difference in the lives of others. This stage is about actively contributing to the well-being of your community and the world, applying empathy and responsibility to real-world challenges.

Learner profile quote: 'You show empathy, compassion and respect toward the needs and feelings of others. You act to make a positive difference in the lives of others.'

In action:

- Seek out and engage in community projects or causes that align with your values, and use your academic skills to make a meaningful impact.
- Consider how you can support others in your community, whether it's through volunteering, leadership roles or organizing events.
- Reflect on how your learning can contribute to social good and how caring actions can support personal and collective growth.

3.8.5 Summary of skills, contexts and concepts

Table 3.25 What have we explored in this section?

Skills developed	Contexts explored	Key concepts
• Self-advocacy • Critical thinking • Collaboration	• Personal • Community engagement • Professional	• Perspectives • Systems • Connections

Learning journal

Portfolio work: Evidence of learning

Throughout this section, you have documented your learning through:

- reflections on experiences where you can extend your learning beyond the classroom
- artefacts from inquiries that take place outside of the classroom
- images from experiences explored in your out-of-school experiences.

As you step beyond the classroom, remember that hands-on experiences are some of the richest sources for authentic portfolio artefacts. Every time you apply a skill in a new setting, organize a project or reflect on your growth, you are building meaningful evidence of your journey. All you do—inside and outside of school—can help develop your portfolio with artefacts that are relevant, applicable and a true reflection of your personal and professional skills in action. Think of your portfolio as a living record of how you bring your learning to life.

3.8.6 Summary

- Academic skills are life skills; practising them in situations and scenarios beyond the classroom is critical to your development.
- Thinking about different contexts in your life can help you to see the connection between academic skills and practical examples.
- Reflection is a critical tool to help you improve your academic skills in different situations.

3.9 Dealing with failure and finding balance

INQUIRY QUESTION

- How do you handle setbacks and learn from failure?

3.9.1 The importance of failure

Failure happens to everyone—but it doesn't define you. In fact, it's often the first step towards your greatest growth. Learning to bounce back from life's challenges is a skill you can build, and it's one that will serve you in every part of your personal and professional journey.

Experts, including those from the UK National Health Service (NHS) *Every Mind Matters* campaign, highlight that resilience is not something you are born with—it's something you create. It involves recognizing your past strengths, planning for the future, staying flexible and celebrating progress instead of perfection. Whether it's handling academic setbacks, personal struggles or professional challenges, every experience you face can become part of a bigger, stronger you.

Remember: every challenge, every mistake and every comeback you experience can help build and develop your portfolio with authentic, relevant and applicable artefacts. True growth doesn't come from staying comfortable—it comes from getting back up, learning and trying again. This section will guide you through turning failures into stepping stones for success, making resilience one of your most powerful skills. It will also highlight the importance of balance so that you can successfully manage areas of your life, especially as you work through setbacks.

Failure is an inevitable and necessary part of growth. It is not a sign of weakness, but a critical tool for learning and personal development. This section will help you develop strategies for improving resilience, balance and critical thinking, and emotional intelligence. To learn more about practical strategies for bouncing back, you can also visit 'Bouncing Back from Life's Challenges—NHS Every Mind Matters' at **www.nhs.uk/every-mind-matters**.

Every meaningful achievement is built on a foundation of setbacks, mistakes and re-tries. Understanding that failure is not final, but formative, allows you to reframe challenges as opportunities for development. Building a healthy relationship with failure and balance in your life strengthens your leadership, adaptability and lifelong learning.

In this section, you will explore two examples of students who faced setbacks and used them to grow. You will also engage in activities that help you develop your own strategies for resilience, balance and self-reflection, capturing these experiences in your portfolio.

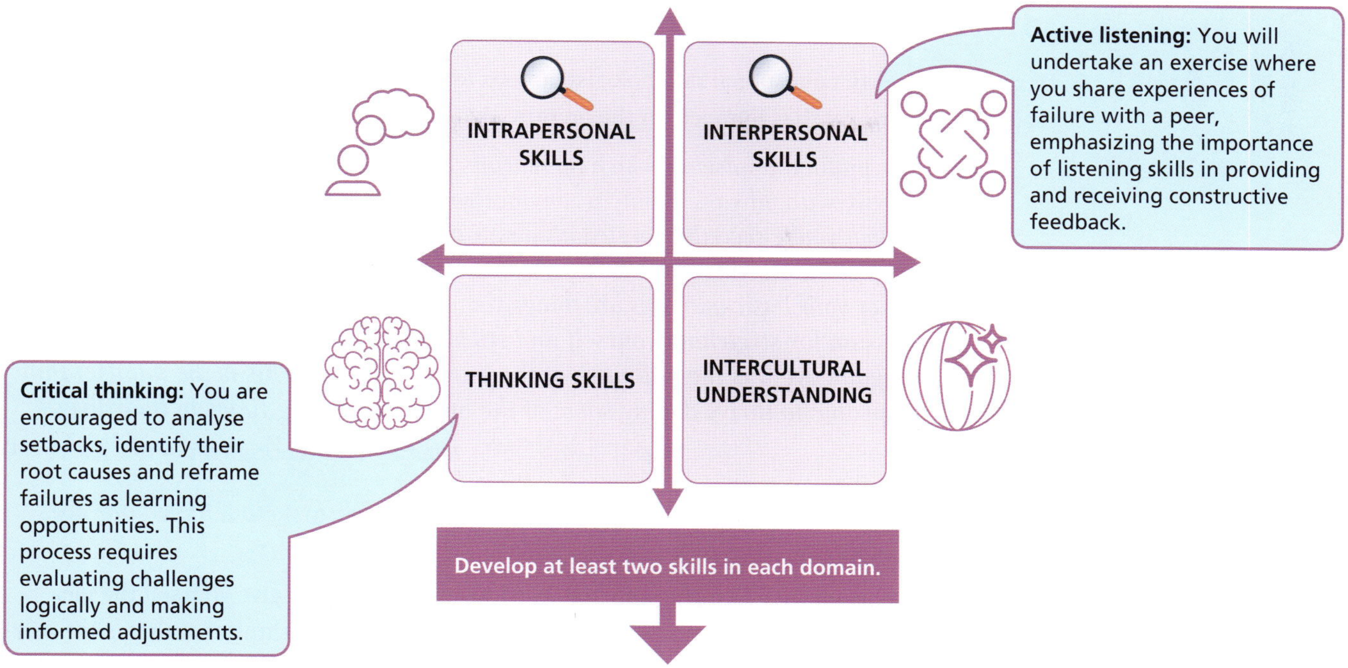

■ PPS skills focused on in Section 3.9

Whether we like it or not, we will all fail at things. This is not just normal, it is completely essential to growing as a well-rounded and self-aware human being taking on the world. This section will explore ideas and strategies not only to be able to deal with setbacks when they occur, but also incorporate them as an essential part of your learning journey, rather than sit in fear that something at some point might go wrong. (Plot spoiler: it will.) The good news is that putting the learning into failure actually makes you smarter.

'I have not failed, I've just found 1,000 things that won't work.'

(Thomas Edison, scientist and inventor from the US)

Learner profile

Risk-taker

We often talk of risk-taking, which can be difficult as risk-taking for one person is different for another. The easiest way to see the role risk-taking plays in your life is to think about the opposite. What will you gain from playing it safe and not stepping out of your comfort zone? We are not talking about 'end of the world' consequences, but we are visualizing an approach to learning that is fearful and limited in impact. The only real way to learn about and extend your capabilities is to ask more questions that start with 'What if ...?' and acknowledge that you may well *not* get things right ... *yet*.

3.9.2 Growth mindset

Carol Dweck is an educational psychologist famous for her work on 'growth mindset'. Her science-based research is founded on the premise that the brain is a muscle.

> *'There's another mindset in which these traits are not simply a hand you're dealt and have to live with, always trying to convince yourself and others that you have a royal flush when you're secretly worried it's a pair of tens. In this mindset, the hand you're dealt is just the starting point for development. This growth mindset is based on the belief that your basic qualities are things you can cultivate through your efforts …* ***The passion for stretching yourself and sticking to it, even (or especially) when it's not going well, is the hallmark of the growth mindset. This is the mindset that allows people to thrive during some of the most challenging times in their lives.'***
>
> (Carol Dweck (2016), *Mindset: The New Psychology of Success*, p.4)

Do you find yourself making statements like 'I've never been able to do that'? Everyone does this at some point.

But why does this matter? Defining yourself, even just internally, can give yourself the idea that this is set in stone and can never change. It can be reassuring to think that that is the way life is, but actually it stops us from growing and keeps us in a fixed mindset. Furthermore, it makes us think 'well, if these are the things I am good at, then I have to be the best and never get it wrong'. We become fixated on getting it right and, if we get it wrong, then we feel like we are showing ourselves up.

LEARNING ENGAGEMENT

Self-awareness

How you see yourself now influences how you will turn out in the future. Ask yourself whether you have a clear idea of what you can do and cannot do. Self-awareness like this can be very helpful.

1. Make a list of ten things you feel you cannot do. Use the sentence starters 'I cannot', 'I can't', 'I don't', etc. You can use any context to explore this. Examples could be:
   - 'I'm not a morning person.'
   - 'I can't bake.'
   - 'Sports aren't for me.'
   - 'I can't do quadratic equations.'
   - 'I don't understand art.'
   - 'I don't read.'
2. Now put the word 'yet' at the end of each item on your list. How does that change your outlook? You are on your way to discovering what Carol Dweck famously phrased as 'the power of yet'.

Science of the brain

Being willing to fail and learning from failure makes you smarter.

REAL-WORLD EXAMPLE

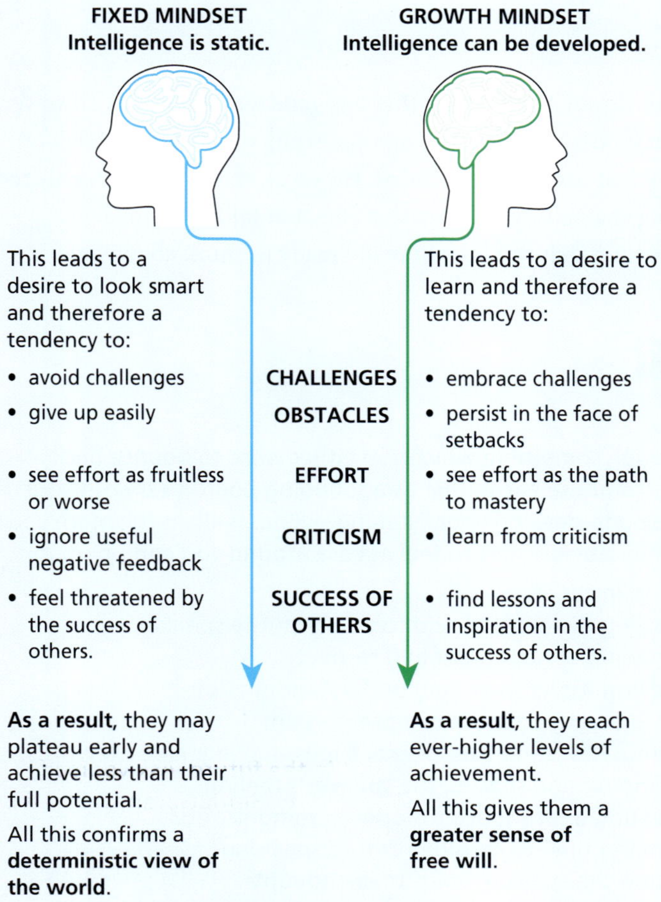

■ How a fixed or growth mindset affects the way we view the world (Based on a graphic by Nigel Holmes, in Carol Dweck, *Mindsets*)

The power of 'yet'

Carol Dweck is noted for her work on growth mindset and her powerful phrase 'the power of yet'. This small word can make the difference between a student thinking they have failed and can do nothing about it (a fixed mindset) to realising that they are on a learning journey and there is a clear road ahead (a growth mindset). In her TEDx talk 'The power of believing that you can improve', which you can find online, Dweck talks about how the phrase 'not yet' can give you 'a path into the future'.

Dweck has examined throughout her career how children cope with challenge and the impact it can have when students realise that they are always on a learning curve and practice makes progress and not perfection. When you understand that your abilities can be developed, you are more willing to take risks and grow; without this, you become fixated on controlling the outcome and comparing yourself to others.

The most important point, however, is illustrated in the visual on the left; scientific research reinforces that a growth mindset makes your brain alive with activity as you consider the possibilities of what is next and yet to come. Embrace making mistakes and learning from them and who knows what you can achieve.

Failure is an inevitable part of growth, but how you respond to it defines your journey. This section equips you with strategies to build resilience and adaptability, turning challenges into opportunities for learning. When faced with setbacks, it's important to pause and reflect on what went wrong and why. Was it a lack of preparation? A misstep in execution? Or perhaps an external factor beyond your control? Identifying the root cause is the first step toward improvement.

Resilience is about staying proactive in the face of adversity. For instance, if a project doesn't go as planned, view it as a chance to learn rather than a definitive end. Adaptability allows you to pivot your approach and try new methods. Consider how you can reframe setbacks as opportunities to grow stronger and smarter. Use reflection exercises to analyse your experiences and extract lessons that can guide you moving forward.

For example, after a setback, it can be difficult to bounce back or get to a place where you feel confident again. Consider the following reflective strategy, designed to support your ability to bounce back after failing at something.

Steps to bounce back

1 Start with what you're good at.
2 Think about difficulties you have overcome.
3 See how you can apply this elsewhere.
4 Find an image or metaphor to help you in difficult times.
5 Take some time to plan ahead.
6 Reflect, recognize and reward.

Now might not be the time to work through something that has gone wrong for you. However, this is a really useful tool for when it does. There is also an opportunity here to look back on something that went wrong and look at how you responded. However, this is a judgement-free process and it is not about thinking shamefully about past events, but taking a broader view of them. So do not pick something that you are not really ready to think about yet without emotion.

LEARNING ENGAGEMENT

Skill: Active listening

Pair up with a peer and talk through something which you either *want* to bounce back from or you *have* bounced back from. Use each other as a sounding board to try out your ideas on. As a bonus, you are going to develop your listening skills as well, as the more you learn this, the more you realize it enables others to feel at ease around you and open up.

Some examples of active listening include:

- **Paying full attention:** Minimizing distractions and focusing on the speaker.
- **Maintaining eye contact:** Showing engagement and respect.
- **Nodding and using verbal affirmations:** Signaling understanding ('uh-huh', 'yes').
- **Asking clarifying questions:** Ensuring accurate comprehension.
- **Paraphrasing and summarizing:** Restating the speaker's message in your own words.
- **Showing empathy:** Understanding and sharing the speaker's feelings.
- **Being non-judgemental:** Creating a safe space for open communication.
- **Responding thoughtfully:** Taking time to consider before speaking.
- **Avoiding interruptions:** Letting the speaker finish their thoughts.

Links

You will find an extension of this exercise in Section 4.8 (on the RP), as developing listening skills is a crucial part of giving and receiving peer feedback successfully.

3.9.3 Finding balance

Sometimes we can become overwhelmed by all of the responsibilities we have in both our personal and professional lives. For example, you may have school commitments, extra-curricular activities, work responsibilities, family obligations, social outings and the list goes on and on. Finding a balance is extremely difficult, but applying the skills you've learned in PPS can help you develop strategies to maintain a healthy balance in your life.

Learner profile

Balanced

Balancing different aspects of our lives—intellectual, physical and emotional—to achieve well-being for ourselves and others is a critical skill.

Balancing your life's responsibilities can feel a lot like juggling multiple balls in the air. Each ball represents a responsibility in your life. Good jugglers are able to throw one ball up in the air while focusing on another; however, if they do not give attention to each ball from time to time, one or more balls can fall to the ground. This is the same with thinking about your life's responsibilities. Finding a way to prioritize which ball to focus on at different times in life is a critical skill. So how can you use the skills developed in PPS to help build balance and keep all of your life's balls in the air?

There are different strategies you can use to create balance in your life.

■ Balancing responsibilities can feel like a juggling act

Reflect and adjust

- Reflect often on your daily actions, including how you spend your time.
- If you notice that one of the balls in your life has fallen, ask straightaway for help from a trusted friend, family member, mentor or teacher. Don't wait!

Prioritize and plan

- Use a planner, digital calendar or app to schedule everything: classes, homework, extracurriculars, social events and even downtime.
- Break down large tasks into smaller, manageable steps.
- Identify and prioritize tasks based on deadlines and importance.

Learn to say 'no' when appropriate

- It's okay to decline commitments that overload your schedule, especially ones that might bring additional stress into your life.
- Prioritize activities that genuinely align with your interests and values.

Establish a routine

- Creating a consistent daily and weekly routine can help you manage your time and reduce stress.
- Be mindful to schedule time for your interests, hobbies and maintaining relationships in your life.

Set realistic goals

- Avoid setting unrealistic expectations for yourself.
- Focus on progress, not perfection.

Reflection and reflexivity

Take a minute to write down all of your tasks, responsibilities and events for the next week. Be sure to include school, work, family and social activities. Using an app, like Google calendar, or a paper calendar, begin to schedule time for each of these events and colour-code them (e.g. red for school, blue for work, green for family, etc.).
Then reflect:

- How balanced is your schedule?
- Do you feel like one thing is taking too much of your time, or not enough?
- Do you have any space for downtime?
- What actions might you take to create more balance in your life?

3.9.4 Student sample inquiries

Below are inquiries that students like you have developed to explore overcoming obstacles and leveraging the power of 'yet'. As you read through them, consider if any of them are inspiring your own independent inquiry that would enable you to embrace the power of 'yet'.

INQUIRY 1

Bouncing back in leadership

Scenario: Naomi was elected president of her school's eco-club but struggled to motivate her team. Several projects failed to launch and Naomi doubted her leadership ability. Instead of giving up, she reframed the experience as an inquiry into resilience and leadership development.

Focus question: How do leaders motivate their team, especially when they've failed in the past?

List the concepts, contexts and skills that will be explored and developed in this inquiry:

- Concepts: Identities, systems
- Contexts: Informal learning, personal
- Skills: Reflection, communication, leadership, adaptability, resilience

Why am I undertaking this inquiry? What are my learning outcomes?

Aligned with PPS learning outcomes:

- Research leadership styles that focus specifically on motivation. (**LO1:** Take initiative and responsibility for independently researching and gathering relevant information.)
- Interview leaders to gain practical advice on strategies that leaders use to motivate their teams. (**LO2:** Communicate effectively and collaborate with others to gather perspectives and insights.)
- Develop a plan to apply new leadership strategies and reflect on the outcome. (**LO4:** Reflect critically on experiences and apply learning to personal growth and future actions.)

How will I explore these topics?

Activities:

- Research different leadership models and case studies.
- Interview experienced leaders about overcoming setbacks.
- Organize a small project to apply a new leadership style.
- Facilitate structured feedback sessions with the team after activities.

How will I reflect on my learning?

- How does leadership style affect team motivation?
- What role does resilience play in leading during challenges?

How will I share my learning?

- Create a leadership reflection guide for future club officers.
- Present lessons learned to the next eco-club leadership team.

Portfolio integration (artefacts to include):

- Leadership reflections and analysis.
- Notes from interviews with mentors.
- Feedback forms from team members.
- Updated inquiry tracker matrix entries reflecting skill development.

INQUIRY 2

Redefining success in academic research

Scenario: Daniel spent months preparing a research paper for a prestigious competition, but was not selected as a finalist. Initially disappointed, he used the setback as an opportunity to explore the idea of resilience in academic pursuits.

Focus question: What are some strategies I can use to overcome an academic setback?

List the concepts, contexts and skills that will be explored and developed in this inquiry:

- Concepts: Change, perspectives
- Contexts: Academic, personal life
- Skills: Critical thinking, resilience, reflection, communication

Why am I undertaking this inquiry? What are my learning outcomes?

Aligned with PPS learning outcomes:

- Analyse the feedback from the judges and seek additional feedback from trusted teachers and mentors on the essay. (**LO2:** Develop and apply communication and interpersonal skills in a variety of contexts.)
- Research other opportunities to submit or showcase my work. (**LO3:** Develop and apply thinking skills in a variety of contexts.)
- Revise and resubmit my work for a new opportunity. (**LO1:** Develop and apply intrapersonal skills in a variety of contexts.)

How will I explore these topics?

Activities:

- Analyse feedback from judges and identify improvement areas.
- Research strategies for revising and resubmitting academic work.
- Revise the original paper based on feedback and best practices.
- Submit the revised paper to a different publication or contest.

How will I reflect on my learning?

- How does receiving and applying feedback transform work?
- In what ways does failure encourage deeper learning?
- Personal reflections on the process of revision and resilience.

How will I share my learning?

- Share a before-and-after portfolio, showing the evolution of the research project.
- Create a reflection essay on resilience and redefining success.

Portfolio integration (artefacts to include):

- Original research paper and judge feedback.
- Revised research submission.
- Personal reflections on resilience.
- Inquiry tracker matrix updates showing the growth journey.

Top tip!

Failure and setbacks are not just challenges; they are powerful learning moments that deserve a place in your portfolio. Remember: everything you experience, including mistakes and growth, can contribute authentic, relevant and applicable artefacts to your portfolio. Reflection after difficulty shows resilience, adaptability and critical thinking—all essential skills for your future. By documenting both successes and setbacks, you are creating a full, honest picture of your personal and professional development.

3.9.5 Embracing imperfect balance

As you continue to build resilience and balance in your life, it's important to remember: no one can give 100% to everything all the time. In an interview for *Chief* magazine, writer and producer Shonda Rhimes reminds us that succeeding in one area often means letting go in another—and that is okay. Choosing to focus on what matters most in a given moment, whether it's your career, school, family or personal health, is part of living a full life.

Remember the balls we talked about earlier? Even with your best efforts in juggling them all, you will drop a ball from time to time or shift your attention away—and that's not failure. It's reality. What matters is your ability to recognize when something needs care, to forgive yourself and to redress the balance when you can. This honest approach to resilience acknowledges that thriving doesn't mean being perfect; it means staying flexible, self-aware and true to your priorities.

Another key part of building resilience is recognizing the importance of small wins. Facing setbacks can sometimes feel overwhelming, but taking the time to notice and celebrate even small steps forward can rebuild your confidence. Every achievement, no matter how minor it seems, is a reminder that progress is possible and that you have the tools to move through difficult times.

Resilience also involves learning to adapt to change rather than resisting it. Life will bring unexpected challenges, but viewing these changes as opportunities for growth helps you stay flexible and solution-focused. Instead of aiming for complete control, resilience teaches you to shift your mindset toward managing what you can, adjusting where needed and trusting your ability to find a way forward.

For more, you can visit 'Bouncing Back from Life's Challenges – NHS Every Mind Matters' on **www.nhs.uk/every-mind-matters**.

Learner profile

Risk-taker

Why it connects: This focuses on the importance of stepping outside of your comfort zone to embrace challenges and new opportunities. As a risk-taker, you are willing to take calculated risks in order to grow and learn. This attribute encourages resilience, courage and the ability to handle uncertainty in a positive way.

Learner profile quote: 'You approach unfamiliar situations and uncertainty with courage and determination; you work independently and cooperatively to explore new ideas and innovative strategies.'

In action:

- Take on new challenges that push you outside of your comfort zone, whether academically or personally.
- Be open to making mistakes and learning from them, seeing failures as opportunities for growth.
- Work collaboratively with others to tackle difficult problems and try new approaches.

Learner profile

Balanced

Why it connects: This discusses the importance of maintaining a healthy balance between different aspects of life, such as academics, personal interests and well-being. As a balanced individual, you prioritize both your intellectual and physical health, recognizing the importance of self-care and well-being for sustained growth.

Learner profile quote: 'You understand the importance of balancing different aspects of your life—intellectual, physical and emotional—to achieve well-being for yourself and others.'

In action:

- Organize your time effectively, balancing your academic responsibilities with physical activity and relaxation.
- Reflect on your emotional well-being and engage in activities that support your mental health.
- Seek opportunities to practise mindfulness or other techniques to maintain your overall balance and well-being.

3.9.6 Summary of skills, contexts and concepts

Table 3.26 What have we explored in this section?

Skills developed	Contexts explored	Key concepts
• Reflection • Resilience • Self-management	• Personal • DP courses/academic • Professional	• Change • Well-being • Perspectives

Learning journal

Portfolio work: Evidence of learning

Throughout this section, you have documented your learning through:

- your growth mindset statements
- the colour-coded calendar showcasing your efforts in balancing your life
- reflections on setbacks in your life and ways you've learned from them.

3.9.7 Summary

- Failure and setbacks are a catalyst for growth and development.
- Developing a growth mindset, reflecting and creating balance in your life can enable you to have a resilient approach when setbacks occur in life.
- Perfection is not the goal, nor is it realistic. Learning from setbacks is a marker of a successful person.

3.10 Curating your portfolio

INQUIRY QUESTION

- How does curating and reflecting on a portfolio deepen your understanding of personal growth and future aspirations?

3.10.1 Your portfolio is personal

Your portfolio tells the story of who you are and who you are becoming. It is more than a simple collection of work; it is a reflection of your growth, your values and your aspirations. Through careful curation, thoughtful annotation and deep reflection, you can transform your portfolio into a powerful narrative of personal and professional development.

Experts highlight that reflection and synthesis are not just academic exercises, but also essential skills for lifelong learning. Curating your portfolio invites you to step back, see the bigger picture of your journey and identify the threads that connect your experiences to your goals. It's a process of making meaning—of seeing not just what you have done, but how it shapes who you are.

A well-curated portfolio doesn't just document your learning—it reveals it. Organizing and reflecting on your experiences allows you to see patterns in your growth, understand your strengths and identify areas for continued development. It helps you make intentional connections between your skills, aspirations and future career paths. A strong portfolio is not only valuable for academic or professional applications, but also acts as mirror that helps you understand yourself more deeply.

This section will guide you through practical strategies for selecting meaningful artefacts, writing insightful annotations and synthesizing your learning into a cohesive and personal story. You'll engage in activities that encourage reflection, critical thinking and self-awareness, helping you create a portfolio that is not only comprehensive, but also transformative.

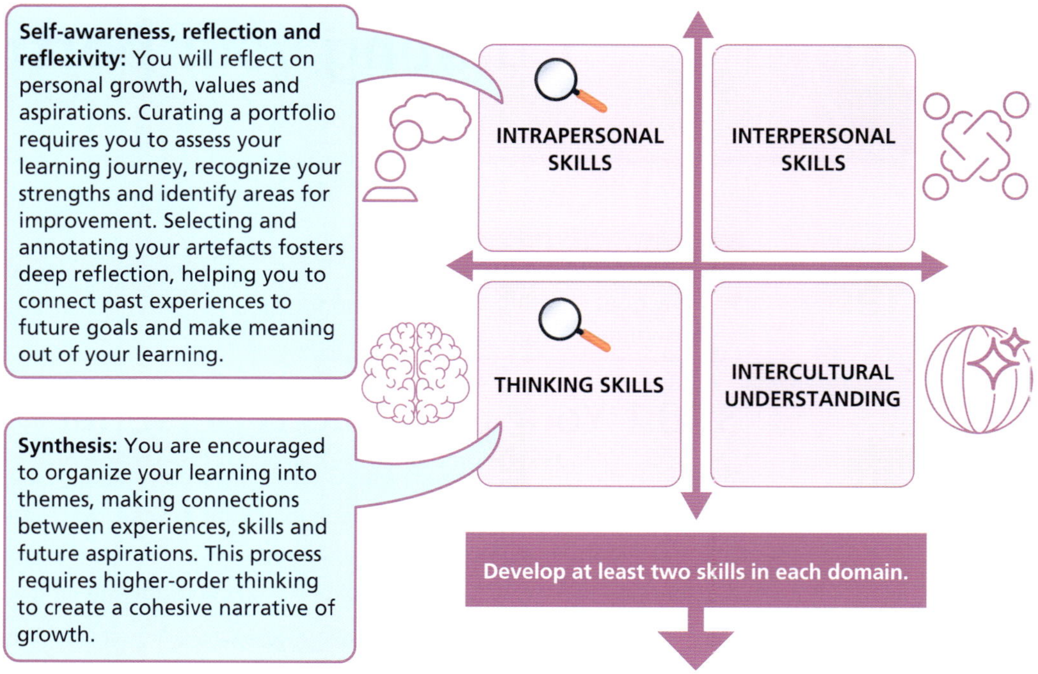

■ PPS skills focused on in Section 3.10

3.10.2 Curating your portfolio

Imagine your portfolio as a canvas, where each artefact represents a brushstroke that paints the picture of your learning journey. This section focuses on how to select, annotate and synthesize your learning artefacts to create a portfolio that is not only comprehensive, but also deeply personal. Let's explore the steps to create a portfolio that effectively showcases your progress and achievements.

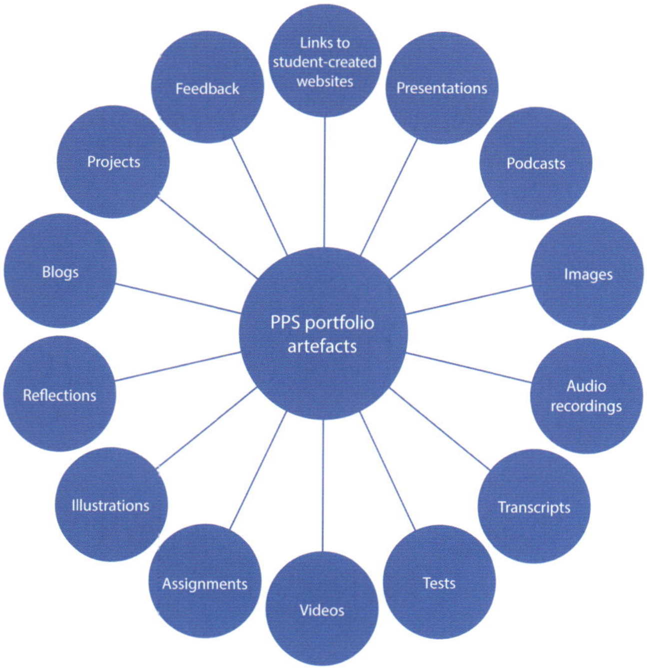

■ Examples of artefacts you can use in your portfolio (Source: IB PPS TSM, p.36)

■ Tips for artefact selection

When selecting artefacts for your portfolio, think about the diversity of evidence you include. A strong portfolio showcases a range of learning engagements—reflections, projects, feedback from mentors and creative works—that highlight different aspects of your journey. It's important to align each artefact with the PPS learning outcomes, such as demonstrating ethical awareness or developing communication skills. Choose artefacts that resonate with your values and goals, even if they highlight areas where you've faced challenges or setbacks. These are often the most powerful indicators of growth.

■ Crafting meaningful annotations

Annotations are the voice of your portfolio, offering insights into the why and how of your learning. Each annotation should explain why you chose the artefact, what it taught you and how it contributes to your personal and professional growth. For example, an annotation might describe how a group project helped you build teamwork skills or how a reflective journal entry deepened your understanding of resilience. By framing your annotations in this way, you add depth and context to your portfolio, transforming it from a simple collection of artefacts into a meaningful narrative of your development.

Synthesizing your learning

Your portfolio is more than a collection of artefacts; it's a cohesive story of your growth. To create this narrative, identify themes that emerge across your artefacts, such as adaptability, ethical decision-making or collaboration. Organize your portfolio to reflect these themes, showing how your experiences connect to the PPS concepts, such as 'connections' or 'identities'. This approach allows you to demonstrate the broader impact of your learning and its relevance to your future goals. By synthesizing your learning in this way, your portfolio becomes a powerful tool for reflection and self-discovery.

LEARNING ENGAGEMENT

The impact of PPS

Create a vision board that captures the key skills you've acquired and the accomplishments you're most proud of from the work in PPS. Think about the challenges you've overcome, the new abilities you've developed and the moments where you felt a sense of achievement. Use your vision board to reflect on your growth throughout the course and to celebrate the progress you've made. What were your biggest takeaways? What skills surprised you the most? Use this board as a way to identify areas that you will want to include in your portfolio.

Pitfalls and challenges

Creating a portfolio is not without its challenges. You might struggle with selecting the right artefacts, balancing your responsibilities or finding the time to annotate and reflect meaningfully. Growth often involves stepping outside your comfort zone, which can feel uncomfortable or overwhelming. It's important to approach these challenges with a growth mindset, seeing them as opportunities to build resilience. If you feel stuck, revisit your focus, seek feedback from peers or mentors and remember that every obstacle is a chance to learn and improve.

Reflection and reflexivity

Reflection is the bridge between experience and growth. It allows you to evaluate what worked, understand what didn't and refine your goals. In PPS, reflective practices connect to other Core components of the CP, such as CE and the RP. For instance, reflecting on a community project might enhance your understanding of ethical decision-making, while considering your approach to the RP can deepen your skills in critical thinking and research. Reflection also helps you understand yourself and others, fostering greater empathy and self-awareness.

3.10.3 Core connections

In this process, it is also valuable to connect your PPS learning to the other components of the CP Core:

- language and cultural studies (LCS)
- community engagement (CE)
- reflective project (RP).

For example, communication skills developed in PPS may be showcased through projects in LCS, ethical decision-making could be tied to experiences in CE, and critical-thinking skills may directly support the development of your RP. Curating your portfolio with these Core connections in mind strengthens the cohesion of your learning journey and highlights your growth across multiple dimensions.

LEARNING ENGAGEMENT

Updating your portfolio

As you have covered many topics, experiences and inquiries throughout this book, go through these 'Core connections' prompts and see what you can add or change for your portfolio.

1 **Core connection prompt: LCS**
How have your experiences with language learning or cultural exploration enhanced your communication or global-mindedness? How can you showcase this growth in your portfolio?

2 **Core connection prompt: CE**
Think about a community project you participated in. How did your PPS skills, like leadership, collaboration or ethical thinking, help you engage meaningfully with others? Which artefacts could highlight this?

3 **Core connection prompt: RP**
Reflect on the inquiry and research skills you've developed through PPS. How are these skills helping you plan, research or reflect in your RP? How can you capture this connection in your portfolio?

Links

Curating your portfolio is also a chance to highlight how your growth in PPS connects with the other CP Core components: LCS, CE and the RP.

Examples of Core connections

Here are a few examples of how students made meaningful connections across their learning.

REAL-WORLD EXAMPLES

LCS: Building global understanding

Lola realized that the communication strategies she developed in PPS helped her confidently engage in discussions during her LCS course. By reflecting on cultural perspectives and practising empathy, she strengthened her ability to collaborate across languages and cultures. Lola chose to annotate a group project presentation where she explored cultural identity, highlighting how PPS and LCS worked together to develop her global competence.

CE: Ethical leadership in action

Miguel participated in a local sustainability initiative for his CE project. He recognized that the leadership and ethical decision-making skills he learned in PPS directly shaped his approach to organizing team meetings and ensuring community voices were respected. Miguel selected an artefact from his project—a reflection journal entry—and annotated it to show how PPS skills supported ethical leadership.

RP: Researching with purpose

Amina noticed that the critical thinking and resilience she practised throughout PPS were essential as she tackled challenges during her RP research. When she faced obstacles finding reliable sources, she drew on her PPS inquiry strategies to stay focused and adaptable. Amina included annotated research notes in her portfolio, demonstrating how her PPS foundation strengthened her ability to manage a complex, long-term project.

Remember: Each artefact you choose, each annotation you craft and each theme you weave together strengthens your ability to reflect, connect and grow. Curating your portfolio is an act of self-discovery, helping you recognize the progress you've made and the future you're building.

Reflection and reflexivity

- After reading these examples, what stands out most to you?
- How might you be able to highlight the connections to the Core in your own portfolio?

Voices from fellow students

Hearing from peers who have navigated similar journeys can inspire and guide you. One student shared how curating a portfolio helped them see their growth more clearly:

> *Keeping a portfolio was like building a scrapbook of 'aha!' moments. It helped me connect the dots between my experiences and my goals.*
>
> **Juno**

Another student reflected on the power of guided inquiry, saying:

> *Exploring leadership skills through projects showed me that leading isn't about being the loudest voice but about listening and empowering others.*
>
> **Amir**

These insights remind us of the transformative potential of reflection and intentional learning.

3.10.4 Student sample inquiries

Below are inquiries that students like you have developed to explore ways to better curate and organize their portfolios. As you read through them, consider if any of them are inspiring your own independent inquiry that would support the curation of your own portfolio.

INQUIRY 1

Building a personal narrative

Scenario: Malik realized that while he had many projects and activities documented, his portfolio felt disconnected. With guidance, he began curating artefacts thematically, showcasing growth in leadership, resilience and ethical awareness. Through reflection, he transformed a random collection into a cohesive personal narrative.

Focus question: How can the thematic curation and reflective annotation of past experiences within a portfolio create a cohesive personal narrative that highlights skill development and supports future personal and professional goals?

List the concepts, contexts and skills that will be explored and developed in this inquiry:

- Concepts: Identities, connections
- Contexts: DP courses, academic, career-related
- Skills: Self-awareness, reflection, communication, critical thinking

Why am I undertaking this inquiry? What are my learning outcomes?

Aligned with PPS learning outcomes:

- Identify and develop skills that support personal and professional goals. (**LO1:** Take responsibility for personal development by recognizing and building relevant skills.)
- Develop strategies for self-management and reflection. (**LO4:** Demonstrate self-management skills and engage in reflective practices to improve learning.)
- Create a cohesive, well-developed portfolio. (**LO1 and LO5:** Organize and present evidence of learning effectively to showcase progress and achievements.)

How will I explore these topics?

Activities:

- Review examples of curated portfolios.
- Analyse how themes are woven across different artefacts.
- Select and annotate three artefacts around a common theme.
- Organize a draft portfolio focusing on synthesis.

How will I reflect on my learning?

- How does curating artefacts around a theme deepen my understanding of my growth?
- What does my portfolio reveal about my journey and goals?
- Write a reflective piece on the process of creating a cohesive narrative.

How will I share my learning?

- Present my portfolio draft to a peer for feedback.
- Write a reflective piece on the process of creating a cohesive narrative.

Portfolio integration (artefacts to include):

- Thematic artefact collections.
- Annotated reflections showing personal growth and future aspirations.

INQUIRY 2

Growth through reflection

Scenario: Priya struggled to see the impact of her service project at first. After curating her reflections and project feedback into her portfolio, she recognized how much she had developed empathy, adaptability and ethical leadership.

Focus question: How does engaging in service learning and employing reflective practices foster the development of ethical awareness, empathy and adaptability, and how can a portfolio showcase this personal and community impact?

List the concepts, contexts and skills that will be explored and developed in this inquiry:

- Concepts: Perspectives, well-being
- Contexts: Community engagement, personal
- Skills: Reflection, reflexivity, ethical awareness, communication, collaboration

Why am I undertaking this inquiry? What are my learning outcomes?

Aligned with PPS learning outcomes:

- **LO2:** Develop and apply communication and collaboration skills.
- **LO5:** Recognize and develop ethical awareness.

How will I explore these topics?

Activities:

- Research best practices in reflective writing.
- Study examples of portfolios that highlight service learning.
- Write reflective annotations connecting my experiences to ethical decision-making.
- Update my inquiry tracker matrix to show growth.

How will I reflect on my learning?

- What ethical challenges have shaped my learning?
- How has reflection helped me see the broader impact of my actions?

How will I share my learning?

- Create a visual representation of my growth through service learning.
- Share reflections with a mentor or small group.

Portfolio integration (artefacts to include):

- Annotated service learning reflections.
- Personal growth map connecting experiences and future goals.

Reflection and reflexivity

1 Take a moment to ask yourself:

- What does your portfolio say about who you are and who you want to become?

Consider how each artefact and reflection contributes to this narrative. By curating your portfolio with care and purpose, you create a tool that not only demonstrates your achievements, but also captures your aspirations and values.

2 Pause and consider these questions:

- How do the artefacts in your portfolio demonstrate your growth?
- What connections can you make between your learning in PPS and other areas of your life?
- How has reflection shaped your understanding of your values and goals?
- What steps can you take to deepen your reflective practice?

By addressing these questions, you strengthen your ability to connect, reflect and grow in meaningful ways. This moment of reflection is not just a pause, but a step forward in your journey of self-discovery.

Learner profile

Reflective

Why it connects: This emphasizes the importance of reflection in personal and professional growth. As a reflective learner, you regularly evaluate your experiences, actions and progress, helping you gain deeper insights into your strengths, areas for improvement and overall journey. This attribute promotes critical thinking, self-awareness and continuous improvement.

Learner profile quote: 'You give thoughtful consideration to your own learning and experiences; you are able to assess and understand your strengths and limitations in order to support your learning and development.'

In action:

- Regularly reflect on your experiences, both successes and challenges, to identify key lessons learned.
- Use reflection as a tool to set new goals and adjust your approach when necessary.
- Seek feedback from others to improve your understanding and performance, recognizing it as a vital part of your growth.

Learner profile

Communicator

Why it connects: This underscores the value of communication in curating a portfolio that reflects your growth. As a communicator, you express your thoughts clearly and effectively, whether in writing or speaking. This skill is essential for sharing your reflections and showcasing your learning journey to others.

Learner profile quote: 'You express yourself confidently and creatively in more than one language and in a variety of modes of communication. You collaborate effectively, listening carefully to the perspectives of others.'

In action:

- Actively engage in discussions and share your learning engagements with others, both in academic and personal contexts.
- Use multiple forms of communication, including written reflections and presentations, to convey your ideas clearly.
- Listen to and learn from the feedback and perspectives of others to enhance your own understanding.

3.10.5 Summary of skills, contexts and concepts

Table 3.27 What have we explored in this section?

Skills developed	Contexts explored	Key concepts
• Reflection • Reflexivity • Critical thinking	• Personal • Professional • Informal learning	• Connections • Perspectives • Well-being

Learning journal

Portfolio work: Evidence of learning

Throughout this section, you have documented your learning through:

- developing a vision board of PPS learning, accomplishments and achievements in PPS
- adding inquiries and artefacts to your PPS tracker
- reflecting on the curation of your portfolio.

3.10.6 Summary

- Your portfolio is not simply a collection of tasks, it is a story of your growth and development.
- Creating a portfolio with a variety of artefacts, experiences, achievements and learning will best communicate your journey.
- Carefully selecting items and thinking about them helps you see your growth and connect experiences to your aspirations.
- Organizing and reflecting on your work demonstrates your understanding and growth, which is valuable for your academic and professional future.

3.11 A future-oriented mindset

INQUIRY QUESTION

- How has PPS prepared you for the future?

3.11.1 How has PPS shaped you?

Personal and professional skills (PPS) is not just about preparing for today's challenges—it's about building the mindset and tools you need for the future. As you complete your PPS journey, you are stepping into a world that requires adaptability, resilience and purpose. Your experiences, reflections and growth throughout this course are just the beginning of your lifelong journey of learning and leadership.

Experts agree that a future-oriented mindset is rooted in reflection, action and continuous self-improvement. It means seeing every opportunity, every challenge and every connection as a step toward something greater. It's about using what you have learned to build not only a successful career, but also a meaningful, impactful life.

A future-oriented mindset empowers you to approach change with confidence, to adapt when challenges arise and to pursue your goals with clarity and resilience. In a world that is constantly evolving, having a vision—and the skills to act on it—is essential for personal and professional success. Reflection, ethical awareness, collaboration and communication will continue to be your tools as you navigate new pathways.

This section invites you to reflect on how PPS has shaped you, to identify your next steps and to commit to purposeful action. You'll engage in activities that help you recognize the skills you've developed, set future goals and build the mindset necessary for lifelong learning and growth.

Remember: the end of PPS is not a finish line. It is the launchpad for everything that comes next!

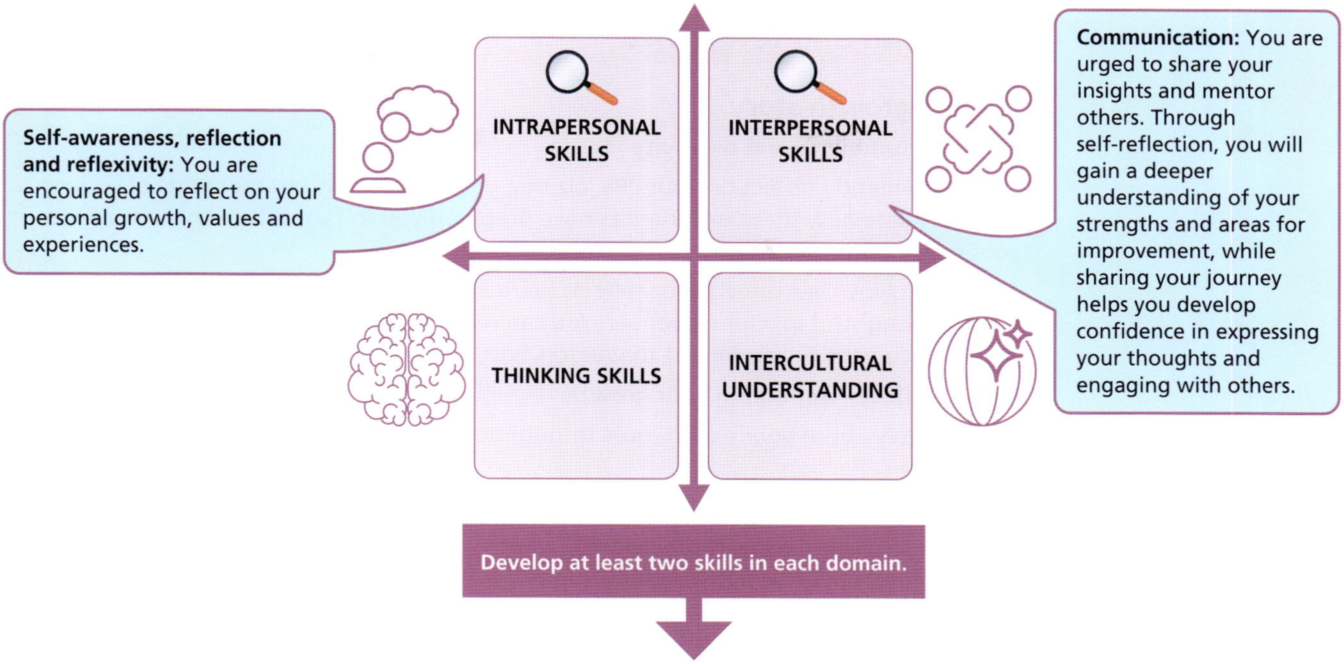

■ PPS skills focused on in Section 3.11

3.11.2 Reflect, share, act

As we reach the conclusion of your journey through PPS, it's important to recognize that this is not an ending but a beginning. You have explored new ways of thinking, collaborated with others and developed a toolkit of skills that will serve you in every aspect of your life. Now is the time to reflect on what you've learned, share your experiences and insights with others, and take meaningful action toward your future goals. By doing so, you solidify your own growth and also inspire and support those around you, creating a positive ripple effect that extends beyond your own journey.

- *Reflect* on how PPS has prepared you to face challenges with confidence and creativity. Think about the moments where you stepped outside your comfort zone, tried something new or overcame a difficulty. Each of these experiences has contributed to your growth. Perhaps you discovered the importance of ethical decision-making, learned to appreciate diverse perspectives or honed your ability to adapt to change. These are not just skills for the classroom; they are tools for navigating life's complexities.
- *Sharing* what you've learned is equally valuable. Your journey is unique and your story has the power to inspire others. Whether it's presenting a project, mentoring a peer or simply reflecting with friends, your insights can spark conversations that encourage growth and understanding in others. When you share, you're not only reinforcing your learning, but also contributing to a community of learners who support one another.
- Finally, it's time to *act*. PPS has given you the foundation to set meaningful goals and pursue them with intention. What are your next steps? Perhaps you want to apply your skills to a community project, take on a leadership role or explore a career pathway that excites you. Whatever your goals, approach them with curiosity, determination and the understanding that learning is a lifelong journey.

Reflection and reflexivity

My PPS growth story

Building confidence and creativity

To independently reflect on your PPS journey, you can identify key moments of growth and articulate how these experiences have prepared you to face future challenges with confidence and creativity.

This activity involves three parts: reflect, share and act. Take your time with each section and be thoughtful in your responses. You can record your reflections in a journal, a digital document or any format that works best for you.

Part 1: Reflect—Unpacking your growth

Think deeply about your experiences throughout PPS. Consider the following prompts to guide your reflection:

1. **Stepping outside your comfort zone:**
   - Describe a specific instance in PPS where you intentionally stepped outside your comfort zone. What was the situation? What made it challenging?
   - What did you learn about yourself or your abilities in that moment?
   - How has this experience influenced your willingness to try new things or face unfamiliar situations now?
2. **Trying something new:**
   - Recall a time during PPS when you engaged in a completely new activity or learned a new skill. What was it?
   - What were your initial thoughts and feelings? What challenges did you encounter during the learning process?
   - How did this experience contribute to your creativity or problem-solving skills?
3. **Overcoming difficulty:**
   - Think about a specific obstacle or difficulty you faced during your PPS journey. What was the challenge?
   - What strategies did you use to navigate this difficulty? Who or what supported you?
   - How did overcoming this challenge build your confidence and resilience?
4. **Key learnings from PPS:**
   - Identify one significant insight you gained related to ethical decision-making. How has this understanding shaped your perspective?
   - Describe a moment where you learned to appreciate diverse perspectives. How did this broaden your understanding of a situation or topic?
   - Reflect on a time when you had to adapt to change within PPS. What did you learn about your flexibility and resourcefulness?

Part 2: Share—Articulating your insights

Now consider how you might share your reflections and insights with others. Choose one of the following options:

1. **Written reflection for a peer:** Write a short letter or message to a peer who is just beginning their PPS journey—perhaps a student in CP. Share one or two key lessons you've learned and explain how these insights can help them navigate their own experiences. Consider sharing your reflection directly with CP students to provide authentic support and encouragement.
2. **Informal conversation starters:** Jot down three key takeaways from your PPS journey that you could share during a casual conversation—perhaps at your dinner table with family or friends—to spark a meaningful discussion about personal growth.

3 **Visual representation:** Create a visual (e.g. a mind map, a short comic strip, a series of images with captions) that represents your growth journey in PPS and highlights the key skills you've developed. Consider sharing your visual with early stage CP students or the incoming cohort to inspire and guide those just beginning their own journeys.

Part 3: Act—Planning your next steps

Building on your PPS foundation, think about your future goals and how you can apply what you've learned. Answer the following questions:

1 **Meaningful goals:** Identify one or two meaningful goals you want to pursue in the near future (e.g. a community project, a leadership role, exploring a career interest).

2 **Applying your skills:** For each goal, describe at least one specific skill or insight you gained from PPS that will help you achieve it. Explain *how* that skill will be beneficial.

3 **Embracing lifelong learning:** How will you continue to approach new experiences and challenges with curiosity and a growth mindset, understanding that learning is an ongoing process?

Key takeaways

Throughout PPS, you've gained essential tools for personal and professional growth. You've learned to reflect on your values and actions, connect with others and adapt to change. These takeaways will not only guide your decisions, but also help you build relationships and contribute meaningfully to the world around you. Remember:

- Reflection deepens self-awareness and helps you learn from experiences.
- Ethical thinking shapes decisions that align with your values and impacts others positively.
- Appreciating multiple perspectives fosters empathy and collaboration.
- Transversal skills like critical thinking, adaptability and teamwork are vital for lifelong success.

3.11.3 Student sample inquiries

Below are inquiries that students like you have developed and explored in PPS to think about their futures. As you read through them, consider if any of them are inspiring your own independent inquiry that would help you envision your future.

INQUIRY 1

Shaping my future vision

Scenario: Jamal realized that through PPS, he had developed a strong passion for ethical entrepreneurship. He decided to create a personal action plan connecting his learning to future business ventures that prioritize social impact.

Focus question: How can I integrate my passion for ethical entrepreneurship, developed through PPS, into a personal action plan that guides my future business ventures and prioritizes social impact?

List the concepts, contexts and skills that will be explored and developed in this inquiry:

- Concepts: Systems, connections
- Contexts: Personal and career-related study
- Skills: Ethics and personal value, leadership, communication

Why am I undertaking this inquiry? What are my learning outcomes?

Aligned with PPS learning outcomes:

- **LO5:** Identify and develop skills that support personal and professional goals.
- **LO1:** Recognize and develop ethical awareness.

How will I explore these topics?

Activities:

- Research future career trends and emerging industries.
- Investigate examples of ethical entrepreneurship.
- Draft a personal vision statement.
- Create a future action plan connecting skills to career goals.

How will I reflect on my learning?

- How have my values shaped my future goals?
- In what ways can I make a positive impact through my career?

How will I share my learning?

- Present my vision and action plan to a mentor or peer group.

Portfolio integration (artefacts to include):

- Vision statement and future action plan.
- Reflections on ethical leadership and personal growth.

INQUIRY 2

Sharing my journey

Scenario: Leah realized that sharing her PPS journey could inspire others. She created a podcast episode reflecting on her growth, the challenges she faced and the lessons she wants others to carry forward.

Focus question: How can I effectively share my PPS journey through reflective storytelling to inspire others and foster a community of growth?

List the concepts, contexts and skills that will be explored and developed in this inquiry:

- Concepts: Identities and connections
- Contexts: Personal, DP/academic, community engagement
- Skills: Reflection, empathy, creative thinking

Why am I undertaking this inquiry? What are my learning outcomes?

Aligned with PPS learning outcomes:

- **LO2:** Develop and apply communication and collaboration skills.
- **LO1:** Develop strategies for self-management and reflection.

How will I explore these topics?

Activities:

- Listen to examples of reflective storytelling (e.g. podcasts, TEDx talks).
- Analyse the elements of effective narrative sharing.
- Script and record a short podcast or video reflection.
- Share my journey with my school or community.

How will I reflect on my learning?

- What lessons have been most meaningful to me?
- How can my story inspire and support others?

How will I share my learning?

- Publish my podcast or reflection through school channels.
- Invite others to share their journeys and create a community of growth.

Portfolio integration (artefacts to include):

- Podcast or video reflection artefacts.
- Reflections on mentoring and communication growth.

Learner profile

Principled

Why it connects: This emphasizes the importance of ethical decision-making, responsibility and integrity as you prepare for the future. Being principled means making decisions based on strong ethical values, understanding the impact of your actions and consistently doing what is right. This mindset is critical as you navigate personal and professional growth and engage with the world around you.

Learner profile quote: 'You act with integrity and honesty, with a strong sense of fairness and justice. You take responsibility for your actions and their consequences.'

In action:

- Reflect on your values and ensure that they guide your decisions, both personally and professionally.
- Act with integrity in all situations, even when faced with challenges or pressure.
- Make ethical choices in your career and personal life, considering their long-term impact on others and the world.

Learner profile

Thinker

Why it connects: A future-oriented mindset requires the ability to think critically, solve problems and innovate. As a thinker, you are equipped to approach complex situations with an analytical mindset and come up with creative solutions. This ability will help you adapt to new challenges, set future goals and make thoughtful decisions in your career and life.

Learner profile quote: 'You think critically and creatively to analyse and take action on complex problems. You approach problems with an open mind and are willing to try new approaches.'

In action:

- Use your critical thinking skills to assess situations and make informed decisions that align with your long-term vision.
- Approach challenges as opportunities for creative problem-solving and continuous learning.
- Set future goals that are based on a thoughtful analysis of your strengths, values and the opportunities ahead.

3.11.4 Scenario-based sample inquiries

To deepen your understanding of PPS in different contexts, this section includes scenario-based inquiries designed for early stage CP students. These inquiries provide an opportunity to apply key concepts like perspectives and cultural intelligence in practical, meaningful ways. Over a six-week period, students engage with authentic materials and case studies to explore complex topics, reflect on their learning and develop skills relevant to professional life in a globalized world.

SAMPLE INQUIRY 1

Teacher class: Early stage CP

Duration of inquiry: 6 weeks

Inquiry title: Bridging cultures: Understanding perspectives in a globalized world

Entry point: A video documentary showcasing cultural misunderstandings in international workplaces. This entry point helps students recognize the real-world impact of cultural perspectives and systems.

Concept: Perspectives

Context: Professional life—International work environments

Content:

- Cultural intelligence and communication strategies.
- Case studies of multinational companies navigating cultural differences.
- Ethical dilemmas in intercultural interactions.
- Impact of technology on cross-cultural communication.

Skill development: Interpersonal skills, thinking skills, intercultural understanding

Learning outcomes:

- **LO2:** Develop and apply communication and interpersonal skills in a variety of contexts.
- **LO4:** Develop and apply intercultural understanding in a variety of contexts.
- **LO5:** Demonstrate awareness of ethical implications of one's choices and actions on self and others.

Connection to prior knowledge and skills:

- Students may have prior experience interacting with people from different cultures through social media, travel or school projects.
- Students need to learn about frameworks like Hofstede's cultural dimensions and strategies for effective intercultural dialogue.

Resources needed:

- Case studies of global businesses.
- Interviews with international professionals.
- Interactive simulations or role-playing activities.
- Articles on cultural competency in the workplace.

Differentiation strategies:

- Visual learners: Infographics on cultural differences.
- Kinesthetic learners: Role-play different workplace scenarios.
- Auditory learners: Podcast interviews with multicultural professionals.

Assessment:

- Formative: Group discussions on case studies and journal reflections on personal biases.
- Summative: A presentation analysing an intercultural workplace conflict and proposing solutions.

Inquiry activities:

- Explore:
  - Research cultural communication styles in different regions (e.g. Asia versus Western Europe).
  - Analyse case studies of miscommunication in global businesses.
- Act:
  - Conduct interviews with professionals who work in diverse teams.
  - Participate in a cross-cultural role-playing activity.
- Reflect:
  - Journal reflections on biases and cultural misunderstandings.
  - Group discussion on how to apply learning in future careers.
- Share:
  - Create a video or podcast episode discussing key takeaways.
  - Present findings in a virtual panel discussion.

Reflections on learning:

- How has my perception of cultural differences changed?
- How will I apply these skills in my future career?
- Did my learning influence my peers or family discussions?

SAMPLE INQUIRY 2

Teacher class: Later stage CP

Duration of inquiry: 6 weeks

Inquiry title: The science of well-being: A global perspective

Entry point: A short film or TEDx talk about how different cultures define and achieve happiness and well-being. The Edge of Happiness' by Helen Russell (TEDxOdense) or What happiness looks like around the world by Helen Russell)

This entry point engages students by contrasting different cultural perspectives on well-being.

Concept: Well-being

Context: Personal life—Mental and physical health strategies

Content:

- Psychological theories of happiness (Maslow's hierarchy, PERMA model).
- Cultural differences in well-being (e.g. Denmark's Hygge versus Japan's Ikigai).
- The impact of technology on mental health.
- Socio-economic influences on well-being across different regions.

Skill development: Intrapersonal skills, thinking skills, interpersonal skills

Learning outcomes:

- **LO1:** Develop and apply intrapersonal skills in a variety of contexts.
- **LO3:** Develop and apply thinking skills in a variety of contexts.
- **LO5:** Demonstrate awareness of ethical implications of one's choices and actions on self and others.

Connection to prior knowledge and skills:

- Students have personal experiences with stress, happiness and emotional well-being.
- Students need to explore how different cultural and scientific approaches shape well-being.

Resources needed:

- Articles on global happiness indexes.
- Documentaries on mindfulness and lifestyle differences.
- Interviews with people from different cultures on their definition of happiness.
- Research studies on social media and mental health.

Differentiation strategies:

- Visual learners: Infographics on well-being strategies in different cultures.
- Kinesthetic learners: Practice mindfulness and physical activities from various traditions (e.g. tai chi, yoga).
- Auditory learners: Listen to podcasts on mental health in different societies.

Assessment:

- Formative: Class discussions on cultural approaches to well-being and self-assessment of personal well-being strategies.
- Summative: A comparative research project on well-being strategies across cultures and creation of a well-being action plan based on personal reflection and cultural insights.

Inquiry activities:

- Explore:
  - Compare happiness rankings from different countries.
  - Analyse well-being strategies from different traditions (e.g. Mediterranean diet, Indigenous storytelling).
- Act:
  - Keep a personal well-being journal using strategies from different cultures.
  - Conduct surveys on what well-being means to different people in their community.
- Reflect:
  - Discuss how cultural background affects one's approach to stress and happiness.
  - Write a personal reflection on which well-being practices resonate most.
- Share:
  - Present findings in a 'global well-being expo' showcasing different practices.
  - Create a social media campaign promoting a well-being practice.

Reflections on learning:

- What well-being practices were most surprising to me?
- How will I apply my learning to improve my own well-being?
- Did this inquiry challenge any of my preconceptions?

3.11.5 What's next for you?

What's your next step and how will you take it? Set a specific goal for the coming weeks or months and think about how you will hold yourself accountable. Remember that every small step forward is progress. Whether it's reaching out to a mentor, starting a new project or committing to daily reflection, your actions today lay the foundation for your future.

Reflection and reflexivity

Pause to consider these final questions:

- How has PPS changed the way you see yourself and your future?
- What moments of growth stand out most to you, and why?
- What skills or values do you want to continue developing?
- How can you use what you've learned to make a positive impact on your community?

This is your time to celebrate your journey, honour your achievements, and look ahead with confidence. Remember, the end of this course is just the beginning of your story. Carry what you've learned with you and continue to grow, share and act with purpose. The future is yours to shape.

3.11.6 Summary of skills, contexts and concepts

Table 3.28 What have we explored in this section?

Skills developed	Contexts explored	Key concepts
• Reflection • Self-awareness • Creative thinking	• Personal • Community engagement • Career-related study	• Change • Well-being • Connections

Learning journal

Portfolio work: Evidence of learning

Throughout this section, you have documented your learning through:

- creating a plan to reflect, act and share your learning from PPS
- developing a plan to celebrate and share your growth in the PPS course
- listing your key takeaways from the PPS course.

3.11.7 Summary

- Reflection is a key component to growth and development; it is critical to pause and reflect on your successes in PPS.
- Using skills developed in PPS—like reflection, critical thinking, empathy and self-awareness—will provide you with insight into your next steps for your future.
- Sharing your successes is an important way to celebrate your accomplishments.

4 Reflective project (RP)

4.1 Introduction to the RP

INQUIRY QUESTIONS

- What is the purpose of the reflective project?
- Why is the reflective project useful?
- How does the reflective project link with the whole CP?
- What are the requirements of the reflective project?

4.1.1 Purpose of the RP

The reflective project (RP) is an in-depth body of work focused on an ethical dilemma in a career-related area. The area you choose can be one you are studying now or one you are interested in exploring to a greater extent. Furthermore, the whole process allows you to show development over an extended period of time and gives you a place to illustrate just how much you have learnt in terms of knowledge, experience and skills over the course of the whole CP. You can choose the mode of communication you use to present your work, be it written, verbal, visual or audio–visual.

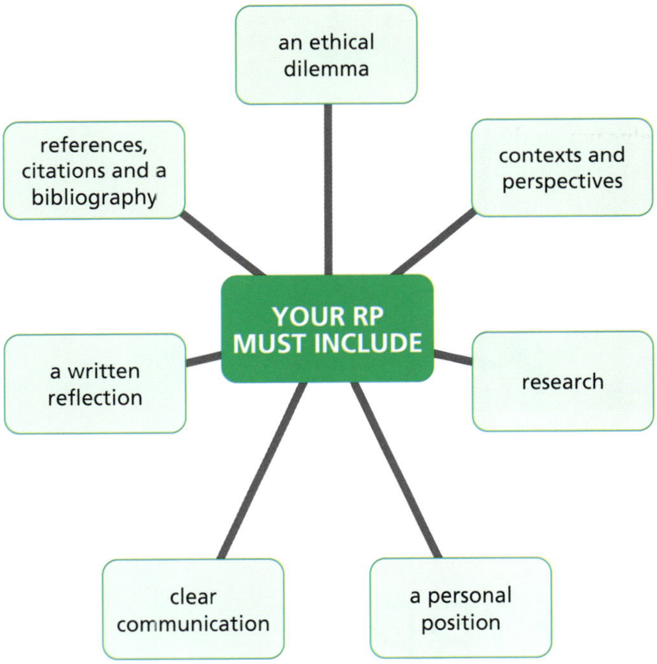

What does each RP need to include?

There are three key things that make the RP stand out and really worth doing. Firstly, *you* drive the process; it is all about your voice and the choices you make. This might be daunting but think about how much it allows you to grow as a learner. Secondly, you will make connections with other aspects of your studies throughout the process and when this happens, you will appreciate how your knowledge, skills and attitudes transfer to other areas of your personal, school and professional life, both now and in the future. Lastly, the RP is designed so that you are assessed in a way that is authentic to the world around you and your future career. It's common for students generally to question how assessments can be of any use practically, and is really worth remembering that the whole experience of the RP has been designed to have real-world meaning and application.

LEARNING ENGAGEMENT

RP skills for your future

With the RP, you will use skills needed in your future career development. These are captured by the questions in the table below. For each question, think of your whole CP course (the CRS, DP subjects, CE, LCS and PPS) and your previous experience and come up with two examples where you have already had to think of these ideas.

■ **Table 4.1**

Questions	Examples
How can you produce detailed, accurate research efficiently?	
How can you critically evaluate the effectiveness of your research and its impact on your thinking?	
How can you communicate with peers and adults professionally and sensitively, as well as present research effectively?	
How can you explore the full impact of an ethical dilemma, taking into account multiple perspectives?	
How can you push the limits of your own creativity and formulate a personal position on an ethical dilemma?	
How can you think in innovative ways that challenge what you think you know and believe?	

4.1.2 How does the RP link with the whole CP?

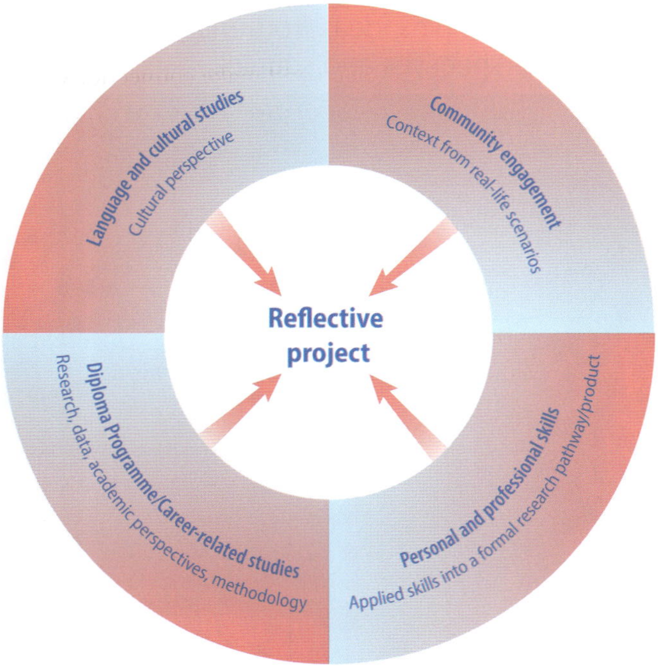

■ How do the elements of the CP relate to the RP? (Source: IB RP guide, p.11)

All the elements of the Core connect and each, in turn, helps you make connections relevant to your RP. Take some time to look at the image on the left and Table 4.2 (on the following spread), which show how each Core element links to the RP. It's important to note that you do not start the RP on day one of the CP. As you explore the course, you will notice that each of the Core elements gradually enables you to be more independent in your application of skills. The RP is the ultimate opportunity to see the value in transversal skills. Your CP course is a bank of valuable skills you can draw upon to complete it.

As shown in the visual, every part of the CP is a potential resource of skills for your RP—it's up to you to identify the intentional connections. We explore some of those connections in the following table.

Top tip!

Put this image in your learning journal as a reminder of the places you can draw inspiration from in the course when you need it.

Table 4.2 How will the other elements of the CP help me?

CP element	Overview	Specific examples of skills you transfer to the RP
PPS	In PPS you develop personal and professional skills that are transversal. So you can expect to draw upon lots of useful tools and skills from your course to support the RP.	Collating, verifying and analysing research; reflective and reflexive skills; self-monitoring, organization and presentation skills; creating a valid and convincing argument. Furthermore, ethical thinking runs throughout the PPS course, so you will already have experience of considering multiple perspectives as well as expressing what you think, what course of action you would take and what your personal position might be.
CE	The combination of community engagement, DP courses and your career-related studies means you can have real experiences of the impact of ethical issues and dilemmas on different communities. CE asks you to understand what community means by placing yourself directly in a community.	Meaningful and targeted research; flexible communication strategies; reflexivity to make complex and ethical choices; understanding and empathizing with complex issues from different perspectives; connecting and considering the implications of complex ideas from multiple perspectives and sources.

CP element	Overview	Specific examples of skills you transfer to the RP
LCS	LCS encourages you to have agency and an excellent perception of your own relationship with language and culture. In this element of the course, you forge a sense of identity and how language and culture can influence it. You will see the word 'positionality' a lot in this process, and the way you use reflection in LCS can give you an appreciation for multiple perspectives and a confidence about your own position about ethical dilemmas that is crucial for the RP.	Developing a position with confidence; awareness between yourself and your relationship with culture; how to identify cultural influences and what shapes culture; critical understanding of how cultural perspectives play a role in ethical dilemmas; communication skills in adapting language for different contexts.
DP subjects and CRS	DP subjects and CRS can provide you with inspiration for the ethical dilemma at the centre of the RP, as well as the self-management and communication skills to develop your ideas. One aspect that differs from school to school and, often, from student to student is the choice of CRS and DP subjects.	Understanding multiple contexts in the wider world; contextualizing ethical dilemmas; understanding ethical issues in career-related contexts; research skills; analytic and evaluative skills; decision-making and problem-solving processes; forming a perspective based on evidence.

Reflection and reflexivity

Why is reflection so important?

In short, the process of reflection is such an important skill to develop that this element of the CP Core was named after it. It might seem strange to start this process by discussing a word often associated with looking back on something that has finished, but a good understanding of what reflection entails at the very start of the RP will get you into the mindset and working habits needed for success far beyond the parameters of the project itself.

Top tip!

Remember, you cannot reuse any assessments from your DP and CRS for the RP.

What does it mean to be reflective and reflexive? Why is this important?

As you know from the Introduction, the RP is a piece of work which asks you to analyse the multiple perspectives and evidence surrounding an ethical dilemma and come to your own conclusions. However, it is also about your understanding of the long process you went through to create your work, and this is assessed separately from the rest of your project in Criterion E. As the skills you need for this project are developed over the entire CP course, you could say the RP directly and indirectly showcases how you have developed in every aspect of your course.

Definitions of 'reflection' and 'reflective'

When you suspect certain words are going to be used endlessly (and the words 'reflection' and 'reflective' are definitely two of them), it helps not only to revisit the definition, but also to consider its synonyms. This creates a fuller view of what that word can mean and all its implications.

- **Reflection** involves thinking about action and impact—what, how, why and with what effect we and others do what we do.
- **Reflexivity** involves thinking about beliefs and values—what, how, why and with what effect we and others think what we think.

The first definition is possibly the one you are most familiar with. However, if you take a close look at the second, you will start to realise something important—that, actually, the whole RP is about your analysis of other people's reflections as well as your own.

LEARNING ENGAGEMENT

Cultural perspectives

As a pair or in a group, create a mind map together. With one person acting as a scribe, discuss the following questions:

1 How do you know when a culture is being represented negatively?
2 How do cultural misunderstandings take place?
3 Now think of any negative stories in the local, national or international news. Consider what role cultural misunderstanding, ignorance or miscommunication played in these stories.

You might feel comfortable discussing stereotypes that you have experienced yourself, but do so only if you want to. Remember as well that your experiences are valid and someone else might have a different experience and that is also valid. This is an important aspect of international-mindedness. Being able to demonstrate how different perspectives hold value without cancelling out each other is a crucial step in becoming a critical thinker and developing a position yourself.

International-mindedness and the IB mission statement

To be internationally minded is to have a mindset that values the perspectives of all cultures. Read the mission statement from the IB:

> *'The International Baccalaureate® aims to develop inquiring, knowledgeable and caring young people who help to create a better and more peaceful world through intercultural understanding and respect.*
>
> *To this end the organization works with schools, governments and international organizations to develop challenging programmes of international education and rigorous assessment.*
>
> *These programmes encourage students across the world to become active, compassionate and lifelong learners who understand that other people, with their differences, can also be right.'*

(Source: IBO, The reflective project, p.4)

Reflection and reflexivity

- Reflect on how the mission statement encourages you to be internationally minded.
- Look at the very last line and think about how it might relate to being a critical thinker.

4.1.3 What are the aims of the RP?

The reflective project is assessed on the *process* as well as the *output*, which is why this book is designed to help you use your initiative and benefit from every step of the process and not just focus on the final piece.

Through the RP, you can expect to:

- work for a minimum of 50 hours on an extended piece of work
- drive a personal inquiry into a specific ethical dilemma through to action and reflection
- learn how to structure a coherent argument in written, audio, visual or audio–visual modalities
- understand topics that have implications for local and/or global communities
- build high-level research, communication, and critical and creative thinking skills
- submit your work to be marked by your school and externally assessed by the IB.

What are the requirements of the RP?

The IB's RP guide (p.7) tells us that:

- The RP **must focus on an ethical dilemma in a career-related area** which can be one you are already studying or one you are interested in.
- The total RP is 4,000 words, which can be submitted in a choice of formats. This 4,000 words includes a reflective statement of 1,000 words maximum, provided on the RP/FRF.
- The RP is an independent extended project that will take you a minimum of 50 hours to complete. You have a supervisor to support you for 3–6 hours.
- During the process, you will present your research findings to your peers and supervisor so you can receive guided feedback.
- At final submission, you will take part in a *viva voce* with your supervisor, which is a moment to celebrate the end of the RP process and show the extent of your understanding, thinking and just how far you have come. Through an interview, you explain your learning process to your supervisor, which reinforces the authenticity of your RP and the process you have been on.
- All RPs are submitted to the IB for external assessment and are assessed using five assessment criteria that align with the four assessment objectives.
- You must achieve a D grade or higher for the RP to be awarded the CP certificate.

(Source: IB RP guide, p.7)

What will the process look like?

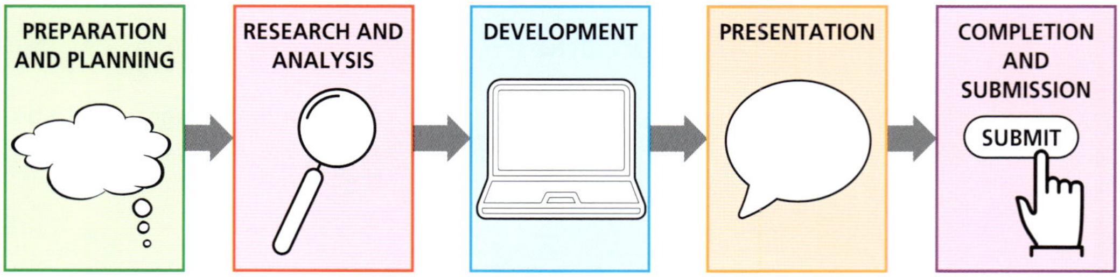

Reflective project process

■ **Table 4.3**

Phase of RP	Detailed steps involved
Preparation and planning	● preparation and building of background knowledge ● identification of an ethical dilemma ● peer discussions ● research plan and project proposal ● peer/RP supervisor feedback and reflection point
Research and analysis	● conduct research ● reflection point ● supervisor feedback ● reflection point
Development	● initial project draft
Presentation of findings	● presentation ● reflection point
Completion and submission	● revision and final project ● *viva voce* ● final submission

Top tip!

Remember that you are completing this project over an extended period of time, so as well as choosing an ethical dilemma that interests you, it is important to think about how the format will keep you engaged too.

What format can the RP take?

Researching and choosing a format for the RP is explored in detail in Sections 4.6 and 4.10, as you will start considering formats in phase 1 (preparation) and developing this in detail in phase 3 (development). Briefly, you will need to choose a format from these options: written, visual, audio or audio–visual. For example, a magazine article as a form of expository essay would be a written format, a photo-essay would be a visual format, a podcast would be an audio format and a 'TEDx' style presentation would be an audio–visual format.

It is your choice and you are encouraged to be open-minded. You might choose a format because it relates to your future career field or because it is particularly relevant to the ethical dilemma you are researching. You could choose it because it is familiar to you or because you are simply interested in it. You will see in Section 4.10 that each option's requirements are as accessible as the other, so it is a chance to think creatively.

4.1.4 How is the RP assessed?

Your RP is assessed with four objectives in mind that reflect the way you will build your RP over time into its final product. Think of Table 4.4 as a flow chart going from one step to the next as you build up your skills and knowledge.

■ **Table 4.4** The four RP assessment objectives

Assessment objective		What will you have to do?
AO1	Knowledge and understanding	You are going to build up knowledge and understanding directly about an ethical dilemma related to a career of your choice and the concepts and terminology related to it. The more your knowledge and understanding of your chosen area grows, the easier you will find it to navigate big ideas and use career-related language.
AO2	Application and analysis	When you apply research methods, you will reveal differing perspectives associated with your ethical dilemma and be able to analyse why this matters, and what the impact is on individuals and/or groups in multiple contexts. Think of the perspectives, implications and impact as a tree with many branches growing as your understanding increases.

Assessment objective		What will you have to do?
AO3	Synthesis and evaluation	You will be able to synthesize research, which means making connections between ideas and linking ideas to evidence. This allows you to create an informed and justified personal perspective on the ethical dilemma—what we refer to as a position. You will consider the impact of your position and use reflective and reflexive thinking skills to reason and justify your thoughts. It's not just the RP itself that you evaluate—it's also your entire learning journey and how much you have grown.
AO4	Communication of research	All of your knowledge, understanding, application, analysis, synthesis and evaluation needs to be communicated effectively for the most impact. You have lots of choice about how you might do this, so you can communicate in a way that is organized, coherent, appropriate and structurally/stylistically accurate for your career field and selected format.

LEARNING ENGAGEMENT

Thinking about the AOs

Look at the four assessment objectives for the RP in Table 4.4. Use your learning journal to note:

1. Where have you explored these skills in the past? (Maybe you did the MYP, maybe not.)
2. Which courses are you doing right now that connect to these objectives?
3. What challenges do you see here? Make a note of anything that you have questions about.

The AOs will be assessed through marking criteria which you and your supervisor will use as a tool to help you through the process and assess your final work for a predicted grade. All the sections that follow this one will explore the skills needed to demonstrate these assessment criteria. What's important to notice at this stage is how evenly distributed the marks are, so the skills are very balanced, with ethical, critical, reflective and reflexive thinking all having a similar weight, and communication and research skills playing important roles.

Table 4.5 The RP marking criteria

Marking criteria	Key elements
A: Focus on the ethical dilemma (6) 'This criterion assesses the extent to which the work submitted for assessment identifies and explores a career-related ethical dilemma by focusing on differing perspectives and varied contexts.'	• Defined ethical dilemma related to career area. • Balance of differing perspective on ethical dilemma. • Sustained focus and effective examples and contexts.
B: Knowledge and understanding through research (6) 'This criterion assesses how effectively the work submitted for assessment uses research to develop and demonstrate understanding of issues related to the ethical dilemma and their impact.'	• Research is broad in range and deep in understanding. • Extensive knowledge and understanding of issues relating to the ethical dilemma. • Understanding of how contexts, individuals and groups are impacted.
C: Critical thinking (8) 'This criterion assesses how effectively the work submitted for assessment analyses the ethical dilemma and synthesizes research to propose and justify a personal position, taking into consideration the impact on, and implications for, various contexts and groups.'	• Research is analysed and findings are connected together (synthesised). This leads to an identified, supported and reasoned personal position. • Impact and implications have been considered in the justification of the personal position.

Marking criteria	Key elements
D: Communication of ideas (6) 'This criterion assesses how effectively the work submitted for assessment uses appropriate organization, terminology and structural elements to support the clear, cohesive and effective communication of ideas.'	• The structure of the RP helps to communicate ideas clearly. • Appropriate style and conventions of formats are used which helps clarity. • Ideas are well-developed and presented logically.
E: Reflective practice (8) 'This criterion assesses how effectively the work submitted for assessment demonstrates planning, research and implementation of reflective practice during the project completion process.'	• Reflections include explanations for decisions, actions and thinking surrounding the project and its effectiveness or limitations. • Reflections also consider and discuss the impact of this learning engagement on you.

How do I keep a record of the process?

A critical requirement of the RP is that you keep a reflective journal throughout. You will have seen above that the term 'reflection point' appears multiple times throughout—this is an indication of how and when the learning journal becomes important. The reflective journal is a documented witness to your whole research process and how your thinking has been challenged. Therefore, it is also a way to ensure your work is your own, with clear academic referencing.

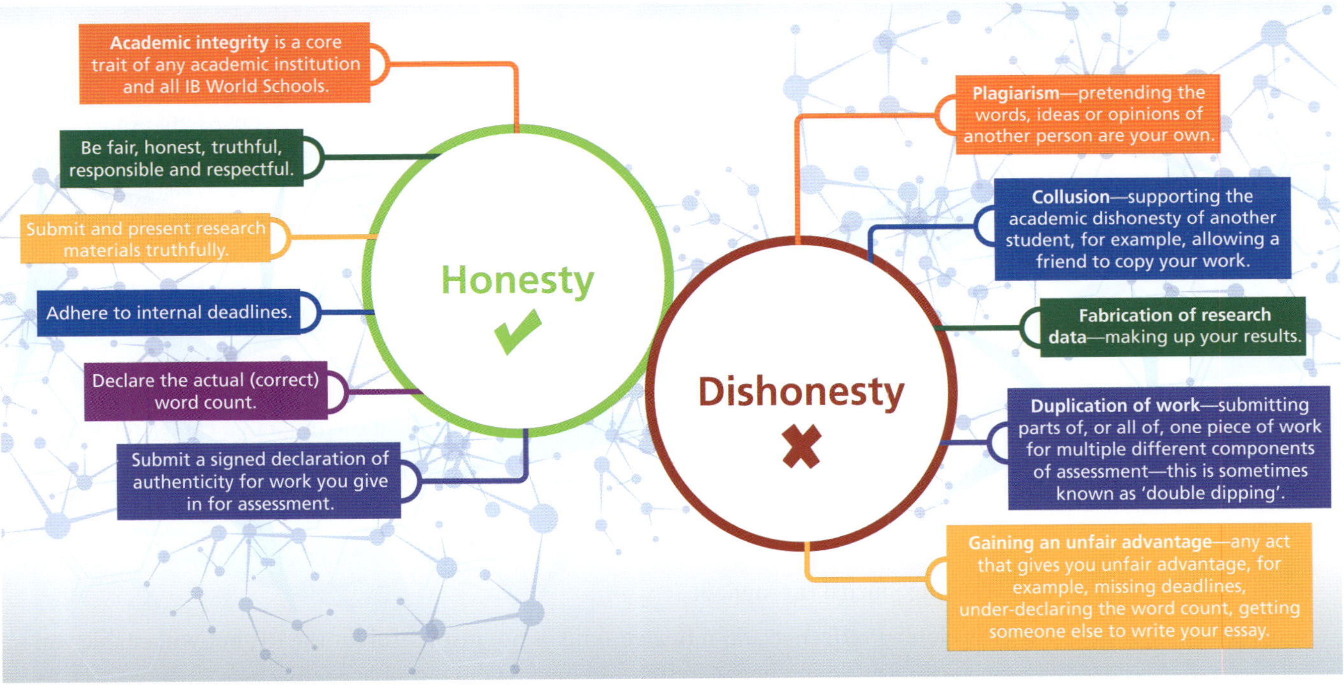

■ Academic integrity means keeping honest throughout the RP process

Academic integrity and using technology

> **Key term**
> ◆ **Plagiarize:** To take someone else's work or idea and (accidentally or deliberately) pass it off as your own.

We started this section by stating that '*You* drive the process; it is all about your voice and the choices you make.' So, you must make sure your voice is yours alone. Be explicit as to where your sources, perspectives and ideas come from. You need to take care not to accidentally **plagiarize** content from other places and ensure you always record where quotes, images and ideas have come from. You might think you will remember where something came from, but noting your sources (e.g. books, websites, videos) at the time you first come across them means you won't mistakenly think it was your own idea later or be unable to give details of a source.

LEARNING ENGAGEMENT

Academic integrity and the learner profile

The following descriptions incorporate the learner profile attributes and could be applied to the RP process. Use the details in this section and create a table with at least one example of how the RP enables you to develop each of these IB learner profile attributes. You may find the examples given in the opening section under these same headings helpful as a starting point!

- Ethical and internationally minded thinker
- Adaptable communicator
- Open-minded risk-taker
- Principled, balanced inquirer
- Reflective researcher

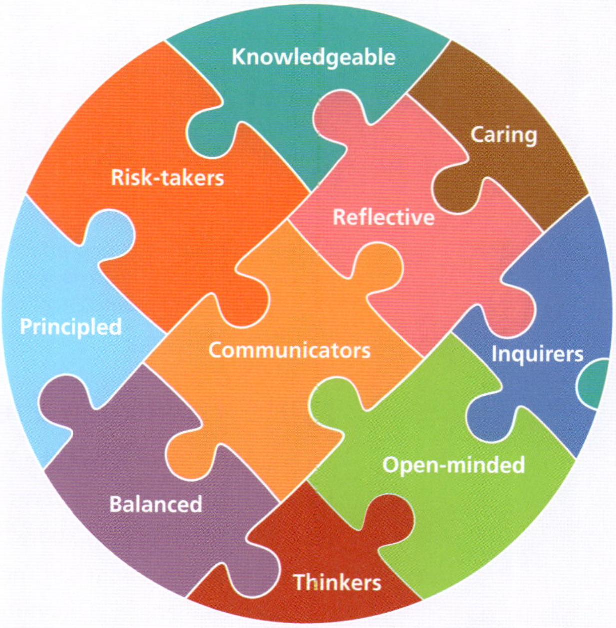

■ Learner profile attributes

Common pitfall

You might be reading about the learning journal and think 'I don't need that' or 'that sounds like a lot of effort'. Putting aside the fact that it's a compulsory part of the RP process and is needed to confirm that your work is actually yours, a common mistake is not realizing its value in tracking how your ideas are developing as you go along. The final written reflection is up to 1,000 words and you cannot write it without your reflections from the process.

4.1.5 Summary

- The RP is an in-depth body of work focused on an ethical dilemma in a career-related area.
- In the RP, you will use skills needed in your future career. Every element of the CP can inspire your RP.
- The RP process involves five phases. You can create it in a range of formats and you keep a learning journal throughout.
- Developing reflective and reflexive skills is not just useful for the RP, but will enable you to navigate new contexts in your life and understand multiple perspectives.

4.2 Becoming an ethical practitioner

INQUIRY QUESTIONS

- How does thinking ethically matter to the RP?
- What does it mean to be an ethical, internationally minded practitioner?
- What are ethics and why do they matter in the world of work?
- What part will ethics play in the RP process?

4.2.1 Defining a clear goal and taking ownership

Taking ownership of your reflective project (RP) starts with choosing an ethical issue and dilemma that interests you in a career area that you find fascinating. This may or may not be the career-related subject that you are actually studying right now for the CP, which also adds to the flexibility. You have a responsibility to get this right as you are the student at the centre of all this; however, the good news is that there is plenty of time to get it right.

The RP allows you to understand that ethical decision-making is around us all the time in a deeply interconnected world. Yes, at the heart of it is an exploration of an ethical dilemma in a career that interests you, but ethics is not just contained to the project itself. The way you carry out your research, interact and communicate with others, commit to deadlines and apply reflective and critical thinking processes all involve a good understanding of ethics and ethical behaviour and the role they play in the wider world.

Ethics in the whole Core

What does ethics really mean?

Ethics and ethical thinking run through all elements of the CP Core. You will find connections regarding concepts, experiences and transversal skills by consistently using an ethical lens. For example, in CE, you actively experience the impact of issues on individuals and groups in the local community and beyond. In LCS, you are encouraged to be self-reflexive by exploring identity and how your values and beliefs are inextricably linked. In PPS, you also share the concepts of ethics, identity and intercultural understanding, but develop many skills that will support you in the RP, such as communication, critical thinking, information literacy and ethical decision-making. All these connections enable you to be open-minded by considering and evaluating multiple perspectives.

Why is an ethical education so important?

Perhaps the right way of phrasing this is, 'Why is an education that includes exploring ethics important?' The short answer is that you have already been developing steadily into an ethical human being through all sorts of influences in your life. When it comes to the education you receive as you prepare to live, work and study in the world beyond school, it pays to have a deep understanding of how and why people act the way they do in different contexts.

The ethical, internationally minded practitioner

As you deepen your understanding of ethics as an IB student, you will build a position of where you stand on many issues and dilemmas. It's important to really think about the lens with which you are looking through to other cultures. There are some terms that can help you be aware of the approach you take and on which the RP is built.

- *Ethnocentrism* involves understanding another culture through the values of one's own culture; this can lead to a bias where one cultural group is deemed more important and superior to another.
- *Cultural relativism* dictates that a person's beliefs and activities should be understood and make sense in terms of the culture within which they work and live and not from an outsider's view. Whether something is right or wrong is analysed within the moral norms of a specific culture. Different environments mean different lifestyles, which in turn means that everything is relative.
- *Ethical pluralism* (or *value pluralism* or *moral pluralism*) is a philosophical view that acknowledges that there are many valid ethical values but that these can conflict with each other; in other words, there is no one moral principle that applies to everyone. It might be that individuals and different cultures all hold particular values, and the more you can understand that, the easier you can find out what you think yourself.
- On the other hand, *ethical universalism* is the concept that there are ethical principles that are always valid and apply to everyone, regardless of context.

Reflection and reflexivity

Thinking about ethics

To get an idea about how you are already learning, living and working in an ethical way, consider the research question with an ethical dilemma below. There are questions that follow to help you consider it. Don't worry if you do not have answers to some of the questions yet or are not even sure how to answer them. However, use the terms above to help you think about the different contexts you work in. Record your thoughts in your learning journal.

Research question: Should all students be required to take a course in ethical thinking before leaving school?

- How do you make ethical decisions in a diverse and interconnected world?
- Can you think critically about how ethics work in different contexts?
- Can you investigate and analyse an ethical dilemma and the perspectives of multiple stakeholders?
- What roles do cultural, social, historical, economic and other influences play?
- Can you consider the impact of an ethical dilemma on different stakeholders, their communities and beyond?
- Do you understand how individuals and communities are interconnected on a global scale?
- What does this tell you about your own values and beliefs and how they connect to others?
- Can you challenge your own assumptions and be open-minded to changing your mind?
- Can you take your understanding, knowledge and skills from your RP to communicate a position and where you stand personally with this ethical dilemma?

Key terms

◆ **Ethics:** The study of right and wrong, as well as any system or code of moral rules, principles or values. Understanding why something is right or wrong helps to inform and guide our choices, actions and behaviours. (RP guide, p.65). (Synonyms: right-minded, right-thinking, principled, irreproachable, unimpeachable, blameless, guiltless, righteous, upright, upstanding, good, lawful, honest, trustworthy, admirable, praiseworthy.)

◆ **Morals:** This relates to the standards of good or bad behaviour, fairness, honesty, etc. that each person believes in, rather than to laws. (Cambridge Dictionary Online) (Synonyms: moral code, code of ethics, moral standards, moral values, principles, principles of right and wrong, rules of conduct, standards/principles of behaviour, standards, morality, sense of morality, scruples, ideals.)

4.2.2 What are ethics and morals?

Now that we have the 'why' of an ethical education and considered 'how' you might already be thinking about ethics in the way you act and think, let's go back to the start and look at the 'what'. And for that let's look at a number of definitions in the field of ethics that are particularly relevant to the RP (in the key terms box on the left). The reason to do this is that there is a danger in your studies that you will use words such as 'ethics' and 'ethical' so much that you lose sight of what they actually mean, so it is a good idea to consider synonyms to give you a wider vocabulary as well as understanding.

Top tip!

When approaching any ethical angle, you are thinking about both how individuals act and also how wider groups of people/whole institutions act and believe as well (such as governments, schools, religions). These will link together and that relationship can be really interesting when they differ!

Is the distinction between ethics and morals important?

> *'Ethics and morals relate to 'right' and 'wrong'. While they are sometimes used interchangeably, they are different: ethics refer to rules provided by an external source (e.g. sources of conduct in workplaces or principles in religions); morals refer to an individual's own principles regarding right and wrong.'*
>
> (Source: www.diffen.com/difference/Ethics_vs_Morals)

Can you see this distinction? In terms of the RP, you will be exploring a range of individuals' moral perspectives in relation to how they are challenged by a particular ethical context.

It can be interesting to distinguish where a person's personal moral values conflict with the ethics of the context in which they are working. For example, a journalist might hold moral principles that you should always tell the truth, whatever the circumstance. However, when they are working on a confidential story, the ethics of journalism tell us that you should protect your source's identity. They might abide by the ethics of journalism but this conflicts with their personal set of values.

What is an ethical issue and dilemma?

Further to understanding the difference between ethics and morals is the distinction between an ethical issue and dilemma. An ethical issue is a situation that requires moral or ethical frameworks to work out what to think and what to do about it. They can be encountered in all areas of life (e.g. personal, social, professional, economic, environmental) and may be related to questions of fairness, honesty, justice or human rights.

To look at the area of environment alone, there are vast amounts of ethical issues: for example, fast fashion, food waste, deforestation, water usage, single-use plastics, fair trade, GMO foods, factory farming, endangered species, land rights, responsible tourism, renewable and non-renewable energy. These are just a few and clearly cross over into other topic areas.

Ethical issues and dilemmas often become seen together. However, an ethical dilemma is where you have a choice between two (or more) conflicting values or courses of action, where each alternative has its own drawbacks or may lead to undesirable consequences. Because neither alternative provides an ideal solution, there is no clear-cut answer and an ethical decision is difficult to make.

Top tip!

Look for a clash and conflict of principles to see whether it is truly an ethical dilemma.

Take the ethical issue of 'responsible tourism' given above. The dilemma here can be captured by the pursuit of economic gains through tourism clashing with protecting the well-being of the local environment and community.

Recognizing communities and contexts

What will make your RP even more interesting is if you choose dynamic examples from communities and contexts that relate to your ethical dilemma. It is also an important step in enabling you to analyse an ethical dilemma from multiple perspectives and impact, as well as cultural factors that create those perspectives in the first place.

LEARNING ENGAGEMENT

Following the trail of the ethical issue and dilemma of *over-tourism*, take some time to do some initial research into Venice, Barcelona, Santorini, Bali or Machu Picchu and you'll start getting an idea of the complexities of this ethical dilemma. Look for the similarities and differences of an ethical dilemma in different contexts.

4.2.3 Choosing an ethical dilemma for the RP

You might have already chosen an area to explore and have direct experience from your CE, CRS or experience that provides an example from a community close to you, or it might be an example of a community on the other side of the world experiencing something similar or different to what you have come across in your initial reading. Whatever the examples, make them original, as these will reinforce your ideas and help you consider your ideas from new angles. Furthermore, examples that are focused and appropriate to your study will develop your critical understanding far more.

Although we aren't far into this section, skills have already been mentioned a lot! It's worth reading through the different stages of the RP (given in the flow chart below) and thinking about the skills you will need, as this will prepare you directly for the challenge ahead and help you be in charge of your own learning.

Recognizing potential challenges before they happen is part of managing a project. However, so is overcoming challenges you hadn't anticipated.

The RP process

Table 4.6 Steps in the RP process (Adapted from the IB RP guide, p.32)

1	Develop a research question appropriate to the ethical dilemma.
2	Include a timeline and potential resources in the research proposal.
3	Evaluate resources for relevance and bias.
4	Use reasoning to identify a personal position on the ethical dilemma.
5	Record all reflections throughout the research and development process in the learning journal.
6	Organize any findings and ideas into a structured first draft that includes all of the key elements required.
7	Use the assessment criteria as a guide to ensure all descriptors have been addressed.
8	Cite and reference all sources used in the project properly.
9	Prepare a presentation, based on the research and initial draft, to present the findings and personal position to peers, RP supervisors, mentors and/or other appropriate community members.
10	Receive and provide feedback after the presentation to reflect and develop further or revise the RP.
11	Reflect on the feedback provided and make any revisions or decisions.
12	Use the assessment criteria to self-evaluate the RP.
13	Submit the final RP to the RP supervisor.
14	Reflect on the entire RP experience and engage in dialogue with the RP supervisor through the *viva voce*.

Learning journal

The RP process

Use your learning journal to reflect upon the RP process with these three questions:

1. Where have you used these processes and skills before? Think about PPS, CE, LCS, DP subjects and CRS.
2. What thinking, social, communication, self-management and research skills do you imagine using for some aspects of the RP process?
3. How do you think the following aspects of the RP process encourage you as an *ethical* learner?

4.2.4 Summary

- Thinking ethically matters to the RP as this is how you will unpack the ethical dilemma related to your chosen career area and focus.
- An ethical, internationally minded practitioner is someone who navigates the world with clear, ethical decision-making processes and an outlook that acknowledges that people can differ in perspectives and attitudes and still be right.
- In the RP, you will develop your ethical thinking to form a position on your chosen ethical dilemma and explore the impact and implications of this.

4.3 Documenting the journey

INQUIRY QUESTIONS

- Why do you have to keep a learning journal for the RP?
- How do you start the learning journal?
- What could you include in each phase of the RP process?
- What sorts of ways can you respond in your learning journal?

Learner profile

Reflective, principled, thinker

International-mindedness: 'others with those differences can also be right'

ATL: Self-management, thinking skills

The leaner profile characteristics that you will explore in particular in this chapter are 'reflective', 'principled' and 'thinker'. However, these all link to a central theme in IB education, which is being 'internationally minded'. This means recognizing that even if we the think differently to others, it does not mean they cannot be right as well. You will also notice these characteristics link to ATL areas, such as self-management and thinking skills.

4.3.1 Making the most of the learning journal

The learning journal is a compulsory part of the reflective project (RP) and, despite it not being formally assessed, it is the heart of your whole process. In your learning journal you will keep:

- an ongoing record of where you are in your research practically, with clear referencing and citation
- all your reflective thoughts on the whole process, from choosing an ethical dilemma and researching it to developing your critical thinking and formatting
- your responses to questions, thinking routines, activities, feedback and advice that you have discussed with your supervisor or classmates that are designed to help you with the process.

By keeping evidence throughout the process, you make it possible to do two things:

1. Prove that the work is entirely yours and demonstrate the complex understanding that led you to the position you hold about your ethical dilemma.
2. Provide the basis for your presentation, your final written reflection and what you will discuss in your *viva voce* with your supervisor at the end of the RP process.

The learning journal is the place where you not only keep track of your research, but you also interact with your findings. By using the learning journal in multiple ways, you create an accurate record of your RP. If you take a look at the assessment criteria A–E here, you can get an idea of how you use the learning journal to support your process:

- A: focus on the ethical dilemma (6)
- B: knowledge and understanding through research (6)
- C: critical thinking (8)
- D: communication of ideas (6)
- E: reflective practice (8).

So, do you want to know what you need to talk about with your supervisor? To prepare your final written reflections? And prepare your *viva voce*? The answer is the same: use all the ideas, research and reflections you have recorded throughout the process, accounted for in your learning journal.

Links

CE, LCS, PPS, DP and CRS

You will find that by the time you come to document your RP journey in your learning journal, you will be very familiar with this process. Learning journals are used in both CE and LCS in similar ways. You also will have been documenting your PPS journey and curating your experiences in the PPS portfolio. Lastly, your main CRS and DP subjects will also employ systems to document and reflect on your learning throughout your two-year course.

How the learning journal works

This might seem new but, actually, by the time you come to keep a learning journal for the RP, you have already had some experience of consciously keeping a record of your experiences. PPS, CE and LCS all have a journal or portfolio so you can continue using all those skills you have already developed.

4.3.2 Being an ethical researcher: AI and AI

Let's talk about 'AI' in two ways. The most important principle to have throughout the RP (and any other piece of work as it happens) is one of *academic integrity*. By seeing the learning journal as a constant companion throughout your RP process, you are allowing it to fulfil its most important role: keeping you honest. As an IB student, you are promising to be clear and honest in the way you carry out and produce your work. You should be clear at all times where evidence, ideas and perspectives come from and never put yourself in the position where you might pass off someone else's ideas as your own. You may well be thinking that you would never do that as, of course, people can do this intentionally. However, it is a lot easier than you think to plagiarize and accidentally pass someone's idea off as your own if you do not have clear note-making and organizational skills.

The second 'AI' we need to talk about is *artificial intelligence* and how using technology is an important part of your research process. To some extent, nothing has changed in terms of citation and referencing AI if you have used it as a source. However, it is worth considering how else you use AI in your work and what you consider ethical and unethical. Your school will almost certainly have a clear policy on how to use it. Make sure you are familiar with that and use it as your guide. You should also use your learning journal to note down exactly how you are using AI.

Top tip!

A bibliography is a must for your final project, although not theoretically necessary for your learning journal. However, you will thank yourself hugely at the end of the RP process when you are finalizing your bibliography if you make it a habit of recording your sources accurately as you go along.

LEARNING ENGAGEMENT

Make yourself a key code so that you can quickly code and identify what sort of entries you need to make or have already made in your learning journal. For example, you could start with colour coding (or using symbols to indicate) different contexts, sources, evidence, perspectives, reflections and opinions you are forming. Then see what else you can add as you work through the process.

4.3.3 Starting the RP learning journal

As you should know by now, the learning journal is there to help you do two things: inquire and reflect. There is no set number of times you have to use the learning journal, but if you use it regularly, you become increasingly aware of your growing ability to inquire and reflect.

By keeping a learning journal, you can:

- define your research purpose, objectives and the research question
- collect primary, secondary and tertiary research
- clearly differentiate between types of texts
- identify interesting and original sources
- use tools to read a text effectively
- ask meaningful questions
- make notes that matter
- collect and analyse data
- evaluate bias in sources
- carry out a literature review
- prepare to present to your peers and supervisor
- spot connections between sources
- synthesize information in your notes
- recognize growth and gaps in knowledge
- create a successful bibliography
- continuously reflect on your process and positionality.

How will I know I am reflecting properly throughout the RP?

In Section 4.4, we explore the different types of reflection and reflexivity in detail, so you can be more intentional in directing your thinking. However, to get us started on the learning journal, let's look at what you can use it to reflect on in the simplest terms.

- The research you are carrying out and your thoughts on your discoveries (metacognitive reflection).
- The ups and downs of your process and any changes you are having to make in order for the project to be successful (process reflection).
- The impact of what you are learning about your actions and beliefs on yourself and how it is shaping you as a person (self-reflection and self-reflexivity).
- The impact of what you are learning about, your actions and beliefs on the world around you (critical reflection and critical reflexivity).

(In brackets are references to the types of reflection or reflexivity you are demonstrating through these activities, so you can make this link later on.)

Using your learning journal to support the RP process

Keeping a learning journal with a system of clear sections or coding allows you to build your RP in a clear and supportive way. This will help you to develop your self-management skills and enable you to:

- see your progress linearly
- go back and forth between phases of the RP as you revisit and reflect on ideas.

> Don't forget both parts of this process—success is not straightforward or on an upward trajectory. Success is self-awareness about the thoughts you are developing *and* your relationship with the skills you are using. Get the system right and the learning journal will become the backbone of your RP process.

The learning journal supports the RP process, which is divided into five distinct phases. Throughout these phases you are going to actively explore cultures, contexts and perspectives so you can develop your ethical, analytical, critical and reflective skills, and communicate a personal position effectively.

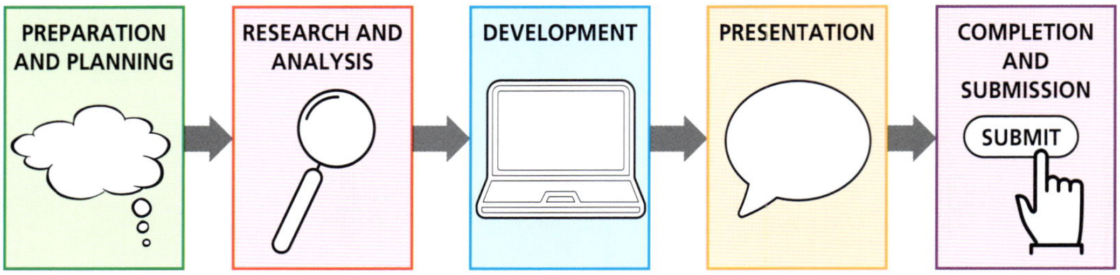

The RP learning journey

Preparation and planning phase

In this phase, you will reflect on how you prepare for the RP and build your background knowledge. You will build on your reflections to consider how you identify an ethical dilemma and create a research plan and project proposal. Furthermore, you will discuss this with your peers and supervisor and reflect on their feedback as well.

Things you could include in your learning journal:

- Questions you have about any part of the process.
- Ethical issues and dilemmas that have interested you from your career-related studies or a career you find interesting and why this has captured your attention.
- Reflections about how your ethical dilemma relates to you, your career aspirations and your personal views on the ethical dilemma.
- Examples of ethical frameworks and thinking tools from your PPS course and RP foundational unit/workshop that help you identify your ethical dilemma and explore it from different perspectives and contexts.
- Transcripts or audio recordings of discussions and group chats you have had with your peers about your ethical dilemma and the feedback they have given you.
- Lists, collations and reflections on any sources.
- Checklists of good research questions and your thoughts on how your question measures against it. Include feedback from conversations with your peers about your research question.

- Ideas on formats that could suit the research question.
- Your initial position on the ethical dilemma now and your justification with evidence.

Research and analysis phase

In this phase, your research analysis and feedback from your supervisor will form the basis of your reflections.

Things you could include in your learning journal:

- Questions you have about any part of the process.
- Citations and bibliography—start collating and recording these. There are many good, free apps that can help you keep tabs on your bibliography and can easily be a part of your learning journal.
- Examples of ethical thinking tools from your PPS course and RP workshops that help you break down the ethical dilemma and start to see the strengths and limitations of different perspectives.
- Your opinion on what you are researching and analysing, as this builds towards creating a strong, informed personal position.
- Mind maps you've created on how you are starting to see the impact of the ethical dilemma on different communities, or how the ethical dilemma is viewed differently by different cultures.
- Notes on the different tools you have available that help you spot and evaluate the impact of bias and ask and answer critical questions. (For example, you can use the acronym RAVEN to explore whether a source is biased by looking at the reputation, author, vested interest, expertise and neutrality of the writer/platform. We'll look at this in more detail in Section 4.7.2.)
- Further ideas on what formats might suit your question, narrowing down your ideas.
- Your growing/changing position on the ethical dilemma now and your justification with evidence.

Development phase

This phase is where you will develop your initial project draft, so your reflections will include your decisions about formats as well as your development of your personal position.

By this phase, you should be used to including your opinion throughout the process as you build your research. This phase is a good chance to signpost how your thinking is changing or being reinforced through your process, as you know so much more about the topic now. This is a messy process! But in the development phase, you can start connecting your ideas.

Things you could include in your learning journal:

- Voice notes you've created on your personal position's impact on you and, potentially, on those around you and the wider world. What would happen if others thought like you?
- A visual where you explore the pros and cons of different formats for your research question.
- Evidence of your reflective abilities as well as analytical and critical thinking. Allow yourself to say exactly what you think and feel, however formal or informal, fully formed or nonsensical it might sound at that moment.
- Explorations of different formats and how open-minded you are being about your communication preferences.

- Research into different stylistic conventions of different formats that have caught your attention.
- And remember, keep the questions coming!

Presentation of findings

This phase comes upon the completion of your initial draft, when you deliver a presentation to your peers and supervisor. Their feedback will form the basis of your reflections and help you redraft your work for the final submission.

Things you could include in your learning journal:

- Notes on what to include in your presentation and any questions you have.
- Your thoughts on the feedback you received from your peers and supervisor.
- Further questions you have and how you will go about finding the answers.

Completion and submission

In this last phase, you use your learning journal to collate, curate and create your final reflection of up to 1,000 words to accompany your final revised RP. Your learning journal, final project and written reflection will also form the basis of your *viva voce* with your supervisor, where you discuss the whole process.

4.3.4 Reflecting consistently

With all the suggestions on how to use the learning journal, you will notice plenty of opportunities to constantly incorporate your thinking throughout. It is good to signpost these regular reflective moments and the tools you are using, as you will find them easier to find and understand when you are building your final 1,000 word reflection.

For example, one student who kept a digital journal often used comment boxes or colour coding to flag particular moments in their learning, such as a great source discovery, a change of mind, a setback or another perspective that adds to their understanding. This could be done in a physical journal too. Another student kept a separate set of voice memos where they made a note of particular 'aha!' moments that could go into the final reflection. This kept the process clearer for them in this instance.

Like the RP itself, you can keep a learning journal in various formats. You should choose a format that allows you to work in a way you find the most comfortable. In short, choose a format that makes it easy to keep up to date. You may also find that a mixture of digital, physical, audio and video formats work for you, but you must ensure that you are organized, with a central place for keeping your responses. Digital, audio and video responses can all be stored digitally, but it's always handy to have a physical notebook to write ideas down spontaneously. The more your learning journal is shaped to how you work best, the more likely you will use it effectively and stay engaged in the process. Furthermore, the wider the variety of tools you use, the more confident you will feel about exploring interesting formats and deeply considering the best way to present your RP.

Top tip!

The more detailed you are with your reflections along the process, the more you can incorporate excerpts straight from your learning journal into your final reflection, or at least make this final part so much easier.

LEARNING ENGAGEMENT

Learning journal toolbox

1 How do you communicate your ideas best? For this learning engagement, you will think individually before comparing with your classmates. You could have both an individual reflection and/or a small group discussion to identify how you could work and which of those methods you think would work best for you. Firstly, create your own mind map of the benefits or pitfalls of keeping a digital, physical, audio or audio–visual learning journal, or using digital, physical, audio or audio–visual responses in your learning journal.
Then compare your list to the following table and discuss with your classmates.
Next, make a note of what you would like to put into your learning journal toolbox.
This is a way of identifying the ways to communicate that suit you best.

Table 4.7 Different ways to communicate ideas

Format	Possible tools	Examples of entries	Benefits
Digital	Personal website School learning management system Cloud-based folders	Photos Videos Documents Hyperlinks Blogs	Easy, speedy feedback Varied ways of responding Easily stored and less easily lost Sharing settings for private and public audiences
Physical	Journal, folder	Written notes and longer entries Mind maps Drawings	Spontaneous, unedited thoughts and portable Reduces screentime Easy for feedback but difficult to replace if lost
Audio	Phone app for voice recordings	Spoken reflections Spoken memos about research Recordings of discussions with peers and supervisor	Verbal expression and easy for feedback and storage Spontaneous thoughts that can be organized easily Develops articulation of ideas and therefore communication skills
Audio–visual	Phone with video recording equipment	Filmed research, evidence and interviews Vlogs	Can be audio and non-verbal Personal, spontaneous way of responding which develops presentation skills

2 Now create a vision board, either digitally or physically, of how you will keep your RP learning journal. Use it as a reminder of all the varied ways you can respond when you are looking for inspiration. Go back to the bullet lists on each phase of the RP learning journey and pick two that you are going to try this week.

If you use social media, how much could you say you are keeping a journal already?

The learning journal is a way for you to see explicitly how managing a project works. Wherever you work, you must adopt the process and project-management system or systems in that industry. Technology, manufacturing, engineering and administration are to name but a few. They may already be familiar to you or you will receive training in their use. There are many variations, but what remains the same is the use of a central system to map out the sequence of a process when decisions are made, the people involved and the time it takes to do it. Getting experience of this sort of accountability is a valuable part of the CP's real-world relevance.

Common pitfall

Some students could consider the learning journal as an optional extra and not a compulsory part of the project. Do not make this mistake!

4.3.5 Summary

- Keeping a learning journal for the RP is compulsory and, while it is not assessed by the IB with your RP, it proves that the project is your own work.
- Keeping a learning journal is an important part of developing reflection and reflexivity skills, and that will ultimately inform the content for your final written reflection which is assessed.
- Find a way of keeping the learning journal that works best for you as a learner and use a variety of tools to help you.

4.4 Being reflective and reflexive in the RP

INQUIRY QUESTIONS

- What is the difference between being reflective and reflexive? And why does it matter?
- What does a successful learning process look like?
- What is a successful learning process meant to look like?
- Why does reflection and reflexivity matter so much?
- What are the different forms of reflection and reflexivity?

4.4.1 The importance of reflection

The process of reflection is such an important skill to develop that this element of the CP Core was named after it. It might seem strange to start this process by discussing a word that is often associated with looking back on something that has finished. Still, it is important to understand that reflection and reflexivity go much further than that.

This section will reintroduce you to tools that enable you to develop and understand yourself dynamically. As the skills you need for this project are developed over the entire CP course, the RP directly and indirectly showcases how you have developed in every aspect of your course. The consistency also expected of you in how you use reflective tools will create a mindset and working habits that reach far beyond the parameters of the project itself.

As you know from the introductory section, the central focus of the RP is to analyse and evaluate the multiple perspectives and evidence you have researched surrounding an ethical dilemma and demonstrate your understanding through your own **positionality** on the dilemma. However, there are two more strands to add to our central focus: the first is reflecting on the process itself and the second is reflecting on yourself as an ethical practitioner, and how you change and develop throughout the project. It's important not just to come to your own perspective in conclusion to the RP, but also to observe how you got there.

Key terms

◆ **Positionality:** This represents a person's perspective or attitude towards something; for example, a person's position on a controversial issue. In the RP, students must determine and justify their position on an ethical dilemma. (Source: IB RP guide, p.60)

The learning journal as a reflective tool

Learning can be a long and winding road

As you discovered in the last section, the learning journal is a compulsory part of the RP process and something you will need to complete your final reflection successfully. The reflections you keep about the process and your own position will inform your final reflection of up to 1,000 words (final reflection form) and will be assessed by Criterion E, worth nearly 25% of the total marks. We also learnt that keeping the learning journal helps contain your research but, more than that, what you think about your research and how you are forming a complex and critical position on your ethical dilemma. The learning journal is a place where you can ponder your topic and how it is developing.

But why is reflection so important? And what is reflexivity?

REAL-WORLD EXAMPLE

How reflection and reflexivity play a role in the wider world

However senior you are within your chosen career, the day you believe reflection is no longer necessary is the day you should consider retiring. Reflection on all aspects of your job is essential and shows you care not only about the work itself, but also about those you work with, their perception of you and ultimately, therefore, your own self-worth.

Emma, lawyer

As the busy world spins frantically, time to reflect feels like a gift—ancient cultures have known this and made meditation part of their day. For me as an educator, reflection is when the learning happens. What did I do, how well did it go and what would I do differently next time?

If you don't reflect, you repeat mistakes and don't learn. And when my reflections are confusing or unclear, then I know I've hit the learning zone!

Carolyn, educator

Reflection and reflexivity

What is a successful learning process meant to look like?

Reflect on the picture below, which has something to say about what it's like to go through a learning process. Think about your learning engagements so far in your schooling, as well as your whole CP experience. How do you relate to this? What message is being communicated here? Does this challenge your existing position on what progress means?

What people think success looks like.

What success really looks like.

- Which of these represents a successful RP?

4.4.2 Defining reflection and reflexivity

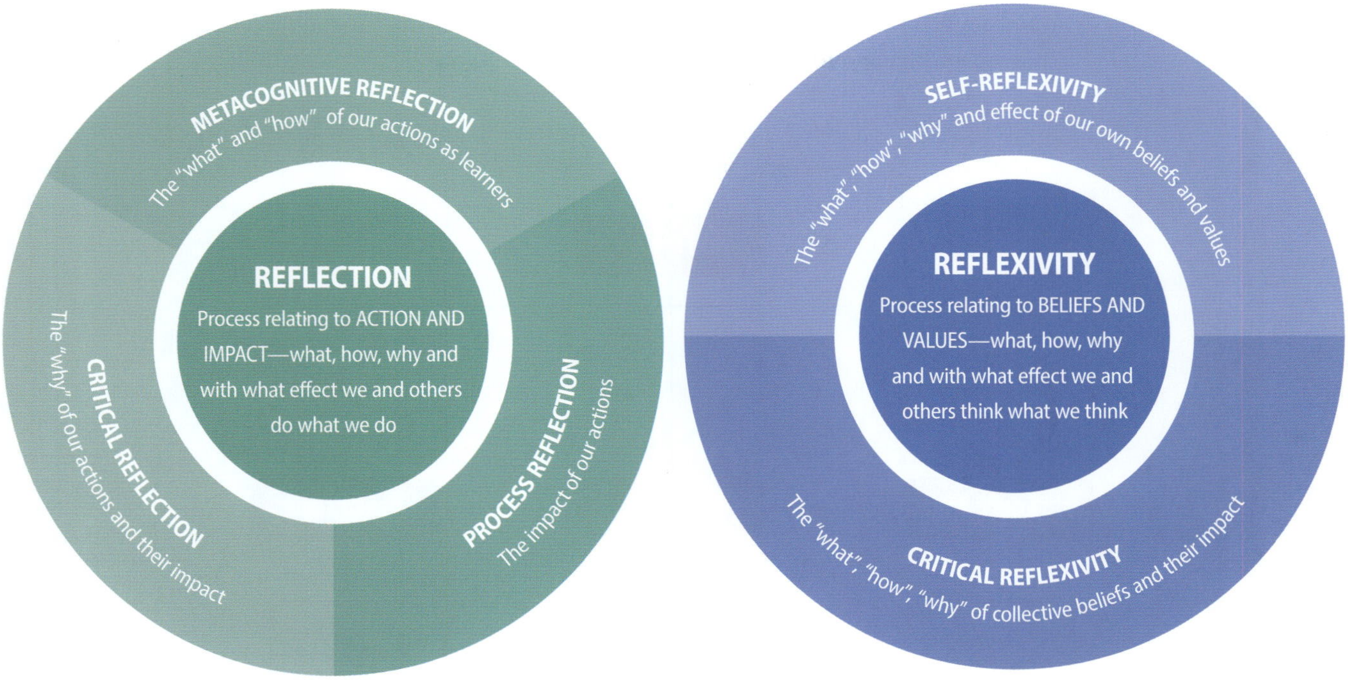

■ Reflection and reflexivity (Source: IB RP TSM, p.37)

Many IB students are familiar with reflection, as it makes up one of the learner profile characteristics. However, get used to the adjectives 'reflective' and 'reflexive' as two words that will accompany you throughout the RP process.

We have already had a look at their definitions in Section 4.1.2 (and you have been taking part in your own 'reflection and reflexivity' exercises throughout this book). No doubt you encountered a lot of information about them initially, but your understanding of the significance of each term will grow with your thinking as you embark on the RP project itself.

You may also find it helpful to refer to the introduction to remind yourself of some examples of reflective and reflexive questions (Table 4 on p.xxvii).

Remember that reflection is a process relating to *action* and *impact*—what, how, why and with what effect we and others do what we do. On the other hand, reflexivity is a process relating to *beliefs* and *values*—what, how, why and with what effect we and others think what we think. In order to explore this, carry out the following learning engagement.

Learning journal

Exploring reflection and reflexivity

1. Create your own visual which shows the *difference* between reflection and reflexivity. A good starting point is if you think of 'reflection' as associated with action and 'reflexivity' as associated with beliefs.
2. Now use the definitions in the text and from your answer to question 1 to explain in your own words to a partner what reflection and reflexivity mean to you, and where you have already had experiences of using these thinking skills. Keep your explanation relatively simple at first, and add any other information from the text as you develop your response. Share with your partner and discuss any differences in your explanations.

Types of reflection and reflexivity

Reflection asks you the 'what' and 'how' of your actions; you look closely at past experiences and actions to improve what you do in the future. There are three types of reflection here: **metacognitive**, **process** and **critical reflection**.

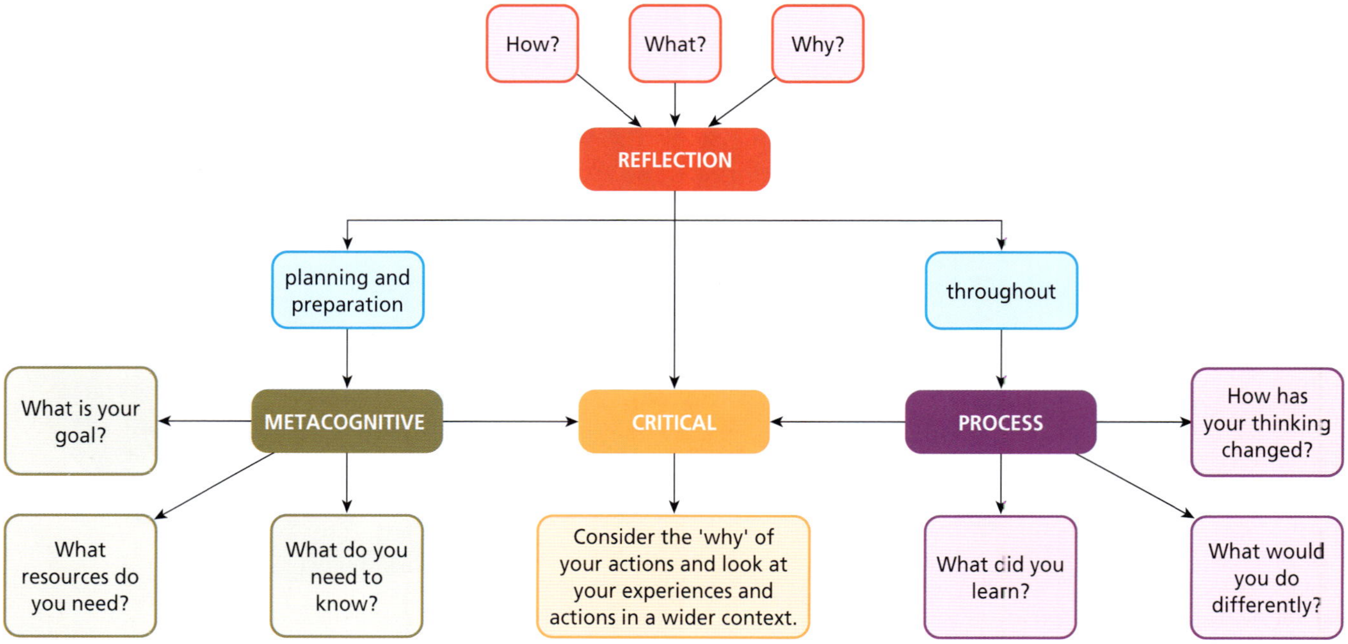

Types of reflection

> **Key term**
>
> ◆ **Metacognitive and process reflection:** These involve examining past experiences and actions to improve future practice (focused on the 'how' of actions). Reflection as a metacognitive skill enhances awareness of one's own cognitive/learning process. It involves examining one's thinking, actions and goals, leading to self-regulated learning. Process reflection starts with an experience and leads to new or changed understandings, insights and/or actions.

Reflexivity, on the other hand, relates to our beliefs and values; how and why we form our thoughts and the effect these thoughts have. There are two types of reflexivity here: **self-reflexivity** and **critical reflexivity**.

The following section takes you through the different types of reflection and reflexivity.

METACOGNITIVE REFLECTION

In metacognitive reflection, you focus on yourself and reflect on your skill development. This means you can become increasingly independent as your abilities increase.

Phases of the RP where it is most prominent:

- planning and preparation.

Possible questions: What is your goal? How will (might) you approach this … (project, topic, research, challenge, process)? What resources do you need to support your learning for this … (project, research, process)? What do you need to know (or do) to be successful?

PROCESS REFLECTION

Process reflection looks at the effects that evolve; think about your starting points and observe how your understandings change over time. Process reflection takes place throughout the RP.

Phases of the RP where it is prominent:

- research and analysis
- development
- presentation of findings
- completion and submission.

Key terms

◆ **Critical reflection:** This links reflection with analytical and critical thinking, encouraging students to focus on experiences and actions within a broader, systemic context. (Source: IB RP guide, p.60)

◆ **Self-reflexivity:** This involves considering one's positionality, identifying and questioning one's own assumptions, biases and attitudes, understanding how they influence one's own responses and actions, and how they impact others, given the complexity and interconnectedness of roles and relationships.

◆ **Critical reflexivity:** This involves critically examining and challenging collective assumptions, values and frames of reference, understanding their contexts (e.g. cultural, societal, historical), how they shape perceptions and actions, how they impact others, and how they might change in the future. (Source: IB RP guide, p.60)

Possible questions: What did you learn from this ... (research, feedback, mistake, project)? How has this ... (research, information, project) changed your ... (thinking, perspective, understanding)? What went well? If you did this again, what would you do differently? Why? What are your next steps?

CRITICAL REFLECTION

Critical reflection deepens your thinking to consider the 'why' of your actions and look at your experiences and actions in a wider context.

Phases of the RP where it is relevant:

- development
- presentation of findings
- completion and submission.

Possible questions: Why did you choose this particular ... (ethical issue, ethical dilemma, resource, format, project)? Why did you take this ... (action, decision)? How has it had an impact on your ... (thinking, perspective, project)? What choices did you make? Why? How did that have an impact on your ... (learning, understanding, result)? What else could you have done? How might that have changed the result?

SELF-REFLEXIVITY

Self-reflexivity means understanding the effect of your beliefs on yourself and others. You look closely at and question your own positionality and the assumptions, biases and attitudes that contribute to your responses and actions and impact others.

Phases of the RP where it is relevant:

- presentation and findings
- completion and submission.

Possible questions: How did your values, assumptions or biases affect your approach to this ... (project, solution, activity)? How did your (or others') values, assumptions or biases influence your choice of this ... (topic, ethical dilemma, format, activity)? How might your ... (values, assumptions, biases, choices, actions) affect others?

CRITICAL REFLEXIVITY

From self-reflexivity you move to critical reflexivity, where you consider how/why these beliefs came about, and how/why they have the impact that they do. For this you will have to understand different contexts and the influence they have to shape the future.

Phases of the RP where it is relevant:

- presentation of findings
- completion and submission.

Possible questions: Where do you think your bias about this ... (perspective, context, issue, solution) might come from? How has your new understanding changed your thinking? What do you think has influenced your perspective? How might your perspective change in the future?

(Adapted from the IB RP TSM, p.58)

The visual you created in response to the learning journal activity above might be something like this. You might be interested to know that this was created by two teachers in response to the same information!

Reflection is a process relating to action and impact — what, how, why and with what effect we and others do what we do.

Reflexivity is a process relating to beliefs and values — what, how, why and with what effect we and others think what we think.

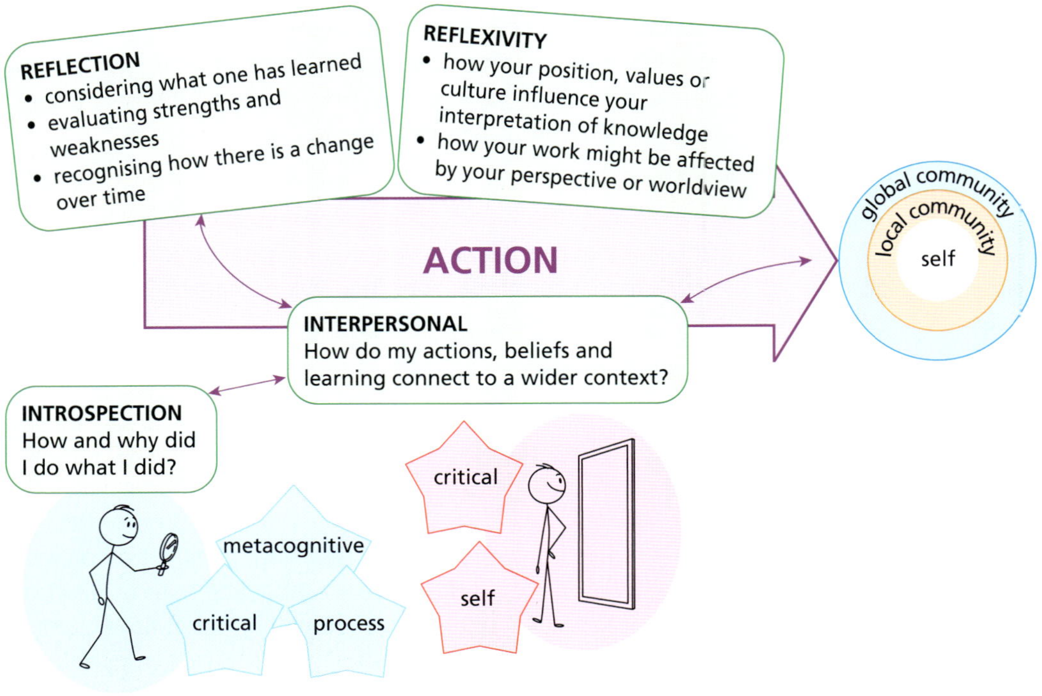

■ Example of a visual on reflection and reflexivity

LEARNING ENGAGEMENT

Create your own database of questions that will help you reflect along the way in your learning journal, which take into account the different types of reflection and reflexivity you are going to engage in. Use the table below to create questions based on the starters and topic ideas. Some have been given to help get you going.

■ **Table 4.8** The learning process and examples of reflection points along the way

Question starters	Question topics	Your question ideas
What …	Initial ideas	What are my initial ideas about the ethical dilemma and why do I think this way?
When …	Predictions	
Why …	Sources	
How …	Surprises	
Where …	Disappointments	
If …	Successes and setbacks	
Should …	Impact	
Could …	Adaptations	Could the way I think about this ethical dilemma impact those around me?
What if …	Strengths and limitations	
What next …	Personal obstacles	
So what …	Influences	
	Assumptions and bias	
	Beliefs	
	Society/history/culture	
	Feedback	

It might be that, as you have explored the different types of reflection and reflexivity so far, some of these skills sit more comfortably with you than others. Often, looking at one's actions and process can be a little less daunting than analysing what influences you to think a certain way.

The following exercise takes a thinking routine and helps you explore what self- and critical reflexivity can mean, with some process and metacognitive reflection afterwards. The important thing to do here is to be open-minded about what you might discover, but with that comes not being judgemental too.

LEARNING ENGAGEMENT

■ What story do you see?

1 Look at the image and think about these questions:
- What is the story?
- What is the untold story?
- What is your story?
- What is his/her story?
- What is our story?
- What is the bigger story?
- What is the smaller story?
- What is the scientific/historical/cultural story?

2 Then reflect on the process itself:
   a How did you find this process?
   b What does each of these questions make you consider?

(Adapted from critical thinking tools available at www.harvard.edu)

The following table provides an overview of the different types of reflection and reflexivity you will engage in over the entirety of the RP process.

■ **Table 4.9** Types of reflection and reflexivity involved in the RP process

Phase of RP	Detailed steps involved	Reflection/ reflexivity type
Preparation and planning	● preparation and building of background knowledge ● identification of an ethical dilemma ● peer discussions ● research plan and project proposal	reflection
Peer/RP supervisor feedback	● reflection point	
Research and analysis	● conduct research ● reflection point ● supervisor feedback ● reflection point	process reflection
Development	● initial project draft	process reflection critical reflection
Presentation of findings	● presentation ● reflection point	process reflection critical reflection self-reflexivity critical reflexivity
Completion and submission	● revision and final project ● *viva voce* ● final submission	process reflection critical reflection self-reflexivity critical reflexivity

4.4.3 The learning journal and final written reflection

When it comes to reflection, the ideal outcome for the whole RP process is that you learn not only to use reflection and reflexivity as a habit, but you also see the benefits of doing so. You will certainly thank your earlier self, when it comes to the final reflection, if you have reflected the whole way through the process, as you can directly use and shape these excerpts in your final reflection for the RP and written reflection, as well as help you prepare for the *viva voce* with your supervisor.

Criterion E assesses how effectively your project demonstrates your planning, research and reflective practice throughout the process. Here are some guiding questions to help you evaluate how well you are meeting the criterion:

- Have you demonstrated reflective practice?
- Have you reflected on your learning process?
- Have you reflected on your learning and how it has had an impact, or might have an impact in the future, on yourself or others?
- Have you critically examined your own and others' thinking, actions or decisions?

(Source: IB RP TSM, p.56)

Top tip!

Become familiar with Criterion E to give you focus for what your written reflection is all about. Put the guiding questions for Criterion E somewhere you will see them often. If you are keeping a digital learning journal, you would put it as a header so you will always see it. If you are keeping a physical learning journal, then you can write it on card and use this as a bookmark continuously.

■ **Table 4.10** Explanation for Criterion E (Source: IB RP guide, p.53)

	Reflection on process	Reflection on project	Reflection on learning
Descriptors from the highest markband in the guide	Reflections include thoughtful explanations.	There is a detailed evaluation of the project's effectiveness. Relevant strengths and limitations are explained.	Reflections on how learning and new understandings have an impact on the student or others are thoroughly considered and discussed.
What this might look like	• You explain any important decisions or actions you took during the planning, research and development process, why you made them and how they had an impact on your project or thinking. • If you received important feedback and acted on it, you explain how, why and its impact on your work.	• You explain how effective you think your overall project is, and why. • You identify your project's strengths and explain why you felt they were successful. • You explain what you would have liked to improve on, why and how you would improve it.	• You explain the impact of your learning or new understanding from the project on your thinking, actions and personal growth. • You explain how your learning or new understanding from the project did, or might, have an impact on others.

You will notice from Criterion E that you are assessed on three areas of reflection: process, project and learning. The image below gives some examples of what these might look like in a learning journal entry. Look at the colour coding—they don't necessarily just relate to the Criterion E, but project, progress and learning run throughout it. This learner has used these colours where they are in the process (yellow), giving reasons why their choices were valid (green), showing critical thinking (blue) and, crucially, what their next steps will be (purple) and a plan of action for their research (orange).

Today we discussed ethical dilemmas in our CRS that we might want to explore in our RP. My top three interests are: embryonic stem cell research, assisted dying and DNR orders. I think all three topics have the potential for different perspectives and will have different views around the world. Some problems might be that these topics have more to do with the legal system than the health care system. I found it pretty easy to think of these possible dilemmas because we had discussed them already in lesson, so I know these are all relevant in my CRS in today's society. The class was pretty divided on our opinions, so I think there will be a good opportunity to explore both sides. Next, I want to begin to research all three topics to make sure there are academic sources available and that there is a balance in perspectives. I plan to use online academic sources as well as asking our librarian about books about these topics.

Detailing what step and activity this journal entry relates to

Providing rationale for the merits of the choices

Thinking critically about a flaw of some of the options

Specific focus for next steps; thinking critically about what to look for

Specific plan of action; demonstrates understanding of reliable academic sources

■ Excerpts of learning journals (Source: IB RP TSM, p.60)

Defines what the ethical dilemmas are, rather than considering merits or flaws

Balanced assessment of perspectives, but it's not necessarily relevant to the purpose of the journal entry as it is part of the definition rather than an evaluation of the student's process

Today we discussed ethical dilemmas in our CRS that we might want to explore in our RP. My top three interests are: embryonic stem cell research, assisted dying and DNR orders. Embryonic Stem Cells are cells from embryos that aren't developed into fetuses yet, so the cells have the potential to become any cell in the body. Research could mean finding cures for diseases like cancer. Assisted Dying is when a person who is terminally ill chooses to die in order to save themselves from pain, but for the doctors to help them would be considered murder in a lot of countries, so making it legal would save the patients pain. DNR order means Do Not Resuscitate order. This is an ethical issue for doctors because they take an oath to "do no harm" and letting people die can be considered doing harm. On the other hand, some people think that keeping people alive is doing harm too. I'm leaning towards Embryonic Stem Cells, so I'm going to start looking at some websites to research that.

Detailing what step and activity this journal entry relates to

Evidence of student bias, but not recognized by student

Plan of action in place but limited to only one focus and plan is vague

■ Excerpts of learning journals (Source: IB RP TSM, p.60)

In this example, you can see there is not the same self-awareness of the learner on the process or their project. They are explaining parts of their research and not looking closely at their thoughts for bias. They also comment on different perspectives which is great, but not necessarily relevant here to the learning journal, where we want to focus on the learner themselves and their process, project and learning. It's important to make a plan with detailed next steps rather than be vague.

Process, project, learning

By reflecting on your process, project and learning you will provide explanations for your actions and thinking, how effective the actual project is and the impact of the project on yourself and others. The overall impact is a reflection that is thoughtful, detailed and gives a real sense of growth. You will be in a different place by the end of the process and you have made it really clear how the process, project and learning influenced this.

LEARNING ENGAGEMENT

Identifying what you need

Look back through your learning journal and find evidence in terms of process, project and learning using the following descriptors for the top band of 7–8 marks for Criterion E: Reflective practice (IB RP guide, p.54).

You can do this exercise at two different times:

1. At the start of your RP process, use your learning journals and PPS portfolio to do this exercise to see how you have been reflective already on process, project and learning.
2. As you go through the RP process, use this to review your learning journal as you prepare for the written reflection.

The key here is to be very clear about new understandings you have gained from the process. This might be new understandings about yourself and the way you learn.

GUIDING QUESTIONS

Reflect on process:

> *'Reflections include thoughtful explanations for decisions, actions and thinking, and most are justified.'*

- What do you think were the most successful parts of your process? Why?
- What problems did you have during the research and development and how did you overcome them?
- Would you change anything about the way you did the process? Why do you feel this way?
- What would you take forward from this project in terms of skills to future projects? Why?
- How did you use peer and supervisor feedback in the process? Was it helpful in decision-making? Why?

Reflect on project:

> *'There is a detailed evaluation of the project's effectiveness. Relevant strengths and limitations are explained.'*

- Looking back on your research, what new questions came out of it?
- What new ethical considerations did you make and did any of your research surprise you? Why?
- What do you think is particularly strong about your project and what areas do you think you could improve? Why?
- What were the highs and lows in finding reliable sources? Why?

Reflect on learning:

> *'Reflections on how learning and new understandings have an impact on the student or others are thoroughly considered and discussed.'*

- What was your original perspective of the ethical dilemma and why did you think this?
- How did your perspective change and what made it change?
- How do you think about the ethical issue differently now at the end of the project? Why?
- What impact has this ethical issue and dilemma had on you? Think now and in terms of your potential future decisions.
- How might your position, informed by your learning, impact others?

(Adapted from the IB RP guide, p.54)

Think of yourself as an individual with beliefs and growing or changing opinions about your ethical dilemma. Now think about how you came to have those beliefs and the assumptions and biases you hold (we all have them, don't worry!). What is the impact? To be more critically reflexive, look out to the wider world and find out what influenced your beliefs in the society around you, both now and in the past. Being reflexive ultimately includes thinking about the impact of your beliefs and being open to changing your position on yourself and the world around you.

Learning journal

Create a learning journal entry to identify changing ideas.

When you are ready, find an image that captures your ethical issue and dilemma. Record your ideas, attitudes and assumptions at the start of the project. Later, revisit them and repeat the exercise. You should be able to see clearly how your ideas, attitudes and assumptions are changing and developing over the project.

4.4.4 Summary

- The RP requires you to develop skills in reflection and reflexivity throughout the process. This means process, self- and critical reflection as well as self- and critical reflexivity.
- The learning journal is a reflective tool you use to support the development of your process, project and learning throughout the learning journey.
- Criterion E asks you to reflect on process, project and learning so that you think about your actions, how effective you are and the impact of your learning.
- Realizing the power of questions and having a question bank in your learning journal can really support your use of reflective tools, so that you look at your thoughts and actions and become more self-aware.

4.5 Applying ethical thinking

INQUIRY QUESTIONS

- How do you identify an appropriate career-related ethical dilemma?
- How can you explore the ethical dilemma from multiple perspectives?
- How do you sustain focus on the ethical dilemma with relevant examples from varied contexts?
- How do you build knowledge of multiple perspectives?
- How do you apply ethical thinking to real-world ethical dilemmas?

4.5.1 Where in the RP process is ethical thinking relevant?

Learner profile

Open-minded, thinker, principled

Arguably, navigating ethics requires employing all the IB learner profile attributes. However, 'open-minded', 'thinker' and 'principled' are at the heart of what it means to be an ethical thinker in different contexts.

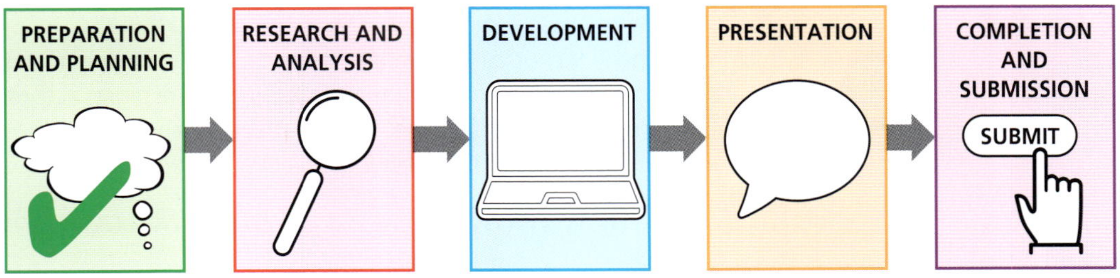

■ The RP process

■ **Table 4.11** Steps involved in the preparation and planning phase

Phase of RP	Detailed steps involved

Preparation and planning	• preparation and building of background knowledge
	• **identification of an ethical dilemma**
	  ◦ Research issues related to a career field to identify an ethical dilemma of interest.
	  ◦ Identify which groups are impacted by the dilemma and how.
	  ◦ Consider the various contexts and perspectives that might inform further research for the project.
	• **peer discussions**
	  ◦ Discuss important topics related to the RP process with peers and supervisor.
	  ◦ Give and receive feedback early in the RP journey.
	  ◦ Topics for discussion might include how to move beyond researching an issue to identify an ethical dilemma; how to construct a research question; different approaches to the learning journal; how to use technology effectively and ethically; format options; clarification of requirements; sharing of research plans; current progress and thinking.
	• research plan and project proposal

Remember that:

> *'Ethical thinking involves thinking critically about and applying ethical values to navigate our personal and professional lives. It fosters moral development and enables us to make responsible choices and be accountable for our decisions.'*
>
> (Source: IB RP guide, p.59)

Finding your own issue and dilemma

There are many CP educators around the world who have been helping students for years through the ethical dimensions of careers and finding their own point of view. What is their top advice for understanding ethical dilemmas?

Be prepared to sit in the grey; that's where the magic happens. Unpack why something feels uncomfortable rather than sprint to solutions.
A, Hong Kong

Ethical thinking isn't about the right answer; its a process of decision-making.
G, India

Also, look at the power dynamics at play and clash of values. But also look for whose voices are missing from the conversation.
B, USA

Don't play it safe; be prepared to wrestle with complexity.
R, UK

Links

Just like in the PPS course, you are also going to lead your own inquiry in the RP. In PPS you create inquiries by finding a focus, then following the explore, act, reflect and share process. It is similar here but you will find the words 'reflection' and 'reflexivity' occurring more often! We have explored their role in Criterion E: Reflective practice, but let's explore the impact they have in other criteria as well.

Identify prior knowledge

It has already been stressed that you must choose an area that interests you for your reflective project (RP). However, you do not necessarily need to start from scratch. Consider what you already know and build upon it. In terms of skills, your PPS course is just one place where you will have already familiarized yourself with ethical thinking prior to this process; this will give you a background in applied ethics and intercultural understanding.

'Criterion A: Focus on the ethical dilemma' assesses your knowledge and understanding of the ethical dilemma. How you identify and describe the ethical dilemma shows your knowledge and understanding of both your subject and career field. Furthermore, how you contextualize the ethical dilemma and discuss related issues and multiple perspectives also shows your knowledge and understanding, as well as impact on individuals and groups.

- You already have a sizeable amount of subject-specific knowledge retained from your career-related subject (CRS), and this learning connects with other areas of knowledge and influences to form your unique perception of it. The learning we retain the most is often what we find most interesting.

- Equally, you will have collected other experiences from other careers that interest you as well as your CE, PPS course, DP subjects and possibly professional work experience. These all might point towards an area of interest for you.
- You might connect your current CRS or career you are interested in directly with other subjects you already have an interest in. For example, your CRS might be business or art and design, or you might take business studies or art for your DP subject. How might these communities and interests connect?

One of the features of a good ethical dilemma to explore for an RP is how many different perspectives you can see it from. We are not looking for a story with two sides. The world we live in is far more complicated than that. To explore this further, let's take a photo and look at how complex perspectives can work.

LEARNING ENGAGEMENT

Place yourself in the ethical dimension and consider different perspectives.

1 What is happening in the photo?
2 What assumptions can you make?
3 Why do you think that?
4 Where do your sympathies lie?

Place yourself in the shoes of two or three people in the picture. Try and see matters from their perspectives, even if you do not agree.

Without revealing the origin of the photo to you, reflect on this final question:

5 Which teachers in your school might give you further insight into this photo? (Go past the obvious!)

Now, research the origin of this photo using the internet.

Being willing to look from different perspectives is being open-minded and employing empathy. You are not bound to it. You never know what you might find. It's like trying on clothes in a shop before you buy, and you are entitled not to buy them at all!

How do you build knowledge of multiple perspectives?

Change your lenses for a different perspective.

Finding new perspectives means that you need to look at the familiar from different angles. Looking at an ethical dilemma through a specific lens gives you a sharp focus of analysis.

Take a *cultural lens*, for example; this is somewhat of an umbrella term that can explore a number of societal perspectives and the influence they have on how we perceive an ethical dilemma. Examples of cultural lenses are racial, political and religious. What is also interesting is considering your own bias when exploring these views, as you aim to understand a culture in context and not by your own cultural biases.

An *environmental lens* means looking at the link between humans and the natural world. More than that, it considers the interconnection of all living things and the impact humans have on them.

Links

This is a fascinating insight into systems thinking and the relation between the individual and the wider world. You may well have come across this in CE and also when you are employing self- and critical reflexivity throughout your CP subjects.

A *social and historical lens* means you look to see what was happening in society at the time that might impact how you see something, and you might need to look back in history to understand it even further.

A *feminist lens* encourages you to consider the role of gender in an issue and how much conventional stereotypes of gender roles play a part in understanding and impact. However, this lens might also encourage you to think about the notion of inequality in general, and how traditional systems can reinforce inequalities related to wealth, age and race.

REAL-WORLD EXAMPLE

An interesting example of looking at inequality in film is the 'Bechde test'. The key takeaway from this is to consider the impact of looking at something from a specific angle and the new understandings it can bring you.

This actually started out as a joke by its author, Alison Bechdel, who first used it in her comic strip—she never intended for it to become mainstream—but it does provide us with a really interesting example of looking from a feminist perspective. The Bechdel test is a way of looking at a film to measure the quality of representation of women in film and other media. The Bechdel test uses three simple rules:

1 The story has to have at least two *named* women in it.
2 The two women talk *to each other.*
3 The two women talk to each other *about something besides a man.*

An *economic lens* means looking at an event or thing's economic/financial aspect. For example, you might analyse the impact of a war from an economic perspective to see who benefited the most financially, to give you another angle on the event.

An *industrial lens* is employed when considering how a product, process or service is designed, manufactured, distributed and, ultimately, used within the industrial landscape. For example, it might be that you are considering the ethical implications of a product aimed at teenagers, so it makes sense to consider the design process and its eventual impact from the perspective of the designers and industry itself.

A *technological lens* means you consider how technology can influence how we perceive and understand the world. You take on the perspective that technology shapes how we see reality. You could use this lens on an ethical issue, such as the connection between social-media companies and politics, or you could look at the impact of social-media algorithms.

LEARNING ENGAGEMENT

Build up your perspectives

Companies in many industries face ethical challenges and need to take a holistic approach to solving them, which means considering a lot of different angles. An interesting take is to look at different industries connected with your CRS. You could take a particular example and mind map your research in response. Each of these prompts invites you to look at the company from a different perspective and through a lens:

- What are their attitudes towards diversity, equity and inclusion? (societal/feminist lens)
- How have they changed over time? (historical lens)
- What are the values they hold about their products or processes? (economic/industrial lens)
- What are their attitudes towards the environment? (environmental lens)
- How do they treat individuals? (societal/environmental lens)
- How does the whole system work together? (environmental lens)

LEARNING ENGAGEMENT

Discovering your dilemma

This activity has three stages. Either working by yourself or in a small group with people from other career-related subjects to your own, cover some wall space with a sizeable amount of paper. Now fill it with as many of your interests and thoughts as possible, no matter how unconnected you think they might be to your CRS or any career you are interested in. This is about creating and you will select and refine your ideas later. If you are working with others, take turns talking through your ideas.

Stage 1: Circles of interest

1. Draw three circles within each other—small, medium and large.
2. Beginning in the centre circle, mind map the different areas of your CRS you have studied and any subtopics that come to mind. Also include any other professional areas of interest you might have explored in the PPS course or within your CE experiences, for example.
3. In the next circle, put in the areas you find particularly interesting—you do not need to know why yet—and be sure to use a different colour for each person.
4. In the outer circle, put in areas connected with your CRS that you may not have studied yet but are interested in.

Circle the areas that interest you the most. Different global or local contexts or real-life situations might interest you. Chat to your group about the mind map you have produced. Please note, if you do work with others, that they are from different career-related contexts, as it can be challenging to remain academically honest otherwise. Remember to take a photo for your learning journal, which you can annotate with further thoughts.

Stage 2: Exploring ethical issues

■ Look for the controversy

Sometimes it just takes one word to get you to an important matter associated with your CRS or career interest. To uncover ethical issues, you might want to explore more. See how the following words might connect with your ideas from the Stage 1 exercise.

■ **Table 4.12**

responsibility	duty	protection	conflict	control
freedom	equality	authority	law	money
funding	education	government	charity	censorship
age	love	prejudice	hate	loyalty

Stage 3: Identifying dilemmas

Differentiating a dilemma from an issue can be difficult. However, if you can find at least two perspectives that show different moral points of view connected with the topic you have uncovered, you are on your way.

Expand on the ideas you developed in Stages 1 and 2 that you like the most by considering:

1 What do you already know about this?
2 What questions do you have? (You might have a lot of questions!)
3 Are there two or more stakeholders and who might they be?
4 What might be the different perspectives of these stakeholders?
5 What is your initial perspective?

Top tip!

Be open-minded about working with and talking to your peers, as you will be giving and receiving feedback with each other a lot.

The secret to identifying the ethical dilemma is to look for the clash of ethical principles underneath it. There will be multiple stakeholders a l having something to say about it. Remember that dilemmas are puzzles—there should not be one easy answer. Remember the analytical ethics iceberg metaphor that we explored in the introduction (p.xxii)? Think about the explicit and implicit values that make up this ethical dilemma.

LEARNING ENGAGEMENT

A five-minute analysis of an ethical dilemma

You can work on this as a pair or a group. This is an activity to see how quickly you can identify the key features of a dilemma.

Look at the following dilemma and answer the questions underneath. You have five minutes to do this before sharing your ideas.

Ethical dilemma: Should there be more legal ramifications for the use of misinformation and 'deepfake' media?

Clash of ethical principles: Freedom of speech versus principle of truth.

1 **Think about:**
   a What are your initial questions?
   b What information do you need?
   c Who are the individuals and communities involved and what perspectives might they have?
   d What are the implications and potential impact of this issue?

2 **Take your thinking further:**
   Consider how this ethical dilemma might be perceived in different contexts:
   - politics and elections
   - personal relationships
   - business and finance
   - media and journalism
   - your own career of interest.

4.5.2 The nature of ethical thinking

So far in this section, you have had the chance to try different lenses to find out new perspectives and start to develop your own thoughts on ethical dilemmas connected to your career of interest.

Where do you stand ethically?

For your RP, you need to find an ethical dilemma that you can feel passionate about and can sustain your interest. As human beings, we know we feel strongly about issues such as human rights, euthanasia, war and globalization, or at least hold opinions on them, but we don't often reflect about how we came to that stance. And when we don't know why we think something, it becomes hard to justify or expand on our ideas.

Discussion and debate can come to a grinding halt when someone falls back on a defensive stance of 'well, it's my opinion'. As a CP student, thinking deeply about *why* you think the way you do is not necessarily a comfortable process. However, when you ask questions and consider even just a few philosophical theories in their application to ethical dilemmas, you will not only come to a new understanding of *what* you think and *why* you think it, but you might also find new ideas. You will find your voice.

Top tip!

Remember that your RP is all about applying ethical decision-making in different contexts. You can take different approaches to explore the ethical dimension of a dilemma that can lead you down new avenues of thinking, and this all adds up to you finding your own personal position on your dilemma. Keep your focus at all times on the wider world, with your ethical dilemma at the centre.

Framing your ethical thinking and ethical decision-making

Ethics is a subject that can be explored in many different ways. However, the ethics we are concerned about throughout the CP is driven by action and how you apply it in the wider world—not learning about some theories that often lie inactive in a dusty old book. Looking at different ways other people have framed making ethical decisions is not you changing yourself to their way of thinking; it's a way of finding a centre in an ethical dilemma and having tools that enable you to find out what *you* think about it.

Deep thinking takes time. To be a true critical and creative thinker about an ethical dilemma in the RP, you need to explore different perspectives and why they exist, weigh up their strengths and limitations, and build up to finding possible solutions. Exploring different ethical frameworks and their relevance beyond the classroom can help us develop and flex these critical muscles, and the more we do that, the more adaptable and confident we will be at navigating this ourselves.

Here we will look at some of the ways you can consider ethical dilemmas to develop your thinking. You will find that these tend to have one of three foci; the person, the act and the consequence. This relates very well to the development of our reflection and reflexivity skills, as you have considered your own actions and the impact on those around you and the wider world.

Most of the time when we make ethical decisions, we simply do what feels best at the time or instinctively act in a way we learnt from our family, school or other experiences. It's sometimes hard to know what we think and why we think it. Using ethical frameworks can suggest perspectives that we can use to explore ethical dilemmas. They can give us a lens to understand the scope of the ethical dilemma we are looking at and explore different perspectives, including what it reveals about our own position.

Focusing on the person and their character

You might take the approach that the people and their well-being are the most important factor to consider in ethical decision-making. Humans just need to practise the right tools to be ethical people and you can make decisions based on the best way for a human to develop their values. This approach is often referred to as *virtue ethics*.

What could be the drawbacks? While it is important to focus on individuals and the best way for them to act, society works differently and we need to think about people en masse. Also, not all humans can behave the same; there are huge cultural distinctions and what might be seen as right and true in one country might be very different in another. In fact, *situational ethics* tells us exactly that—we can only make ethical decisions on a case-by-case basis because there is so much diversity in the contexts that humans navigate.

Learning journal

For your ethical dilemma, think about how far the individuals associated with your dilemma have values that impact how they act and what they believe. Write your thoughts in your learning journal.

REAL-WORLD EXAMPLE

'Living in truth' and Havel's greengrocer

Vaclav Havel (1936–2011) was a famous philosopher, poet and playwright who was imprisoned for his beliefs during the Communist Era. After its fall, he became president of Czechoslovakia, which then became the Czech Republic. He wrote throughout his life on the nature of human freedom, and his analogy of a Prague greengrocer in his political essay, 'The power of the powerless', in his book, *Living in Truth*, has become famous and is well worth researching as an individual, group or class. You could read the essay itself or find shorter secondary analysis for an overview of the essay. There are obituaries for Vaclav Havel that consider his work, as well as how he lived his life.

Focusing on action

A *duty-based ethics* approach to ethical thinking places people's actions as the most important aspect to measure when considering an ethical dilemma. If you act in a morally good way to start with, then the consequences are of far less importance. Intentions are everything and there are few exceptions. The most famous proponent of this was Immanuel Kant in the eighteenth century, but let's leave him there and look at how thinking in this way has had its influence around us today.

Rights-based ethical thinking is the twenty-first century version of duty-based ethics, and you will see examples of rights- and rules-based ethical approaches all around us. An ethical framework that uses a rights-based approach means that the rights of all individuals are recognized, and also the responsibilities that come from these rights. Certain rights should be respected to the extent that there are no exceptions, no matter the consequences.

REAL-WORLD EXAMPLE

The Universal Declaration of Human Rights

> *'The Universal Declaration of Human Rights (UDHR) is a milestone document in the history of human rights. Drafted by representatives with different legal and cultural backgrounds from all regions of the world, the Declaration was proclaimed by the United Nations General Assembly in Paris on 10 December 1948 (General Assembly resolution 217A) as a common standard of achievements for all peoples and all nations. It sets out, for the first time, fundamental human rights to be universally protected and it has been translated into over 500 languages. The UDHR is widely recognized as having inspired, and paved the way for, the adoption of more than seventy human rights treaties, applied today on a permanent basis at global and regional levels (all containing references to it in their preambles).'*

(Source: www.un.org/en/about-us/universal-declaration-of-human-rights)

LEARNING ENGAGEMENT

The Universal Declaration of Human Rights

Look up the UDHR. Which rights mean the most to you personally? Taking the idea that there are no exceptions, no matter the consequences, have any of them been controversial in the world?

Learning journal

Are there human rights to consider in your ethical dilemma? Does the protection of these rights matter more than any other factors? Write your thoughts in your learning journal.

Focusing on consequences

This approach to ethical thinking sees the outcome as the great decider of whether something is right or wrong. So no matter what the intention, if the outcome benefits the most amount of people possible, then how people have acted is not important. You may have heard of the phrase 'the end justifies the means'. Jeremy Bentham, a key proposer of this way of thinking, said that something was good based on whether it provided 'the greatest good for the greatest number of people'.

LEARNING ENGAGEMENT

A school decides to ban the use of technology and mobile phones in school for ages 7–17 to protect the greatest possible number of students' mental health and online safety. What might be the different perspectives at play surrounding this decision?

Empathetic ethical thinking

Now you may have read the examples so far of approaches to ethical thinking and thought, 'Where is the emotion?' You are right. Those approaches do recommend that ethical decisions need to employ reason and remain unemotional. However, are humans not emotional beings?

You might feel that leading with empathy is a crucial part of the decision-making process. When you make ethical decisions, you consider the relationships between friends and family members, individuals and their communities.

An example of this is social justice, which impacts individuals and the relationships they have in their communities. You only have to look on the news to see people acting with empathy irrespective of cultural differences. You could also look at international non-governmental aid organizations.

LEARNING ENGAGEMENT

Research and explore the work of Amnesty International and ask yourself:

- How does a big organization such as Amnesty International decide who to support?

Context-based ethical thinking

We started this discussion with the notion that you might make ethical decisions based on the situation at hand, and that you treat each circumstance as unique with no hard and fast rules. You decide what is right for the complex situation in front of you. That is an approach to ethical thinking in its own right!

You might approach ethical thinking from a religious perspective; for example, frameworks such as 'situation ethics' hold that the Christian principle of *agape* (love) needs to guide any ethical dilemma, irrespective of other factors. Or you might approach it from a more global angle—what we call *ethical relativism*—where there is not one set of correct principles and that we can only, as different cultures and societies, try to decide what is right or wrong.

Remember, this isn't a history or philosophy lesson. You can look more into the philosophers behind the ideas if you want to, but what matters is developing different approaches to ethical thinking and the impact it can have on *your* thinking. The aim is that all of this should give you a perspective on finding out what *you* think.

Reflection and reflexivity

Taking a personal position on your ethical dilemma

How do you develop your own ethical decision-making? You might apply this process to a stance you have taken in a class debate, or to your actual ethical dilemma as you form your own position on it. Take your learning journal and mind map your current position on your ethical dilemma. What could the following questions reveal to you?

- Does your perspective respect the rights of all stakeholders? Is that possible?
- Does your position treat everyone fairly? Is that possible?
- Have you considered what helps the whole community and not just a few people?
- Does your position reflect you as the way you want to act as a person? If not, why not? (This is not a judgement!)

Now take your reflection further to a metacognitive level:

- How did you find this process?
- What did it reveal so far about your thinking?
- What might you take away from this to act upon?

4.5.3 Exploring ethical dilemmas

In this section, we are going to explore different ethical dilemmas that are present in the world right now and appear to be long-lasting. Firstly, though, as a way to deepen our thinking when we look through the lens of the twenty-first century, it's worth considering certain concepts that can help frame our ethical thinking. For example:

- social and ecological justice
- sustainability
- individual and shared responsibility
- accountability
- power
- care
- choice
- agency
- post-truth.

For example, post-truth relates to circumstances in which objective facts are less influential in shaping public opinion than appealing to emotion and personal belief.

Links

Consider how you have come across these concepts already throughout your course—especially in your DP subjects and CRS. This would make a good entry for your PPS portfolio!

LEARNING ENGAGEMENT

Ethical thinking about architecture

Architecture has often been connected with aesthetics rather than ethics, but this has shifted completely in the twenty-first century. Nowadays, architecture must navigate ethical principles that place human well-being and community as a priority.

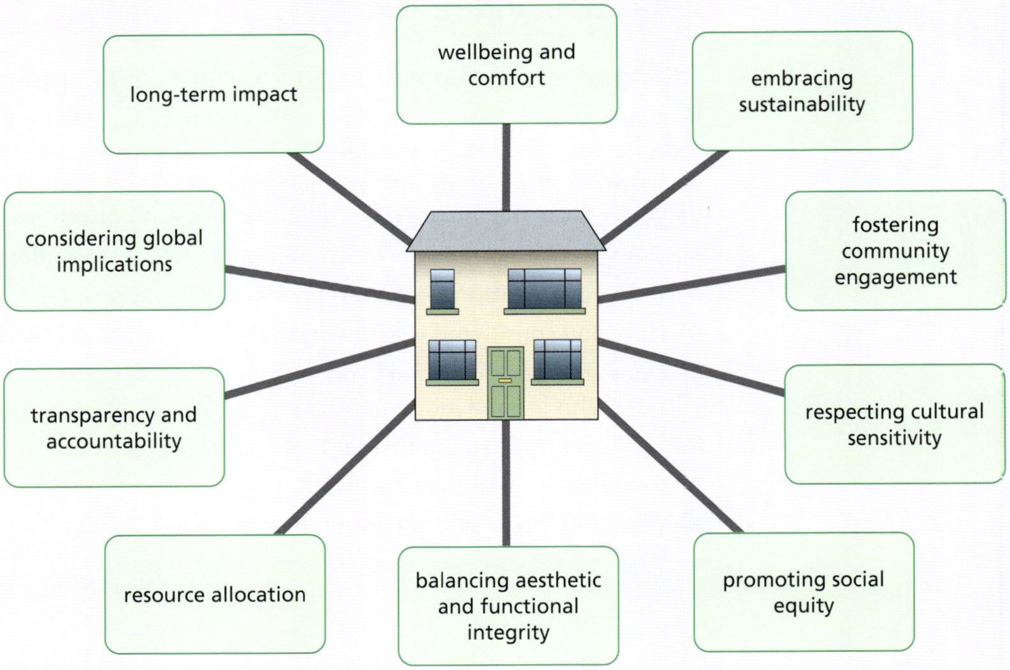

■ Concepts considered for ethical architecture

1 Look at the diagram above and consider which ethical principles matter most to you as an individual and which do you think matter most to living in a community. You could do this through chatting with a partner or debate in class.

On the other hand, the term 'hostile architecture' refers to the design of public spaces for the purpose of deterring people from using them for long periods of time or even at all.

2 Consider examples of architecture that intentionally seek to discourage community engagement. Reflect on why this type of architecture exists. What behaviour do communities want to stop happening? Can the way something is designed stop certain behaviour? And why is this controversial? Should public spaces always be designed for sociable purposes?
3 Think about a simple bench in a public place. Research examples of hostile designs of benches and draw a mind map in your learning journal of the impact of one of the designs you find.
4 Understandably, hostile architecture has come to have associations with being unsympathetic to those who are homeless. Use your learning journal to create a balanced mind map of perspectives on this issue. Share with a partner or group, remembering that sharing perspectives can sometimes be difficult for controversial topics. What is your position?

LEARNING ENGAGEMENT

Ethical thinking about technology companies

For this dilemma, we are going to go straight in with a question and break down how you could respond using what you have learnt in this section.

Should a school accept sponsorship from a tech company known for unethical data practices to fund under-resourced programmes?

The first step is thinking about what the conflict is here.

1 Use the following prompts to help you articulate an initial response using your communication skills. Feel free to use your learning journal space to map out some ideas, but try risk-taking and talking through what role these words might play in this dilemma.

Table 4.13

digital ethics	equity	privacy	'good of the many'	'compromise of values'

2 Think of the perspectives of those involved. Consider the students, the teachers, the parents, the company, the community and the government.

3 Work with a partner to break down the potential impact example this ethical dilemma.

4 Research real-world examples to help you contextualize this and see how many different directions this could go in.

Learning journal

In this section, you have explored multiple ways of building ethical understanding and forming multiple perspectives on issues and dilemmas. Make a list of words that you can keep in your learning journal to help you explore your ethical dilemma at the heart of your RP.

4.5.4 Summary

- Your main learning journey with the RP starts with the ethical dilemma connected to a career field of your choosing. You have a wealth of experience and prior knowledge from different contexts to inspire you, so never think you are starting from scratch!
- What makes an ethical dilemma truly a dilemma is that it does not have an easy solution and it has multiple perspectives surrounding it. Take time to explore ethical issues from different lenses and look for the clash of ethical principles.
- Developing your ethical thinking can include trying out particular ethical approaches, such as looking at the person, the actions and the consequences surrounding ethical dilemmas. This can enable you to find ways to take a stand or be flexible in your thinking.
- As you grow through the RP learning journey, so will your voice. One of the most important features of your RP is that you take a position on your ethical dilemma and suggest solutions—more than just considering the impact and implications too.

4.6 The research question and project proposal

INQUIRY QUESTIONS

- How do you develop a research question?
- How do you avoid a descriptive question?
- How do you put together a project proposal?
- How do you start to think about formats?

4.6.1 Creating and refining a research question and project proposal

In the preparation and planning phase, you will focus on the research plan and project proposal.

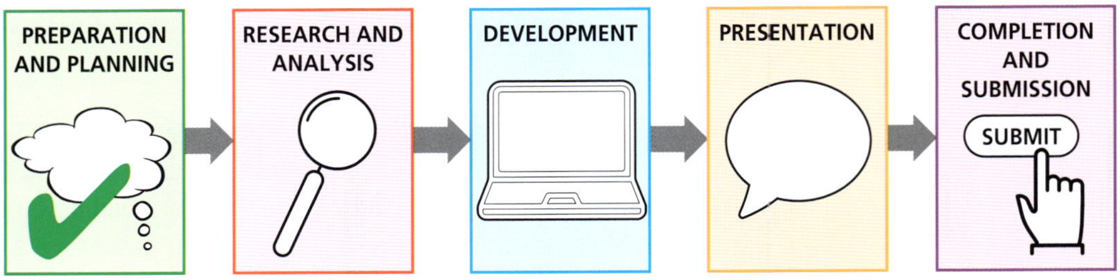

■ The RP process

■ **Table 4.14** Steps involved in the preparation and planning phase

Phase of RP	Detailed steps involved

Preparation and planning	● preparation and building of background knowledge
	● identification of an ethical dilemma
	● peer discussions
	● **research plan and project proposal**
	  ● **Refine the ethical dilemma/research question.**
	  ● Consider and articulate approach to the RP through the creation of a research plan and submission of a proposal to the supervisor.
	  ● Determine a research approach and potential resources.
	  ● Decide on a project format.

Let's look at what is meant by 'Refine the ethical dilemma/research question' in the process. For your research question to work, the ethical dilemma must be completely clear in the question, so you will need to refine it. To do this, work through the following steps:

1. Identify the ethical dilemma you want to investigate related to either your CRS or specific career field of interest.
2. Make sure that the dilemma you have chosen will allow you to carry out an in-depth investigation.
3. Develop your research question related to the ethical dilemma. It is important that your research question is suitable, clear and will provide a guide for you to follow in researching, writing and developing your RP.
4. Put together a project proposal to discuss with your supervisor and choose the format you want to use for your project.

In the previous section, you looked in detail at choosing an ethical dilemma connected with a career field of interest. Now you need to find out whether you can make a suitable research question from it.

4.6.2 Developing a research question

Without the right question, there is a limit to how successful your reflective project (RP) can be. The question will provide you with the ethical, contextual and cultural framework, in terms of scope and depth, in which you are arguing. Get the question right and you will have a forum to explore ideas, debate their strengths and weaknesses, find your own voice and understand why you think that way, as well as how your thinking has changed. Get the question wrong and it will be like setting out for a run with just one shoe on. You might think it would be ideal if the perfect question just came to you in a moment of inspiration, but actually working at getting the question right is an excellent exercise in critical thinking. It therefore makes sense for you to spend time at the beginning to develop your research question.

> You don't have to start a project process immediately excited and impassioned about what you are exploring; you can work on this. Your confidence grows with your knowledge and skills. As you find out more about areas that interest you, start to refine your focus and talk it through with your peers and supervisor, your motivation and engagement will generally increase. Be patient.

Research question checklist

Can you answer 'yes' to each of the following questions when you look at your proposed research question? If you do not have a research question yet, don't worry. You could use the following question against the checklist below to map out how it could work.

Example research question: *Should students prioritize loyalty to a friend or their responsibility to report plagiarism?*

- ☐ Is it an evaluative question? (This means there needs to be alternative viewpoints/interpretations that you can assess throughout, rather than a purely descriptive or explanatory account.)
- ☐ Is the question clear in its relation to a career that you are studying or a profession that interests you?
- ☐ Does the question suggest that what will follow is a well-researched and balanced exploration of a specific dilemma?
- ☐ Is the ethical dilemma clear in your question? (There should be a clearly identifiable clash of ethical values or principles.)
- ☐ Is the question not too narrow, but also not too general?
- ☐ Does the question indicate that you are taking on a valid dilemma with a range of perspectives to evaluate? Does there appear to be more than one solution?
- ☐ Does the question work when applied to different contexts?
- ☐ Does the question indicate this RP can be done within the time and word limit required?

There must be sufficient academic resources around your chosen title to sustain your research. The RP accounts for approximately 50 hours of your time, so you need to ask yourself whether your question lends itself to this amount and depth of work.

How to avoid a question that leads to a descriptive RP

Descriptive projects, no matter how interesting, do not fulfil the requirements of the RP. With a descriptive RP, we are talking about a project that only goes so far in its thinking. You know when you have a descriptive question as it prompts you to describe an event as though you are retelling a story. You will find yourself concentrating on what happened, who was involved and when it occurred rather than investigating the how and why.

For example, a descriptive question might be, 'How do different cultures typically handle issues of euthanasia?' There is a clear ethical issue undoubtedly, and you have lots of space to think about different cultural views, but it doesn't push you to think about why people act the way they do, believe what they do and the impact of this. In short, it is not set up for you to explore the consequences.

> Your initial question may be a descriptive one. That is fine as a starting point—a good question does not appear like magic. It is an exercise in problem-solving and perseverance.

A good question promotes different viewpoints on a socially significant matter that is in an ethically grey area. There should not be a clear solution, but almost a motion for a debate. For example, 'Should spouses be protected legally in cases of assisted dying?'

This question is not quite right as it is contextually vague and very broad. However, it does tick the box of being open, debatable and inviting multiple perspectives. Crucially, it is an ethical dilemma as there is no clear-cut solution. Don't forget that ethical dilemmas can be emotive and controversial.

> We explore critical thinking in lots more detail in Section 4.8, but it is a good test of a question to see whether it gives you the opportunity to explore an ethical dilemma analytically and evaluatively, as you see here.

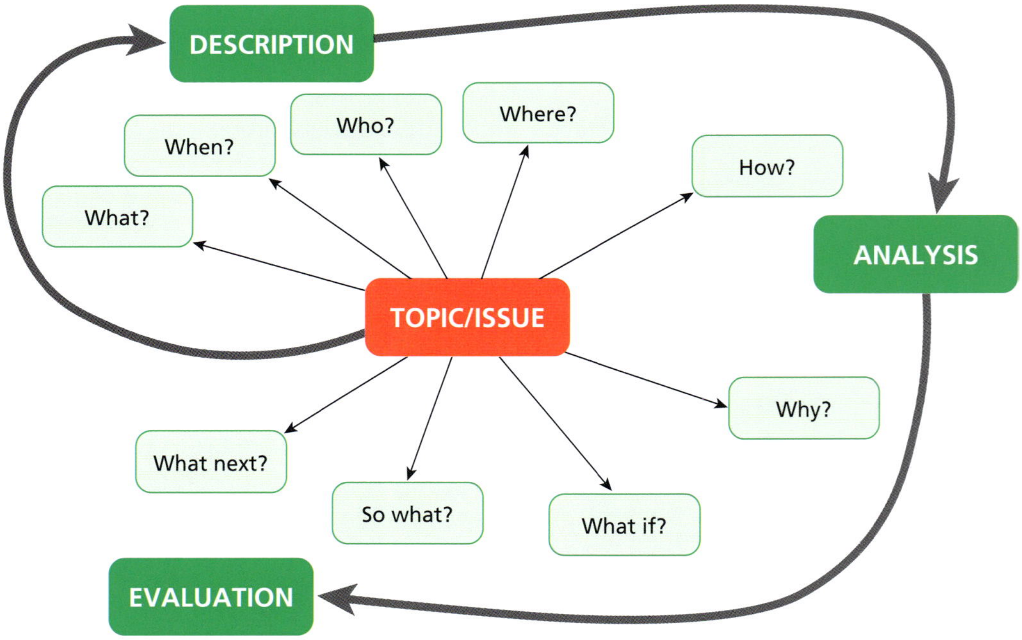

The journey from descriptive to critical thinking (Based on the 'Model to generate critical thinking' by John Hilsdon, University of Plymouth)

So, a good question allows you to explore all sorts of issues and build your thinking. You might successfully establish the context of your ethical dilemma with the questions: *What? When? Who?* and *Where?* For example, *What happened? When did it happen? Who was involved?* and *Where did this take place?* But you need to then break that down into *How?* and *Why?* So *How did it happen?* and *Why did it happen?* However, you cannot stop there, because you want to be able to evaluate it critically with your own independent voice, position and possible solutions. Note that these questions increasingly enable you to have a voice and consider the impact of what you are studying.

Simple steps to a question

In Section 4.7 we look into research skills in more detail, but there are five essential steps to developing a research question. Here we take a topic and see how this might lead to a final research question.

1. Find an issue relating to your career-related study or a career area that interests you.
   Social media and the impact it has on self-esteem in young people.
2. Create a question that allows you to describe what you already know.
   How might social-media algorithms affect young people's self-esteem?
3. Redraft this question so it asks for a solution.
   How have mental health issues associated with social-media platforms been tackled by its hosts?
4. Now try and think of the ethical dilemma that is actually in question. You have the issue but what is the element that presents differences of perspectives?
   Should there be harsher penalties for people who use social-media platforms to body-shame other users?
5. Now focus on the ethical dilemma and widen it so that the actual question goes beyond the limits of the original observation in step 2. Your question should prompt multiple suggestions as to the right answer and therefore require the use of argument.
   Should social-media platforms do more to protect their teenage users from mental-health issues arising from content they have viewed?

Examples of reworked questions

The following table explores potential questions and how to shape them into questions suitable for the demands of the RP. Before reading the explanations, you could assess whether you think the questions would work by using this checklist and, if not, suggest revisions.

- ☐ Is it an evaluative question?
- ☐ Is the question clear in its relation to a career that you are studying or a profession that interests you?
- ☐ Does the question suggest that what will follow is a well-researched and balanced exploration of a specific dilemma?
- ☐ Is the ethical dilemma clear in your question?
- ☐ Is the question not too narrow, but also not too general?
- ☐ Does the question indicate that you are taking on a valid dilemma with a range of perspectives to evaluate? Does there appear to be more than one solution?
- ☐ Does the question work when applied to different contexts?
- ☐ Does the question indicate this RP can be done within the time and word limit required?

Table 4.15 Shaping initial questions into suitable questions for the RP

Initial question	Revised question
Why do aging members of society not work more? This is certainly interesting but would lead to a description with research rather than an exploration of conflicting perspectives. The clash of ethical principles is not clear.	*Should businesses do more to diversify the age of their workforce to include more above 'retirement age'?* Clear relation to a career area. The possibility of a balanced exploration of an ethical dilemma is suggested with the potential of multiple perspectives. The clash of ethical principles is clear. The question is quite broad so the student will need to be careful about contextualizing this. However, many contexts could work here which makes the possibilities exciting. The question can work within the parameters of the RP word limit and different format parameters.
Why cannot people identifying as transgender play football in the Football Association? This question has a clear context to explore and is certainly based within an ethical issue and related to a career area of sport. However, phrased as it is, the clash of ethical principles is not clear and all signs point towards this leading to an explanation and potentially a history lesson.	*Should people who are transgender be allowed to play football competitively?* There is a clear relation to a career area—potentially multiple here for sport, health and social care, and business. This is a controversial area demanding sensitive handling of multiple perspectives. There are many contexts that could be relevant here and care will need to be taken on a polarizing topic; however, the impact that a balanced approach could bring here captures the power an RP can have as a process and a product.

LEARNING ENGAGEMENT

Peer check-in

Checking that your research question captures a dilemma clearly is worth doing early in the process, before you take part in your first review meeting. You will need a partner for this activity and should already have an idea for your research question.

1 Discuss each other's questions and how successful they are. Record your conversation for later reference.

Now reflect upon the following question in your learning journal:

2 Does your research question capture an ethical dilemma effectively?

You can tell if your question is complex by how you are talking. You might find yourself getting excited, like you are watching fireworks, as you realize it's both a complex question and controversial. Also, you might move between confidence and hesitation in your voice as you talk through it, which can indicate there are lots of ideas surrounding the question and that you are not sure what your position might be. All of these are good signs of a complex and difficult dilemma present in your question.

Top tip!

Write your own responses to points 1–5 as a draft proposal and share them with your supervisor, who will give you feedback. Then keep it in your learning journal, revisit it and reflect on it throughout. This is a good way of keeping focused, but if you do find your focus changing, you can review and refine your original proposal and track those changes.

4.6.3 Completing your project proposal

Completing a project proposal is an important part of the RP, as it enables you to refine your ideas and state what you want to do at this stage of the process. Sharing this with your supervisor and peers also allows you to get helpful feedback to make it better.

What goes into your project proposal?

1 An outline of your dilemma.
2 What you want to achieve through your research and how you are going to carry it out.
3 Any perspectives or contexts you are interested in exploring at this moment.
4 Your ideas for the format you have chosen at this stage and your reasons for doing so.
5 A timeline and any resources you have found so far.

Designing a project proposal

Your project proposal does not have to be a specific form, though there are templates available from the IB and there is a completed example on the next page. The important thing here is the content of your project proposal's framework and that it can be a useful tool throughout your RP process.

Prompts to consider as sections in your project proposal:

- dilemma
- research objectives
- research methods
- perspectives
- contexts
- impact
- formats
- feedback.

Learning journal

Use your learning journal to mind map your RP proposal and identify where the gaps are in your thinking. Do not worry about how messy your thinking is at this stage. Colour-code your responses and identify where the gaps are. Then move to the learning engagement to see how you might develop this area further.

LEARNING ENGAGEMENT

Creating a research proposal

Use the following questions as a way of mapping out your research proposal in your learning journal and seeing where the gaps are. This will also help you put together your proposal.

1 Explain the ethical issue you want to explore and the reasons why you chose it.
2 Now explain how this ethical issue relates to a career-related field.
3 What is the ethical dilemma? What are the ethical considerations? For this, you must clearly show the clash of ethical principles.
4 Identify *at least three* contexts where this ethical dilemma has an impact. What is the impact? What considerations could be researched?
5 Identify *at least three* individuals or groups who are affected in some way by the ethical dilemma and what their perspectives might be. What considerations could be researched?
6 What format will your RP take, and why?
7 What are your next steps?

An example proposal

The following example has a commentary to guide you on how you might approach filling out your own project proposal.

Name:	Date:

See comment 1.

Explain the ethical issue you want to explore, and the reasons why you chose it.

Issue: Regulation of emissions to reduce environmental impact

I am very concerned about the environment and what can be done to reduce the negative impact caused by humans and industry. I also live outside of London and my parents are impacted by the Ultra Low Emissions Zone (ULEZ).

See comment 2.

How does this ethical issue relate to your career-related field?

It relates to BTEC Law.

We studied bylaws versus national laws.

See comment 3.

What is the ethical dilemma? What are the ethical considerations?

Ethical dilemma: Should ULEZ be expanded to other cities?

Environmental protection and health versus personal freedom.

'Class tax' and government regulation versus personal freedom.

Environmental responsibility of current generation versus environmental needs of future generations.

Identify at least three contexts where this ethical dilemma has an impact. What is the impact? What considerations could be researched?

See comment 4.

Contexts	Impact	Considerations for research
Very large populated and heavily congested urban areas (e.g. large urban cities, heavily populated countries like China or India)	Urban residents, particularly poorer urban residents, are subjected to heavy air pollution. Commuters to urban areas could be financially impacted and inconvenienced by the expansion of ULEZ.	Connection between pollution and population size
Large geographic areas where people work in urban locations but live outside the city, where there are very limited means of public transport (e.g. London is the initial context, but it could apply to many large urban cities in Canada and the USA, where public transit is less common)	Transportation for commuters is necessary, but lack of public transit requires extensive use of personal vehicles—this causes heavy emissions in the cities and negatively impacts the environment.	Current government regulations related to transportation and reduction of environmental impact Lack of public transport Affordability of housing versus availability of jobs
Smaller geographic areas but largely dense urban areas; people live and work in the cities (e.g. Singapore, Japan)	With a lack of living space, everyone must live and work in the same urban setting; rural living is expensive. Since public transit is available, there is less congestion, but there are still emissions from the public transit system.	Urban design Emissions output of public transit versus personal vehicles
Smaller geographic areas with efficient public transit and a culture of cycling versus driving (e.g. the Netherlands)	Commuters have a choice to use public transit or to use bicycles. While public transit may still have emissions that impact the environment, the common use of bicycles reduces the environmental impact compared to other contexts.	Efficiency and effectiveness of public transit Benefits of a bicycle culture

See comment 5.

See comment 6.

Identify at least three individuals or groups who are affected in some way by the ethical dilemma and what their perspectives might be. What considerations could be researched?

Affected stakeholders	Perspectives	Considerations for research
Commuters	They want to drive their car for convenience, but would be required to pay extra to avoid the ULEZ.	Lifestyle preference and personal convenience versus the common good
Poorer communities in inner-city London (or other large urban areas)	These residents have limited ability to change neighbourhoods/fewer options for affordable housing. If they do commute, they often have older cars and can't afford a new one with lower emissions.	Financial and health impacts
Taxi companies/ professional drivers	Driving and individual vehicle is their livelihood. They can't necessarily afford more environmentally suitable cars.	Impact of regulation costs to commuters/consumers
Cyclists	Cyclists help to reduce pollution, but may still have to breathe in polluted air caused by others. City infrastructure accommodates bicycles. They may receive tax reductions or other financial benefits from cycling instead of driving or using public transport.	Environmentalism Government incentives to comply with regulations
People with mobility needs	They may not be able to use public transit or be able to afford an environmentally suitable vehicle if it does not accommodate their mobility needs.	Health

What format will your reflective project (RP) take, and why?

Newspaper article: Investigative/editorial—for a public audience as this issue affects the wider public.

What are your next steps?

1. Research how other cities have treated traffic congestion and air quality.
2. Research the reasons ULEZ was implemented in the first place.
3. Research the effects ULEZ has had on air quality and public transit.
4. Identify sources to learn more about the contexts and perspectives outlined to understand if expansion of ULEZ-type regulation to other contexts is economically, politically or socially feasible.

RP supervisor:

Approval date:

Example proposal analysis

Comment 1: Note that the issue is clear and brief. The reasons for choosing it are connected to the student personally and contextually.

Comment 2: The student here has related it to their CRS directly and one of the topic areas that is connected to the ethical issue. Remember that this could be a career field that you are *not* studying.

Comment 3: Note the clear research question which is debatable and open. The ethical dilemma and context are also clear. The student frames the ethical considerations by looking for the clash of ethical principles and responsibilities.

Comment 4: Notice here the range of contexts that this student has chosen. They start out with London as an initial context of a large, urban city, but also consider the transference of issues potentially to other major cities as well as smaller but equally dense examples—they are thinking globally and giving diverse connected contexts. Their impact suggestion is clear with initial concise ideas. They have given possible leads where they could research connected ethical issues, which gives the research scope. Some considerations might turn out to be more impactful in terms of research than others, but they have set the parameters of their research area which they can now develop. Notice the balance between considering the larger and smaller geographic areas and that they are not limiting themselves to three contexts in this circumstance.

Comment 5: The outline of contexts has revealed the individuals and groups who are affected by the ethical dilemma, and the student here has empathetically considered the ethical dilemma from their perspective in a concise way. Notice that at this stage, there are more suggestions for some individuals, groups and others which is fine. Again, this might reflect how much the student knows at this stage or indeed pre-empt the biggest impact of the ethical dilemma. However, they will probably notice where the gaps are in their ideas and set an intention for their research to close these gaps.

Comment 6: With the student's initial ideas for a format, the details are brief but they have considered purpose, audience, language and structure already. Their next steps remind us of the inspiration for their RP ethical dilemma and their initial context, but they are already thinking of how what is happening locally affects the global context and given themselves a number of avenues to explore.

4.6.4 Choosing a format for the RP proposal

In Section 4.10, there is a detailed exploration of different formats and how you might choose from them. At this stage of the process, you might feel like doing one of the following:

- You want to get an idea about formats for your project proposal but not overwhelm yourself with information right now. If this is the case, stick to this section's information for now and move on to explore Section 4.10 as the project progresses.
- You are happy to explore the formats in detail now. If this is the case, use this section's outline and cross-reference it with Section 4.10.
- You have a really good idea already for a format you want to explore. If this is the case, then explore the information in this section and Section 4.10 for more information. When you have an overview of the choices and opportunities you have, then focus in on the mode that has captured your attention.

Learner profile

Balanced, open-minded, reflective

Creating a research question and project proposal involves juggling a range of skills. The learner profile characteristics that are most relevant here are 'balanced', 'open-minded' and 'reflective'. All of these characteristics combined will enable you to be open to what you do not know yet, and to reflect on the assumptions and biases you and others might have that stand in the way of being balanced.

Learning journal

Whichever option you pick, remember to reflect on your ideas in your learning journal. Reflect on how you used the learner profile attributes of 'balanced', 'open-minded' and 'reflective' to make a decision. If you think you have not been balanced, open-minded or reflective, then it might suggest that further research is needed.

An introduction to the formats

You will start thinking about what format to use when you are creating your project proposal. A summary of the four different options you can choose from is given in Table 4.16 below.

Table 4.16 Types of format for your RP

Format	Description/examples
Written	The written option takes the form of an essay, but this can be in any style. Expository is best, which means having an intention to explain, educate and support with facts rather than entertain or persuade. This could be (but is not limited to): • an investigative newspaper or magazine article • a personal blog post • a formal letter to an organization about an ethical dilemma and your position • a business proposal that poses a solution to a dilemma • a dissertation-style essay, such as an academic report or case study.
Visual	This includes a variety of images that, when put together, make a statement or tell a story about the ethical dilemma in your chosen career area. You can create the images or collect and curate them or do a mixture of both. This could be (but is not limited to): • a storyboard for a film • a media campaign • a graphic novel • a photo-essay.
Audio	An audio format could be (but is not limited to): • a recording of an interview • a speech • a podcast (these vary hugely in style).
Audio–visual	This format combines the audio and visual choices. This could be (but is not limited to): • a documentary • a short film (live or animated) • a video recording of an interview • a video recording of a speech or presentation (e.g. TEDx talk) • an animated presentation with recorded voiceover • a video podcast.

LEARNING ENGAGEMENT

Create a mind map of a career pathway. Think about your chosen career pathway and what sort of formats might be particularly appropriate, for example:

1 How would a practitioner in that career area choose to communicate?
2 Would there be expectations of good oral or written communication?
3 What sort of tasks would they be expected to complete?

This mind map will give you clues as to what might be an appropriate format for your exploration of an ethical dilemma in this particular career.

Reflection and reflexivity

Consider the PPS, CE and LCS courses as well as DP subjects. What formats and communication styles have inspired you within these areas?

Take time to explore the different format options, even if you think you have a preference already. Have an open mind. This is an exercise in balance and giving an equitable amount of time to exploring different options.

Have a look at the figure below. Your starting point is, 'My career options require skills and knowledge that are more reliant on …' This allows you to consider your career field of interest in terms of written and non-written communication. You can then take into account your preferred learning and assessment styles before considering your preferred resource type. All of these will give you ideas on how you might communicate in both written and non-written formats.

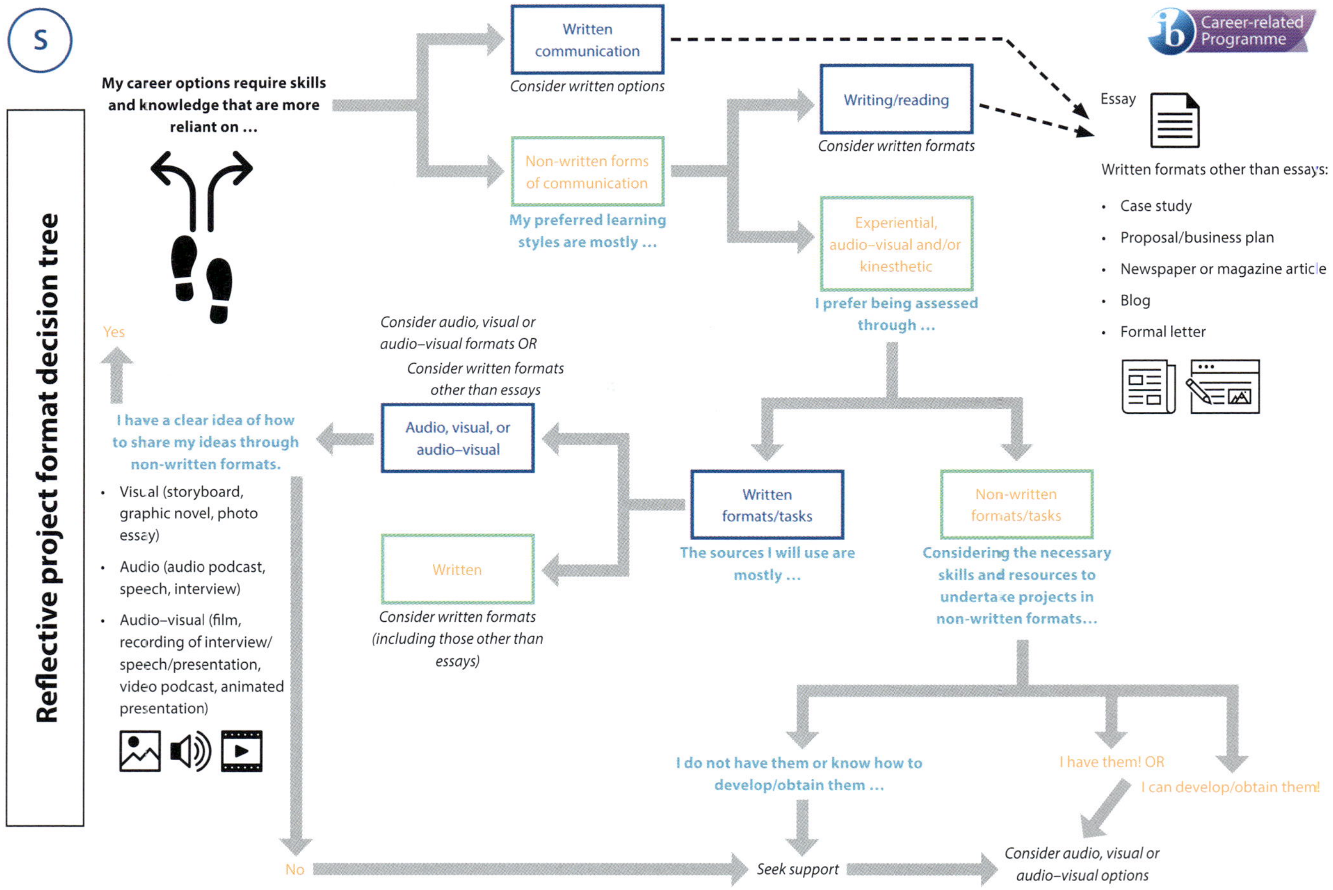

■ Decision tree to help with deciding on your RP format (Source: IB RP TSM, p.46)

PALS

Let's explore further. It's one thing to have preferences and interests within the format options, but it is another to understand their style and conventions. One way to map this out is by looking at purpose, audience, language and structure (PALS). This means keeping the rationale behind your RP central in your mind, along with who your intended audience is, the language you might use to address them and the structure you will use to build your exploration.

■ **Table 4.17** Using PALS to help you decide on the format of your RP

Purpose	Keep the point of your RP at the forefront of your mind. **Ask yourself:** How can I present and explore an ethical dilemma in this format as well as include different perspectives, various contexts and a personal position?
Audience	Consider who it is you are aiming your RP at. Often we can assume it's our teacher or the examiner, but that does not have to be the case with the RP. **Ask yourself:** Is my audience the general public or is it a specific group or organization linked to my career field? How can I communicate my ethical dilemma and personal position to this audience?
Language	What is the best way of communicating your ideas in your RP? Consider what is best for you as a communicator, as well as what will convey your ideas and perspectives most effectively. **Ask yourself:** How can I make the language I use appropriate to the audience, format and my ethical dilemma? Does my format choice use language in a specific way? For example, the use of terminology, style and tone could be formal, descriptive, educational, conversational, informative, concise, detailed, elaborate, technical, etc.
Structure	How will you build your RP brick by brick? Consider how you will construct your RP to best convey your research and critical thinking and how you can use the specific conventions and style of different formats to help you. **Ask yourself:** How can I structure my reflective project in this format so it makes sense? How does this differ depending on the format I choose?

Learning journal

Become PALS with the formats: purpose, audience, language and structure. Your first stop is to look for authentic use of different formats—look for its use elsewhere, whether that be television, film, podcasts, online or print. Once you have an example in front of you, use your learning journal to reflect on the questions in Table 4.17 above. Create a number of mind maps that show your thinking in response to different formats.

You can also use PALS to analyse the effectiveness of your chosen format—have a look at the examples in the following figure.

FORMAT	PURPOSE	AUDIENCE	LANGUAGE	STRUCTURE
Audio product Podcast "You're wrong about"	To entertain and inform about fact-checking popularized 90s media stories	English-speaking audience in their 30s and 40s	Informal register Anecdotal Factual Humorous Sympathetic	Question and answer Intro and outro music Recurring segments Dialogue
Audio product Podcast "Andes. 72 días en la montaña"	To inform about the Andes 72 accident, 50 years later	Spanish-speaking audience interested in learning more about the Andes 72 incident	Factual Sympathetic Formal register	Intro and outro music Monologue Interview
Audio product Podcast "Lorete de Mola"	To inform about current Mexican political events	Primarily Mexican citizens interested in learning more about contemporary political issues	Informal register Conversational tone Figurative language Critical Factual	Intro and outro music Recurring segments Monologue and dialogue

■ Using PALS to analyse the appropriateness of a project's format (Source: IB RP TSM, p.46)

4.6.5 Creating the research proposal

Once you have understood the requirements of the RP, narrowed down to a particular focus and arrived at a research question, you are well on your way. You are then prepared to create the project proposal, as we explored in the previous section.

■ **Table 4.18** Steps involved in the preparation and planning phase

Phase of RP	Detailed steps involved

Preparation and planning	• preparation and building of background knowledge
	• identification of an ethical dilemma related to the CRS or career field of interest
	• peer discussions
	• **research plan and project proposal**
	  • Refine the ethical dilemma/research question.
	  • **Consider and articulate approach to the RP through the creation of a research plan and submission of a proposal to the supervisor.**
	  • Determine a research approach and potential resources. (The act of determining a research approach and potential resources involves a review of the literature surrounding your ethical dilemma.)
	  • Decide on a project format.

■ **Table 4.19** Steps involved in creating and submitting a research proposal

Create and submit a research proposal	• Outline the project's dilemma, research objectives, methodology, perspectives and contexts to be explored, and reasoning for the format chosen in the research proposal. • Include a timeline and potential resources in the research proposal. • Ensure that the research adheres to ethical guidelines. • Refine or adjust the approach to the RP following feedback and guidance from the RP supervisor.

Once you have decided on the topic, you can then decide whether there are enough resources out there to support a potential research project before you finalize your proposal. This is called a 'literature review' and the methods for doing this are explored in the following section. You will use this literature review to create your research proposal. As you embark on the research process, you will keep a detailed list of sources and their relevance and reliability. We call this an annotated bibliography.

The more you read, the more you will spot particular themes and perspectives emerging and the way that different sources may or may not support these. To review your sources, you don't need to go through each source individually and mark it out of ten, as that would be tedious. However, using a thematic approach, such as taking certain perspectives, individuals, cultures or communities that have struck you as interesting, and using tools to analyse where sources are relevant and how far they might support a certain theme will help you greatly. You can then see whether you lack credible sources in particular areas or in the overall research area, and you might also start to see how your whole structure might unfurl.

What to do with a disappointing research proposal

If you have a question in mind but have found limited (or maybe too many) sources or ideas surrounding it, this is the time to stop and revise your focus. It might feel disappointing, but proceeding with a question that you know deep down does not really work will set you up for a frustrating and difficult time. However, your work is not wasted; changing direction and adapting is crucial to reflection. You might need to refine or refocus your search area just a little to get the question on the right track.

For example, your first research proposal could emerge like this. Say you are interested in the sports industry as a career (this may or may not connect with your CRS). You centred your topic on the doping laws surrounding the Olympic Games. However, your first research proposal highlighted an overwhelming wealth of sources all related to this topic, with no real dilemma identified. This is not a disaster, however, as you noticed that some of the sources you uncovered pointed towards a potential controversy in acceptable testosterone levels in athletes of both genders in the last Olympic Games. Yes, you need to review your research proposal, but none of your initial research has gone to waste.

4.6.6 Summary

- Developing a research question deserves time. Use the checklist in this section to make sure it is suitable.
- A good question generates the possibility of exploring multiple perspectives and not just describing the history of an ethical dilemma.
- The last stage of the preparation and planning phase is creating a project proposal with an outline of your dilemma, your intention for research, perspectives and contexts.
- Your research proposal will also get you exploring the best way to communicate your RP in terms of formats. Consider the communication styles and formats that relate most to the career field of interest that your ethical dilemma is based in.

4.7 Developing research skills

INQUIRY QUESTIONS

- Where do you start becoming a researcher?
- What research methods can help you?
- What sort of evidence are you looking for?
- What is the assessment criteria asking you?
- How can you synthesize and analyse sources?
- How can you use AI for research?

Learner profile

Principled, balanced, inquirer, thinker

Developing research skills means working with academic integrity, so the learner profile characteristic of 'principled' is central. To research means to be curious and to be an 'inquirer' and the more you research, the more you must aim to present your research of the ethical dilemma with fairness, accuracy and depth. This is where the characteristics of 'balanced' and 'thinker' become important.

4.7.1 Embarking on the research journey

In the last section, you explored how to create a good research question and communicate your research plan in a project proposal to discuss with your supervisor. This section helps you move from the preparation and planning phase to the research and analysis phase of your reflective project (RP). It might be that you have already dipped into this section to explore research methods ahead of discussing your research plan and project proposal with your supervisor.

The learning journal comes into its own in this part of your RP journey, as your initial thinking begins to change. Be ready to see this coming out of your reflective and reflexive moments.

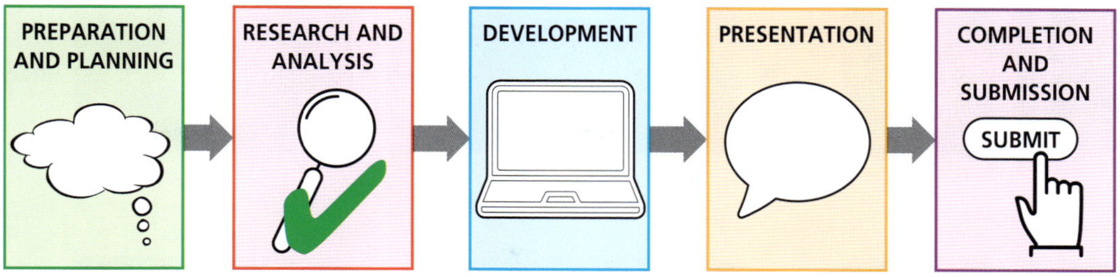

■ The RP process

■ **Table 4.20**

Phase of RP	Detailed steps involved
Research and analysis	● **conduct research** ● Use the research methodology determined with the RP supervisor. ● Conduct research. ● Record notes in the learning journal for use in creating the project. ● **reflection point** ● Reflect on the understanding of the information found in the research. ● Develop a personal and critical position on the ethical dilemma. ● Record reflections in the learning journal. ● **supervisor feedback** ● On completion of the research, meet with the RP supervisor to explore current thinking and progress. ● Receive guidance and feedback. ● **reflection point** ● Reflect on the RP supervisor feedback. ● Determine whether any action is appropriate. ● Record reflections and any actions taken in the learning journal.

The importance of academic integrity

Research is the process you go through to collect information and data in an academically honest way. Making your knowledge, understanding and thinking completely visible throughout your RP is at the heart of keeping academic integrity at the heart of the whole process. The marking criteria and the project's design as a body of work with a separate reflection make it clear that it is not just about what you know, but how you have constructed your ideas and why you accept or reject specific perspectives. In a technological world that is constantly changing, the way we learn is also changing and it is hard to know how to use sources. By consistently learning and applying research skills, you will see how knowledge is constructed, its ideas and values, and how you construct your knowledge and find your voice.

> Research enables you to find out what you think. If you lose sight of this at any point then you know that you need to re-evaluate how you are researching. For example, AI can be a great tool to help you get your research going, but don't let it take over.

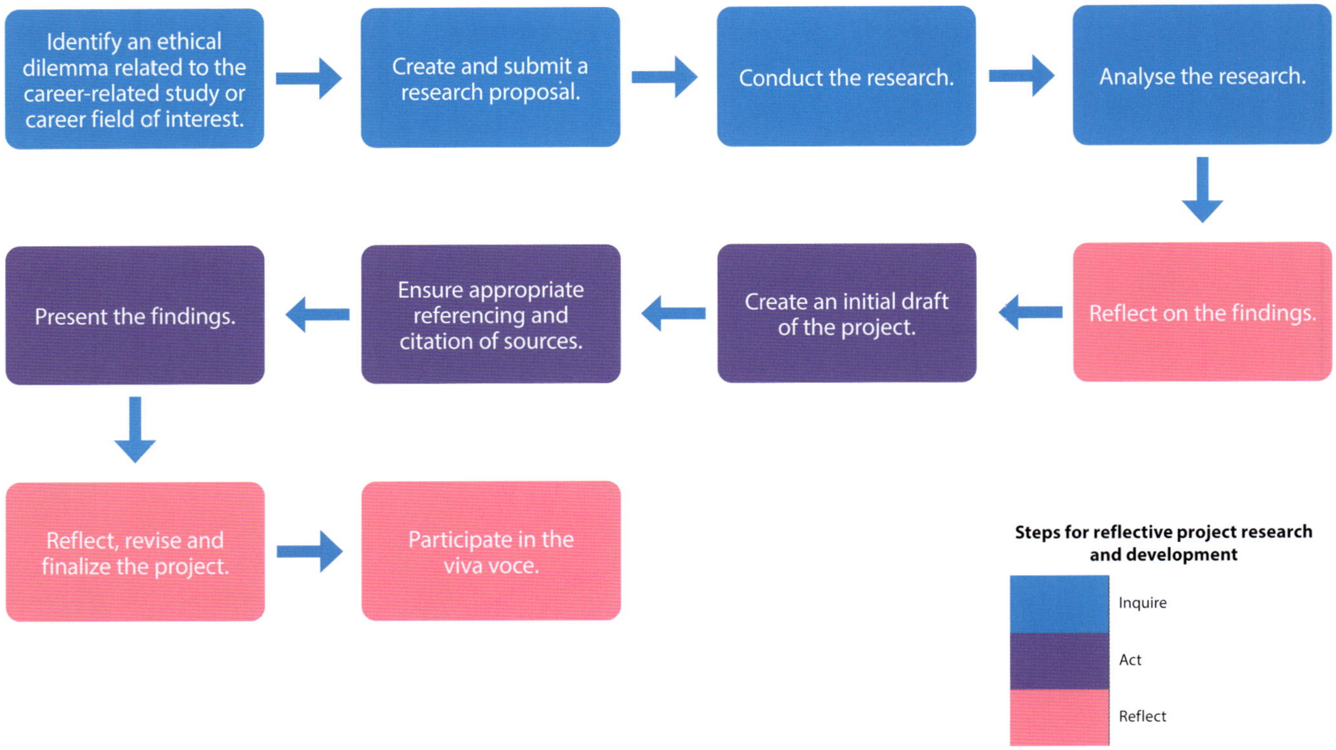

■ Remember to use all stages of the inquiry cycle continuously. Don't forget to reflect! (Source: IB RP TSM, p.31)

Understanding research in the marking criteria

You need to be aware of the different criteria you will be assessed against that link directly to the research process. The questions below will help you to check whether you are exploring the criteria in the right way.

■ **Table 4.21** Exploring the research criteria (Source: IB RP guide, p.32)

Criterion	Description	Questions to ask
A	Excellent career-related ethical dilemma, balanced range of perspectives and variety of contexts.	• Is my ethical dilemma clear, controversial and the main focus throughout? • Does it relate to a career-related field? • Do I explore different perspectives in a balanced way? • Have I used examples from a range of contexts?
B	Quality research, range of resources, knowledge and understanding.	• Have I demonstrated that my research is both broad in scope and deep in detail? • Have I used a range of resources? • Can I demonstrate the knowledge and understanding I gained from the research?
C	Analysis and synthesis of research, discussion of relevant findings, justification of personal position, thinking supported by reasoning and linked to research, impact of the dilemma and own position.	• Have I analysed and synthesised my research? • Have I identified and justified a personal position? • Have I clearly given reasons for my thinking and linked this with relevant and quality evidence? • Have I considered the impact of the dilemma and my own personal position?

Begin your research

When undertaking your research, the IB guidelines suggest that you:

- conduct a literature review to understand the contexts and perspectives related to the ethical dilemma
- evaluate resources for bias and relevance
- keep notes and create an annotated bibliography to ensure correct citations and to document key findings
- collect data for primary research, according to the chosen research methods (e.g. surveys, interviews, observations.

(Source: IB RP guide, p.32)

Keep an annotated bibliography as an active document

Whether you keep a digital or physical learning journal, keep a document running for the entirety of your research process where you consistently record the sources you are using in alphabetical order.

An annotated bibliography is a list of accurately cited sources in alphabetical order. However, in your notes you can also annotate each source with a summary of how the content connects to the ethical dilemma and an evaluation of its relevance and reliability.

An annotated bibliography can:

- allow you to keep track of research and whether you are accessing enough sources
- encourage you to think critically about the sources
- allow you to spot early on if you have concerns about certain sources
- help you to see quickly if a source is of use to you
- help you to justify your use of particular sources, both to your supervisor and to the examiner
- save time
- enable you to develop critical thinking skills in selecting and evaluating source material.

4.7.2 What is the difference between primary, secondary and tertiary research?

Actually, the process starts in reverse with tertiary research! Since tertiary sources synthesize information gathered from other sources and are often in easily accessible and concise formats, they are a great place to start. Tertiary sources include encyclopedias, chronologies and textbooks. They are good for an information overview and finding out some of the key words at play, but not for getting to the heart of an issue. However, looking at the bibliographies that accompany them may give you the names of experts you could research later.

The research you may be most familiar with is the use of secondary sources, as you have probably already read some journal or newspaper articles in preparation. These texts analyse, review or restate information in primary resources or other secondary sources. Examples include biographies, scholarly articles, review articles, historical studies or literature reviews. However, you need to be aware that secondary sources vary greatly in quality (see the learning engagement later in this section for tips on how to test the usefulness of a source).

Primary research is conducted by someone directly. You can quote or refer to primary research that someone else has created or conduct your own primary research. Types of primary research might vary more than your think. Scientific primary research could be data sets, technical reports or experimental research results. However, primary sources in other fields could be diaries, narratives, autobiographies, memoirs, speeches, novels, plays, poems, works of art and popular culture.

Potential useful data

> **Key term**
>
> ◆ **Data:** Facts and statistics collected together for reference or analysis.

As you can see from the definition, **data** does not just mean numbers, graphs and charts in the form of statistics. In philosophy, data can mean things that are known or assumed as facts, which make the basis of reasoning or calculation. Data can therefore also mean information and facts, and these can come from multiple places and not just essays, books or articles, such as:

- an interview with an expert on your issue in question that has been published in an online or print form
- an interview that you have conducted yourself with a reputable authority
- statistics from credible governmental, non-governmental and professional organizations
- documentaries
- internet sites from reputable authorities such as universities, museums and non-governmental organizations.

See further on in this section about how you can use technology and AI as a tool in how you sort and present your data.

Common pitfalls

Primary and secondary research pitfalls:

- Make sure you use the data you find. This might sound obvious, but the information you collect should back up and synthesize with your ideas in your main project. Examiners are not necessarily obliged to read the appendices, so do not put anything important to your main analysis in there.
- Avoid using long quotes. More importantly, avoid using long quotes and then not analysing them. If the quote is over 3–4 sentences then it really needs to be set apart on its own as a block quote. This is really just copying and plagiarism software will pick up on it.
- Avoid conducting small surveys where you ask your classmates or immediate community a few questions. Although this can be good for gaining an insight into some initial perspectives, it is not proof enough to add any sense of depth or weight to your main argument.

Producing your own primary research

To produce your own data, it must be scientifically valid, which means it must be conducted on a convincing scale and be representative of the community you are studying. If you would like to carry out your own primary research then consider the following tips to help you succeed:

- First, decide what the purpose of carrying out your own primary research is and confirm that your own research is absolutely necessary to the issue and dilemma you are exploring.
- Work out who you will ask, what you will ask them and why you will ask them it.
- Make the questions count; take time to create the questions using the Socratic method detailed in Section 4.8.2.

- Know the difference between the types of data. Quantitative tends to be numerical and more scientific, with structured data collection and statistical analysis; qualitative tends to be non-numerical data, such as interviews, case studies and open-ended surveys.

Critically examine your research from the very beginning

Research needs critical examination. As you start to read, remember you are in charge. Have a simple colour-coding process for key areas you are looking for and write down any key words, phrases or ideas that might be helpful in future research and/or relate to the RP guidelines.

You will also need to assess every source for bias. Take time to reflect in your learning journal about the literature you have uncovered. You can also use the tips and activities in this section to help you with this reflection before you present your literature review to your supervisor.

LEARNING ENGAGEMENT

Scan reading

Practise scan reading to help you work out if a source will be useful. This can often be done quicker than you think. (Later in this section we'll look at how technology can be used as a tool to help you work out if a source is relevant for you.) Find a text source such as a journal article and follow the steps below:

- First, flick through—scanning.
- Look at the index.
- Look at the headlines.
- Look at the pictures.
- Look at any summaries at the beginning or end of sections.
- Stop and glance at anything that interests you.
- Jot down anything you already know—key words.
- Produce a mind map to develop the ideas further.
- Always make notes and ask yourself questions.
- Don't forget to colour-code!

Finding interesting, diverse and useful sources, and identifying validity and bias

As you look at sources more deeply, you need to interrogate the author and ask questions as you are reading. The questions below will help to make you a more active reader and might give you more confidence in how to use a text. Ask yourself:

- How do I know this is true?
- If it is true, what else follows?
- Is the conclusion justified? How do I know?
- What is being presumed or assumed here?
- Is this fact or opinion, and what evidence do I have?
- If it's fact, is it always true? If it's opinion, can I trust the source?
- Are there any (better) examples to illustrate this argument?
- Is this logical?
- What is my personal opinion and has it changed? Can it be justified?
- What new points have been made for my topic?
- What is essential to know and what is just padding?

Contextualize and synthesize your sources

Two important parts of the research process are contextualizing and synthesizing:

- To contextualize something means to analyse a word or event in terms of the words or concepts surrounding it. The issue you have chosen is not in isolation; by considering local, global and cultural influences currently connected to it, you are contextualizing it.
- We synthesize when we combine ideas from a range of sources in order to group and present common ideas or arguments, as well as develop and strengthen our own arguments. Once you have read a range of sources, you will start to notice ideas that connect in some ways and this is when you can start to synthesize this information.

Recognizing growth and gaps in knowledge and understanding

You will need to maintain the same level of focus on your dilemma while you research as you will while you are writing. It is important to organize your ideas as you go so you can start to see your arguments emerging, as well as spot where you need more help.

- Keep to the topic at all times and keep going back to your question.
- Gather together all the research you have done—notes from books, sources from the internet, etc. When you have your notes together, try mind-mapping the key ideas.
- Now start to add to the mind map, putting ideas together in groups and consider how they connect.
- Check: Are your points focused on the question or even suggesting a solution?
- Check: Have you considered the significance of local, global and cultural influences?
- You might be able to see the introduction, middle and end of your RP emerging already.

Assessing the credibility of sources

Here's a way of building on your understanding of bias and assessing the reliability of a source, as well as developing your critical thinking by using the mnemonic 'RAVEN':

R **Reputation:** The reputation of the publication/author. How might this affect, positively or negatively, the reliability of the source? Has the source been reliable in the past or has it distorted the truth?

A **Ability to see:** Is it a primary or secondary source? Is the author, or their own sources, in a position to know what they are talking about?

V **Vested interest:** Does the source have a 'hidden agenda' in presenting one side of the argument as more compelling than the other? Do they have anything at stake personally or professionally in the issue?

E **Expertise:** What are the author/publication's credentials? Are they an expert in the field on which they are writing? Have they used expert witnesses?

N **Neutrality:** Is there any reason to suspect bias? For example, newspapers have a 'leaning' towards a political stance.

(Adapted from R. Brink-Budgen and J. Thawaites (2012), *OCR AS Critical Thinking*)

LEARNING ENGAGEMENT

Now use RAVEN to look at a source you have chosen:

- What is it claiming?
- What information are you using from it?
- Is it fact, opinion or speculation?
- How did you make this judgement?
- If it is factual, how do you check the accuracy of the facts given?
- If it is opinion or speculation, how reliable is it and why?

Learning journal

The project proposal quadrant

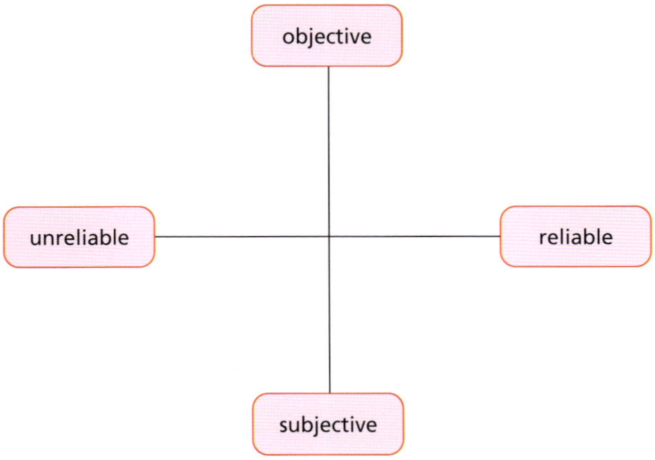

Project proposal quadrant

Using 'The quadrant' is a good way of evaluating the strengths and weaknesses of your sources and deciding where you might need more information. Draw the quadrant on a large piece of paper for your learning journal and consider each of the sources you have used so far: look at how relevant they are to your topic and their reliability using the criteria in this section. This will give you an overview of your work as you go along and inform your next steps.

You could project the quadrant onto a screen or wall and use sticky notes with your sources on them so you can move ideas around and make decisions about which sources to remove—this is a great discussion to have with your supervisor.

Remember to take a photo for your learning journal.

LEARNING ENGAGEMENT

Research skills presentation

Working with a partner or a small group, see how much you have understood about research. Below are research skills discussed in this section that you will need in this research process. Discuss all of them together and make a poster with tips on how to be successful in 3–5 of the skills you think are the most important.

- Collect primary, secondary and tertiary research.
- Differentiate between types of texts.
- Find interesting and original sources.
- Read a text effectively.
- Use technology ethically as a tool.
- Ask meaningful questions.
- Make notes that matter.
- Collect and analyse data.
- Evaluate the bias.
- Carry out a literature review.
- Make connections between texts.
- Use sources to contextualize an issue.
- Synthesize information in your notes.
- Recognize growth and gaps in knowledge.

4.7.3 Using technology and AI safely, responsibly and effectively

It is hard to put in writing exactly how we should be using technology when it has become apparent how quickly it all changes. However, there are some things that are always true when it comes to transparent and ethical research, and the emergence of AI just means we need to be even clearer with our use.

Learner profile

Principled

Part of being an IB student is upholding the values in the learner profile, so being principled is crucial here.

You will need to have the mindset of a young adult who actively places themselves in their learning engagement, having agency and confidently demonstrating your academic integrity and ethical use of technology along the way. The responsibility is yours to demonstrate your authenticity and not the responsibility of your school to prove your lack of it.

The advice from the IB is clear here on how to research, cite and reference honestly. Look at the following description and note that many of these expectations existed before AI began to take the spotlight.

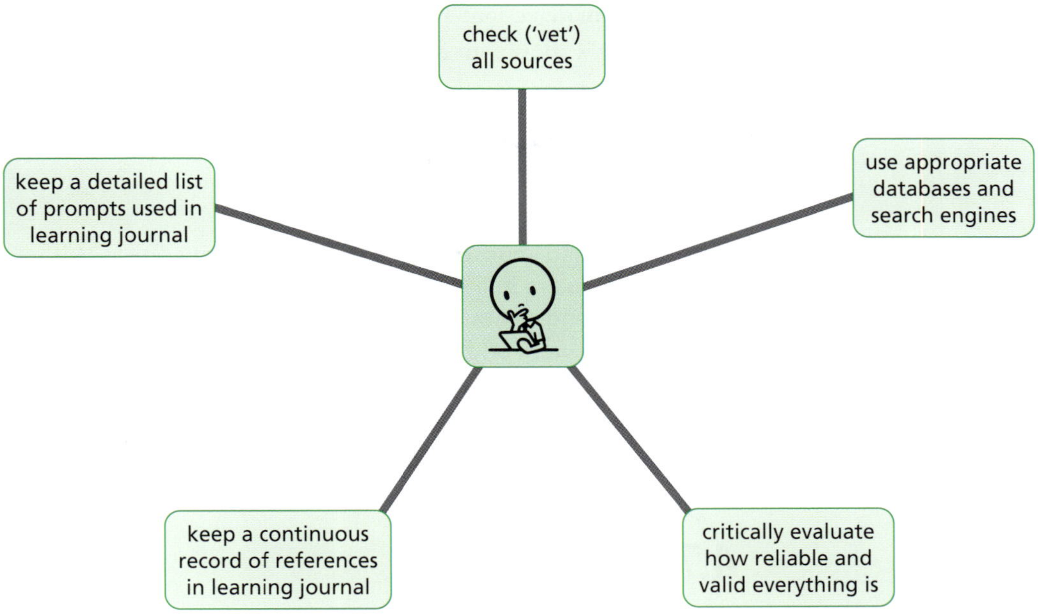

■ Using AI effectively

Using AI for research

Remember that, unlike print sources and other resources made by humans, you do not know where the information from AI has come from or if it is accurate. Also be aware of the role that bias plays. Seven key skills when using AI for research are outlined below:

1 **Prompt engineering:** It is important to consider how you are using prompts and you should research tips on doing this effectively.

2 **Generating ideas at the start:** Use internet search engines or generative AI tools to find ethical issues related to your career interest. You can build from here to connect ethical dilemmas and potential contexts and perspectives you might consider. Remember though, this is just the very start and you have to do the analysis and critical thinking of research yourself.

3 **Summarizing research:** You may find a lengthy academic article with no abstract that summarizes the whole piece. AI tools can be helpful here to work out if a source is worth further investigation. Using it this way can also help you create an annotated bibliography for your literature review.

3 **Language support:** You may be looking at research that is not in your first or best language, so using AI translation tools can be helpful.

4 **Data analysis:** If you are conducting your own primary research, then AI can help you visualize this in a supportive way. You might think about this in particular for your presentation, but also with your choice of format, which might be particularly visual.

5 **Writing and editing:** Communication is an important part of the RP and is assessed in Criterion D. Many of us already use writing assistants to help us with grammar, punctuation, structure and word choice. However, you might consider using this tool further if you are working in a particularly creative format to present your RP, as you can research particular stylistic conventions you might use in your writing or audio–visual presentation. Tread carefully though, as although you can use a tool to make creative suggestions you might use, you may not use generative AI to write or create your project.

6 **Project management:** You might be finding the RP process daunting and hard to manage, so there are AI project management tools that can help you stay organized.

7 **Plagiarism detection:** This is not new in schools and you already know that you must prove that your work is your own. You can use plagiarism software yourself to check you are citing sources correctly and not leaving them uncited by accident.

LEARNING ENGAGEMENT

Creating your own school AI policy

First of all, read your school's academic integrity policy. With a partner, group or as a class, you are going to consider how you might add instructions on how to use technology and AI ethically, so that students, parents and teachers might understand. Present your work and what you believe is the best practice for effective technology and AI use to a new audience. Your teacher could organize a presentation to a younger school year or another staff member. Fill your presentation with tips for using technology as a tool and how to be clear when you have used it.

4.7.4 Summary

- At the heart of all research methods is honesty and accuracy. Your learning journal is intended as a system that, when used regularly to reflect on your research, can prove your RP is your own work.
- Break up the research process into manageable chunks. This is an essential part of all project management, whatever the context.
- You can see the impact of your research through the assessment criteria, especially A, B and C.
- Find a system for evaluating the credibility of sources, such as RAVEN, build up your annotated bibliography and discuss them with your supervisor.
- Be very clear about how you can use AI tools to help you with your research and record your use of them clearly.

4.8 Giving and receiving feedback

INQUIRY QUESTIONS

- How can you give feedback to your peers and act upon feedback yourself?
- How can your supervisor help you and how can you get feedback from them?
- How can you receive feedback from your peers and give feedback yourself?

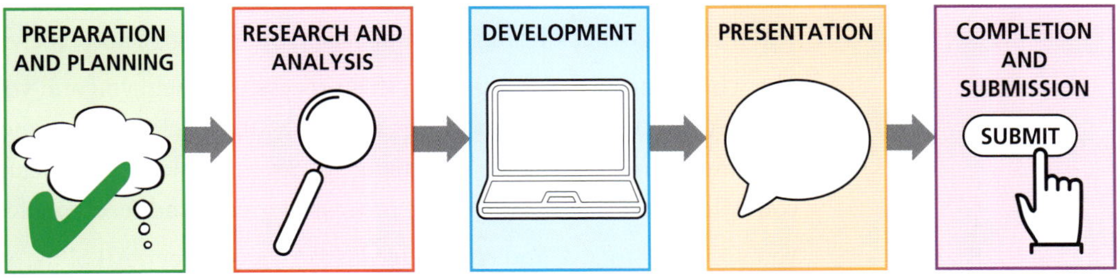

■ The RP process

■ **Table 4.22**

Phase of RP	Detailed steps involved

Preparation and planning	● **preparation and building of background knowledge**
	  ● Develop research and self-management skills.
	  ● Establish foundational knowledge for applied ethics and intercultural understanding.
	  ● Learn how to give, receive and respond to feedback.
	  ● Explore and practise different types of reflection and reflexivity.
	  ● Confirm understanding of the requirements and criteria for the RP.
	● identification of an ethical dilemma
	● **peer discussions**
	  ● Discuss important topics related to the RP process with peers and supervisor.
	  ● Give and receive feedback early in the RP journey.
	  ● Topics for discussion might include how to move beyond researching an issue to identify an ethical dilemma; how to construct a research question; different approaches you might take to update your learning journal; how to use technology effectively and ethically; format options; clarification of requirements; sharing of research plans; current progress and thinking.
	● research plan and project proposal

Peer/RP supervisor feedback	● **reflection point**
	(The feedback points identified in the guide should be considered as the minimum expectation; however, additional opportunities may be added.)
	  ● Meet at an appropriate point after the initial planning and research.
	  ● Peer and/or supervisor conversations on relevant topics allow for feedback, reflection and progress towards successful completion of the project.
	(Topics for discussion and feedback at the reflection point might include the project proposals, planning, research methodology, contexts and perspectives relevant to identified dilemmas, and format choices.)

4.8.1 The importance of feedback

What does feedback mean to you? When we talk about meaningful feedback, we mean the act of giving helpful information about how to make something better. In this case, feedback will help you develop your reflective project (RP) plan, refine your research question, work out your research methods, develop your whole project and reflect on your learning.

> Really supportive feedback involves criticism as, in this context, criticism is a balance of communicating both the strengths and drawbacks of a piece of work.

This section will help you understand why giving and receiving feedback is an essential part of the RP—both knowing how to give feedback kindly and how and when to respond to it. You will receive feedback from your supervisor, but also give and receive feedback with your peers.

The whole purpose of feedback in this process is to help you and your peers improve your work. ATL skills play a part in this too, as the feedback you give and receive generally requires focusing on areas of self-management, research, thinking and social communication skills, and you will use all those skills in the process of giving and receiving feedback too.

You will need to give and receive feedback in any career. All of us, at one time or another, have experienced feedback in a negative way (if you haven't, then this is very unusual!). So we already know, first-hand, the impact it can have if you do not prepare and lead with kindness.

4.8.2 How to give and receive feedback

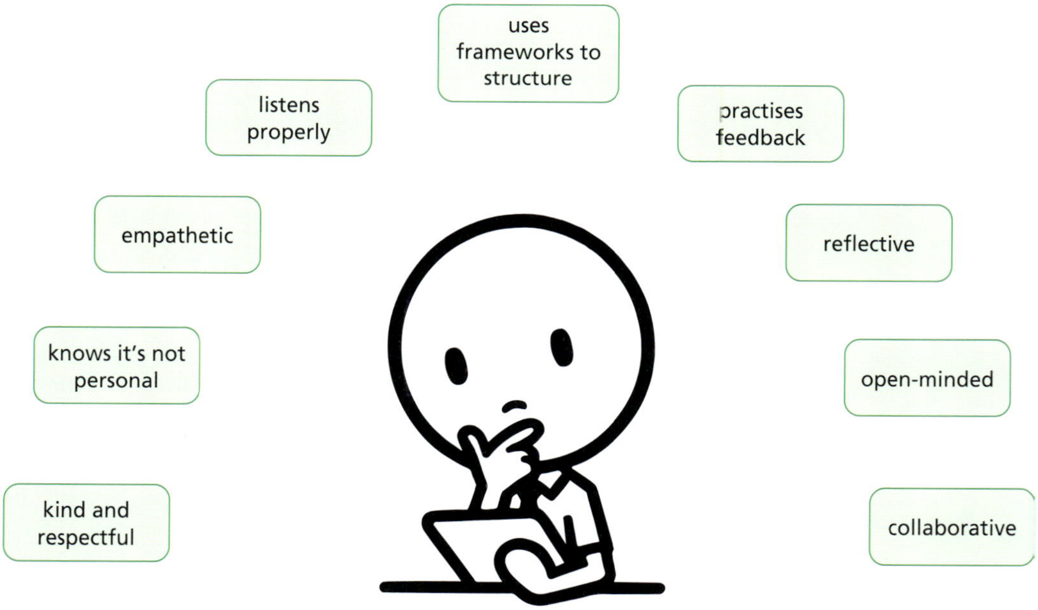

■ The supportive peer

The general rules

It's important to establish clear expectations with each other at the start. As Brene Brown famously stated, 'clear is kind, unclear is unkind'. So we are leading with the idea that honesty does not mean being brutal with your thoughts. This leads to another understanding in that learning can only happen when you feel safe in the space you are working in, so work with your class to agree on the mindset and manner in which you will give and receive feedback. It is important to follow these general rules for feedback to be constructive:

Top tip!

Assume the best intent and be open-minded!

- Lead with kindness.
- Being helpful is being specific; being specific is being helpful.
- Suggesting improvements does not have to be delivered in a negative way.
- Always clarify that it is your perspective and you offer suggestions, rather than dictating how someone else's work should be done.
- Being all positive and giving no suggestions is as unhelpful (albeit a softer approach) as being negative and overly critical. True criticism is balanced.

LEARNING ENGAGEMENT

Structuring your thoughts

This thinking routine of 'protocol' from Harvard Project Zero can be used anywhere you are asked for feedback and is not unique to the RP. Start from the bottom and climb up the ladder. The more you practise, the more confident you will be in your communication skills. Try it out for a few minutes—pair up and swap pieces of recent schoolwork and give feedback to each other using this ladder.

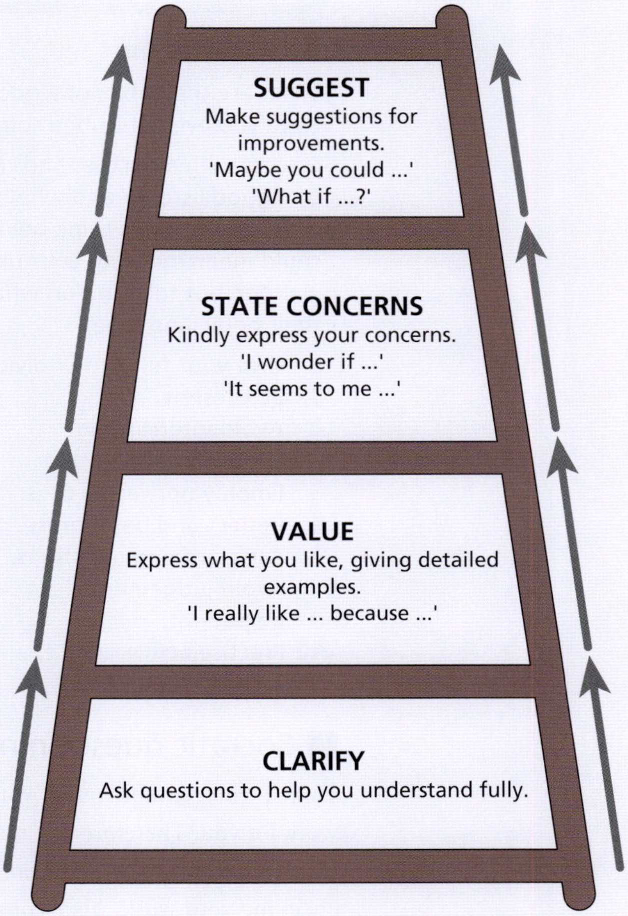

The ladder of feedback (Adapted from Harvard Project Zero)

Learning journal

'Clear is kind; unclear is unkind.'

Research this saying from Brene Brown. Reflect on how her ideas about feedback are relevant to your RP experience, and how giving feedback well is an important part of being a leader. Make a note in your learning journal of how you can implement some of her advice.

Top tip!

During feedback (whether you are giving or receiving feedback), create a positive and kind atmosphere and use active-listening strategies. This way, you will be more open to other ideas and others will be more open to you.

How to make the most of feedback from your peers

When you are preparing to receive feedback, it's good to remember that this is not an exercise in being right or wrong, but in being open to suggestions. Everything you hear will be suggestions with your best interests at the centre. Nothing is set in stone so there is no need to be defensive. You may listen to feedback and feel wholeheartedly that you have been misunderstood or that it is incorrect. You could not listen properly and concentrate on what you want to say in response. Or you could take a step back, reserve judgement and listen. There is always something to take away in someone else's suggestions, no matter how you might initially feel about them.

LEARNING ENGAGEMENT

Active listening

What are the habits of a good listener? How do you know if you are a good listener? Have you ever described someone as a terrible listener? What did they do?

Discuss with a partner and create a 'compare and contrast' table of the characteristics of a good listener and what they do and don't do. Use the suggestions below and develop what you think being a good listener would look like. For example, 'be present' could mean ignoring your phone if it buzzes, and being aware of not letting your mind wander, but focusing on what the speaker is saying both verbally and non-verbally (with their body language).

1. Give your full and undivided attention.
2. Be present.
3. Avoid interrupting.
4. Show empathy.
5. Employ nonverbal cues.
6. Reflect and paraphrase.
7. Ask clarifying questions.
8. Avoid judgement.
9. Be patient.
10. Practise active silence.

Socratic questioning model

To help you get more out of your peers' suggestions, it helps to know how questions can work for you. Therefore you might employ the 'Socratic questioning' model, which contains six types of questions. You can also use this in discussions with your supervisor and when checking your work. Also, consider the actions you might take if your peers ask you these types of questions.

For example, let's say you have been given feedback by another student that your chosen question is too descriptive, but you disagree with them. You could ask them, 'Why do you say that?' and you could also ask yourself, 'What would be the consequence of assuming that the question is actually too descriptive?'

Table 4.23 The Socratic questioning model

Questions you could ask …	
… for clarification	• Why do you say that? • How does this relate to our discussion?
… that probe assumptions	• What is being assumed here? • How can you verify or disprove that assumption?
… that probe reason and evidence	• What might be an example? • What is … analogous to? • What do you think causes this to happen? Why?
… about viewpoints and perspectives	• What would be an alternative viewpoint? • What is another way to look at it? • Would you explain why it is necessary or beneficial, and who benefits? • Why is … the best? • What are the strengths and weaknesses of …? • How are … and … similar? • What is a counterargument for …?
… that probe implications and consequences	• What generalizations can you make? • What are the consequences of that assumption? • What are you implying? • How does … affect …? • How does … tie in with what you have said before?
… about questions	• What was the point of this question? • Why do you think I asked this question? • How does … apply to everyday life/different cultures/global and local context?

Top tip!

Just as you are exploring multiple perspectives in the RP, remember you can always look at feedback from multiple perspectives too.

LEARNING ENGAGEMENT

Filtering the feedback

You can give and receive feedback with your peers at various points of the preparation and planning phase. However, it can be difficult to know how to respond to feedback; not everything suggested will be helpful or actionable. You can do two things with feedback: first, consider it properly and sincerely; second, be very honest with yourself about your answers. Leave your ego at the door.

In this activity you can take the feedback you have been given and consider what has merit. Follow these steps:

1. Form a small group and each discuss a piece of research you have found, how it connects to your project and whether you plan to use or not.
2. Give 2–3 pieces of specific feedback to each other about the way you made that decision, your research methods and suggestions for next steps.
3. Then individually reflect on the feedback given, filtering it using these criteria:
    - Does the feedback ring true with concerns you already had? Is there something more to investigate here?
    - Is the person who gave feedback in a position to know about this ethical dilemma and context? (This is not an essential—actually, a fresh perspective from someone without the subject expertise can be very insightful.)
    - Can you try out any of the ideas suggested?
    - Are there credible and relevant sources that endorse anything that has been suggested?
    - Could this provide another angle or perspective and bring new complexity to your ethical dilemma?
    - Does this make you want to reconsider your focus?

4.8.3 Your RP supervisor

First of all, let's discuss what being a supervisor means. Your supervisor's main role is as a guide and mentor. They act as a sounding board, motivator and monitor of progress. They not only help keep you on track, but they also become so familiar with what you are doing that they can sign off your work as yours to the IB. Most importantly for this section, they also give you consistent and timely feedback and help you to be reflective.

What a supervisor is required to do:

- Give you 3–6 hours of supervision. There are clear benchmarks to be met in your process but you will also have more informal meetings.
- Comment on one completed draft.
- Conduct a *viva voce* (final interview) with you as a last reflection.

What your supervisor cannot do:

- Edit or massively annotate your draft.
- Correct spelling or punctuation mistakes.
- Correct information, data or statistics.
- Rewrite, reorder or reproduce any of your RP draft.
- Correct your bibliography or any citations.

Unsatisfactory and unhelpful relationships with a supervisor happen when you:

- assume they will chase you for meetings and wait for them to contact you
- assume they will teach you and lead the way in your project
- go to a meeting without preparing ahead and without showing motivation.

If you want a useful and supportive experience with your supervisor:

- Make sure you know, early on, what to expect and how you are going to work together.
- Find the best times to meet and best methods to communicate with each other.
- Understand that if you do not fulfil your side of the agreement, the supervisor will have to discuss your lack of progress with the RP or CP coordinator and seek wider support.
- Equally, do not be scared of making sure you get the support you need and, if it is not there, then do talk to your mentor, CP coordinator or wider support network.

The RP supervisor role

The RP supervisor plays a pivotal role in supporting and guiding students throughout their RP learning journey. They help students understand the nature of the RP and its requirements. They help the students to plan their research, recommend appropriate research methods and sources, and provide timely feedback as students develop their project.

Students are expected to complete the RP in a self-directed manner, but as it is a longer-term, in-depth project, a key aspect of the supervisor's role is to keep students engaged and motivated over this extended length of time.

While each phase of the learning journey includes specific opportunities for RP supervisor support, throughout the learning journey and during every phase supervisors should:

- ensure that students are responsible for their own work
- reinforce and cultivate all five types of ATL skills
- encourage students to ask for guidance and feedback
- ensure that students comply with the ethical guidelines for the RP

- monitor the progress of their students' RPs to offer guidance and confirm the authenticity of student work submitted for assessment
- encourage students to reflect meaningfully during the process and to keep their learning journal updated
- promote a learning environment where students offer and receive respectful feedback.

(Source: IB RP TSM)

Preparation and planning

- Check that the students understand ethics and its relation to their career-related field or subject of study.
- Discuss with students:
  - the nature of the RP
  - the most appropriate research methods to use
  - the formal requirements.
- Host review point(s) to help students complete a reflective project proposal form by devising a well-formulated and focused research question through discussion.
- Advise student planning for collecting resources, contemplating research methods and critically evaluating research methodologies.
- Provide feedback on the project proposal.
- Check that the students understand the assessment criteria and academic integrity.
- Guide and facilitate peer feedback.
- Discuss the different RP options and encourage students to choose the format that best fits their interests and skills.
- Promote agency and self-management skills by explaining the RP pathway and help students design an outline and timeline for their project.

Research and analysis

- Ensure that students comply with ethical standards of research.
- Ensure that students understand the academic integrity policy.
- Ensure that students are responsible for their own work.
- Ensure that students have access to exemplars, guides, and resources on referencing and writing.
- Guide students to evaluate the reliability and bias of sources.
- Help students with challenges they may face as they conduct research.
- Monitor students' progress to keep them on track with their research plan and aware of their timeline.
- Ensure that students understand the assessment criteria as they relate to research and analysis.
- Host review point(s) with students to check progress and provide feedback.

Development

- Ensure that students are aware of all requirements for the RP.
- Ensure that students understand the academic integrity policy.
- Ensure that students are responsible for their own work.
- Ensure students are aware of the structural and stylistic conventions of the format they have chosen.
- Monitor students' progress.
- Ensure that students understand the assessment criteria and use them to self-assess their progress.

Presentation of findings

- Ensure that students understand the assessment criteria and academic integrity guidelines.
- Ensure that students are responsible for their own work.
- Facilitate peer feedback after their presentation of findings.
- Provide students with feedback based on their presentation of findings.
- Ensure that students are on track for completion and submission.

Completion and submission

- Read and comment on only one draft of the RP.
- Ensure that students complete the *Reflective project—Final reflection form* (RP/FRF).
- Report any suspected plagiarism to the Career-related Programme (CP) coordinator.
- Ensure that the final version of the project is submitted before the viva voce takes place.
- Conduct the viva voce with the student upon completion of the final project.
- Confirm authenticity of student work and complete the RP/FRF.
- Determine a predicted grade using the RP grade descriptors.
- Support the RP coordinator or CP coordinator as needed with the submission of the project.

■ Responsibilities for the role of a supervisor (Source: IB RP TSM)

How to make the most of feedback from your supervisor

You can expect feedback from your supervisor on your project proposal, ethical dilemma, research question, methodology, analysis, format choice, quality of research, coherence of argument, your perspective, findings, communication, reflections and reflexivity.

It's useful to know what sort of feedback you can receive during each phase of the RP. You can anticipate the sort of questions you or your supervisor could ask and what this specifically addresses about the criteria.

It's interesting to consider the support you will get throughout the RP process in terms of ATL skills. Look below at all the ways your supervisor will support you and think about how they assist the development of research, thinking, social, communication and self-management skills.

Your supervisor will:

- check you understand ethics and its relevance to your chosen career field
- discuss with you the whole RP process, research methods and formal requirements
- help you complete a project proposal by reviewing it and discussing it with you
- advise you on how you might plan your research and how you work out if your methods are effective
- give you feedback on your project proposal
- help you understand the assessment criteria and academic integrity
- guide and facilitate the feedback you get from your peers
- discuss the options available to you and how you go about choosing a format that suits your interests and skills
- help you develop self-management skills along the RP process
- help you create your own outline and timeline.

Preparation and planning phase

In this phase, your supervisor can give you feedback on the focus of your project proposal. When it comes to your focus, make sure that you are specific about your research and career interests. Also, be honest about your opinions and position on the area you are interested in already.

You can discuss with your supervisor how clear, relevant and complex your ethical dilemma is in terms of the perspectives surrounding it. They will look for the opportunities available in your ethical dilemma to explore a conflict of ethical principles, multiple contexts and perspectives, as well as possible solutions with no clear answer.

Research and analysis phase

In this phase, you can discuss with your supervisor the research methods you might use and how you collect data.

When it comes to analysis, your focus should be on how you are analysing bias and validity of sources, what conclusions you are coming to and then reflecting on your own personal biases and how this might be impacting your analysis. You might discuss how your position is shaping up or changing as your research progresses and how to account for different perspectives.

All these areas are important in deepening your thinking, so be patient with the time it takes.

Development phase

In this phase, you can discuss your format choice with your supervisor, such as whether the format allows you to address the ethical dilemma and criteria successfully. How can you account for the conventions of your format option? Also discuss the format you have chosen in terms of any creative techniques you might be anticipating. Do you want to explore those first or problem-solve as you create your RP?

You also might discuss with your supervisor the quality of your research in terms of how relevant and connected your evidence is. Have you integrated your research into your project and is it balanced?

Overall, you want to concentrate on the coherence of your own voice. How well-expressed and supported is your personal position? How well structured is your argument and how deep is your reflection?

Presentation of findings phase

Along with your peers' feedback, you can expect feedback on the conclusions you make in your presentation and the clarity of your argument. This will enable you to complete the final drafting process.

Completion and submission phase

In this stage, discussions will concentrate on the depth of your reflection and reflexivity. In terms of reflection, focus on discussing your actions, process, project and learning. In terms of reflexivity, consider your thinking, positionality and impact and how it has changed and/or strengthened.

Making sense of your supervisor's feedback questions

When you submit your initial draft to your supervisor, they are only allowed to see and comment on one draft. You then consider their feedback and make final revisions, such as improving your analysis and completing your final reflection. Questions are a vital part of the feedback process, and having an idea of the type of questions your supervisor might ask you throughout each phase of the RP can help you prepare your responses. Some examples of these are given below.

Table 4.24 Questions your supervisor might ask

Project proposal	• What are you interested in researching, and why? • How does this area connect to your career interest? • What personal biases, perspectives or positions do you already have on this subject?

Ethical dilemma	• Does the ethical dilemma you have identified:
	    • involve conflicting values or principles
	    • occur in multiple contexts or are there broader implications
	    • have an impact on multiple stakeholders
	    • present more than one alternative with no straightforward solution?
	• How might you clearly articulate the dilemma as a research question?
	• How relevant or significant is the ethical dilemma to the professional field?
	• Is the dilemma based on a real-life or hypothetical scenario?
	• Does the dilemma involve two or more perspectives?
	• Is one perspective more predominant or are you able to balance competing ethical considerations?

Methodology	• How might you go about undertaking this research? • Is the research design clearly outlined? • How are you identifying your sources? • Does the research design align with your research question and the nature of your ethical dilemma? • Does your planned research method conform to ethical research principles? • Will your selected method and sources help you analyse the ethical dilemma?
Data	• Are your methods of collecting data appropriate for the research method? • Does this research method provide a better understanding of your ethical dilemma than another?
Validity/reliability	• Are your sources appropriate/sufficient? Will they inform your understanding of the ethical dilemma from multiple perspectives? • Are you using a range of resources and analysing them for bias and reliability? • Have you acknowledged potential biases, and do you have a plan to mitigate their impact?
Conclusions	• Is there sufficient information to analyse differing perspectives on an ethical dilemma? • What conclusions can you draw from your research? • Do the conclusions you've drawn include the implications and impact of the ethical dilemma on different individuals or groups, and in different contexts? • Are additional questions emerging for you? • Do you need additional sources, or should you continue researching to further clarify the ethical issue?
Reflexivity and positionality	• Do you have sufficient data/information to begin formulating a personal position? • How has any personal bias been considered? • Has the research on different perspectives or different contexts changed your thinking?

Reflection and reflexivity

Reflect on what you have learnt about feedback and what you will take forward in the process when supporting your peers in their presentations. What skills will benefit you in your future career or education?

4.8.4 Summary

- An essential skill not only for the RP, but also beyond the classroom, is knowing how to give and receive feedback.
- Practising using the language and structure of a routine such as the 'ladder of feedback' can give you confidence in giving valuable, clear and kind feedback.
- Become an active listener so you can make the most of feedback, whether you are giving or receiving it.
- Use Socratic questioning to understand and respond to feedback.
- Understand the role of your supervisor and how they can support you in every phase of the RP learning journey.

4.9 Developing critical thinking

INQUIRY QUESTIONS

- How are you already a critical thinker?
- How can you build on prior learning?
- How can you deepen your thinking about your research?
- What does the assessment criteria say about critical thinking?
- What are the steps to forming a personal position?

4.9.1 Engaging with critical thinking

As is important in IB education, we start by thinking about what we know already. We are not starting from scratch. You have not got to this stage of your school career, or indeed this part of the CP, without employing critical thinking skills at some point. It might be that you want to get better at them—that's one thing. But we are not starting from a place of zero knowledge. The key is to know what to look for. You don't have to look far because if you have been practising your reflective and reflexive skills, this is the foundation of critical thinking.

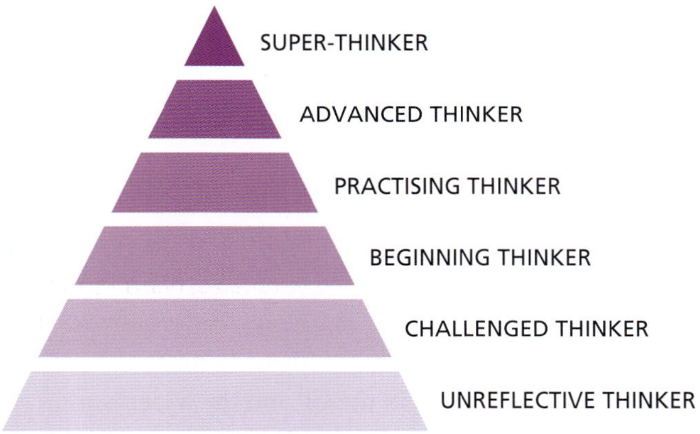

■ The six types of thinker (Source: Paul and Elder, *The Miniature Guide to Critical Thinking Concepts and Tools*, 2008)

The educational psychologists Richard Paul and Linda Elder are renowned for their work in the field of critical thinking. Becoming a successful critical thinker requires effort and is something we can all work at. Paul and Elder refer to six types of thinkers in a pyramid—unreflective thinker, challenged thinker, beginning thinker, practising thinker, advanced thinker and super-thinker. If you are this stage of the RP, and indeed the CP, and you have been consistent with your learning journal across the Core, then you can probably say you are already a practising thinker.

> Becoming a critical thinker demands a growth mindset and an understanding that this is not a skill we are born with, but a skill that we can develop and get better at, the more we practise.

A well-cultivated critical thinker:

- raises vital questions and problems, formulating them clearly and precisely
- gathers and assesses relevant information, using abstract ideas to interpret it effectively, comes to well-reasoned conclusions and solutions, testing them against relevant criteria and standards
- thinks open-mindedly within alternative systems of thought, recognizing and assessing (as needed) their assumptions, implications and practical consequences
- communicates effectively with others in figuring out solutions to complex problems.

(Adapted from Paul and Elder, *The Miniature Guide to Critical Thinking Concepts and Tools*, 2008)

Learning journal

Look at the above definition of critical thinking, adapted from Paul and Elder (2008). Look back through your learning journal and identify a place for each bullet point where you have demonstrated critical thinking in your RP process.

Links

Look across your CP now and the different components. Find examples from your CRS, DP subjects and other Core elements where you are already demonstrating the characteristics of a critical thinker.

Top tip!

There are many approaches to critical thinking out there—too many to include in this book. But the key is to understand the intended purpose of any approach you might use and its possible outcome.

Understand the role of critical thinking

The next logical step for your well-researched ethical dilemma is to break down your emerging ideas, evaluate the strengths and challenges of different perspectives and also spot the connections between different areas of your thinking. This is the essence of analysis, evaluation and synthesis. We do this to widen and deepen our thinking and the more we commit to this, the more informed our own perspective is on the ethical dilemma and possible solutions we might suggest.

There are lots of thought processes and routines you can use to do this, and all the reflective and reflexive habits you have established through PPS, CE, LCS and already in the RP process will stand you in good stead for being a great critical thinker.

Building on prior experience

The RP process is designed so you can plan, monitor and evaluate your progress as you go along. So if you are reading this at about half-way through the project, chances are you have been employing a number of critical-thinking skills already.

Let's take a moment to see how you have already been employing skills to navigate complex thinking in the CP. We're going to look at various scenarios in the CP and the wider world, where critical-thinking skills can have a big impact. For each one, notice why the approach was taken and what it enabled the student/employer/staff member in question to achieve. You will notice that in terms of ATL skill areas (or indeed the skill domains in PPS), critical thinking crosses over into communication, self-management, social and research and is not just in the domain of thinking skills.

Critical thinking impact 1: Local to global

Applying critical and creative thinking enables us to recognize patterns, make generalizations, and evaluate perspectives from a local and a global context.

REAL-WORLD EXAMPLE

You are a business owner and someone relatively new is not yet working at their best in the organization. As their line manager, you are considering their situation. They seem very quiet and withdrawn, but rather than just assume that the individual themselves holds the answer or what is happening in their life, you are also prepared to consider the environment within which they are working, and whether elements of the whole system in which everyone works could be contributing. For example, who are they working with, where are they working and how are they being supported? You consider whether they had a long enough induction to the organization and if there could be further opportunities for feedback and encouragement.

Applying this consideration of the 'local' to the 'global' in the RP and the ethical dilemma, you can start seeing that it is essential to evaluate both the role of the individual and the systems within which they are working, and be prepared to evaluate much bigger influences. So an ethical dilemma can be analysed from the perspective of an individual, but also from the culture and society within which the ethical dilemma sits. This is what we mean when we talk about taking 'the local to the global' or 'the micro to the macro'. When you look at it this way, you can often find interesting tensions and points of conflict as well as patterns.

Critical thinking impact 2: Social skills

It is interesting that critical and creative thinking also connects to other skill areas, such as social skills. For example, when you empathize with others and collaborate, you can gather multiple perspectives and adjust your behaviour accordingly. This is another reminder that learning is a social process.

REAL-WORLD EXAMPLE

A school is considering introducing a new programme—the CP—in their school. Before implementing this, they survey staff, governors, parents and students about how they might interpret this decision and this survey gives valuable feedback about when the right time to introduce the new programme might be. The initial survey shows a lot of support so the school embarks on the authorization process. They meet a problem when the first CRS suggestions are not appealing to the students, though have been suggested by a range of parents, so they speak to the students to understand what they want. Still, not many people sign up to take the CP and there seems to be some misunderstandings about it and what it can help you to do when you leave school. So with a small cohort signed up, the school decides to increase the amount of communication on the CP to the school community and also to the wider community.

REAL-WORLD EXAMPLE

In CE, you have found a particular project that you are really enthusiastic about working with. It's a charity connected to the school that's run by the parents of some students. You have some ideas on how you think the school could work more closely with the charity but have been advised to research how your peers, parents and the local community might feel about this decision. The charity's management like some of your ideas for improving communication about the purpose of the charity and events to the local community, but would like to see a plan of your campaign first before they agree in full. One of their stipulations is that they want you to include more students from other year groups in your plans. You can now amend your plans accordingly.

Critical thinking impact 3: Self-management skills

You need critical thinking tools to plan, monitor and evaluate your progress within your CRS, DP subjects and Core areas. When you start the CP, your teachers support you in developing the processes for this, but as the course progresses, you are expected to do more yourself.

REAL-WORLD EXAMPLE

In PPS, you have been co-creating inquiries with your class and your teachers, which has been supportive as you have all been doing the process together to start with. Now the course is progressing, you are beginning to form your own inquiries, which is a little daunting as you have not done it alone before. However, learning how to do this in PPS has been great, as it gave you the confidence to create your own CE project in coaching some of the younger years students in preparation for a football tournament for schools in the local area. You plan to get feedback from the students on each session to help you plan for the next ones.

Critical thinking impact 4: Reflective thinking

Throughout the CP, you are encouraged to reflect on your actions and decisions. This ability to evaluate the effectiveness of your decisions and where the areas for growth are means that you can make purposeful adjustments, rather than make unnecessary major changes or no changes at all.

REAL-WORLD EXAMPLE

You don't do so well in a test in one of your DP subjects. Rather than revising the entire module immediately, you reflect on the reasons why you may not have done well. Thinking back to the weeks in the run-up to the test, you remember that you were away for one of the formative preparation assessments because of ill health, when everyone worked with a classmate to give feedback to each other. You discuss this with your teacher and because the absence could not be helped, it is agreed that you can retake the preparation stage and receive feedback on this from your teacher. You then take the test again and, while the results aren't perfect, it is certainly an improvement.

REAL-WORLD EXAMPLE

After delivering a presentation following your initial draft of your RP, you receive feedback from your peers and supervisor. In the feedback, you notice a particular pattern in response to one of the perspectives you explored and whether the sources you used were biased. Looking at the sources, you realize there was an imbalance in the articles you used. To address the feedback, you research and find further more balanced sources. Just changing this one area has a significant impact on the strength of the whole argument in the essay.

4.9.2 Critical thinking for the RP

Through all these scenarios, you should start to recognize that you have been employing many thinking skills already in the RP process and in your other subjects. In that last example, however, you may have spotted that the RP presentation can only happen when you are further ahead in the process and have applied your critical-thinking skills to your ethical dilemma. So let's explore how you might do this successfully.

■ How do we deepen our critical thinking for the RP?

Learning journal

You may start this section feeling a little uncertain about the phrases 'synthesizing', 'analysing' and 'evaluating for critical thinking', which are associated with this part of the RP process. The key to doing these successfully is by developing excellent reflective and reflexive skills and, in order to do this, make sure you are keeping up with your learning journal.

Good reflection skills lead to good metacognition, and being able to analyse how our brains find patterns and form ideas is essential to critical thinking.

In Sections 4.6 and 4.7, as you developed research skills, you were introduced to the ideas of synthesis, analysis and evaluation of sources.

Here's a quick recap of what we mean by these terms:

- **Synthesis of sources:** This is the combining of information from multiple sources to create a new whole, which offers insights or perspectives rather than just summarizing each source individually.
- **Analysis of sources:** This is breaking down a source by understanding where it has come from, its content, context and purpose.
- **Evaluation of sources:** This is assessing the credibility, accuracy, bias and authority a source might hold in relation to your ethical dilemma.

The route to critical thinking

In this section, we are going to break down Criterion C of the RP assessment criteria and see what you need to do to demonstrate critical thinking well and how you might go about doing this. Throughout this we are going to remember the definition of a critical thinker we established earlier and relate this to the assessment criterion. This means bringing it back to considering what questions you should ask to check you are on the right path, what to do with all the information you have gathered, exploring the ethical dilemma and its impact from multiple angles, and being able to use reason and justification to communicate your own personal position.

What does the criterion say?

Criterion C: Critical thinking—in detail

'This criterion assesses how effectively you have analysed the ethical dilemma and synthesized your research to determine and justify your personal position on the ethical dilemma, and that you have taken into consideration your position's impact on and implications for various contexts and groups.'

(Source: IB RP guide, p.51)

A critical thinker 'raises vital questions and problems, formulating them clearly and precisely.'

(Source: Paul and Elder (2008), p.4)

To understand the impact questioning can have, you need to understand how far questions can take you. Remember the model we met earlier (in Section 4.6.2) with different question stems to use? Which question stems have you used already in the process so far?

Top tip!

Make a note of these questions and use them to check your RP when you read through your draft and final piece.

In terms of critical thinking, Criterion C asks the following questions to assess how successful you are as a critical thinker in the RP. Let's use these as a guide:

- Have you analysed the research and synthesized the information?
- Have you used reasoning to identify a personal position on the ethical dilemma?
- Have you justified your position?
- Have you taken into consideration the impact or implications of your position?

Have you analysed the research and synthesized the information?

A critical thinker 'gathers and assesses relevant information, using abstract ideas to interpret it effectively, comes to well-reasoned conclusions and solutions, testing them against relevant criteria and standards.'

(Source: Paul and Elder (2008), p.4)

During your research process, you have gathered a lot of information. The word 'abstract' in the description above might be a little off-putting, but all it means is that we are using ideas we cannot see in concrete form in the world around us. For example, in the research process, if you used the process of RAVEN to evaluate the value and relevance of a source, this is applying abstract ideas to understand something better. It's also a way of 'testing them against relevant criteria and standards'. When you look at sources through an ethical lens and consider what they add to your ethical decision-making process, this is also using an abstract idea to think critically about your ethical dilemma. Your conclusions and solutions from interpreting your sources are leading you towards a position, which we know is an important part of critical thinking in the RP.

Learning journal

Look back at your research notes now and consider how you have explored bias in one of your sources. You may already have used the process of RAVEN, as mentioned above and in Section 4.7.2. If not, you can try it now using the summary below (refer back for the full version of this exercise, as below is just a summary).

- **R** **Reputation:** What is the reputation of the publication/author?
- **A** **Ability to see:** Is the author, or their own sources, in a position to know what they are talking about?
- **V** **Vested interest:** Does the writer have a personal or professional stake in the issue?
- **E** **Expertise:** Is the author an expert in the field on which they are writing?
- **N** **Neutrality:** Publications such as newspapers can have a 'leaning' towards a political stance. Is there any sign of this?

(Adapted from R. Brink-Budgen and J. Thawaites, *OCR AS Critical Thinking*)

Have you used reasoning to identify a personal position on the ethical dilemma?

> *A critical thinker 'thinks open-mindedly within alternative systems of thought, recognizing and assessing ... their assumptions, implications and practical consequences.'*

(Source: Paul and Elder (2008), p.4)

■ Have you looked at your ethical dilemma from all angles?

One of the three areas of critical thinking that you are assessed on is how well you analyse and synthesize your research. You need to make sure you do this consistently enough that you are able to look at your dilemma from all angles. This could mean:

- what the ethical dilemma looks like in different contexts
- a variety of perspectives surrounding the ethical dilemma
- the impact of what you have found on the individuals and communities in question
- any other related ethical issues that stem from what you have found.

Most of all, it means that all the ideas and examples you use are tightly connected to your ethical dilemma, its impact and the conclusions you have come to. As you have analysed your research, you have spotted patterns emerging and explained how ideas connect together. This is the key to synthesis.

Top tip!

This is not only a good area where you can assess yourself in your drafting process, but also an area you can ask for feedback on. Ask yourself, 'Are all my examples relevant, connected and balanced?'

Have you justified your position?

> *A critical thinker 'communicates effectively with others in figuring out solutions to complex problems.'*
>
> (Source: Paul and Elder (2008), p.4)

To communicate your own voice effectively in the RP, you are going to use the following words in order: reason, evidence, justification, impact.

The next two sections are about the importance of your 'personal position' in the RP. By following the research process and being reflective and reflexive continuously throughout, you will be able to identify and support your own position on the ethical dilemma.

> How do you know you have a personal position? When you have personally answered your research question with your own justified and supported point of view on the ethical dilemma. So focus on doing this as well as you can.

The process of creating a full personal position goes:

Table 4.25 Creating a full personal position

You are clear about your personal position and show how clear, connected and well-selected evidence led you to it.
You justify your personal position by explaining how you got there and why it's acceptable.
You consider the positive and negative impact of your personal position in a balanced way.
You explain why other alternative solutions might not work as well as yours.
All of this you explain in a thorough way.

LEARNING ENGAGEMENT

Finding a personal position

This can be a sociable learning activity with a partner and small groups, as you can use each other as a sounding board for ideas.

Use the following question stems to create questions specific to your work. The idea is that using creative questions will help you look at your research and analysis so far in a different way, which will help you to find a personal position. This involves thinking beyond your research and predominantly asking 'what if ...?'

The way to change the questions is to consider adding in or subtracting certain factors. For example, what if the contexts were different, such as the age/gender/religion of the individuals and communities involved?

- What would it be like if ...?
- How would it be different if ...?
- What would change if ...?
- How would it look differently if ...?
- Suppose that ...

1. Make a list of 12 questions and put a star next to the ones that are the most interesting to you.
2. Once you have explored these, then focus on the following question:
   What new ideas do I have about my RP that I didn't have before?

LEARNING ENGAGEMENT

Self/peer assessment to build a position

This learning engagement makes a good piece of self-assessment of your own work, but is equally good to do with a peer or your supervisor. It's a simple exercise that creates a habit of the mind that leads to greater depth in your justification of a position. The best time to do this learning engagement is when you have begun articulating what your personal position is in answer to your research question. This could be done as a mind map, voice note or as a written paragraph.

1. Having read through your research notes and reflections up until now, put two minutes on a timer and, without over-thinking the process, just start talking, writing or drawing your own answer to the research question. If you are doing this verbally, be sure to record it.
2. Now take a small section of about three statements (you might want to transcribe your voice note to make this easier). After each sentence, ask yourself, 'What makes me say that?' and note down the evidence that you have that each statement is true. If you cannot find evidence then put a question mark next to it. If you have supplied some evidence, then look to see whether you can make it stronger by connecting it to further proof.
3. Now repeat the first step with two minutes on the clock again, but this time incorporate your further evidence and justification to back up your points.

Have you taken into consideration the impact or implications of your position?

As part of being a critically reflective and reflexive student, you have had opportunities to explore the impact of actions and beliefs throughout your CP course and, more specifically, through this RP process. As you are building you personal position, you want to keep your thoughts clear and logical. The following exercise is intended as a reflective way of taking a step back and considering the local and global impact of your ethical dilemma and the position you have taken.

Reflection and reflexivity

Exploring impact

What is the impact of your ethical dilemma and the personal position you have taken:

- on yourself (strengthening or changing of actions and beliefs)
- on your inner circle (of friends, family, the people you know)
- in your community (your school, neighbourhood)
- in the world (beyond your immediate environment)?

Learning journal

Remember that thinking locally and globally is not just about geography, but also about the breadth and scope of ideas. Look at the following definitions and see where you have been using them already. Could you deepen your use of them? What could you use further? Write down an intention in your learning journal.

> *'Local contexts refer to specific geographical, social, economic, environmental, cultural and political dynamics that characterize a particular place or community at a given moment in time.'*
>
> *'Global contexts encompass worldwide dynamics emphasizing interconnectedness, interdependence and shared challenges faced by humanity as a whole.'*
>
> (Source: IB RP guide, p.66)

4.9.3 Summary

- You have been becoming a critical thinker throughout your school career and will be consciously building on this experience throughout the RP process.
- Critical thinking is a vital skill in navigating personal and professional life, as it enables you to understand the impact of ideas, employ empathy and reflect on your actions and decisions.
- To build your critical-thinking skills, you need to analyse and synthesize your research, break down how it is relevant and reliable, and then see how different sources connect.
- Forming a personal position is the key indicator in the assessment criteria that you are a critical thinker. This involves answering your research question with an explanation of why your stance is acceptable, the potential impact of having such a perspective and why other solutions won't work.

4.10 Exploring and choosing a format

INQUIRY QUESTIONS

- How can you use a format and word count for the greatest impact?
- How can you explore what is meant by written, audio, visual and audio–visual formats?

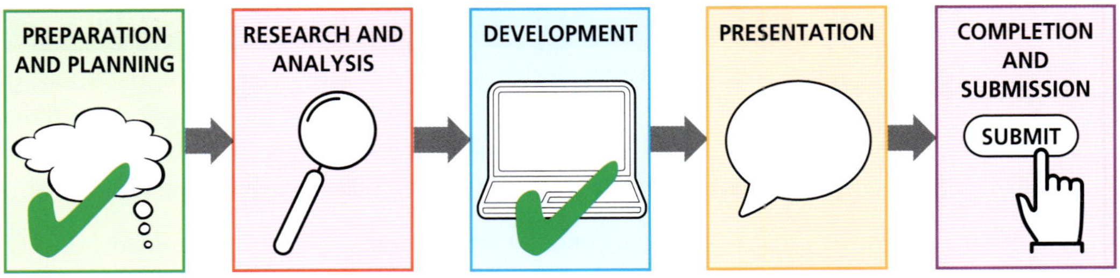

The RP process

Table 4.26

Phase of RP	Detailed steps involved

Preparation and planning	• preparation and building of background knowledge
	• identification of an ethical dilemma
	• peer discussions
	• **research plan and project proposal**
	  • Consider and articulate approach to the RP through the creation of a research plan and submission of a proposal to the supervisor.
	  • Refine the ethical dilemma/research question.
	  • Determine a research approach and potential resources.
	  • **Decide on a project format.**

Development	• **initial project draft**
	  • Organize research and ideas.
	  • Create an initial project draft.
	  • Include all required elements.

4.10.1 Formats for the RP

We explored formats briefly in Section 4.6.4, as you developed your research proposal. It might be that you have popped into this section to explore formats a little more for your research proposal, which is great—this book was never meant to be linear and you can jump around as your ideas and needs develop! However, so far we have looked at formats quite generally and linked it to what we want the formats to be able to achieve for your reflective project (RP) in terms of purpose, audience, language and structure.

Now, it's time to go deeper. You will notice in the RP assessment criteria that Criterion D is about communication. You have already done so much to develop your communication skills throughout your school career, but during your CP, you have probably noticed that your course and individual subject areas explicitly concentrate on your self-awareness of skill development and, of these, communication skills is a significant one. Sometimes with courses and the assessments you have to complete, it can feel like you have to respond in a way that does not suit your communication strengths. You also might question how relevant it is to what you want to do in the future. With the RP, within the four formats of written, audio, visual and audio–visual, your choices are wide open and you can really consider the questions:

- How do I prefer to communicate?
- How does communication work in the career field I am interested in?

Common pitfall

Many students think that their RP must be in written form and that the written form must be an essay. This is not the case!

Identifying formats that work well with exploring ethical dilemmas

As you will see below, the four format options of written, visual, audio and audio–visual can mean many things and there is no one right way, and nor is one way easier than another. Yes, some might have more technical requirements, but the format options are specifically designed to represent communication styles that are current and future-facing. By that we mean that the skills you develop in creating and delivering any of these formats are ones that can have direct relevance in your chosen career field.

You may make your format choice based on:

- appeal, experience and preference
- the best format to explore your chosen ethical dilemma
- formats that link directly to your chosen career field.

To make a decision, ask yourself, 'What will help me explore my ethical dilemma and show my positionality, but also keep me interested and be relevant for my future?' Be honest in your answer!

Researching formats

You can't just watch one documentary, listen to one podcast or read one magazine article and think that you now know that format. You may think you are more familiar with some formats over others, but do you really know what goes into them? Let's look first at the different requirements for each format before going into more detail at how each format can showcase a personal exploration of an ethical dilemma.

Learning journal

When you planned your research proposal to share with your supervisor, you explored the format decision tree. What were your findings in both this process and your proposal? Have these changed since then?

4.10.2 Consider the criteria

You will need to think about how the format you select enables you to meet Criterion D: Communication of ideas—in detail. This criterion looks at how you clearly communicate your ideas and the way your format explicitly and implicitly impacts this. Namely, it determines whether:

- you have used terminology that is both relevant to your ethical dilemma but also the codes and conventions of the format you are using
- you have structured your ideas so they can flow, but also used features for structuring that are relevant to your format
- your ideas develop in a coherent way that enables you to look deeply into your ethical dilemma, as well as make connections between your ideas.

The format options are summarized in the IB RP guide (p.20) as follows:

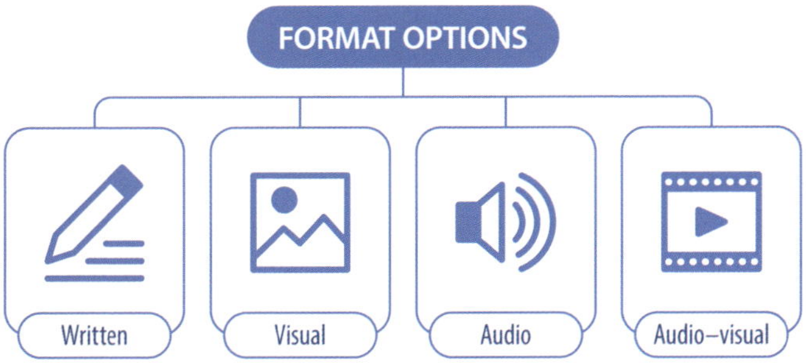

Summary of the format options (Source: IB RP guide, p.19)

Written options are products that convey ideas and information in forms that can be read. They do not move or produce sounds.

Visual options are products that convey ideas and information through still and/or moving images.

Audio options are products that convey ideas and information through recorded sound.

Audio–visual options are products that convey ideas and information through a combination of visual and audio modes.

Requirements for written formats

- A total of 4,000 words maximum (including 1,000 words maximum for the written reflection).
- A maximum of five labelled graphs, tables or still images may be included, if appropriate, to support text content.
- Whichever essay style is selected, students should use structural elements and conventions appropriate for the style, and ensure that the ethical dilemma is thoroughly explored to achieve all aspects of the criteria.
- Sources must be properly cited.
- Submissions should be in DOC, DOCX, PDF (non-editable) or RTF file types.

(Source: IB RP guide, p.20)

Requirements for visual formats

- Total equivalence of 4,000 words maximum (including 1,000 words maximum for the written reflection.
- A minimum of 5 images and maximum of 15 images with a description or annotation of a total minimum of 500 words and maximum of 2,000 words.
- The description/annotation should include an explanation of what the images are, why they were chosen or created, and how they contribute to the project.
- Sources must be properly referenced for any images not produced by the student.
- Images should be in JPG, JPEG or PNG file types. Images can be copied/pasted into a document to include annotations and submitted as a DOC or PDF (non-editable).

(Source: IB RP guide, p.21)

Requirements for audio formats

- Total equivalence of 4,000 words maximum (including 1,000 words maximum for the written reflection).
- A minimum of 10 minutes (approximately 1,500 words) and maximum of 15 minutes (approximately 2,250 words) with any additional explanations, annotations or context provided in writing.
- For any music or sound effects that are used, you should explain why they were chosen and how they contribute to the project.
- A transcript should be attached as an appendix to all audio products. It will not be marked or included in the word limit, but serves to support the recording in case of technological difficulties.
- Audio submissions should be in MP3, M4A format.

(Source: IB RP guide, p.21)

Requirements for audio–visual formats

- Total equivalence of 4,000 words maximum (including 1,000 words maximum for the written reflection).
- A minimum of 10 minutes (approximately 1,500 words) and maximum of 15 minutes (approximately 2,250 words) with any additional explanations, annotations or context provided in writing.
- For images, music and sound effects that are used, students should explain why they were chosen and how they contribute to the project.
- A transcript should be attached as an appendix to all audio–visual products. It will not be marked or included in the word limit but serves to support the recording in case of technological difficulties.
- Film/video/screencast submissions should be in MP4, MOV (codec H264) or M4V format.

(Source: IB RP guide, p.22)

Making the most of the requirements

1. Don't put anything in an appendix that is crucial to understanding the arguments or perspectives in your RP, as there is no guarantee the examiners will read them.
2. Remember for visual, audio and audio–visual, you will want to include additional explanation, annotation and context in writing about your project. This also must include your explanations for any technical choices (e.g. images, music and sound effects) and how they contribute to the project.
3. You must include a transcript of visual, audio, and audio visual formats as a back-up in case there are problems with the file you upload.

4.10.3 Making the most of each format

Audio–visual presentation

This might be a format that you are arguably most familiar with if you are a social-media user and digest a lot of your media this way. Whatever career area you are interested in, it's good to consider the impact that audio–visual communication can have. After all, the combination of these terms creates a multi-sensory experience and can be very engaging for an audience.

Audio–visual communication happens everywhere, including:

- live performances and events within performing arts, creative industries and marketing/PR industries
- educational materials that could include interactivity and/or animations for charities, education boards and research think-tanks
- conferences within many industries, such as corporate businesses
- content for social-media presence and campaigns within the sporting industry
- presentations where graphics are used in an update to a team or pitching for new business.

You might look into how an audio–visual presentation can take different forms, including a TEDx talk, documentary film, a short live or animated film, and a video podcast. There are many forms this can take, but we are going to look at an example in detail to explore how to make the most of this format, both in how you can structure your ideas and how you present them.

GREAT PUBLIC SPEAKING

Chris Anderson's 'TED's secret to great public speaking' reminds us all that the most powerful public speaking centres around something quite simple—an idea. Consider the following takeaways from Anderson's speech and how this applies to the position you are developing on the ethical dilemma at the centre of your RP.

- Your number one task as a speaker is to transfer into your listeners' minds an extraordinary gift—a strange and beautiful object that we call an idea.
- An idea is a pattern of information that reshapes our worldview, offering new lenses to navigate the complexities of life.
- Ideas sculpt our worldview; a speech must convey one potent idea effectively, altering perceptions and inspiring action.
- To truly captivate, an idea must not only benefit the speaker but also offer a tangible, positive shift in the audience's perspective.

(Source: Chris Anderson (March 2016), 'TED's secret to great public speaking' [Video], TEDx Conferences)

There is no prescribed way to structure your presentation, but there are some important elements that you can keep central.

Firstly, introduce yourself and your topic. You are here to communicate your ideas, so start with the intention of capturing the main theme of your speech. Secondly, be consistent with your evidence throughout your speech. You have spent many hours researching, evaluating, analysing and synthesizing your ethical dilemma, so remember to explore your ideas from different perspectives and use evidence to back up what you are saying. Thirdly, remember you are in charge. Assume the best intention of your audience: that they want to know what you have to say and that you have a voice that is worth listening to. Furthermore, if you choose to use slides, do not let them take attention away from what you are saying with lots more text to read; consider how you use visuals to complement what you are saying and create impact. Lastly, when finishing your speech, try to say something new. You have been weaving your positionality throughout your presentation, but conclude strongly. Keep the critical thinking criteria in mind here and use it as an opportunity not just to establish your position, but to communicate why your ideas could work better than other potential solutions.

Top tip!

It's good to research how other people deliver presentations, such as TEDx talks, but remember you are not trying to be like someone else—just be yourself. The tips we extract from what makes good practice is one thing, but thinking you have to copy an exact style to be successful is not the aim of the game.

Learning journal

Read through the extract above and take notes on the advice given. Identify the areas that you would want to focus on personally.

Podcasts

A podcast could fall into either the audio or audio–visual format, depending on whether it is audio only or a video podcast. You may watch or listen to podcasts regularly and have never thought about creating one yourself. A welcome addition to the RP formats is the ability to create a podcast, which is a form that has grown in popularity over the last ten years.

Here let's look at what a podcast actually is according to 'How to start a podcast: The creator's step-by-step guide' from Creators: Spotify.

WHAT IS A PODCAST?

In its simplest form, a podcast needs two things: an idea, and a voice to bring it to life.

Let's be real. Most of us have a general understanding of what a podcast is (a collection of digital audio or video files that are made available for audiences), but as we enter the podcast world ourselves, more questions start popping up.

A podcast can be many different things—and it all depends on you, the creator. A podcast can be:

- one person speaking into a microphone (or even their phone's mic) alone in their apartment or podcast studio
- a video podcast with the cameras turned on
- a pair of friends or a group of five
- serious, funny, boisterous, cerebral, quirky, sarcastic, or a little bit of everything.

So what can be a basic format to plan your ideas around?

Take a moment to evaluate what makes your perspective unique and write it down on a piece of paper. Get clear on why you want to start a podcast. Is it to connect with people? To have great conversations? To express your ideas?

(Source: https://creators.spotify.com/resources/how-to/start-a-podcast)

Plan your podcast

1 Choose your topic and define your why.

2 This is the story only you can tell, so in RP terms, this means being clear about your own positionality.

3 Determine a podcast format suitable for your RP. Some possibilities include:
- solo podcast (just you speaking)
- interview podcast (you interview 1–2 people as part of your podcast)
- round-table podcast (more people and even more discussion focused)
- narrative non-fiction podcast.

4 Who is your audience?

5 What is your structure? Create a plan you will follow. This is very much part of your learning journal work, so do use the assessment criteria to check you have covered everything you need to.

6 Consider branding to an extent—you might include an intro or outro (don't spend too much time on this).

7 Equipment. Keep it simple and work out what you actually need as opposed to equipment you would really like. If you are doing a solo podcast then you can speak directly into your computer. If you are interviewing or creating a roundtable podcast then it is worth looking into microphones to assist you. A decent pair of closed-back headphones to monitor your recordings and help with editing is a good idea.

Before you record, check that your recording equipment is ready and your devices are charged. Your script or outline should be positioned somewhere you can read it clearly. Check your Wi-Fi connection and, if you have guests you'll interview remotely, check in and make sure they are ready, in a quiet environment and a strong WiFi signal too. If you're filming a video podcast, make sure you are happy with the placing of your lights and cameras.

8. Now you can record. Before you do that, check what you sound like before you start.
9. Editing. Before you start this, have a plan. Have your original intended structure for the podcast in front of you and listen through everything you have recorded. In your learning journal, you can have a structure in mind for a clear and cohesive argument thread, and then review this consistently throughout the process.
10. Include any other creative sound effects that will enhance your project. Remember to think about the explanations you will give the IB for why they are there to make sure they add something to your podcast.

Top tip!

While this process has a podcast in mind, the main structure also works for planning of any format.

4.10.4 Getting familiar with codes and conventions

For any of the formats, the requirements make it very clear that you need to communicate in the most appropriate way. You may be choosing a format specifically because it relates to your career field and what you anticipate will be one of your communication styles in the future, so you can see that using the codes and conventions of your chosen format is really important.

Here we are going to use the audio–visual format of documentary to explore how you plan a film in your learning journal and incorporate the codes and conventions of film-making, even if this is a new area to you.

Audio–visual format: Documentaries

Look through this process and consider how each step could support conveying the ethical dilemma well. You do not want to spend all your time editing and end up losing sight of the ethical dilemma and research question, so use your learning journal to keep notes on the key features of this audio–visual format that you need to employ in conveying your ideas clearly.

First, there are four main types of documentary to choose from:

- **Interview-led** documentaries are based on interviews with key people involved in the topic of the film. This type of documentary is typically used to explore a particular issue or event in depth.
- **Presenter-led** documentaries are narrated by a presenter, who guides the viewer through the story. They can be used to tell any kind of story, from historical dramas to travel vlogs.
- **Observational-led** documentaries are filmed entirely as if the viewer is an unseen observer, with no voiceover narration or interviews. This type of documentary is often used to capture reality in unscripted situations.
- **Narrator-led** documentaries use a narrator to guide the viewer through the film, often providing additional information and insights that wouldn't be possible in an observational or interview-led documentary.

PLAN YOUR DOCUMENTARY

1 Do your research.
2 Decide on your narration style. Documentaries often make use of more than one, so don't limit yourself to sticking to just one.
3 Use a three-act structure. Think in terms of set-up, development and resolution, and plan those sections individually.
4 Get a crew. More than likely you will need some help with this, so plan this and ask for support.
5 Create a 'treatment'. This is simply the filmic term for how you plan to explore the ethical dilemma through film. You should think about themes you want to convey, what footage you need and the most important information you want to get across. This should go alongside your research in your learning journal.
6 Create a schedule and stick to it.
7 Organize equipment. You will know that you can shoot a film on your phone quite easily and there is great editing software available that you may already be using. This is not a project that calls for an expensive camera when it is completely possible to master the skills you need on much more accessible equipment.
8 You have relatively little time for your documentary, so you will want to use some variety of shots to make it as dynamic as possible. The Documentary Film Academy (DFA) makes this suggestion for five shots to create interesting documentaries:
   - Film a close-up of your subject's hands to show what is being done.
   - Film a close-up shot of your subject's face.
   - Film a wide shot to show where the scene is taking place.
   - Film an over-the-shoulder shot of your subject.
   - Film an unusual shot to show the scene unfolding—it's up to you what camera angle you use. (Source: www.docfilmacademy.com/blog/how-to-make-a-documentary)

   However, do make sure you keep this safe! Risk-taking is an important part of the learner profile, but not in terms of physical safety!
9 Paper-edit your film. This means getting your original plan and watching your recordings back, making notes against each section for how you might edit it. It might take a long time but you will thank yourself later.
10 Edit your film. You will want to choose an editing software that you feel comfortable using. Upload everything you have and become really familiar with it all before you think about how you will put it altogether into your three-act structure.
11 Edit colour, sound and effects. Once you have your edit, it's time to add on effects that will really enhance what you have created. For example, think about how you can use music to emphasize any aspect of the film. Remember, in the RP requirements, you must provide written explanations for your technical choices, so be clear with yourself about what the features you are using are actually adding to your film.

4.10.5 Visual formats

You will have seen throughout this section that the four modalities of written, audio, visual and audio–visual can overlap in many ways. It's good to look at visual by itself and what it can mean as, just like the other options, it is part of the communication preferences for all career fields. The key thing is knowing how it applies to you.

You might hear the word 'visual' and think it just applies to the creative industries, such as design and advertising, but it really depends on what the information is you are conveying. Consider the role of visual communication in scientific research, for example, and the role that graphics play in conveying information such as data and complex concepts. Visual communication allows people to access difficult ideas in new ways and improve their understanding of them. When you think about it, this plays a part in every career field.

Photo-essay

Through the photo-essay, we are going to explore the idea of expressing ideas visually with accompanying written text.

Let's be clear; a photo-essay is not a pile of images and some words put together with no passion or cohesion. It is a storytelling format that should have the same level of structure and continuity as any other. Your task is to consider how the visual works with the written word to create a narrative.

Read the box below to find out if you are a visual storyteller. This process works for any creative media and not just photo-essays. The following is suggested by Shorthand:

GET INSPIRED

No matter how compelling the vision in your head is, you can still benefit from a little inspiration. If you're looking for photo-essay ideas, consider:

- focusing on a single subject for a day (known as 'a day in the life' photo-essay)
- documenting local events, such as art shows, protests, or community gatherings—this is an endless source of photo-essay topics
- capturing social issues from your local area
- starting a photo series, in which you document the same specific subject over a period of time
- researching the great photo-essayists from history, such as W. Eugene Smith and James Nachtwey
- diving into the archives of the great photo-essay magazines, such as *National Geographic* and *Life*
- doing some research on your potential subject. This will help you formulate different angles from which to approach your photo-essay.

(Source: https://shorthand.com/the-craft/compiling-an-engaging-photo-essay)

Reflection and reflexivity

Revisiting the format decision tree

A lot of time has passed since your first project proposal. How do you feel about the formats now? Look below at the format decision tree which you saw earlier (in Section 4.6.4) and reflect on where you stand now.

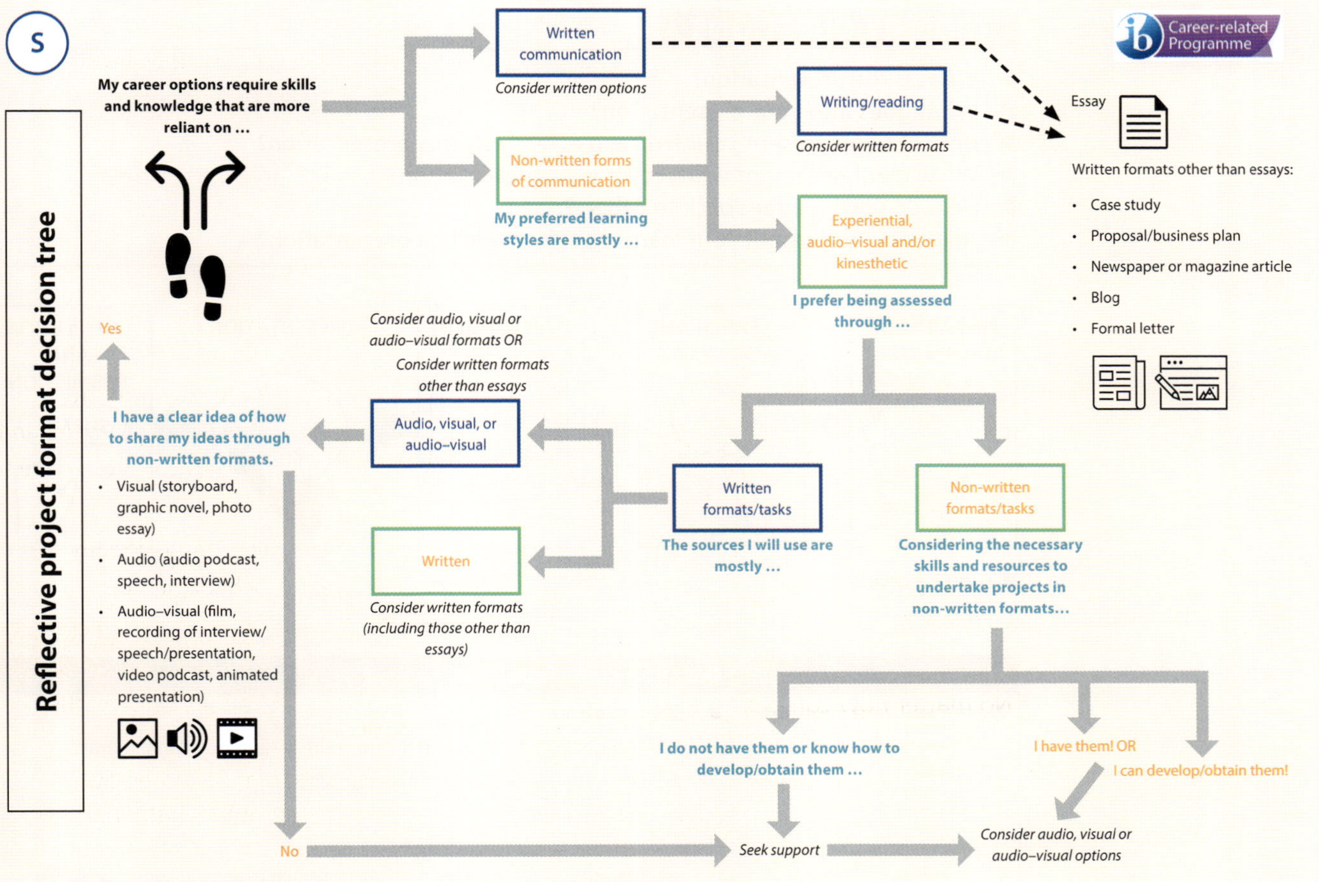

■ Decision tree to help with deciding on your RP format (Source: IB RP TSM, p.46)

4.10.6 Summary

- The RP can be created in written, visual, audio and audio–visual formats.
- You are encouraged to think about the communication styles you are most comfortable with, and also what will be most useful to your chosen career field of interest.
- All formats are the equivalent of 4,000 words, including an up to 1,000-word written reflection. Be clear on what this might look like in terms of visual formats, or how long this might be in terms of audio and audio–visual formats.
- If you choose visual, audio or audio–visual, you will need to consider using additional explanations, annotations or context in writing, as well as an accompanying transcript.
- Just as you did in phase 1, revisit the format decision tree to ensure you are using the best format for you.

4.11 Creating and delivering a presentation

INQUIRY QUESTIONS

- What is the presentation?
- What goes into your presentation?
- How can you present your learning effectively in a presentation?
- What feedback might you get for your presentation?
- How do you give feedback to others?
- How can you present your learning effectively in a presentation?

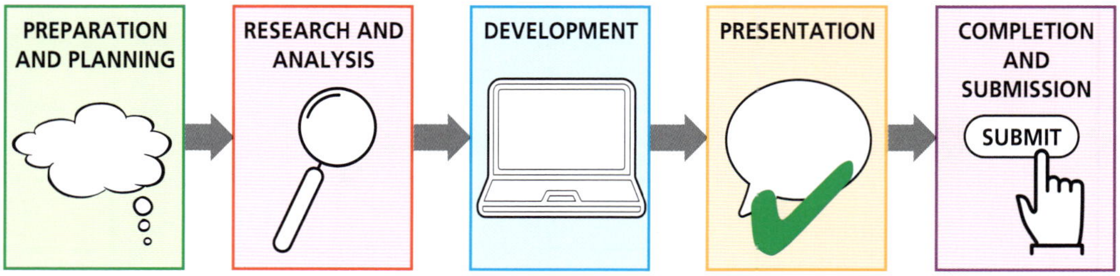

■ The RP process

■ **Table 4.27**

Phase of RP	Detailed steps involved

Presentation of findings	• **presentation**
	  • Share the findings and ideas from the research and initial draft.
	  • Demonstrate oral communication skills.
	  • Receive feedback.
	  (Topics for feedback might include the clarity and coherence of the argument; the quality of the research; the inclusion of required elements; the effectiveness of the organization and communication of ideas.)
	  • The presentation happens early enough for students to make additional changes based on feedback or further thinking.
	• **reflection point**
	  • Reflect on the status of the current draft and the feedback provided.
	  • Determine how to finalize the project.
	  • Record reflections and any actions taken in the learning journal.

4.11.1 The RP presentation

As you can see from the RP process here, the next step after completing your initial draft is to present your findings and current thinking. The presentation is a compulsory part of the RP process and it is not formally assessed.

This is a chance for your peers to learn about your ethical dilemma, contexts, research, personal position and its impact on you. For your supervisor, it's important to check the quality of the work you have done as well as how much you have done. However, the most important part of the presentation, apart from building your communication and social skills, is the way it will bring clarity to your thinking and keep the momentum going in

Top tip!

Set your mindset. For example: 'By preparing and delivering this presentation, I will receive feedback from my peers and supervisor to help me clarify what I think and strengthen my ideas and arguments so I can finish the process with a strong final RP.'

the RP process—so there's no chance to procrastinate! It's an opportunity to sort out your thoughts before proceeding to the final drafting stage. By the time you complete this stage, you will be far more experienced in giving and receiving feedback to and from your peers, so you should find this a useful stage.

You have probably found that there are several stepping stones throughout the process that are designed intentionally to help you structure your RP experience. It's important to remember that they would not be there without a reason, so keep in mind that each stepping stone will reveal something more about your RP process, the development of your skills and your own ethical position. Lead with purpose and the intention that this will help you grow.

A few requirements:

- You must make your presentation to your peers and supervisor. You could also include the wider school community, such as your mentor or the CP coordinator.
- You will present your current place of understanding with your RP at the point of having completed your initial draft. This will include your findings, current thinking and positionality.
- After your presentation, there will be an opportunity for you to address questions.
- The format of your presentation is flexible. You can use visual aids or presentation software (remember, there is huge variety here), but you don't have to use any at all.
- Your presentation should not last more than ten minutes. When you first think about this, you might think ten minutes is a long time. Once you start preparing for this, however, you realize how quickly time passes!
- You should have no more than five minutes for questions after your presentation.

4.11.2 What to put in your presentation

Learning journal

Consider how you feel about giving a presentation. Are you excited, nervous or unbothered? Record your initial thoughts in your learning journal.

The focus of the presentation should include:

- the ethical dilemma and how it relates to a career field
- the contexts and perspectives explored
- what research has been undertaken
- what research findings have been gathered
- how your ideas or understanding changed through analysing the research
- your personal position on the dilemma, how you arrived at it and how it might have an impact on yourself or others
- how your learning/new understanding might have an impact on your future career/education.

(Source: IB RP guide, p.24)

One way to plan your presentation is to use a visual tool, such as an Ishikawa or fishbone diagram. An outline of how to do this is given on the next page. Place the main problem or issue you want to address (your ethical dilemma) at the head of the fishbone diagram. Then consider what categories you can to branch off as the larger 'bones'. You could use the points above (contexts, research, personal position, impact on career plans) or other points that are relevant to you. There are plenty of other planning tools, visual or otherwise, that you could also use—this is just one example.

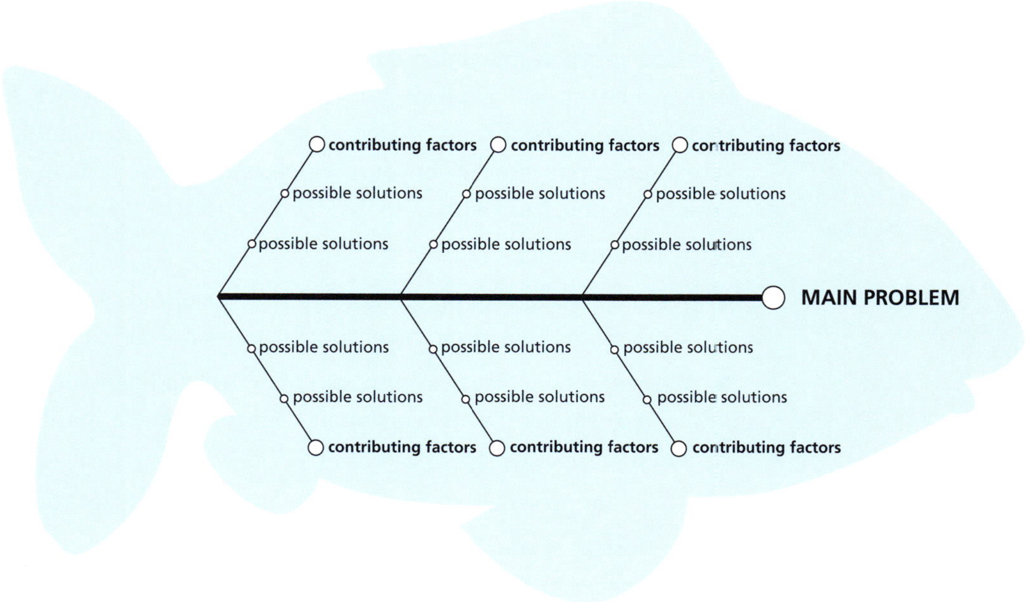

■ An Ishikawa or fishbone diagram

LEARNING ENGAGEMENT

1. Plan your presentation using your learning journal and initial RP draft. You could choose to create a diagram or a mind map.
2. Consider the Ishikawa diagram as a way of thinking about all the different factors that contribute to the ethical dilemma and their impact.

4.11.3 How to give a presentation comfortably

You may find the detailed description in Section 4.10.3 on presentations as a format option helpful to you in developing your presentation. The focus here is how to be at ease with giving a presentation. After all, this is about a topic you know far more about than anyone else in the room, so you can feel at ease showcasing your learning. However, the idea of a presentation can be stressful, so let's make it manageable.

Links

This presentation might also be appropriate for use as evidence in your PPS portfolio, as you curate your experiences throughout your CP course.

Build on prior knowledge acquired from a range of contexts

A confident presentation will come from building on your experience of previous presentations. Look back through your PPS portfolio and note when you have made presentations before. It might have been a presentation you made in PPS or within another context, such as your CRS, your DP subjects, CE or perhaps work experience. What are the skills that you developed most when doing this?

You might start with the skill domains of intrapersonal skills, interpersonal skills, thinking skills and intercultural understanding. Within those, you might see examples of developing skills such as self-management, communication, social awareness, problem-solving, information-literacy, social awareness and empathy. Which ones are most relevant to you here?

Think also about presentations you have attended. There is no denying that presentations which are read out word for word from a script can be a little uninspiring. Sometimes the person reads too fast and it can be difficult to pick up on all the ideas they have. However, the thought of not having a script can be stressful, so this is where structure and practice come in.

Consider using a PowerPoint or Google Slides presentation as an aid (but remember not to rely on it too heavily!). You can then use your slides as prompts which can really help you structure your presentation. However, don't put lots of information on the slides which you then read out verbatim. Instead, aim to create a visual that complements what you are saying.

Top tip!

Watch some TEDx talks to see how different people approach a presentation.

Remember that you do not have to use slides at all. You have your knowledge, speaking voice and, armed with some well-planned and practised notes, you can deliver your presentation very well without.

LEARNING ENGAGEMENT

Building communication and social skills

Practise: Break down your presentation into sections, with a clear purpose in each one. Map out what you are going to say and then record yourself practising the different sections of your presentation.

Peer practise: With a partner, talk through your plan and see how you can support each other to expand your ideas. You may find looking back on the different types of reflection in Section 4.4 helpful, as well as the questions you used for peer feedback in Section 4.8.

Speaking in front of people: If this is something that bothers you, then deliver your presentation by concentrating on one person in the audience who you know will encourage you. This might be your supervisor or a trusted classmate. This is a technique that is used by many people and can help calm your nerves at the start of a presentation. Remember, everyone is in the same situation so everyone wants you to do well.

4.11.4 What feedback might you receive for your presentation?

You will receive feedback from two sources: your peers and your supervisor. They will comment on areas such as:

- how clear and coherent your argument is
- how relevant, clear and explorative your research is
- how appropriate the contexts and perspectives you have explored are
- if you have included all the required elements for the RP and your format choice
- how well-organized your project is so far
- how successfully you communicate your ideas
- how your ideas have changed or developed
- the impact of your ethical dilemma and how you have approached the RP.

The feedback may be delivered using a feedback form like the one below.

■ **Table 4.28** Example of feedback rubric for presentations (Source: IB RP TSM, p.49)

Student name:				**Date:**			
	Ethical dilemma and relation to career field	**Contexts and perspectives explored**	**Research findings**	**Change and/or development of understanding**	**Personal position on the dilemma**	**Impact**	**Communication**
Level	**Is the ethical dilemma clear? Is it linked directly to an identified career field?**	**Are various contexts and perspectives explored thoroughly and with intention?**	**Is the research broad and deep enough to fully support the project? Are the sources reliable?**	**Is there identification of changes and/ or development in thinking or understanding?**	**Is the personal position clearly identified? Is the personal position adequately supported?**	**Has the impact of the dilemma, personal position or student learning been explored?**	**Is communication clear? Are ideas cohesive and well organized?**
1	Dilemma is unclear. Unclear link to career field.	Various contexts and perspectives are not explored.	Insufficient research.	There is no identification of changes and/or development in understanding.	Unstated or implicit personal position.	No exploration of the impact.	Ideas are unorganized and not communicated clearly.
2	Partially clear dilemma Implicit link to career field.	Various contexts and perspectives are partially explored.	Research is adequate but reliability of sources is unclear.	There is some identification of changes and/or development in understanding.	The personal position is stated but unclear.	There is some exploration of the impact.	Ideas are organized and presentation is generally clear.
3	Clear dilemma. Clear link to career field.	Various contexts and perspectives are explored thoroughly and with intention.	Appropriate research. Sources are reliable.	There is sufficient identification of changes and/or development in understanding.	There is a clear personal position.	There is sufficient exploration of the impact.	Ideas are well organized, cohesive and clearly communicated.

■ **Table 4.29** Possible content for feedback form

Notes on ethical dilemma and relation to career field	
Notes on contexts and perspectives explored	
Notes on research findings	
Notes on change and/or development of understanding	
Notes on personal position on the ethical dilemma	
Notes on impact	
Notes on communication	

LEARNING ENGAGEMENT

Understanding the criteria

With your peers, create your own traffic-light feedback form by using the following headings and questions. Decide what the traffic-light descriptors would be (red, amber and green) for achievement in those areas. The first one has been done for you.

1 **Ethical dilemma and relation to career field:**
Do I think the ethical dilemma is clear? Can I understand a clear link to a career field?
- **Red:** Dilemma is unclear. No clear link to career field.
- **Amber:** Dilemma is partially clear. The link to the career field is partially explored.
- **Green:** Clear dilemma. Clear link to career field.

2 **Contexts and perspectives explored:**
Are there a variety of contexts and perspectives explored? And how far are they explored?

3 **Research and findings:**
Do the sources seem reliable? Are there enough sources to support the project?
4 **Change and/or development in understanding:**
Is there evidence of a change in thinking about the ethical dilemma in this process so far? How much change is evident?
5 **Personal position on the dilemma:**
Can I tell what the speaker's personal position is? Is this implicit or explicit?
6 **Impact:**
How far has the impact of the dilemma, personal position or speaker's learning been explored?
7 **Communication:**
How well does the speaker communicate their ideas? Is the presentation well-organized?

This section has focused a lot on building a presentation and what kind of feedback you might receive from your supervisor and peers. Do refer back to Section 4.8 for ways to respond to the feedback you receive but, hopefully by now, you are well-versed in not taking this personally. You will be more able to spot helpful feedback and more open to balanced criticism that expands your thinking. Remember, this is a skill to develop over a lifetime, so don't be too harsh on yourself if you find this hard.

4.11.5 Summary

- The presentation is a compulsory part of the RP process and is not formally assessed.
- In ten minutes or less, you will present where you are in the RP process with your findings, current thinking and positionality, and will have the chance to answer questions and gain feedback to assist you in your next steps.
- You can use visual aids and/or presentation software if you wish.
- You will give feedback to your peers, and receive feedback from your peers and supervisor based on the assessment criteria.

4.12 Using the assessment criteria

INQUIRY QUESTIONS

- What is being asked in each criterion?
- How can you use the assessment criteria as a tool for redrafting successfully?
- What might evidence look like for each criterion?

It can be easy when working on an assessment (within any subject in your CP) to worry about what you have not done yet, or feel that you are not doing everything exactly right. However, it is important to reframe this so you can concentrate on what you are doing well, and this positive approach also reflects how examiners approach the marking of your RP. Remember that when your work is assessed by the IB, they look for what you are doing rather than what you are *not*. So when using the marking criterion descriptors, they start at the bottom and move upwards until they find the highest level of achievement for your work.

Although we will examine the part of the process where the assessment criteria are applied formally, remember that the assessment criteria are there to support you throughout the project.

4.12.1 The RP assessment criteria

This section explores different ways of interacting with the criteria so you can assess your own progress, find ways to improve different aspects of your work and use the criteria as a checklist for your final reflective project (RP).

All of us have been using assessment criteria for years, whether we realize it or not. As you get further on in your studies, and particularly in the CP, you will use the criteria more and more as a tool. However, it's important to be honest and say that our history with marking schemes can induce feelings of frustration, confusion, anxiety and even boredom as we perceive the sea of words in front of us. That is why it is important to build up your understanding gradually and take it step by step. There are various tools suggested in this section—some might work for you particularly well. Find what works best for you and gives you those lightbulb moments.

Let's start off with the headings before we delve into the detail.

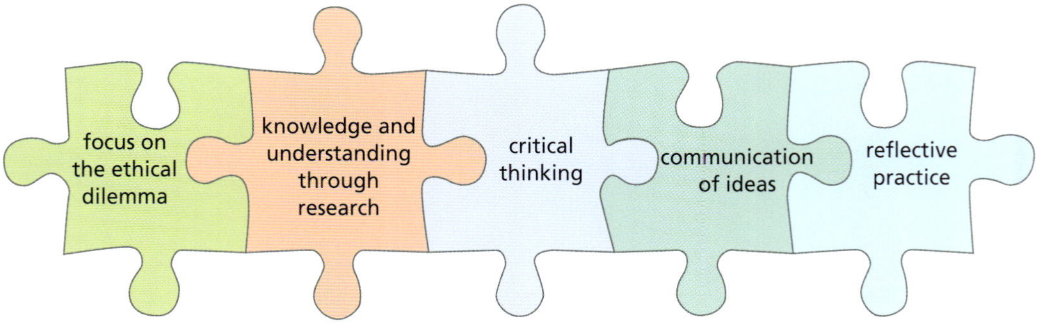

■ The RP assessment criteria

What is being asked in each criterion?

Table 4.30 (Source: IB RP guide, pp.50–53)

Criterion	Description	Key terms of assessment
A: Focus on the ethical dilemma	'This criterion assesses the extent to which you identify a career-related ethical dilemma and explore it by focusing on differing perspectives and varied contexts.'	Nature of the ethical dilemma, perspectives, focus and context
B: Knowledge and understanding through research	'This criterion assesses how effectively you have used research to develop and demonstrate your understanding of issues related to the ethical dilemma and their impact on different people or groups in different contexts.'	Research, understanding, impact of ethical dilemma
C: Critical thinking	'This criterion assesses how effectively you have analysed the ethical dilemma and synthesized your research to determine and justify your personal position on the ethical dilemma, and that you have taken into consideration your position's impact on and implications for various contexts and groups.'	Analysis and synthesis of research, personal position: reasoning and evidence, personal position: justification and impact
D: Communication of ideas	'This criterion assesses how effectively you organize your ideas and use appropriate terminology and structural elements to clearly, cohesively and effectively communicate your ideas.'	Terminology, structure, development organization of ideas
E: Reflective practice	'This criterion assesses how effectively your project demonstrates your planning, research and reflective practice throughout the process.'	Reflection on process, reflection on project, reflection on learning

Top tip!

- If you temporarily colour-code your project according to the criteria in Table 4.30, you will soon see where the gaps are in your RP.
- You can also assess your learning journal by using the guiding questions from Criterion E to see how you are using your reflective and reflexive skills. You might find some elements of reflexive practice particularly difficult and may not have developed your ideas as far as they could possibly go.

Links

You may be reading this page at different times of the RP process. If you are in the early stages of your RP, read through the summary above and think about what is already familiar. Maybe you have explored ethical dilemmas and positionality in PPS. Perhaps you have explored potential impact and implications on different groups in CE. You may have had a learning engagement in LCS where you have considered how you organize your ideas and use appropriate terminology with cultural impacts in mind.

4.12.2 Guiding questions for each criterion

This is a great list of questions for checking your final project. However, why wait until then? Use this to look through your initial draft before you submit it, as well as your learning journal.

Remember, these questions are only suggestions so there may be lots more!

Criterion A

- Have you identified an appropriate career-related ethical dilemma?
- Have you explored the ethical dilemma from multiple perspectives?
- Have you sustained focus on the dilemma by providing relevant examples from varied contexts?

Top tip!

Trace your ethical dilemma. Do you identify, explore and sustain your focus? Temporarily colour-code your RP if you like.

To achieve the highest level in this criterion:

- **Nature of the ethical dilemma:** An ethical dilemma is clearly and precisely defined, and could lead to several possible resolutions. The relation of the ethical dilemma to a specified career is clearly stated.
- **Perspectives:** The work balances the exploration of differing perspectives on the ethical dilemma.
- **Focus and context:** There is a clear, sustained focus on the ethical dilemma. The examples and variety of contexts provided are effective.

(Source: IB RP guide, p.50)

Criterion B

- Have you effectively conducted research?
- Have you demonstrated knowledge and understanding of issues related to the ethical dilemma?
- Have you considered the implications and impact of the ethical dilemma in different contexts and on different individuals or groups?

Top tip!

Trace the effect of your research with colour coding. Look for knowledge and understanding of your ethical dilemma, and implications and impact on individuals and groups.

To achieve the highest level in this criterion:

- **Research:** The scope and depth of the research are comprehensive. An extensive range of resources is used.
- **Knowledge and understanding:** The work indicates extensive knowledge and understanding of issues related to the ethical dilemma.
- **Impact of the dilemma:** The work demonstrates excellent understanding of how identified contexts, individuals or groups are impacted by the issues explored.

(Source: IB RP guide, p.51)

Criterion C

- Have you analysed the research and synthesized the information?
- Have you used reasoning to identify a personal position on the ethical dilemma?
- Have you justified your position?
- Have you taken into consideration the impact or implications of your position?

Top tip!

Trace your position. Do you state and give reasons for your personal position? Do you justify it and explore its impact and implications?

To achieve the highest level in this criterion:

- **Analysis and synthesis of research:** Analysis and synthesis of research are thorough. Relevant findings are effectively discussed.
- **Personal position (reasoning and evidence):** A personal position is identified and supported by clear, focused reasoning, which is synthesised from and explicitly linked to well-selected evidence.
- **Personal position (justification and impact):** There is a clear and concise justification of a personal position. There is substantial evidence that the impact or implications of the personal position have been thoughtfully considered.

(Source: IB RP guide, p.52)

Criterion D

- Are your ideas coherent and organized in such a way as to communicate clearly and effectively?
- Have you used terminology and structural elements appropriately and effectively to support the communication of your ideas?

Top tip!

If you have written your RP, then read it out loud and check the communication is clear. If you have presented an audio or audio–visual, jot down the argument and ideas down as you hear them. If you have used a visual format, then visually trace your ideas and talk through out loud as you do. Then with whatever format you have chosen, mind-map the terminology and features you have used that are particular to that format.

To achieve the highest level in this criterion:

- **Terminology:** Relevant terminology and/or appropriate stylistic conventions are consistently and accurately used to support the communication of ideas.
- **Structure:** The project is effectively structured, which supports the clear and coherent communication of ideas.
- **Development and organisation of ideas:** Ideas are well developed and are presented in a logical and coherent manner.

(Source: IB RP guide, p.53)

Criterion E

- Have you demonstrated reflective practice?
- Have you reflected on your learning process?
- Have you reflected on your learning and how it has had an impact, or might have an impact in the future, on yourself or others?
- Have you critically examined your own and others' thinking, actions or decisions?

Top tip!

In your final written reflection, go back to your original understanding of metacognitive, process and critical reflection, and self- and critical reflexivity, and check you have included features of these—process, actions, beliefs and impact on self and others.

To achieve the highest level in this criterion:

- **Reflection on process:** Reflections include thoughtful explanations for decisions, actions and thinking, and most are justified.
- **Reflection on project:** There is a detailed evaluation of the project's effectiveness. Relevant strengths and limitations are explained.
- **Reflection on learning:** Reflections on how learning and new understandings have an impact on the student or others are thoroughly considered and discussed.

(Source: IB RP guide, p.53)

It's important to recognize that these lists of questions might cause you confusion at points, which is a frustration worth pushing through. When this happens, it will highlight areas of your process that you might need more support with or need to increase your understanding of. Remember to ask your supervisor and peers for clarification and help.

Learning journal

Use your learning journal to reflect on the criterion questions above.

4.12.3 What evidence do I use to demonstrate each criterion?

It's one thing to understand what the criteria are asking; it's quite another to know what that actually looks like in reality. Everyone's RP will be such a personal response in a wide variety of formats that it's important to know how you can show you have achieved the criteria.

Criterion A

The research question should clearly define an ethical dilemma, and its connection to a specific career field should be clearly stated. There should be a clear, sustained focus on the ethical dilemma throughout the project. This can be shown by:

- contextualizing the dilemma within relevant issues in the career field
- using examples from a variety of contexts (e.g. local, global, historical, cultural)
- explaining how it has an impact on various individuals or groups whose perspectives are explored and discussed in a balanced way. (This also demonstrates that differing views have been taken into consideration as students develop their own personal positions.)

Criterion B

The project should demonstrate what students have learned from their research on the issues and perspectives related to the dilemma. This can be evidenced by:

- the range of resources used
- a thorough discussion of issues related to the ethical dilemma and its impact on different individuals or groups
- the variety and quality of examples used.

Criterion C

It should be clear to the reader that students have thoroughly analysed and thoughtfully reflected upon their research. This can be demonstrated through clear and relevant connections between conclusions drawn and evidence from the research.

Students must use reasoning from their findings and reflections to clearly state a personal position on the ethical dilemma. The personal position should be justified by explaining their reasoning. The justification should demonstrate that students have considered the potential impact or implications of their position.

Criterion D

The project should be structured in a way that supports clear communication of the student's ideas. This can be shown by:

- ensuring a clear and cohesive organization of ideas
- using structural conventions (e.g. headings, labels for graphs or tables, transitions, bullets, quotations, introduction and outro/conclusion sections that are appropriate to the format used)
- correctly using terminology that is specific to the topics being discussed
- using appropriate stylistic conventions for the chosen format (e.g. imagery, sound, visual effects, word choice, tone, formatting, gestures or body language in a presentation or film).

Criterion E

Several areas for reflection should be included in the final written reflection:

- reflection on the planning and research process
- reflection on feedback and any meaningful action taken (if appropriate)
- evaluation of the project's execution and final result
- reflection on how the student's learning and any new understandings from the project have had an impact on their thinking or decision-making.

The reflections recorded throughout the RP journey can be used as a starting point for developing the final written reflection, as students should have already reflected authentically on these aspects of their project.

(Source: IB RP guide, pp.33–35)

LEARNING ENGAGEMENT

Can you use these assessment criteria for different purposes? See how many you can tick off throughout the RP process.

- ☐ Discussing individual criterion with your supervisor as your RP develops.
- ☐ Discussing the difficulties you are having with your supervisor and finding where that is represented in the criteria.
- ☐ Using the criteria as a checklist before you submit your initial draft.
- ☐ Reflecting upon the criteria while preparing your presentation to your peers and supervisor.
- ☐ Reflecting on your initial draft once you have implemented feedback, and looking for the strengths and areas for development.

4.12.4 What am I aiming for in each criterion?

Table 4.31

Criterion	Aim	Explanation
A	The key terms you are looking for here surrounding your ethical dilemma in context are clarity, focus, variety and balance.	**Clarity:** Your ethical dilemma and its relation and importance to your chosen career field is absolutely clear, and this focus is sustained throughout your whole project. **Variety:** You want the ethical dilemma to offer various possible solutions that will each impact individuals, people and/or communities. You also balance a variety of perspectives, all with their own unique influences, without letting any dominate your exploration. Lastly, you explore a variety of contexts that can differ greatly from each other but are all connected to the ethical dilemma and the impact it has.
B	The key terms you are looking for here surrounding knowledge and understanding through research are scope, depth, knowledge and understanding, cause and effect, impact.	**Scope and depth:** Your research is wide in variety and appropriate depth. You explore enough that you can connect ideas and lead to understanding cause and effect. **Knowledge and understanding:** Your research has enabled you to thoroughly understand your ethical dilemma and connected issues from multiple perspectives. **Cause and effect, impact:** You explore how the ethical dilemma impacts different groups and the causes of it in different contexts. You explore the role of context, values and beliefs in shaping perspectives.
C	The key terms you are looking for here surrounding critical thinking are analysis, synthesis, reasoning, evidence, justification and impact.	**Analysis and synthesis of research:** This is thorough and you discuss your findings effectively in terms of how and why they are significant in relation to your ethical dilemma, and explain how ideas connect together throughout your project, from multiple angles. **Reasoning and evidence:** You have your own personal position—you have answered your own research question and backed it up with evidence. **Justification and impact:** You explain how you got to your personal position, understanding that there are no ideal solutions, but you can weigh up the positive and negative impacts as a result of your solution. You also give alternative solutions and explain why they are not as effective as yours.
D	The key terms you are looking for here surrounding communication are terminology, structure, development and organization.	**Terminology:** You utilize appropriate topic-specific terms throughout your project and use the style and conventions of your chosen format. This could include word choice, tone, formatting, use of imagery, sound and visual effects. **Structure:** There is a clear structure that enables ideas to flow. You might use headings, sections, clear labelling for diagrams, graphs and tables, clear quotations, etc., all in line with what is appropriate for your chosen format. **Development and organization of ideas:** All this combines to allow your ideas to develop logically and build on each other. Your communication allows you to go deep into your ethical dilemma, connect your ideas and be clear in your explanations.
E	The key terms you are looking for here surrounding reflection are process, project and learning.	**Reflection on process:** This includes explaining important decisions or actions you made throughout the process, the impact they had and the feedback you got. **Reflection on project:** You explore how effective your project is and the strengths and areas to improve on. **Reflection on learning:** This is where you consider the impact of your learning and any new understanding you have gained in terms of actions and your personal growth. You also think about the impact your RP might have had or still could have on others.

Reflection and reflexivity

Take a moment to look at how you have developed from being guided through the RP process to being able to independently assess your own work for strengths and areas for development. Can you see anywhere else in your CP process where you have transitioned from being guided and supported to working by yourself?

4.12.5 Summary

- Your RP will be assessed using five assessment criteria: focus on ethical dilemma (6 marks), knowledge and understanding through research (6 marks), critical thinking (8 marks), communication of ideas (6 marks) and reflective practice (8 marks).
- Using the questions in this chapter and your learning journal will help you reflect on how you are developing against each criterion throughout the process.
- Table 4.31 will help you self-assess your RP draft and help you improve.

4.13 Completing your RP

INQUIRY QUESTIONS

- How do you complete your final written reflection?
- What is a *viva voce* and how do you prepare for it?
- How do you make final checks before submitting your RP?
- When completing your project, how can you use your learning journal for the final written reflection and *viva voce* with your supervisor?

Learner profile

Balanced, risk-taker, reflective, caring, open-minded, communicator, knowledgeable, principled, inquirer, thinker

What part have all the learner profile attributes played in this process?

Each phase of the RP process demands particular characteristics of the learning profile to play their part. In the final part of the RP, as you complete and submit your hard work, it is rewarding to look back and consider how all characteristics of the learner profile contributed to your success.

4.13.1 Revision and final project

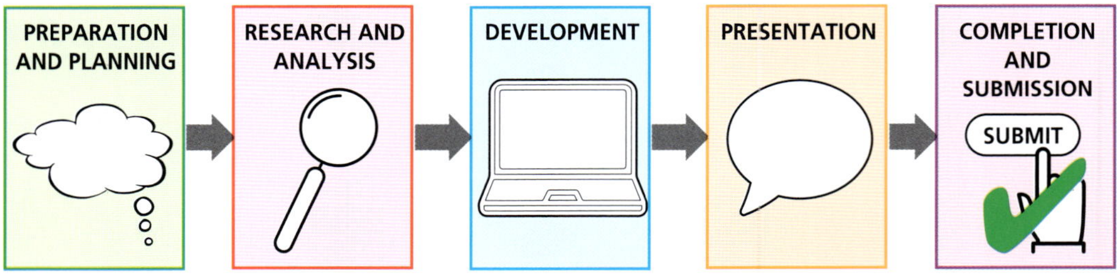

■ The RP process

This part of the process is the final flourish before submitting all your hard work to the IB. You have completed the majority of the reflective project (RP) and this is the final part before submission. By the time you get to this part of the process, you truly are in charge of your own learning, so be proactive in finishing this last part with a bang and not a damp firework.

■ Table 4.32

Phase of RP	Detailed steps involved
Completion and submission	● **revision and final project** ● Revise and finalize the project based on reflections and any further actions taken. ● Share a draft of the project with the supervisor for feedback. (**Note:** The supervisor can only review one draft. Additional revisions can be made after supervisor feedback before final submission.) ● Ensure that all required elements are included. ● Use the assessment criteria to self-evaluate the project. ● Develop the written reflection for the RP—final reflection form (RP/FRF). ● *viva voce* ● Complete the final project. ● Submit the final project and RP/FRF. ● Take part in the *viva voce* with the RP supervisor to discuss and reflect on the process, the final project, the learning journey, any new understandings, personal growth and impact. ● **final submission** ● Student authenticity confirmed to IB by RP supervisor. ● RP supervisors provide predicted grades. ● RB projects are uploaded to the IB.

In this final stage of the RP process, you are advised to:

- Use your feedback and reflections to finish your written reflection for the RP—final reflection form (RP/FRF).
- Take advantage of your familiarity with the assessment criteria and self-evaluate your project to make further improvements.
- Check the requirements for formats in Section 4.10 to ensure you have got the word count, structure and file format (that you must save and submit your RP in) correct. Then submit your project!
- Take part in a *viva voce* with your supervisor once you have completed and submitted your final project. This is an interview where you meet to reflect on your process and project, and to discuss your learning journey as whole, including the wide-ranging impact your RP has had.
- Once you have completed the *viva voce*, your RP supervisor will provide a predicted grade and confirm that your work is all yours when they upload your final project to the IB.

4.13.2 The learning journal and final written reflection

Your learning journal has accompanied you throughout this process, and you will still need its support. This is where your efforts with your learning journal pay off. You can take a moment to thank yourself for your commitment to this process because, if you have been using the learning journal regularly and as intended, you will find this final part of the RP quite straightforward.

For you will now use your learning journal to write your final written reflection and prepare for your *viva voce* (final discussion). Excerpts from your learning journal can actually be used as the basis of your *viva voce* with your supervisor.

The written reflection should include evidence of metacognitive and critical reflection, as well as critical and self-reflexivity, which you have been building your understanding of throughout the RP process and in your learning journal. Therefore, this section is an extension of Section 4.4 on the written reflection and expands your thinking on how to complete it.

Links

Remember that you have not just been developing your research skills in the RP. Reflection and reflexivity, as you know, is an essential part of LCS, CE and PPS, so you have lots of experience of using these skills in other contexts.

Just like the learning journal itself, there is not one single approach to the written reflection. Consider what Criterion E states is required in the written reflection in the top-mark band (below). The indicators of a successful written reflection are:

- **Reflection on process:** Reflections include thoughtful explanations for decisions, actions and thinking, and most are justified.
- **Reflection on project:** There is a detailed evaluation of the project's effectiveness. Relevant strengths and limitations are explained.
- **Reflection on learning:** Reflections on how learning and new understandings have an impact on the student or others are thoroughly considered and discussed.

(Source: IB RP TSM, p.59)

Top tip!

Start slow and let yourself get the hang of the exercise. If you get stuck, this would also make a great chat with your supervisor. However, you will probably notice that you have done much better at this than you first anticipated! Once you have some momentum, let yourself add three more places where you identify your reflective skills.

LEARNING ENGAGEMENT

Explore the indicators given above for a successful written reflection. Which words stand out to you?

If you have kept a physical learning journal, you might take some colourful index tabs or sticky notes, write down phrases from the process, project and learning points above. Look back through your learning journal, placing them where you think you might have achieved this aspect of the criterion.

If you have used a digital platform for your learning journal and created non-written responses, you can colour-code or highlight them with comment boxes or digital sticky notes.

Find three places in your learning journal where you feel you have achieved the criterion to start with. You might expand this to include something else from each area of process, project and learning, once you've got the hang of it.

What you need for the written reflection

By now, you should have thoroughly reviewed your learning journal for evidence of your reflections on process, project and learning.

Remember, there is no prescribed way of presenting your written reflection, although it must remain under 1,000 words. These following questions will guide you to the areas that really need expanding upon in your work. In other words, the more perceptive and self-aware you are in your written reflection, the more successful your reflection will be.

We are now going to dig deeper into what you need for your written reflection and how you will use the learning journal to develop it. It's important that you have done the learning engagement above before you proceed to this activity. For this we are going to return to the guiding questions that have supported your process that we first looked at in Section 4.4 and, you've guessed it, reflect upon them further. This can form the basis of your written reflection.

GUIDING QUESTIONS

- What do you think were the most successful parts of your process? Why?
- What problems did you have during the research and development and how did you overcome them?
- Would you change anything about the way you did the process? Why do you feel this way?
- What would you take forward from this project in terms of skills to future projects? Why?
- How did you use peer and supervisor feedback in the process? Was it helpful in decision-making? Why?
- Looking back on your research, what new questions came out of it?
- What new ethical considerations did you make and did any of your research surprise you? Why?
- What do you think is particularly strong about your project and what areas do you think you could improve? Why?
- What were the highs and lows in finding reliable sources? Why?
- What was your original perspective of the ethical dilemma and why did you think this?
- How did your perspective change and what made it change?
- How do you think about the ethical issue differently now at the end of the project? Why?
- What impact has this ethical issue and dilemma had on you? Think now and in terms of your potential future decisions.
- How might your position, informed by your learning, impact others?

(Adapted from the IB RP guide, p.53)

You might be tempted to copy and paste excerpts of your learning journal into your written reflection. It might be that you feel your excerpts make perfect sense in your written reflection straight away, but it is more than likely that you will have to adapt it to work properly. The question to keep in mind is, 'How cohesive is my reflection when I read it out loud?' This means that all the parts fit together to work well as a whole. Your reflection should flow well and each part should clearly connect to the next. Make sure that you adapt your learning journal material as needed to preserve this flow.

Reflection and reflexivity

Reflecting on reflection

When you are reading through your written reflection, check that you have the types of reflection and reflexivity you have developed skills in throughout this process:

- self-reflection
- critical reflection
- self-reflexivity
- critical reflexivity.

4.13.3 Preparing for the *viva voce*

Check in with your well-being. The *viva voce* can sound a little intimidating and, while you naturally want to do as well as possible to do justice to your hard work, it is important to remember just that: you have done the hard work. You have been part of a thorough process, had support and feedback from a variety of sources and most certainly had ups and downs. Have the mindset of celebrating and showcasing what you have done, rather than feeling you are defending yourself in court.

Viva voce

A *viva voce* is a process that has been used for a long time in academia, where a student is interviewed by their supervisor to discuss their thesis. In this case, you will meet with your supervisor who has supported you the entire way through the learning journey, and reflect upon what you have learnt. It is a final authentication that the entire work is your own and you can be proud of this.

Your final RP is the product of being able to analyse research critically, reflect on your discoveries and learn about yourself throughout your learning journey. It is these skills that you want to communicate in the final task of the process—the *viva voce*.

While the supervisor plays a guiding role by asking questions to prompt conversation, the *viva voce* is a dialogue and can be led by you, with excerpts from the learning journal serving as launching points for discussion. The discussion is not about discovering what you don't know; it's a positive exercise in exploring your learning journey.

Top tip!

When preparing your thoughts for the *viva voce*, think about how all the different parts of your RP process connect and the reasons behind your choices.

LEARNING ENGAGEMENT

Joining the dots for your *viva voce*

Use the following part of this section to prepare thoroughly for your *viva voce*. Have a copy of your RP to hand as well as your learning journal. Take time to mind-map or create voice notes to track your thoughts on the following questions, and make a note of any questions you need to think about in more detail. These written/verbal notes will provide you with a clear summary to look at before you start your *viva voce*. And remember, your supervisor cannot ask you every single question here!

Think through how you might make the following connections or provide explanations about the content of your RP:

- how your focus of your RP links with your career interest
- what caught your eye about your ethical dilemma and how this links with your initial thoughts
- the approach you took with your research and how that links to the quality of resources you collated
- how your understanding of your ethical dilemma grew and how you see this in your final product
- how your position about your ethical dilemma has changed and/or developed throughout the process
- your format choice and what influenced you to choose this
- what skills you feel you developed during the process and how this connects with your own assessment of your performance
- how the ethical dilemma impacts you and also how it impacts the wider global context
- how you can take your learning from the RP and use it in your future career or education.

Topics and questions your supervisor could ask

Your supervisor may well ask questions connected with content, like the exercise above, but they could also go deeper into the process, critical analysis, personal development and future impact.

Whatever your supervisor might ask you, if you look at the questions below, they all have one thing in common: they take you from where your associated thinking was at the start of the process, through how it developed to the point where it is at the end.

So, prepare to answer questions such as:

Table 4.33 What questions could your supervisor ask?

Topic	Questions
Content	• How did your focus of your RP link with your career interest? • What caught your eye about your ethical dilemma, and how does this link with your initial thoughts? • What approach did you take with your research, and how does this link to the quality of resources you collated? • How did your understanding of your ethical dilemma grow, and how is this reflected in your final product? • How has your position about your ethical dilemma changed and/or developed throughout the process? • What additional discoveries did you make that made you curious about further investigation?
Process	• Reflecting on your RP journey now, what challenges did you have in the process and how did you overcome them? • What approach did you take with your research, and what were the successes and setbacks associated with this? • Were there any surprises during your research process that led to a rethink of your methodology? • Would you do anything differently, looking back now?
Critical analysis	• What ethical frameworks did you find particularly helpful when analysing your findings? How did they challenge and/or develop your thinking? How did they help you reach the position you hold now? • If you were to undertake any further research, what would you do? • What did you learn about the complexities of ethical dilemmas in your chosen career field? What surprised you? What did not surprise you?
Personal development	• How has the RP process developed how you see ethics in your career field? Has your approach to these topics changed? • What impact has the RP process had on you, and what have you learned about yourself? • What skills have you developed that you feel are the most valuable for your future or education?
Future impact	• What has been the most rewarding aspect and/or most challenging aspect of the RP? • How will your understanding of ethics in your career field impact you in the future? • If you could go back and give yourself advice at the start of the project, what would it be?

Links

Think about all the skills you are not just using, but showcasing in these final stages of the RP. Chances are that you are completing your RP towards the end of your CP course. What experiences and transversal skills can you draw upon in your whole CP experience to support you here and give you confidence? Think about your CRS, DP subjects, LCS, CE and PPS.

Top tip!

A way of ensuring you are prepared for your *viva voce* is to take a deep breath and think through how you would fill in the blanks here:

'In terms of my RP, I used to think … but now I think …'

REAL-WORLD EXAMPLE

Viva voces are actually far more common in the world of work than you might first think. Consider the scenario in many industries of reviewing an employee's performance with their boss, or reflecting on the success of a project with a work team or a client. These discussions involve self-awareness, knowledge, reflection, critical analysis and honesty about the work involved and the progress that has been made along the way.

4.13.4 Project submission to the IB

What happens to your RP once you have completed it?

The RP is externally marked, which means that your RP is uploaded by your school and sent to the IB, and they will mark everyone's reflective projects globally. Your school will also put a predicted grade alongside your upload.

Before you submit your project, take the time to work through this checklist.

REFLECTIVE PROJECT CHECKLIST

Cover page (title page):

- ☐ Have I included the research question?
- ☐ Have I stated my personal code?
- ☐ Have I included the word count?

Declaration of authenticity:

- ☐ Have I included a signed declaration of authenticity?
- ☐ Have I dated the declaration of authenticity?
- ☐ Have I submitted the declaration of authenticity to my supervisor?

Research question:

- ☐ Is my research question clearly stated?
- ☐ Is my research question consistent throughout the project and does not change?
- ☐ Is the ethical issue in my research question clear?
- ☐ Is the ethical dilemma in my research question clear?
- ☐ Is there no bias implicit in my research question?
- ☐ Is the topic area clearly relevant to my chosen career field?

Format requirements (these will vary depending on your format):

- ☐ Have I included a contents page?
- ☐ Have I used section headings?
- ☐ Have I included page numbers?
- ☐ Have I checked the page numbers are accurate?

Research methods:

- ☐ Have I used a sufficient range of appropriate sources?
- ☐ Is there evidence that I have selected and assessed sources carefully?
- ☐ Have I provided evidence that I have considered the implications of different sources?

Synthesis, analysis and critical thinking:

- ☐ Have I used subject-specific terminology appropriately and consistently?
- ☐ Have I explained the significance of the data and information I collected?
- ☐ Does my evidence support my points?
- ☐ Have I evaluated different perspectives and the influence of contexts?

Conclusion:

- ☐ Have I come to my own positionality on the ethical dilemma and made this clear?
- ☐ Do I provide possible solutions to my issue and dilemma?
- ☐ Do I provide further questions that have come from my analysis?

Written reflection:

- ☐ Have I used my learning journal to put my final reflection together?
- ☐ Have I written about the process, project and learning throughout my written reflection?
- ☐ Do I provide evidence of my thought processes and decision-making?
- ☐ Have I considered challenges I faced or changes of direction?
- ☐ Have I used a readable font, such as Arial or Times New Roman?
- ☐ Is my work in font size 12?
- ☐ Are all my pages numbered?
- ☐ Are my graphs/charts/images/illustrations numbered?
- ☐ Are my graphs/charts/images/illustrations captioned?
- ☐ Are my graphs/charts/images/illustrations referenced appropriately?
- ☐ Do my page numbers in the table of contents match up with the pages themselves?
- ☐ Have I proofread all my work for spelling, punctuation and grammar errors?
- ☐ Have I used a consistent system to cite and reference my sources?
- ☐ Have I used quotation marks properly and consistently?
- ☐ Have I cited the source of every quotation?
- ☐ Have I checked I have attributed every quotation explicitly?
- ☐ Have I clearly shown where I have used the ideas of others?
- ☐ Does the appendix (if used) contain only relevant and necessary information?
- ☐ Does the appendix (if used) have a title and an appropriate source?
- ☐ Are each of the appendix items (if used) clearly mentioned in the text of the essay?
- ☐ Are all references to items in the appendix clearly cross-referenced, including the relevant page numbers?

Bibliography (works cited or references):

- ☐ Have I included a bibliography, containing all my sources used to research and create the RP?
- ☐ Has the bibliography been produced in alphabetical order?
- ☐ Do my citations in the body of the essay match the correct references in the bibliography?
- ☐ Does my bibliography list every source used in my RP?
- ☐ Does my bibliography use a referencing system consistently?
- ☐ Does my bibliography specify at least author(s), title, date of publication and the publisher for every reference?
- ☐ Is my punctuation consistent?

Others:

- ☐ Have I submitted a copy of my RP to my supervisor?
- ☐ Am I ready to submit my RP?

Your work here is done. Be proud.

4.13.5 Summary

- Your learning journal helps to draw together your reflections on process, project and learning throughout the learning journey.
- Your learning journal also helps you prepare for the viva voce, where you will discuss the whole learning process and demonstrate the authenticity of your work to your supervisor.
- The checklist in this chapter can be used to make final checks before submitting your RP.

5 Career-related studies (CRS) and the Diploma Programme (DP)

5.1 Career-related studies

INQUIRY QUESTIONS

- How can you make the most of your career-related studies?
- What do we mean by 'competencies'?
- What is meant by 'career' and what will working be like for you?
- How can the Core help your career-related studies?

While much of this book is devoted to the core elements of the CP, it's important to remember that the aims of the Core programme include career-related studies (CRS) and DP subjects too. After all, they make up most of your course. Interconnecting with the Core, the CRS and your choice of DP subjects enable you to develop a wide range of competencies.

You will read and hear a lot about skill development throughout this chapter (as you already have in the other sections) and in the world outside this book's covers. It's important to recognize that skills go hand in hand with other factors that enable you to navigate and self-advocate in the twenty-first century. 'Competencies' refers to a combination of skills, knowledge, attitudes and values that enable you to contribute to the world responsibly and effectively; to fall back on a cliché, they help you to make the world a better place for yourself and those around you, locally and globally. This sentiment is captured in the IB mission statement, so very much drives the CP.

5.1.1 What is meant by a 'career'?

Applied learning, vocational and technical education, industry-specific education ... There are many terms globally for what the CP calls career-related studies, and this takes a central part of the CP.

The CRS element of the CP has an important role in steering the direction of your two-year course and influencing your future career choices and pathways. There is a high chance that one of the reasons you chose the CP is because the CRS was particularly appealing and you could specialize in certain DP subjects. You may think that the CP looks similar in other schools and that all CP students take similar courses to you. In reality, the CP differs from school to school and there is a huge range of subjects available, as schools choose what makes sense for their unique context.

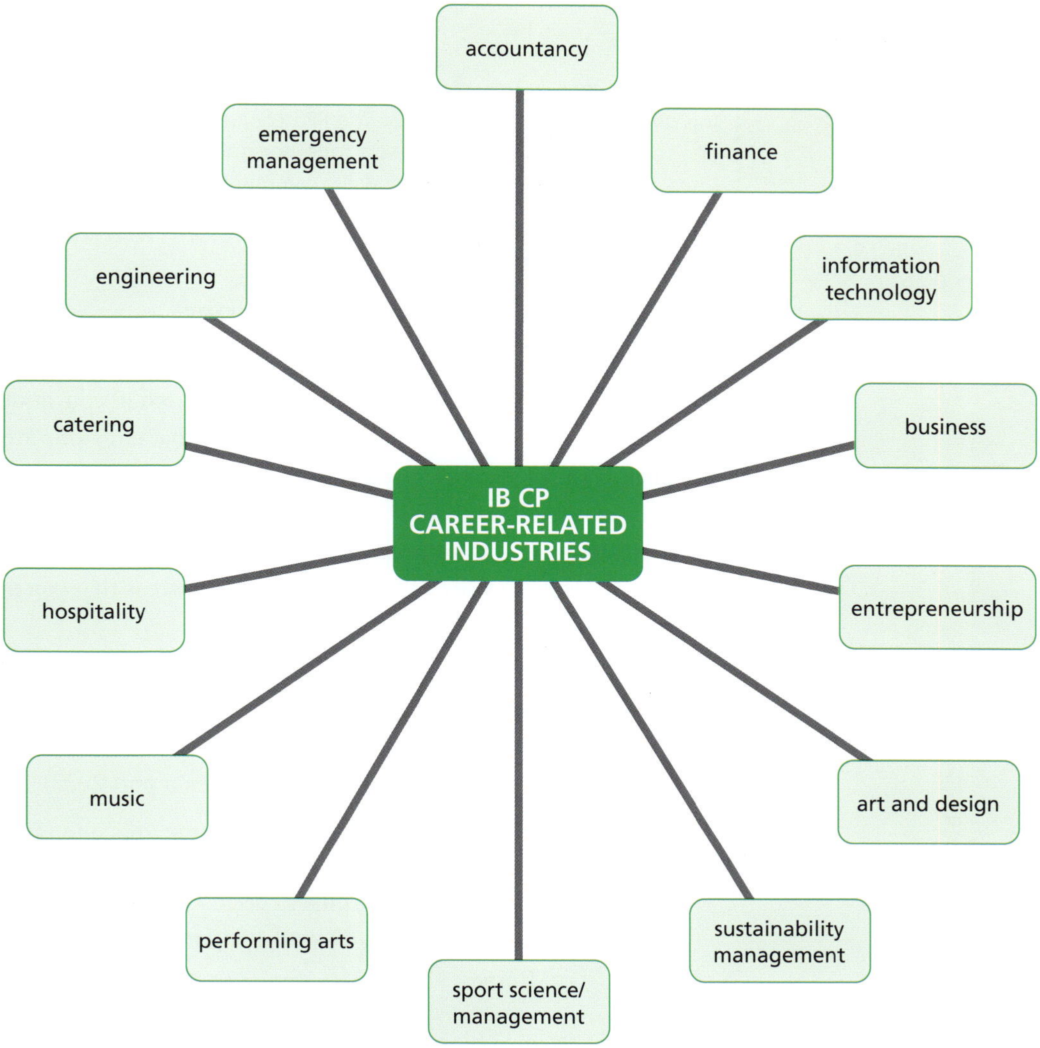

A snapshot of career-related industries associated with the CP in 2025

You may choose to continue a career pathway from your CRS in the future. You may not. The design of the CP is such that it will give you the skills, self-awareness and self-advocacy to adapt to whatever direction you want to pursue. Many people now and in the future will have portfolio careers (which means they pursue multiple income streams simultaneously) or will change career many times. The chances of anyone starting and finishing their career in the same role, field or area of interest are small. This might seem daunting but is all the more reason to focus on what you enjoy and feel strong and curious about right now—this will open you up to opportunities that you might not have seen otherwise.

What am I preparing for?

Many different sources—from the news and parents to research reports and teachers—tell us that we do not know yet what future jobs and careers look like, so we must be adaptable and concentrate on transferable skills. It can therefore be somewhat overwhelming trying to plan for the future. The good news is that by choosing the CP, you have a course designed with the intention to align with what a range of trusted and peer-reviewed research says young people need for future readiness. And the key? Not just developing your skills, but knowing how your skills can transfer to different contexts for different purposes.

Links

Early on in your course, start looking for connections between subjects and how you are using the same skills in different areas. The PPS course will explore transversal skills in detail, but one tool that links all your subjects together is the approaches to learning (ATL) categories of research skills, self-management skills, communication skills, social skills and thinking skills, as a general way of seeing how everything connects.

Embrace being a lifelong learner

You have a head start by studying the CP, as this course will help you understand your skillset with a growth mindset. This term is often used in education, but it is important when considering oneself as a lifelong learner. It means that our skills are not talents determined at birth; such is the physiological way the brain works that skills can be developed constantly. Obviously, we are all different and find our ability to develop skills easier or more difficult in different areas. In this section, we are going to look at a variety of sources that help you to creatively think about your CRS right now and the areas that you might be interested in, in the future.

We are right in the middle of a shift in the way we work. As we saw in the introduction to this book, the World Economic Forum's research in 2023 predicted that 23% of today's jobs will change because 'technology is expected to create 69 million new job roles and displace 83 million current roles' (Source: WEF, Future of jobs report 2023).

> *'The days of learning one trade for a lifetime are gone. To stay relevant in today's job market, workers need to embrace continuous learning and reskilling. With 44% of job skills expected to change within five years, it's essential that both individuals and companies invest in lifelong learning.'*
>
> (Source: WEF, www.weforum.org/stories/2024/10/jobs-skills-work-digital-economy)

As a response to the WEF's report, *Forbes* magazine published an article 'From jobs to skills: What the future world of work will look like'. Table 5.1 contains examples from the article of what researchers, educators and people in industry think about the future of work. What do you think?

Table 5.1 Some predictions about the future of work (quotes from *Forbes* magazine, 'From jobs to skills: What the future of work will look like' by Dan Tynan)

Forbes predicts …	Experts respond …
Skills are the only preparation	'Disruption will strike each discrete role—skills are the only way to prepare.'
Organizations will change how they work	'Instead of a strict hierarchy of employees with fixed roles and responsibilities a skills-based organization will likely function more like a revolving talent pool, with teams assembled project-by-project based on the skills they bring'.
Jigsaw approach to recruitment	'I'm not looking for one person who can do 15 things … I might want to find four people who can each do two or three things and put them all together.'
Be prepared to collaborate with AI	'You need to start designing with AI as part of the workforce'.
The lifelong learner	'Reskilling and learning never ends'/'Organizations need to think about delivering training in bite-sized pieces during the flow of work'
Companies are preparing to thrive with skills	'Companies that put skills-based workforce planning in place will have tested, connected and invested in skills and be in a position to win.'

Top tip!

Ask your teacher to complete the learning engagement and join in the conversation. You might find you have different reactions to each other! Who do you think would be the most prepared for the future?

LEARNING ENGAGEMENT

Review Table 5.1 with a partner. If you have time, look up and read the article it draws on. Then discuss these questions together:

1 What could be the reasons behind these thoughts about the future?
2 What further questions would you like to ask the person saying each one?
3 Do anyone of them surprise you? Which ones do you agree or disagree with?
4 Do these predictions appeal to you?

Remember, at all stages of your CP, you are encouraged to have a voice!

5.1.2 What does your generation look like?

Careers advice and guidance counselling has changed a lot in schools since the turn of the century, with many schools taking a comprehensive approach to it at the very start of your secondary school experience. After all, how do you know what you would like to do if you don't see examples of it around you? Exposure to different areas of work not only develops character, but also a sense of aspiration.

Schools adapt to the needs of their students and these needs have changed over the years due to the climate that you have grown up in. You may also have heard of the terms 'Gen X' and 'Millennials'—it's more than likely these are your parents' generations! You may assume you are 'Gen Z'; however, if you were born after 2010, then you can call yourself 'Gen Alpha'. (This term was coined by the social analyst and demographer Mark McCrindle, and it's well worth looking up McCrindle's comprehensive 'Gen Alpha' infographic on his website.)

Why do any of these terms matter? Well, the way your generation has grown up enables predictions to be made about your future and how the future workforce will need to adapt. In terms of the CP, this matters because no longer do we discuss having one or two careers in a lifetime. You can expect to pivot into new jobs and career areas fairly regularly, and the reason why you can do this is because the focus will be on *how* you can use your skills in multiple contexts.

Interestingly, this book's life will span a crossover of generations, and the last Gen Z students will use this in 2028.

Be curious and open-minded to careers

It's good to explore early on just how many different roles are out there that can be part of your career pathway. It might be there are some career ideas that interest you but seem quite far off in terms of training and upskilling. That might be true, but there is no reason not to consider it as part of your career journey. Then you can trace backwards the different ways of getting there.

In this section, we will take a sample of popular career-related studies that CP students take globally and explore the careers that can stem from them in the present day. The aim is to help you realize the breadth and possibilities of careers and to find the possible connections to what you are doing right now. Look at the suggestions below and then do the learning engagements that follow. While the CRS areas have been separated out for ease of reading, remember that all these areas can interconnect.

- **Performing arts:** Actor, teacher, coach, singer, musician, artist, comedian, therapist, agent, community arts worker, screenwriter, arts administrator, sound engineer, costume designer, set designer, choreographer, stage manager, theatre manager, director, producer.
- **Visual arts and creative media:** Art education, therapy, consultant, fashion designer, illustrator, 3-D artist, makeup artist, set designer, concept artist, web designer, graphic designer, photographer, textile designer, furniture designer, curator, animator, interior designer, exhibition designer.
- **Sustainability management:** Be prepared to work in lots of different industries; for example, head of sustainability for an organisation. Further roles could include supply chain manager, recycling officer, energy engineer, waste management officer, geographical information systems officer, countryside officer, sustainability consultant, sustainability manager, green finance, ecologist or scientist.
- **Business and entrepreneurship:** The very notion of a business means it crosses over into many different sectors and can go hand in hand with entrepreneurship. The following include suggestions of the different ways you can work and do not specify the context. For example, you could be a business or start-up owner but also go in very different directions. Other areas include social entrepreneur, independent consultant, business analyst, marketing/sales manager, management consultant, freelancer, corporate entrepreneurship, start-up employee.
- **Engineering:** There are general engineering fields such as mechanical, electrical, civil, chemical and software. There are specific engineering fields such as aerospace, biomedical, environment, nuclear, petroleum, materials, industrial and computer. There is also a design and manufacturing engineer. Within these industries there are engineering roles for biomedical scientists and production/process/project managers.
- **Medical sciences:** Biomedical scientist, clinical research associate, research scientist, forensic scientist, biotechnologist, histology technician, science writer, nurse/doctor/paramedic/surgeon, physiotherapist, higher education lecturer.
- **IT and digital technologies:** Software developer, web developer, network engineer, IT technician, database administrator, systems analyst, cybersecurity analyst, data analyst, data scientist, AI/machine-learning engineer, cloud engineer, DevOps engineer, product manager, IT consultant. There are also industry-specific roles such as medical/financial/government/educational IT.

For all these careers, the same or similar roles could exist in a variety of settings. For example, a data scientist could work in art galleries, museums, government agencies, design firms, media companies, photography studios, architecture firms, theaters, production companies, universities, private companies, big industry settings, small start-up companies, hospitals, healthcare settings, hospitality, charities and environmental fieldwork—to name but a few!

LEARNING ENGAGEMENT

What interests you?

Review the CRS areas listed and the examples of careers associated with them. Choose one CRS area that interests you and the careers linked to that area. Consider the following questions:

1. What skills will you need to enter those careers?
2. Are those skills you are developing right now? Or could there be a possibility of training in the future?
3. Now broaden your perspective and consider the idea of competencies. What knowledge, attitudes and values accompany those skills?

Looking at engineering as an example, in terms of skills, knowledge, attitudes and values, the following play a role: knowledge of engineering science and technology, mathematical design, analytical skills, computer proficiency, technical expertise in specific field, communication skills, problem-solving, teamwork, attention to detail, leadership, lifelong learning disposition, creative and innovative, resilience and self-direction, strong work ethic and commitment to changing the world.

LEARNING ENGAGEMENT

Creative thinking about careers

You should also consider how careers are connected to the challenges that we are all facing, now that we live in an increasingly digital world, with climate change being a very difficult reality. Let's take the concepts of well-being and sustainability and see how they play a part in your CRS. There are also suggestions of some industries that will very much play a part in the future.

1. What do the terms 'well-being' and 'sustainability' mean to you?
   Discuss with a partner or in a group and settle on some definitions that you connect to personally. Decide on one that you are going to explore in more detail first.
   You may decide to use AI as part of this discussion, but be sure to discuss and critique what AI has to say. Connect it to examples you have thought about yourself.
2. Let's look at four industries that will continue to play a big role in our future:
   technology healthcare renewable energy finance
   How do well-being and sustainability connect with these industries? You can do this part of the learning engagement as a discussion with your classmates and teacher.
3. Now put your CRS in the centre of a page (digital or physical) and mind-map how you think well-being or sustainability connect to your CRS or a career that interests you. (This might be different to your current studies and that is fine!) Once you have created your initial mind map, research further on how it connects with your chosen focus.
   For example, you may be studying sport science as your CRS. Here well-being is not just something that is considered in a business' code of ethics for its employees, but is an entire industry in itself.

5.1.3 Creating a career-related vision

From the examples so far in this chapter, you can see that your career can absolutely parallel your journey as a lifelong learner and take you in all sorts of directions, and that is hopefully reassuring. To think at age 16–19 that you are choosing a career to last most of your life would be somewhat daunting and would inevitably lead to worry, rash decisions or no decisions at all.

Furthermore, by exploring different perspectives on what the term 'career' means in the future, you will appreciate the importance of the term 'career-*related*' in the CP. This term has the flexibility to envisage multifaceted pathways which might weave through several different career-related areas in your lifetime.

Learning journal

A vision of competencies

We started this chapter talking about forming 'competencies', which goes beyond just skill acquisition—it is a combination of skills, knowledge, attitudes and values.

In your PPS portfolio, create a visual of competencies you would like to develop in connection to your CRS or a career you are interested in. You do not have to limit yourself to one career—you can start with what you are studying now and then revisit this as you find career areas you are interested in throughout the course. To get the most out of this exercise, stagger it over time, which will help you develop an attitude of curiosity long-term.

1. Write down your own thoughts or make your own voice note on the knowledge, skills, attitudes and values needed in your future career.
2. Speak to people who know. Rather than reaching for the search engine, there is nothing better than asking people who are in the position to know. Many teachers have worked in other industries. You must also be curious when you take on work experience or work on projects for CE.
3. If step 2 is not immediately possible, then do your own research online. It's good to look for sources of first-hand accounts from particular industries rather than what AI generates first.

Remember that your CRS is a launchpad for all sorts of opportunities, and the boundaries of a subject do not confine you.

How your CRS supports and is supported by the Core

Another important way to make the most of your CRS is to look at how it connects with everything around it. We are going to start by looking generally across the whole of your CP and the way it is designed, so you can use concepts, contexts, content and skills as a way to connect your learning. Being aware that you can make connections in this way will make this much easier than you think. Let's get a better idea of what we are talking about first.

Concepts

Concepts are broad, abstract ideas that organize and connect learning and information. Concepts can be transferred and applied across multiple contexts, so a big idea you explore in your CRS might look very different in another context and will give you another perspective on it. This is great for critical thinking.

For example, if you are studying business or entrepreneurship in your CRS, you might come across concepts such as change, creativity, ethics and sustainability as common threads. However, whatever you are studying for your CRS, consider how those concepts could play a part in your CP too.

Links

Examples of concepts in DP/CRS/Core components are conflict, perspective, identity, well-being, unity, connections, pattern, space, time, communication, representation, transformation, culture, creativity, community, power, diversity.

Context

Your CRS provides a rich context for you to explore in multiple ways. In PPS, you will have the opportunity to take a step back from your CRS and reflect on the ways you are developing transversal skills. Having the time to engage in the skill domains of intrapersonal skills, interpersonal skills, thinking skills and intercultural understanding allows you to understand the reality of your CRS. It might also be that your CRS provides the context for a CE experience, such as internships or work experience.

Content

When schools choose CRS, they will consider what is most relevant for their students. And when teachers create their courses, even if following a globally recognized curriculum model, they will select the content that is the best fit for you and the intended assessment. There will be a lot of content in your CRS and, at times, you might find areas you would like to explore in more detail or from further perspectives. This can provide the foundation for a great RP where you critically explore an ethical dilemma over an extended period of time that you were not able to do in your CRS. (There is more on the RP, CRS and DP subjects below.)

Skills

The skills you learn in your CRS enable you to learn, complete tasks and develop new ideas. Throughout your CP, you will learn skills that enable you to understand and manage yourself, work with other people, think and learn how to contribute to the world in an ethical way. Below we explore in more detail the transversal skills in the four skill domains of PPS that you can connect to your CRS and track throughout your course. However, it's good to remember the ATL skill areas that connect all your subjects—research, thinking, social, communication and self-management.

5.1.4 Connecting your CRS and the rest of the CP

It's time to consider how the course you are studying right now connects to all this exploration about the current and future career climate. We have referred to transferable skills and the variety of careers, and it's important to reiterate that the CP sets you up to tackle the future as a self-advocating, self-aware, lifelong learner.

Exploring ethics in CRS and DP subjects

Your CRS and the DP subjects make up a substantial part of your CP and, whatever you choose, this is a rich resource for developing your ethical-thinking skills and exploring real-world examples of ethical dilemmas. After all, there is nothing better than seeing that something you are studying has a direct application in the world locally as well as globally. Because it is likely that every CP student studies something slightly different and has a very different personal response to what they are studying, this creates a treasure trove of inspiration.

Top tip!

Wherever you keep your CRS work, in digital or physical folders, keep an ongoing record of the ethical issues and dilemmas you have explored. It doesn't have to take much time at all.

Perhaps you study business, healthcare, sport or engineering as your CRS. It's possible you will encounter ethical dilemmas where you get to employ ethical decision-making processes that are appropriate within that career field.

In your CRS, there may be ethical issues that are very broad in nature concerned with gender, culture, race, age and equity. Take gender, for example; you may come across the disparity in pay between female and male athletes or the ethical issue of gender equity in the gaming industry. You may not spend long on the topic in class, and it's important to remember that you cannot reuse work from your CRS for your RP. Still, it can give you the inspiration to take this study further and explore it in far more detail, applying it to different contexts.

Links

The more ethical dilemmas you explore in your CRS, the more ideas you will get for your RP and the ethical dilemma you will choose to explore. Your PPS course and RP process will also enable you to develop the skills and knowledge you need to develop the RP.

How can I connect my CRS to the Core elements?

The CP course is designed for interconnection. The most meaningful connections are subjective and down to you as the individual—that is why, excitingly, everyone's CP experience is different. The following section takes you through some of the ways the CRS connects with each Core element, both in the nature of the subject and the ways you will be studying it. There is an activity connected to each Core element for you to undertake when you have embarked on the CP for 1–2 months, and then revisit it throughout your CP so you can build up the sense of connection. What is most satisfying about doing it in this way is that a little work over a long time builds a complex picture of connection and will be a rewarding journey to look back on.

Personal and professional skills

The PPS course asks you to explore at least four concepts and apply them in a minimum of two contexts to encourage transferability. You must develop a minimum of two skills from the four skill domains. Your CRS becomes immediately relevant because it is one of the six suggested contexts. You curate a portfolio throughout the PPS course. Therefore, it is wholly likely that you will use your CRS as inspiration throughout your PPS course, as it is such a fruitful and rewarding place to explore skill development.

Although you won't yet have decided what to focus on in detail in the PPS course, it is a good idea to keep a note in your CRS learning space or folder of the skills you are developing across intrapersonal skills, interpersonal skills, thinking skills and intercultural understanding. You will also co-create inquiries with your teacher that may well include and build on your experiences in your CRS.

■ **Table 5.2** The skill domains and transversal skills

Skill type	Examples
Intrapersonal skills involve self-awareness and the understanding of our own emotions.	Reflection and reflexivity, resilience, self-advocacy, self-awareness, self-management
Interpersonal skills are the behaviours and strategies we use to interact effectively with others. Communication, collaboration and teamwork to navigate a complex world.	**Change management and conflict mediation**, collaboration and networking, communication, leadership
Thinking skills involve cognitive processes that we use to solve problems, make decisions, ask questions, plan, organize and create.	Critical thinking, creative thinking, **ethical decision-making**, **information literacy**, problem-solving, reflection and reflexivity, systems thinking
Intercultural understanding involves knowledge and understanding of our own culture, other cultures and the similarities and differences between cultures. These skills enable students to be effective and ethical participants in diverse settings.	Civic and social responsibility, empathy, ethics and personal values, **reflection and reflexivity**, **self-efficacy**, social awareness

LEARNING ENGAGEMENT

Discuss with a partner or in a small group the table of skill domains and transversal skills. Which ones do you most associate as important in your CRS? Which ones would you need to find out more about?

Lastly it's important to remember that when you frame your learning through concepts, you make more connections and think more deeply. Your DP courses all have concepts running throughout them and so does the Core—you will find that these concepts undoubtedly play a role in your CRS.

In PPS, the concepts are well-being, change, perspectives, identity, connections and systems. There are many different ways of connecting these to your CRS, but here are a few ideas below to get you started.

Community engagement

Community engagement is all about learning in, from and with communities, as well as applying your knowledge and skills that you acquire through your involvement with communities to other areas of your learning. Since your CRS will inevitably have communities associated with it, connecting your CRS with CE emphasizes the relevance and importance of what you are studying. On a practical level, making the most of work experience and internships, and developing a CE project connected to it, deepens your understanding of your CRS as well as the interconnectedness and complexity of what community can mean. Obviously, not all of your CE projects have to be connected with your CRS, but it is a great context to explore.

The principles that CE is founded upon are dialogue, reciprocity, reflection and reflexivity, and these are also just as important in the approach you take to your CRS.

- The principle of dialogue involves listening actively, holding different perspectives and questioning assumptions, and creating understandings with your classmates and colleagues as you are all collaborating on a similar goal.
- Reciprocity is all about contributing to creating an environment where everyone can work together. Your CRS will also branch out from the walls of your classroom into the community, and how you build relationships there in a fair and equal way is also really important. During your CRS, you will build your understanding of ethical

decision-making, which contributes to being an ethical practitioner within a professional community. Most of all, through your CRS and experiences, you will be held accountable for your decisions, plans and goals; essentially, you will have both individual and shared responsibility in the projects you undertake. So how you work in your CRS will influence your CE experiences and vice versa.

- Reflection and reflexivity is everywhere in your course and is the gateway to being a successful critical thinker. The more opportunity you have to use it in different contexts, the more adaptable and able to deal with complex thinking you will become. In both your CRS and CE you will think critically, out of your comfort zone and learn how to take action. By being able to analyse your actions and beliefs, as well as the actions and beliefs of different individuals and communities within which you live and work, you will better understand the complex way people and systems work. This can only lead to being a more confident thinker and communicator.

The learning outcomes of CE closely align with whatever CRS you are taking; indeed your CRS will often be a context that you choose to develop CE experiences around. In CE, you have the chance to explore how the term 'community' works in a personal, relational and systems way. This has a great connection with not just the nature of your CRS, but also the approach you take to working.

Learning journal

1 A few months into your CRS and CE courses, take your learning journal and write the words 'personal', 'relational' and 'systems' in the centre of the page. These terms all relate to the way community can be understood and they are intended to be connected. But what do they mean to you?
2 Take your understanding of personal, relational and systems from your CE introductory unit and consider how these terms relate to your CRS. It might be that you have already explored this to an extent in your CE classes, so take time to see how your understanding has grown in each area.
3 Create a visual to reflect your current understanding. Are some areas more developed than others? What opportunities can you see for possible CE engagements that could connect to your CRS?

Language and cultural studies

In language and cultural studies, after the introductory unit you will choose an area of exploration, which can be community, career or personal. You may potentially have very close links between LCS and your CRS, as the latter gives you a very practical forum to develop your language skills as well as intercultural understanding.

For example, you may concentrate on your professional use of a language during an internship arranged for the end of your first year of CP. Equally, you might want to develop your professional use of a language that is different from the language of your host country in order to gain more global experience. Conceptually, it's good to take advantage of the four LCS concepts to support your thinking—perspectives, power, communication and identities.

REAL-WORLD EXAMPLE

Bella and her classmates were studying performing arts for their CRS, specifically focusing on the dance industry. Some of the class found the language of instruction challenging whereas for others, this was either their first language or one in which they were fluent. After the introductory unit, all the class had a very clear idea of their language and cultural repertoire through their language and cultural portraits and also how this course could support their future aspirations.

Students explored the language and culture associated with the performing arts. Many of the class decided to pursue the area of exploration of 'career' with each looking at different languages. Some were very keen to develop the language of instruction, so it helped them with their CP right now, whereas others were keen to explore working in different areas of the world and industry—namely, the understanding of languages and cultures that would help them there. Students were interested in developing English, French and Russian, but this very much depended on them as individuals. The course enabled them to look at workplace etiquette, finding a job in another country and practical tools such as navigating auditions, creating CVs and making applications.

What was the effect?

The focus on language and culture in this way enabled the students to broaden their employability skills in an industry that could potentially take them across the world. However, the focus for LCS was rooted in the language students were utilizing every day in their CRS, so the CRS teachers and LCS teacher worked closely together. For example, the LCS teacher took time to understand the CRS and the needs of the students so they could assist in suggesting resources and directions the students could take. Language acquisition also played a part, with students exploring grammatical structures and vocabulary relevant to their industry, and how culture influences the performing arts area in their chosen language. The LCS teacher noticed an increase in confidence with the students over the course of the CP, as they undertook learning engagements that stretched their communication skills and willingness to take risks. All of these learning engagements had a real-world application and a connection to the students as individuals. As the course progressed, what seemed daunting at first, became second nature.

Learning journal

Perspectives, power, communication and identities

Undertake this task once you have been working on the CP for several months and you have completed your introductory unit of LCS.

1 In your learning journal, draw two overlapping circles as the start of a Venn diagram. Make sure there is plenty of space in the overlapping section to write. Label these circles 'LCS' on the left and 'CRS' on the right.
2 Add to the circles how you have explored the concepts of perspectives, power, communication and identities in LCS and CRS. Then move to the overlapping section and add in how LCS and CRS connect through these concepts.

Reflective project

CRS is a springboard of inspiration for the reflective project (RP), in which you will independently explore a research question framed by an ethical dilemma over an extended period of time. Your RP can be based on an ethical dilemma stemming directly from your CRS or it can be a career field in which you are interested. Either way, your CRS is crucial in providing the context and, in some cases, the initial content that inspires the action for your RP. Over the course of your CRS, you will come across multiple ethical issues and dilemmas which will enable you to build your understanding, not just of what ethics is all about, but also how it impacts you as an individual, the actions you take and the beliefs you hold.

Remember that you cannot reuse any of your CRS in your RP. You are reminded of this several times in this book because it is a really important point to note.

Learning journal

There are key terms associated with the RP which each hold meaning for any CRS. Create a glossary of these terms and what they mean in your CRS as you build up the skills that are connected with them.

Below are a few examples to get you started. You will find most of these in the glossary at the end of this book, which you can also use for reference to help you create definitions for yourself in your own words.

Table 5.3

bias	context	ethical thinking	ethical issue	ethical dilemma
local context	global context	modalities	perspectives	position

Your school will have a full RP process in place, where they enable you to build up the skills you need to fulfil the aims of the RP independently. For this, they will draw upon a number of transversal skills that you are developing across your CRS, DP and Core components. However, for CRS, because it influences the course so explicitly, you can build up preparation for the RP in two key ways from the start of your course—by building up an understanding of both ethical thinking and communication skills.

REAL-WORLD EXAMPLE

Bella's CRS are in creative media and she has an ambition to use this directly within the sports' industry, which is a firm passion of hers. She decided to use the RP process to develop her audio–visual skills and made a podcast connected to an ethical dilemma facing the soccer/football world. This gave her the chance to gain expertise in a communication style very relevant to her future ambitions, while also developing her critical-thinking skills and understanding of the ethical issues and dilemmas facing the sporting industry.

Top tip!

Keep a record of communication styles that are most useful in connection to your CRS. In the RP, you can choose from written, visual, audio or audio–visual formats and the reason behind this is so you can develop communication skills most connected and relevant to your future career. If you are considering a career in journalism, then you might want to create a photo-essay or an article for your RP as a way of showcasing your written communication skills and building up your portfolio.

LEARNING ENGAGEMENT

Ethical thinking habits

Every time you explore an ethical issue in your CRS, ask these four things out of habit. Even spending a couple of minutes on this can help get the habit firmly in place.

1. What could be a dilemma that stems from this?
2. What different perspectives might there be on this dilemma?
3. What examples are there?
4. Do I want to explore this further?

5.1.3 Summary

- Making the most of your CRS is realizing its connection with everything else you are studying. Your DP and Core components influence your CRS and vice versa.
- It's important to think about how you are developing, not just in skills but competencies. By competencies we mean knowledge, skills, attitudes and values that make us into an adaptable, ethical and professional worker.
- The landscape of future careers is changing and is at an exciting time with the emergence of AI. You can expect to work in a variety of career fields and jobs in your lifetime, so being adaptable and understanding of your competencies is important.
- Connecting your CRS to your Core components allows you to develop an explicit understanding of how your skills are transversal along with how you might independently explore the role your CRS has in the community. You might broaden your opportunities by developing your linguistic and cultural repertoire in your CRS, and independently exploring over an extended period of time how ethical issues and dilemmas are relevant in your area of interest.

5.2 DP courses and the Core programme

INQUIRY QUESTIONS

- What part do the DP courses play in the CP?
- How might you choose your DP courses?
- What does teaching and learning look like in the CP?
- How do ATL skills in the DP courses connect to the Core?
- How can you connect your DP subjects in your own Core inquiries?

The word 'academic' can be a little confusing. People often use it when describing the Diploma Programme (DP) courses to communicate that they can be complex and demanding, which might give the impression that they are hard to access. Sometimes the word 'academic' can also be associated with being somehow 'better' than career-related or practical courses. None of this is very helpful when preparing to start and manage the DP courses—they are demanding and rigorous but accessible. The important part to remember is that by studying a mix of different courses (academic and career-related), you are learning early on to be an adaptable thinker and worker, which increases your choices in employment, apprenticeships and further study.

As the CP is a baccalaureate course, it has several components that will differ from student to student. The career-related studies (CRS) and DP subjects you choose are down to what your school offers and this can vary greatly between schools. This gives brilliant flexibility, but the nature of some of the courses can differ, and this can catch you unprepared if you are not careful.

Learner profile

Balanced, risk-taker, reflective, communicator, open-minded, caring, knowledgeable, principled, inquirer, thinker

You may be familiar with the IB learner profile already if you have studied the PYP and/or MYP. Take time to discuss with a partner how these characteristics might play a part in your studies for both the DP and CRS.

This section focuses on the DP subjects. DP courses are challenging and will require you to push yourself and your thinking as you step out of your comfort zone. However, what is the alternative? Playing it safe and not seeing what you can achieve? That might seem appealing at times, but actually, it gets dull rather quickly.

5.2.1 How should I define my DP courses?

Let's talk about the DP courses. Combined with the CRS and Core components, you will study a minimum of two DP courses at Standard Level. Many students study more than this, and at Higher Level, which means the DP courses can make up a significant part of your course. Whatever you choose to study, your teachers or CP coordinator will have guided you, so it will be right for you. It is likely you will have discussed where you see yourself after you finish the CP with your counsellor or coordinator, such as in employment, apprenticeships or university, which all contribute to what your CP looks like.

The learning journey

This section is designed to help you find connections between your DP courses and the rest of your CP and to see how accessible the DP courses are. We will also look at tips and tricks for managing your learning process, just like you manage your other CP courses. So let's identify the unique opportunities the DP courses offer before considering what connections you can find with your CRS and Core areas, such as the RP, LCS, PPS and CE.

The first thing to remember is that learning in the DP courses is all about the process, just like your Core and CRS. You are not just working towards final exams as though nothing else matters; you are building skills every step of the way that can be transferred to other contexts. Therefore, we need to explore the DP courses the same way we have for all the other areas of the CP. Ask yourself, what is it you enjoy about learning? Or is that too difficult a question? If so, we need to narrow it down. Explore the following pages, which will not only give you an overview of the DP subjects, but also ask you to reflect on what it is you enjoy learning about.

LEARNING ENGAGEMENT

Let's reflect on where you would like your learning to take you. Listed below are six lines of inquiry you might be curious to pursue in relation to your learning. Follow the three-step process:

1. Skim read these inquiries. Pick out two or three that sound most appealing to you:
   - How can I broaden my worldview and capacity for compassion?
   - How can I sharpen my mind through communication and international-mindedness?
   - How can I understand the how and why of human behaviour?
   - How might I wonder at the universe and contribute to its future?
   - How might I master mathematics as a universal language for understanding the world?
   - How can I shape my identity through creative and critical thinking?
2. Now take time with each of the six inquiries and think of how you have already enjoyed (or not!) exploring them in your education so far.
3. Now revisit your initial response to step 1. Do you want to add to your initial response or change any of your choices?

DP subjects you might take

To be able to provide the CP, a school thinks very carefully about the DP courses that will most appeal to their students, so they might not offer every subject available. Some students can be under the impression that there is a small selection of DP subjects because they only have access to the DP courses their school has provided. Sometimes, a school already offers the complete Diploma Programme as a separate course, so students can access a wide range of subjects. Whatever your reality, you will have been advised to approach your selection of DP courses by considering how they complement and connect with your CRS.

In Table 5.4 (on the following spread) we explore a range of DP courses available in each group of the Diploma Programme. We do not go into detail on every DP course, but we do detail the nature of that group of subjects and provide some examples to explain this further. You might choose a subject that you already have experience in or that you need experience in. However, there are also subjects that you will not have studied before which might also be appealing.

Table 5.4 IB Diploma Programme courses

	Title	Nature of group	Courses	Description
1	Studies in language and literature	Broaden your worldview and capacity for compassion	Literature, language and literature, literature and performance, language and culture (in pilot phase in 2025)	The study of literature and this group of courses, complements any other CRS or DP subjects with its focus on communication skills, critical thinking, empathy and open-mindedness. This area makes you question, reflect upon and reimagine the world in which we live and broadens your repertoire of understanding and connecting the political, historical, economic, social and cultural influences and the impact of the texts we read and write.
2	Language acquisition	Sharpen your mind through communication and international-mindedness	Language *ab initio*, classical languages	Communication and social skills drive studying language *ab initio* and classical languages, and increase your intercultural understanding and capacity for empathy. Studies show how learning languages sharpens your decision-making, memory function and brain capacity. Studying languages widens your horizons by giving you more options for where you might work.
3	Individuals and societies	Understand the how and why of human behaviour	Business management, digital society, environmental systems and societies, geography, global politics, history, philosophy, psychology, social and cultural anthropology, economics, world religions, language and culture (in pilot phase in 2025)	Individuals and societies focus on human behaviour, culture and society, so if you are curious about the human experience and why people act the way they do, then this is your subject area. Individuals and societies cover so many different areas that they cannot help but connect and complement CRS and deepen your understanding of it. For example, students studying business or sustainability might also study psychology or ESS and find that it gives new perspectives on their CRS.

4	Sciences	Wonder at the universe and contribute to its future	Environmental systems and societies, biology, chemistry, physics, computer science, sport exercise, health science, design technology	Studying the sciences enables us to understand the world from the smallest particle to the largest galaxy. The scientific field is also a career area of great innovation and change, dedicated to problem-solving, creative and critical thinking, and working towards solutions. This is a strong group of subjects that complements whatever you are thinking of for your CRS, emphasizing methodology, evidence, and analysis.
5	Mathematics	Master the universal language for understanding the world	Analysis and approaches, applications and interpretations	Mathematics is the foundation for technology, science and engineering careers. The emphasis on problem-solving, logical reasoning and analysis transfers to many career areas. It is also proved to strengthen the mind; its memory and capacity for problem-solving.
6	The arts	Shape your identity through creative and critical thinking	Dance, film, literature and performance, music, theatre, visual arts	First and foremost, you enjoy creativity and expression. You also like critical thinking and problem-solving as you analyse your own and others' work in different media. The arts subjects develop many transferable skills, but particularly communication, adaptability, empathy, and the ability to work with others with cultural sensitivity. Most of all, this group of subjects helps you develop a distinct sense of identity and confidence.

LEARNING ENGAGEMENT

You might have noticed that each of the six DP subject groups was accompanied by a statement that captures something significant about its nature.

For this exercise, look at all these statements below and consider how they might be true for where your learning could take you in the DP subjects you are interested in studying.

- 'Broaden your worldview and capacity for compassion.'
- 'Sharpen your mind through communication and international-mindedness.'
- 'Understand the how and why of human behaviour.'
- 'Wonder at the universe and contribute to its future.'
- 'Master the universal language for understanding the world.'
- 'Shape your identity through creative and critical thinking.'

5.2.2 Approaches to teaching and learning in the DP

Whatever you study, no matter how varied the courses, there is a shared approach to teaching and learning which is defined by specific skills areas. Your CRS will be delivered by another provider but, while the courses will be different, it does not mean that there will not be similarities with how you are taught and how you learn. Both the DP courses and your Core are part of the DP and CP curricula, so it is a good opportunity to explore what you can expect from an IB education and what sets it apart from other education systems. Once you know a little of how this works, you start to see how it plays a part in all areas of your studies. If you have taken an IB programme before, such as the Middle Years Programme, then you might well be familiar with this already.

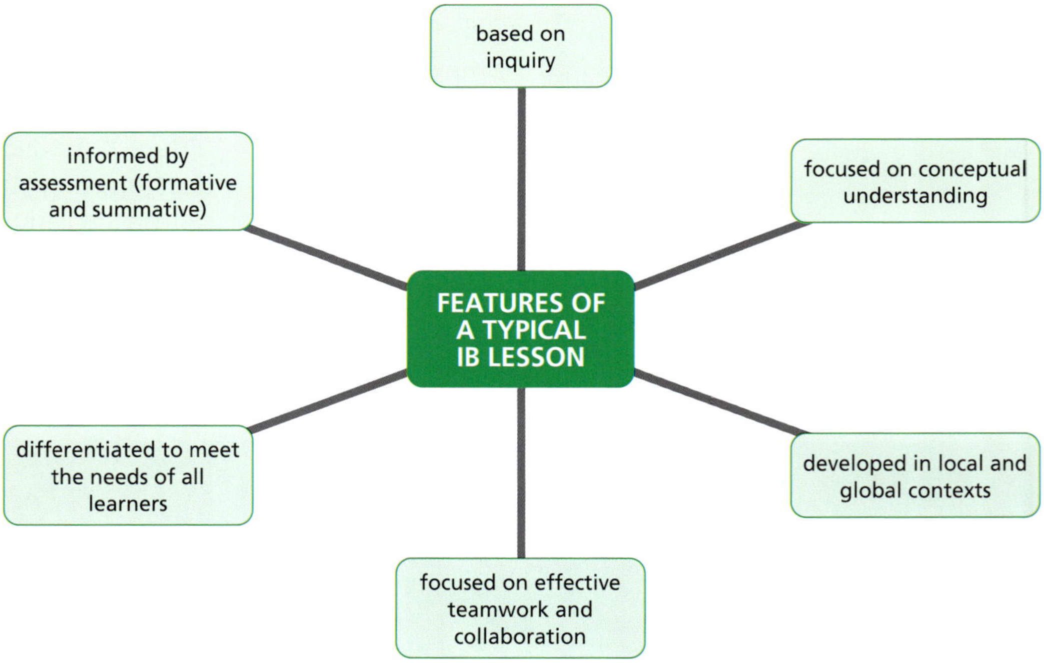

■ What are the features of a typical IB-programme lesson?

When you take part in inquiry-led learning, you have the chance to put your own curiosity at the centre and build your own learning around it. It can all start with asking a question which then opens the doors to building knowledge. This is because inquiry-led learning is a cycle and starts with a question, followed by a period of action and then reflection, which tells you what and how you have learnt and, importantly, what your next steps will be. The more you practise this, the more skills you develop. You might notice that your DP teachers lead and instruct you more through inquiries at the start of your course than they do at the end, because by then you should be more independent and able to create your own inquiries.

Links

You will notice that a number of your Core components follow an inquiry cycle, although it may look different in each area. However, inquiry cycles tend to start with a focus, lead to action and always have a place for reflection.

Focused on conceptual understanding

Learning how to connect your ideas

You will have come across the word 'concept' a lot already. In the IB, it's important that subjects make use of big ideas (called concepts) as these enable you to make connections within the subject and between subjects. You will notice that all your DP subjects have concepts identified that are key to understanding the true nature of this course. The second thing you will notice, early on in your course, is how your other subjects overlap and share many concepts. Accompanying concepts are contexts, content and skills. When you can make connections between your learning, soon you move from just knowing something to understanding it deeply. Rather than just knowing the features of a topic in a particular subject and being able to recount them, you can explore a subject through different perspectives, which gives you a more complex understanding of it. In short, when you explore universal ideas connected to your subject and others, you become a deeper thinker.

Links

Courses such as LCS and PPS explicitly refer to concepts. However, you will find concepts throughout your CRS too.

Developed in local and global contexts

Linking local and global contexts

When you learn about concepts, they can feel quite abstract and remote, so another essential element in your IB education is that you are encouraged to connect your learning to the wider world. This might be in a specific way or in the immediate world around you, or through a wider lens and a global perspective. By doing this, you can see how your learning is relevant to you as an individual, to those around you, your community and further afield. This is another way of being able to see how your education answers the questions: 'How does this matter to me? To my family? To my community? To the world?'

Links

You will notice that the RP asks you to contextualize the ethical dilemma and choose contexts in which to explore its impact. Furthermore, in CE you can explore the impact of yourself as an individual working in a local context, and the impact you might have on the wider community as well as global significance.

Focused on effective teamwork and collaboration

Working with others and as a team

Learning is a social process. Your learning is shaped by your prior experiences and by constructing an understanding with those around you. Learning does not happen when you pass knowledge from one individual to another, but when you build understanding together. This way you are exposed to different perspectives, multiple ways of problem-solving and working towards a common goal. You will learn how to work successfully in a team, which will almost certainly be important in your future work. Ultimately, working with others requires the ability to empathize with different viewpoints and realize the impact and implications of your actions.

Links

In your PPS course, you will co-construct inquiries with your teacher and class and learn together. In your CRS, you may well take part in work experience or an internship, which will directly introduce you to working with others outside the classroom. In CE, you will explore how working with others involves understanding the needs of everyone involved in a project, not just your own.

Differentiated to meet the needs of all learners

Removing barriers to learning

One of the barriers for students to learn successfully is having a fixed mindset. This means you think that your talents and skills are set in stone and you cannot do much to change that. Some sections of this book will refer to having a growth mindset and the idea that, through effort and embracing challenge, you will improve and change. So your DP and CP subjects will purposefully enable you to build up your understanding of yourself as a learner, so that you are confident. Also, you will always explore what you know already before you build more understanding; when you do things this way, it makes you feel safe and more likely to take risks and extend your learning. Another way of building confidence as a learner is knowing how to scaffold the steps to practising a skill and being able to see your growth. All these steps allow you to access your learning. You bring the open-mindedness and effort!

Links

In PPS, you directly participate in inquiries to increase your self-awareness as a skill practitioner in different contexts. The aim is for you to know and understand yourself, your ability to adapt and manage change, and speak up for yourself.

Informed by assessment (formative and summative)

Assessing the journey and not just the destination

You will be assessed in your course. (This is a qualification after all!) However, there are different types of assessment and not just end-of-course exams. There is an assessment *of* learning, which we are most familiar with—called the summative assessment. This takes place after an inquiry or a course. For DP subjects, official summative assessments that count towards your final grade take two forms: internal assessments (IAs) and final exams. Your teachers tend to mark your IAs and these are externally moderated by the IB to check the marking criteria have been used correctly. Final exams are assessed by the IB. However, to get you to the exams successfully, we need other types of assessment too. Assessment *for* learning means assessing how you are doing *throughout* the learning process so you can get feedback to help you reach your goals. Assessment *as* learning means leading your own evaluation and judging your work and that of your peers in order to work out your next steps. For example, you will build your ability to mark your work and understand mark schemes throughout your course. The critical thing to remember about assessment throughout your course is to know that there is a learning journey, not just a learning destination.

Throughout the CP Core, you will use a learning journal (or in the case of PPS, a portfolio) which places your own assessment of your learning process at the centre of your courses.

Approaches to learning

Many more traditional academic courses will make the content of their course the primary focus. The IB way of doing things is slightly different; while content is essential, it holds hands with concepts, contexts and skills. This should sound very familiar if you have already explored the PPS course and other Core areas. If not, let's say they are designed using those features too. Don't worry if you are unsure of their significance, as we explore this below.

First, however, let's start with ATL, which are skills in five different areas: thinking, communication, social, self-management and research skills. Below you can see how the ATL skills are represented in the four skill domains in PPS. There is a lot of terminology flying around here, but do not be dismayed. The 'transversal' part is ensuring that you see how you can move them around and apply them in all situations.

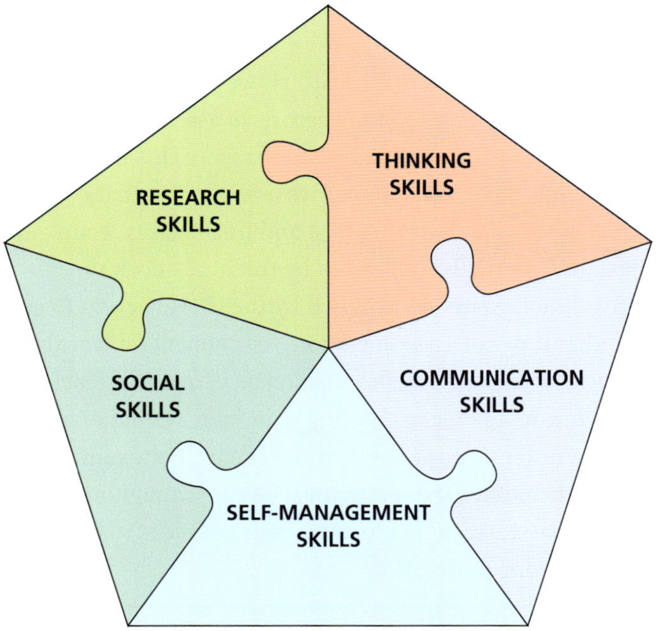

■ ATL skills are transversal skills.

Here is a summary of the ATL skills:

- **Thinking skills** encompass a wide range of processing skills, varying in difficulty from how you acquire and understand knowledge to being able to critically evaluate. Arguably, every skill involves thinking!
- **Communication skills** are vital for advocating for yourself and to incorporate how you speak, listen, read and write, as well as present and argue your ideas.
- **Social skills** are closely aligned with communication skills. These are essential for working and collaborating with your peers and teachers with kindness and respect.
- **Self-management skills** mean both organization skills (managing time and tasks effectively) and affective skills (managing state of mind, self-motivation and resilience, etc.).
- **Research skills** means the ability to gather, critically evaluate and use information for different purposes in an academically honest and effective way.

You don't have to work too hard to find the link between the ATL skills and the Core. Years ago, PPS used to be called 'approaches to learning', so you can see its influence!

5.2.3 Connecting your DP subjects and the Core

It is important not just to focus on how your Core contributes to your DP subjects, but also how your DP subjects connect to your Core. When you transfer and use your learning from your DP subjects and use it in your Core explorations, there is the potential to create your own completely open inquiries that you lead.

■ Personal and professional skills

All the ATL skills are transversal skills. The best way to see how your DP subjects and PPS interrelate is to consider the skill domains and transversal skills at the heart of the DP and how you have been using them already. Let's look at the four PPS skill domains of intrapersonal skills, interpersonal skills, thinking skills and intercultural understanding and the skills contained within them.

■ **Table 5.5** The four PPS skill domains and the skills they contain (Source: IB PPS guide pp.21–25)

PPS skill domains	Skills contained
'Intrapersonal skills involve self-awareness and understanding of our own emotions. Students explore their own traits, behaviours, emotions and abilities to develop an awareness of their own interests, goals, strengths and areas for improvement.'	Adaptability, reflection and reflexivity, resilience, self-advocacy, self-awareness, self-management
'Interpersonal skills are the behaviours and strategies we use to interact effectively with others. Students practice communication, collaboration and teamwork skills to build confidence in relating to others. These skills enable students to influence, manage and respond to change in a complex world.'	Change management and conflict mediation, collaboration and networking, communication and leadership
'Thinking skills involve cognitive processes that we use to solve problems, make decisions, ask questions, plan, organize and create. Critical and creative thinking, problem-solving and information literacy skills consistently top the list of skills necessary to successfully navigate our ever-changing world in a variety of contexts.'	Critical thinking, creative thinking, ethical decision-making, information-literacy, problem-solving, reflection and reflexivity, systems thinking
'Intercultural understanding involves knowledge and understanding of our own culture, other cultures and the similarities and differences between cultures. It relies on a variety of interpersonal and intrapersonal skills, such as ethics, values and collaboration across cultures, as well as the social awareness and responsibility required to be an effective global citizen. These skills enable students to be effective and ethical participants in diverse settings.'	Civic and social responsibility, change management and conflict mediation, empathy, ethics and personal values, reflection and reflexivity, self-efficacy, social awareness

LEARNING ENGAGEMENT

With a partner, complete the following:

1 Talk through how the descriptors in the first column of Table 5.5 link to what you do in your DP subjects.
2 Then take the ATL skill areas (self-management, research, thinking, social and communication skills) and think about how the transversal skills in the second column link with these areas. How do you see the connection?

By focusing on transversal skills in PPS, you will be enhancing your experience in your DP subjects by being able to understand how, where and why you are developing as a learner.

Community engagement

Threaded throughout your DP subjects are many real-world examples that directly show you how relevant they are. CE gives you the framework to directly connect topics that have interested you in your DP subjects to the wider world and identify the opportunities and challenges associated with communities.

LEARNING ENGAGEMENT

Consider some of the DP subjects below and make a list of CE projects that might stem from them:

- Language and literature
- Spanish B
- Business management
- Environmental systems and societies

We have explored how ATL skills transfer between your subjects, and your PPS course is explicitly about how this happens. However, don't forget that you can use your knowledge from a DP subject and the research methods you learn as a great foundation for a CE project.

Top tip!

Remember to look for the potential community partnerships you can make to develop your projects and what it will bring to everyone for you to work together. For example, a student studying film might consult with students and teachers with the aim of starting a film club for younger years in their school. They could also plan to create a short film festival at the end of the school year.

Language and cultural studies

Making connections between your DP subjects and LCS depends on what is interesting and meaningful to you. Students can choose to enhance their language and intercultural capabilities for academic purposes. LCS can expand your academic language skills and cultural understanding of a career field connected to your DP subject.

After the introductory module, you will have a choice of three areas of exploration to choose from: career, community and personal. From here you might consider the role your DP subject plays in your learning. It is not that you have to use your DP subjects as a connection, but it's worth remembering what a rich resource of inspiration they are. For example, let's say a CP student is considering a career in the field of global politics (by studying first for a degree and then moving into journalism). By focusing on the 'career' area of exploration, they could decide to create a glossary of media-related linguistic and cultural references and influences. This would lead them to a deeper understanding of their subject and the direction they want to take their career in.

LEARNING ENGAGEMENT

Consider the following activities and how you could use your DP subjects to develop your understanding of language and culture:

- translating text from one language to another
- speaking to employers
- creating a campaign for environmental issues
- developing a multimedia experience for a community event.

Reflective project

Your DP subjects are also great inspiration for your RP, which asks you to explore an ethical dilemma either in the CRS you are taking or a career you are interested in. It might be that your DP subjects have given you fascinating insights into careers in that context and this is the chance to explore it further. Here we explore some of the career fields that you might explicitly hear about and study in some capacity during your DP courses and some which you might not have thought of.

Here are some examples of the connections you might make in some popular DP subjects that inspire your decision:

- health and social care + psychology + biology = mental health therapist
- business + environmental systems and societies + art and design = sustainable product designer
- engineering + physics + sports and exercise science = sports equipment engineer (technologies for enhancing performance)

LEARNING ENGAGEMENT

Look at the following career fields, which may or may not be connected to your CRS. How might they be connected to your DP subjects?

Table 5.6

accountancy	finance	information technology	business	entrepreneurship
art and design	sustainability management	sport science	sport management	performing arts
music	hospitality	catering	engineering	emergency management

Many graduates work directly in a field connected with their DP subjects. You will also find graduates who see particular subjects as part of their career development, especially in connection with other sectors. There are some obvious careers, but also ones you may not have thought of.

Table 5.7 Expertise and opportunities connected to studies in different areas

Studies	Expertise and opportunities connected to those studies
Language and literature	Writing and content creation, teaching, communication and public relations, cultural administrator of programmes and events, research and analysis, editing and proofreading
Language acquisition	Translation and interpretation, journalism and media, diplomacy and international relations, business, marketing, law, human resources, charities and NGOs, governmental civil service
Individuals and societies	Social worker, therapist, teacher, researcher, policy analyst, psychologist, journalist, economist, environmentalist, lawyer, public relations, sustainability manager, archivist, librarian
Sciences	Research scientist, healthcare practitioner/researcher, educator, engineer, pharmacist, dentist, paramedic, forensic scientist, psychiatrist, data scientist, veterinarian
Mathematics	Financial analyst, insurance underwriter, mathematician, programmer, accountant, meteorologist, economist, game designer, financial trader, software tester, statistician
The arts	Curator, fashion designer, actor, musician, graphic designer, illustrator, concept artist, arts administrator, educator, therapist, curator

LEARNING ENGAGEMENT

Choose some of the career opportunities suggested in Table 5.7 and consider the ethical issues and dilemmas that are possibly associated with them.

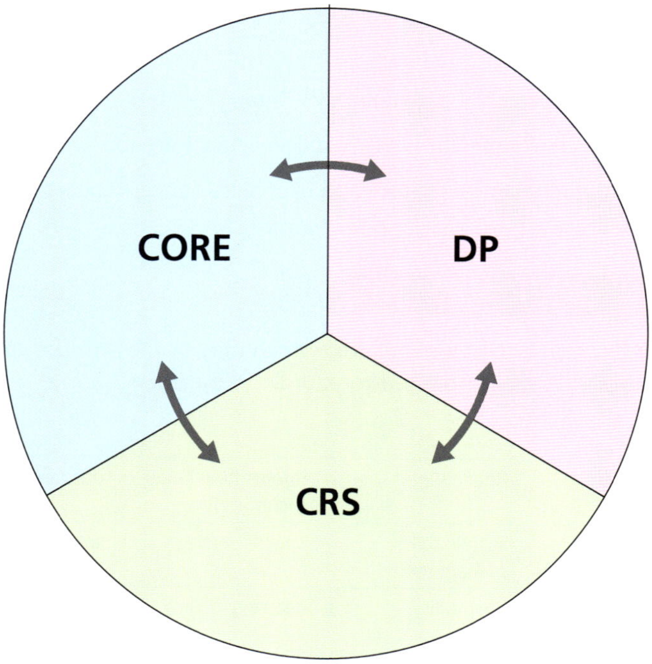

The interconnection of every component of the CP makes it unique.

5.2.4 Summary

- The DP courses are an essential part of the CP, and studying academic courses in conjunction with your CRS and Core components makes you an adaptable, critical and creative thinker.
- Your school will advise you what subjects to choose and how many are possible. It's worth considering Higher Level subjects, especially if you want to study that subject in the future.
- Teaching and learning in the IB, which you will experience directly in your DP subjects, is very active and places you at the centre of your learning. It is not like traditional 'chalk and talk' types of teaching and learning, and involves being able to connect all aspects of your education.
- Your PPS course directly develops transversal skills that incorporate the ATL skill areas of thinking, communication, social, self-management and research skills that you explore in your DP courses.
- The CP Core is a great opportunity to explore aspects of your DP courses freely in your own open inquiries, whether that is by exploring specific transversal skills, working in the community, deepening your linguistic and cultural repertoire or developing your understanding of a career field you are interested in and the associated ethics.

Glossary of key terms

Active hope: Authentic, action-oriented hopefulness that combines criticality and a clear view of reality with identification of what we truly long for and the determination to act and move in that direction. Active hope is about becoming active participants in bringing about what we hope for. It is a practice—something we do, not something we have.

Agency: A philosophical, sociological and psychological idea that acknowledges humans as active participants in their own lives with the capacity to initiate intentional action. (Adapted from IB LCS guide, p.50)

Anthropocentric: The belief that the needs of humans are the most important beings on the planet, and that their needs are more important than the needs and rights of non-humans, ecosystems and the rest of life on the planet.

Biocentric: The belief that non-human beings have inherent value, and that their welfare should be considered as equally important to that of humans. This belief focuses on the well-being and rights of non-human life as a moral imperative for humanity.

Care ethics: Making decisions by caring for others and focusing on relationships, empathy and compassion.

Communication: The expression and exchange of meaning through language or any other mode. Communication is often multimodal, including non-linguistic elements such as body language, gestures and images. The success of communication depends on the negotiation of meaning and cooperation between individuals within a given sociocultural and situational context. (Source: IB LCS guide, p.17)

Compassion: The ability to appreciate the forces that influence people's feelings, thoughts and actions; the capacity to both understand conceptually and empathetically what it is like to be an actor in a system, combined with the intention to act in support of others who might be impacted by the unintended consequences of human behaviour within larger, interconnected systems.

Complex systems: A system made up of many connected parts that influence each other. These systems can change over time, and small actions in one part can lead to big or unexpected changes in the whole system. Examples include ecosystems, communities and societies.

Complexity theory: 'Complexity theory helps to grasp the non-linear nature of [...] processes, including how [...] choices have unintended consequences or how small [actions] can cause large-scale systemic changes.' (IB Global politics TSM 2024, p.18)

Critical reflection: This links reflection with analytical and critical thinking, encouraging students to focus on experiences and actions within a broader, systemic context. (Source: IB RP guide, p.60)

Critical reflexivity: This involves critically examining and challenging collective assumptions, values and frames of reference, understanding their contexts (e.g. cultural, societal, historical), how they shape perceptions and actions, how they impact others, and how they might change in the future. (Source: IB RP guide, p.60)

Criticality: The ability to analyse, assess and evaluate information, ideas or situations in a thoughtful and objective manner. It involves examining different perspectives, questioning assumptions and evaluating evidence and arguments in order to form well-reasoned judgements and conclusions. In essence, criticality encompasses the process of thinking critically and applying critical-thinking skills.

Cultural repertoire: The full range of resources and tools (such as skills, styles, ways of understanding the world) that individuals have at their disposal and which they can select from, and deploy, in order to act and interact adaptively and responsively in various social and cultural contexts. (Source: IB LCS guide, p.52)

Culture: Shared understandings within a group of people and the interpretive lenses that they bring to any interaction. Through these lenses, they interpret, create and exchange meanings. (Source: IB LCS guide, p.50)

Curate: To prepare materials for an audience to communicate meaning. In the context of PPS, this refers to the collection of evidence for students' portfolios in a way that communicates students' learning.

Data: Facts and statistics collected together for reference or analysis.

Deontology: Doing what is right based on rules or duties, no matter the outcome.

Dialogic: A reciprocal style of communication where different perspectives and viewpoints can arise, people can openly respond, and inquiry and the co-construction of knowledge are centred.

Ecocentric: The belief that the welfare of ecosystems must be protected for the sake of all life on Earth. This belief focuses on the interconnectedness of ecosystems, including living and non-living elements, and prioritizes actions that will bring about overall ecological health and balance.

Ethic of care: An ethic of care places caring relationships at the centre of what it means to lead an ethical life. Rather than a strict adherence to universal principles, the focus is on compassionate, reciprocal and caring relationships that are grounded in relevant contexts.

Ethic of community: An ethical framework emphasizing the importance of contributing to the well-being of the larger community. Loyalty, responsibility, compassion, social justice and the wellbeing of the greater good are central themes.

Ethical concepts: The core ideas or 'ingredients' of ethical thinking, such as identity, integrity and power, that help you explore what is right or wrong in a situation.

Ethical dilemma: A choice between two (or more) conflicting values or courses of action, where each alternative has its own drawbacks or may lead to undesirable consequences. Because neither alternative provides an ideal solution, there is no clear-cut answer and an ethical decision is difficult to make.

Ethical issue: A situation or topic that raises questions of what is right or wrong for individuals, organizations, communities or society as a whole, and which requires consideration from an ethical or moral perspective. Ethical issues may be encountered in all areas of life (e.g. personal, social, professional, economic, environmental) and may relate to questions of fairness, honesty, justice, human rights or the rights of nature.

Ethical lenses: The perspectives or values you use to interpret ethical situations. Like a pair of glasses, different lenses can help you see an issue in a new way and lead to different decisions.

Ethical paradigms: The broader cultural or philosophical systems that shape how you understand ethics. Your paradigm influences which voices you prioritize and how you align you values with your actions.

Ethical thinking: Ethical thinking involves thinking critically about, and applying, ethical values to navigate our personal and professional lives. It fosters moral development and enables us to make responsible choices and be accountable for our decisions. Self-reflexivity supports ethical thinking as it enables us to identify and examine our personal values to guide us in our actions and decisions.

Ethics: The study of right and wrong, as well as any system or code of moral rules, principles or values. Understanding why something is right or wrong helps to inform and guide our choices, actions and behaviours. (RP guide, p.65). (Synonyms: right-minded, right-thinking, principled, irreproachable, unimpeachable, blameless, guiltless, righteous, upright, upstanding, good, lawful, honest, trustworthy, admirable, praiseworthy.)

Growth mindset: When you have the belief that your capacities and talents can be improved over time with effort.

Heritage languages: There are languages with which one has historical, cultural and/or personal connections. Heritage languages often exist alongside the dominant/official languages in your context. Heritage language speakers might also be able to read and write in the language, or they might speak and understand the language to varying degrees. Alternative terms include 'community language', 'home language', 'home background language' and 'minority language'.

Identities: This refers to the particular combinations of backgrounds, dispositions and experiences that define individuals, groups, communities, organizations, objects, eras and places. Identities are complex and dynamic. They can be shaped through internal and external, present and past influences. Individual and collective identities are manifested in both tangible and intangible ways, and these identities influence our view of the world and how others view us. (Source: IB LCS guide, pp.17–18)

Independent inquiry: An inquiry that you initiate, develop and execute on your own based on something you want to explore or learn about. You can use the tools provided by your teacher or the PPS toolkit to guide you in developing independent inquiries.

Inquiry: The process of exploring a topic by asking questions to deepen understanding.

Interculturalism: The reciprocal act of negotiating understanding of meaning in diverse situations within and across languages and cultures; coming to understand and appreciate the mediating role of languages and cultures in identity formation.

Interpersonal skills: The behaviours and strategies we use to interact effectively with others.

Intrapersonal skills: Intrapersonal skills involve self-awareness and the understanding of our own emotions.

Language and cultural portrait: A way to represent your linguistic and cultural repertoire. Your portrait can be represented as a diagram, a mind map, a timeline, a piece of writing, a spoken reflection or presentation, a performance, a video, a blog or any combination of any modality. Your portrait changes over time as your repertoires expand and develop, as well as when you gain new insights into your portrait. Your portrait has a key role in your learning journal and should be regularly updated, annotated and referred to.

Language ideologies: The beliefs, opinions, biases and feelings (conscious or unconscious) that people have about different languages and ways of speaking. These ideas influence how we use language and how we view others based on their speech. (Adapted from IB LCS guide, p.51)

Language variety: Different versions of a named language (e.g. American English, Gulf Arabic).

Language: The primary means by which people construct, share and maintain understanding and meaning. Language is not understood only as code and system (words and grammar), but also as social practice; it includes language use in the contexts of situation and in the context of culture. (Source: IB LCS guide, p.50)

Linguistic repertoire: The totality of linguistic resources (such as words, sounds, structures, styles, genres, registers and their respective norms) that individuals have at their disposal in all of their languages/language varieties (irrespective of their level of linguistic competence) and which they can select from, and deploy, in order to create and communicate meaning in various contexts. (Source: IB LCS guide, p.52)

Metacognitive and process reflection: These involve examining past experiences and actions to improve future practice (focused on the 'how' of actions). Reflection as a metacognitive skill enhances awareness of one's own cognitive/learning process. It involves examining one's thinking, actions and goals, leading to self-regulated learning. Process reflection starts with an experience and leads to new or changed understandings, insights and/or actions.

Morals: This relates to the standards of good or bad behaviour, fairness, honesty, etc. that each person believes in, rather than to laws. (Cambridge Dictionary Online) Synonyms: moral code, code of ethics, moral standards, moral values, principles, principles of right and wrong, rules of conduct, standards/principles of behaviour, standards, morality, sense of morality, scruples, ideals.)

Multilingualism: The availability of two or more languages/language varieties in an individual's linguistic repertoire, regardless of stage of acquisition or degree of proficiency.

Named languages: Such as Polish, Arabic, Zulu, Thai.

Narrative assessment: A way to monitor, evaluate and share your progress over time. It combines storytelling and reflection to show you how you are learning and changing. It often includes your thoughts and feelings, making it a more personal and meaningful way to reflect on your learning in relation to the four LOs.

Perspectives: This refers to the positions from which we view situations, objects, facts, ideas and opinions. Perspectives may be associated with individuals or groups, and they may be influenced by social, cultural, disciplinary, political or historical contexts. Different perspectives often lead to multiple representations and interpretations. (Source: IB LCS guide, p.18)

Plagiarize: To take someone else's work or idea and (accidentally or deliberately) pass it off as your own.

Positionality: This refers to the stance or positioning of individuals or groups in relation to overlapping cultural, social, historical and political contexts and relations of power, and how identities (including the perspectives, biases, assumptions, values and experiences we hold) shape frames of reference and, therefore, the way we understand and engage with the world. It also aims to highlight both how individual identities are created by social constructs, how they are malleable and change over time. (Source: IB LCS guide, p.51)

Power: This refers to the hierarchical structures, relations and processes that are formed by social, cultural, political, economic and historical factors, and that involve a person's or group's capacity to exert influence, domination or control over other individuals and groups. Power is not equally distributed in all contexts. Individuals' and communities' choices and actions can influence, or be influenced by, power structures and relations. (Source: IB LCS guide, p.18)

Privilege: A social advantage that only one person or group of people have, usually as a result of their social, economic, sexual, racial, identity, position or viewpoints.

Qualitative: Measuring by the quality of something, rather than its quantity (the size or number).

Quantitative: Measuring by the size or number of something.

Reciprocal: Reciprocal communication and relationships are built on respectful, shared efforts with mutual, two-way contributions that benefit everyone involved.

Reflection: Metacognitive and process reflection involve examining past experiences and actions to improve future practice (focused on the 'how' of actions).

Reflective and reflexive practice: An intentional, active and ongoing process of reviewing one's thinking, practice and actions, examining views and assumptions, and being open to having one's own perspectives challenged and changed. (Source: IB LCS guide, p.52)

Reflexivity: Critical and self-reflexivity involve examining our thoughts and beliefs, where they come from and the impact they have.

Repertoire: The full range of linguistic resources and cultural tools that you possess, so you can effectively communicate and interact in different contexts. (Adapted from IB LCS guide, p.52)

Self-reflexivity: This involves considering one's positionality, identifying and questioning one's own assumptions, biases and attitudes, understanding how they influence one's own responses and actions, and how they impact others, given the complexity and interconnectedness of roles and relationships.

Systems iceberg: A visual tool that helps support deeper explorations of systems issues through understanding the underlying causes of events. The systems iceberg model consists of four levels: events, patterns and trends, underlying structures and mental models.

Systems: Sets of interacting or interdependent elements that use processes or procedures to work towards a common purpose. Social, economic, political and ecological systems provide a lens for exploring structure, interdependence, complexity and change in the human and natural worlds.

Thinking skills: These involve cognitive processes that we use to solve problems, make decisions, ask questions, plan, organize and create. Critical and creative thinking, problem-solving and information literacy consistently top the list of skills necessary to successfully navigate our ever-changing world in a variety of contexts.

Transversal skills: These are not specifically related to a particular job, task, academic discipline or area of knowledge, but can be used in a wide variety of situations and work settings. These skills can be transferred and applied to different contexts.

Utilitarianism: Doing what creates the greatest good for the greatest number of people.

Virtue ethics: Making choices based on being a good person with strong character traits (e.g. honesty or courage).

Well-being: Well-being generally refers to one's physical, emotional and mental state of being, which influences overall quality of life. Individual well-being exists in conjunction with the well-being of communities, as well as with ecological and planetary well-being.

Index

The abbreviations CE (community engagement), LCS (language and cultural studies), PPS (personal and professional skills) and RP (reflective project) are used to refer to the main components in subheadings. Subheadings for major course related main entries are provided in two sequences: the first sequence of *'course features'* is arranged in a non-alphabetical logical list; the second following sequence of *'other aspects'* is arranged alphabetically. Page numbers in **bold** indicate definitions.

Acknowledgements

We are grateful to the rightsholders for permission to reproduce the following:

p.173—'Entre' by Werber, B. (1993). *L'Encyclopédie du Savoir Relatif et Absolu*, Albin Michel

We are also grateful to the IBO for allowing us to quote, adapt and reference their Career-related Programme Core publications throughout this title, details of which are given in the references section below.

Artworks

We are grateful to the IBO for allowing us to reproduce their illustrations throughout this title.

Illustrations on pp.56, 360, 361, 362, 377 and 394 by Aptara Inc.

Photo credits

Section opener images on pp.1, 133, 231, 351 and 479 © Melita/stock.adobe.com

Background image on pp.xxiii–xxxiv, 8–9, 138–139, 242–243, 354–355 and 496–497 © JBLANCO_PHOTO/stock.adobe.com

p.ix © Hurca!/stock.adobe.com; p.xiii © Oleg/stock.adobe.com; p.xxix © Charles stockio/stock.adobe.com; p.3 (top left) © SDI Productions/E+/Getty images, (top right) © Monkey Business/stock.adobe.com, (bottom left) © Dragana Gordic/stock.adobe.com; p.15 (top) © Mediaphotos/stock.adobe.com, (bottom) © K.A./peopleimages.com/stock.adobe.com; p.27 © Berit Kessler/Shutterstock.com; p.46 © Batuhan toker/stock.adobe.com; p.50 © Seventyfour/stock.adobe.com; p.52 © Tawna Brown/Alamy Stock Photo; p.55 © Mediaphotos/stock.adobe.com; p.134 © Kittiphan/stock.adobe.com; p.137 © GoodIdeas/stock.adobe.com; p.149 © A. Zeitler/stock.adobe.com; p.152 © ARIF MIFTAHUL ANWAR/stock.adobe.com; p.156 (top) © Fabio Principe/stock.adobe.com, (middle) © Seventyfour/stock.adobe.com, (bottom) © CHRISTOPHE PETIT TESSON/EPA-EFE/Shutterstock; p.157 (left) © Pingebat/stock.adobe.com, (middle) © Jesadaphorn/stock.adobe.com, (right) © HridoyAhmed/stock.adobe.com; p.160 © Kazi/stock.adobe.com; p.165 © 5second/stock.adobe.com; p.166 © WONG SZE FEI/stock.adobe.com; p.167 © Pixel-Shot/stock.adobe.com; p.178 © Gaulois_s/Shutterstock.com; p.179 © SimoneO/stock.adobe.com; p.180 © Mypokcik/Shutterstock.com; p.246 (top left) © Monkey Business/stock.adobe.com, (top right) © A.S.peopleimages.com/stock.adobe.com, (bottom left) © Andrey/stock.adobe.com, (bottom right) © Monkey Business/stock.adobe.com; p.256 © Rawpixel.com/stock.adobe.com; p.291 © ImageFlow/stock.adobe.com; p.312 © Kris Black/stock.adobe.com; p.325 © R. Gino Santa Maria/stock.adobe.com; p.356 © Scottiebumich/stock.adobe.com; p.377 © Rafaila Gheorghita/stock.adobe.com; p.383 © Jiri/stock.adobe.com; p.391 © Horace Cort/Associated Press/Alamy Stock Photo; p.392 © Click_and_photo/stock.adobe.com; p.394 © Sdecoret/stock.adobe.com; p.395 © Flavijus Piliponis/stock.adobe.com; p.442 © Miha Creative/stock.adobe.com; p.494 © Wayhome.studioe/stock.adobe.com

References

Ahenakew, C. R. (2017). Mapping and Complicating Conversations about Indigenous Education. *Diaspora, Indigenous, and Minority Education*, *11*(2), 80–91. https://doi.org/10.1080/15595692.2017.1278693

Amagoh, F. (2016). Systems and complexity theories of organizations. In A. Farazmand (Ed.), *Global Encyclopedia of Public Administration, Public Policy, and Governance*. Springer. https://doi.org/10.1007/978-3-319-31816-5_73-1

Ball, J., Caldwell, W., & Pranis, K. (2010). Doing democracy with circles: Engaging communities in public planning. Living Justice Press.

Bohanon, J. P. (2006). *The talking circle: A perspective in culturally appropriate group work with Indigenous Peoples*. Southeastern Oklahoma State University.

Brink-Budgen, R. and Thawaites, J. (2012). *OCR AS Critical Thinking*. Hachette UK.

Cajete, G. A. (2015). *Indigenous community: Rekindling the teachings of the seventh fire*. Living Justice Press.

Chaves, M., Macintyre, T., Verschoor, G., & Wals, A. E. J. (2018). Radical ruralities in practice: Negotiating buen vivir in a Colombian network of sustainability. *Journal of Rural Studies*, *59*, 153–162. https://doi.org/10.1016/j.jrurstud.2017.02.007

Clarkson, L., Morrissette, V., & Régallet, G. (2001). *Our responsibility to the seventh generation.* International Institute for Sustainable Development. www.iisd.org/publications/our-responsibility-seventh-generation

Darling, J., Horrigan, S. (2012). A dynamic peacemaking method: Restorative circles. In D. Forbes, J. Lin, & E. Losh(Eds.), Education in action: Experiential learning in higher education (pp.169–176). UCSD.

De Swaan, A. (2001). *Words of the World*, Polity.

D'Eon M. F. (2022). The Ladder of Inference re-visited: 'Don't jump to confusions!'. *Canadian Medical Education Journal, 13*(5), 1–5. https://doi.org/10.36834/cmej.76000

Diffen. *Ethics vs. Morals*. www.diffen.com/difference/Ethics_vs_Morals

Elder, L. & Paul, R. (2008). *The Miniature Guide to Critical Thinking Concepts and Tools*, Foundation for Critical Thinking Press.

Elder, L. & Paul, R. (2016). *Critical Thinking: Concepts and Tools*. The Foundation for Critical Thinking.

Ermine, W. (2007). The ethical space of engagement. Indigenous Law Journal, 6, 193–203. https://kinasevych.ca/2017/09/14/ermine-2007-the-ethical-space-of-engagement/

Fischer, M., Maxwell, K., Nuunoq, Pedersen, H., Greeno, D., Jingwas, N., Graham Blair, J., Hugu, S., Mustonen, T., Murtomäki, E., & Mustonen, K. (2022). Empowering her guardians to nurture our Ocean's future. *Reviews in Fish Biology and Fisheries, 32*(1), 271–296. https://doi.org/10.1007/s11160-021-09679-3

Fonseca, S. T., Souza, T. R., Verhagen, E., van Emmerik, R., Bittencourt, N. F. N., Mendonça, L. D. M., Andrade, A. G. P., Resende, R. A., & Ocarino, J. M. (2020). Sports injury forecasting and complexity: A synergetic approach. *Sports Medicine, 50*(10), 1757–1770. https://doi.org/10.1007/s40279-020-01326-4

Furman, G. C. (2004). The ethic of community. *Journal of Educational Administration*, 42(2), 215–235. https://doi.org/10.1108/09578230410525612

Gade, C. B. N. (2011). The historical development of the written discourses on Ubuntu. *South African Journal of Philosophy*, 30(3), 303–329. https://doi.org/10.4314/sajpem.v30i3.69578

Gram-Hanssen, I., Schafenacker, N. & Bentz, J. (2022). Decolonizing transformations through 'right relations'. *Sustainability Science, 17*, 673–685. https://doi.org/10.1007/s11625-021-00960-9

Grim, J., & Tucker, M. E. (2014). *Ecology and Religion*. Island Press.

Gudynas, E. (2011). Buen Vivir: Today's tomorrow. *Development*, 54(4), 441–447. https://doi.org/10.1057/dev.2011.86

Hilsdon, J. (2008). 'Model to generate critical thinking', *Study Guide 8: Critical thinking*. Learning Development, University of Plymouth.

Hunter, L.M., Logan J., Goulet, J. G., & Barton S. (2006). Aboriginal healing: Regaining balance and culture. *Journal of Transcultural Nursing, 17*(1), 13-22. https://doi.org/10.1177/1043659605278937

International Baccalaureate Organization. (2025). *CE toolkit.*

International Baccalaureate Organization. (2025). *LCS toolkit.*

International Baccalaureate Organization. (2025). *PPS toolkit.*

International Baccalaureate Organization. (2025). *RP toolkit.*

International Baccalaureate Organization. (2025a). *CE guide.*

International Baccalaureate Organization. (2025a). *LCS guide.*

International Baccalaureate Organization. (2025a). *PPS guide.*

International Baccalaureate Organization. (2025a). *RP guide.*

International Baccalaureate Organization. (2025b). *Community engagement teacher support material.*

International Baccalaureate Organization. (2025b). *Language and cultural studies teacher support material.*

International Baccalaureate Organization. (2025b). *Personal and professional skills teacher support material.*

International Baccalaureate Organization. (2025b). *Reflective project teacher support material.*

International Baccalaureate Organization. (2025c). *What is an IB education?: Support material*. https://resources.ibo.org/ib/works/edu_11162-412365?lang=en&root=1.6.2.8.5

Johnstone, C. (July 2020). *Keynote address: Active hope: Nourishing personal and collective resilience in a time of overwhelming disasters*. [YouTube video]. 45th Annual Natural Hazards Research and Applications Workshop, Boulder, Colorado, United States. https://hazards.colorado.edu/workshop/2020/keynote?row=8

Kahui, V., Armstrong, C. W., & Aanesen, M. (2024). Comparative analysis of Rights of Nature (RoN) case studies worldwide: Features of emergence and design. *Ecological Economics, 221*, 1–19. https://doi.org/10.1016/j.ecolecon.2024.108193

Kimmerer R. (2013). *Braiding sweetgrass*: *Indigenous wisdom, scientific knowledge and the teachings of plants*. Milkweed Editions.

Kothari, A. (2018). Eco-Swaraj vs. eco-catastrophe. *Asia Pacific Perspectives*, 15(2), 49–54. https://doi.org/10.4314/sajpem.v30i3.69578

Little Bear, L. (2000). Jagged worldviews colliding. In M. Battiste (Ed.), *Reclaiming Indigenous voice and vision* (pp.77–85). University of British Columbia Press. https://doi.org/10.59962/9780774853170-009.

Littlechild, D., & Sutherland, C. (2021, March). *Enacting and operationalizing ethical space and two-eyed seeing in Indigenous protected and conserved areas and Crown protected and conserved areas*. Indigenous Circle of Experts. https://y2y.net/wp-content/uploads/2022/04/Operationalizing-Ethical-Space-in-IPCAs-and-Crown-Protected-and-Conserved-Areas-FINAL.pdf?utm_source=chatgpt.com

Lyman, R. K. (2024). *How to increase the odds of people paying attention to your communication*. University of North Carolina. https://execdev.unc.edu/how-to-increase-the-odds-of-people-paying-attention-to-your-communication/#:~:text=George%20Bernard%20Shaw%20said%2C%20%E2%80%9CThe,they%20are%20not%20being%20heard.

Macy, J., & Johnstone, C. (2012). *Active hope: How to face the mess we're in without going crazy*. New World Library.

McCabe, A. (2025). *Learning and reflecting on the African 'spirit of Ubuntu.'* https://ecampusontario.pressbooks.pub/teachingnelsonmandela/chapter/12/

McCandless, K., & Lipmanowicz, H. (2014). T*he surprising power of liberating structures: Simple rules to unleash a culture of innovation*. McCandless & Lipmanowicz.

McCrindle, M. (2025). 'Gen Alpha' infographic, https://mccrindle.com.au/app/uploads/infographics/Generation-Alpha-Infographic-2025.pdf

Miller, C. (n.d.). The intersection of Indigenous knowledge and Western science (Module 3). In J. Brooks, E. Gilpin, B. Cougler Blom, R. Cox, K. Lambert, & B. Forssman (Eds.), *Indigenous knowledges and perspectives on climate adaptation*. Resilience By Design Lab, Royal Roads University. https://pressbooks.bccampus.ca/indigadapt/chapter/the-intersection-of-indigenous-knowledge-and-western-science/

Mogyoros, J. (n.d.). *Guided inquiry prompts: Weaving Indigenous and Western sciences*. Defining Moments Canada. https://definingmomentscanada.ca/education/etuaptmumk/guided-inquiry-prompts/

Mustonen, T. (2019). Meaningful engagement and oral histories of the indigenous peoples of the north. *Nordia Geographical Publications*, *47*(5), 21–38. https://nordia.journal.fi/article/view/79929

National Research Council. (1992). Neem: A tree for solving global problems. *The National Academies Press*. https://doi.org/10.17226/1924

Ngubane, N., & Makua, M. (2021). Ubuntu pedagogy: Transforming educational practices in South Africa through an African philosophy: From theory to practice. Inkanyiso: *Journal of Humanities and Social Sciences*, 13(1), 12. https://doi.org/10.4102/ink.v13i1.9

Nikolakis, W., & Hotte, N. (2021). Implementing 'ethical space': An exploratory study of indigenous-conservation partnerships. *Conservation Science and Practice*, 4(1). https://doi.org/10.1111/csp2.580

Noddings, N. (2016). *Philosophy of education*. Routledge.

Owolabi, K. A. (2022). *Because of our future: The imperative for an environmental ethic for Africa*. IFRA-Nigeria. https://doi.org/10.4000/books.ifra.3617

Pashby, K., Sund, L., Corcoran, S., & Wicker, C. (2022). Teaching for sustainable development through ethical global issues pedagogy: Participatory research with teachers. *Impact*. https://my.chartered.college/impact_article/teaching-for-sustainable-development-through-ethical-global-issues-pedagogy/

Pranis, K. (2005). *The little book of circle processes: A new/old approach to peacemaking*. Skyhorse Publishing.

Royal Road University. (2025). *Indigenous Knowledges and perspectives on climate adaptation: Module 3: The intersection of Indigenous Knowledge and Western science*. British Columbia/Yukon Pressbooks. https://pressbooks.bccampus.ca/indigadapt/chapter/the-intersection-of-indigenous-knowledge-and-western-science/

Sapega, M. *How to create a photo essay*. https://shorthand.com/the-craft/how-to-compile-a-photo-essay/index.html

Schroeder, J., & Rowcliffe, P. (January 2021). Compassionate Systems Leadership. www.compassionatesystemsleadership.net

Snow, T., Bandaranayaka, A., Fyfe, R., & Wolff, L. (2025a). *Storytelling for systems change: Listening to understand*. Centre for Public Impact. https://centreforpublicimpact.org/resource-hub/storytelling-for-systems-change-listening-to-understand/

Snow, T., Murikumthara, D., Dusseldorp, T., Fyfe, R., Wolff, L, & McCracken, J. (2025b, February 7). *Storytelling and systems change*. i2Insights. https://i2insights.org/2023/02/07/storytelling-and-systems-change/

Sodi, T., Bopape, D., & Makgahlela, M. (2021). Botho as an essential ingredient of African psychology: an insider perspective. *South African Journal of Psychology*, 51(3), 441—452. https://doi.org/10.1177/0081246320985259

Solberg, S. *How to make a documentary: Step-by-step guide for beginners*. www.docfilmacademy.com/blog/how-to-make-a-documentary

Stein, S., Ahenakew, C., Valley, W., & Evans, S. (2024). Toward more ethical engagements between Western and Indigenous sciences. *FACETS*, 9, 1–14. https://doi.org/10.1139/facets-2023-0071

The rights of nature. (2022). *We are the African Hub of GARN!* www.garnafrica.org/about-us/

Truth and Reconciliation Commission of South Africa. (1998). *Truth and Reconciliation Commission of South Africa report* (Vol. 1). Truth and Reconciliation Commission of South Africa. https://www.justice.gov.za/trc/index.html

Tūhoe. (2025). *Our Rohe*. www.ngaituhoe.iwi.nz/our-rohe

Tutu, D. (October 2010). *Archbishop Desmond Tutu on 'dignity'.* Amnesty International. www.amnestyusa.org/blog/archbishop-desmond-tutu-on-dignity/

Tynan, D. (June 2023). 'From jobs to skills: What the future of work will look like', *Forbes* magazine, www.forbes.com/sites/guild/2023/06/28/from-jobs-to-skills-what-the-future-of-work-will-look-like/

Unesco (2022). 'Cutting Edge | Indigenous languages: Gateways to the world's cultural diversity', https://unesco.org/en/articles/cutting-edge-indigenouslanguages-gateways-worlds-cultural-diversity

United Nations Declaration on the Rights of Indigenous Peoples, 13 September 2007, A/RES/61/295 [UNDRIP]. www.un.org/development/desa/indigenouspeoples/declaration-on-the-rights-of-indigenous-peoples.html

United Nations Universal Declaration of Human Rights, 10 December 1948. www.un.org/en/about-us/universal-declaration-of-human-rights

van Wessel, M. G. J., Ho, W. W. S., & Tamas, P. A. (2021). Narrative Assessment: A new method for monitoring, evaluating, learning and communicating about advocacy. *Wageningen University & Research*. https://edepot.wur.nl/564132

Viscogliosi, C., Asselin, H, Basile, S., Borwick, K., Couturier, Y., Drolet, M-J., Gagnon, D., Obradovic, N., Torrie, J., Zhou, D., & Levasseur, M. (2020). Importance of Indigenous elders' contributions to individual and community wellness: Results from a scoping review on social participation and intergenerational solidarity. *Canadian Journal of Public Health, 111*, 667-681. https://doi.org/10.17269/s41997-019-00292-3

Visible Network Labs (2023). *Community engagement 101: Ultimate beginner's guide.* https://visiblenetworklabs.com/guides/community-engagement-101/

WEF (April 2023). 'The Future of Jobs Report 2023', www.weforum.org/publications/the-future-of-jobs-report-2023

WEF (January 2025). 'The Future of Jobs Report 2025', www.weforum.org/publications/the-future-of-jobs-report-2025

WEF (October 2024). 'Skills for the future: 4 ways to help workers transition to the digital economy', www.weforum.org/stories/2024/10/jobs-skills-work-digital-economy

Wood, S. (2023). *Rights of nature: What are they? A plain language legal guide for earth citizens.* Centre for Law & the Environment, University of British Columbia. www.allard.ubc.ca/cle, Available at SSRN: https://ssrn.com/abstract=4919708 or http://dx.doi.org/10.2139/ssrn.4919708

Yao, Xinzhong. (2014). An eco-ethical interpretation of Confucian 'tianren heyi'. *Frontiers of Philosophy in China*, 9(4), 570–585. https://www.jstor.org/stable/44156919